Institutional Economics

PROPERTY, COMPETITION, POLICIES

SECOND EDITION

Wolfgang Kasper
Emeritus Professor of Economics, University of New South Wales, Sydney, Australia

Manfred E. Streit
Emeritus Professor, Max-Planck-Institute of Economics, Jena, Germany

Peter J. Boettke
Professor of Economics, George Mason University, Fairfax, USA

Edward Elgar
Cheltenham, UK • Northampton, MA, USA

Published by
Edward Elgar Publishing Limited
The Lypiatts
15 Lansdown Road
Cheltenham
Glos GL50 2JA
UK

Edward Elgar Publishing, Inc.
William Pratt House
9 Dewey Court
Northampton
Massachusetts 01060
USA

Paperback edition 2013
Cased edition reprinted 2014
Paperback edition reprinted 2018

A catalogue record for this book
is available from the British Library

Library of Congress Control Number: 2012940998

ISBN 978 1 78100 662 7 (cased)
        978 1 78254 012 0 (paperback)

Typeset by Servis Filmsetting Ltd, Stockport, Cheshire
Printed and bound in Great Britain by the CPI Group (UK) Ltd

Institutional Economics

Contents in brief

Full contents

Figures

Tables

Foreword to the second, revised edition

The first edition of *Institutional Economics*, which was published nearly 15 years ago, was received with gratifying reviews by prominent fellow economists and – gradually – gave us helpful feedback from academic teachers and students. We were particularly pleased with the response – and sales figures – of the Chinese translation and the amazing impact the book had on the thinking of a growing circle of Chinese professional economists.[1]

Over the past few decades, institutional economics and an evolutionary, individualistic perception of economic life have gained much wider influence in teaching, research and policy advice (Boettke, 2012). As we shall make clear in the *Epilogue*, the simplistic neoclassical model, which is based on unrealistic assumptions of knowledge and motivation, has been in retreat – except for the sudden re-emergence of paleo-Keynesian and interventionist responses to the global financial crisis since 2007.

The growing acceptance of the institutional-economics approach, as described in this book, helps to understand the new need to promote openness, freedom and prosperity as well as to adapt economic structures to changes in the old and new industrial economies alike:

- At a time, when the greatest fear of most citizens in mature economies is *anome* – to use the Greek word for 'disorder and hence loss of confidence' that has assumed a new popular meaning in the European debt crisis – it is advisable to think again about what creates social order and trust. Taking institutional economics seriously will also help a generation of disaffected youths to come to grips with a worldview that has, time and again in the past, offered hope for a promising future.
- The increasing economic and psychological problems in mature Western societies, with their ageing populations and government-run social-security systems and infrastructures, make it urgent to reassess the rule systems and inherited cultural foundations that underpinned the rise of the West. Competition, capitalism and self-responsibility within the rule of law have delivered unprecedented prosperity, freedom, justice and

prosperity over the past three centuries. Yet, the very foundations of our technical-capitalist civilization are now again coming under attack from within and without. The Marx-and-Lenin brand of collectivism may have come to naught (Chapter 13.1), but concerns about environmental issues and fears of change have given the advocates of a new collectivism a growing audience. It seems to us appropriate to reconsider the insights of, for example, David Hume and Adam Smith, which benefited a generation 200 years ago when it faced the problems of an incipient knowledge revolution and the advent of the industrial revolution. Only a flexible, competitive economy will be able to reconcile worthwhile environmental conservation, the rise of new industrial countries and global structural adjustments with sustained and widespread prosperity.

- Since the onset of the global debt and financial crisis in 2007, the interventionist top-down approach has again become fashionable in public policy. Do our time-tested rule systems have to be reaffirmed or adjusted? Do demographic changes, the emergence of new industrial locations and the unrelenting advances of technical progress make a renewed reflection of the institutional underpinnings of material progress necessary? Printing more money, emergency meetings of political leaders to control international trade and capital flows and the growing sway of international bureaucracies are unlikely to advance sustainable solutions. Institutional economics, by contrast, offers insights into how order can be restored nationally and internationally. Earlier experiences and the logic of individual action have shown that macroeconomic engineering fails if the microeconomic incentives and the rules that shape them are overlooked.

- For a long time, modernity and prosperity had been the almost exclusive possession of Western nations (with the notable exception of Japan). Over recent decades, however, globalization has spread the aspiration to prosperity and modern individualism to an ever-widening circle of communities and nations. The rule system of the market economy – property rights, prices, incentives – has now to be grafted onto diverse cultures and world views. We have learnt that not all cultural traditions lend themselves equally to serving as a foundation for prosperity-creating market institutions. What is needed – figuratively speaking – is the presence of the right 'cultural Velcro surface' onto which the 'Velcro surface of the market economy' can be fastened. In some parts of the world, cultural change has favoured this. Thus, the long cultural traditions of the Confucian orbit or the Indian bazaar economy have been rather readily adjusted to bond constructively with the institutions of the modern market economy (Chapters 12 and 14). In other parts, for example the Islamic world, the necessary cultural changes have proved more elusive. What is now emerging is a multiplicity of modernities, in which markets, technical dynamism and useful learning are bonding to a greater or lesser degree with the cultural foundations of diverse civilizations. The concepts of institutional economics lend themselves both to understanding these epochal changes and to fostering supportive policies.

● After the demise of totalitarian socialism in 1989, the old model of supposedly value-free neoclassical economics failed to provide useful answers to new generations of East Europeans, Asians and others, who rejected central command and control, wanted freedom and sought ways to live in a prospering, peaceful and just society. For many, this has been fundamentally a moral issue. They have embraced institutional economics because of its value content and the ability to analyse the material consequences of alternative rule sets.

● At a time when the freedom ratings in the world as a whole have been consistently in decline (according to Freedom House, 2011) and when ever-denser government regulations constrain individual economic freedoms in many countries, it is worthwhile to look to institutional economics to evaluate the likely consequences of this trend.

•••

It is with such considerations in mind that we went about revising the first edition of *Institutional Economics* and preparing this second edition.

We inserted a more explicit discussion of economic development along the lines of the late Lord Peter Bauer in the new edition and drew on insights about culture, migration, evolution and social cohesion by such friends as Tom Sowell and Eric Jones. The detailed discussion in the first edition of diverse reform strategies in post-Soviet Eastern Europe has been replaced by a more long-term analysis of the 'treadmill of Soviet reform' – or rather non-reform. We have also addressed more explicitly the question of whether governments can and should stabilize the business cycle and expand aggregate demand by incurring increasing debts, almost irrespective of what price movements, productivity trends and profits do to individual decisions.

We have placed a number of quotations at the head of each chapter, not only as an appetizer about the topic area, but also as an indication that many others before us have thought about the same issues. Numerous academics, other observers and practitioners of politics and business have recognized the importance of institutional arrangements, even if they did not explore institutional theory in systematic detail.

•••

Advancing years and the transition of the two original authors into the blessed status of professor emeritus suggested that we should coopt a third, younger and like-minded co-author, who had been using the first edition in his teaching: Peter J. Boettke. The extra pair of hands was particularly welcome because poor health prevented Manfred Streit from actively contributing to the new edition. A major benefit of working as a wider team has been that the book now can draw not only on experiences in Europe and the Asia-Pacific, but also more on American dimensions and materials. As the three authors reside, respectively, in Australia, Europe and America, we had to communicate across three time zones. The Internet, our shared view of basic economic philosophy and the stimulus of interaction not only kept our task manageable, but turned it into an exhilarating, enriching experience. We trust that this will be conveyed to our readers.

We acknowledge with thanks permissions to reproduce materials, as cited, by the Foundation of Economic Education in Irvington-on-Hudson, NY; the Fraser Institute in Vancouver, Canada; the Centre for Independent Studies, Sydney, Australia; the Institute of Public Affairs, Melbourne, Australia; and Weidenfeld & Nicolson, a division of Orion Publishing Group Ltd., London (covering excerpts from Paul Johnson's *Birth of the Modern*).

Special thanks go to Professor Nils Karlson of the Ratio Institute in Stockholm for help with the account of the institutional reforms in Sweden. We are also indebted to Matthew Boettke, David Currie, David Hebert, Peter Lipsey, Caralynn Reddig, and Liya Palagashvili at George Mason University for critically reading chapter drafts. Last but not least, we acknowledge Edward Elgar's personal encouragement to write this book and the competent support of his editorial team in expediting it into the marketplace.

Thus, this has become – as our team-internal working title went – a 'tricontinental edition' of *Institutional Economics*. We commend it to our readers wherever in the world they may be.

Wolfgang Kasper, Australia
Manfred E. Streit, Germany
Peter J. Boettke, United States of America

NOTE

1 Kê Wŭg--ang and Xi Manfei (2000), *Zì Dù Jing Ji Xúe – Sè Hùi Zhi Xù Yu Gong Gòng Zèn Cè* [Institutional Economics: Social Order and Public Policy]. Beijing: Commercial Press.

Foreword to the first edition

This book introduces the student – and others with a basic understanding of economics – to the rapidly evolving discipline of institutional economics. The central tenet of this discipline is that a modern economy is a complex, evolving system whose effectiveness in meeting diverse and changing human purposes depends on enforced rules, which constrain, possibly opportunistic, human behaviour (we call these rules 'institutions'). Institutions protect individual spheres of freedom, help to avoid or mitigate conflicts, and enhance the division of labour and knowledge and thereby promote prosperity. Indeed, the rules that govern human interaction are so decisive for economic growth and other fundamental aspirations of mankind – whose numbers are bound to keep increasing for some time yet – that its very survival and prosperity depend on the right institutions and the fundamental human values that underpin them.[1]

Institutional economics differs greatly from standard, orthodox neoclassical economics, which is based on narrow assumptions about rationality and knowledge and which implicitly assumes the institutions as given. Institutional economics has important connections with jurisprudence, politics, sociology, anthropology, history, organization science, management, and moral philosophy. Because institutional economics is open to intellectual influences from a wide range of social sciences, this book recommends itself not only to the economist interested in economic growth and development, technical innovation, comparative economic systems, cultural change, and political economy, but also to students of the above-mentioned disciplines.

The realization that institutions matter has spread rapidly over the past thirty years. One may compare this ongoing shift to the new institutional economics with the Copernican Revolution: the focus of economics is being turned from specific processes and outcomes to universal, abstract rules The trail blazers of this approach were writers such as Friedrich von Hayek and others writing in the Austrian tradition, Ronald Coase who alerted economists to the consequences of transaction costs, James Buchanan and others in the 'public choice' school, economic historians such as Douglass North who discovered the importance of institutions by analysing past economic development, and economists such as William Vickrey who showed the consequences of people having limited, asymmetric knowledge. The fact that all these authors received Nobel Prizes in Economics in 1974 (Hayek), 1986 (Buchanan), 1991 (Coase), 1994 (North) and 1996 (Vickrey) also indicates that the study of institutional economics is in the ascendancy. The shift to a focus on institutions has also been furthered by theories of complex systems, such as chaos theory and fuzzy logic, which show that actions frequently have unforeseeable side effects. Case-by-case process interventions therefore often produce inferior outcomes to reliance on uniform, general rules.

Although a growing number of scholars are grappling with the consequences of the complexity of economic life, their insights have, in many countries, not yet filtered through to public opinion, nor for that matter influenced many university courses. To be sure, the consequences of complexity are now widely understood in other areas, such as ecology. [The] public now understands that ecological systems are complex and evolving – and in many respects beyond human comprehension – so that interventions can have unpredictable and dangerous side effects. Yet, when it comes to policy interventions in equally complex economic systems, similar caution is rarely advocated. Indeed, side effects are routinely ruled out by economics teachers who make the assumption of *ceteris paribus*.

The recent revival of institutional economics owes much to events, too. In the mature Western welfare states with electoral democracies, the traditional economic order under the institutions of capitalism has been decaying gradually, often imperceptibly, under the load of proliferating interventions and an increasingly politicization of economic life. This has led to slower economic growth, given rise to a widespread cynicism about public policy and now gives rise of fear from new competitors, such as China and India. These experiences have triggered more or less consistent attempts at economic reform from the late 1970s onwards (for example privatization and deregulation). Increasingly streamlined legal-institutional arrangements are seen as crucial to better economic and social outcomes and it is accepted by many policymakers that institutions need to be cultivated. Observers in the ascendant industrial countries and a growing number of less developed economies have also realized that conventional theories of economic growth exclude important, indeed essential dimensions of the problem of economic development, in particular institutional development to achieve freedom, economic prosperity and security. Even international organizations have in recent decades begun to research the effects of institutional reforms and have advocated them in more differentiated, sophisticated form than the former 'Washington consensus'.

Globalization has certainly drawn attention to the role of institutions. The intensifying international competition amounts, to a considerable extent, to a competition between different institutional systems. Some rule systems have proven successful in keeping the transaction costs of doing business low, attracting growth-promoting capital and enterprises. Countries, such as China, who were losing out have begun to emulate the institutions of their successful neighbours.

The arguably most powerful impetus to reintegrate the study of institutions and institutional change into economics came with the spectacular failure and collapse of the centrally planned, socialist economies in the late 1980s. The institutions of socialism had long discouraged citizens from drawing fully on their knowledge and resources. As a consequence, the socialist countries failed to keep pace with the capitalist market economies. The transformation of the formerly socialist societies focused the minds of many economists in the East and West on the importance of institutions to encouraging initiative, enterprise and exchange.

To understand the arguments of political reformers around the world, one has – in the first place – to integrate institutions explicitly into one's economic theories. It is, for example, simply not possible to explain satisfactorily why (re-)privatizing government activities, such as welfare provision, promises to lead to overall gains and why deregulation has advantages, if one tacitly eliminates the explicit analysis of institutions from one's research.

We belong to those economists who see the search for and testing of useful knowledge as the major driving force behind modern economic growth. Therefore, social devices which help us to economize on the cost of knowledge search are of central interest to economics.

When we began to teach economics from this standpoint, we could not find a fully satisfactory introductory text. To be sure, there is no shortage of relevant literature, but most textbooks still suffer from the birth defect of assuming 'perfect knowledge'. This text is an effort to fill the gap.

•••

This book begins with an introductory discussion why institutions matter. We show that the extraordinary and continuing growth of the world population and living standards this century, as well as the dramatic differences between national growth rates, have a great deal to do with certain types of institutions, values and social orders. In Chapter 2, we define key concepts, such as 'institutions', 'economic order', 'coordination costs' and 'public policy'. We then discuss fundamental assumptions about human behaviour and acknowledge that people who act as agents for others sometimes may behave opportunistically and against the interests of the principals (Chapter 3). Although individuals tend to pursue their own purposes, they nevertheless share certain fundamental values with others, for example freedom, security, justice and material wellbeing. These fundamental values underpin social cohesion. They are discussed in Chapter 4. Then, we proceed to discuss the nature and role of institutions and the order that certain institutional arrangements facilitate (Chapters 5 and 6).

Whereas Chapters 2 to 6 are intended to lay the theoretical foundations for an understanding of institutional economics, the remaining chapters deal with more applied aspects of institutional economics. In Chapter 7, we analyse the foundations of the capitalist system, in particular private property and the freedom of contract. The following chapter is focused on competition, a dynamic process in which entrepreneurial buyers and suppliers discover, develop and test useful knowledge. We shall differentiate between economic competition among sellers and buyers for the favours of the other side of the market, and political competition for political influence. We then look at institutional arrangements that underpin economic organizations, such as business firms (Chapter 9). In Chapter 10, we look at the functions of government and problems that arise when economic problems are addressed by collective, political action. We shall also discuss the precautions that need to be taken to prevent politicians and bureaucrats from acting against the interests of the citizens.

What has been learnt up to that point is used to discuss international economic exchanges and how national governments can be restrained from suppressing competitive challenges, and how institutional systems evolve (Chapters 11 and 12). In the final two chapters, we apply the institutional-economics approach to a discussion of some of the most topical issues in contemporary economics: why socialism failed, how the socialist system can be transformed, how the heavily administered, mature welfare states might be reformed to meet the competitive challenges from the new industrial countries, and why the continued spread of prosperity around the world will ultimately depend on fostering appropriate institutions.

The development of the main themes in this book from basic premises demands a somewhat patient reader. Impatient readers may want to jump straight to Chapters 7 to 14, if they wish to find out quickly why property rights and free markets matter for prosperity and innovation, what is essential to the functioning of business and government organizations and how institutional economics is applied to pressing policy issues. We urge impatient readers to revise the Key Concepts throughout the earlier chapters, which we have put in focus by placing them in framed 'boxes'.

•••

This book is a joint venture of two friends who began their academic careers as 'apprentices' in the same workshop in the mid-1960s as PhD students and associates of Prof. Herbert Giersch at Saarbrücken University, Germany and as staffers with the German Council of Economic Advisors. Over the past quarter century, our careers have taken us to far distant places and through differing experiences: the European and the East Asian-Australian life experience respectively. Yet, most of our conclusions, and the way in which we reshaped our basic philosophies and the economics we once learnt, moved along similar trajectories. It was therefore not all that hard to engage in the dialogue in which this joint textbook was developed, despite the fact that we probably had very different types of student before the eye of our imagination when conceiving the various chapters. We happily admit that writing this book was even fun!

The reader will learn that it is often useful to make value judgments about what is desirable and what is not, when discussing public policy. It behooves us therefore to declare explicitly up-front that we hold certain preferences, which some of our readers may not share or with which they clearly disagree. We place a high personal preference on individual freedom and see the individual as the ultimate reference point for all public policy. We do not attribute purposes separate from the individual to some abstract community such as 'the nation', or non-human phenomena like Nature. We also prefer growing prosperity to contentment with modest material achievement, and hold the view that justice and equity refer to formal rules about treating people in equal circumstances equally – not equal outcomes irrespective of one's effort or good luck.

It seems to us that one cannot help but take such a position when one observes the transformation of the economy and society in East Germany, where much of this book was first conceived and drafted. The material and moral outcomes of the alternative collectivist position, and of fuzzy institutional arrangements, become painfully evident when one shuttles between various countries and societies. This is also obvious when one compares the quality of life for the broad mass of people in developing countries with differing economic systems, or when one observes the climate in collectivist welfare states and in those regimes that are based primarily on self-reliance, responsibility and initiative. These conclusions of course reveal our personal preferences and value judgments.

Leaving our own value judgments aside, we should also note at the outset that institutions reflect specific values and are instrumental in their pursuit. Values therefore have to be identified and explored as part of institutional economics. This should enable us to arrive at scientific statements about values which may be assessed critically as to their consequences – as distinct from value judgments with which one might agree or disagree.

• • •

Since most of institutional economics depends on complex verbal reasoning and reference to diverse disciplines, the reader may find the book harder to follow than a standard text in mainstream economic theory, which relies on, by and large, simple mathematics. To make it easier for the reader not to lose the 'red thread', we employ several didactic devices:

- At the beginning of each chapter, there is a short 'Primer' to serve as an appetizer and to draw the reader's attention to the main issues and their relevance.
- At the end of each chapter, we invite the reader to review the material by posing a number of provocative questions. They are intended to help readers to check whether they have understood the most important elements of our argument.
- We highlight Key Concepts by placing them in 'boxes'. The intent is not to offer encyclopedic definitions but rather to ensure that the reader pays due attention to the key ideas which were developed in the preceding paragraphs and which constitute the major tools of institutional economics.

• • •

A book of this kind is built on the work of many scholars, not all of whom could ever be acknowledged by citing their work. Indeed, we owe much to intellectual giants who preceded us; and the only justification for attempting this work is that even a dwarf can see further when he stands on the shoulders of giants. In writing this book, we ran up a particularly heavy debt to one class of scholars whom we did not quote sufficiently: the many analysts – past and present – of the German economic tradition who paid more attention to institutions than mainstream Anglo-Saxon economists. The great masters of the past have of course been translated into English and can be cited. But German economics offers a sophisticated and differentiated strand of modern institutional economics whose findings and subtleties have not, as yet, been fully received on the global academic stage. We exploited our comparative and absolute advantages of being able to read German, but did not assume that our average reader would have access to German sources and decided not to make our full academic debts explicit by citing much of the German-language literature.[2]

A particular word of thanks goes to the *Foundation for Economic Education* in New York for permitting us to reprint Leonard Read's classic piece on the division of labour and knowledge, "I, Pencil", which is reproduced in the Appendix.

For a part of the time spent on drafting this book, Wolfgang Kasper benefited from a special studies programme of his employer, the *University of New South Wales*, which freed him from lecturing and administrative routines and gave him a travel grant. On two occasions, he enjoyed the hospitality of the new *Max-Planck-Institute for Research into Economic Systems* at Jena, Germany, where much of this book was conceived and developed. Both authors owe a debt of gratitude to all those scholars at the Institute who took an active interest in the project, in particular Daniel Kiwit, Stefan Voigt, Oliver Volkart, Antje Mangels and Michael Wohlgemuth. The latter two gave generously of their time and knowledge when they commented in detail on an earlier draft. Anna Kasper in Sydney, Mathias Drehmann in London and John W. Wood at Lincoln University in New Zealand also contributed useful comments and criticism. We also owe thanks to Prof. Fred Foldvary of the Kennedy School of Business in California for critical comments on an earlier draft. On a more practical level, this book owes much to Mrs. Uta Lange in Jena and in particular Mrs. Firzia Pepper in Canberra who assisted ably and with great dedication in the production of the manuscript.

The major theme pervading this book is that human knowledge is limited, as is, of course, our own knowledge. We therefore accept the usual responsibility for all remaining oversights, mistakes and misinterpretations.

We hope that the reader will enjoy the book and adopt the novel way of looking at life from the angle of economic and social institutions.

Wolfgang Kasper and Manfred E. Streit
Canberra and Jena, February 1998

Note on language:

'Liberal' and 'liberalism' are used throughout in their original sense, namely implying freedom of information, thought, association movement, exchange and so on, rather than the North American sense of 'redistributive-interventionist'.

NOTES

1 Throughout the book, we shall use the term 'institutional economics'. In the 1960s and 1970s, when the importance of institutions for economic analysis was rediscovered by a growing number of authors, the term "new institutional economics" was used to differentiate these modern efforts from the earlier, normally much more descriptive treatment of institutions, both by the German 'historical school' and the American institutionalists in the late nineteenth and early twentieth century.

2 Readers with access to German are, in the first instance, referred to the journal *ORDO*, which has, over the decades, been the main market place for German *ordo* liberal writing.

In addition to Streit (1991 and 1995, cited in the Bibliography), the following books would have been cited repeatedly, had our book been written for German speakers: W. Eucken (1952/90), *Grundsätze der Wirtschaftspolitik*, Tübingen: Mohr-Siebeck; F. Böhm (1980), *Freiheit und Ordnung in der Marktwirtschaft*, edited by E.-J. Mestmäcker, Baden-Baden: Nomos; E. Streißler and C. Watrin (eds) (1980), *Zur Theorie marktwirtschaftlicher Ordnungen*, Tübingen: Mohr-Siebeck; W. Stützel, Ch. Watrin, H. Willgerodt, ND K. Hohmann (eds) (1981): *Grundtexte der Sozialen Marktwirtschaft*, Stuttgart–New York: Fischer; V. Vanberg (1982), *Markt und Organisation*, Tübingen: Mohr-Siebeck; A. Schüller (ed.) (1983), *Property Rights und ökonomische Theorie*, München: Vahlen; D. Cassel, B.J. Ramb, and H.J. Thieme (eds) (1988), *Ordnungspolitik*, München: Vahlen; G. Radnitzky and H. Bouillon (eds) (1991), *Ordnungstheorie und Ordnungspolitik*, Berlin, Heidelberg, New York: Springer; E.-J. Mestmäcker (1993), *Recht in der offenen Gesellschaft*, Baden-Baden: Nomos.

1

Introduction: why institutions matter

People cannot survive, let alone thrive for long without interacting with their fellows. And they cannot work together without a degree of predictability. Individual actions become more predictable when people are bound by enforceable rules (which we shall call institutions). Indeed, the type and quality of institutions make a decisive difference in how well members of a community are able to satisfy their economic aspirations and improve their economic condition. In other words, institutions significantly determine how fast living standards grow.

Beginning with an empirical dimension, one can see the unprecedented record of global economic growth and the role institutions have played in it. During the second half of the twentieth century, real per-capita incomes have grown faster and the experience of rising living standards has reached more people on earth than ever before. Unfortunately, the experience of rising living standards was far from uniform. While some societies managed to realize rapid growth, others grew at a constant low rate for hundreds of years. One might ask for an explanation of the differences, for example, between the fast growth in East Asia and the slow growth (or even decline) in Africa and the former Socialist bloc: Why did people in fast-developing economies marshal resources more successfully, and why were they more enterprising in grasping economic opportunities? This is one of the first questions economists asked: Why have some countries become rich and others stayed poor?

A brief survey of theories of economic growth will show that economic growth is a complex phenomenon. Standard neoclassical theory could only identify proximate conditions of growth, such as capital accumulation and the growth of the labour force. To really understand *why* people save, invest, learn and search for useful knowledge, we have to look at the different institutions and value systems behind the successes and failures. We will also see that while some institutions erect barriers to growth, other 'rules of the game' help in motivating people to overcome existing obstacles to material betterment.

Man's behavior in the market relationship, reflecting the propensity to truck and barter, and the manifold variations . . . that this relationship can take; these are the proper subjects for the economist's study.

James Buchanan, 'What Should Economists Do?' (1964)

[After having deposited a considerable sum of money in a bank in a foreign country:] It hit me that I'd handed over my [funds] to a total stranger in a bank I knew nothing about in a city where I knew almost nobody . . . in exchange for nothing but a flimsy paper with a scribble in a language I didn't understand. What I had going for me, I reflected . . . was a great web of trust in the honesty of business. It struck me with awe how much that we take for granted in business transactions suspends from that gossamer web.

Jane Jacobs, *Systems of Survival* (1992)

Economic growth will occur if property rights make it worthwhile to undertake socially productive activity. . . . Governments take over the protection and enforcement of property rights because they can do it at a lower cost than private volunteer groups. However, the . . . needs of government may induce the protection of certain property rights which hinder rather than promote growth; therefore we have no guarantee that productive institutional arrangements will emerge.

Douglass C. North and Robert P. Thomas, *The Rise of the Western World* (1973)

When measured by decades, the economy is always in upheaval. For the past few hundred years, every generation has found more efficient ways of getting work done, and the cumulative benefits have been enormous. The average person today enjoys a much better life than the nobility did a few centuries ago. It would be great to have a king's land, but what about his lice?

Bill Gates, *The Road Ahead* (1993)

1.1 Why do institutions matter?

The reader may wish to learn up-front what is meant by 'institutional economics', and the two constituent elements: 'economics' and 'institution'.

Economics is the field of study that deals with the fundamental fact that humanity has to live with scarcity; individuals tend to have unlimited wants, but limited means for satisfying those wants. Scarcity has nothing to do with material wealth per se. Even Bill Gates copes with scarcity every day as he makes choices. Scarcity necessitates choice, and choice entails the economic meaning of cost – the highest foregone alternative in making a choice. In other words, all decisions involve trade-offs and decision makers in all settings require various aids to help negotiate those trade-offs. The aids to human actors in their effort to negotiate the complex trade-offs of life come in a variety of forms in a political, social and economic context. Within the market economy we speak of the incentives of profits and losses in using private property, the information of prices, and the innovations that are spurred on by the lure of expected profit (as well as the disciplinary feedback of loss). In democratic politics, the currency of the realm is votes and the exchange is largely over public policies, while in society the currency of the realm is trust and reputation, and the exchange often relates to community status and the network of friendships and connections that enable us to negotiate trade-offs and come to live better together (Heyne et al., 2012).

When economists speak of resources, they refer not only to natural resources (land, water, climate, minerals) but also to all scarce ingredients that are needed to produce the goods and services that we want. Both labour and capital are important resources; capital goods are tangible things that one may call the 'hardware of the economy'. Implements, machinery, buildings, and infrastructures make labour more productive but frequently require skills, or *human* capital, to be operated properly. In addition, a lot of technical and organizational knowledge is either built into or needed to manage the capital goods. It is also important to know how flexible the structural composition of the capital stock and the skill base is: rigid structures lend themselves to less adaptation when wants and other resources change than flexible ones. Economists sometimes refer to knowledge and structural flexibility as 'third production factors', that is, factors (or resources) other than labour and capital.

The various resources are combined in production processes, which can be compared to what happens in a kitchen: ingredients are mixed together and exposed to energy by someone who – one hopes – has the required knowledge. Knowledge is the key to the culinary outcomes.

But neither a meal, nor other goods and services come about automatically. This requires entrepreneurs; people with energy and vision to initiate the production process, tap into the available resources, and find additional ones. Entrepreneurs often imagine and then implement new ways of combining the ingredients; they also often try to stimulate human wants (by advertizing, for example) and try out new methods of production and new products (innovation).

Producing all those countless, diverse goods and services that people want in different places and at different times is an unimaginably complex task. Even a simple department store stocks 50,000 different items, in different sizes and colours. And to put an airliner into service, there are tens of thousands of components that thousands of different people have to design, produce, and transport to where these components are needed. Even producing a simple pencil requires the cooperation of countless people who never meet or know each other (see Appendix "I, Pencil").

Enterprising people are not engaging in all these complicated and costly actions simply because of their enterprising nature. They have to be motivated. Coordinating millions of partly ignorant people, who often struggle to find out pertinent facts, to do what millions of others want is unimaginably complex – and all these activities must ceaselessly adjust to changing circumstances (*idem*).

This is where institutions come in: institutions – customs, laws, and the like – are known, enforceable rules of behaviour that come with penalties for not obeying the rules of the game (called sanctions). Institutions can make the actions of individuals more predictable and help enormously with the difficult coordination problem. In particular, institutions help in situations where enterprising people try out new factor combinations, new products or new ways of producing existing products.

It is the mission of this book to explore the role and effects of various types of institutions on people's economic behaviour – what they produce and what they want to consume.

•••

Humans are social beings. To survive and thrive for any length of time they must interact with their fellows. However, one person cannot interact with another without some shared understanding about how the other will respond and be sanctioned for responding arbitrarily or contrary to previous agreement. Individuals and businesses can only buy, sell, employ labour, invest, and explore innovations if they can have some confidence that their expectations will be met.

Much of the exchange between individuals and firms is based on repetitive operations. We prefer these to be predictable because that reduces frictions and uncertainties. Just imagine, if your next bill at the check-out in the supermarket came to ten times what you paid for the same basket of goods on the last visit! Or if the bank where you deposited your savings suddenly refused to honour your cheque! Human interactions, including in economic life, depend on some sort of mutual trust that is based on an order facilitated by institutions that sanction unpredictable and opportunistic behaviour.

In our daily lives we interact with numerous people and organizations whom we scarcely know, but in whose predictable behaviour we place great faith. We hand over our hard-earned money to a teller clerk, whose face we may not remember five minutes later, in a bank, about whose reserves and management we know nothing. We allow ourselves to be operated upon by surgeons we have hardly met, in hospitals we had never seen from the inside before. We prepay for the delivery of a car made in a foreign country by workers we never meet. Yet, in all these situations, we trust that we will get worthwhile service and that promises made will be kept. Why? Because all these people are bound by constraints on their opportunistic temptations not to deliver or to short-change us we are able to assume that selfish breaches of the contracts we enter will incur sanctions of one sort or another.

Modern economic life therefore depends rather precariously on numerous written and unwritten rules. If they are widely violated – as in cases when society collapses after a lost war or during internal chaos – many of the human interactions that we depend on are no longer possible; living standards and the quality of life then plummet. The institutions that normally prevent this are therefore the very foundations on which our material wellbeing and sense of security are built.

KEY CONCEPTS

Economics is the study of how people who face scarcity satisfy their diverse wants by finding and testing useful knowledge. Scarcity results from the fact that people tend to increase their wants faster than they are able to increase their knowledge and other resources to satisfy them. Consequently, scarcity is a pervasive and prevalent trait of the human condition.

Institutions are rules of human interaction that constrain – possibly opportunistic and erratic – individual behaviour; they make the actions of others more predictable, thus facilitating the division of labour and knowledge and therefore wealth creation. Institutions, to be effective, always imply some kind of sanction for rule violations. The terms 'institution' and 'rule' will be used interchangeably in this book.

The institutional deficit in economics and public policy

The mainstream of twentieth century neoclassical economics has, by and large, assumed that institutions are exogenously given and that economic actors have perfectly adjusted to them. At best, it has treated institutions as a complication in economic modelling; at worst, economists strove to develop an institutionally antiseptic theory. The standard assumption of orthodox economics is that people transact business without frictions and transaction costs. In defence of this stance, it is argued that all theorizing is necessarily based on abstractions and that observers abstract from phenomena that do not matter to what they wish to analyse. The pre-occupation with equilibrium theorizing has thus resulted in an analytical focus on a frictionless end state, where economic forces have already done all their work.

However, this defence is wholly inappropriate. Institutions reduce the costs of coordinating human actions and therefore are of central importance to understanding human interaction. The frictions of everyday life require the work of economic forces to reconcile conflicts and coordinate economic activities. Economic life is about exchange and the institutions within which exchange takes place. The frictions of human existence give rise to institutions, which in turn produce patterns of predictable behaviour that lower the costs of coordination. We can demonstrate this either by plausible, everyday examples, or by showing that assuming institutions away has led to critical deficits in economic knowledge and misguided public policies.

At the level of everyday life, institutions already matter in the nursery: when children are given their toys as their own personal property, it can be observed that they take care and can be encouraged to be generous in lending their property to playmates. When, on the other hand, everything belongs to all of them and no one in particular, children tend to neglect their 'assets' and fight over the possession of specific toys (Alchian, in Henderson, 2008, p. 424). Another example that can show how an institution helps people obtain their goals more effectively is money. When people have to rely on barter to obtain the goods and services they want to consume but do not produce, they face narrow limits on what they are able to obtain, as well as uncertainty regarding what is attainable. Will they find a taker for the vegetables they have grown? Who wants to exchange these for the computer program they need? More importantly, they may not even find out what they are able or want to buy. If, on the other hand, there is an asset, which is generally accepted as a medium of exchange (one of the functions of money) and whose supply and uses are bound by institutions, people can have much greater confidence that they will be able to obtain what they desire. Their search and transaction costs are much lower than with barter. Money thus helps to economize on coordination costs.

Assuming institutions away 'for simplicity's sake' has also had important consequences for practical economic policy. Standard neoclassical mainstream economics has repeatedly failed in recent years to explain or predict real-world phenomena because it excluded institutions and the reasons for their existence from its models. The downfall of standard economics became evident in explaining the process of economic growth. Policy advice to developing countries was often misplaced, because economic advisors made the habitual assumption that institutions do not matter. Many of the imported development concepts foundered because the existing institutions in developing countries differed greatly from those being prescribed; in order for policy concepts to stick, the indigenous cultural institutions have to adapt to the new rules of the game or the imported concepts have to be adapted (for example Boettke et al., 2008; Boettke, 2012).

After the implosion of Soviet-style central planning, it also became clear that the core task in reviving economic and social life in the former Soviet bloc was to create appropriate institutions, including informal customs and habits of the population. The demise of socialism posed the challenge to create and foster such fundamental institutions as private property rights, contract law and the rule of law in general. The institutional framework, in which modern production and trade can flourish, must therefore not be taken for granted. Western economists trained in a tradition that does so are ill-prepared to diagnose why sustained growth does not materialize in certain places and civilizations and what might be done to remedy the situation (Olson, 1996).

Another way of making the same fundamental point about the importance of institutions is to draw attention to the high and rising share of coordination costs in the total cost of producing and distributing the national product in modern economies. A large part of the service sector – which now accounts for over two-thirds of the total economic product in affluent countries – is concerned with facilitating transactions and organizing human interaction. The 'coordination sector' of the modern economy is necessary to facilitate the growing division of labour and knowledge, on which high living standards are based. To assume, as orthodox neoclassical economics does, that transaction costs do not matter and hence that there is no need for rules to economize on them, pushes more than half of all productive endeavours in advanced economies aside – namely the large and rapidly growing segment of the service sector, which deals with transactions and coordination, for example legal and financial services, advice and design. By underrating the significance of the coordination problem, neoclassical economics thus biases the analysis towards physical production and distribution. The neoclassical approach therefore becomes less relevant for much of modern business, which is concerned with organizing and coordinating decisions of suppliers and buyers.

A similar blind spot of orthodox mainstream economics is the source of failure in diagnosing why the heavily administered welfare states experience slow growth, high unemployment, growing distrust, and widespread voter cynicism. The gradual erosion and decay of essential institutions (such as reliable property rights, self-responsibility and the rule of law) in lobby-dominated democracies has often gone unnoticed. Ways to reform were not readily discovered, as institutional reform was not part of what most economists analyse.

Economic historians discovered long ago that institutional change is an important and exciting part of their discipline (Gibbon, 1996/1776–88). Nobel Prize winner and economic historian Douglass North put it well in the 1990s when he wrote: "the neoclassical paradigm is devoid of institutions . . . The currently fashionable growth models of economists do not confront the issue of the underlying incentive structure that is assumed in their models. These lacunae in our understanding have been forcefully brought to the attention of economists by the events in Central and Eastern Europe . . . where the challenge is to restructure the economies . . . in order to create a hospitable environment for economic growth. Can that restructuring be done without deliberate attention to institutions? Delineating the institutional characteristics of such markets is a first step in answering these questions" (North, 1994, p. 257; also see North in Drobak and Nye, 1997, pp. 3–12).

It has also become clear that standard economic theory is only of very limited value to business economics. Many practitioners of business rightly find economic theorizing barren, abstract and of little relevance to their pursuits. Moreover, economic models that leave no room for the costs and possible mishaps in coordination automatically eliminate jurisprudence and lawyers from the field of investigation. As a result, many law faculties around the world have dropped economics from their syllabuses, to the detriment of the discipline. The lack of studying costs and problems with coordination in mainstream models explains why some of the recent revival in institutional economics has originated in the study of business history, economic sociology, the 'new organization science' and 'law and economics'. These disciplines have explicitly incorporated institutions into their models to offer more realistic analyses and advice.

The renaissance of institutional economics

Because of mounting dissatisfaction with standard economics and its abstract, torrid models, many scholars are now (again) taking up the central proposition of institutional economics: institutions play a crucial part in stabilizing expectations and thus helping the coordination of individual decision makers. The analysis of the foundations, evolution, content, consistency and enforcement of rules can tell us a lot about central economic phenomena, such as economic growth or how markets function. It is now being increasingly realized that institutions constitute critical social capital – they are, so to speak, the 'software' that channels the interaction of people and the development of society. Indeed, we are finding ever so often that the software is normally more important than the 'hardware' – tangible phenomena, such as natural resources and physical capital.

As a consequence of these insights, the interest in institutional economics has been growing since the 1970s. Fewer economists now focus merely on the conditions of allocation of *given* resources to satisfy *given* wants (though numerous university courses still are built on this unrealistic assumption). As we shall see in Chapter 2, institutional economics does not take resources or human wants as given, but rather focuses on the discovery and utilization of new wants and new resources.

1.2　The record of economic growth

The long-term view

Since institutions are critical to economic growth, we will, in the remainder of this chapter, show that the extraordinary economic growth experience over the past two generations cannot be satisfactorily explained without an understanding of institutions.

It is important to keep in mind throughout this discussion that growth rates are merely an imperfect proxy for a variety of measures of human wellbeing, such as life-expectancy, educational access, environmental quality, and personal liberties. The *Economic Freedom of the World* project run by James Gwartney and Robert Lawson has demonstrated that – though we cannot 'eat growth rates' – institutions guaranteeing economic freedom are highly and positively correlated with per capita income and the "good things" in life, such as health, longevity, life satisfaction and so on. (Gwartney and Lawson, *passim*). Our task is to analytically explain the mechanisms underlying these correlations.

The first step in explaining the simple mechanics of long-term economic development is to recognize that the only way to increase real income of a community is to increase the real productivity of its people. Increasing real productivity is a consequence of improvements in physical capital (better machines), human capital (better learning capacity), and the rules of the game under which human actors interact with one another as well as with nature. The countries that grow rich are those where increases in real productivity takes place, while those that languish behind do so because no matter how much foreign aid they receive, real productivity does not improve.

Until not so long ago, mankind's long-term economic experience has been characterized by very slow or non-existent progress in productivity and living standards. Population growth normally matched technical and economic advances, so that average living standards remained almost stationary over many centuries. Basic material living conditions (such as longevity, basic health, child mortality, the incidence of famine and major epidemics) did not change much for the average citizen between the neolithic revolution, which heralded the beginning of agriculture and animal husbandry nearly 12,000 years ago, and the seventeenth century, when the industrial revolution began in Western Europe (Kahn, 1979, pp. 7–25; Rostow, 1978). European peasants lived with the reality of cold, grime, hunger, disease and early death almost to the same extent as their forefathers had in Roman times; and the average Chinese peasant in the first half of the twentieth century was hardly any better off than his forebears during the Han dynasty 2000 years earlier. Historians often focus on the rulers and the few rich, but remind us infrequently of the living conditions of the average man or woman.[1]

We have to remind ourselves of the long-term economic experience of mankind in order to appreciate the more recent growth revolution and see how growth-facilitating institutions have been central to the rise and spread of sustained prosperity. First, England, then Northwest Europe and North America witnessed sustained rises in the living standards of the *average* citizen. This process began in the eighteenth century and gathered steam during the nineteenth: three countries – Britain, the US and Germany – were then producing two-thirds of the world's manufactured output. During the nineteenth century, one country after the other embarked on industrialization and sustained economic growth. Towards the end of the nineteenth century and in the first half of the twentieth, per-capita incomes in the countries now known as OECD countries, that is, the old industrial countries with essentially capitalist market economies, grew on average at an unprecedented 1.4 per cent annually, despite the destructions of two world wars during the first half of the twentieth century (Table 1.1). As the twentieth turned into the twenty-first century, the growth experience had become common throughout most of East Asia and was spreading in Latin America, South Asia, and even in parts of Africa and the Middle East. Major economies, such as China, India and Brazil, now seem set to catch up with the West, offering the old industrial countries new competition and new markets. There is much scope for catching up with the most productive parts of the world economy, since the most productive one-fifth of the world population is – according to the International Monetary Fund – still producing four fifths of measured world output (gross world product).

Table 1.1 Modern economic growth – Per-capita income adjusted for inflation, in % p.a.

Period	Old industrial countries (OECD)	Less developed countries
Up to early 19th century	Virtual stagnation (some takeoff)	Virtual stagnation
1820–1870	+0.6	Virtual stagnation
1870–1913	+1.4	Virtual stagnation
1913–1950	+1.3	(some take off)
1950–1973	+3.5	2.7 (great divergence)
1973–present	+2.2	+2.9 (great divergence)

Source: Maddison, 2001, 2007, own updates.

At the end of the Second World War, many observers depicted the growth record of the nineteenth and early twentieth centuries as a passing phenomenon and predicted secular stagnation. They were wrong. Not only did average per-capita incomes in OECD countries rise by an unprecedented annual average of 3½ per cent from 1950 to the onset of the oil crisis of 1973, but economic growth also began to spread to the rest of the world. Before 1950, only a few industrial centres had existed outside the West (for example in Japan or Shanghai). Now, modern methods of production were adopted in numerous new locations; trade and investment flows between the old and new industrial locations intensified (globalization).

Between 1950 and 1973, the amorphous group of developing countries recorded an unprecedented average annual growth rate of 2¾ per cent. A subgroup, the 'new industrial economies' of East Asia, grew much faster, attracting producers from rich countries and capturing world markets for their exports. In the process, they narrowed the gap to Western standards of technology, productivity and income in record time (World Bank, 1993; Kasper, 1994). After the oil crisis of 1973, global economic growth slowed a little, to 2½ per cent per annum on average in the old industrial countries (OECD), but it accelerated in other places, most notably China. In the East Asia-Pacific economies, where society and governments placed a high priority on material progress, average real per-capita incomes have risen from a very low level at the end of the First World War to 2010 at a breath-taking pace. Within less than two generations, East Asians have, on average, achieved a 12- to 15-fold rise in real per-capita incomes, even if some doubt remains about the quality of official income statistics. Such a dynamic growth experience, affecting nearly 2 billion people, is unprecedented in human history!

If one can make long-term comparisons of living standards, as economic historians have long tried to do (Rostow, 1978; Maddison, 1995; 2001; 2007), one has to conclude that present-day living standards in India have surpassed those in Britain after the Napoleonic wars, and that average living standards in China in 2010 compare with US American income levels after the First World War. The average inhabitant of the most dynamic East-Asian market economies (the city states of Hong Kong and Singapore, as well as Taiwan) now enjoys a living standard comparable to, or even higher than the average West European.

Demographic transition

The rise in living standards went along with an unprecedented rise in world population. When modern industry first started in England (around 1750), the total world population stood at an estimated 790 million. Whereas the number of people on earth is estimated to have risen by 68 per cent during the nineteenth century, it went up by no less than a further 370 per cent during the twentieth (Rostow, 1978, pp. 1–44). By late 2011, there were 7 billion people on earth.

Historically, human life expectancy was short. For example, women in France in the 1740s could expect to live only about 25 years. Now, the average life span of French women is 81 years. This has much to do with economic growth. It ended the ever-present threat of starvation (there had been 16 general famines in France in the eighteenth century alone) and enhanced medical resources (in eighteenth century London, 10 per cent of all deaths were from smallpox, a disease that was defeated completely by general vaccination). About one quarter of children born in pre-Revolution Paris were abandoned by their mothers, and childbirth was an unbelievably dangerous event for mother and child. Ordinary people's diets were monotonous and unbalanced. When living standards rose, the gains were often channelled into better health care, famine relief and improved nutrition, so that fewer people died early (Clark, 2007). After the onset of economic development, mortality rates dropped rapidly in one country after another, whereas birth rates declined with a lag and more gradually, leading to a temporary population explosion. This phenomenon is called 'demographic transition'.

Likewise, the rapid rise in living standards in the Asia-Pacific region since 1960 was accompanied by rapid decreases in mortality rates. Thus, on average of the 1 75 billion population of this region, infant mortality dropped from 77 per thousand in 1970 to 40 per thousand in 1995 (World Bank, 1997, p. 225). This is typical; human life expectancy has invariably risen with living standards. Economic growth has increased human life spans, a fact that can be illustrated both by data from the US, which run parallel to experiences in many other now affluent countries.

	1913	2010
Income level (in constant US$, per capita)	100	597
Average life expectancy (years)	59	78.3

... as well as with more recent data from China:

	1970	2010
Income level (in constant US$, per capita)	100	850
Average life expectancy (men and women, years)	59	73

Sources: Maddison (2007), World Bank, UN.

The rapid acceleration in population growth tends to subside with continuing economic growth, better education and rising material aspirations (Freeman and Berelson, 1974, pp. 36–37; Kahn, 1979). Indeed, the transition to slower population growth comes with a 'demographic prosperity bonus': the share of working-age people in the population goes up (fewer dependents, both under-age and of retirement age), so that economic growth is likely to accelerate.

The most remarkable aspect of the global economic experience in the twentieth century has been that most of the rapidly increasing numbers of people on earth are better fed, clad, housed, educated, and entertained than their forebears (Ridley, 2010). In fewer and fewer areas, the long-term human experience of dire misery persists or material living conditions are deteriorating. This is, however, unfortunately still the case in parts of South Asia, Africa and some of the formerly centrally planned economies.

The secular and global shift from stagnation to growth during the twentieth century has of course not created Utopia on earth. However – in most places and for most of the time – higher income levels have proven to be compatible with the other fundamental values to which people aspire, such as freedom, justice and security (Chapter 4).

KEY CONCEPTS

Economic growth is measured by a sustained rise of the per capita *flow* of valued goods and services in real terms, that is, after elimination of the effects of inflation. When allowances are made for international differences in purchasing power, we obtain ➡

⬅

per-capita incomes at purchasing-power parity (GDP [PPP] per capita).

Some economists have argued for making allowances for other factors, such as environmental amenity or the assumed exhaustion of a *stock* of natural resources. The GDP measure deals with flows of production, incomes and expenditures in a given period, and not with a stock of assets at a given point in time. Therefore, valuations of the stock of environmental assets are not included. Besides, the measurement difficulties are so intractable that per-capita income (or per capita gross domestic product) is the most widely used measure of growth.

The term **demographic transition** refers to the temporary acceleration of population growth that occurs after take-off into sustained economic growth. It results from the coincidence of a fairly prompt drop in death rates and a lagged fall in birth rates.

Some country experiences

The global growth experience, sketched so far, was far from uniform. On the whole, countries that were ahead at the beginning of the twentieth century – the USA, Great Britain, and Australia – still rank amongst the world's most wealthy nations: Indeed, the societies that were most affluent and productive in 1820 managed to achieve the steepest increase in living standards during the nineteenth century. Many of the countries that were poorest nearly 200 years ago are still at the bottom of the income pyramid.

In Figure 1.1, we depict the rise in real living standards (per-capita incomes adjusted for inflation and international price differences) for a number of major regions and a few selected countries.[2] It can be seen that:

- Two thousand years ago, even 500 years ago, there was a high degree of equality around the world: everyone was equally poor; even relatively well-off Europeans and Mid-Easterners lived below the present-day income levels of average Bangladeshis and were probably as poor as the inhabitants of the poorest African countries today;
- from the European Renaissance onwards (ca. 1500AD), people living in Western European civilization, first Holland (not shown) and the United Kingdom, experienced massive and sustained improvements in material living conditions; as always, when growth takes off, inequality increased;
- overseas off-shoots of Western civilization, most notably the United States and Australia (not shown in Fig. 1.1), attained even higher living standards, although the Latin American countries, which had made an early growth start, fell back during the nineteenth century;

Figure 1.1 World economic growth

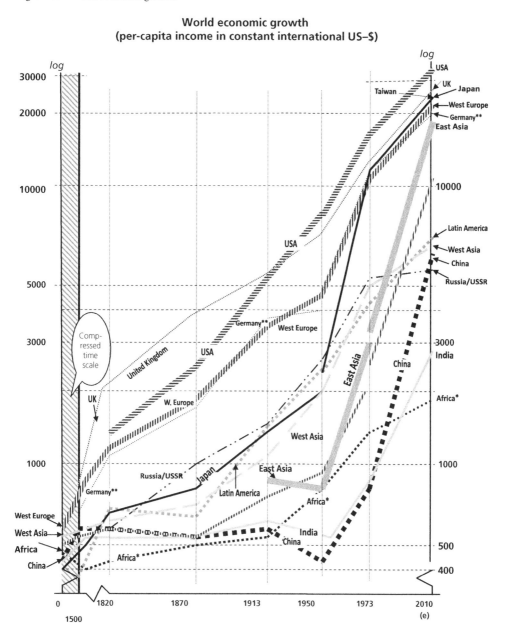

**World economic growth
(per-capita income in constant international US–$)**

*Africa south of the Sahara. **1950 and 1973: West Germany

Note: Logarithmic scales, as used here, show a steady rate of growth as a straight line and an acceleration as a gradient. The steeper the gradient, the faster the growth.

Source: Maddison, (2007) updated by authors.

- during the first half of the twentieth century, the Western leaders kept growing, although west Europeans, most notably the Germans, suffered set-backs during the 'long war of 1914–1945'; the Soviet Union closed the gap, although it still remained far behind;
- after 1950, remarkable things happened first in Japan (already the Asian growth leader at the time) and the small East Asian economies along communist China's fringe, who became the 'economic growth tigers' (see South Korea and Taiwan in Figure 1.1), the most productive and ambitious of which have by now caught up with the West; more recently, China joined this growth league;
- even regions that have stayed behind (South Asia, West Asia and even Africa) have by now been swept up in the global growth experience; and
- the former USSR experienced an absolute decline in real living standards after the 1980s, although many parts have more recently re-embarked on economic growth.

These fundamental economic facts require an explanation. Why did sustained economic growth begin in the West, in particular the Anglo-Saxon countries? Why, for example, did living standards in China and India stagnate for some four centuries after 1500 and decline in absolute terms during the first half of the twentieth century? Why did the 'Confucian East' begin to catch up from the 1960s onwards? Why were others left behind? Are growth conditions now changing for the better in all countries on earth?

In some cases, the consequences and answers seem obvious. For example, Russian per-capita incomes were estimated by the World Bank to have fallen by 40 per cent between 1985 and 1995, before new growth impulses took over (World Bank, 1997, p. 215). This has had deleterious social consequences, for example on life spans and health. To cite but one example, the incidence of diphtheria cases, negligible in Russia in the 1980s, rose to about 50,000 in the early 1990s. The answer to the question why obviously lies in the fact that the old, though deficient set of institutions (coercive central planning) was jettisoned, but new, better rules were not invented and enforced quickly enough (for more on the transition problems, see Chapter 13).

The uneven, fickle economic growth record goes to show that economic growth is far from automatic. The conditions of economic growth need to be cultivated.

Economic stagnation and decline, it would seem on a priori grounds, are associated with closed economies, civil and international strife, disruptive changes to economic systems, and heavy constraints on private initiative and ownership (lack of liberty), whereas fast, sustained growth is associated with secure property rights, competition, openness and economic freedom (Chapter 14; Gwartney and Lawson, *passim*; Lawson, 2008). This hypothesis deserves detailed exploration and explanation.

More generally, the question arises what 'explains' economic growth, which is the long-term economic concern that towers over all others.

1.3   Explaining economic growth

The mobilization of production factors

When economists tried to explain the remarkable record of sustained growth in productivity and incomes, they discovered more and more explanatory factors for this complex phenomenon.

In the 1940s and 1950s, economists emphasized the importance of mobilizing capital (K) for long-term growth, assuming that growth depended on capital accumulation (savings and net investment).

Central factor of growth: K

In modern economies, capital accumulation requires two separate acts by (normally) different people: (a) the postponement of consumption from current income, the 'savings sacrifice', and (b) the borrowing of such savings by enterprises coupled with the acquisition of productive machinery, buildings and other items of physical capital (investment). The process of capital formation has often been depicted as potentially unstable (Harrod-Domar theory).

Many economists of the 1940s and 1950s, such as British star economist John Maynard Keynes, considered growth a temporary phenomenon, because they assumed that growing amounts of capital would lead to a declining marginal productivity of capital. In that respect, they echoed the nineteenth century prediction by Karl Marx (1818–1883), who forecast the eventual downfall of the capitalist system because investors would sooner or later run out of ideas for profitable uses of capital; the rate of return on capital would drop and the capitalist system would then collapse. As we now know, Marx was completely wrong.

In the 1950s, the economics profession became uncomfortable with the narrow focus on capital as an explanation of the growth process. This happened at a time when growth in the developed countries resumed vigorously. Economists now drew on the notion of a national production function, a relationship in which inputs such as capital, labour (L) and technology (TEC), are related to predictable amounts of output. Nineteenth century theories, which had asserted that population growth has a key influence on economic growth, were now also revived and related to the growth of the labour force.

The rapid growth of labour supply was normally seen as a positive influence on economic growth. All inputs of production factors were assumed to have positive, but decreasing returns to scale (Solow, 1988, summarizes earlier writings by himself and others on this type of theory):

Central factors of growth: K, L, TEC

This 'neoclassical growth theory' had the advantage of demonstrating that the growth process need not be unstable or run inevitably into declining rates of increase, as Marx had asserted. By introducing the notion of growing technical knowledge, economists also changed thinking about growth from a focus on things (hardware) to a focus on ideas (software) (Schumpeter, 1908/1961; Scherer, 1984; Romer, 1990; 2008, pp. 129–130; Jones and Romer, 2010). Technically speaking, economists no longer thought in terms of a *given* production function, but realized that better technology shifted the production function upwards. This means that better technology, for example, enables given inputs of capital and labour to be translated into more output. The theory also allowed for the obvious fact that factor prices can change – for example when growing capital surpluses reduce capital interest rates. This induces factor substitution: cheaper capital can, for example, be used in greater proportions to save on expensive labour. Such labour-capital substitution of course requires changing technologies and free markets. Indeed, from the 1960s, technical innovation became one of the focal interests of researchers when they explored the reasons for economic growth.

The hardware and the software of growth

That quest received a further boost in the 1960s when economists began to stress the important influence of better education and skill acquisition (SK) – processes that add to what has come to be known as 'human capital', that is, knowledge, skills, and habits (Bauer, 1957; Becker, 1964).

Central factors of growth: K, L, TEC, SK

This line of inquiry underlined the insight that better technical knowledge and better skills were needed to ensure that growing capital stocks are used more productively. It soon became apparent that improvements in the 'software of development' (skills, technical and organizational knowledge) ensured the better efficiency of the 'hardware of development' (labour, capital). More recently, Paul Romer has highlighted the importance of *'meta* ideas', concepts that facilitate the production and application of useful knowledge (Romer, 1990; 2008). Examples for such *meta* ideas are the German and later American research universities, industrial research laboratories and agricultural extension services as invented in Australia and the United States, and the concept of free-market think tanks invented in various Anglo-Saxon countries from the 1940s and 1950s onwards.

During the 1960s and since, other observers emphasized the contribution of natural resources to growth and pointed to a possible eventual exhaustion of some natural resources [NR] (Club of Rome, see Meadows et al., 1972). They echoed the theories of Robert Malthus, who had (wrongly) predicted in the late eighteenth century that mankind was condemned to perpetual poverty because of limited natural resources. Around the turn of the millennium, concerns about climate change led to renewed assertions that economic growth has limits, so that the freedom to use natural resources, in particular fossil-fuel energy, ought to be politically controlled. Yet, economists with an understanding of knowhow and technology held the optimistic view that rising scarcity prices for some natural resources would, yet again, mobilize new knowledge of how to obtain more such resources or how to economize on available resources. This will open new avenues of growth (Hahn and Matthews, 1969; Beckerman, 1974; Matthews, 1986; Simon, 1995; Kasper, 2005a, 2007; Klaus, 2008; Ridley, 2010).

More recently, cultural pessimists have seized on aspects of natural resource scarcity to cast doubt on the desirability of economic growth and the possibility that all of mankind can attain high levels of material comfort and a high life expectancy. They maintain that one consequence of spreading wealth is a rise in unwanted by-products, most notably higher emissions from the consumption of energy, which is central to enhancing productivity, leisure and human wellbeing (IPCC, *passim*). Although much of this debate lies beyond the scope of this book, we will have to ask whether better institutions can assist in attenuating feared climate change, whether natural or man-made – and if not, what consequences this has for the quality of time-tested institutions.

To return to the history of growth explanations, which economic analysts have offered: statistical data for the 'software factors' were hard to get. But it was shown in many quantitative analyses of economic growth (based on the assumption of a neoclassical production function and competitive markets) that these factors were indeed very important. Often, half or more of the measured rise in living standards could be plausibly attributed to 'third factors', that is, inputs other than labour and capital (Denison, 1967). In particular, it was found that the differences between slow- and fast-growing economies could often be explained by such 'third factors' (Denison, 1967; Abramovitz, 1979; Barro and Sala-I-Martin, 1995, pp. 414–461).

However, while offering a useful quantitative perception for what mattered to the long-term growth performance, the analysis did not really explain why certain societies accumulated more physical and human capital than others. All the above-mentioned analyses offered only proximate explanations of growth. One still could not tell *why* people save and invest, exploit natural resources, acquire skills, innovate or fail to do so (Hahn and Matthews, 1969; Giersch (ed.), 1980; Harberger, 1984).

Other economists who analysed economic growth in old and new industrial countries focused on an observation already made in the 1930s, namely that the structural composition of economic activity changes systematically with rising income levels. In particular, manufacturing was the 'engine of growth' over a certain range of incomes, growing faster than the economy as a whole (Syrquin, 1988; Rostow, 1978). At high income levels, services tend to grow disproportionately fast. Thus, it was observed that different types of industries flourished at different income levels. Labour-intensive industries have the growth edge when incomes (and wages) are low, and more capital- and skill-intensive industries when incomes rise. The structural composition of the national product highlighted the fact that, behind the summary, macro-economic phenomenon of growth, there are in reality organically evolving microeconomic structures, which are being transformed all the time. Economies with a high degree of price flexibility and high factor mobility tended to grow faster than rigid economies (Chenery and Syrquin, 1975; Chenery et al., 1986; Kasper, 1982, pp. 71–96; Howitt, 2006). The economy was seen as a living organism, whose proportions – like those of a tree or a human body – change systematically during the growth process. Structural change [ΔSTR] therefore is part and parcel of the growth process and artificial structural rigidities (for example when governments subsidize declining industries to stop their natural shrinkage) are an impediment to overall economic growth:

> **Central phenomena of growth: K, L, TEC, SK, NR, ΔSTR**

It was thus found that political choices often do much to rigidify economic structures, both in less developed countries (where established interest groups might rule) and developed, democratic economies (where lobbies and self-seeking power groups might collude with politicians and bureaucrats to resist structural adjustment to new conditions).

Enterprise, knowledge and institutions

This microeconomic focus blended well with a renewed and more sophisticated focus on the central role of knowledge: How is new, useful knowledge best found, tested and applied? What motivates the agents of that process – the entrepreneurs [E] – to mobilize production factors, to risk innovative uses of knowledge and to try out structural changes?

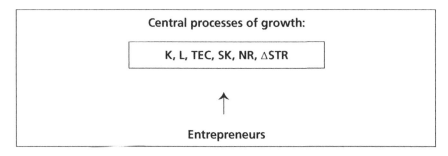

Central processes of growth:

K, L, TEC, SK, NR, ΔSTR

↑

Entrepreneurs

In the 1970s, economic theorists drew on work done in the first half of the century by writers such as Joseph Schumpeter (1883-1950) and the Austrian school of economics (Ludwig von Mises, 1881-1973*; Friedrich August Hayek, 1899-1992). These writers studied the role of the entrepreneur in economic progress and the importance of competition as a discovery procedure for useful human knowledge (Hayek, 1937; 1945; 1978b; Kirzner, 1960; 1963; 1973; 1985; 1997; Kilby (ed.), 1971; Machlup, 1981-84; Blandy et al., 1985). They held that the evolution of knowledge, technology, and the economy was driven by risk-taking agents of knowledge discovery – but only

---

* We plead to pronounce his name as 'Meeses".

if they faced a material incentive to be on the alert and to innovate and if they were exposed to the ongoing challenge of competition.

Knowledge can only be exploited and multiplied if people with specialist knowledge cooperate. A better division of labour – which is in reality a division and coordination of knowledge – is thus the real source of economic progress. This insight is not new. Scottish economist-philosopher Adam Smith wrote over 200 years ago: "It is the great multiplication of the productions of all the different arts in consequence of the division of labour which occasions, in a well-governed society, that universal opulence which extends itself to the lowest ranks of the people" (Smith, 1776/1976, p. 10).

Since the mid-1970s, the quest for explaining economic growth has also received considerable impulses from long-term economic history (North and Thomas, 1973, 1977; North, 1992; Jones, 1981/2003; 1988; Rosenberg and Birdzell, 1986; Hodgson, 1988; Bernholz et al., 1998; Mokyr, 2004; Clark, 2007). These analyses showed why great advances in technical and organizational knowledge had been made in the industrial revolution. These advances did not come about suddenly, but depended crucially on the gradual evolution of institutions favourable to capital accumulation and exchange in markets (individual civil liberties; property rights; effective protection of contracts under the law; limited government). They demonstrated that capitalist entrepreneurs had not been able to produce sustained economic growth where there was no trust. Entrepreneurship flourished under economic, civil and political liberties, as well as under favourable institutional frameworks that underpin mutual trust and view individual entrepreneurship in a positive light (Nelson and Winter, 1982; Scully, 1991, 1992; Porter and Scully, 1995; Mokyr, 2004; McCloskey, 2010).

A related line of enquiry asked why potentially very useful technical ideas in non-European civilizations had not led to an industrial revolution. In particular, it had long been a puzzle of economic history why China's excellent technology, especially in the Sung dynasty (960-1278), was never translated into an industrial revolution. These analyses pointed to the lack of certain social, political and legal preconditions – in short, institutions – in China and other huge Asian economies. In those large, closed economies, the rulers did not have to compete to attract or retain entrepreneurial, knowledgeable people in their jurisdiction (as was the case in many of the rivalling jurisdictions of post-medieval Europe; Jones, 1981/2003; 1994). After examining alternative explanations for the failure of a sustained Chinese industrial revolution, a team of economic historians came to the conclusion that "[the individual members of Chinese] society could reduce transaction costs only so far, not far enough to put the economy on a course for sustained intensive growth . . . Little was provided [by government] in the way of infrastructure or services. Notably, there was no independent legal system, no protection for valuables carried over the roads, no policeman to guard the standing crops . . . There were formal courts of law, but they lacked systematic procedures involving such nuisances as real evidence. Contracts were not enforceable . . . Business dealings tended to be face-to-face or confined to groups with which the merchants or artisans were already affiliated for non-business reasons" (Jones et al., 1994, p. 33). In other words, lacking institutional development in Asia negated the reaping of the fruits of technical progress and a potentially large market. Douglass North concluded in the same vein: "The historical study of economic growth is a study of institutional innovations that permit increasingly complex exchanges to be realized by reducing the transaction (and production) costs of such exchanges" (North, in James and Thomas, 1994, p. 258). Sustained differences in economic growth rates cannot be explained without reference to institutions (Olson, 1982; 1996; Roll and Talbot, 2001; de Soto, 2001).

Institutions – to which Adam Smith already referred in the above quote when he spoke of 'a well-governed society' – have more recently again been identified as crucial to the coordination of dynamic economic life by the theory of evolving, complex systems (Section 6.1). This is relevant because uncertainties dominate economic and business life. Fairly regular patterns on which people may rely are therefore important to facilitate business decisions. If these are disturbed by frequent, hard-to-understand policy interventions with unforeseen side effects, it may become impossible to plan outcomes, and potentially useful ideas might not be pursued. This is why the coordination of modern, complex, changing business life depends so much on general, abstract and adaptive rules of interaction and coordination – in short, institutions and underlying values (Parker and Stacey, 1994).

These various strands of inquiry added empirical substance to the teachings of the neo-Austrian school, as well as Continental European researchers in the *ordo* liberal school and writers in the public-choice tradition. These scholars emphasized the crucial importance of institutions for entrepreneurship in discovering useful knowledge and in marshalling the resources of capital, labour, skills and raw materials, so that new and growing outputs are created (Hayek, 1960; 1967a; 1967b; 1973–79a; Eucken, 1992/1940; Buchanan, 1991; Casson, 1993; Berggren et al., 2002). Growth is then the statistically measured reflection of the millions of actions of entrepreneurs, consumers, savers, producers and traders to obtain what people value more highly.

Empirical research has also pointed to a further, related aspect, namely the importance of preferences for material betterment, as well as widely shared preferences for a number of fundamental values, such as freedom, peace, justice, and security. Appropriate institutions are a necessary, but not sufficient condition for growth. Entrepreneurs, and people generally, also need to have a preference for honest cooperation and material advancement (for example choosing work over leisure). Entrepreneurs and the pursuit of wealth also have to be valued and respected in society (McCloskey, 2010). In the long term, there is a complex interrelation between peoples' fundamental values and institutions: if institutions enable wealth creation, people are more likely to develop a taste for the experience and if they experience growth, they value trust-enhancing institutions.

US economist Deirdre McCloskey in particular has recently argued that standard economic models cannot adequately explain economic growth, because they fail to acknowledge the critical role played by the shift in values as reflected by 'the talk' and 'rhetoric' within the specific time and place under investigation with respect to the activity of the entrepreneurial class or bourgeoisie. In short, as the activity of everyday commerce was afforded respect, which was previously denied, entrepreneurial activity increased. Scientific and technological innovations dovetailed with business acumen, and an institutional environment of private property rights, free pricing, and the pursuit of profit was culturally legitimated. It has been this combustible combination of scientific enlightenment within a commercial culture that has produced the great burst in productivity, which has enabled mankind to reap the blessings of sustained modern economic growth.

Growth is thus driven by entrepreneurs using knowledge in a deepening division of labour (specialization). This is only possible with appropriate 'rules of the game' governing human interaction. Appropriate institutional arrangements are needed to provide a framework for free and responsible individuals to cooperate predictably in markets and within organizations. A coordinative framework is, for example, provided by cultural conventions, a shared ethical system, and formal legal and regulatory stipulations (for details see Chapters 5 and 6). The result is an understanding of the growth process that ties the macroeconomic analysis to the microeconomics of structural change and the microeconomic foundations of motivation and institutional constraints and that relates economic growth to sociological factors, such as preferences and value systems.

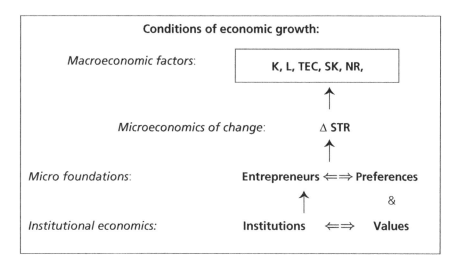

The notion that institutions are crucial to the long-term growth process has been spreading gradually since this hypothesis was explicated in the first edition of this book (Kasper and Streit, 1998). Thus, Charles I. Jones and Paul M. Romer wrote in a 2010 survey article (based on summary neoclassical growth theory): "There is very broad agreement that differences in institutions must be a fundamental source of the wide differences in growth rates" (Jones and Romer, 2010, p. 238), recognizing that "the quality of institutions is a key factor that shapes economic evolution and that institutions are more complicated and matter much more than the neoclassical model once suggested" (*idem*, p. 228). Even the World Bank, whose contributions to economic growth theory and policy prescription ignored institutions for so long, has become more open to the view that institutions matter crucially to economic growth (for example Acemoğlu and Robinson, 2012, which is based on their earlier report for the World Bank, Acemoğlu and Robinson, 2008). While institutional factors are now widely acknowledged as highly relevant, exact definitions are nevertheless still somewhat at variance with what is discussed in this book (see *Epilogue*).

Some authors have gone beyond the institutional focus of growth theory, emphasizing the underlying cultural values. Thus, Deidre McCloskey – as mentioned, in her book *Bourgeois Dignity* (McCloskey, 2010) – discusses different explanations of growth and challenges the purely institutional story. Instead, she focuses on ideas, namely the shift in attitudes toward a wide acceptance of the bourgeois value system. Nevertheless, her analysis also upholds the key role of the institutions that underpin private property and free markets. Economic historian Joel Mokyr and others also demonstrated that the industrial revolution owed much to a combustible combination of scientific enlightenment and the rise of a commercial culture, that is, specific institutions and values of the sort discussed in this book (Mokyr, 2004; Taverne, 2005).

In many respects, the focus on the institutional aspects in explaining economic growth amounts to a rediscovery of what early thinkers such as the Scottish social philosophers David Hume and Adam Smith had said. They taught us that at least three institutions are fundamental to human progress and civilized society: the guarantee of property rights, the free transfer of property by voluntary contractual agreement, and the keeping of promises made (Hume, 1965/1786; Hodgson, 1988; 1998). The ideas implicit in this explanation of economic growth had always been part of popular American thinking, though not necessarily of formal mainstream economics. Thus, American writer Henry Grady Weaver (1889-1949), 1938 'Man of the Year' on the cover of *Time* magazine, explained economic progress with reference to economic freedom and limited government (Weaver, 1974/1947) and the ever-active *Foundation for Economic Education* in New York persevered with the same message. It is doubtlessly important to know where the prevailing value system in a society lies on the scale from collectivism and individuality. Another fundamental societal quality is the extent to which people, or at least the elites, believe in passively accepting fate (fatalism) or believe that it is the role of the human race to improve its condition in this world – measured against the fundamental values discussed here and in Chapter 4 (Kasper 2011b).

We may therefore conclude that contemporary economic growth theory is returning to the traditional tie-up with philosophers of freedom, who had emphasized it as the mainspring of economic progress, before abstraction and economic modelling took hold of the central economic issue of explaining growth.

We conclude this introductory chapter by saying that institutions underpin the complex web of human interaction across nations and continents, as human interaction depends invariably on very tenuous links of trust – indeed a 'gossamer web', as it was so aptly put by Jane Jacobs in one of the quotes at the head of this chapter.

KEY CONCEPTS

Physical capital consists of tangible assets that have the potential of raising the capacity of other production factors, such as labour, to produce goods and services. In modern economies, the process of capital formation requires acts of **saving** (not consuming income generated) and acts of **investment** (borrowing to install capital assets).

The term **human capital** sometimes relates only to those assets that are embodied in individuals (skills, knowledge, knowhow); other authors have a wider conception of human capital, including shared, disembodied knowledge, such as shared values, shared conventions, rules, and laws – what we shall cover in this book with the term 'institutions' (see following chapter). Human capital therefore goes far beyond explicit knowledge or what intellectuals know, covering implicit, informal knowhow, aptitudes and basic values, as well as socially shared rule systems.

Entrepreneurs are people who are on the alert for opportunities and are ready to exploit them. Economic entrepreneurs are on the look-out for new, useful knowledge and are prepared to risk as-yet-untested combinations of production factors in the hope for material gain.

NOTES

1 A noteworthy exception is the graphic, insightful description of average living conditions in Europe before the onset of the industrial revolution by Braudel (1981-84).

2 The graph is based on data collated by the experienced observer of long-term economic history, Angus Maddison (2001; 2007). They are based on inflation-adjusted national incomes, translated into US-dollars with purchasing-power equivalents (that is, , reflecting how many real goods and services people can buy in their respective countries). Clearly, such long-term international comparisons are based on many assumptions, so that the data can only serve as a general guide. Nonetheless, these are the best data available to document how different societies fared in their long-term quest for material betterment.

Part I

Foundations

2

Definitions: economics, institutions, order and policy

In this chapter the reader will learn what exactly an institution is, how institutions come into existence and how they facilitate the emergence of order (a confidence-inspiring, predictable pattern of behaviour). The reader will also see how institutions and order help in coping with the economic problem, namely overcoming scarcity and discovering new wants and resources. We shall see that institutions assist members of a community when they wish to cooperate, since institutions make it more convenient, less costly and less risky for individuals to rely on each other, in particular when developing and using new knowledge.

We also learn that institutions and their economic consequences are now attracting growing interest – although the basic ideas are not new. Property rights, the freedom of contract, stable money, and other confidence-inspiring certainties, are based on sound institutions. These areas have already been analysed by the classical moral philosophers and economists. The writings of David Hume and Adam Smith, the Austrian school and 'public-choice economics' can all be considered precursors of modern institutional economics. Their contributions will be reviewed briefly.

In building up a scientific picture of the economic world, definitions play an important part.

Walter Eucken (1992/1940)

Law is reason without wishes.

Aristotle (384-322BC)

[T]here . . . are certain super individual schemes of thought, namely institutions, which . . . serve . . . to some extent the coordination of individual plans.

Ludwig Lachmann (1977/1943)

2.1   Basic definitions

This book is about economics: the science that aims to explain how people satisfy their diverse wants by drawing on scarce resources and how people discover new wants and resources – specifically the role that institutions play in this. Before we can begin to discuss the issues, it is necessary to spell out how we define the most important terms. Note that other people, and researchers in other disciplines, do not always attach the same meanings to the terms that we do.

Institutions

Institutions are defined here as man-made rules which constrain people's (possibly arbitrary and opportunistic) behaviour in human interaction. Institutional economics reflects a move to broaden the research and teaching of economics to not only the analysis of choice within constraints, but also to choice between the constraints on choice. Institutions are the formal and informal 'rules of the game'. In our definition, institutions are shared in a community and are always enforced by more or less established social sanctions for violators of the rules. Institutions without sanctions are useless. Rules with effective sanctions channel human actions in reasonably predictable paths, creating a degree of order. They serve a normative purpose. Only if sanctions apply will institutions make the actions of individuals more predictable. If various related rules are consistent with each other, the confident cooperation between people is facilitated so that they can take good advantage of the division of labour, knowledge and creativity. For example, traffic rules – a set of institutions – impose constraints on individual drivers, but allow people on the whole to travel more speedily and safely. In a similar way, the institutions that establish protected individual property rights enable people to buy, sell and grant credit to others.[1] The web of trust within a vibrant economic society, which we mentioned at the end of Chapter 1, does not reside necessarily in any one individual, but in the institutions that govern social interaction between individuals. We trust strangers not because we know them (we do not, by definition), but because we interact with strangers within an institutional setting that we trust.

The general presumption is that institutions have great impact on how well people attain their economic and other objectives, and that people normally prefer institutions which enhance their freedom of choice and economic wellbeing. But institutions will not always serve these ends. Certain types of rules may have deleterious consequences for general material welfare, freedom and other fundamental values. Indeed, the decay of the rule system can lead to economic and social decline. One therefore has to analyse the content and effect of institutions on the freedom of choice and prosperity.

Order and economic life

In Chapter 1, we already defined institutional economics as the two-way relationship between economic life and the various coordinative rules individuals utilize and enforce. The key function of institutions is, as we noted there, to facilitate order – a systematic, non-random and therefore comprehensible pattern of actions and events. In social chaos, interaction with others is excessively costly, confidence is shattered and cooperation disintegrates. The division of labour and knowledge, which is the major source of economic wellbeing, is difficult and may be next to impossible. In such a world where the social gains from cooperation would go unrealized, as Thomas Hobbes famously wrote, life would indeed be nasty, brutish and short. Nature is red in tooth and claw, and we humans are not well equipped to survive in isolation from others. We survive and thrive only because of our ability to cooperate with others and to form social networks. We shall therefore focus here on how institutions promote order in economic interaction: patterns emerge when individuals try to come to grips with the scarcity of resources. Order inspires trust and confidence, and reduces the costs of coordination. When order prevails, people are able to make predictions; individuals are then better able to shape their own plans, cooperate with others and feel enough confidence to risk innovative experiments of their own. Institutions can also make it easier for people to find specialists with whom they can cooperate, guess what such cooperation is likely to cost and estimate what benefits it might bring. More useful knowledge will then be discovered and used.

As noted previously, economics deals with scarcity. This means that a decision in favour of one course of action inevitably implies rejection of alternative actions. We call the most-valued alternative use of a resource the 'opportunity cost'. Each reader of this chapter is foregoing other uses of her or his time and attaches different costs to reading this. Such decisions are always subjective – different individual decision makers evaluate alternatives differently. For example, one reader's opportunity cost may be the attendance at a lecture, and another's a flirt with a friend or time on the beach (Buchanan, 1969, Foreword). Even where the alternative foregone by a certain choice is technically the same – for example, that we cannot listen to a rock concert because we read this book – the value of the sacrifice will differ between us. You may bear much higher opportunity costs than we do. This point is fundamentally important: economic decisions should be left to individuals, as individuals know their own subjective opportunities. Collective decision makers are less informed about the diversity and subjective values of the opportunities people face.

When people with different aspirations and capabilities make choices and assess their opportunity costs, order and trust are greatly appreciated, since information is then easy to convey to others and a sophisticated division of labour is possible. The content of order-supporting institutions is therefore of great relevance to economic outcomes that satisfy diverse people in their ever-changing environments.

KEY CONCEPTS

As economics is concerned with choices in the face of scarcity, the concept of **opportunity cost** plays a key role. It highlights that any choice 'costs' the next best alternative that has to be foregone. In practice, the opportunities foregone are anticipated and evaluated by individuals differently, depending on their subjective appreciation (subjective opportunity costs). Thus, one person's opportunity cost often completely differs from another person's.

To repeat: **Institutions** are rules of human interaction that constrain – possibly opportunistic and erratic – individual behaviour; they make the actions of others more predictable, thus facilitating the division of labour and knowledge, and hence wealth

creation. Institutions, to be effective, always imply some kind of sanction for rule violations. The terms 'institution' and 'rule' are used interchangeably in this book.

Order prevails if repetitive human interactions follow some kind of discernible pattern. Such patterns can emerge when certain institutions exist: the 'rules of the game' must be sufficiently cohesive in order to channel human actions so that they are non-random, and hence essentially predictable.

Institutional economics covers the two-way relationship between economics and institutions. It is concerned with the effects of institutions on the economy, as well as how institutions respond to a dynamic world.[2]

The origins of institutions

What causes institutions to come into existence? One possibility is that rules and entire rule systems are shaped by long-term human experience. People may have serendipitously stumbled upon certain arrangements that allowed them to better meet their aspirations. It may have proved useful, for example, to adopt the custom of greeting the people one meets. It may have made the traffic flow better when everyone stayed on the same side of the road. Useful rules tend to be perpetuated and become a tradition; if adopted by sufficient numbers of people to create a critical mass, rules are eventually followed by everyone in the community. The rules will be spontaneously enforced and emulated, as they emerge gradually and become known throughout a community. While rules that ameliorate human interaction are reinforced, arrangements that fail to satisfy human aspirations will be rejected and abandoned. Thus, most of the rules that matter to our daily lives have evolved within society in a process of gradual feedback and adjustment. The precise content of most institutions will evolve gradually along a steady path. We call such rules internal institutions, as they arise within the community and are enforced internally, that is, by spontaneous reaction from the people who are directly affected. In analysing how internal institutions come about, institutional economics can draw on the insights of moral philosophy, anthropology, psychology and sociology.

Other types of institutions come into existence because they are designed by someone with authority, are made explicit in legislation and regulations and are formally enforced by an authority outside society, such as a government. Such rules are designed and imposed by agents who may have acquired this role by force, inheritance or as the result of a political process. Although there tends to be much voluntary compliance, these institutions are ultimately enforced by legitimated means of coercion, for example through the police and the judiciary. We call these rules 'external institutions'.

As soon as institutions are imposed and enforced externally by rulers, parliaments, or bureaucracies, a fundamental problem arises: the political agents, who should act in the interest of the citizens, lack perfect information and often tend to exceed their mandate; they often use rules and enforcement to their own benefit. For this and other reasons, political processes themselves need to be subjected to certain rules. The effectiveness of external institutions depends greatly on whether they are complementary to the internally evolved institutions – for example, whether legislation supports a society's morality, its cultural conventions, customs, and manners. External institutions cause agency and compliance costs and are normally much more costly than corresponding internal institutions. When analysing external institutions, one has to draw on political science and jurisprudence.

KEY CONCEPTS

Internal institutions evolve from human experience and incorporate solutions that have tended to serve people best in the past. Examples are customs, ethical norms, good manners and conventions in trade, as well as natural law in Western society. Violations of internal institutions are normally sanctioned informally by those directly affected – when people with bad manners discover that they lose respect or are not

➡

←

invited again – but sometimes formal sanctioning processes are also relied upon to enforce internal institutions (see Section 5.2).

External institutions are imposed and enforced from above, having been designed and established by agents, who are authorized by some political mechanism. An example is legislation. External institutions are coupled with explicit sanctions, which are imposed in formal ways (for example law courts following procedures of due process) and may be enforced by legitimated uses of force (for example the police). External enforcement normally suffers from information problems, and the costs tend to be considerable.

The distinction between internal and external institutions thus hinges on the origin of the rules and the mechanism of enforcement.

Normative content and public policy

In institutional economics it is often appropriate to analyse values and the effects of fundamental values; institutions are often decisive for how people attain their own personal objectives and are able to realize their own aspirations. Institutions also impact on the values that people hold and the purposes they pursue. Institutions thus reflect subjective notions of the relation between one individual and others in the community. Their acceptance and enforcement depend crucially on cultural notions of what society stands for. A community's shared fundamental values support cohesion and motivate people to act within the institutional framework. Institutional economics therefore has to analyse human values explicitly – more precisely statements about what people appreciate as valuable – and participate in moral discourse (Palmer, 2011). In this respect, it draws on moral philosophy, the origin of modern economics.

Fundamental values are deeply anchored in the traditions of civilizations and are not easily changed. They form part of a community's identity and may even be tied to firmly held religious beliefs. This has the potential of posing huge obstacles to economic and cultural change when economic development takes off in a hitherto stationary society. The institutions of the market economy (Chapters 7 and 8) then have to be grafted onto the fundamental values of a particular society. Some civilizations come with values and social attitudes, which easily mesh with the 'rule book' of the market economy, or at least readily adjust, so that private property rights, competition and the rule of law are easily adopted. Other civilizations, however, come with value systems that reject the enjoyment of material welfare, reward for individual effort and the equality of all before the law. Smaller groups, such as indigenous tribes, then often lose their identity. Bigger groups then experience cultural distress and great difficulties in embracing modern economic growth (Bauer, 2000; Bauer and Sen, 2004; Boettke et al., 2008; Kasper 2011b). These adjustments to the institutional infrastructure of values and basic attitudes ensure that the institutions that make the market economy will differ from one society to the next, so that 'multiple modernities' emerge (Chapter 14).

Institutions – the rules that are informed by the underlying, shared values – define a community, be it a family, a neighbourhood, a nation or an international professional association. Institutions constitute the 'social cement' that makes and defines a society (to employ the term American sociologist John Elster used in the title of a well-known book, Elster, 1989). Individuals may of course belong to a great variety of different, overlapping communities, obeying differing sets of institutions; some they share with their neighbours in the same geographical area, others with people far away. In the same vein, institutions have an inter-community dimension. Systems of economic institutions may also be more or less open to others. Openness here means that exchanges of goods and services and flows of people, capital and ideas are possible between different communities. In this respect, institutional economics shares common ground with sociology, international law and politics.

We must also distinguish between the theory and the policy of institutional economics. Institutional theory describes, explains, and predicts the emergence and the effects of rules; it also discusses how changes of certain rules may help or hinder certain outcomes or classes of outcomes. In this respect, institutional economics belongs to the realm of positive science and contributes to economic policy.[3] Depending on how well institutional theory works, one may go beyond this and be able to derive policy-oriented knowledge that helps to shape institutions in the real world according to certain objectives (economic reform, Chapters 13 and 14). Economists, as scientists, may give policy advice on how given objectives could be more effectively pursued under alternative sets of institutions. Public policy – the systematic use of political means in the pursuit of certain objectives – will normally proceed within given institutional constraints, but policy actions may also alter institutions, either in explicit ways or as a side effect of experiences. Institutional economists tend to focus on the interactions between public policy and institutions.

Beyond this, economists, like any other citizens, may of course articulate what they consider to be desirable, good or bad. When they do so, they should reveal their personal values and preferences, because they then adopt a normative posture.

KEY CONCEPTS

(Fundamental) values are defined as high preferences revealed, time and again, in human choices and public actions. They are accorded – by most people most of the time – a high rank order and are frequently seen as the 'stopping points' for discussions of what is good or bad. Other preferences are subordinated to them. Examples of such values are freedom, justice, security, and economic welfare.

Public policy is the systematic pursuit by political, collective means of certain objec-

tives. Public policy is not only conducted by government agents (parliamentarians, politicians, administrators), but also by representatives of organized groups. Labour unions, industry associations, consumer and welfare lobbies, bureaucracies and certain individuals (industry leaders, academics, media representatives) may influence collective actions, that is, actions that involve agreements between more than two partners (often implicitly between millions of people in a community).

2.2 The precursors of contemporary institutional economics

The Scottish Enlightenment

This brief overview of the key concepts of institutional economics needs to be rounded off by at least some references to the history of ideas and the precursors of contemporary institutional economics. As noted, institutions have, over recent generations, not been explicitly analysed in most of mainstream economics. Their importance was largely overlooked because of the assumptions commonly made by neoclassical economists. In particular, analytically convenient, but peculiar assumptions about 'perfect knowledge' and hyper-rationality (rational choice between given, known objectives and available, known means), and the pre-occupation with equilibrium end-states made the explicit treatment of institutions superfluous.

Different from contemporary economic theorists, the classic social scientists of the eighteenth and early nineteenth centuries understood the central importance of institutions. The Scottish moral philosophers and economists of the eighteenth century were particularly aware of institutions. Adam Smith's famous 'invisible hand' mechanism – which describes how self-seeking individuals are coordinated by competition in markets – cannot be comprehended as anything other than an ordering institutional system. Adam Smith's Scottish contemporary Adam Ferguson stressed the evolution of institutions over time, and his friend David Hume explored the institutional foundations on which the capitalist market economy is built, and how these foundations are placed into the intellectual, cultural, and political life of a nation. Both Ferguson's focus on institutions 'of human action, but not of human design' and Hume's identification of the institutions of property, contract and consent as providing the foundation for civilized society are still of great relevance in contemporary institutional economics.

A slightly under-appreciated aspect among contemporary institutional economists, but an idea fundamental to the moral philosophers of the Scottish Enlightenment was that of developing a robust political economy – a concept revived recently by Boettke and Leeson (2004), as well as Boettke (2012). Smith and his contemporaries sought to develop a political economy where bad men could do least harm if they were to rise to power. The institutional system of checks and balances should be so strong that it would hold the ambitious and rapacious in check. Rather than empower the good and the wise to rule, as the French Enlightenment thinkers sought, the Scottish Enlightenment argued that the institutions of government should be designed, as Hume put it, with the presumption that all men are knaves.

Human nature, from this perspective, was treated as neither benevolent nor omniscient, but instead as sometimes good and often bad; sometimes smart, but more often stupid. And the question is what institutional configuration could utilize man's basic instincts and channel them in a productive direction to realize the gains from social cooperation by the division of labour. The great eighteenth century discovery of the Scottish moral philosophers, and then developed during the eighteenth and nineteenth centuries by classical political economists, was that private property and free markets provided such an institutional configuration (Boettke and Leeson, 2004; Leeson and Subrick, 2006).

The Austrian school

More recently, institutional economics received mighty impetuses from the 'Austrian School' – from Carl Menger and Ludwig von Mises to 'neo-Austrians', such as Ludwig Lachmann, Friedrich von Hayek, Murray Rothbard and Israel Kirzner. Even 'Chicago economists', such as George Stigler and Milton Friedman, initiated a discussion of institutions (see references to these authors in the Bibliography at the end of this book). The Austrian contribution placed the analysis of rules into the context of limited human knowledge; methodological individualism, the insight that only individuals act (never abstract collectives, such as nations, races, or social classes[4]); constantly changing circumstances and the dynamics of processes of adjustment and adaptation to those changes; and subjectivism, the insight that individuals read the world subjectively and therefore differ in their ability to understand it and relate it to their value judgments.[5] From this follows that interpersonal differences have to be respected and cannot be easily aggregated into collective goals.[6] The Austrian contributions present important analytical and philosophical challenges to orthodox mainstream economics and suggest a cautious treatment of what we mean by rationality and equilibrium (Huerta de Soto, 1998; Kasper, 2010). Ludwig von Mises produced an early critique of the institutions of socialism, which has yet to be fully absorbed into the mainstream of political and economic thought (Butler, 2010, pp. 88–92). His line of argument was carried further by Hayek, Kirzner, Buchanan and Rothbard. Their inspirational influence on economic institutions and orders will be evident throughout this book.

Institutional economics is also based on the conception of the economy as a complex, evolving system. The notion of equilibrium as a durable, or even a desirable, condition is alien to this approach. Instead of such ahistorical notions as equilibrium, economic life is seen as in the process of gradual evolution; some elements appear and others disappear as people select what suits their diverse purposes (Shackle, 1972; Witt, 1994; Metcalfe, 1989).

KEY CONCEPTS

The term **Scottish Enlightenment** refers to moral philosophers and economists (such as David Hume and Adam Smith) who wrote predominantly in the eighteenth century. They explored what basic institutions a functioning capitalist economy needs; namely the rule of law, private property, and the freedom of contract. They castigated the deleterious consequences of Mercantilism (selective trade protectionism and the preferment of specific groups, reliance on public enterprise, powerful coalitions between ruler and established merchant interests). They advocated a minimal state and self-responsibility of the individual citizen.

Neoclassical economics has become the dominant orthodoxy in economic analysis during the twentieth century. It centres on the conditions of economic equilibrium and is normally based on the simplifying assumptions:

- that economic agents have 'perfect knowledge';
- that people pursue their purposes rationally and maximize some target variable subject to budget constraints;

➡

←

- that it is possible to describe representative households, producer-investors, and governments;
- that business transactions, for example in markets, are frictionless and cost-free; and
- that the individual preferences of the members of society can somehow be expressed in a social welfare function.

In contradistinction to evolutionary economics (see below), the analysis typically begins with an equilibrium – understood as a situation in which everybody's plans and expectations are mutually compatible. This equilibrium is disturbed by an isolated event; the analysis then shows the new equilibrium to which the system moves (comparative static analysis, assuming all other things to be equal, the famous *ceteris paribus* clause of economic textbooks). It is often assumed that policy makers are able to design a line of rational actions, which achieve their objectives. These assumptions facilitate the formulation of mathematical models and econometric analyses. In turn these models suggest that economic policy should be conducted in terms of predetermined goals and instruments, with policy makers pulling deftly at 'the levers of the economy'.

Austrian economics is a tradition of analysing economic phenomena, which began during the late century in Vienna, but is now gaining growing influence in business and policy making, particularly in developing countries. It is based on the understanding that knowledge is imperfect and that people interact in dynamic market processes so that time and evolution are important. Its cornerstones are:

(a) **methodological individualism**: economic phenomena are explained by the actions of individuals who try to acquire costly information and engage in purposeful action,

(b) **subjectivism**: economic phenomena have to be explained by the decisions of people who bring to bear their unique perceptions of reality and hence their unique values, aspirations, knowledge and assessments of costs and benefits, and that people act rationally in their own distinctive self-interest, and

(c) an emphasis on complex, open-ended **processes of trial and error** which happen in historic time and occur in an environment of uncertainty; economic actions therefore tend to have many unintended and unpredictable side effects.

Austrian economists concentrate on how people coordinate their individual pursuits and what institutions evolve so that they can better cope with lacking knowledge to reach their individual goals. Different from the 'instrumentalist approach' of neoclassical economics, Austrian economists counsel caution in policy interventions and suggest a focus on cultivating and setting universal rules which channel market processes.

For an introduction, see 'Austrian Economics' in *The Concise Encyclopaedia of Economics*, Boettke in Henderson (ed.), 2008, pp. 23–27; Boettke (ed.) 1994 pp. 1–6; and Kirzner (1997).

Ordo liberalism, public choice and other sources

Another tradition in law and economics that focused on institutions is the 'Freiburg School', sometimes also called the German *ordo* liberal school. It was inspired for decades by Walter Eucken and Franz Böhm, who showed the deleterious effects of the decay of the basic rules of competition in the Weimar Republic (1919-1933) and Nazi Germany. They adapted the basic institutions described by the Scottish philosophers to modern industrial mass society with multi-party democracy, self-seeking bureaucracies and organized interest groups (Section 10.3).

New Anglo-Saxon impulses to contemporary institutional economics began arguably with the path-breaking work of Ronald Coase; more recently his ideas were taken up by 'public choice economics' in the works of writers such as James Buchanan, Gordon Tullock, Harold Demsetz, Elinor and Vincent Ostrom, and Mancur Olson. Other insights, which added much empirical content to institutional economics, have been contributed by long-term economic historians such as Douglass North and Eric L. Jones whom we quoted in Chapter 1. They showed how the competition amongst communities and jurisdictions led to the evolution of more citizen- and enterprise-friendly rules, such as limited, rule-bound government, property rights, due process and the rule of law. Economic and business historians have had great influence in turning economics again from a comparative-static to an evolutionary discipline. The 'new organization science' has also added analyses of the effect of institutions on the shape and effectiveness of particular organizations (see authors such as Armen Alchian, Harold Demsetz, Oliver Williamson, Yoram Barzel, and Louis de Alessi in the Bibliography at the end of this book).

Since the 1970s, institutional economics has developed into a dynamic, broad field of research that focuses on the central importance of institutions in motivating economic action. In many respects, the growing numbers of free-market think tanks around the world have been standard bearers for a freedom-oriented institutional worldview (for example Palmer, 2011). A challenge was put to the economists working to develop modern institutional economics early on in this effort by the German sociologist Hans Albert. Albert had identified the fundamental problem that plagued modern economics in the 1950s, 1960s and 1970s as that of 'model Platoism'. As such, the effort to repair economics, Albert warned, would never work until economics addressed this fundamental flaw. As he put it, neoclassical economics will never repair its institutional deficiency until it repairs its behavioural deficiency. In other words, the closed model of choice and the single-exit model of interaction evident in the scientific programme of optimization against given constraints and general competitive equilibrium can never truly capture the role of institutions in economic life (Albert, 1979; 1985).

The field of institutional economics subsequently split into two camps: one group of analysts comes from traditional neoclassical economics and organization science; they have recognized the importance of institutions (and transaction costs) and have tried to graft these phenomena onto traditional mainstream economics (for example, Eggertson, 1990; Furubotn and Richter, 1991). A second group, to which we belong, has found that fundamental assumptions of institutional economics are incompatible with the constituent assumptions of the neoclassical orthodoxy, such as 'perfect knowledge' and objective rationality. We have taken the hard step of writing off much of our old 'knowledge capital' in order to develop institutional economics afresh from basic presumptions about fundamental values, cognition, and behaviour.

This book is an attempt to make the, albeit imperfect, results of this new intellectual venture teachable and to show the far-reaching consequences for public policy

KEY CONCEPTS

***Ordo* liberalism** (also known as the *Freiburg School*) refers to a specifically German tradition that began in the 1920s and 1930s. It attributed the economic (and political) failures of the Weimar Republic to interest-group-driven political rent-seeking and the government's tolerance of the closure of markets to competitors. The *ordo* liberals recommended that the key institutions that the Scottish Enlightenment had identified (private property, freedom of contract, rule of law) be supplemented by an active defence of competition by government to counter the influence of the opportunism of political parties, organized groups, and bureaucratic egotism. They also demanded that policy should help to create stable expectations and desist from stop-go policies (for an introduction, see Kasper and Streit (1993)).

Evolutionary economics designates a school of thought that focuses on market processes of change and progress, restructuring and innovation through competition, rather than on static equilibrium, the focus of neoclassical economics. It analyses economic phenomena in historic time, that is, on the knowledge that one cannot turn the clock back and that certain events are irreversible. One therefore has to look at historic paths, for example in technical change. Evolutionary economists reject the unrealistic notion – common in neoclassical analysis – that economic actors make decisions completely anew at the beginning of every period. Evolutionary economics also deals with open-ended systems, which allow individual experimentation by variation, selection and imitation of what people value highly. Thus, evolutionary economics focuses on change, diversity, learning and creativity, and the complex interplay between technical, societal, organizational,

➡

←

economic, and institutional change. It pays great attention to the role of creativity and entrepreneurship. Competition is seen as the device that sorts what is deemed useful from what is considered not worth the cost.

In distinction to comparative-static analysis, it is assumed:

(a) positively that 'disequilibrium' is the normal state of affairs, and

(b) normatively that people thrive in disequilibrium processes ('equilibrium is death!').

The evolutionary approach is to analyse a path-dependent sequence of events, where the decisions in earlier periods have great (though not exclusive!) influence over what can happen in the next.

To illustrate the point: the standard neoclassical assumption would be to assume that a music student in her first semester chooses to learn the piano, in semester 2, she starts afresh and decides to learn the trombone, in semester 3, it may be the violin. By contrast, **path dependency** in evolutionary economics assumes that, normally, music students build on their first-semester skills. In contrast to comparative-static neoclassical economics, which suggests the pursuit of perfection, the evolutionary policy stance is to look out for pragmatic, ongoing improvement (for an introduction see: Witt (1994), also Witt (1991), Metcalfe (1989), and Nelson (1995)).

Public choice is originally an American tradition, which applies economic principles to the analysis of political decision-making. It is based on the observation that politicians and administrators – like all other people – pursue their own goals, which are not necessarily those of their electorate. In other words, public choice economists operate on the assumption that, when one turns self-seeking knaves into elected officials or bureaucrats, they do not turn into white knights in shining armour. Public choice analysis thus highlights **rent-seeking,** that is, the reallocation of property rights by political intervention, rather than untrammelled market competition. Government agents and industrialists are understood to frequently pursue particular interests through redistributive political interventions. Public choice has shown the limits of what can be achieved by political, collective action. It may be labelled the 'economics of politics and collective decision making'. (For an introduction see the following short articles in Henderson (ed.) (2008): 'Public Choice', pp. 427–430, and 'Rent-Seeking', pp. 445–446; and Buchanan (1991), pp. 29–46; Buchanan and Tullock (1962), or for a book-length exposé: Mitchell and Simmons (1994), esp. pp. 195–222.)

The **old institutional economics** covers the contributions of American and European economists who wrote mainly in the early decades of the twentieth century, analysing institutions and rejecting classical economic theories. In Germany, the 'Historic School' – authors such as Gustav Schmoller – described economic reality by incorporating the rules of human interaction in their descriptions of economic and social evolution. In the United States, Thorstein Veblen, John Commons and Wesley Mitchell studied the economic role of institutions (for more detail, see articles on "Institutionalism, 'Old' and 'New'" in Hodgson et al., 1994, pp. 397–402; and Hodgson, 1998). The new institutional economics, as defined in this book, has little in common with the old institutionalists in the US and their Historical School counterparts in Europe.

NOTES

1 The term 'institution' has numerous and conflicting definitions in the literature. Social scientists from different disciplines and ages have imbued the term with so many alternative meanings that it does not seem possible to give a generally valid definition beyond a loose association with regularity in behaviour. However, the definition that we shall use consistently in this book – in the sense of rules with sanctions that have normative influence on human behaviour – appears by now to have emerged as the consensus definition amongst contemporary institutional economists (see for example North, 1990, pp. 3–6; Drobak and Nye (eds), 1997, pp. xv–xx).

   Common English usage often confuses institutions, as defined here, with 'organizations', which are systematic arrangements of resources aimed at achieving a shared purpose or purposes (Chapter 9). Thus, firms, banks and government administrations are purposive organizations, whereas the Ten Commandments and the traffic code are sets of institutions.

2 A century ago, the term 'institutional economics' came into use thanks to authors such as Torstein Veblen, and was, for a while, the dominant body of economic analysis in American universities (Hodgson, 1998). Others have identified the term with a branch of Marxian economics. While all these antecedents have made the important point 'that institutions matter' to economic performance, the way we shall use the term here focuses on the quality of the rules that underpin secure individual property rights and their free use within the framework of the rule of law.

3 Positive economics extends also to the analysis of the consequences of different sets of human values, which are related to institutions. In this case, the economist produces scholarly statements about the consequences of certain values, as opposed to making his own value judgments.

4 The founder of Austrian economics, Carl Menger (1840-1921), drove the point home when he wrote (in 1883): "the phenomena of 'national economy' are by no means direct expressions of the life of a nation as such or direct results of an 'economic nation'. They are, rather, the results of . . . innumerable individual economic efforts. [They] must . . . be theoretically interpreted in this light" (cited after Boettke, 1994, p. 11).

5 For a survey of the contributions of the Austrian School of Economics, see Boettke (ed.) (1998), The Elgar Companion to Austrian Economics, and for an introduction to the writings of the contemporary generation of scholars working in the Austrian tradition, and developing it in new directions, see Boettke, (ed.) (2010), The Handbook of Contemporary Austrian Economics.

6 The reader is invited to become alert to often-heard collectivist statements such as 'the nation has the desire to . . .', 'the international community should attend to this problem', 'the government ought to decide', 'the nation requires a population of 100 million . . .', 'the world community must solve the problem of hunger', 'world history will explain', or references to undefined collectives, such as 'poverty should be eradicated by 2020'. It is very educational to ask in each case who specifically the intended individual decision makers are, what their subjective motivations might be and why they are hidden, or hide themselves, in faceless collectives.

3

Human behaviour

Here we discuss a few basic, but far-reaching assumptions about human nature. We shall see that the central problem to overcoming scarcity is ignorance (the knowledge problem). This is at variance with the assumption of 'perfect knowledge', which is still often made by economists.

Bits of useful knowledge and useful skills are dispersed among individuals throughout the community. People pursue their own, self-set purposes by drawing on their own knowledge and that of others, if they can be found. In the process, more useful knowledge is discovered, despite the fact that each and everyone has a limited capacity, limited resources and limited time to acquire and evaluate new information and to compound it into knowledge. This is a costly process. People therefore tend to make decisions within the bounds of their limited information and learn by trial and error. We shall also see that certain institutions assist economic agents to reduce the costs of knowledge search and inspire confidence in cooperating with others, for example through exchanges in the market place.

We will also try to find out what motivates human beings to act to the benefit of others. In the family, among friends and in small groups, people frequently act out of love, solidarity or altruism. However, what works well in the small group cannot be transferred to modern mass society or collective action in an entire nation. At the level of modern mass societies, we act in the interest of strangers normally only if we are either coerced or see an advantage for ourselves, for example when strangers offer us a payment in exchange for our efforts.

We conclude this chapter by pointing to the pervasive problem of how to motivate agents, who act on behalf of others and who are often much better informed than the principals. In other words, we shall look at the pervasive 'principal-agent problem' in human interaction.

Man is truly altered by the coexistence of other men; his faculties cannot be developed in himself alone, and only by himself.

Samuel T. Coleridge, British poet-philosopher (1818)

The worth of knowledge cannot begin to be asserted until we have it. But then it is too late to decide how much to spend on breaching the walls to encourage its arrival.

George Shackle (1972)

Even 200 years after Adam Smith's *Wealth of Nations*, it is not yet fully understood that it is the great achievement of the market to have made a far-ranging division of labor possible, that it brings about continuous adaptation of economic effect to millions of particular facts or events which in their totality are not known and cannot be known to anybody.

Friedrich A. Hayek (1978b)

Before we can discuss institutions in detail, it seems appropriate to investigate some basic traits of human behaviour. The need to foster institutions arises from certain intrinsic qualities of human nature, such as our limited capacity to absorb and evaluate information and to retain knowledge. 'Information' is used here to designate an item of explicit knowledge that everyone can learn. Bits of information are evaluated and amalgamated into a body of knowledge, in which ideas are systematically related and which should remain open to revisions and new insights. The word 'information' frequently relates to the act of informing and the *flow* of information, whereas 'knowledge' refers to the personal holding of a *stock* of knowledge in one's mind. People with much information may not necessarily be able to use it in interactive, applied and creative ways (information junkies). Knowledgeable people are able to make use of what they know, often in novel and creative ways. When we complain of 'information overload', we speak of the problem of too many bits of information coming our way and our intellectual capacity to make sense of them by integrating them into a system of knowledge. The science, which deals with knowledge and how people arrive at new insights, is called 'epistemology' (after the Greek term *episteme* – knowledge, insight, understanding).

We will also have to discuss how individuals share and use knowledge in a world where the coordination of individual actions is not cost-free.

3.1   The knowledge problem

On epistemology

We saw in Section 1.2 that economic growth is limited by a lack of knowledge, although competing buyers and sellers help to utilize existing, and to develop further, knowledge. Despite this cooperation of the many to obtain mutually beneficial outcomes, the problem of limited knowledge is a central tenet of human existence. It is the ultimate cause of scarcity: since we do not know everything, we cannot satisfy every human want with available material resources. We do not live in Utopia – and therefore have to study economics. Human ignorance and processes to overcome it – albeit imperfectly – are thus central to economics, the science of how to tackle scarcity. The concept of the 'knowledge problem' was introduced into economics by Friedrich August von Hayek who spoke of 'constitutional ignorance' as an essential aspect of human existence (Hayek, 1937; 1945, esp. p. 530; also see reference in Henderson (ed.), 2008, pp. 540–543). In his 1974 Nobel Prize lecture, entitled the 'Pretense of Knowledge', Hayek returned once again to the theme to show that much of the economic profession pretended to know what was in reality unknowable. The profession therefore risked giving irrelevant advice (Hayek, reprinted in Nishiyama and Leube (eds), 1984, pp. 266–280). The knowledge problem is the central theme of the Austrian critique of orthodox mainstream economics (see *Epilogue*).

When developing a theory about complex reality, one has, admittedly, to make simplifying assumptions – just as a map depicts a simplified model of reality and omits much confusing detail. However, we must also avoid over-simplifications that inhibit our ability to understand. Just as we do not have or need a map that is a 1-to-1 correspondence of the local landscape in the glove-compartment of our car, we also do not just have a napkin with arrows pointing North-South and East-West. In theorizing, we always strive for an adequate level of abstraction. In that theoretical quest, it is not permissible to abstract from *constitutional* criteria, which are essential to what one wants to explicate. The lack of knowledge is such a constitutional condition if one wants to explain scarcity and other economic phenomena. Assuming it away for simplicity's sake leads to nonsense models. To illustrate the point: when one develops a theory of ballistics, it is acceptable, in the first instance, to abstract from air temperature and humidity. One can then derive a simplified model, which can later be made more realistic by dropping these assumptions. However, one is bound to arrive at nonsensical conclusions, if one begins by assuming away the constitutional element of gravity. Likewise, it makes no sense to start developing a theory of human medicine by assuming blood circulation and the nervous system away, or an economic theory assuming that people have 'perfect knowledge'.

In reality, human beings suffer from two kinds of incompleteness in their knowledge when interacting with others:

- First, they have uncertain knowledge about the future ('future uncertainty'), but they have to make guesses about the future to act. They will appreciate being given help that reduces uncertainty and inspires confidence.
- Second, they have 'sideways uncertainty' about resources and potential exchange partners, as well as important details about the type of

resources and their potential exchange partners. Such 'sideways uncertainty' arises in particular, when people want to engage others to act on their behalf. They will often not know whether those agents will act honestly, reliably and to the best of their capability, or whether the agents will try to shirk obligations.

The assumption is often made in conventional economics textbooks that there is an 'economic man' who has perfect knowledge of all available means and his own ends. This enables *homo oeconomicus* (or *femina oeconomica*) to make rational choices that maximize his (or her) utility now and in the future. Analyses based on this narrow kind of end-means rationality turn economics into a mere computation exercise. However, such model exercises fail to convince practitioners in business, because business people simply know that no one ever has all the requisite knowledge of all available means and that people are often unsure of their own objectives. Normally, it is an essential part of their jobs for business people to chase better information about these matters. Business practitioners have to operate daily on the premise that individuals have a limited capacity to absorb information, to digest, convey and apply it – expressed technically: human beings suffer from limited cognitive capacity. This is a constitutional element in economic and business life.

People carry some of the knowledge they need in their own heads, but – most of the time – they can utilize what they know only in cooperation with others. In the modern world, the knowledge that individuals have does not go very far to help them meet their aspirations. An individual would not even be able to produce something as simple as a pencil. Indeed, no single person on earth has ever made a pencil all by himself. It takes graphite miners in Bolivia, wood cutters in Canada, glue makers in Taiwan, tool makers in Germany, traders in New York, and thousands of unknown others to cooperate and contribute (see Appendix). Much of people's knowledge is specific to the place where they live and work and much consists of highly specialized knowledge. For everything else, they have to rely on what past generations developed, for example complex tools and ways of organizing work and trade. The connections between numerous experts, who will never meet or even know of each other, are necessary for as commonplace an item as a pencil to arrive into our hands (and all this for the price of a few cents!). Does this seem like a miracle? If producing a pencil seems a task of mind-boggling complexity, think of a standard motorcar, which contains about 5000 components made in many different factories in different countries, or a modern jet fighter that contains some 3/4 million highly specialized bits and pieces!

For most of what is required to meet our wants and aspirations, we thus have to rely on cooperation with others, frequently uncountable numbers of unknown others who have knowledge of which we have not the slightest inkling. To satisfy our wants we depend on the division of labour amongst specialized producers, which means on the division of specialist knowledge (Boulding, 1968/1962). This specialization is so complex that it cannot be understood completely by any one human mind. The big question therefore is: How can all these diverse people around the world be coordinated to produce the desired end result, namely millions of different goods and services?

Knowledge and coordination

When individuals interact to draw on the specialized knowledge of their fellows to satisfy their aspirations (or, for that matter, to find out whether their aspirations are at all feasible), they are uncertain about how others will respond to their initiatives. They may, in the first instance, not even know whom to approach as potential partners and how. What material conditions are important to meeting their own aspirations and those of others? At the same time, they are uncertain as to who will approach them, with what demands and how. They will also be unclear how they themselves might respond to new demands made by others. In other words, they face strategic uncertainty.

In this context, we have to distinguish between two different types of knowledge, or rather ignorance:

(a) Economic actors may lack certain kinds of supplementary knowledge, but be roughly aware of the character and content of the information they still need. For example, suppose that I told you in which suburb I live, but not in which house. In trying to find me, there are more or less effective search processes – for instance referring to a map, using a tom-tom, driving around, asking people. Institutional arrangements can help in the search process, for example the rule that houses should be numbered sequentially. In these cases it is appropriate to speak of 'information search'.

(b) A totally different type of ignorance exists when we do not even have an inkling of what we do not know. When such knowledge is discovered, the discoverer is totally surprised. In retrospect, the new idea is obvious. Indeed, we are often surprised that, prior to the discovery, we did not know. Since people do not know what to search for, they cannot go about this in rational ways, for example by trying to minimize the costs of finding out (about something which they cannot know). An example of this was Columbus chancing upon the New World. He (probably) had no prior knowledge that America existed. Often people are convinced that they have the complete knowledge and then, one day, have to learn that they have been totally ignorant of pertinent facts. In such cases, it is appropriate to speak of a 'discovery' (Kirzner, 1997; Popper, 1959).

The knowledge-search-and-coordination problem is complicated by the fact that the knowledge we carry in our heads is the result of evolutionary selection. People (other than new-born babies) possess knowledge that they have acquired and validated by subsequent experience. If old knowledge is not useful or turns out to be counter-productive because circumstances have changed, it will be forgotten or revised. The world changes all the time: people's tastes change, different and more people are born, resources become scarce or are newly discovered, new production technologies are put in place, and so on. In the process, everyone has to cope with uncertainty about how the world will change and how others will react to new circumstances. Most relevant knowledge is thus the result of learning by doing and is acquired by innumerable different human beings in a decentralized selection process of trial and error. It is therefore crucial that we keep an open mind to new developments and opportunities. Even facts that have been verified thousands of times should not be taken as the eternal, unchallengeable truth. For thousands of years, Europeans *knew* that all swans are white – until the first black swans were brought back from Australia (Taleb, 2010)! Whether for reasons of mental inertia or fatalism, it behooves to reject a closed mindset and sacrosanct doctrines.

A central tenet of epistemology – and of Western civilization – is that knowledge is not static. It is always specific to a particular time. People acquire most of their knowledge by a process of *catallaxis*, that is, by interacting with others and exchanging ideas and assets. This concept was probably first explicitly formulated by British economist Richard Whately (1787–1863) and has more recently been revived by Ludwig von Mises. These scholars were able to draw on the pioneering work of British social philosophers John Locke (1632–1704) and David Hume (1711–1776) who had analysed the problems of human cognition, that is, how human senses receive impressions (sensation) and digest them through thought processes of internal relation-building (reflection).[1] They investigated how a person's ideas are developed by the digestion of impressions in the brain to generate that person's body of knowledge. When people interact and cooperate, they continually discover new sensations. They will be torn between a conservative instinct to retain familiar knowledge, which they share with others, and an experimental instinct to explore new ideas and overturn what is familiar to them and others. Thus, producers of a certain good or service have an interest in replicating what they have been producing in the past. That saves effort. But this conservative interest may be challenged by the need to take account of customer feedback about deficiencies and hence the need to redesign the product. The wish to beat the competition drives producers, time and again, to yield to the experimental urge and modify their existing knowledge. Thus, they keep learning. Personal preferences and real-life circumstances of course play a key role in what knowledge is being selected and retained in individuals' minds. As a result, different people possess different knowledge. It is a fundamental mistake to assume that everyone knows the same.

KEY CONCEPTS

Epistemology is the science, which investigates how humans acquire and convey knowledge. One of the main branches of philosophy, it is concerned with the nature, origin, scope, and limits of human knowledge. The name is derived from the Greek terms *episteme* (knowledge) and *logos* (theory): the theory of knowledge.

We speak of **information search**, when the general context is known and details have to be found out. This is, for example, done by software developers who want to improve a computer program. By contrast, we speak of **discovery** when totally new knowledge is found and the discoverer is genuinely surprised. It takes good luck and a certain quality of enterprise to make such discoveries.

New knowledge often comes about by marginal adaptations and variations of existing knowledge. As people interact, marginal tinkering and small creative steps occur here and there, so that stepwise improvements accumulate over time. Thus, much of the improvement in aircraft design since the Wright brothers took off in 1903 is owed to numerous small improvements in aeronautic technology, propulsion and management, and much of it emerged in the interaction between aircraft users and aircraft builders. The broad stream of such steady, adaptive improvements is sometimes overshadowed by major breakthroughs when completely new concepts emerge. Thus, the emergence of electronic data processing and communications technology has revolutionized many fields of computation, management and entertainment. Such creative breakthroughs capture the imagination and are recorded in the history books, but their contribution to economic progress has been much less than the broad, gradual adaptive advancement of knowledge across the many areas of human endeavour (Schumpeter, 1961/1908).

Sometimes, knowledge is put together by systematic design, such as in organized industrial research and development or in architectural planning. Here knowledge does not evolve pragmatically by trial and error inside society, but is constructed systematically by a group that observes and plans matters from the outside. Groups of such planners are motivated to find perfect 'or-all-eternity solutions', based on precise and stable information. They then construct an ideal design. As long as the framework for the design remains unchanged, such knowledge may indeed be consistent and effective, but problems arise as soon as the framework conditions evolve. When that happens, yesterday's perfect solution may turn out to be tomorrow's dud.

Knowledge may emerge either in a creative act, out of curiosity and inspiration when people spontaneously try out a new idea or when they engage in systematic research and design to find something new. An example of planned knowledge search is the invention and commercial utilization of nuclear power; an example of a spontaneous act of creativity, which was not planned by a designer, was the painting of the Mona Lisa, which probably reflected how Europeans viewed the human condition in the Renaissance. Much knowledge has been uncovered serendipitously, that is, by chance, by sheer inspiration or as a by-product of a search for something else. Thus, the modern lifestyle drug Viagra was not discovered because the pharmaceutical company wanted to find something like it, but as a fortuitous by-product of other research. What is important is that people are alert, open-minded and prepared to make discoveries. This is even true in the modern world in which much research and development is organized and conducted by research professionals.

Thus, much progress is owed not to an emergent, major breakthrough, but to adaptive change, to creativity by trial and error, by tinkering and improvement in response to new demands and changing conditions. Adaptive tinkering is often underrated or even overlooked by general observers, who tend to be fascinated by the more conspicuous big innovations. The far-distant ancestor who invented the wheel changed human knowledge by a big and creative step. However, since then, that basic idea has been improved upon by millions of users of wheels in thousands of adaptive changes – from tiny wheels in watches to giant wheels on huge dump trucks in mining. Of course, in the process of ceaseless trial and error, numerous ideas fail and are abandoned. For every successful oil well, there are, for example, probably dozens of 'dry holes'. Exploring the unknown and widening our stock of useful knowledge is risky. But it may often turn out to be profitable business (Boulding 1968/1962).

Implicit and explicit knowledge

Another aspect of human knowledge worth discussing relates to how relevant knowledge is retained in people's minds and passed on. Certain types of knowledge can easily be put in words, written down and passed on in the form of manuals or textbooks. Most scientific and technical knowledge can, for example, be made explicit to be passed on in schools and university lectures. It can also be described in patent applications and sold to businesses that want to utilize it. But such explicit knowledge is far from all that we know and use to enhance our living standards. There is much implicit knowledge, on which we rely tacitly in our daily lives and our work routines. We often refer to it as 'knowhow' and 'skills'. It is often surprisingly difficult and costly, if at all possible, to make knowhow explicit: just try to write down an instruction how to tie shoelaces for someone who has never done it!

Implicit (or tacit) knowledge can be acquired through 'learning by doing'. It is internalized in the human mind so that people then use it without reflection (Polanyi, 1966). Much learning is concerned with practicing and internalizing tacit knowledge. Just think of the young fellow who learns skateboarding with alacrity by imitating friends and going through the same routines time and again, until he is a master skateboarder! It would be near-impossible to convey all relevant knowledge in explicit form to a teenager by handing him manuals about gravity, friction, velocity and centripetal forces! Or, to cite another example, would you entrust your life to a surgeon who has studied all the relevant knowledge for open-heart surgery from books and professors, but without ever acquiring the necessary routine skills by operating on frogs and pig hearts? Yet, the leaders of many post-colonial developing countries kept foreign experts and multinational companies out who could have conveyed implicit knowhow and skills. Instead they relied solely on the acquisition of explicit industrial knowledge. The industrial record of such countries suggests that underrating the importance of practical routines, skills and knowhow has costly and far-reaching consequences. For the same reason, industries that stress hands-on work in apprenticeships and engineering studies tend to use technical knowledge better than industries where explicit knowledge is overrated and implicit knowhow, skills and efficient work routines are ignored or neglected.

KEY CONCEPTS

Knowledge consists of symbols and relations retained in the human mind. Knowledge may be made explicit and communicated formally. Or it may consist of implicit knowhow – informal, petty knowledge, often of great complexity and specificity to place, circumstance and time – which can probably be acquired only by practice (**learning by doing**). Much relevant knowledge is in tacit (or implicit) form, often called **knowhow**. It is acquired by imitating routines in which all the many petty, complex bits of relevant knowledge are absorbed. Whilst some bodies of implicit knowledge can be made explicit (for example written down in manuals) much still depends on tacit knowhow.

Knowledge is often generated spontaneously by the interaction of people. It may also be created by conscious design when people get together in an organized, systematic way and develop new knowledge following a plan of research and development.

The **knowledge problem** derives from the fact that human beings have only a limited capacity to develop, test and apply knowledge. Ignorance therefore is a constitutional element of human existence, including in economic pursuits, that is, in how to overcome scarcity. 'Constitutional' here means that it is an essential part of the human condition and must not be assumed away.

The sum of human knowledge is contained in the diverse brains of all the people who live on earth. Only tiny fractions of it can be concentrated in any one mind. Knowledge therefore is used effectively only if mechanisms can be found to draw on the diverse, specialized knowledge of large numbers of people. The **division of labour and knowledge** allows people to specialize, but requires them to cooperate. Thanks to specialization, communities are able to acquire more knowledge and use it to solve problems. With experience, they are likely to chance upon more knowledge. Over time, they become more effective in meeting their own and other peoples' wants, as they learn new and adapt or discard old knowledge. The division of labour and knowledge therefore is a dynamic, evolving concept.

One has to distinguish between **emergent and adaptive additions to knowledge:** emergent knowledge refers to major creative breakthroughs (for example, the splitting of the atom), whereas the adaptive development of knowledge refers to the steady flow of creativity in which small, stepwise improvements are made in response to opportunities of supply and demand (for example, the gradual improvement of computer software programs). Emergent additions are often the result of **discovery** of ideas that were previously completely unknown, whereas adaptive additions to knowledge are often the result of systematic **information search**.

Knowledge evolves in a tension between:

- a conservative instinct, which aims to retain what has proved useful and has been appreciated by others, and
- an experimental instinct, which derives from curiosity and the desire to better meet one's aspirations by matching (often changing) circumstances.

Knowledge specific to space and time refers primarily to knowhow, which differs from place to place and evolves over time. It is essential to effective human interaction. In economics, it relates primarily to commercial knowledge: Where is the cheapest source of supply? Who has the skills and connections this year to produce a specific product? How can one obtain a specific service by tomorrow, and so on?

'Economic man' is an unrealistic fiction

As noted, the orthodox neoclassical economics that one finds in many introductory textbooks has pushed the knowledge problem aside by simply assuming that economic agents have 'perfect knowledge'. This assumption tends to be made cursorily on page 1 of many textbooks, so that the authors can begin with logical deductions from this and other premises (see *Epilogue*). What this implies in practice is that the preferences of millions of people for trillions of goods, services and satisfactions, are known, as well as all the resources on earth and billions of relevant production techniques! With that sort of knowledge, it is of course possible to reduce economics to a simple computing exercise of how known resources are transformed by known technologies to meet the pre-existing, known preferences of a standardized 'economic man'. The elegant neoclassical model thus shirks the quintessential question of economics. The assumption of perfect knowledge is the birth defect of neoclassical theory, which often deprives it of relevance to the real human existence, namely the constant struggle to test existing knowledge and know more.

The approach to institutional economics in this book is not based on the unrealistic assumption of perfect knowledge. Rather, the lack of knowledge – ignorance – is accepted as part and parcel of the human fate. It must not be eliminated, as it is constitutional. But – as we shall see – deficient knowledge can be overcome in part by appropriate institutional arrangements, which guide individual decision makers through a complex and uncertain world. Certain institutions can help us to economize on the need and cost of acquiring knowledge. This approach may make economic analysis more cumbersome and less elegant, but – we trust – more relevant to understanding reality and more convincing to the practitioners in business, law and public policy.

3.2   Types of behaviour, cognition and bounded rationality: deciphering reality

Of symbols and images

We acquire a 'world view' and decipher the complex reality around us by attaching meanings to symbols and by relating these symbols, one might say by operating with 'images' (Boulding, 1997/1956). Thinking with symbols is not a purely private, individual matter. What the human mind constructs as an image of reality is influenced by social, cultural experience, so that different people and people from different civilizations may well perceive the world in different ways. Upbringing and cultural experiences influence a person's cognition, as does language, since some thought processes make use of linguistic symbols. This sometimes complicates communication between members of different cultures, because certain 'images of the mind' are not shared and need to be explicated before they are understood (Redding, 1993, pp. 72–77). A problem in this context is what neuro science calls 'cognitive bias': different people are disposed to recognize certain facts and opinions more than others, because previous experience makes them receptive to some insights, but not others (Gigerenzer, 2006). Information that can be easily integrated into one's prior knowledge tends to be more readily accepted than information that challenges preconceived ideas. This makes what is objective and rational less clear-cut than most would assume.

Because they create meaningful symbols and relate them in their minds, humans are able to interact with the world in ways that go beyond reflexive behaviour (such as the response of the pupil of the eye to bright light), conditioned reflexes (such as our mouths salivating when we see delicious food) and instrumental behaviour (such as the use of a club to propel a golf ball). The human mind is able to attach non-intrinsic, abstract meanings to signals and turn these into symbols, which often represent meanings that have nothing to do with the original signal. Thus, early systems of writing depicted real objects, but the letters, characters and other symbols acquired abstract meaning to convey words or part of words. Symbols frequently depend on a complex context to be read correctly (for example, a red light may indicate the need to stop the car, or it may signal a red-light district). It is this capacity to work with abstract symbols that forms the "mental gulf that divides the lowest savage from the highest ape", as the renowned British anthropologist Edward Burnett Tylor once put it (Tylor, 1883; Kasper 2011b).

Symboling constitutes the largest part of the knowledge and information we acquire. It then influences the more primitive types of behaviour (reflexive and instrumental behaviour). Much learning takes the form of 'internalizing' concepts that are first consciously acquired as symbols and then, through repetition, turned into conditioned reflexes. Thus, we first absorb a chain of symbols to learn how a car is steered. Then, we practice – again and again – until the various actions become almost automatic, conditioned reflexes. Skills and much specific knowledge are acquired in such a way to become 'implicit knowledge'. In similar processes of internalization, we acquire moral standards which one might call 'ethical skills'. They are most effectively learnt by repeat practice (observing adults in the family for example). As a result, we are normally honest, not because we carefully analyse a specific situation whether we can get away unpunished with dishonesty, but rather in a conditioned-reflexive way. Such reflexive behaviour speeds up decision processes and enhances the effectiveness of human interaction.

KEY CONCEPTS

Cognition is the invisible (re-)construction of reality as perceived by our five senses. It takes place in the mind, which operates almost imperceptibly in thought processes and which helps people to decipher the real world. Cognition is to some extent culturally conditioned, so that people from different cultures decipher reality differently. The human mind is informed by social experience, so that reality for one person may be at variance with reality as perceived by another who has had different experiences.

We can distinguish between the following **types of behaviour** (moving from primitive to more highly developed forms):

- reflexive (example: contraction of a muscle when pain is inflicted);
- conditioned-reflexive (example: a shudder when you think of being beheaded);
- instrumental (example: use of knife and fork to eat);
- symbolizing (the creation, combination and digestion of symbols, example: developing an architectural design and using it to construct a building).

A **symbol** is a mental abstract, an image of the mind, which represents a more complex whole.

The information paradox

Rational decision making requires knowledge and willful choice between known alternatives. However, resources and time to obtain information about alternatives are scarce and costly; endless information gathering before we can make a decision would lead to paralysis by analysis. It is just not feasible. Economics Nobel Prize winner George Stigler once remarked: "Information costs are the costs of transportation from ignorance to omniscience, and seldom can a trader afford to take the entire trip" (Stigler, 1967; p. 297). We often choose to remain ignorant because it is simply too costly to be fully informed. The question therefore arises to what point people should carry their information search: to the point where the expected marginal cost is equal to the expected marginal benefit (Stigler 1971), or to a point where experience suggests to decision makers that they probably know enough to decide?

The answer is that individuals cannot know the expected costs and benefits of obtaining certain types of information, before they have acquired it. Consequently, they are unable to maximize net returns from knowledge not yet acquired. Paradoxically, they would need the very information before they have acquired it, as British economist George Shackle (1903-1992) pointed out in the quote at the head of this chapter. This logical insight has been called the 'information paradox' (Arrow, 1971/1962). Unlike the production of goods and services, where one has the knowledge about costs and benefits beforehand so that one can optimize resource use, the production of new knowledge cannot be subjected to such a rational calculus.

We can illustrate the point by thinking of a student who wonders whether it is worth $10 of his money to watch a specific movie. The only way to really find out is to spend the money and watch it! Although the risk can be reduced by reading film reviews, it is always possible to conclude with hindsight that the money would have been better spent on something else, whatever a film review conveyed by way of partial knowledge of the movie. In short, when searching for new knowledge, one never knows what one will find and whether the information is of as much value as expected. Often, one is even completely ignorant of what one misses until one makes a discovery.

There is another peculiarity in the production of knowledge: the costs for knowledge search have to be considered as 'sunk costs'. This means that the costs for knowledge production – once incurred – have no relevance to the extent to which the knowledge is used, whereas the costs of producing goods have a direct bearing on the amount which can be profitably produced (Streit and Wegner, 1992). In practice, people engage in the search for information until they perceive that they have incurred sufficient expense and then make a decision within the bounds of what they have been able to find out. Experience and individual inclination will guide them in acquiring information until they think they have informed themselves sufficiently to make a choice. Experience will prevent them from wasting excessive effort on information gathering. This does not, of course, mean that they will not, in specific instances, make decisions that turn out to be wrong.

We make decisions all the time that we may regret *ex post*. A classic example of this is going out to eat at a new restaurant – *ex ante* we expect to enjoy the evening of good food and drink, but if our meal does not meet our standard, we often wish we had gone instead to the older, more reliable restaurant. The critical issue for economic activity is not our regret per se, but how that disappointment plays into our decision calculus in the future. It is the very discrepancy between our *ex ante* expectations and our *ex post* realizations that spur our learning. This is, at least in part, what Shackle (1972, p. 156) means when he writes that "*being* consists in continual and endless fresh *knowing*."

Information economics with its core idea of optimal search runs into the information paradox that we referred to above. Because obtaining and analysing new knowledge is costly in terms of time, effort and resources, no one on his own will acquire all the knowledge needed for complex operations. People will rather seek to exploit the knowledge of others by interacting with them. Indeed, it is rational for people to acquire only certain bits of information and to remain ignorant of other information, given the high costs and uncertain outcomes of knowledge search (rational ignorance).

CH 3 – CASE ONE

Known Unknowns and Unknown Unknowns

Then US Secretary of Defense, Donald Rumsfeld, when talking about unknown military threats, elicited much mirth among ill-informed media commentators, when he distinguished between 'known unknowns' and 'unknown unknowns'. Yet, he made a very important epistemological point: Often people know that there is information which is (yet) unknown to them and which they hope to discover by systematic search and analysis. We are often aware of such gaps in our knowledge. But often we are not even aware that we are ignorant. We may occasionally make surprising discoveries, of which we had no prior knowledge at all – the (yet) unknown unknowns! Thus, early Portuguese explorers of the coastline of West Africa did not know its precise shape before they drew their charts, but the coastline was not a complete surprise. Matters changed fundamentally when Vasco da Gama rounded the Cape of Good Hope – an unknown that he could probably not have anticipated. Europeans had not even known that they had been completely ignorant about the 'door to the Indian Ocean'.

Similar, genuine discoveries by genuine pioneers of technologies that had previously not even been imagined by anyone were the printing press, the steam engine and the transistor (emergent innovations). Once these mega inventions were known, they gave rise to numerous follow-up applications, triggering waves of innovation (adaptive innovations).

Different kinds of rationality

What has been said so far has a further important consequence: people who incur the costs of searching for useful knowledge under conditions of uncertainty cannot be all-knowing and will often not be able to make absolutely rational choices. They will normally even find it hard to stick rigidly to pre-conceived, set objectives and aspirations. In the process of interacting with others, their aspirations will evolve. If people are frequently disappointed, they tend to peg back what they aspire to. If objectives are reached easily, they may become more ambitious and hope to attain new wants. In other words, people will often display adaptive behaviour, recognizing the bounds of what they can attain. This is, however, not invariably the case. At other times, enterprising people will act to break through constraints which they normally accept as given, or they may discover new opportunities by chance.

We therefore have to distinguish between three kinds of rationality:

(a) end-means rationality where the ends and the means to attain them are known, for example from earlier experience;

(b) bounded, adaptive rationality; and

(c) entrepreneurial-creative rationality that, on occasions, breaks out of recognized bounds or exploits chance discoveries.

Instances of end-means rationality can be observed where agents have set themselves fixed goals, or where others have set those goals for them, and where people use available resources and techniques to maximize the attainment of these goals. When you enter a marathon race, your objective may be to finish in the shortest possible time. You employ all your resources of physical strength and willpower, as well as your knowledge of how to pace yourself, towards attaining that goal. Another example may be a business company that employs all available means to achieve the highest-possible return on their assets. This sort of rational behaviour underlies conventional neoclassical textbook analysis.

However, frequently the other kinds of rationality are prevalent. What if you are not a top-rated long-distance runner, but nevertheless want to compete in marathons? You will rationally adjust your objective to your own capacity in the light of past performance and get great satisfaction from running at a speed commensurate to your capability. Instead of following absolute goals, people gradually discover what they can achieve and handle their goal-attainment rationally in an adaptive way. This is so because people are frequently limited in their capacities to absorb and evaluate more information. American economist-sociologist Herbert Simon called this 'bounded rationality' or 'procedural rationality' (Simon, 1957; 1959; 1976; 1982; 1983). Instead of optimizing given objectives, people and businesses 'satisfice', he wrote; they adjust their aspiration levels in the light of past experience.

CH 3 – CASE TWO

The knowledge problem and the concept of efficiency

One important consequence of the knowledge problem is that one has to be extremely careful in using the term 'efficiency'.

It is valid to say that a car, which runs 100 km on six litres of petrol, is more efficient than

CH 3 – CASE TWO *(continued)*

one that consumes 10 litres. Here, we compare physical outputs (travel over 100 km) with inputs (litres of gas) between simple technical systems and make statements about **technical efficiency**.

Economic choices, however, require that we put valuations on inputs and outputs, for example market prices for the input of petrol and a value on the performance of a 100 km trip. This gives us information about **economic efficiency**. Such statements are valid, as long as one is clear about the valuation and understands the system in which inputs are converted to outputs when making interpersonal utility comparisons.

Frequently, however, the term 'efficiency' is applied by planners and managers to more complex, evolving systems, where the valuation of diverse inputs and outputs is not clearly understood and where implicit, invalid interpersonal utility comparisons are made, about whose basis one really has no knowledge. It has to be recognized that different observers will attach differing values to inputs and outputs and consider their own, subjective opportunity costs. Then, comparisons to the effect that 'A is more efficient than B' are not valid, because one simply does not know how other people would value inputs and outputs. The point may become clear to the reader when you are asked: Which is the most efficient motorcar in the world? What is the best book? What is best depends on individual, subjective valuations. A complex machine that can serve a myriad of differing purposes cannot generally be called the best or most efficient. This is why it is frequently wrong to assume that 'one size fits all'. Mao suits for everyone may be technically efficient to dress people, but this method makes for poor satisfaction. Frequently, diversity is wealth.

The problem of deciding what is most efficient becomes even more intractable when one deals with unknowable inputs and outputs. A statement to the effect that 'this is the most efficient way to defend the security of our nation' is invalid, because the output 'security' is inherently not known and hence not measurable. Rough-and-ready assumptions that some assumed proxy measures a nation's security, so that one can decide on efficiency are likely to lead to dangerous errors. More likely than not, such assumptions will turn out to be wrong.

When considering complex systems, such as national economies, one can only legitimately say that one system is capable of generating more economic growth than another, or more innovations than another. This is a statement about the **dynamic efficiency** of a system, an inherent quality to adapt, respond or develop new knowledge.

The term efficiency becomes meaningless when its use implies comparisons between complex reality and an abstract, ideally functioning economic model. Model decisions are often made on the basis of perfect knowledge which allows decision makers, somehow, to evaluate all possible outcomes of using given production techniques and given resources. Such a reference system can nowhere be realized. It is utopian. Hence it is not a valid reference standard for judging the efficiency of operations in the real world. It has been aptly characterized as the 'nirvana approach to economics' (Demsetz, 1969). (See also Cordato, 'Efficiency' in Boettke, 1994, pp. 131–137).

At times, people do not act rationally in the sense that they maximize ends and means or adapt aspirations in view of past experience. People, who normally accept given constraints and act within them, may at certain junctures decide to tackle these constraints head-on in order to widen or bypass acknowledged obstacles to their goal achievement (Schumpeter, 1961/1908). Thus, the Wright brothers, and many before them, refused to accept the known constraints of gravity. They finally managed to fly in a heavier-than-air contraption. Or, in the Renaissance, some exceptional Europeans refused to accept the man-made constraints over the supply of spices from the East (the supply being constrained by Muslim intermediaries): They sailed south to discover the sea routes to India and chanced upon America in the process. In these cases, individuals act out of a creative and entrepreneurial motivation and overcome technical or other constraints. Acting in creative-entrepreneurial ways sometimes also involves the breaking of institutional constraints, for example by violating established conventions and customs, or by political lobbying to gain support for the change of a certain rule. We therefore have to recognize creative rationality, which propels people to take risks and break new paths and keeps them on the alert for new discoveries, as a third type of rational behaviour, and one that is apt to enhance human knowledge. It would be plain wrong to describe entrepreneurs who try to market a new product as irrational, although they do not optimize known ends and given means.

One may go further and acknowledge that a considerable part of our daily behaviour is not rationally and logically targeted at any specific, identifiable objective. Much action is coordinated by habits which cannot be explained in any one specific instance by rational calculus: Why do people vote at elections, when this has patently no measurable effect on policy, let alone their own lives? Why do people give tips to waiters whom they will never see again? Often people simply follow habitual patterns or imitate others.

KEY CONCEPTS

Rationality refers to purpose-directed action, guiding all actions towards the attainment of a goal or a set of goals (or ends).

We can distinguish between:

(a) **'end-means rationality'**, when the end is given and actions are taken to attain that given end (example: pursuit of a rate of return by a firm);

(b) adaptive, **'bounded rationality'** which relates to (in practice frequent) situations when people do not all-knowingly maximize their given objectives, but adapt their aspirations (goals) in the light of experience to what is feasible for them;

(c) **'entrepreneurial-creative rationality'** which relates to an approach in

➡

> ← which agents try to overcome existing constraints, be it of resource supplies, technological limits or institutional constraints (example: humans overcame the pull of gravity, a physical constraint, eventually in entrepreneurial-creative ways by exploring the lifting capacity of gasses and fluid dynamics around fixed wings).
>
> **Rational ignorance** is the behaviour of people not to acquire certain types of knowledge in the face of the costs and uncertainties of information search.

3.3 Motivation: by love, convincing, command, or self-interest

The individual and social bonds

At this juncture, we have to remind ourselves of the obvious fact that human beings interact with others; all human behaviour has to be seen in a social context. Indeed, very few people can function effectively if left on their own for more than very limited periods of time. They need the stimulation and control of how their fellows respond. Humans thrive intellectually, morally, culturally, and emotionally only thanks to their personal connections with their fellow men. Indeed, most people are at their worst when they are isolated, anonymous and alienated from others.

By definition, the student of institutions rejects a position of 'isolationist individualism', that is, a position of seeing the individual as an island. Rather, one conceives people as 'social animals' who pursue their own ends in cooperation with others. To adopt a position of individualism, as we have here, therefore does not mean that one studies people as stand-alone individuals. Individualism means instead that individual aspirations are the ultimate objective of social and economic study, but of course of individuals who live in a social context and are constrained by institutions that largely define what is 'social'. The institutional-economics approach therefore acknowledges that individuals establish reciprocal relations and indeed need lasting communal bonds. Associations with others give us a sense of belonging, but also impose institutional strictures. Such associations are perceived as deeply satisfying and give people a sense of identity and security (Hazlitt, 1988/1964, pp. 35–43). Social connections serve, so to speak, to keep our selfish, atavistic, opportunistic and cognitively biased individual instincts on a leash; institutions form a central part in constraining instinct-driven opportunism.

What has been said about social bonds between individuals also applies to groups. If various social groups are sharply delineated and in conflict with each other, sustained economic development is unlikely (Powelson, 1994). What is needed is an open, tolerant society, in which the poor have a share in power and obey the sane rules as the rich and powerful (Popper, 1945). Eric Jones, who studied episodes of economic growth in history, spoke in this context of the 'relative connectedness' of the community as a precondition to creative and effective interaction (Jones, 1988, p. 128).

It does not, of course, follow from recognizing these facts of human existence that the 'herd' has to be organized by a leader, commanded from the top down and directed to serve some predetermined goal(s). Frequently, social bonds evolve because people discover spontaneously that they share interests. People normally belong to numerous, overlapping groups, associations and networks that are governed by differing institutions (pluralist society). Thus, we may be members of a family, various clubs, a religious community, different regional entities, such as a local neighbourhood, a city, a province, a nation state, and a transnational cultural community. We normally feel that such diverse and multiple associations best serve us to realize our potential.

The social aspect of human behaviour is no doubt deeply embedded in the human heritage. Paleo-anthropologists believe that the gradual evolution of our ancestors from bands of *Australopithecus*, who probably fended for themselves in hordes like baboons, had much to do with social interaction when hunting, gathering or sharing the loot in camps. Humans trained their differentiated cognitive abilities by social interaction; they gained evolutionary advantages in coordinating activity with others in order to survive better (Leakey, 1994).[2] Evolution thus favoured people with good interactive and coordinative abilities who functioned well in social groups. And tribes, which developed institutions and ensured that scarce food resources were shared evenly within a closely-knit, small group under a circumspect leader, had better survival chances. Thus, a 'tribal mentality' based on social bonding and sharing evolved over millions of years and got deeply embedded in the human psyche (Hayek, 1976, pp. 133–152; Jacobs, 1992; Giersch, 1996).

When studying human behaviour, we therefore must not assume that humans are isolated individuals, but rather that they are social creatures whose interaction is essential to them. This leads us on to the next question: namely, what motivates individuals to act for the benefit of others?

Four types of motivation

It is a basic premise of human behaviour that individuals normally act in their own self-interest. They may pursue their aspirations in whatever way possible, whether this harms the aspirations of others or not. Thus, the aspiration not to go hungry may be pursued by planting food, by buying and selling, or by theft. Experience shows, however, that theft (and other types of opportunistic behaviour) leads to costly conflicts and is wasteful: a society of thieves reaches lower satisfaction levels than an honestly cooperating community. One therefore has to ask how individual autonomy to act should be constrained so that such opportunism is controlled. We of course already know that constraining opportunistic behaviour is the function of institutions.

In principle, there are four ways in which people can be induced to make an effort in the interest of others (Boulding, 1969, p. 6; Hazlitt, 1988/1964, pp. 92–107):

(a) They make the effort to benefit others out of love, solidarity, or other variants of altruism.
(b) They are coerced by someone who threatens them with the use of force (command).
(c) They act out of their own free will, but are motivated out of enlightened self-interest because they can expect a sufficient reward. What they do for others is then the side effect of their selfishness.
(d) They act voluntarily for the benefit of others because someone has convinced them by rational argument to do so. This latter case can, however, be subsumed under one of the first three categories: it may appeal to love and solidarity, may be backed up by a threat of force or be based on an explanation of long-term, enlightened self-interest.

The first type of motivation works well in small groups such as a family, a small tribe and among friends. Such behaviour deserves social recognition and is often rewarded by respect, honour or prestige. It enables the division of labour and knowledge in small communities, without inflicting high coordination and monitoring costs. As noted above, this type of behaviour has been so essential for the survival of small bands of our distant ancestors during hundreds of thousands of generations that most humans have been instinctually conditioned to consider altruism as noble and praiseworthy.

But what works well in the small group – because of good knowledge about the others and direct mutual control that is tempered by personal empathy – cannot be transferred to the large group, such as the modern macro-society with industrial mass production and mass communication.[3] Some may regret that large communities such as nations do not function like a big family. They may regret that the baker does not simply provide the bread because he loves his hungry customers. They may regret that the Christian maxim of 'love thy neighbour' cannot be extended to millions of distant people whom we do not know. Yet, the evidence is clear: when interacting with complete strangers, people usually need a motive other than love and solidarity.[4]

This becomes apparent when the solidarity model of the small group is transferred to society at large under the doctrine of idealistic socialism. The promise of communal sharing under the slogan 'from each according to his ability, to each according to his need' ineluctably leads to massive shirking of contributions of effort, massive claiming of benefits, and hence poor living standards. Efforts to reform human nature and to create the new socialist man, who toils selflessly for others out of mere altruism, have failed abysmally. Consequently, people under socialism had to be coerced. Authorities, however selected, assumed the power to punish others who did not produce to the targeted norm. Coercion and fear thus became the main motivation under socialism to get people to produce something that benefits others – and dissimulation and shirking wherever people could get away with it then became widespread.

In the Western Christian tradition and the Eastern Confucian and Buddhist traditions, education and preaching are relied upon to encourage people to treat others with solidarity. This may have worked in small groups in early Christendom or small village communities in Asia, but it failed to ensure adequate living standards in bigger societies where solidarity inevitably declines with social distance.

The third possible motivation is self-interest. It works, for example, through voluntary exchange in the market place. People share their knowledge and assets to help others because they want what the others have to offer in exchange. The veterinarian, who gets up in the night to attend to a cow having trouble calving, does so normally for the money. But the beneficial side effect of his selfish action is that cow and calf survive. It may be shocking to young people who are educated in the solidarity mode of the family to discover that, in anonymous mass society, others do things that benefit them as a by-product of a selfish pursuit of money. But at least many different people, with different skills and assets, act to their benefit, even if they do not care personally for the people they serve. People are thus guided as if by 'an invisible hand' to work for the benefit of others. The invisible hand of the market mechanism has of course to be supplemented by institutional constraints, such as an understanding of professional duty (for example in the medical profession) and the effort to keep a reputation of the profession intact out of a long term, extended self-interest.

Clearly, people will only be motivated to perform a service for others out of self-interest if they can keep the reward and if they are not coerced to share what they have earned with others. This means that people must have the right to private property, including to their own labour and skills. Without a respected and protected right to own property – which also means the right to exclude others from its use and to dispose of the property as one decides – there would be insufficient motivation for the many specialists in a modern society to produce the goods and services that we want. The useful knowledge that is held in millions of different human brains can only be exploited to the best of peoples' abilities, if a set of institutions (rules) protects private property and its free use.

The long-term President of Uganda, Yoweri Museveni, expressed the motivation issue brilliantly when he remarked: "I think that [collectivism] was a strategic mistake. They [the Marxists] chose a tool, which would not get human beings to produce. Do you make ... [the people] ... produce by appealing to the altruism which was very much in short supply? Or do you make them produce by making use of their selfishness, which was in abundance?" (reported in *Time*, 14 April 1997, p. 43).

Motivation in micro and in macro societies

At this juncture in our discussion, we have reached several important conclusions:

- Love and altruism, which have a very important place in motivating people in small groups, do not work among people in modern mass societies who do not know and cannot control each other directly.
- The alternative of relying on coercion has the important drawback that those in authority often do not have the knowledge necessary for utilizing all available resources and that people who are coerced try to shirk their duties when they think they can get away with it.
- The system of utilizing available knowledge and accumulating new information, which is at the heart of the economic growth process, requires incentives that appeal to self-interest and rely on voluntary action. The desirable outcomes of such action are often unintended by-products of the selfish pursuit of people's own purposes.
- Rational argument and education to convince people to do what others want can be important to improve the likelihood that we produce what benefits others.

KEY CONCEPTS

The **information paradox** arises when one wants to assess how many resources should be invested in information search. Whereas one can calculate beforehand what resources to use in order to obtain a desired output from a farm or factory, given one has all relevant information on how the farm or factory functions, such a calculus of optimization cannot be made for the production of knowledge. One simply does not have the necessary information before one has incurred the expense of acquiring it! One can normally only go by past experience and seek limited information before making a decision how much to invest in information search. And once one has acquired the knowledge, the costs of the search are sunk costs: they have no effect on the further use of the knowledge.

Opportunism describes the short-term maximization of human satisfaction without regard to the impact of such behaviour on others and without regard to the accepted norms of behaviour in the community. Such forms of behaviour have disintegrating, hence harmful long-term consequences; they make human actions less predictable over the long term. Thus, it is opportunistic to satisfy one's appetite by stealing from others, or to forget repaying one's contractual debts. "By opportunism I mean self-interested seeking with guile. This includes, but is scarcely limited to, more blatant forms, such as lying, stealing, and cheating" (Williamson, 1985, p. 47). It is the role of institutions, which must include sanctions for violations, to suppress opportunism.

Small-group coordination, for example within the family, is based on much implicit knowledge and informal, mutual behavioural control. People with authority often find their power tempered by sympathy for the less powerful members of the group. By contrast, **macro-group coordination** requires general institutions, because a large number of people cannot be coordinated by personal knowledge and empathy and no-one can possess all the specific knowledge and the capacity to control everyone and everything by prescriptive command.

Altruism is an attitude that places the interests of others above one's own. It contrasts not only with egotism (ruthless self-seeking), but also with a rational extended self-interest in pursuing own goals in preference to the poorly known aspirations of others.

3.4　The principal-agent problem

Agents and principals

Since motivation by altruism is normally limited to small groups and coercion is wasteful and ineffectual, problems arise when people act on behalf of someone else to whom they are not very close. In other words, people act as agents for principals. For example, the owners of a firm employ staff to do work for them; managers run the day-to-day operations of a business that belongs to shareholders; citizens elect politicians to make certain decisions on their behalf. In these cases, agents may be tempted to act opportunistically in the knowledge that they will get away with it, since the principals are often not well informed or remain 'rationally ignorant' about the details of the agent's actions. Principals may incur high monitoring costs if they want to find out what the agents are really doing, as information is asymmetric: the agent knows more than the principal. Consequently, workers may get away with shirking some of their duties although they could work harder. Business managers may prefer the good life and satisfice, whereas it would be in the interest of the owners of the business (the principals) if they behaved in more risky, creative-entrepreneurial ways. And the citizens, who are the principals in a political community, often do not get from government officials what they really want, because parliamentarians and officials pursue their own selfish purposes. This is known as the 'principal-agent problem'. It is a consequence of the knowledge problem and the natural limits of solidarity with others.[5]

When people feel they can get away with opportunistic behaviour, because those whom they short-change do not know and will not find out, they fall prey to 'moral hazard'. This term was first used in insurance: The insured fail to take proper precautions to avoid damage and only they know what full precaution could achieve in particular circumstances. Thus, agents are exposed to moral hazard when the principals are ignorant or the agents are not constrained by appropriate rules.

The principal-agent problem is considerable in big business and government organizations. Agents then tend to busy themselves with activities they themselves find agreeable, but not necessarily activities that serve the purpose(s) of the enterprise to sell at a profit for the owners or achieve other objectives set by the principals. To deal with this, high organization costs may have to be incurred. Managers of a firm may come up with plans for numerous meetings in pleasant places, interesting research projects, in-service courses and coordination committees, which detract from their obligation to shoulder responsibilities for risk-taking. They may justify a need to travel and a whole host of other seemingly 'essential' activities that amount to 'on-the-job consumption'. There are many ways which occupy work time pleasantly and add to overhead costs without making sufficient contributions to the profit. Yet, outsiders, including the owners of the firm, do not know which of those costs are necessary and which not (for more see Chapters 9 and 10).

How to motivate agents

Wherever people employ agents to act on their behalf, the motivation of the agents requires attention. The types of motivation, which we discussed above, may be employed by the principals to ensure that their agents act to the best of their capabilities.

(a) Agents can be inspired to make the principals' goals their own out of solidarity. Where only few people are involved, say in a small firm, collaborators can be very loyal to the owner or owners. They may use direct appeals to their colleagues to perform well; and even in bigger operations collaborators can be educated in habits of loyalty to the principals, which then saves on monitoring and other transaction costs.
(b) Agents can be controlled by direct supervision and direct commands. They may be guided by instructions and subjected to penalties if they do not follow the instructions, as long as the principals keep themselves informed about the agents' actions and potential scope for improvement.
(c) Agents may be required to follow general rules, which create incentives for them to pursue the principals' interests. Thus, businesses may offer their workers performance pay to promote profitability or investment funds give their managers a share in improved asset values. These are ways to draw on the agents' self-interest (indirect control).

An example of direct control of possibly opportunistic agents is the supervision of workers in a factory to see whether they meet targets and produce the output quantities and qualities that the management has planned. This requires much detailed knowledge on the part of the principals and supervisors and may cause high monitoring costs, especially when the production task becomes complex. The alternative is to appeal – as far as possible – to the self-motivation of the agents by rules and incentives which induce them to do the principals' bidding voluntarily, for example by paying the workers piece rates or rewarding quality output. Important indirect controls of agent opportunism also derive from competition, which demonstrates to the agents that they risk losing their jobs if they do not perform to the best of their ability in promoting the principals' purposes. This can be made explicit, for example, by benchmarking and competitions between different work teams.

Massive principal-agent problems arose under socialism, a doctrine that claimed the moral high ground, rejecting motivation by selfishness (that is, by competing to earn a high return in a market). Alas, solidarity with 'society' turned out to be rather limited in practice. The principals therefore had to rely on coercion, but found themselves confronted with insurmountable information and monitoring costs. The principals were simply unable to know what production was possible, what innovations might be feasible and what resources could be saved. Their capacity to coerce and punish 'their' workers was extremely limited. Shirking became almost universal (Gregory, 1990 and Section 13.1). In the end, the system collapsed in the Soviet Union, because of the failure to cope with the principal-agent problem, but the command-and-control approach is still relied upon in many places, from socialist production in Venezuela and Cuba to the provision of health and education services in Western welfare states.

The principal-agent problem is a central concern of institutional economics. As we shall see, it may often be addressed by appropriate rules. Much human effort has gone into finding ways of tackling it (Jensen and Meckling, 1976; Arrow, 1985). In later chapters, we will discuss the problem in business organizations, which are typically run by managers on behalf of the owners, and in government, where politicians and administrators need to be motivated to do the citizens' bidding in circumstances where the citizens simply do not know much about the business of government and often prefer to remain ignorant.

KEY CONCEPTS

The **principal-agent problem** arises whenever people act as agents for others, whom we call principals, and when the agents have better knowledge about the operation than the principals (asymmetric information). It is then possible that agents act in their own interest and neglect the interests of the principals (shirking, opportunistic behaviour). This problem is prevalent in big business and big government and presents a major management challenge.

When people act opportunistically, we say that they fall prey to **moral hazard**. The term was first used in the analysis of insurance to describe cases where insured individuals failed to undertake all possible steps to avoid damage, knowing that they would be compensated for possible damage. In a more general sense, moral hazard is now used to describe situations where self-interested individuals are tempted to violate general standards of honesty and reliability because circumstances allow them to get away with it.

NOTES

1 John Locke in particular was far ahead of his time. Recent physiological research has confirmed how sensations lead to short-term connections in the brain and are committed to the short-term memory. As a given sensation is reaffirmed by repeat sensations or reflection, hormonal bursts convert the short-term impressions into 'hardwire' connections in our brains, associations that we remember long term.

2 The theory of biological evolution, which Charles Darwin developed, differs from the evolution of human knowledge and ideas in that new knowledge can be learnt and passed on to other people, whereas biological evolution does in all probability not contain a mechanism of incorporating what has been learnt in the genes which are passed on to future generations. Insofar as a close analogy between biological and social evolution would be misleading.

3 In Western society, most people think of a continuum of ever-wider communities, from micro to macro groups to which they belong – the nuclear family, the extended family, the local community, the province, the church, the professional group, as well as other intermediate, voluntary groupings of civil society, the nation, the West, the global community. In other societies, perceptions differ. Thus, traditional Chinese society had a much less continuous perception of belonging. One was the member of a distinct, strongly bonded and self-administering micro-society called family and of the macro society of the nation (Redding, 1993). However, Chinese emigrants quickly developed many voluntary associations that form layers between the micro level of the family and the macro universe of the nation and developed a corresponding gradient of solidarity.

4 This does of course not preclude charity towards strangers. Indeed, affluence promotes voluntary giving and acts of generosity by some. However, charity cannot be relied upon to coordinate the trillions of acts of production and distribution, which keep the millions of people in modern society fed, clothed, cared for and entertained.

5 One aspect of the principal-agent problem, which is not often dealt with, concerns the opportunistic sheltering of principals behind their agents: Sometimes the boss hides behind the agents – think of the Mr. Big in drug trading or absentee landlords – to escape responsibility for his actions. This point will not be pursued further in this book.

4

Fundamental values

Most individuals aspire to certain universal, fundamental values, such as freedom, justice, security, peace and prosperity. These are general, overriding preferences to which most people in most civilizations attach a high priority, to which they subordinate other pursuits and which serve as 'ultimate stopping points' when discussing what is desirable or not. These values underpin societal bonds and motivate people in their life's pursuits. We incorporate considerations about basic human values in our analysis, because they underpin social structures and institutions.

In this chapter, we shall also discuss the meaning of freedom, justice and equity, as well as security, peace and material welfare. We will see that certain interpretations of justice and equity have the capacity to undermine freedom and security. Next, we shall discuss the conservation of a livable environment and recent attempts to place environmental goals above the human-centred values just mentioned.

The point will be made that only human values can serve to coordinate people. Moreover, the pursuit of one or several absolute objectives, which are not related to the other shared values, is likely to undermine a free society. We acknowledge that conflicts arise when these fundamental values are pursued, but we shall also argue that conflicts can be attenuated or even turned into complementarities if one thinks long term and relies on general rules rather than arbitrary ad hoc interventions.

One may rob an army of its commander-in-chief; but one cannot deprive the humblest man of his free will.

Confucius (ca. 551-479BC), *Analects*

We regard happiness as the fruit of freedom, and freedom as the fruit of courage.
Pericles, reportedly in his funeral oration for the dead of the Peloponnesian war
(431BC)

Political liberty consists in the power of doing whatever does not injure another. The exercise of the natural rights of every man has no other limits than those which are necessary to secure to every other man the free exercise of the same rights; and these limits are determined only by law.

French National Assembly, *Declaration of the Rights of Man* (1789)

All men are created equal . . . endowed by their Creator with certain inalienable rights; that among these are Life, Liberty, and the pursuit of Happiness.

Bill of Rights, adopted 1790 in the US Constitution

An economy of course, does indeed consist of technologies, actions, markets, financial institutions and factories – all real and tangible. But behind these, guiding them and being guided by them on a sub-particle level are beliefs: . . . They shape in aggregate the macro economy . . . They are the DNA of the economy.

B. Arthur, *Complexity* (1995)

To preach morality is easy; to give it a foundation is hard.

A. Schopenhauer, German philosopher (1788-1860)

4.1 Shared, underlying values

Universal values

When individuals pursue their own specific purposes, which will of course differ from those of others and will vary over time, their actions tend nevertheless to be informed and supported by largely similar underlying values. Whatever their background and the civilization they hail from, most human beings, when given the choice, place a high priority on attaining a number of fairly universal, fundamental values, even at the expense of other, more specific aspirations. The values that we discuss in this chapter are ultimate purposes to which most people aspire and most consider as being desirable. These fundamental values constitute powerful motives for human action and have pervasive influence over daily activities. Visible economic phenomena are influenced by these values in ways analogous to how invisible DNA carries genetic information, which informs all visible physiological and psychological traits (see the quote from Brian Arthur at the top of this chapter). Moreover, one can observe that these values are central to what most citizens would consider the good society (Boulding, 1959; Hazlitt, 1988/1964; 35-43 and 53-61).

They are:

(a) Individual freedom from fear and coercion is spelled out in specific civil, political and economic liberties. Freedom means that individuals can enjoy a safe-guarded sphere of autonomy to pursue their own, self-chosen purposes, a domain where they are in control of their decisions and actions, but of course within constraints set by physical-technical and socio-economic conditions, particularly the institutions that serve to protect the freedom of others. Freedom without the constraint of rules would be license, and license inevitably destroys social harmony and effective cooperation.

(b) Justice means that people in equal circumstances are treated equally and that restraints are placed on all in equal measure, irrespective of class or person (no discrimination). In practice, this relates normally to the demand for the rule of law, rather than the (arbitrary) rule of men. This kind of procedural (or formal) justice is closely related to equity, namely that all have the opportunity to pursue their self-set goals without artificial hindrance. Some observers stipulate different interpretations of justice and equity, implying some degree of equality of outcomes irrespective of the starting position, luck or effort (see Section 4.2 below).

(c) Security is the confidence that people will be able to enjoy their life and freedom into the future without experiencing violent and undue interference and unexpected and unmanageable changes in their circumstances. Security is thus the inter-temporal dimension of freedom. It may refer to one's own personal appreciation of security or to someone else's appreciation of other people's security. Some observers (though decidedly not the authors of this book!) give a different meaning to security, relating it to the protection of acquired socio-economic positions and of certain conditions over time irrespective of changing circumstances and new challenges.

(d) Peace is the absence of strife, terrorism and violence inflicted by powerful agents, both within the community (internal peace) and from the outside (external peace). Peace is closely related to security according to our preferred meaning (in the above paragraph (c)). By contrast, security in the sense of conserving acquired socio-economic positions frequently is detrimental to peace.

(e) Economic welfare (or prosperity) relates to material betterment and some measure of security of material achievements over time. Prosperity defines to what extent people's wants are satisfied by the use of scarce resources.

(f) A livable natural and man-made environment is another fundamental value that most people aspire to. This may be thought of, to a considerable extent, as a sub-set of security (for example, avoiding future environmental catastrophes that could harm human wellbeing). Other observers, though not the authors of this book, nowadays postulate nature preservation as an absolute objective, which should overrule all other human aspirations.

These fundamental values take varying concrete form, depending on experiences and cultural circumstances. They have universal appeal only in their general, abstract content. As far as we know, human beings have hardly ever striven to be deprived of freedom, to forego justice, and so on, unless they saw a worthwhile trade-off with another of the afore-mentioned fundamental values. Of course, there are, for example, individuals and groups that avoid enhancing their economic welfare, either because they hold a fatalistic worldview or because they seek salvation in this life by abstinence from material satisfactions. Generally, however, these fundamental human values – these universally shared preferences of a very high order – are revealed in frequent choices. "Where an individual sets the 'stopping point', what 'ultimate' values he adopts, is solely his responsibility, not that of society, although the values prevalent in a given society influence the individual who has grown up there or lives there" (Radnitzky, in Radnitzky and Bouillon, 1995a, p. 7).

If one studies different civilizations in history and across the world today, it also becomes obvious that not all societies and groups pursue these fundamental values with equal energy. Earlier in history and now still in less developed countries, one can observe that many with political influence are not committed to improving the human condition by realizing the values discussed here. Indeed, it is a distinguishing feature of the European, Judeo-Christian tradition that men could and should seek salvation by advancing their material welfare, freedom, justice and so on in this life (Némo, 2006, Kasper, 2011b). Many in other civilizations have accepted conditions as they are and have even made a virtue of fatalistic compliance (for example in many versions of the Hindu-Buddhist and Islamic traditions and in traditional Amerindian civilizations). It is, however, also apparent that, during the broad sweep of history, many communities have become less otherworldly, more individualistic and more eschatological (that is, aware that life on earth can and should be improved). The spread of modernity around the world has much to do with these fundamental shifts in basic attitudes. It is also evident that powerful elites have promoted the fatalistic worldview among the 'masses', in order to better control them and conserve their own advantageous social position. Many social and political conflicts in the present era have to do with the fact that important sections of the population realize that they, too, can embrace eschatological aspirations and need not tolerate passively a continuation of the poor fate of their forebears. Better information about the wider world and the example of a growing number of success stories in economic growth is making it more likely that fatalistic acceptance wanes and that the active, resourceful pursuit of fundamental, universal values spreads.

As most human beings pursue these values through their actions, it seems appropriate to incorporate the analysis of values – and of how these values affect action – in the discussion of institutional economics. This also extends to normative deliberations. Confining ourselves to a value-free analysis – in the sense of the analyst not referring to his values – would deprive the theory of much relevance, as it could not properly explicate reality.

Interdependencies in multi-value systems

When people pursue various fundamental values concurrently, as they normally do, they may discover a complex interdependence between them. Sometimes, there are complementarities between values, which means that an advance in one fundamental aspiration also advances the achievement of another. An example of such a complementarity would be a situation where greater prosperity leads to more security because more material resources can be invested into ensuring future freedom. In other cases, there are conflicts, for example when greater individual freedom means less peace within the community.

The trade-offs between the various values are often hard to assess because they change with circumstances and because the interdependencies are many and complex. It is therefore important not to single out one particular value as superior to all others. Admittedly, a single-value approach may often be appealing and easier to understand, which makes this tempting in political action. However, this only leads to the total neglect of the other values, and ultimately a worsening of the human condition. If, for example, the preservation of peace were given absolute priority, individual freedom, material progress and widely shared notions of justice would in all likelihood soon be violated. Likewise, the claim to accord absolute priority for environmental conservation over all other fundamental values is bound to lead to the neglect of freedom, prosperity and justice. This would sooner or later lead to a backlash and a costly reversal of policy. The pursuit of specific aspirations is therefore always circumscribed by trade-offs between the costs and benefits in terms of the multiplicity of other values.

One good example of complementarity between fundamental goals has played a big role in the literature: Adam Smith and other economists and philosophers have argued for the freedom to trade. They focused not only on the efficiency and welfare gains that result from the exploitation of comparative advantage, but also on the civilizing characteristic of trade. It promotes peace and satisfies other fundamental aspirations. After all, the Greek term for exchange – *catallaxy* – also means turning a stranger into a friend. As Voltaire famously argued, the Jew, Gentile and the Muslim may violently dislike each other, but they meet in the market place cooperatively to exchange goods and services. This ability to realize cooperation in anonymity is one of the great, beneficial mysteries to be explained by the logic of economics. This is the moral of Leonard Read's "I, Pencil" (Appendix). The power of self-interest can overcome ethnic, linguistic and geographic distance. The Liberal International Order of free trade is built on Kant's dream for a system of "Strangers Nowhere in This World" (Chapter 11). Rather than allowing differences to divide, they are the source of the great gains to be had from exchange in terms of goods and services that are realized through peaceful and cooperative trade. It is the vision of peaceful social cooperation among diverse and distant individuals that has animated the arguments for free trade from Adam Smith to Mises, Hayek, and Friedman.

Conflicting values tend to be more frequent when one thinks short-term. What is a conflict over the short run may fortunately turn out to be a complementarity over the longer run, for example:

- Constraints on individual freedom may promote short-term prosperity, for example when the freedom to invest abroad is limited. But, over the long run, prosperity is promoted by the freedom of choice of how and where to invest, and growing prosperity is in turn likely to promote liberty, as the experience of many nations over recent decades shows (for example, the spread of political freedom and democracy in the emerging Asian economies).
- In the short run, security often conflicts with prosperity, for example when scarce resources are diverted from private investment and consumption to defence spending. But, over the long run, prosperous countries are more secure, and secure countries attract more capital and enterprise, which in turn is conducive to growing prosperity.

This has the practical implication for public policy that a long-term time horizon promotes conflict-avoidance and a better realization of people's aspirations and that it pays in short-term conflicts to plead for a measure of tolerance.

KEY CONCEPTS

Fundamental values are defined here as universally held, high, abstract preferences of individuals. More specific aspirations tend to be subordinated to them. Fundamental values take different concrete shape in different civilizations, but are in principle universally pursued irrespective of culture. Examples of such fundamental values are freedom, justice, peace, security and prosperity.

Two fundamental values (or goals) are in **conflict** when the promotion of one ➡

←

detracts from the other (example: greater security coming at the expense of freedom). They are **complementary** when the promotion of one value also furthers the attainment of the other (example: more freedom promotes prosperity). Relationships between fundamental values are not static, but depend on the means chosen to attain them and on the time horizon over which the values are pursued. With longer time horizons, conflicts frequently turn into complementarities.

What defines a decent society?

One may judge various societies by the extent to which its members are able to enjoy these fundamental values and by the extent to which the majority of the population adheres spontaneously to them. It also seems appropriate to apply these fundamental, widely held standards as a measuring rod to judge a particular government's policies and actions. Sets of such values are the norms by which institutions and policies are normally judged. They describe what can be considered the good society from the viewpoint of the individual; they reflect a vision that turns human wellbeing over the longer term into the yardstick for assessing institutions and public policy.

Policy makers sometimes adopt these values as explicit policy goals, even enshrining them in constitutions and political programmes. However, it must be noted that fundamental values are not just abstract ends in themselves. They are always anchored in individual aspirations. To be quite explicit: They are not some societal, communal goals that represent solely what the rulers want. The fundamental values cannot be separated from what individual citizens – even the poorest – want. They must always reflect what the members in the community value highly and universally.

The high and universal preferences that we call fundamental values are often internalized. This means they have been deeply ingrained in the human psyche by practice and experience; they often influence behaviour without explicit reflection. The process of internalizing fundamental values probably begins with education at a young age. Similar to conventions such as honesty, they are practiced within the microcosm of the family before they are applied and refined in contact with the macrocosm of the wider community. They become part of 'culture' and the identity of a society.

If the fundamental values of a society are shared strongly and consistently and – if necessary – are defended resolutely, they constitute a support for that society's institutions, enhancing the chance of social order (Radnitzky and

Bouillon, 1995a, 1995b; Scully, 1992). Comparisons of men's fundamental beliefs and expectations with the DNA information that shapes the physical appearance of the body seem appropriate, as diverse human actions are guided by these universal preferences in the same manner in which the specifics of biological evolution are guided by invisible chromosomes. Reasonably stable, universal values and beliefs make an intractably complex world more manageable for us. They are therefore part of the 'social capital' that enables the community to prosper thanks to the division of labour and growing material resources. In that sense, fundamental values may be considered a production factor, which is often more important than physical items, such as machines or transport facilities. They underpin how smoothly the members of society cooperate. The importance of fundamental values becomes also evident when we look at societies that do not share a commitment to them. For example, parts of the Middle East are suffering from gross violations of peace and justice, and in numerous African societies personal security is endangered by ethnic and political violence, organized crime, high murder rates and repressive regimes; around the world, billions of people see their individual liberties curtailed by force and guile. This is of course a consequence of poor and poorly enforced institutions. It is related to poorly defined and defended fundamental values.

The relationship between human values and economic life is not a one-way street. Communities with a prospering, open economy, in which most people are largely self-reliant, demand the defence of fundamental values (as Adam Smith already observed). A prospering economy tends to form part of a social environment in which fundamental aspirations to freedom, justice, security and the like are constantly practiced, tested and asserted, so that they are held more firmly and uniformly. This can be best seen when we observe what happens in economies that are not competitive and in societies that are subject to totalitarian rule, as is still the case in sub-Saharan Africa and parts of North Africa and the Middle East. Here, subservience, dissimulation of basic aspirations and toleration of gross violations of basic values are common. The community's institutions are then not well anchored in shared fundamental values. When traditional, hitherto stationary societies are swept up by dynamic changes that carry them towards modernity (openness to trade and factor flows, openness to technical and social changes) often challenge engrained value systems, which derive from shared history, culture and mores, on which their social cohesion was built and which underpin the institutions (rules) of conduct. In the social-science literature, the essential foundation for rules in the inherent values, traditions and customs of society is sometimes described by the term '*metis*' (from Greek 'inherited wisdom, skill and craft'). In Stoic Greek philosophy, the term was given the meaning of prudence or wise counsel, and it is now used to signal caution against social engineering, that is, the imposition of external institutions that have no counterpart in a community's tradition and informal social norms (Boettke et al., 2008). A shared, deeply anchored set of values ensures that proposals for new rules and ways of doing things are not always readily accepted, but that the rule system is 'sticky' and path dependent. *Metis* can be understood as a kind of social DNA that informs a society's institutions. It may reject constructs, which do not mesh with it. Some traditional societies have value systems that can be easily adapted to mesh with the 'superstructure' of a market economy; figuratively speaking they have or develop 'Velcro surfaces' that lock onto the 'Velcro surfaces' of market capitalism (Section 12.2). Other societies are imbued with underlying value infrastructures, which are less adaptable or lend themselves less to adopting modern market institutions and therefore find it harder to realize modern economic growth and participation in the open, global civilization that is now evolving (Bauer, 2000). Imported rules, especially rules designed by outsiders, often do not function well in coordinating behaviour.

As we shall also see later, one of the legacies of totalitarian regimes with grossly discriminatory institutions and little economic freedom is that basic human values are held and practiced in a poorly defined manner. The internal and external institutions are then not well supported by the citizens and few are prepared to defend them spontaneously when the rules are violated.

4.2 Freedom, justice and equity

'Freedom from' and 'Freedom to'

The United Nations human rights declaration begins with the statement that all human beings are born free, reflecting an insight of the philosophers of the European Enlightenment and other thinkers. Freedom depends on a community consensus that certain actions (by fellow citizens or by governments) must be tolerated and others are prohibited by general, enforced rules. It is the liberty *from* something, such as coercion or fear (negative liberties), not the freedom *to* do something or lay some claim *to* something (positive liberties). The prohibitions that ensure freedom are directed against all actions that might impede others in their legitimate pursuit of their own happiness. On a related tangent, one may define freedom in the words of German philosopher Immanuel Kant (1724–1804) who wrote that freedom relates to the "conditions under which the arbitrary decisions of the individual are made compatible with the arbitrary decisions of others by a universal law of liberty". Thus, the protection of the autonomous domain of citizens to the maximum possible extent is the guarantee of freedom.

Institutions (laws) that proscribe actions, which have in past experience proven to be incompatible with the freedom of all, serve to promote overall freedom. Such institutions have to be universal in that they apply equally to unknown numbers of people and cases (Hayek, 1988, pp. 62–63; also see Section 5.5 in the following Chapter).

The classical definition of freedom is freedom *from* interference: To what extent can individuals enjoy protected domains of autonomous decision and self-responsibility? But in the course of the twentieth century, another definition of freedom has been made popular in certain circles: the freedom to claim resources, to have a job, to health services, and so on. In contradistinction to the classical notion of negative freedom (denying others control and ensuring self-responsibility), this second notion relates to positive freedoms, claims to the resources that belong to others. The argument in favour of positive freedom is that negative freedom cannot be exercised without resources; poor or unemployed people are not 'free'. This notion has given rise to the contemporary American meaning of 'liberal', which differs from the classical European meaning of the term. The proliferation of open-ended, liberal claims on the community's resources requires coercion, destroys incentives that come with self-reliance and leads to cynicism, that is, it diminishes freedom in the classical meaning of the word.

In this book, the terms 'freedom' and 'liberal' are confined to the classical definitions, American readers are invited to substitute 'libertarian' when they read 'liberal'.

Power and freedom

When people are free, they are able to pursue their self-set goals as they see fit. But a person may also exercise his or her free will by trying to influence others so that they support his or her goals. Such an influence may be voluntarily accepted – for example out of personal empathy or under a contract – or because of a threat of force (coercion). In the first case, the freedom of the other party is not impeded, whereas it certainly is when coercion comes into play. The distinction between voluntary compliance and coercion is, however, less clear-cut than it may appear at first glance. Coercion represents merely the extreme case in which the coerced party does not have a chance to resist or escape the threatened use of force.

Below a certain threshold, more or less subtle means to exercise coercive power over others exist, even in situations in which people eventually submit in more or less voluntary ways. Power over others – whether exercised by individuals or organized groups, such as industry cartels, unions or government authorities – is a consequence of limited or inferior choices at the disposal of those subjected to persuasion. The alternatives to submitting (more or less freely) may be unattractive, for example when there is a psychological dependency on the holder of power. In economic life, power is the result of a lack of competition, that is, a lack of close substitutes between which one is able to choose. Suppliers may, for example, have market power in the form of a monopoly thanks to a successful innovation, which prevents potential buyers from choosing realistic alternatives. Such limitations of the freedom of choice for buyers tend to be temporary. More durable limits to economic freedom exist when a supplier's market power is the result of public restraints of competition, for example when government protects an industry cartel or interferes with free trade. Such public restraints are based on the power of government to coerce. These few examples should suffice to demonstrate what difficulties arise when one deals with the phenomena of power and freedom.

Two important consequences of individual freedom, which we shall discuss in more detail later, are that free people are more creative, which is conducive to economic growth, and that they are more resilient to external shocks, when circumstances change (Quigley, 1979/1961). Western civilization, which aspires to a high degree of individual freedom, has overcome periodic challenges better than more collectivist civilizations that have arisen and declined again. It seems that long-term prosperity and freedom are complementary and that coercive collectivism leads to cultural rigidity that eventually brings about overall cultural decline.

Procedural justice versus 'social justice'

The discussion of freedom and power also touches on justice. Private coercion is not only incompatible with individual freedom but is also considered as unjust (de Jasay, 2002). One of the major justifications for the existence of government is to ensure that all citizens are protected from coercion by powerful individuals and groups. Where human interactions are determined by the violence potential of thuggish people or groups, ordinary people experience injustice. Most communities therefore accept the exercise of collective force by certain officials (the 'violence professionals', such as police officers, judges and jailers) as legitimate, because experience has shown that the exercise of individual power by violent means leads to injustices and a 'brutish state' of society – as British philosopher Thomas Hobbes (1588-1679) put it. Indeed, to prevent abuses of power is a central concern of collective action (Chapter 10).

Justice may be measured by one of the following standards:

(a) justice of individual behaviour – namely that individuals and author-
    ities should treat others equally in equal circumstances (no discrimina-
    tion; procedural justice; de Jasay, 2002); or

(b) justice as a social norm – namely that social positions and outcomes of
    interaction should be equal ('social justice' or 'equality of outcomes',
    which is at the basis of the welfare state and which will be discussed
    more fully in Chapter 10).

Like 'positive freedom' (claims), 'social justice' is at loggerheads with the
attainment of freedom and prosperity, as we shall see below.

The principle of non-discrimination

When discussing institutions such as the law, one may ask what content
the institutions should have to ensure that the actions of individuals and
governments are considered just. At least in the Judeo-Christian social tradition, which is based on the notion of the equality of individuals before God,
justice in the procedural sense is tied to the concept of equality before the
law. Justice is that kings and beggars are subject to the same laws (a key
aspect of the rule of law) – a concept that is far from universal and that is in
practice widely violated around the world. Some religions explicitly advocate
inequality and the tolerance of it. Procedural justice requires the guarantee
of equal basic rights irrespective of gender, race, religion, wealth or connections. It always relates to 'negative liberties', freedoms from unnecessary and
unequal restraints – and not to 'positive liberties'. In economic life, justice
in this sense means that all have, in principle, the same liberties to compete
with their diverse assets and be treated as equals. It does not mean equal
good luck or equal outcomes from that competition.

When discrimination is proscribed and individuals are not allowed the use
of force, then people are compelled to rely on voluntary cooperation with
others through contracts. The aim of the (private) law is to ensure that all
citizens enjoy equal opportunities to act out of their own free will without
unnecessary legal constraints. This is procedural justice. It is the only form
of justice, which the state can guarantee – equal outcomes can, in any event,
never be guaranteed since chance has a hand in determining most outcomes
and since different people have different levels of talent and commitment to
achieve. In this context, it is also important to recognize that high achievers
enhance the life opportunities for less talented and less committed fellow
citizens. Pulling high achievers down thus may well have the unforeseen
side effect that the less eager and fortunate also lose out (Sowell, 1990).
Another reason why government cannot guarantee social justice in the sense

of ensuring equal outcomes is that, in modern mass society, a great number of other human beings influence outcomes, many of whom are unknown to the individual actor or the government. Equal outcomes are therefore impossible to imagine, as long as people are free to act and react, and as long as that has a bearing on what they earn and own. Like 'positive liberties', policies to realize greater equality of outcomes (social justice) require that governments infringe individual property rights, an important part of economic freedom. Redistribution policies always rely on confiscating the property of some for the purpose of giving it to others. It must in any event be noted here that inequality is not injustice (Flew, 1989).

'Social justice' – attained by redistribution of property and opportunities to achieve greater outcome equality after interaction in the market place – relies on collective action to realize a pre-conceived standard of equality. Social justice therefore conflicts with the principle of justice in the sense of equal treatment of persons and circumstances, as well as the principle of freedom. The pursuit of social justice thus poses several fundamental questions: If formally just treatment of people leads to unequal outcomes, should people then be treated unequally to ensure outcome equality? What should be done if different people enjoy differing unequal starting positions in competing and if these unequal starting conditions persist? Then, redistributive government interventions have to discriminate against some citizens. The fundamental value of negative freedom is also pushed aside when (positive) outcome equality is pursued. 'Social justice' always implies that the traditional concept of procedural justice is violated, as the law is then used to discriminate between formally equal citizens. Then, the equality before the law gives way to a state of affairs that many consider unjust (Hayek, 1976, pp. 62–88; Sowell, 1990; de Jasay, 2002).

When government redistributes wealth and incomes, it can therefore not treat all citizens with formal equality. The classical role of government was only to protect the law and the peace. But when redistribution became a major concern of Western governments, individual liberties and the rule of law were being undermined (for a more detailed analysis of the consequences of the pursuit of social justice see Section 10.4).

The conclusion is that outcome equality (that is social justice) cannot be achieved by political action over the long term. This is borne out by the persistence of begging on the streets of even the most elaborate Western welfare states. The evidence shows that income inequalities persist irrespective of average income levels (Gwartney and Lawson, passim; Sowell, 1990).

Despite this logical and empirical insight, gross inequalities in incomes and living standards are considered unacceptable to many in Western societies, partly because people identify to some extent with their most vulnerable fellow human beings and partly because they fear deleterious consequences for internal peace and the attainment of other fundamental values (Kliemt, 1993). There is certainly a role for private, voluntary charity by the affluent for the poor. Such voluntary redistribution, instead of coercive state intervention to reallocate property rights, has beneficial effects, including for those who do not participate. It therefore deserves societal acclaim.

4.3 Security, stability, peace and prosperity

Security: the inter-temporal dimension of freedom

Security can be endangered not only by external threats, but also by domestic infringements of freedom and by unforeseen events. It is the inter-temporal aspect of freedom, namely the confidence that future freedom will not be endangered.

When we deal with security from external coercion or attack, the goal of external peace is closely related to security, the future freedom from violence and coercion in international relations. Internal security and peace cover not only the absence of civil war, but also the absence of violent confrontations, such as widespread crime, violent strikes and riots, and the prevalence of social harmony.

Security and peace are defined in relation to violent and arbitrary behaviour of people with power. The transition from the normal daily conflicts and disputes, which are inevitable in any living society, to a situation of genuine insecurity is gradual. Small interpersonal conflicts are the inevitable consequence of differences in human values and aspirations. Everyone's pursuit of happiness, of course, often has external consequences for the wellbeing of others. The dividing line, where security and peace are genuinely endangered, lies where violent, deceptive and arbitrary means to obtain personal objectives are used, where conflicts are no longer resolved by discourse, private negotiation or the mediation of third parties and where generally accepted rules are violated. It is apparent that violations of security and peace – not only by civil wars, but also lesser conflicts and crime – are prevalent in poor countries in Africa, the Middle East and Central America (World Bank, 2011).

When discussing security, one has to establish who assesses security – individuals personally assessing their own security, or a third party assessing someone's or a group's security. As the future is inevitably uncertain, assessments of security vary greatly between individuals; some will be confident that they can master risks, others will be risk-averse and easily feel insecure. Security assessments always require much information search and forecasting, as well as an evaluation of the capability to respond to unforeseen eventualities. It follows then that security is impossible in a changeable world. The only way to prevent all airplane crashes would be to ground all planes – but such absolutist approaches to security would be unrealistic and at the expense of economic welfare. The pursuit of absolute security would thus only endanger other social values and would be unsustainable. In an evolving world, security must therefore not be equated to rigidity. Indeed, attempts to avert adaptive changes are only likely to produce greater insecurity in the long-term as changing reality gets further out of kilter with aspirations to secure the status quo. Frequently, the best one can do for one's security is to maintain a capability of alertness, flexibility and responsiveness in dealing with unforeseen developments.

As security relates to the future, it always has a time dimension, which at times complicates the definition of what it means. As just noted, the pursuit of security for the short term can easily imperil long-term security. Thus, if people elect political leaders who only emphasize securing material living standards for the next few years and who refuse to take longer-term considerations into account, they opt for great risks to their security in the long term. A proper understanding of security therefore requires a variable time horizon and conscious trade-offs between short- and long-term aspirations to security, as well as deductions from maximalist interpretations of what is considered subjectively secure.

When members of societies place their security above all other objectives, they are bound to discover that – after a time – conservation replaces experimentation and evolution. Then, alertness and adaptability to change get lost and consequently, the means to secure future freedom get eroded. When people have lost all taste for change and the capabilities to cope with it constructively, they begin to feel subjectively insecure and lose confidence. They may then try to control competition and openness, which are frequent sources of challenge to existing economic and social positions. When their preference for imposed security then grows, this hampers the very adaptations that would guarantee long-term security – as judged by an informed, independent observer. Dealing with aspirations to security therefore requires careful assessment and the readiness to cope with certain sources of insecurity, as and when challenges arise (Hayek, 1960, pp. 397–411).

Stability

Economic activity tends to proceed in cycles. Sometimes, activity and job creation accelerate above the trend, sometimes they fall behind or decline. Before the twentieth century, most considered this a natural fact of life, but from the 1930s onwards, many governments began promising to stabilize production and employment (this policy is sometimes called Keynesianism, after its chief protagonist, British Lord John Maynard Keynes). The public policies proposed often became popular with electorates that did not yet see the limitations and the long-term consequences of such an undertaking, such as rising public debt levels and sustained inflations that destroy the usefulness of money (for more detail see Sections 7.6 and 10.2). Nor was it initially evident that the artificial manipulation of economic activity by governments in the interest of stability benefited some sections of the community more than others and that the prevention of periodic 'cleansing crises' impeded long-term economic growth. Critical voices pointed out that periodic economic crises were needed to adjust production and employment structures to new evolving conditions and to mop up costly, but redundant production facilities.

Counter-cyclical policy (demand management) is based on the assumption that policy makers know all the relevant variables in the open, modern economy. Instead it has been discovered all too often that unintended side effects were triggered, including effects that made the business cycle more pronounced (procyclical effects) because lags between policy intervention and the movements of the economy were misjudged (that is, recognition, decision, implementation, and reaction lags). In modern democracies, Keynesian policies have also introduced an inflationary bias: In recessions, it is popular for central banks to expand money supply and for finance ministers to cut taxes and increase public spending (running budget deficits). It is much less popular and therefore rarer that corresponding restrictive measures are implemented when the economy booms. As a result, there has been a long-term tendency to accumulate costly public-sector deficits, depriving private investors of some of the savings of capital that would serve long-term prosperity and job creation. In addition, it needs to be recognized that living economies have always gone through business cycles. It is a natural rhythm, in which misjudged investments are written off. When macroeconomic activism creates the impression that investors will be protected from such crises and that central banks will drive down and distort interest rates artificially, capital structures get increasingly out of line with evolving demand structures and undue entrepreneurial risk-taking is encouraged (Hayek, 1935; Burton, 1986; Mankiw et al., 1993). We conclude that business cycles will always be a fact of life, but that the intensity of the cycle depends critically on the flexibility of the economy, that is, the intensity of competition. Fiscal and monetary activism – even if politically popular in the short-term – rigidifies economic structures and therefore prejudices long-term economic growth and employment.

The promise of stability has also expanded the role of government and restrictive controls, all too often resulting in limitations of economic freedom. The alternative of fostering a competitive economy would have made producers and employers more alert and responsive to changes in economic circumstances and would have ensured more spontaneous, endemic stability (see Section 10.3), In other words, this is again a case of a conflict between the basic value of security (for influential persons and groups) and the aspiration to freedom and justice for all.

Peace and security: competition depersonalizes conflict

Peace in a community tends to be enhanced when potential conflicts are depersonalized by rules that commit the members of the community to non-violent conflict resolution. One way of depersonalizing inter-personal or inter-group conflicts is to reduce the coverage of what is decided collectively by governments to the minimum, namely ensuring that life, the institutions and material assets are protected, as well as funding the administration of this protective function of government. The allocation of incomes, property and production are then left largely to the impersonal mechanisms of competition. When income and wealth allocation, the stabilization of business conditions and the production of more and more goods and services become the business of government, these matters become politicized. Then, collective antagonism can easily take hold. Once emotions are whipped up by self-seeking political operators, internal harmony and the self-responsibility of citizens suffer. This is conducive neither to internal peace, nor to positive engagement and creativity. It is no coincidence that the massive new government interventions to shore up banks and businesses in the wake of the 2007 financial crises and the subsequent need for budget cuts have led to angry, though poorly informed protest movements, such as 'Occupy Wall Street'.

One important function of market competition is that the power of individual and corporate suppliers and buyers is contested and thereby controlled by other competitors. Competition not only controls economic power, but also political power which ever so often flows from economic monopoly positions. Another function of competition in markets is to make the control of economic effort impersonal: sellers make offers for self-seeking motives, but do so voluntarily; and in doing so, they satisfy potential buyers – a beneficial side effect. Those sellers who cannot obtain prices sufficient to cover their production and transaction costs – in other words, who fail to make a profit – will be inclined to blame the anonymous market forces for their failure, rather than specific competitors or buyers. This means the ever-present conflict between sellers, who want a higher price, and buyers, who want a lower price, is depersonalized and de-emotionalized. This contributes to peace, both within countries and in international relations.

An example of how the impersonal institutions of the market can help to defuse potential conflict is a free, deregulated labour market. If employers are driven by their pursuit of profit, they will hire the workers who promise to offer them the best productive value for the wage cost. As a consequence, employers have to be blind to race, creed or gender. By contrast, those who discriminate, for example on the basis of race, incur a profit penalty and may eventually have to get out of the business. This is typically a more effective way to integrate a diverse society than cumbersome and costly policies to enforce 'positive discrimination', for example on racial grounds, which is a difficult-to-measure quality (Rabushka, 1974; Sowell, 1990; 1996).

People from greatly differing cultural backgrounds, who have little in common, can interact productively and peacefully when they deal with each other in markets. With time, they may learn from each other and even gain respect and a liking for each other. By contrast, political directives and controls often emotionalize interracial relations and create divisions which political agents may well be tempted to exploit (Sowell, 1994). It was revealing that Bosnians, Serbs and Croats, who fought an armed conflict in the 1990s, were able to deal with each other civilly in market places, even when political reconciliation proved unmanageable. The same holds true internationally: Nations whose citizens share growing trading interests and are prevented from imposing political controls (such as tariffs) tend to see advantage in keeping the peace (Gartzke, 2005).

Conflicting economic interests can only be depersonalized if competition is widely accepted as an ordering principle. This also means that all distributive and other consequences of free competition are accepted and political agents are kept from intervening. Once certain agents intervene to constrain the competitive process (for example by forming cartels) or use their power to coerce (for example by setting up barriers to market entry), peace and security is likely to suffer, precisely because conflicts become personalized, emotionalized and politicized.

The philosophers of the eighteenth and early nineteenth centuries were optimistic that the spread of commerce and the shift to motivation by self-interest and voluntary action would enhance morals and the spontaneous adherence to fundamental values, in particular social peace and security (Boulding, 1969; Hirschman, 1977). Twentieth century observers, however, were unable to share this optimism, as the competition they observed was frequently not even-handed, that is, among equals, but among powerful and powerless people or groups. Positions of economic and, consequently, political power were then used to entrench market power further. It is, however, not permissible to conclude from this experience that open competition confers no benefit for peace and security. Rather, the fostering of competition should be seen as an effective means to control concentrations of power, and with it abuses of power that endanger security, peace and freedom.

Well-functioning competition always has consequences for individual security, as market participants are invariably exposed to unforeseen changes in supply and demand. They can never expect total security. Moreover, people face the risks of being unable to be productive for personal reasons, for example because of illness or old age, or because they are hindered by socio-economic conflicts. These risks to personal security have to be met by private wealth buffers and insurance. There may also be a consensus in a community that some of these economic risks should be addressed by collective action (public provision of security, social security). It is, however, not valid to eliminate the insecurities of the market by suppressing competition. That only leads to much greater insecurities in the longer run. It is an empirical fact that ham-fisted political interventions eventually lead to haphazard, costly change, rather than steady evolution.

Nor can governments promise total material security to all citizens, because the entire economic system would rigidify and moral hazard and loafing would spread. The cost for this would have to be borne collectively and anonymously by taxes, whereas the gains in material security are personal. Public guarantees of material security therefore create an asymmetry, which results in limitless, open-ended claims for more and more social provisions of security. In electoral democracies, political interests will then drive policy making increasingly towards a focus on security and away from other fundamental values. This process is illustrated by the experience of late medieval corporatist city states in Europe, China under the Ming and Ching dynasties, the socialist regimes and the welfare states of the twentieth century. In all these cases, the securing of personal income and wealth positions by political intervention led over the long run to unmanageable public debts, societal dislocation, cynicism, burdens on subsequent generations and hence inter-generational injustice. As of the early twenty-first century, most Western governments have made untenable concessions to well-organized public-sector unions (on salary levels, work conditions, pension entitlements and so on), which are now leading to disruptive fiscal deficits and public agitation.

We must conclude that security can only be provided – and should only be demanded and promised – by carefully observing the trade-offs with other fundamental values.

Prosperity

Prosperity (or economic welfare) relates to the command over material goods and services to satisfy wants. It ensures access not only to purely material satisfactions, but also to cultural and spiritual fulfilment, health care, old-age provision and other ingredients of securing a comfortable, enjoyable life. As a first approximation, the attainment of prosperity is measured by real per-capita incomes and wealth. In addition, the security of prosperity over time, such as by the control of inflation and a measure of stability of income flows and asset values, is also part of what people aspire to under the rubric of material welfare.

Prosperity has gained greater priority in the minds of many around the world in recent times with the decline of fatalism, the spread of modernity and the economic growth experience (see Chapter 1). For many, prosperity now appears to have taken even a pre-eminent position, comparable to the pursuit of religious and spiritual salvation in medieval Europe, or in parts of present-day India and the Middle East.

As already noted, complementarities and trade-offs exist between security and the aspiration of most to economic welfare. Prosperity, in particular when it gives people a buffer of wealth against contingencies, promotes individual security and enables communities to shore up their security. After all, insurance, the defence of future freedom against external or domestic aggression and security-building institutions cost scarce resources. As we have seen, there is, however, also a potential conflict when demands for security dominate, endangering future prosperity.

Fortunately, other fundamental values, such as freedom, justice and peace, tend on the whole to be promoted by better material conditions. This does of course not mean that economic prosperity can be equated to happiness, only that it is seen as desirable by large numbers of people throughout the world.

Observers critical of the modern world have said much about the empirical question whether income and wealth go along with greater happiness. Recent research, based on detailed survey data for 126 countries with decent income statistics and over considerable time periods, supports the conclusion that there is a positive correlation between real income and satisfaction with life (Sacks et al., 2010). Alternatively, one might quote the saying: "Money does not make you happy, but it makes misery so much more acceptable."

Sometimes, analysts look at a wider definition of 'economic welfare', rather than only prosperity in the sense of real wealth and income. They then often include price-level stability (average of all prices), a high rate of employment of those willing to work at prevailing labour market conditions, external balance (a sustainable balance between imports and exports of goods and services) and stability of aggregate demand in line with a more or less steadily growing supply potential. These macroeconomic statistics may indeed serve as guideposts for day-to-day economic policy. However, turning these into policy goals has resulted in much policy activism, which has prejudiced long-term prosperity.[1]

KEY CONCEPTS

Freedom is the opportunity to pursue one's own, self-set purposes autonomously within one's domain and to do so without interference. Freedom is of course circumscribed by the equal freedom of others. It implies the absence of coercion or fear of coercion. Freedom (or liberty) is here always defined as the (negative) freedom from coercion and interference.

    Justice means that equal circumstances are treated equally by individuals and authorities and that restraints are placed on all in equal measure (and not according to personal standing or belonging to a particular group). This is the concept of **procedural** (or formal) **justice**, which underlies the principle of equality before the law. It has to be distinguished from **social justice**, which is oriented towards the **equality of** **outcomes** of human endeavour irrespective of starting position, luck, and effort. Social justice aims to even out interpersonal or inter-group differences in incomes and wealth. If it becomes a dominant concern of public policy, it undermines procedural justice and freedom and erodes incentives to compete and perform.

    Equity closely relates to justice, namely that all should have access to similar opportunities. It, too, has to be distinguished from the equality of outcomes.

    Security relates to the confidence that people will be able to enjoy their freedom into the more or less distant future. It is freedom from fear of violent interference by private or collective agents. Appropriate institutions can constrain arbitrary and violent behaviour in some, and are there-

➡

fore able to promote the security of others. In a different meaning, security is sometimes equated with social justice. As soon as security is, however, oriented towards the protection of acquired social and economic positions it clashes with freedom.

Peace means the absence of violence and strife, both within the community (internal peace and harmony) and from the outside (external peace). It relates to security in the first meaning.

Economic welfare or prosperity relates to the availability of goods and services to satisfy (easily growing) material wants. Although one cannot equate prosperity with happiness, we note a positive correlation between real living standards and life satisfaction.

4.4   Conservation of the environment

Intergenerational justice and the environment

In recent decades, as the number of people on earth and in certain areas has increased, aspirations to conserve natural and traditional man-made environments have grown in most countries. Numerous social critics have claimed environmental conservation as a fundamental human value and hence a basic goal of policy, which should be considered equal to, or more important than, individual freedom or prosperity, for example. At one level, this demand can be understood as a reaction to numerous changes in the wake of the unprecedented economic growth over the past two generations, to the exhaustion of known or easily-accessible stocks of natural resources or the accumulation of hard-to-digest residues from growing production and consumption activities, namely polluting effluents, waste, and congestion. The growth of production and consumption has created external costs, that is, burdens on third parties, and has led to the exhaustion of previously free goods, such as clean water in certain locations. However, the growing demand for conservation also seems to reflect Romantic resistance to continuing, even accelerating changes which challenge the individual's capacity to adjust; in a way, conservation also reflects aspirations to fewer challenges for adjustment and greater security (Kasper, 2007).

Some observers have even concluded that economic growth cannot continue, because it runs into limits set by the natural and productive soils, clean air and water, indeed that rising and spreading prosperity has to be stopped in the interest of 'saving the planet'. Modern growth is driven by carbon-based power, so that it is seen by many to increase global temperatures (anthropogenic global warming). This argument is based on the logic of physics, which says that matter is finite and cannot be 'mined' for human use forever.

This closed-system logic is based on a misunderstanding of what constitutes economic growth. Growth is open-ended, which means that the economic system is opened up continually by innovative knowledge. Rising living standards, as reflected in rising real per-capita incomes, do of course require that physical molecules are relocated and transformed. But the more important aspect of economic growth is that physical matter, when relocated and combined in certain ways, is given a higher value by humans. Thus, the iron taken from the ground is valued much more highly when converted into a knife, and the grain of sand, once converted with energy into a silicon wafer, has increased enormously in value. National products grow not so much because natural resources are taken from the ground, but because they are valued much more highly once transformed. Besides, modern economic growth is becoming much less dependent on the extraction of natural resources, because many resources are now recycled and because overall demand is shifting to services which frequently use few natural resources. The computer age is making abundant silicon a key raw material. This is why a survey of long-term social trends and possible resource and environmental bottlenecks by a panel of 64 leading scientists concluded that there was no unmanageable natural resource constraint on economic growth (Simon, 1995). The assertion that possible climate warming is caused by recent industrial and transport activity also remains contentious and problematic (for example, Kasper, 2007; Carter, 2010).

This is not to say that there are not some bottlenecks in the supply of natural resources, in particular in energy supplies and the absorption of waste and emissions from economic activities (Bennett, 2012). But these will be overcome when scarcity prices send out the signal to economize and find substitutes or to test and implement innovative technologies (Beckerman, 1974; Borcherding in Block (ed.), 1990, pp. 95–116; Anderson and Leal, 1991; 1997). Nonetheless, the question arises whether this is the most appropriate solution to specific environmental problems or whether direct policy intervention is more appropriate. We will see later that private and collective solutions – markets or public policy – have to be considered, depending on the specific environmental problem at hand.

Concerns with the natural environment often arise when someone's economic activity imposes costs on others that cannot be easily measured and compensated (externalities). Other environmental concerns address the interests of future generations: How can we ensure that future generations have the freedom to develop without facing sudden, harsh and unmanageable resource bottlenecks or the collapse of the natural system in which they live? This relates environmental issues to security and inter-generational justice. After all, it would be unjust to leave a devastated environment to future generations. It is certainly appropriate to include the likely interests of future generations in some way among our fundamental values and to ask how they can best be looked after. Environmental conservation is therefore a legitimate fundamental concern, but it must be weighed against all other aspirations, such as individual freedom, justice, security and material welfare (Bennett, 2012). To abandon all fundamental aspirations for the sake of environmental conservation amounts to the abandoning reason in the shaping of community life and public policy (Taverne, 2005). Moreover, even if one were to place environmental goals above all others, it is not valid for political organizations with environmental and scientific pretentions to selectively pick data that support a certain, pre-determined point of view and to use biased scientific research to score points in public policy. Giving absolute priority to environmental conservation – as many of the affluent in affluent economies, many international and national officials and many media writers now do – would indeed seem to be one of the biggest threats to freedom, and the prosperity that has come with it, since the threat of Soviet dominance has evaporated (Kasper, 2007; Klaus, 2008).

Can we deal with extra-human values?

In the debate about the natural environment, one sometimes hears an argument that goes beyond what has been said so far. Some in the environmental debate try to place environmental conservation above all other human interests. They see human beings as an integral part of an interdependent physical system and argue in terms of purely quantitative, physical trade-offs between human demands and the demands of animals, plants and other elements of the physical world. Thus, a group of animal-rights activists in the United States of America initiated a court case to declare captive whales that perform in shows as slaves under US law. This school of thought wishes to extend institutional protections, which are designed to enhance human social interaction, to non-human beings, such as primates and whales. This 'eco-fundamentalist' school rejects the argument in this chapter that human concerns and valuations *alone* should be the measure of all human activity. Instead, it tries to place the interests of animals and ecosystems on an equal footing with human interests, if not even above them. This school of thought also advocates an extreme interpretation of the 'precautionary principle' in ecology, namely that no harm should be done to the natural environment, whatever the consequences to other human aspirations, such as prosperity. It is argued that the precautionary principle should automatically apply when damage to the environment is deemed irreversible (for example: extinction of a species), even when the connection between a suspected harmful action and the environmental effect is not (yet) scientifically proven. This kind of thinking has, for example, become dominant in the discussion of global climate change. However, this approach presents fundamental logical difficulties because the design of all policy is a product of the human mind and we can express, assess and compare only human values. Attempts to take away the reliance on human valuations would suppress the very communication and steering mechanisms which coordinate human action, and would empower some political group to assume collective dictatorship. The implication of this type of environmentalism for freedom is now widely recognized (Kasper, 2007; Klaus, 2008; Bennett, 2012).

Once we abandon human valuations as the sole reference system for human action, we have to ask whose valuations are to replace them – maybe the polar bear's, for whom humans are food. Humans have no way of entering into adequate communication with other species. All that happens is that some human agent argues on behalf of another species on the pretence that she or he knows what serves that species. It amounts to a grab for political power. Once one abandons human valuations and reasoned discourse about them, the 'interests of Nature' become an excuse for some self-appointed elite to overrule other human valuations. The protagonists may claim superior knowledge about what is good for nature conservation and then enforce their decisions in undemocratic, interventionist ways against the wishes of the majority of people. The interaction of the many human beings in market decisions – who are concerned with freedom, justice, prosperity, future security, including future resource supplies – is then replaced by the dictatorial directives of an elite, however selected and legitimated. This is an absolutist approach that violates the fundamental individual values, which underpin and inform society.

KEY CONCEPTS

Conservation of the environment is concerned with safeguarding environmental amenities and natural resources with regard to the interests of present and future generations. It relates to prosperity, equity, security and inter-generational justice and is a legitimate concern for moral discourse and public policy.

Eco-fundamentalism demands absolute priorities for nature conservation, which are not related to fundamental human valuations and which are to override human aspirations, such as freedom, prosperity, security and justice. The precautionary principle, often claimed for nature conservation, could then also be stipulated for job security, international peace and prosperity, for example.

This brief discussion of eco-fundamentalism clarifies one important point about fundamental values: they always have to reflect the diverse and conflicting valuations of citizens and relate all social interaction to a humane perspective. A humane society depends crucially on the focus on human values, which are after all the only language in which the members of the community can communicate their aspirations. Foisting non-human values, external to human valuation, on public policy would cause society to disintegrate in discord and poverty. This may empower an elite to override everyone's interests, but it would destroy freedom, justice, prosperity, security, peace and the other aspirations discussed here.

NOTE

1 Readers, who wish to pursue the discussion of fundamental values and the moral issues they pose in practice should look at the essays in Palmer (2011).

5

Institutions: individual rules

Douglas North, the 1993 Nobel Prize winner in economics, argues that institutions are the rules of the social game, if properly enforced. Elinor Ostrom, the 2009 Nobel Prize winner in economics, has studied the rules of governance in a diversity of historical and cultural contexts, examining both the 'rules in form', and the 'rules in use' in the governance of human affairs. Ostrom showed how effective rules of governance limit access, assign accountability, and establish graduated penalties. Following Friedrich Hayek and other Austrian economists, as well as North and Ostrom, we shall discuss in this chapter how these rules have evolved, or been designed, to constrain the behaviour of individuals in their interactions with others and with nature. Appropriate institutions create trust and make it easier for people to cooperate constructively and live together more peacefully, securely and justly. We will also look at rule violations incurring sanctions that may vary widely as to their character and formality.

We shall discuss a wide range of institutions that have evolved within societies – for example customs, good manners, work practices and the manifold institutional arrangements that merchants and financiers have created and apply to facilitate their trade.

Although such internal institutions order much of social and economic life, people in more complex societies have invariably found it convenient and effective to supplement internal institutions with external institutions and formal enforcement. Such external rules are designed in political processes and are enforced by government authorities, carrying out the protective function of government, including by legitimate uses of force.

Appropriate institutions serve to reduce coordination costs in complex systems, limit or resolve conflicts between people and protect individual domains of freedom. To serve these ends, institutions need specific qualities, such as certainty, generality and openness. In other words, they should be universal. Rules that are not universal, but are designed to obtain specific purposes fail in their coordinative, normative function and often overtax the cognitive capacity of the rule makers. Moreover, they overtax the knowledge of those whom they are to influence – in plain English: citizens simply cannot know and obey thousands of complicated, case-specific rules and regulations.

The obedience to learnt rules has become necessary to restrain those natural instincts which do not fit into the order of the open society.

Friedrich A. Hayek, *Political Order of a Free People* (1979)

Civil liberty is the status of the man who is guaranteed by law and civil institutions the exclusive employment of all his own powers for his own welfare.

W.G. Sumner, *The Forgotten Man* (1883)

Certainty we cannot achieve in human affairs, and it is for this reason that, to make the best use of what knowledge we have, we must adhere to rules.

Friedrich A. Hayek, 'Competition as a Discovery Procedure' (1978)

Pacta sunt servanda

Roman saying, second century BC

A deal is a deal.

Anglo-Saxon saying, nineteenth century

5.1   Overview: rules and enforcement

Institutions are defined throughout this book as generally known, enforced rules. They constrain, possibly opportunistic, behaviour in human interactions and always carry some sanction for breaches of the rules (North, 1990, p. 3; Ostrom, 1990, p. 51; 2005). As mentioned in Section 2.1, rules without obligatory sanctions are useless. When sanctions are no longer applied, institutions collapse. It should also be noted that institutions are man-made, not physical constraints on human action.

We will first elaborate on a couple of aspects of institutions to explain their character and then discuss various types of institutions that differ as to how they come about and are enforced.

Prisoners' dilemma

Institutions – and in particular the sanctions attached to them – allow people to have confidence that promises made will be fulfilled. Human nature is such that self-seeking individuals will all too often make promises, but later forget them or shirk on fulfilling them. Our instincts play a big role in this sort of opportunism, and institutions support the control of our innate instincts in the interest of effective cooperation between people over the longer term (Hayek, 1979a, pp. 165–173; 1988, pp. 11–28). Cooperation between people, which is necessary for our survival and prosperity, normally requires a framework of institutions to discourage innate instinctual opportunism. They decrease the risks of shirking and reinforce habits of cooperation for reciprocal benefit, and create trust.

People who cooperate are often better off than when they do not cooperate. This has been explored by game theory under the label of 'prisoners' dilemma'. The term was derived from the case of two prisoners who are held captive and are not permitted to communicate with each other (cooperate). When interrogated, each prisoner faces a dilemma in that he does not know whether to remain silent, hoping that his guilt cannot be established, or whether to speak out to put all responsibility on the other prisoner and claim mitigating circumstances. Both prisoners face this same dilemma, as long as they cannot cooperate with one another. Both would be better off if they could. Then, each would be able to make credible commitments to the other prisoner, for example promising each other that both will remain silent. When they cannot communicate and speak out in self defence, they incriminate each other and are both worse off. The matrix in Figure 5.1 clarifies what is at stake here.

Figure 5.1 The prisoners' dilemma

		Prisoner A	
		Remains silent	Speaks out
Prisoner B	Remains silent	Both go free	B is found guilty
	Speaks out	A is found guilty	Both are found guilty

Such prisoners' dilemmas can arise when people are unable to cooperate reliably. Institutions then enhance the opportunities and chances of mutually beneficial cooperation.

An instructive example that demonstrates the advantages of cooperation based on appropriate institutions was the history of the Cold War and the strategic arms limitation agreements that followed in the 1970s and 1980s. As long as the two super powers did not cooperate, they were tied up in a costly arms race and faced the danger of a nuclear holocaust. Both sides increasingly realized that both would be better off with some kind of cooperation. They entered into negotiations to establish rules, monitoring procedures and sanctioned retaliations for rule violations. Eventually, they established credibility, which made cooperation possible. This solved their prisoners' dilemma and allowed them to reduce the nuclear threat.

However, cooperation is not always desirable. Various suppliers of a product may, for example, find it beneficial to free themselves from the prisoners' dilemma of having to compete by forming a cartel to fix prices at a high level. In this instance, the prisoners' dilemma of the suppliers serves a good purpose from the standpoint of potential buyers and the community at large, just as the classical case of a prisoners' dilemma serves a good purpose from the viewpoint of the interrogator. Whether to facilitate or impede cooperation by appropriate institutions depends on the circumstances and whose interests are included in the evaluation.

Institutions and trust

Institutions are rules of conduct, a means of channelling people's actions. By channelling the structure of pay-offs, incentives and disincentives, institutions effectively rule out certain actions and narrow the range of possible reactions. Thereby they make the actions of others more predictable and give social interaction a certain structure. Institutions provide a kind of 'external scaffolding' for human choice and learning (Drobak-Nye (eds) 1997, pp. 269–290; Leibenstein, 1984). Indeed, by facilitating predictability and preventing chaos and arbitrary behaviour, institutions establish trust and allow people to economize on the costly search for knowledge. Even if rule-bound behaviour does not offer 100 per cent certainty, it can be perceived as more probable and plausible than chaos.

Institutions normally reflect what has proven useful in the past and what is needed for people to interact with others in pursuit of their diverse individual objectives. In that respect, institutions are 'storehouses of knowledge' acquired by past generations. In the face of ever-present knowledge problems, institutions give people a degree of confidence that the interactions in which they are engaged will occur as expected. This lowers the costs of information search, a difficult and risky business. Appropriate rules of conduct reduce the costs of transacting business or cooperating within an organization. Without trust in the wider framework, individuals would often not be able to concentrate on exploiting knowledge in their specialization or to find knowledge in new areas. Numerous useful actions would simply never take place (Hazlitt, 1988/1964, pp. 53–61). This is the reason why some communities have stayed so poor for so long: a better division of labour and knowledge has not been possible, and as a consequence living standards remain low.

Humans often try to cope with the knowledge problem by thinking through an overall strategy that sets a framework of rules for individual actions before they act. Lest people be overwhelmed by ad hoc decisions and mal-coordination in the heat of battle, all bind themselves in their tactical day-to-day decisions by this strategy and keep necessary tactical changes within the overall strategy.

Given cognitive and other limitations of human nature, institutions to be effective have to be easily knowable. To that end they should be simple and certain, and sanctions for violation should be clearly communicated and understood. This is not the case when rules proliferate, when they are purpose-specific, rather than abstract, or when rule systems become inherently contradictory. Nor should institutions discriminate between different people, giving some groups a preference over others. In that case, institutions would be less likely to be obeyed and would less effectively serve their function of economizing on transaction costs. Institutions that are anchored in a community's fundamental values are more likely to be effective than institutions that are foisted on the community from outside or contradict its fundamental mores.

There is also an inter-temporal dimension to effective institutions: rules that change all the time are harder to know and are less effective in ordering people's actions than stable rules. This is expressed in the conservative saying that 'old laws are good laws'. The advantage of stable institutions is that people have adjusted to old institutions to the best of their ability and have acquired a practice of following them almost automatically. Stability reduces enforcement costs, improves reliability, and hence facilitates human interaction. However, excessive stability can become a vice. It may lead to institutional rigidity, even when circumstances change and make institutional adjustment desirable. Hence, there must be some scope for adjustment. Hayek made this argument incisively in his essay 'Why I am Not a Conservative' (Hayek, 1960, pp. 395–411). When rules are open, that is, when they apply to an indeterminate number of future cases, rigidity is less of a problem than if the rules are case-specific. Nonetheless, even open rules may require adaptation if conditions evolve.

To illustrate how appropriate rules establish trust and why this is essential for effective interaction, we can look at football rules: They stipulate certain types of behaviour of the players and obligatory sanctions for rule infringements. The rules are simple and certain (no ifs, ands or buts!), hence knowable. They are abstract in that they do not apply only to one particular game or one player, and they are open-ended in that they apply to an infinite number of future games. Thanks to these qualities, the rules shape the behaviour of the players, or – as institutional economists would say – are 'normative' of their behaviour, making it predictable.[1] Now imagine if these qualities are suspended: the referee rules on every move and goal in a discretionary manner. Instead of abstract rules, he decides case-by-case, giving preference to some players, possibly on the basis of expediency, and changes the implicit rules all the time. The football game would at best end in conflict and total confusion, and at worst could not be played at all. Even a deluge of directives from the referee would not coordinate the players on the two sides. Likewise, case-by-case regulation and intervention in civil and economic interaction destroys trustworthy rules and leads to disintegration of a healthy society and economy. It was a great contribution of the ancient Romans to Western civilization that the praetors of the Roman Republic (the law enforcers) announced rules under which they would act. From this initiative, transparent, stable law evolved, on which people could rely.

Institutions may also be categorized as to how they are framed:

(a) They may be *prescriptive*, instructing people precisely what actions they must take to achieve a specific outcome, for example to move from point A to point B so as not to get a speeding ticket.
(b) They may be *proscriptive*, ruling out certain classes of unacceptable behaviour, for example not to exceed a speed limit or not to steal.

Examples for proscriptive institutions are many of the Ten Commandments, which rule out certain classes of action – 'thou shalt not . . .'. Another example is the well-known Hippocratic oath (named after Greek doctor Hippocrates, fifth century BC), which instructs medical practitioners *not* to harm the patient. Such proscriptive rules do not give purpose-directed commands of what to do. Therefore, they leave people much scope for autonomous judgment and initiative.

Both types of institutions coordinate peoples' actions. Where behaviour is prescribed this is done by a visible hand and according to a leader's plan. Where behaviour is proscribed, people are more likely to respond voluntarily and spontaneously. As we shall see in the following chapter, prescriptive rules are an essential part of a planned, coercive order, whereas rule-bound behaviour, which is guided by proscriptions, is typical of spontaneous orders, such as the rules that coordinate people active in markets by an invisible hand (Sudgen, 1986).

One important difference between proscriptive and prescriptive institutions needs to be underscored. Those who prescribe from the centre what others must do – those who give instructions and directives – need much more specific knowledge than those who only rule out certain types of action. If one prescribes, one has to be aware of the means and capabilities of the actors, as well as of possible conditions for, and consequences of, the prescribed actions. Those who rule out – proscribe – certain types of behaviour only need to know that certain actions are undesirable, but those at the centre are able to leave the specific detail and the evaluation of consequences in the field to the actors who are directly involved. Actors have more freedom when guided by prohibitions of the type 'thou shalt not . . .'.

KEY CONCEPTS

Institutions are widely known, man-made rules that constrain, possibly opportunistic, human behaviour. They always carry some kind of sanction for non-compliance. Institutions should be simple, certain, reasonably stable, abstract, open and consistent with complementary rules to be effective.

Prescriptive institutions instruct and command people, telling them what to do. They create an order of actions from above, by some leader. **Proscriptive rules** leave actors much freedom of what to do; they only rule out certain harmful classes of actions (negative instructions along the lines of 'thou shalt not. . .').

Prisoners' dilemma describes a situation in which two or more parties are worse off if they do not cooperate, but in which each party is tempted to go it alone, as the other party or parties cannot make credible commitments. The term derives from the game-theoretical case where two prisoners are held in separate rooms and are not allowed to communicate. They face a dilemma: should they remain silent and hope that their guilt cannot be established, but risk that the other prisoner will incriminate them? Or should they speak out, incriminating the other and hoping for lenient treatment? The dilemma would be resolved by cooperation between the two prisoners. In other words: what is individually rational behaviour yields inferior results for the group; and cooperation pays off.

A prisoners' dilemma also arises in competition between suppliers who are inclined to underbid each other in order to attract buyers. The suppliers would be better off as a group, if they cooperated, for example by forming a cartel. In this case, the dilemma serves good purposes for the community. We have to conclude that cooperation is sometimes, but not always, socially desirable and institutions are needed to underpin such cooperation, but also to prevent it in situations where non-cooperation deserves to be promoted.

Organizations are not institutions

We should, again, draw attention to a use of the term 'institution' in everyday English, which deviates from our definition. In common usage, 'institution' is frequently applied to the concept of 'organization' (which is defined as a more or less durable combination of property rights to production factors under a leader in order to achieve some shared purpose, see Chapter 9). Institutional economists do not call banks, universities and psychiatric hospitals 'institutions'. These are organizations. Institutions are rules, organizations are players (North, 1990, p. 4).

Certain institutions of course require organizational support and rules may be embodied in organizations. Just as certain types of knowledge are implicit or embodied in (built into) capital goods, so are institutions sometimes implicit in organizational structures. Certain institutions incorporate implicit knowledge and are inseparably tied to certain organizational arrangements. An example is the traditional family, an organization that serves various ends for its members and embodies certain rules of conduct for mother, father and children.

The importance of implicit institutions is made clear when one compares different firms in an industry. One often observes hard-to-explain differences in productivity between the best-practice firm and other firms in the same branch of industry, which can only be attributed to different work practices (Kreps, 1990). These implicit institutions are sometimes given fuzzy labels such as 'corporate memory' or 'organizational culture'. The fact that some institutions are built into organizations makes it often hard to transfer them to other organizational environments, a reason why so many corporate take-overs do not work out. The embodiment of rules also enables the owners of specialized institutional knowhow to claim property rights in their specific institutional arrangements and to extend the use of that proprietary knowhow by taking over other organizations. To give an example, some of the rules on how to run an honest and competent stock exchange are so intimately tied to the implicit knowhow of those who run the stock exchange that it is hard to imagine such knowledge being disembodied from the organizational back-up. There is no manual along the lines of "Running a Stock Exchange for Dummies". In short, organizations are often storehouses of implicit knowledge, which is essential to their functioning.

KEY CONCEPTS

Organizations are purpose-oriented, reasonably durable combinations of resources, which are to some extent coordinated in a hierarchical way by a leader. Organizations may pursue economic purposes, for example in the form of a business partnership or a share company. They may also pursue political purposes, for example in the political organization of local or national governments, party organizations or lobby groups.

Organizations, although partly coordinated by top-down ordering, also require internal rules to function effectively. Many of these rules tend to be implicit because they govern frequently repeated actions between the limited numbers of members of the organization. Examples of **institutions that are embodied in organizations** are established procedures, work practices and business routines. Such implicit institutional wisdom is often hard to transfer to other organizations as the transfer depends on association, imitation and emulation.

5.2   Internal institutions

Internal and external institutions

In Chapter 2, we touched on the important distinction between internal and external institutions. To remind the reader, internal institutions are defined as rules that evolve within a group in the light of experience, and external institutions are rules designed externally and imposed on the community from above by political action. South African economist Ludwig Lachmann made this distinction to show that many rules, which influence our behaviour, are the result of evolution and that communities functioned on the basis of rule-bound behaviour long before government was even invented (Lachmann, 1973; Bernholz et al., 1998, 13-34). The distinction between internal and external institutions relates to the genesis of the rules – how they came into existence. Examples for internal, or evolved, rules are good manners, which tell people to be punctual, and ethical standards that the members of a community follow. Examples for external, or man-made, institutions are the civil law or a traffic code, which a parliament or government authority has decreed. In practice, one can of course observe fluid transitions between internal and external institutions.

Institutions can also be classified as to whether the sanction for non-compliance comes in the form of decentralized, spontaneous social feedback (informal institutions) or by a formally organized mechanism (formal institutions). As we shall see, the distinctions between internal and external, and informal and formal do not always coincide.

What matters is the degree of constraint and discipline that institutions exercise over individual actions. Internal institutions appeal to voluntary compliance, but non-compliance with the rules has consequences. In specific circumstances, it is the individual that decides whether or not to accept the consequences of non-compliance. By contrast, coercive orders, which rely heavily on external institutions and formal sanctioning, leave the individual much less leeway to evaluate the specific situation (Radnitzky, (ed.) 1997, pp. 17–76).

How internal institutions evolve

Human interaction is governed by numerous internal institutions that keep evolving spontaneously in the light of experience. Someone discovered a rule and found it useful, making interaction with others possible in the first instance, and easier, once these rules of conduct were imitated, and gained critical mass to become a norm widely obeyed in the community.

A good example of how such evolved institutions develop and work is language. We order the sounds that we are able to produce and hear into recognizable patterns called words, and, by applying rules of grammar, we order words into sentences. These rules have evolved over time and contain much knowledge how to communicate. No one has designed a living language, which is an ever-evolving system ruling the interaction of millions of people. New words arise, meanings change, and words fall into disuse. Thus, the word 'app' was unknown at the turn of the century, now every iPod and iPad user knows what an app is. Attempts have been made to design languages, such as Esperanto, but the acceptance of such creations has been limited. Even where the internal institutions of language are supplemented by external rules, which are policed by an authority, such as the *Académie Française*, the results are often ineffectual or ridiculed.

Another example of how the internal workings of society produce institutions that no one designs, but that emerge from the interaction of millions of people is the custom that people who do not tell the truth lose respect or are shunned in honest society. The genesis of this habit has no doubt to do with the fact that fibbing to mislead people inflicts costs on others and destroys trust. The rule not to tell lies is sanctioned by the spontaneous exclusion from social exchange, typically in a fairly informal, but nonetheless powerful manner. Internal institutions arise and continue to exist through selection processes within society.

Internal rules also govern economic interaction. Markets depend on some basic rules being respected. For example, people have to be allowed to keep the profit from their exchanges (respected private property rights), and market participants negotiate to narrow the differences between offer and demand price bids. Reversals of price offers, that widen the gap again, are spontaneously punished by a discontinuation of the negotiation (shunning of potential contract partners). For markets to function smoothly the relevant rules have to be widely known and adhered to. Another example of internal market institutions is the convention that a deal, once struck, terminates all further price negotiations. If someone tries to re-open negotiations once a deal has been struck, the sanction will probably be that traders will not deal with him in the future (ostracism). To give a yet another example: work contracts operate satisfactorily for workers and employers only if institutions about many work practices are widely shared, adhered to and violations are sanctioned.

A one-off experience turns into an internal institution only when a critical mass of people imitates and accepts it. Institutions may begin within a small group who benefit from sharing certain arrangements, for example the custom that loans are repaid punctually. Once the benefit of this rule becomes apparent, it is likely that more people will adopt it. Successful institutions spread to bigger and bigger groups of participants. On the other hand, institutions that were no longer found useful – such as the European and American institution that gentlemen defend their honour by dueling – lost critical mass. Nowadays, other ways of sorting out attacks on someone's honour have been adopted. Internal institutions are thus subject to gradual evolutionary processes. They are varied, accepted or rejected (selection), and only some gain critical mass. Traditions that are found to fail when circumstances change are adjusted. In developing countries, the advent of modernity and the impact of globalization have challenged familiar traditions in manifold ways – by "a million little mutinies", as Indian writer V.S. Naipaul once aptly put it.

Philosophers and social scientists have long recognized the importance of internal institutions in structuring social interaction, bridging the gaps between self-centred individuals and forming bonds that hold a society together. As far back as 2500 years ago, the Chinese philosopher Confucius (551-479BC) emphasized the importance of what he called 'ritual' in creating harmonious, predictable human behaviour and in enabling many people to live together in confined spaces and with limited resources. French social philosopher Charles de Montesquieu (1689-1755) went back to the Roman institution of unwritten laws, known as *mos maiorum*, when he wrote about the importance of *mœurs* (customs) in his treatise '*De l'esprit des lois*': "Intelligent beings may have laws of their own making, but they have some which they never made". The Anglo-Saxon philosophers of the Enlightenment who wrote roughly at the same time, such as John Locke (1632–1704), David Hume (1711–1776) and Adam Smith (1723–1790), also saw that the institutional framework of a society rested on evolved internal institutions. Consciously made, legislated rules, and the entire structure of politically determined institutions, they taught us, had to rest on internal institutions. Long before the laws of social intercourse are codified and written down on parchment, they are written on the hearts and minds of men. In modern times, Friedrich A. Hayek has most forcefully made the same point (1973, 1976, 1979a, especially the *Epilogue* to 1979a, pp. 153–208).

Different types of internal institutions

It is useful to distinguish four broad, though sometimes overlapping categories of internal institutions, which differ in the ways in which adherence is monitored and breaches are sanctioned (Kiwit, 1996; p. 10):

- *Conventions* are rules, which are so obviously convenient that people automatically enforce them, by and large, out of self-interest. For example, people adhere to certain word definitions and grammatical rules because it is in their own interest to make themselves understood. Further examples for largely self-enforced conventions are the tacit agreement in the market that interest rates are expressed in terms of a percentage per annum and that prices are quoted in terms of money. A vegetable seller who might try to express all vegetable prices in terms of grams of apples, which is theoretically possible, would soon discover that she does little business. People adhere to conventions because it obviously pays and they easily exclude themselves from profitable interchange by choosing not to stick to the conventions (de Jasay, 1995).
- *Internalized rules* are a second type of internal institution. People have learnt these rules by habituation, education and experience to a degree where the rules are normally obeyed spontaneously and without reflection (conditioned reflex, see Chapter 3). People have turned many rules into more or less automatic habits, which they consider a personal preference and apply fairly consistently. One's morality is, for example, made up of such internalized rules. That you should not lie or not pay your debts punctually are rules of conduct, which people have learnt and now normally obey as a conditioned reflex. Internalized rules are both personal preferences and constraining rules. They operate as rules in the heat of battle protecting people from instinctual, shortsighted opportunism, often saving them coordination costs and conflict. Violations of

internalized rules are typically sanctioned by a bad conscience – in other words, people suffer a psychic cost. But violations may also be met by reprimand; if you hit me, I will hit you! The tit-for-tat rule in the prisoners' dilemma settings is such an example. A variety of simulations on computer and in lab experiments suggest that, rather than a strict tit-for-tat strategy, a strategy, which is more trusting and forgiving of transgressions, yields higher pay-offs. But there is no escaping the need to have retaliatory strategies at one's disposal. Without a credible commitment to punish those who violate the rules of cooperative play, the game will break down. These punishment mechanisms tend to be exercised mildly and with empathy vis-à-vis children, who get often educated in that way. As children grow up, the sanctions are applied more strictly. Where this sort of education is neglected (because it requires patience and is not always pleasant), there is a danger of institutional decay, that is, a danger that harsher and costlier means of mutual control have to be resorted to or certain beneficial acts of cooperation no longer occur. Overall wellbeing then declines (Giersch, 1989).

These sanctions may be reinforced by reference to the transcendental or to certain symbols. For example, the ethical rule that 'you shalt not steal' has – in the Judeo-Christian tradition – become a violation of a Commandment, which displeases God (Hazlitt, 1988, pp. 342–353). As Adam Smith put it: "Religion, even in its crudest form, gave sanction to the rules of morality long before the age of artificial reasoning and philosophy" (cited after Hayek, 1988, p. 135). In the East-Asian tradition, especially the Confucian, great attention is paid to moral education, which makes young people internalize rules of interpersonal conduct. Members of society are then imbued with strongly held moral institutions that make them comply seemingly voluntarily, or at least without much reliance on formal legal rules and processes.

One benefit of internalized rules, which encourage reflexive obedience and a high degree of rule compliance, is that members of society save on coordination costs. In societies, where people are spontaneously honest because they have internalized honesty, agents have lower decision-making costs and risk fewer 'accidents' than their competitors in societies where cheating is habitual and agents speculate all the time whether, in this particular instance, they will get away with cheating, and what possible penalty they risk. This is why widespread corruption – the non-enforcement or uneven enforcement of the rules – makes entire economies uncompetitive and hinders economic growth (Sections 14.3–14.5).

Internalized rules that establish trustworthiness also save costs as against a situation where trust depends on explicit, mutual contracts that have to be negotiated and monitored.

- *Customs and good manners* are a third type of internal institution. Violations do not automatically attract organized sanctions, but others in the community tend to supervise rule compliance informally, so that violators earn a bad reputation, lose respect or even find themselves excluded, in the extreme even banned or ostracized (Benson, 1995, pp. 94–96).[2] Thus, children who misbehave in East Asian families are often not allowed back into the house or apartment. Punishment in the West tends to rely on a different type of exclusion: badly behaved kids are 'grounded' and thereby excluded from their friends outside the home. People with bad manners tend to be lonely, which can be an extremely powerful sanction. For example, an Australian Aborigine or American Indian, who was expelled from his tribe, was most likely condemned to certain death as individuals could hardly survive for long outside the group. Similarly, an international currency trader, who loses his reputation because he repeatedly violates the unwritten rules of the foreign-exchange trade, will not be able to pursue his profession. He will soon fail to find contract partners, because bad reputations are quickly known throughout professional networks. Other types of enforcement for such customary institutions are that misbehaving parties lose the repeat business, normally a serious penalty, because much trade is not one-off. Since the search for contract partners costs considerable resources, much business is conducted in ongoing bilateral relationships. Only in an 'end game' is there no such sanction. Many exchanges are conducted as repeat games for the very purpose of retaining a sanction. Customs can also be reinforced by contract partners who offer up 'hostages' – for example, a down-payment that is forfeited in the case of non-acceptance of a delivery. Another 'hostage' may be one's reputation that suffers if one sells bad products. A borderline case to the second category of internalized institutions is the case where one's bad conscience is reinforced by reprimand or shaming, ensuring that violators face the sanction of losing face. East Asians tend to rely on this type of sanction more heavily than Europeans who have long been able to rely on the formal enforcement of external institutions. Reliance on magistrates and external institutions is still frowned upon in Chinese society even nowadays.

To recapitulate: sanctions may be enforced spontaneously by reprimand ('tut-tut'), by reciprocity ('tit-for-tat'), by exclusion and ostracism ('out!').

- *Formalized internal rules* are a fourth type of internal institution. Here, the rules have emerged with experience, but are formally monitored and enforced within a group. Communities create much law internally but then enforce it among themselves in organized ways relying on outside third parties. These may be adjudicators (people who clarify the rules and spell out possible sanctions) and arbitrators (third parties who make binding decisions on interpretation and sanctions). An example of this is the self-regulation of the professions, such as the medical, journalistic and legal fraternities. Formalized internal rules also regulate most sports. Experience may have shown that the game of soccer requires formalized rules, which soccer clubs and federations apply. They adjudicate disputes and hand down penalties. Football codes are spelled out and enforced formally, but without reliance on outside authorities such as government bodies. Only rarely are these rules enforced in public courts. Instead, sports bodies rely on formal internal procedures and sanctions, such as excluding offending clubs from the competition for a given period. Tribunals ruling on what constitutes a breach of professional standards may enforce internal rules in formalized ways. Trade and finance in most societies are based on similar internal institutions, which the merchants and bankers have created to facilitate their business. Oriental bazaars and European markets have, for example, developed complex trading rules that community leaders or designated market experts interpret and formally enforce. To cite another example of this type of internal rule: international trade relies on merchant-made laws (*lex mercatoria*) that are often enforced by professional associations and arbitrators but not by a court or a transnational authority (Chapter 11).

Formal internal institutions are often much more effective in facilitating the business than externally imposed and government-enforced laws because self-monitoring and formal enforcement by members of the profession are done by people with much knowledge specific to time, place and the profession, whereas outside judges have only limited knowledge. Indeed, their rulings may trigger unintended, deleterious consequences.

Informal and formal internal institutions

The first three categories of internal institutions are informal, in the sense that the sanction for violations of social norms is not defined and is not applied in an organized way. Sanctions occur spontaneously. The fourth category of internal institution is formal in that the sanctions are spelled out and violations are met with sanctions through organized mechanisms. In short, the distinction between formal and informal relates to the manner in which sanctions are applied – organized (formal) or unorganized (informal).

The first two categories of informal internal institutions discussed above tend to impose a degree of self-discipline. They are self-enforcing, be it out of self-interest or because one tries to avoid a bad conscience. As a by-product, individuals behave in ways that take the interests of others quasi-automatically into account. Where these institutional control mechanisms are commonly practiced, the latter two types of internal institutions, as well as formal legal and regulatory controls, are less necessary. Where these norms get neglected, we may end up in a litigious society or with societal disintegration.

Spontaneous adherence to internalized institutions has consequences for individual freedom. When people have been educated to control themselves and abstain from opportunistic behaviour out of self-discipline, they enjoy greater freedom from formal, coercive sanctions. Then, effective interactions are greatly facilitated. A good measure of self-discipline, supported by inter-nalized codes of conduct, pays off.

KEY CONCEPTS

Internal institutions can be:

(a) **informal**, that is, they are not sanctioned by formal mechanisms, namely:
   - **conventions**, that is rules that are of obvious, immediate benefit to the persons, whose behaviour they control, and violations harm their self-interest;
   - **internalized rules**, whose violations are sanctioned primarily by a bad conscience;
   - **customs and manners** which are sanctioned informally by the reactions of others, for example by reprimand, tit-for-tat and exclusion; or
(b) **formalized**, where the sanctions are implemented in an organized manner by some members of society.

To reiterate, the distinction between **internal and external** relies on the genesis of the institution, the distinction between **informal and formal** on the way in which the sanction is applied, spontaneously or in an organized manner. **Third-party enforcement** of formal internal institutions occurs when adjudicators or arbitrators are included in the process of enforcing institutional arrangements. This may occur, for example, when one party does not obey a trading rule and an arbitrator is called in to settle the conflict. (Third-party enforcement of course also occurs in the case of external institutions, since government agencies act as the adjudicating and enforcing third parties.)

Not of human design

Internal institutions can be highly effective and are frequently sufficient to order even very complicated and complex interactions. We have already referred to one remarkable modern example, namely how the biggest network that has ever linked mankind, the Internet, operates. It was originally set up by the US Defense Department as a computer network without a centre or a central authority, so that communications could survive a nuclear attack on a centre. Because this network was not fully utilized, the Internet was opened to universities and later to commercial users. Since 1997, the Internet has linked more and more users around the globe and now reaches into every country on earth. It grows dynamically, but only very few external rules have been imposed (for example, to prevent the duplication of provider names). Despite the lack of outside control, the traffic between users is orderly, because certain internal rules have developed and are generally observed. Some of these internal rules are conventions, which are of immediate usefulness to participants, such as sticking to the protocols of how email addresses are written. Other rules are manners that have evolved spontaneously. Where participants try to disturb the traffic, for example by inserting viruses or distributing noxious SPAM, the free market has provided numerous weapons, for example virus-detection programs and SPAM filters. Is it not a miracle that, by such informal means, billions of people on all continents, who are communicating in all languages of the world through sound and images, are served by simple internal institutions? In a few cases, dictatorial governments have tried to censor the Internet, for example in the People's Republic of China and Arab dictatorships. However, creative new programs available on the Net promptly circumvent many of these outsider controls. Central authorities will never be able to impose controls over free speech and free knowledge search that were once feasible. Big operators – big industry, big government, big unions, big media – will probably never be able to dominate what the great diversity of people are now saying to each other over the Internet.

A very important form of spontaneously evolving rule sets is the common law in the Anglo-Saxon countries. Judges discover rules to adjudicate in certain cases and set precedents that form rules for others to follow. This contrasts with the formal, codified law of the Continental European countries, such as the *Code Napoléon* in France and the German Civic Law code. These creations of expert commissions and formal legislation may advance transparency and 'knowability', but they tend to display more rigidity in the face of changing circumstances. In practice, however, the law in countries with formal codebooks is also evolving through case decisions and precedents, resulting in bodies of evolving rules.

The internal institutions that are crucial to human interaction are not the result of human design and enforcement by an external authority. Yet, they form an important part of our civilization, as Hayek pointed out:

> We flatter ourselves undeservedly if we represent human civilization as entirely the product of conscious reason or as the product of human design, or when we assume that it is necessarily in our power deliberately to re-create or to maintain what we have built without knowing what we were doing. Though our civiliza-tion is the result of a cumulation of individual knowledge, it is not by the explicit or conscious combination of all this knowledge in any individual brain, but by its embodiment in symbols which we use without understanding them, in habits and institutions, tools and concepts, that man in society is constantly able to profit from a body of knowledge neither he nor any other man completely possesses. Many of the greatest things man has achieved are the result not of consciously directed thought, and still less the product of a deliberately coordinated effort of many individuals, but of a process in which the individual plays a part which he can never fully understand. They are greater than any individual precisely because they result from the combination of knowledge more extensive than a single mind can master. (Hayek, 1979b, pp. 149–150)

Internal institutions contain much of the distilled, tested wisdom of our fore-bears. They are sometimes called 'soft institutions' because they leave some scope for variation and because the sanctions attached are at times flexible. As many of them are informal and evolve ceaselessly, they have the advantage of considerable flexibility. They permit experimentation and reinterpretation, as and when new circumstances emerge. Many members of a community test them all the time in decentralized ways. Because many participate, change tends to be gradual, hence predictable. Internal institutions, which have evolved from experience, have the innate advantage of adjusting to changes if sufficient numbers of members of a community violate the old rule and behave according to a different pattern. This enhances their evolutionary capacity.

Internal institutions have the related advantage that they can be applied flex-ibly when circumstances vary slightly. What they sometimes lack in clarity and transparency is often compensated by the ability to tailor the precise interpretation and the sanctions to specific circumstances. When self-enforcement fails, sanctions may range from a friendly chide, to a rebuke or a reproach – long before stricter sanctions, such as ostracism or formal third-party enforcement, are employed.

The sanctions that go along with internal institutions may also be tempered by personal empathy and the realization that all of us are fallible, yet have to be held to certain standards if society is to function. Internal institutions may be seen as an intrinsically humane part of the 'cultural cement' that holds a community together (Elster, 1989). As they evolve, internal institutions are part and parcel of the moral discourse by which institutions and shared social values are kept in tune with circumstances and experiences. Indeed, that evolution is an essential part of the history of civilizations (Radnitzky, 1987).

5.3　External institutions and the protective function of government

External institutions defined: political action to design and enforce rules

External institutions differ from internal ones in that they are designed and imposed on a community by an agent with a political will and the power to coerce, who stands above the community as such. Such agents may claim legitimacy for the role by tradition and inheritance, conquest and force, or because the community elected them. External institutions always imply some form of top-down hierarchy. By contrast, internal institutions are applied horizontally, among equals. The sanctions for violating external institutions are nearly always formal and are often backed by the use of force. In many societies, governments have been given the monopoly on the use of force, which they exercise through the police, the courts and the prison system. In modern democratic societies, governments try to control the 'violence professionals' by non-violent means, namely through formal rules and financial controls. Thus, the defining characteristic of an external rule is that it is designed and imposed and the sanction is in the hands of some body outside the community.[3]

We can distinguish various types of external institutions as to their content and target:

- *External rules of conduct* are intended to constrain the actions of citizens in ways similar to internal rules. They consist of universal, prohibitive rules and are contained in the civil, commercial and criminal codes of most countries (Hayek, 1973, pp. 131–139).[4]
- *Purpose-specific directives* are a second type of external rule. They instruct public or private agents to bring about predetermined outcomes. Some such institutions may be contained in statute law, but in many countries

they are found in by-laws based on more general enabling legislation. Such institutions place high requirements on the knowledge of officials because they are prescriptive (see above).

- External institutions can also be *procedural* or *meta* rules, which target the various agents of government, instructing them how to behave and what not to do (administrative law). Many of these institutions may be aimed at keeping the system of rules inherently compatible (see Chapter 6). Procedural rules can be of great importance to giving effect to the external rules of conduct. For example, the rules that protect the citizens from police violence in general terms will require precise procedural instructions to police officers how to carry out their duties in specific situations, reducing their information and decision-making tasks. Rules of engagement of soldiers instruct them what and what not to do in the heat of battle.

KEY CONCEPTS

External institutions are designed, imposed and enforced from above by a political authority. External institutions are nearly always formal in that an authority is identified to enforce sanctions in organized ways. External institutions often work in open-ended, abstract ways – for example, private laws apply to an indeterminate number of individuals and cases. External institutions have normative effect on the behaviour of the members of society, in particular if they are in harmony with pre-vailing internal institutions and values.

Specific directives are aimed at par-ticular purposes or outcomes; they do not apply universally. An example is the rule that citizens must deliver a certain per-centage of their income to the state in the form of income tax.

Procedural rules are needed for the administration of government to facilitate the internal coordination of the various agents of government. They are contained in public and administrative law and form an important part of most constitutions and bodies of laws. Legislation frames many of these procedural rules, but – dif-ferent from private law – they are directed not at the citizens but the agents of government.

Internal institutions order most of the conduct of the citizens. Yet, despite the great effectiveness of internal rules in most circumstances, all complex societies have also adopted external institutions. This is so because internal institutions in complex mass societies cannot eliminate all acts of opportun-ism. One reason for this is that people frequently interact with strangers whom they will never meet again, so that many informal sanctions (such as tit-for-tat, ostracism and damage to one's reputation) are ineffective in preventing opportunistic behaviour. As there is also more likelihood of prisoners' dilemmas emerging, formal rules are useful to support cooperative behaviour.

External institutions have come relatively late in human history (Benson, 1989; 1990; 1997). It seems no coincidence that the invention of agriculture and animal husbandry – which necessitated respected private property rights in land, animals and the yields from these activities – was soon followed by the emergence of lawgivers, judges and formal government.

Although external institutions depend on political decision processes and governments, this does not mean that government officials invent the institutions. Often, government agencies have only codified and compiled pre-existing customs and laws. This was the case with the great lawmakers of Antiquity. In the Roman Republic, the praetors, who were elected law makers and law enforcers, gradually produced a body of codified laws, which originally evolved much like modern Anglo-Saxon case law now does (Némo, 2006; pp. 18–23). In this context, it is also interesting to note the ancient Germanic concept of *Volksrecht*, the law which is owned by the people. The ruler only protects and nurtures it. The famous medieval law code of eleventh century Catalonia was called *usatges* (usages), hinting at the origin of the code in internal customs. At least in Western civilization, public authority is the guardian of the external institutions, but it is there to serve everyone.

External institutions may also come about by formal political processes, such as when chosen delegates make a constitution or pass legislation; they may also come about by administrative action, for example when governments decree certain regulations on the basis of some more general enabling legislation. In some countries, judges who offer new interpretations of existing laws also shape external institutions. In Anglo-Saxon countries, with its common law tradition, such 'judge-made law' has long been the norm, but in more recent times has been supplemented by parliamentary legislation.

Time and again, history has shown that external institutions normally depend, for their effectiveness and durability, on how well they are in harmony with the internal institutions of society and that the evolution of new rules depends on previous rule sets – that is, 'stickiness' (*metis* – Boettke, 2001; Pejovich, 2003; Boettke et al., 2008). This empirical fact has, for example, been demonstrated by the emergence and durability of Law Merchant in international trade (Section 11.2) and by the experiences of the transition of post-Soviet economies and the economic development of different nations (Section 13.1 and Chapter 14).

Reasons for rule setting by government

One may ask the question: What are the advantages of external authorities in rule setting and enforcement, as compared to an exclusive reliance on internal rules? Collective, political rule setting and enforcement has often a number of comparative advantages:

(a) Popular customs and conventions may be ambiguous. They may not be spelled out clearly enough and may not be widely enough known. External institutions may often be more knowable, saving the people information costs. If internal institutions are officially codified – written down formally and pronounced in edicts – they may become more effective, and more visible sanctions can be laid down. This enhances the normative function of rules. Thus, law-givers such as Hammurabi (ca. 1728–1866BC in Mesopotamia), Moses (who probably lived ca. 1225BC in Palestine), Solon (who codified laws in Athens, 630–560BC), the *decemviri* of Rome (a committee of ten who were asked in 451BC to write down the existing laws), and Ashoka the Great (304-232BC in India) are celebrated for having codified existing internal institutions and decreeing them in the form of external laws. Enhancing the institutions by formalizing them and attaching formal penalties for infringements has often been effective in improving the human condition. Such law-giving made it harder for people to be forgetful, slovenly, dishonest or negligent. American statesman James Madison (1751-1836) comes to mind, as he said as far back as 1788: "If men were angels, no government would be necessary".

(b) The spontaneous application of internal rules by the members of the community may be haphazard, far from dispassionate and unbiased. Enforcement of internal rules may for example favour the rich, the popular or the beautiful. To constrain such arbitrariness and bias, community leaders with a reputation for being 'just', may be elected to become judges. 'Just' here means that they are even-handed in protecting everybody from coercion by others and treat everyone as equal before the law. Judges may then develop and make public the rules which they apply, including procedural rules of the sort that are now known as 'due process'. External rule making responds to the need that justice needs not only to be done, but has to be seen to be done in order to have a normative influence on behaviour.

Such adjudication does not necessarily require a government, but financing the expenses of independent judges frequently makes government funding preferable. There is ample historic evidence that informally emerging judges without financial independence may fall prey to temptations of bribery. On the other hand, the material independence of tax-funded judges has proven a weak bulwark against judicial corruption. Therefore, there will be great advantage in external institutions that facilitate the supervision of judges in the administration of justice (Benson, 1995). One external institutional device to achieve this is the existence of several layers of jurisdiction. Since judges of lower courts do not like to see their rulings overturned on appeal to higher courts, they try to comply with top-down controls. Another mechanism for the control of judiciary decisions is critical public opinion and criticism of judgments by the wider legal profession (Cooter and Ulen, 1997).

(c) When judgments have to be enforced, informal sanctions such as shaming or spontaneous community reactions may prove unsatisfactory – think only of affective, excessive anger, such as mob rule, lynching or spontaneous expulsions from the community. Given the likelihood of thuggery on the part of some, there is advantage in appointing 'violence professionals' (police, jail warders, military and so on), who are licensed to inflict legitimate punishment through penalties that are accepted in the community as commensurate to the crime or misdemeanor. There is of course always a certain danger that the 'violence professionals' will abuse their position for their own purposes (principal-agent problem). Therefore, the agents of law enforcement have to be controlled from acting on their own account. These are arguments for government authorities having the monopoly over the legitimate use of force (except in rare situations of legitimate self-defence) and for subjecting the monopoly to non-violent, institutional means of control by those with political power. Most communities have found that turning the violence professionals into government agents and inventing non-violent processes of supervising them is the best mechanism of control.[5] As James Buchanan (the 1986 Nobel Prize winner in economics for his pioneering work in public choice and constitutional economics) argued, the task is to find a set of institutions of governance that can empower the protective and productive state, and yet restrain the redistributive state.

(d) An important aspect of institutions is – as noted before – that they allow people to make credible contractual commitments. In certain circumstances, third parties are needed to make contractual promises credible. Government agencies can wield the weapon of formal enforcement when they become such third parties.

(e) A fifth argument for collective, rather than private action derives from what was discussed above under the heading of the 'prisoners' dilemma'. It has been said that cooperation, which is often advantageous, requires the back up of government institutions to be sufficiently credible (Buchanan, 1975; North, 1990, p. 13). Clans and tribes, who rival with each other, suffer from being prisoners of eternal conflict. All would be better off by cooperating, subject to some external authority, such as a government. They reap, so to speak, a 'disarmament dividend' by ending conflicts (Buchanan, 1975). Commitments to cooperate are frequently made more credible – and the peace is conserved better – if the deal which dissolves the prisoners' dilemma is supported by an overarching third party, such as a ruler (Axelrod, 1984).

(f) A closely related reason for governments setting and enforcing rules is what has been called 'free-riding' (Olson, 1965). In the real world, certain assets have indivisible costs or benefits. Where others cannot be easily excluded from benefits, we speak of a 'public (domain) good' (Sections 7.2–7.3). For example, if one citizen sets up a force of security guards who keep malfeasants away from the community, all neighbours benefit and no one can be excluded from that benefit. The first citizen has to incur high fixed costs to maintain the security guards, but his neighbours enjoy a free ride without paying (for them, it is a free external benefit). In these circumstances, insufficient provision is likely to be made for security. The argument then is for local government to take over the security service and fund its provision by coercive taxation. This same argument applies to protecting the external peace and sovereignty of a nation by a military force. Here, too, nationalization, sharing the costs through the external organization of government and control by external institutions, prevents free riding and leads to a better provision of the public good, namely protection from external aggression. (Public goods will be discussed in greater detail in Sections 10.1–10.2).

(g) A further, related reason given in the literature why governments become involved in designing and imposing institutions is the 'tragedy of the commons', a situation in which members of the community, if acting in isolation, find themselves in a particular prisoners' dilemma: Members of the group exploit a common asset, for example when their cattle graze on community-owned land. As long as resources are bountiful in relation to the demand, grazing land is not scarce. But as the number of users goes up – for example with population growth – grazing has to be rationed. Internal, informal constraints tend to do the trick in small communities, where everyone knows everyone else and spontaneous castigation of those who overgraze work informally at the interpersonal level. It has been found that informal constraints tend to work satisfactorily within groups of up to 50 or 70 members (Hardin,

1968; 2008/1993, pp. 497–499; Ostrom, 1990, 2005). If the group is bigger, individuals become anonymous, information about individual behaviour is insufficient and informal restraints on individuals (such as damage to their reputation) cannot control the excessive exploitation of the commons. As a consequence, overgrazing occurs and the land deteriorates. Then, some authority administering external rules has an advantage; in our example a government authority could allot limited grazing rights to each member of the community. Another solution would of course be to divide the commons into private properties, which fences can protect.

(h) A final reason why external institutions and collective action may be preferable in certain circumstances has to do with the fact that internal institutions often work by discrimination and exclusivity. Internal institutions often have to discriminate between insiders and outsiders to function. Only then is the sanction of exclusion feasible. Networks of traders or financiers often build complex internal rule systems as a foundation for their business pursuits and enforce the rules by confining the network advantages to the members. Examples for this are the medieval corporations of European traders and bankers who managed the trade between Venice, Florence, Nuremberg, Frankfurt and Amsterdam, the famous Champagne fairs, the Arab merchants who ran the caravan trade, the caravanserais and the bazaars, and the contemporary Chinese family networks in East Asia. These networks cover numerous participants and are based on internal institutions, which allow huge volumes of risky business to be conducted at low cost. But these networks can only function if the number of participants is limited and malfeasants can be excluded. Exclusivity and small size are essential to the functioning of the internal institutions within such networks. This may pave the way for monopolization and eliminate beneficial outsider competition. Experience shows that the informal, internal institutions of personally networked trade and finance carry economic development up to a certain level, but not further. This is the reason that is often given to explain why the Mid-Eastern bazaar trade did not lead to industrialization. Small trader networks were able raise the funds for a caravan, but not the capital to build factories. Beyond certain levels, external institutions and protective government enjoy economies of scale and ensure just, open market access to all comers (North, 1990, pp. 48–53). The infrastructures for modern, open, extended markets often simply require sanctions other than private sanctions. Designed, formal laws and a formal judiciary then prove more effective in bringing about an open order, enabling a wider, more dynamic division of labour.

These arguments give rise to the external imposition and enforcement of institutions by government, to what James Buchanan called the 'protective function of the state' (Buchanan, 1975; 1991). These arguments also hold true with regard to the advocacy of anarchy. Unfortunately, the human condition condemns us to accept some state power and to ceaselessly define and control government agents. Simply advocating anarchy, the abolition of all collective action (all government), is a facile way to avoid the difficult issues of the limits and roles of government, which social scientists must address.[6]

Having said this, it has been shown that most of the institutions, which governments normally design and implement, can in principle also be developed and enforced by internal, non-government institutions (Benson, 1990; 1995; 1997; Radnitzky (ed.) 1997, pp. 17–76). Thus, formal sports bodies that investigate incidents and impose sanctions may effectively control cases of fraud and violence in sport. The points listed above concerning the various reasons for government action in protecting the rules of conduct should not be read as indicating that alternatives to government action are often not feasible. They only indicate that, in certain circumstances, collective action tends to have comparative advantages and allows communities to reap scale economies as compared to exclusive reliance on internal rules and private action.

External institutions normally serve as an essential, coercive back-up to the internal institutions. But they may also replace internal rules. If they are intended to replace *all* internal institutions of a society, problems arise – as was the case in various totalitarian regimes in the twentieth century which imposed more and more external rules at the expense of the internal workings of civil society (Section 13.1). Monitoring and enforcement costs rose steeply, people's spontaneous motivation waned, and administrative coordination capacities were overburdened. External coordination then often leads to government failure. It is interesting to note that even one of the most totalitarian regimes of our day, North Korea, had to tolerate private markets when central planning produced a famine in the 1990s. These problems are of course not new. They were, for example, the reason why Confucius and early Confucian scholars advocated spontaneous coordination and were extremely sceptical of 'fabricated' orders that relied on the rule of kings (external institutions) and the command from above: "Whoever . . . wants to order the state and does not rely on custom, resembles a man who wants to plow without a plowshare", says Confucius in the *Book of Rites* (cited after Habermann, in Radnitzky, 1995b, p. 75). It is not surprising that revolutionary Marxists in China who tried to replace traditional civil society with 'scientifically designed' new institutions after 1949 banned Confucianism, but ultimately failed. Now, they rely again increasingly on the internal institutions and the market economy.

KEY CONCEPTS

Codification means that existing internal rules are formally written down in ways that make them visible and unambiguous, for example by engraving the laws on stone walls as in ancient Assyria, Egypt and India, or the formal promulgation of the laws of Israel by Moses in the form of the Ten Commandments.

Free-riding refers to a situation where the costs of information or exclusion are such as to make it impossible to exclude others from benefiting from a good or service that someone in the community has provided. Thus, it may not be possible to exclude youngsters from taking a free ride on a hay wagon, and it may be too costly to exclude people from accessing the radio waves once someone sets up a station. However, technology may change and allow measurement of use and exclusion, so that the free-rider problem disappears and private production becomes feasible. This has, for example, been increasingly the case in television, where free to air services are supplemented by pay TV.

The **tragedy of the commons** can be observed where a large number of people use commonly owned resources, each of whom can benefit by exploiting the common resource to the fullest for their own benefit. If all act like this, the tragic situation arises that the resource gets destroyed. This may be the case with fish stocks in the open seas. It has also been the case in the Sahel area of Africa where the first Landsat photos taken from space in the 1970s showed that commonly owned land was severely drought affected, whereas private, fenced-off properties conserved a decent vegetation cover. The tragedy of the commons was in this case that starvation set in and desertification took over where the land was not owned privately (Hardin, in Henderson, 2008/1993, pp. 497–499).

Protective government is concerned with designing, imposing, monitoring and enforcing external institutions. It normally supports the internal institutions of civil society and makes the fostering of an order of actions the primary concern of public policy.

Two traditions in external rule setting

In the West European tradition of shaping external institutions, there are two strands: the Germanic/Anglo-Saxon tradition which places great store in the common law, that is, reliance on judges finding, developing and formatting the external rules; and the Roman legal tradition, which is reflected in designed systems of legislation such as the *Corpus Iuris Civilis* of late Roman Emperor Justinian, the French *Code Napoléon*, or the German civil and commercial codes of the nineteenth and twentieth centuries. In practice, no legal system is in a pure form. Formal, parliamentary legislation has gradually supplemented and replaced common law everywhere, and even the most elaborate formal law codes require judge-made interpretations to make them effective.

Judge-found law, which is more prevalent in the Anglo-Saxon tradition, tends to be adaptable to interpretation and learning from experience and open to the feedback to judgments from the judicial fraternity and the wider public. It captures the wisdom of more participants. But, by the same token, it lacks the cohesiveness, clarity and transparency of the designed law codes of the Roman tradition.

High courts also reshape judge-made law. The members of the high court bench are normally not elected, but are politically appointed. The composition of high courts can have a lasting and major influence over the life of a nation. Thus, the majorities of the US Supreme Court have a powerful influence on how the external rules of the United States are shaped and reinterpreted. Majorities may be greatly influenced when judges retire, so that the thrust of the US legal system may change quite dramatically as compared to legal systems where the powers of the highest courts are more bound by constitutions and black-letter law. Similar influences are also at work in other legal traditions since the incumbents of the highest courts always interpret existing laws. Generally, the nation's highest courts have normally been a centralizing influence, whether in a common-law regime such as that of Australia or a country with a more explicit black-letter law tradition, such as Germany.

Another consideration is that the costs of running a common-law legal system tend to be high, because daily practice requires the services of legal professionals and frequent adjudication by the courts, whereas many potential conflicts are averted if transparent and comprehensive civil and commercial codes are on the books. However, formal black-letter codes also have their drawbacks. They have long lost their simplicity and logic cohesion, and experience has shown that reliance on formal legislation by parliaments often introduces rigidities in times of change. Political activists have responded to the growing complexity of social interaction by promulgating more and more complicated legislation and regulations, often at the behest of special interest groups (rent creation and rent seeking). Legislative and regulatory favouritism has undermined the coordinative function of external institutions and has reaffirmed the important insight that a complex world requires simple rules (Epstein, 1995; for an argument in favour of external rules to be 'discovered' by competing judges and courts, see Cooter, 1996; Christainsen, 1989/90).

One has to conclude that external rule setting and enforcement is a complicated business and that an exclusive reliance either on codified law or on the common-law approach would fail to serve the purpose of external rule setting, namely to create order and trust. Therefore, flexible mixes – tested time and again – are the best-possible approach to an inherently intractable problem.

5.4 The functions of institutions

Effective coordination and trust

One function of institutions is to make complex processes of human interaction more understandable for the various participants and more predictable, so that coordination between different individuals is expedited, as we have already pointed out. In social chaos and anarchy, a good division of knowledge and labour is impossible as information gathering, as well as many monitoring and enforcement problems are insurmountable. Credible commitments cannot be made and people remain the prisoners of each other's opportunism. Poor and poorly enforced institutions are a major cause of mankind's history of long-term poverty and economic stagnation.

Institutions serve the key function of simplifying everyone's cognition task by reducing the world's complexity. By making the reactions of others more predictable and hence the world more orderly, institutions make it easier for individuals to thrive in a complex, changeable world and avoid 'cognitive overload'. When there are general, recognizable patterns of behaviour and conditions, economic agents can cope better with specifics, such as producing and marketing a particular car or planning for major investments. As institutions help people to understand the complex, confusing world around them, they protect them to a considerable extent from being confronted by unpleasant surprises and situations they cannot handle. Institutions help us to address our primordial fear of not being able to master life. The trust they underpin enables us to risk experiments, be creative and entrepreneurial and encourage others to come up with new ideas of their own (Buchanan and di Pierro, 1980).

Where institutions constrain the actions of others and rule out certain types of future eventualities, they reduce 'forward ignorance'. They make it a lot easier for people to be alert to entrepreneurial opportunities on the horizon, because they create confidence about the nearby humdrum life routines. Only when human behaviour is stabilized, is it possible to enhance the division of knowledge and labour, which is the foundation of growing prosperity.[7]

The reduction of complexity by institutions may be non-specific. Certain general institutions may be widely appreciated because they give people psychological comfort and security – the feeling that they belong to an ordered, civilized community where coordination costs are low and risks limited, where one can feel at home, where one can have trust in those around. Interaction with others is less exacting than if one lives amongst strangers or in less-well-ordered communities. Institutions create bonds that appeal to a sense of belonging, which most individuals find satisfying.

In other circumstances, the coordinative function of institutions is much more specific. For example, the citizens of a nation, where credible institutions ensure the stability of the value of money, can have greater confidence in saving and investing in monetary assets, as well as in financing the capital stocks essential for economic development. It has been found that the very existence of simple monetary rules tends to exert spontaneous stabilizing influences on aggregate demand. This was pointed out in an article that we consider a classical analysis about the coordinative effect of institutions (Simons, 1948/1936; see also Section 7.6).

Institutions can enhance the effectiveness of production factors – such as labour – in meeting human wants. Good institutions play a role similar to other production factors, for example capital, which makes labour more productive. We may therefore consider a community's institutions a valuable productive asset and can speak of 'institutional capital'.

In short, by facilitating order and helping people to overcome cognitive limitations and developing trust, appropriate institutions improve the use of knowledge and the division of labour. In this way they raise productivity and promote prosperity (material welfare).

Protecting domains of individual autonomy

A second function of institutions is to protect domains of individual autonomy from undue interference from the outside, for example by others who wield power. Institutions protect individual freedom, one of the fundamental human values discussed in Chapter 4. Thus, Western civilization has known and valued the institutional concept of private autonomy since Greek and Roman Antiquity. The concept of *dominium* (domain) in Roman law, which incorporates this notion, might be loosely translated into English as 'my home is my castle' – that people have a sphere of autonomy in their home which is protected by generally respected and enforceable institutions. Under Roman law, the master of the home had great powers within his home, where he was free to act; outside interference was ruled out. A similar rule protects private property in many societies. Property rights protect owners from outside interference with the free use of their assets and create a domain in which property owners are free.

The protection of liberties – spheres of individual autonomy – by institutions is never unlimited. The free pursuit of one's own purposes often affects others, so that freedom must always find its limits in the freedom of others. Without such constraints, liberty would be license, and without appropriate constraints on freedom, society would degenerate into anarchy. We should however be aware that we are discussing a continuum between one extreme of completely unconstrained freedom to act autonomously and the other extreme of total domination by others. In practice, the issue is for people to enjoy as many domains of freedom as is feasible, which means for everybody to have as many acceptable choices as possible. Kenneth Boulding (1959, p. 110) put this idea nicely in a rhyme:

> Freedom is what's inside the fence
> of Morals, Money, Law, and Sense.
> And we are free, if this is wide
> (Or nothing's on the other side).
> We come to Politics (and Sin)
> When Your fine freedoms fence Me in,
> and so through Law we come to be
> Curtailing Freedom – to be free.

We shall return to the important idea of institutions protecting and confining domains of individual freedom when discussing property rights in Chapter 7. They establish important domains of freedom, circumscribe economic competition by imposing controls on the uses of private property and limiting what individual property owners may and may not do with what they own. Further, we shall see in Section 8.4, that the entire system of capitalism depends not only on economic freedoms but also on the control of these freedoms by competition, which needs to be upheld by appropriate institutions.

In short, appropriate institutions protect economic and non-economic freedom, which tends to be beneficial to the attainment of other fundamental values, such as peace, security and justice.

Averting and resolving conflict

A third important role of institutions is that they help to mitigate interpersonal and inter-group conflicts. Conflicts between independently acting individuals are sometimes inevitable. When different people pursue their diverse personal purposes, the exercise of their freedoms often impacts on others and some of these impacts are unwelcome. The question then arises how individual freedom to act is best constrained to avoid costly conflicts and how such conflicts can be solved in low-cost, non-violent ways. Rules of conduct that delineate spheres of autonomous action can often avoid potential conflicts altogether, but – where these nevertheless occur –provide guidance how to resolve them without undue cost. Should conflicts arise, institutions can provide mechanisms of adjudication, which allow for non-violent conflict resolution.

In essence, there are two fundamental ways of dealing with interpersonal conflicts:

(a) The absolute freedom of individuals (license) is constrained in general, preventive ways by rules that limit arbitrary action and reduce the probability of conflict. Examples are: a fence signals the boundary of a private domain, the rule to drive on the right-hand side of the road avoids collisions, the emission of noxious fumes by industry is banned to avoid litigation over damages to others, and so on. In all these cases, institutions prevent conflicts by signalling in advance who will be in the right and who in the wrong, that is, who can expect to be punished for breaking the rule.

(b) If conflicts have nevertheless broken out, institutions are used to adjudicate conflicts in previously agreed, and hence predictable, ways. Examples are the custom of compensating aggrieved parties for damages, or rules to settle torts under formal legal procedures, subject to known formal court practices (Boulding, 1959, pp. 117–125; Tullock, 1992, pp. 301–326).

In short, appropriate institutions help the members of society to reduce and resolve conflicts, advancing the fundamental goals of peace, security and justice.

On power and choice

Potential conflicts arise not only from the freedom of individuals to act, but also when people cooperate. Individuals with wealth or charisma are able to exercise power in exchange relations. A rich man may, for example, be able to hire a poor man to do demeaning work, simply because the poor man needs the money to survive. He may feel that the rich employer has power over him, in the sense that the employment relation serves to impose another's will over his own. This is likely to cause resentment if the poor man does not perceive any alternatives and feels coerced and un-free. In such a situation, the poor man will sooner or later demand influence over the exercise of power, for example through worker co-management councils or political controls, demanding a voice. This situation is also an element of the populist movements of the early 2010s to 'Occupy Wall Street' and engage in street protests against 'corporate greed' and cut-backs in government programmes to benefit certain established groups.

The power relationship is a consequence of a lack of alternatives. When many alternatives to earn money are open, people will feel free and will move to other employment or invest in other projects if they feel oppressed. In other words, choices among alternatives set people free. Alternatives control power, even if none of the alternatives offer brilliant opportunities. Where people are in a position to vote with their feet (exit), they will not feel overpowered and will not be all that interested in exercising a political vote ('voice' – as Hirschman, 1980/1970, called the vote as a means to control power in contrast to mobility, that is, 'exit'[8]). Freedom of choice empowers people in many respects without the need for political guarantees of freedom. Only where individuals have no alternatives that allow them to exit and where people have little scope (or will) to adjust their aspirations in the light of past experience, can they be dominated.

In societies where people wield much power over others (who are then un-free), conflict is likely, with possibly costly consequences, even when strong institutions and coercive controls are in place. Where individual freedoms are safeguarded, including the freedom to move and exit, there tends to be less conflict. Institutions that ensure exit opportunities also limit arbitrary uses of power, which infringe on other people's freedom. People with power, who submit to rules, may also protect themselves from the temptation to abuse their own power in the heat of battle, so to speak. Seen from this angle, rules are the concession of the powerful to reason, and to social peace.

A central function of appropriate institutions in long-term economic and social development is to create a power balance between different social groups, such as the nobility and the peasants, and to ensure that the lower-level groups have 'leverage', that is, they can get support from higher-level power groups. Only when power is diffused will broad-based, sustained economic development take place (Powelson, 1994, especially pp. 4–11).

5.5   The essential properties of effective institutions

Universality

Having repeatedly spoken of 'appropriate institutions' to achieve certain ends, we now need to ask: What characteristics ensure that institutions are effective in coordinating individual conduct, or – as lawyers would say – have normative impact.

A first criterion is that institutions should be general and abstract. In other words, they should not be case-specific or discriminate between different individuals and circumstances without a discernible reason. Hayek defined generality as "applicable to an unknown and indeterminable number of persons and circumstances" (Hayek, 1973, p. 50). The principle of generality is violated where, for example, the nobility or a church are exempted from paying taxes or where violations of the traffic code by the police and the military are not prosecuted. A second criterion is that an effective rule must be certain in a twofold sense. It must be knowable (transparent) and it must give reliable guidance in future circumstances. The maxim of certainty implies that normal citizens should be able to read the institutional signal clearly, know the consequences of rule violations, and should be able to rely on them in shaping their actions. The cryptic utterances of the Oracle of Delphi, for example, failed to do this. Similarly, secret decrees and obscure and ephemeral legislation violate the principles of certainty. Nowadays, Western societies suffer from a proliferation of legislation and regulations that no one can know and understand. Thus, the income tax code of most Western democracies now fills many tomes and is ceaselessly modified, so that no one can know the rules anymore. Another example of uncertain institutions is the Islamic practice of different mullahs giving binding interpretations of the law that contradict each other, so that followers do not know which interpretation to follow (Kuran, 2009, 2011). A third criterion is that institutions should be open. This means they must apply to future cases to allow actors to respond to new circumstances spontaneously and with confidence. These three criteria have been subsumed under the concept of universality (Leoni, 1961).

One must add a fourth criterion, namely that the various rules should not contradict each other, but rather form a compatible whole ('order of rules', Eucken, 1992/1940). When, on the other hand, the various rules are compatible with each other, they reinforce each other in creating an understandable order. Thus, economies work much more smoothly, if capital, labour and product markets are equally free, whereas heavily regulated labour markets in an otherwise free economy are bound to produce unemployment and confusion.

Universality can be safeguarded relatively easily in the case of prohibitive rules. The rule 'thou shalt not steal' is universal, binding everyone, but giving different actors great scope to make their own decisions. It applies to an unknown, open number of people and circumstances. Universality also says that no one should be above the law. It also implies the procedural equality of all individuals, which we discussed in Chapter 4. Universality is part of what people perceive as just. A discriminatory application of rules and sanctions to people according to their status of wealth, influence, race or religion is widely considered unjust.

Infringements of universality tend to undermine rule compliance and transparency, hence undermine the normative, coordinative intent of institutions. If, for example, it is the customary rule that rock stars or wealthy individuals are measured with a different moral yardstick than ordinary citizens, if the police can act dishonestly with impunity or if people apply laxer moral standards to government officials than to ordinary citizens, spontaneous obedience to the institutions is likely to wane. The institutions then fail to fulfil their functions and many fail to attain their fundamental aspirations. Universality is an essential formal attribute of the rule of law, a concept with a long tradition in Western civilization. We shall return to the discussion of the rule of law in the following chapter, after having explored the functions of systematic, cohesive sets of institutions.

CH 5 – CASE ONE

Simple rules for a complex world

In the nineteenth century, many Western countries reformed the laws to simplify the rules, to make rule compliance easier and cheaper and to reduce the costs of applying the law. Since then, the law has been made more complex, often in response to a growing complexity of society. However, epistemology and jurisprudence increasingly demonstrate that complex rules do not work because they overtax human cognition and impose unnecessarily high compliance costs (Schuck, 1992; Epstein, 1995). From an individualist position and based on the recognition of the pervasive knowledge problem, some lawyers propose simple rules so that citizens can cope more easily with the complexity of modern life (Epstein, 1995).

CH 5 – CASE ONE *(continued)*

Peter Schuck (1992) identified four characteristics of dysfunctional complexity in institutions:

- density, namely that the institutions regulate great detail, often in a prescriptive manner;
- technicality, namely that the rules cannot be understood by ordinary citizens, but require professional experts to interpret and apply them;
- differentiation, which means that there is overlap between different bodies of law (for example local, State and national law); and
- uncertainty, which means that there are many rules that are conditional, so that no single question determines the legal outcome.

Richard Epstein pointed out that modern rule systems impose unnecessarily high compliance costs on the citizens. To overcome this, he proposes simple rules, not as an exclusive, but as a dominant approach to guiding human behaviour. He writes (Epstein 1995, pp. 307–308): "[U]nder the dominant constraint of scarcity, insist that every new legal wrinkle pay its way by some improvement in the allocation of social resources." He proposes the following simple rules:

> Individual autonomy, first possession, voluntary exchange, control of aggression, limited privileges for cases of necessity, and just compensation for takings of private property, with a reluctant nod toward redistribution. . . . The first four rules are designed to establish the basic relations between persons and their control of things; the next two are designed to prevent the coordination problems that remain in a world of strong property rights and private contracts. The entire enterprise seeks to minimize the errors arising from these two sources.
>
> The protection of the rich because they are rich, or of vested interests because they are powerful, is no part of the overall plan. If people with great wealth and influence cannot continue to supply goods and services that others want and need, then they should, and will, find their own prospects diminished in a world governed by the legal principles outlined here. . . . This simple set of legal rules shows no favoritism.

Symbols and taboos

As we have seen, a primary function of institutions is to economize on the need for knowledge in coordinating people. To enhance their knowledge-saving quality, institutions are often made more certain by the signal of a symbol. Thus, the symbol of the red traffic light tells us quickly and certainly to stop, the symbols of uniforms enhance the coordination of military action in battle, and the symbol of a banknote signals a certain value. Clearly, the symbol is a material thing (for example, a piece of nicely printed paper), but its functions depend crucially on the institutions that the symbol represents. The symbol conveniently represents and reminds us of complicated rules.

A similar knowledge-saving function is often also attached to taboos. Instead of conveying to people the complicated knowledge that fish in certain areas of the reef are toxic at certain times of the year, Pacific islanders simply declare certain fish *tapu*, prohibited. A similar taboo has long been attached to pork in Judaism and, later Islam, because pork in the Middle East was frequently contaminated with trichinae. Such taboos save people the trouble of learning the reason for the prohibition or understanding why a certain condition may hurt them. The purpose is to obtain quick, unreflected obedience. This may, of course, at times restrict the adaptive capacity of a community and become a barrier to adjusting the institutions to new circumstances, a problem that we shall address in Chapter 12.

Symbols and taboos induce conditioned, often quasi-automatic responses and serve to abbreviate the process of knowledge gathering and evaluation. They also make rule enforcement more straightforward. Of course, this does not preclude that leaders of communities with power sometimes abuse symbols and taboos to control their subordinates in self-serving ways, just as they may abuse institutions as such.

KEY CONCEPTS

Universality of an institution means that it is general and abstract (rather than case-specific), certain (transparent and reliable) and open in the sense that it applies to an unknown number of cases. Rules should also be non-contradictory. Simple rules tend to be more easily understood than elaborate and conditional rules. They serve their functions better (Leoni, 1961; Epstein, 1995).

5.6   The costs of interaction and coordination

Coordination costs

In our time, human cooperation has reached a truly astounding extent. Economic interaction between individuals has become extremely complex. Coordination requires much knowledge and causes considerable costs. Both sellers and buyers in a market have to forego other opportunities when specializing in a particular way and interacting with others through market exchanges (these are the opportunity costs of coordination). These coordination costs have been called "the expenses for running the economic system" (Arrow, 1969).[9] Markets, in which individuals, teams and organizations compete, and the rule of law, which lays down anonymous, universal constraints for all players, are needed to help people to coordinate their plans and actions. In other words, markets inform players what they may be able to do and to what advantage, and the law tells them what they cannot legitimately do without harming others. These arrangements keep a balance, but they can only be operated at a considerable cost.

Thanks to better communications technology and a more effective organization of exchange processes and, in some places, better institutions, the *unit costs* of coordinating the various owners of specialist skills and items of property (for example land, capital or technical designs) have probably dropped over the past one hundred years. To cite only one example, between 1930 and 2010 transatlantic telephone costs per unit dropped by an impressive 9 per cent per annum, and computer communication by email and Skype has reduced unit costs even further. Yet, the *volume* of acts of coordination has risen enormously over the past century, because unprecedented economic growth has greatly increased in the global division of labour. The snowballing of the total volume of coordination costs is part and parcel of the economic success stories described in Chapter 1.

The volume of coordination costs in advanced economies has been estimated at around half of all the costs of producing and distributing a rich country's national product (compare North, 1992, p. 6). It has been estimated that the share of labour dedicated to distribution and coordination in the US has gone up from 11% of all work effort in the year 1900 to no less than 61% in 1980 (Oi, 1990, p. 4). Much of the rapidly growing service sector in the advanced economies deals with the coordination of ever-more complex production and exchange networks; the costs of the service sector are, to a large extent, coordination costs.

At first sight, it may seem surprising that such a large part of our economic effort should be dedicated to coordination, rather than physical production. Yet, a large part of the costs of running a firm consists in reality of costs incurred in coordinating and controlling (a) the agents who work in the firm and (b) the actors with whom the firm interacts in markets. A large part of a business' total costs are for administering the internal organization, marketing research, technical R&D, buying and selling, advertising, borrowing finance, obtaining and using legal advice, and other efforts to coordinate people. If one looks at a national economy as a whole, trade and logistics, business services, finance, government administration and other segments of what has been called the 'coordination industry', take up a large and growing share of the total national product.

In the light of this, it is surprising that the assumption of zero transaction costs is still made regularly in most standard introductions to economics. In neoclassical models of the market, the price that the buyer pays and the price that the producer obtains are, for example, assumed to be equal (market-clearing price). In reality, transaction costs are deducted from the price that the buyer pays, to arrive at the producer price. Indeed, before we can even presume to speak of a market, buyers and sellers have to incur high information costs to find out whether they want to buy and sell a particular product and to find out what they need to know in order to buy or sell. Business people can tell you that their enterprises often remain competitive mainly by economizing on coordination costs, both internally and in their dealings with suppliers and customers, and not on their production costs. We must take these coordination costs explicitly into account and always ask how these costs might be reduced. Appropriate institutions are crucial to economizing on the costs of finding the relevant knowledge and of transacting business. Communication becomes cheaper not only because of technical progress, but very importantly also because of institutional improvements. When the institutions are fuzzy and activist regulators complicate the rule system, coordination costs snowball. For example, in countries where public policy is concerned with numerous specific outcomes, prescriptive rules proliferate and numerous otherwise profitable acts of production and exchange simply never happen. Economic reforms in numerous countries over the past few decades have demonstrated that clear, simple institutions can greatly cut coordination costs and thereby promote prosperity. A good historic example of this truism was the rule by the Han Emperors of China 2000 years ago to standardize the axle length of carts: this enabled roads to be standardized and saved on the costs of road building.

Types of coordination costs

Figure 5.2 gives an overview of the various costs of owning and using property rights in interaction with others. When people hold property passively (that is, without using it in transactions), they incur exclusion costs. They incur coordination costs when they put their property rights to active uses, that is, when they exchange them with someone else or combine them with other people's property rights within an organization. When such uses are coordinated in the market place where independent owners of property rights enter into voluntary contractual obligations and deliver on them, we speak of 'transaction costs'. In the first place, these include costs of obtaining information about what is available, on what conditions, when and where, as well as the costs of negotiating, monitoring and enforcing contracts.

Transaction costs will be discussed in greater detail in Section 7.3.

Figure 5.2 The costs of owning and using property

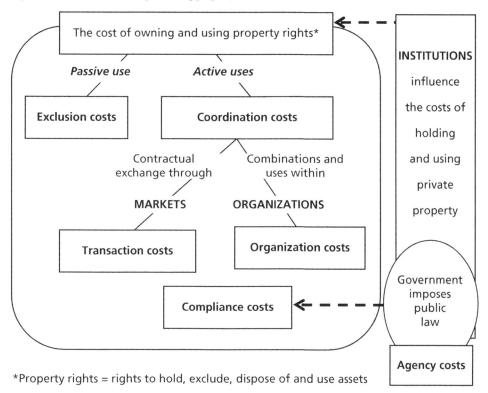

*Property rights = rights to hold, exclude, dispose of and use assets

As an alternative to using their property through market exchanges, people may employ their assets by binding themselves or some of their property rights within an organization. In this case, we call the costs of setting up and running the organization 'organization costs' (Figure 5.2). These will be dealt with in Section 9.2.

Running institutions often requires organizational back-up by collective action, as we saw. In doing this, governments incur agency costs. Operating the external institutions for which government is responsible normally creates very high costs, which are normally covered by fees and taxation (Chapter 10). In the process, governments exercise legitimate political powers mandating certain impositions on business and private citizens. They do so on the basis of public law. This inflicts 'compliance costs' on people who are being regulated. For example, citizens may have to spend much time and effort on red tape to comply with tax legislation, keeping records, collecting documentation, filling in forms and hiring tax agents. They also have to report to government agencies to demonstrate that they comply with the regulations. Such reports may have to be filed on a daily basis, as is the case for example in financial markets. The compliance costs, which have to be borne by private citizens, tend to add considerably to the costs of transacting and organizing business. These private costs come on top of the agency costs of running government, financed through taxes and other levies.

When faced with information costs or, for that matter, other coordination costs, it is often rational for people to remain uninformed (rational ignorance). We must assume that one will always interact with only partly informed partners. Indeed, one easily misjudges reactions if one assumes that others are fully informed, or want to be fully informed.

In concluding this section, the point needs to be made that one man's exclusion, transaction, organization and compliance costs are often another man's income. Those who have to bear these costs have an interest in reducing them, but those who carry out transactions or impose compliance requirements have frequently an interest in keeping these costs high. Much regulation is imposed because it keeps regulators in jobs and earns government authorities incomes and political clout. This conflict of interest plays a role when institutional reforms are attempted to cut coordination and agency costs. It explains the resistance to such reforms by many of the coordinating agents, such as government officials, lawyers and arbitrators.

KEY CONCEPTS

Exclusion costs arise when people want to ensure that no one else makes unauthorized use of their property. The mere passive keeping of property causes such costs, for example for the upkeep of gates and fences, locks, night watchmen and police, share registries, and patent protection.

Coordination costs arise when individuals interact with others to use their property rights, combining them with those of others.

Transaction costs are the resource costs incurred when people use markets to exchange property rights. They include the costs of searching for market information, contracting, monitoring and enforcing the fulfilment of contracts.

Organization costs arise when people try to combine their own resources with those that others own within an organization, such as a business firm, to pursue shared purposes. These include the costs of setting up organizations, communicating, planning, negotiating and monitoring performance of duties within an organization.

Compliance costs burden private individuals and organizations whenever they are subjected to the public-law provisions of government. Individual citizens and organizations have to comply with institutional constraints are imposed by legislation, regulation and taxation. This is, for example, the case when citizens have to spend resources on preparing accounts for tax returns or ➡

when firms have to submit reports that declare that they have complied with government regulations.

The **agency costs** of government refer to the resource costs of running government bodies, including the costs of monitoring what happens outside and inside of government. They are typically financed by taxes, other levies or incurring public debt.

NOTES

1 The term 'normative' here means "shaping behaviour so as to make it more predictable" in contradistinction to the use of 'normative economics' as against 'positive economics'.

2 Ostracism was practiced in ancient Athens from 487BC as a punishment for certain misdeeds. The citizens of Athens had to write the name of a person who was to be exiled for five or ten years on broken pieces of pottery (ostraka), and sufficient numbers of ostraka led to exile.

3 Some authors equate what we call external institutions with formal institutions. This overlooks the existence of internal institutions, which are formalized in the sense that the rules and the sanctions applied in organized ways by a third party.

4 Private and commercial codes of course also contain numerous formal, prescriptive stipulations, which are intended to facilitate transactions.

5 We might note in passing that a commitment of government to protect individuals does not necessarily mean that all aspects of citizen protection have to be under government control. Thus, medieval Iceland (ca. 930–1260) had legislation through a political organization. Parliament laid down many rules externally, and an external judiciary interpreted the laws and decided specific court cases. Both were publicly funded. However, the enforcement of the laws and court judgments was left in private hands: people who had obtained a ruling in their favour could legitimately hire private policemen to execute the ruling (Friedman, 1979, Eggertsson, 1990, p. 311).

6 This is of course not the only function of modern government. Other government activities are concerned with production of public goods and services by government agencies (for example the provision of a judiciary system), the redistribution of property rights as against the way in which they are allocated in the market place and the raising and administering of taxes and other levies to fund the agency and other costs of government. We shall return to these in Section 10.1.

7 Let us note in passing that institutions would be superfluous (a) if everyone lived in isolation, like Robinson Crusoe when he was alone on his island, or (b) if there was 'perfect knowledge'.

8 Hirschman also said that a combination of the suppression of 'exit' (emigration) and 'voice' (democracy) led to a third, and harmful, condition: apathy. Modern history is full of examples where this observation is given empirical content, not only in the Soviet Union and other totalitarian regimes, but also in many countries where milder political and social controls limit exit and voice-participation opportunities, such as Mid-Eastern and African dictatorships.

9 Some authors use the term 'transaction costs' to designate all coordination costs. We prefer to reserve this term to describe the costs of transacting business in markets. We also exclude transport costs (costs of shifting products and production factors in space), because they do not have the information characteristics typical for coordination costs as defined here. But one has to acknowledge that an important cost component in the value-added in the transport services consists of information and transaction costs.

6

Institutional systems and social order

In this chapter, we move from the focus on individual institutions to entire rule systems and the order that such systems can help to create. We begin by looking at what a system is and at hierarchies of rules, which range from constitutions to statute law and administrative regulations.

To make the point that systems of more or less compatible rules have profound effects on economic life, we shall discuss two differing ways of obtaining socio-economic order:

(a) the hierarchical or planned order, which is created by some visible, ordering hand, which, in a command economy, for example, is based on collectively owned property and the allocation of goods, jobs, and investment funds according to someone's plan; and

(b) the spontaneous order, which evolves when people obey certain shared rules, for example in a market economy where decision makers are motivated by private gain and prices emerge from competitive processes to inform them what is valued by others, and what not.

The spontaneous order is based on a vision that perceives the world as an evolving universe. Diverse people with diverse and changing tastes are motivated to pursue, of their own free will, diverse and changing self-directed purposes, using their decentralized knowledge. By contrast, the hierarchical order is based on the assumption that some political agents have both the capability to acquire and use all the knowledge needed to make relevant decisions and the power to coerce all others to follow their commands. Experience has shown that hierarchical ordering does not work well in complex evolving systems, such as the modern economy, and that spontaneous self-ordering promises a better utilization of dispersed, specialized human knowledge.

We shall also see that 'culture' or 'civilization' can be interpreted as a system of rules which are supported by shared values.

We conclude this chapter with a brief discussion of the rule of law. Its primary role is to protect individual freedom and contain conflict. It incorporates sets of rules that constrain individual behaviour, coupled with procedural rules. In many respects it supplements the economic institutions of the capitalist system, which will be discussed in Part II.

Legum servi sumus ut liberi esse possimus – We are the servants of the law, so that we can be free.

Tullius Cicero (106-43BC), Roman lawyer and author

Ubi non est ordo, ibi est confusio – Where there is no order, there is confusion.

Frater Lucas Bartolomeo Pacioli (ca. 1335-1520), *Treatise on Double-Entry Book-Keeping* (1494)

We have never designed our economic system. We were not intelligent enough for that.

F.A. Hayek, *The Political Order of a Free People* (1979a)

No individual is able to comprehend the world sufficiently to give practical instructions.

Martin Heidegger, German philosopher, in an interview with German news magazine *Der Spiegel*, conducted in 1966 and printed posthumously in 1976

Amongst the many other points of happiness and freedom, which your Majesty's subjects . . . have enjoyed . . . there is none which they have accounted more dear and precious than this – to be guided and governed by certain rule of law . . . and not by any uncertain and arbitrary form of government.

From the House of Commons petition to King James I, 7 July 1610

6.1   Social systems and hierarchies of rules

Man-made and self-organizing systems

The focus in the previous chapter was on individual institutions. In reality, institutions serve their purposes not by being observed in isolation but rather by forming constellations of mutually supportive rules. They form rule sets that in turn influence the system of real-world phenomena. In other words, we have to investigate an order of rules, which orders human actions. We have to think in terms of rule systems as well as economic and social systems.

By system we understand a configuration of multiple, interacting elements. Systems can be simple, for example the workings of clock. The system is made by a clock maker and the interaction is mechanical or electronic with regard to a single attribute, time. Other systems are more complex, containing numerous elements, whose interactions are determined by numerous attributes. Influences with regard to different attributes are indicated in Figure 6.1 by different kinds of darts. An example would be an ecological system in which various plants and animals interact with differing characteristics in order to survive.

Complex systems are hard to plan and operate. Many of them are self-organizing and self-correcting. Thus, swarms of fish mill about the ocean and swarms of starlings circle in the sky in ordered ways, and no manager is directing and controlling them, nor has a planner designed the structure of a swarm. Coordination relies rather on the spontaneous actions, reactions and inactions of the various individual animals, who obey simple rules that transmit messages between individuals, which prevent the fish from colliding or dispersing. If we study such ecosystems, we may discover that self-organization depends on the various individual elements following certain rules or regularities, which form a system.

Complex systems may also be open, that is, they can be subject to evolution in unpredictable directions from one period to the next (lower panel in Figure 6.1). Elements and characteristics vary spontaneously; elements appear, mutate or disappear. These variations are tested and selected or rejected. The feedback ensures that the system stabilizes, so that new, recognizable patterns emerge. The evolution of an ecological system over time – for example, how various plants and animals colonize an area – is a good example to illustrate the interacting processes of variation, selection and stabilization. Biologists and ecologists who understand such spontaneous coordination of complex systems also tend to warn us from interfering with such evolving orders, because unforeseen and often deleterious side effects may come about.

Another equally complex and evolving system is the modern economy, in which millions of individuals interact spontaneously with a great variety of different attributes and in which evolution takes place (Anderson et al., 1988; Parker and Stacey, 1995). The various participants do not operate in a chaos but act systematically, taking account of a system of shared rules. They have as little need for a commander or director as the starlings in the sky when the market participants' display ordered patterns of interaction. And the rule system that orders their actions tends itself also to be subject to evolutionary change in the light of experience.

The limited cognitive capacity of people – as discussed in Section 3.1 – makes it often necessary to spell out a number of rules, whose side effects reinforce each other. Individual rules have to be coordinated (ordered) to be effective. Thus, the institutions that protect private property have numerous consequences. One of which may be that propertied people compete with each other to find other property owners with whom they can profitably exchange

Figure 6.1 Types of systems

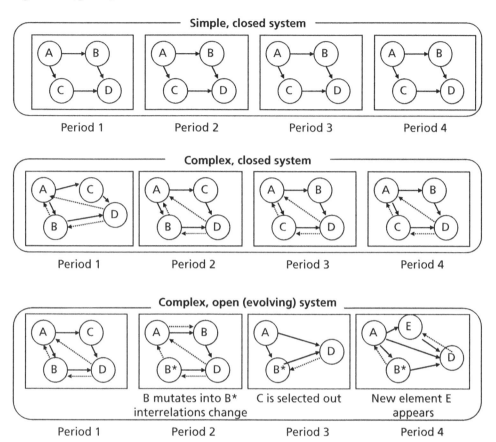

property rights. It will then be useful to spell out rules that ensure free contracting and liability for the promises made in these contracts. Private property, the freedom to contract and liability thus form a system of mutually compatible institutions – an order of rules.

If people enjoy protected property rights, but are not free to contract, contradictions arise: What use does private property have, if the buying, selling or lending of property rights by contract is prohibited or severely restricted? Only when the various rules form a reasonably compatible whole, will they be effective in bringing about order and control arbitrary, opportunistic actions that erode predictability and trust.

Rule systems work better in ordering human actions if they form a hierarchy that runs from general to specific rules. General, universal rules are often

Figure 6.2 A hierarchy of external institutions

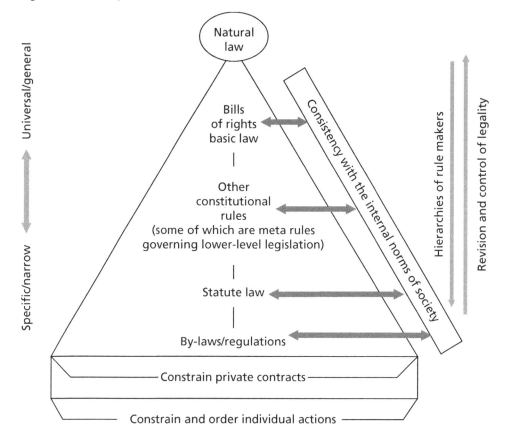

more abstract; they may consist of internalized moral norms (for example, 'thou shalt not steal') or general external institutions that are formally laid down in bills of rights or 'basic laws'. These *meta* rules override more specific institutions if contradictions arise. More specific rules may then explain what constitutes theft in a particular situation. Such rules are typically contained in specific statute laws or by-laws. Overriding rules create a framework for such lower-level rules. Such hierarchical rule systems are in particular typical of external institutions.

Hierarchies of external institutions tend to consist of rules essentially at three different levels, namely constitutions at the apex, statute law in the middle and regulations at the bottom (Figure 6.2). In many legal systems, natural law is often placed on top of this pyramid. This hierarchy constrains what sorts of private contracts can be made legally and how they will be interpreted when doubts arise. Typically, constitutional rules are selected in processes of constitutional choice. Some refer to collective decision-making to establish the legislation and the regulations. These latter institutions govern contracts that are made at the operational and decentralized level. If doubts arise as to legality of specific low-level constraints, this will be assessed from the bottom up, that is, from the specific to the general norms.

Such rule hierarchies make it easier for individuals to understand the rules because they create an order among different rules and maintain consistency over time. If an authority issues a great number of rulings, decrees, edicts, *ukases* (known from the autocratic Czarist and present-day Russian practice of ruling case by case and without reference to consistent general standards), or *fatwas* (known from the Islamic legal tradition in which different mullahs issue binding decrees to suit occurrences of the day), then inconsistency, arbitrariness and randomness will result. The rules cannot be comprehended and are ineffectual in having a normative effect on individual behaviour. They disorient people and create disorder. Such a style of rule making easily tends towards tyranny and discrimination. It is often perceived as unjust and the unsystematic proliferation of rules breeds sullen, outward conformity and dissimulation of one's true thoughts and intentions. This condition is the opposite to the open competition of ideas and the critical assessment of new ideas and experiments: Hence, it is conducive neither to effective coordination and innovation, nor to prosperity and freedom.

Rule systems may consist completely of internal institutions, as is the case with traditional cultures (see Section 6.4 below). Systems of internal rules normally contain only few explicit hierarchical and procedural rules, but we normally understand nevertheless how conflicting rulings are made compatible, for example when we accept that one need not speak the truth in certain extreme circumstances, for example if a white lie saves someone's freedom or life. External institutions and mixes of internal and external institutions require procedural rules to indicate how possible contradictions are resolved. Problems arise when deeply held internal rules of a community conflict with the external rules. A classic contemporary example are the failed US American attempts to foist new external institutions, such as democracy and economic freedom, onto countries defeated in war, if the people concerned have internal institutions and values at variance with those of Western civilization (Coyne, 2007). Then, the costs of monitoring compliance with the external rules and enforcing them limit what governments can achieve by imposing external institutions. It has been estimated that "government can at any one moment in time enforce at best 3 to 7 per cent of all legal norms by compulsion" if the people do not comply spontaneously (our translation; Kimminich, 1990, p. 100). External rules at all levels should therefore always be reasonably consistent with the internal rules and values of society (some of which are embodied in natural law) to ensure that these rules have normative influence on behaviour. In certain situations of conflict among rules, only careful moral discourse can resolve the contradiction.

External rules, to be effective, have to be enforced and also have to be seen to be enforced. With limited administrative and judicial capacity, densely regulated states cannot ensure this. Streamlining of the institutional system then would seem to promise great advantages (Chapter 14). However, there are also instances where the authorities design and impose institutions, although they know from the outset that these cannot be consistently enforced, either because the authorities are materially incapable or too lazy to do so. The purpose of governments here is to use regulations arbitrarily to control and punish political or ideological opponents and to keep challengers selectively under control. Sometimes rules are also made by authorities to extract fees or bribes for waiving them. This of course amounts to gross violations of the rule of law, corruption and expedient, just regulation.

In hierarchies of external institutions, we normally observe clearer statements as to how the various rules are related to each other. Very high-level constitutional rules are often contained in bills of rights, basic laws or preambles to written constitutions. They override all other rules. They tend to be designed by special assemblies and often depend on special criteria of acceptance (for example a two-thirds majority). In some legal systems, these high-level institutions also have to be compatible with natural law, which may be understood as a proxy for deeply held rules and values in the community that protect the inalienable rights of every human being.

The concept of inalienable rights was already known in Europe in Antiquity. It was shaped into codes of fundamental liberties in the modern era. These liberties are now contained, for example, the US Bill of Rights (1789 and later extended by amendments) and the French Declaration of the Rights of Man (1789). In the twentieth century, fundamental liberties from interference with the individual have been supplemented by claims to certain goods and services, such as the 'right to work', for example in the Human Rights Convention of the United Nations and the European Basic Rights Charter.

Other, more specific constitutional rules are subordinate to natural law and basic laws. They often contain procedural public-law rules, which determine how new rules are adopted and applied and which direct the various organs of government, as distinct from rules that guide the actions of individual citizens. We call them *meta* rules.

As one proceeds down the hierarchy of external institutions (Figure 6.2), the hierarchy of legislators also descends, from parliaments with simple majorities in the case of most statute law to administrations that pass more specific by-laws and regulations on the basis of enabling legislation. When such low-level rules are contested, they are subject to revision and control of their legality as against the more universal higher-level rules. High courts are often involved in this process.

Rule systems assist with cognition

Hierarchies of institutions work as follows: Individuals conclude private contracts to cooperate by combining or exchanging their property rights. This may come under specific regulations or by-laws that constrain what the contracting parties are allowed to do and clarifies aspects of the contract, which the contract itself does not spell out. The private contract may, for example, be between an employer and a worker establishing a work relationship. The freedom to enter into such a contract may, for good or bad reasons, be constrained by regulations that prohibit work during certain hours. The contract is of course also subject to formal statute law, which takes precedent over the regulations, should a contradiction become evident. All statutes are of course overridden by the higher-order rules contained in written or unwritten constitutions. If contradictions emerge, constitutional courts are asked to adjudicate how a particular statute law fits in with the constitution. It may find that the statute is invalid because it violates a higher-order constitutional provision. Constitutional rules have in turn to fit into the bill of rights and – at least in the Anglo-Saxon tradition – into natural law. A private contract authorizing slave labour would thus not be a valid, as slavery violates natural law. As mentioned before, the higher-level institutions constitute a framework that offers stability and ensures consistency of the lower-level rules. The hierarchy represents a legal system in the sense defined above. In modern societies, it tends to be complex and evolves, reflecting changes in the real world that the legal system orders. However, the insight applies that complex rule systems are hard to comply with, so that simple rules have much greater effect in ordering a complex world (Epstein, 1995; also Section 5.5).

To return to the example of an employment relationship: a system of rules surrounding the work contract gives employers and employees greater confidence of how future events will be sorted out under their open-ended contracts. A rule system also makes it economical to write employment contracts, since many specific contingencies that might need stipulation by private agreement and may be unimaginable at the time of contracting, are determined by elements in the overall institutional system. If specific adjustments in open-ended employment contracts become necessary, they can be made with regard to these specifics whilst the overall contract continues within the stable, reliable constitutional elements of the system. The coherence, yet flexibility, of a working institutional system enable individuals to make necessary adjustments but to maintain the reciprocal trust relationship between the contracting parties.

Hierarchies of rules assist with managing institutional change

Since the world of private contracts is open-ended and evolves, the corresponding institutional system should also have evolutionary capacity. A key function of a systematic hierarchy of rules is to assist with the evolution of the rule system. Higher-order rules lay down what lower-level rules may and may not stipulate, even when changed. They ensure internal consistency in the rule system and govern procedures for rule adjustment. These *meta* rules differ from institutions that directly affect the actions of private citizens (private law) in that they give directions to those who operate the external rule system (public law). *Meta* rules also lay down procedures how specific lower-order rules may be changed if necessary. Higher-order institutions provide a framework that confines what changes can be made and how these changes are decided. This is essential to the predictable functioning of the institutional system over time. Rules of a higher, constitutional quality keep matters predictable when specific lower-order rules have to be adjusted to new circumstances. Institutional systems that lack such hierarchies of institutions inhibit evolutionary adjustment. They will probably suffer from disruptive discontinuities and become uncertain in the long run.

It is not easy to keep complex institutional systems internally coherent, that is, to maintain the order of rules. Rule makers can avoid incompatibility by being economical in promulgating specific, lower-level institutions and concentrating on fostering simple, general rules. The proliferation of specific, detailed legislation is hardly the sign of a competent parliament. Rather, it is an indication that the general rules are neglected at the expense of interventions to obtain specific purposes. Such a style of rule setting creates insecurities for those subject to them because no-one can know – let alone obey – a large multiplicity of specific lower-level rules. As rules proliferate, the system becomes dysfunctional. In such a situation, simplifying and streamlining the lower-level rules and developing new universal institutions is the best way to making the institutional system more effective again (Epstein, 1995). Enhancing the coordinative power of institutions in this way has been an important aspect of economic reforms around the world. A welcome consequence of simplifying and reforming complicated, non-universal rule systems is not only that people can better understand and obey the rules, but also that contradictions among rules need not be interpreted. Then those with the power to interpret the rules (often arbitrarily) lose power, but this promotes justice, equality and wealth creation.

KEY CONCEPTS

A **system** is defined as a configuration of multiple interrelated elements. We speak of **complex systems** when the elements interact with regard to many relevant characteristics. If the system is open to the future in the sense that elements or characteristics change unpredictably, we call these systems **evolving systems**. Then, variation, selection and self-stabilization interact to produce new recognizable patterns. When we consider cross-connected institutions, we speak of a **rule system**. It may be ordered by experience and evolutionary learning (evolved institutional system) or by design (made, designed institutional system). The **order of rules** can be spontaneous or planned.

Hierarchy exists in a system in which status and authority are ranked vertically, with higher ranks having the right to command and order the lower ranks. In such a top-down system, order is imposed from above.

Natural law is based on the affirmation that all human beings have certain inalienable rights. Aristotle wrote that every human being had certain inalienable, overriding rights irrespective of where they lived and what conventions and laws their community adhered to. Natural law recognizes that all humans are equal in certain fundamental respects. In modern times, the concept of the natural law as a high-order legal principle has gained renewed acceptance in the light of experiences with totalitarian regimes. It is now widely accepted as the source of certain **basic** negative **liberties** (freedom *from* interference by authorities and fellow humans).

Statute law is that part of the system of laws that has been adopted and written down by a formal legislative body (as distinct from common law or case law).

Meta **rules** are procedural rules (or principles), which do not directly affect private citizens, but are intended to keep the external rule system compatible. They govern how institutional changes are made, by whom they can be initiated, by what majorities they are adopted and how conflicts over rule changes are resolved. An example of a *meta* rule is the provision that a constitutional court can review new legislation to establish whether it complies with constitutional principles.

6.2 Two kinds of social order

Two methods of ordering

Human actions can in essence be ordered in two ways:

- either directly by an outside authority that plans and implements order by instructions or directives to achieve a joint purpose (*organized or planned order*),
- or indirectly and in a spontaneous, voluntary way because the various agents obey shared institutions (*spontaneous or unplanned order*).

Spontaneous ordering occurs frequently in nature. To give but two examples: The molecules of a drop of soap water arrange themselves, when you blow into it, in a bubble, a predictable arrangement; and fertilized cells reproduce themselves spontaneously into recognizable living organisms without an outside ordering hand arranging this. We already mentioned swarms of fish that swim in admirable order or starlings that do not collide in mid-air. We also observe much spontaneous ordering among human beings, which allows us to rely on regularities in human conduct: When people visit the beach, they normally distribute themselves evenly in space to attain maximum privacy. When people compete, buyers and sellers are coordinated. In all of these spontaneous ordering processes, the various component parts are equals, obeying the same rules. No one acts as an authority that directs the others.

We can of course also observe that the visible hand of an authority does much ordering in society. Carefully thought-out designs may guide someone to coordinate various actors; one thinking brain may move others, like pieces on a chessboard. This happens in an opera on stage and in a factory in which hundreds cooperate to assemble a car.

The essential difference between these two kinds of ordering human actions can be illustrated by the following comparisons:

(a) The railway system runs on a centrally-planned and supervised timetable that imposes an organized or made order on train movements. When we watch the road traffic flows in a city, we also observe a certain order. But here no one is in control, instructing drivers precisely when to accelerate, brake or turn. Instead, the observed order comes about spontaneously because prohibitive institutions – traffic rules – and the self-interest in making headway and avoiding collisions guide people's actions. Within the constraints of the traffic code, people are free to decide how and where to drive.

(b) Outside our window at a new university campus, we see the coexistence of two kinds of ordering: The planners and architects laid down nicely paved paths, but much of the foot traffic takes short cuts across lawns and flower beds. Obviously, the planned order does not serve the average users who gradually establish their own migration routes. The question then arises: Should the university enforce the made order or tolerate the spontaneous order that emerged from where people want to walk? This leads to the follow-on question: In whose interest have the walking connections been established, those of the students and academics, or those of some planners who have long left campus?

(c) New technology may alter what ordering system is most appropriate. In particular, the electronics and communications revolution has often made spontaneous and decentralized ordering more advantageous. For example, aircraft used to be guided through airspace by central air traffic coordinators, told what routes to fly, whether to ascend or descend and so on. When radar and direct radio communications between aircraft became reliable and were universally installed in all aircraft, central traffic control could be replaced by the spontaneous coordination of flight paths through the participants, who of course obeyed certain general rules. As of the beginning of the twenty-first century, the new technical means of decentralized communication and interaction have, on the whole, empowered dispersed individuals and disempowered central authorities – big government, big unions, big media.

In relatively simple systems, purposive organization and cooperation that is coordinated by top-down command can be the most effective. The more complex the coordinative tasks become, however, the more likely it is that spontaneous ordering has the advantage. This is so in particular when the system is open to unpredictable evolution. Thus, the production of one or several car models is planned and coordinated within a firm, but the coordination with buyers and other suppliers in the world car market occurs spontaneously through competition. Spontaneous ordering engages all participants to be alert for new knowledge and immediately motivates them to respond. This is why this method of coordination is much more robust in the face of new circumstances than centrally planned, made orders. This fundamental fact was the ultimate reason why socialist central planning failed and was thrown in the 'waste basket of history'. The planned ordering of entire economies proved simply too fragile (Boettke and Leeson, 2004; Pennington, 2010).

KEY CONCEPTS

We speak of **spontaneity** in social ordering if predictable patterns emerge independently of the purposive will of actors, as a by-product of individual human actions.

The opposite of spontaneous is **purposive**, the willful action to obtain a planned result from a process of interaction.

Human creations are often arranged along the lines of a carefully thought-out design. At least up to now, human interventions in nature proceed according to a plan, although some analysts now predict that 'nano-engineering', spontaneous self-patterning of matter – similar to the biological ordering of matter or the growth of a crystal – will soon be feasible on an important commercial scale, so that materials and apparatus will be created from the inside out (from its gene information, so to speak), rather than according to an outside design (Drexler, 1986).

We often find spontaneous ordering hard to comprehend because we are so familiar with planned ordering. The order that emerges from a seemingly chaotic process eludes our comprehension unless one is trained to think in those terms. Comprehension, though not existence, of the spontaneous order requires specific scientific training; for example, how new life evolves from a fertilized cell or how markets generate complex new products. Humans have found such phenomena awe- and fear-inspiring and often assumed that there must be an ordering, invisible hand behind it all to reduce the ordering process to a simpler, more comprehensible planning exercise (teleological explanation). Many also probably prefer simple, visible and stable cause-effect relations and feel uneasy about invisible hand explanations. How on Earth is it that the starlings do not collide and crash to earth? How can the pilots of those many aircraft steer freely through the airspace without being policed by air traffic controllers?

The distinction between spontaneous and planned orders of actions and orders of rules (Figure 6.3) was given prominence by Friedrich Hayek, who drew on earlier writers in the Austrian school of economics, most notably Carl Menger (1963/1883, pp. 35–54). As both types of ordering actions and rules exist alongside each other, we have to learn to live with both, for example, the mainly organized, planned order of the family and the firm, and the spontaneous order of the market and the open society. As we shall see below, both these coordination devices require different value systems, attitudes and modes of behaviour, so that moving from a planned, hierarchical to an open, spontaneous order is not easy (Hayek, 1988, Chapter 5).

Figure 6.3 Order of actions and order of rules

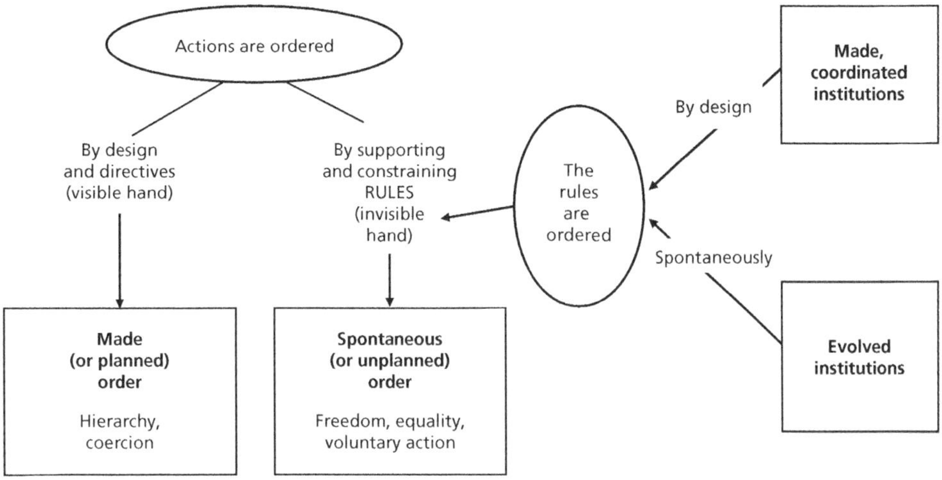

The planned order and its limitations

The planned order presupposes, as noted, some sort of an ordering hand that gives the various actors positive instructions how to act. It always implies some form of design and coordination by specific directives or *prescriptions* – such as an orchestra that follows the instructions of the composer and the conductor, the operations of military units, or the coordination of pro- ductive activities within a factory that follow a production schedule, which assigns specific tasks to the various agents.

The cooperation of human action within designed, hierarchical orders places great demands:

(a) on the availability of knowledge and the capacity of those who coord- inate actions to obtain relevant information,

(b) on the leaders' capability to digest, utilize and communicate such infor- mation, and

(c) on the capacity of the leaders to motivate the agents to make an effort and monitor their own performance (to avoid agent-principal problems).

When a system becomes complex and open, the cognitive limitations of the leaders to plan and implement order can easily become a bottleneck. In complex circumstances, like the coordination of the millions of buyers and sellers of hundreds of thousands of different goods and services, centrally planned coordination from above is bound to falter because of insuperable knowledge problems. Where central coordination is attempted nevertheless, the planners have to pretend that they have the knowledge that enables them to impose an order. In reality, they are tempted to base their plans and commands on averages (the average consumer, the 'representative' firm and so on, under the motto 'one size fits all'). The rich diversity of knowledge and aspirations that makes up the real world is then neglected to the detriment of the many diverse members of society. Following Hayek, we call the persistence with hierarchical ordering in the face of complexity 'constructivism'.

Planned ordering also requires that the followers, who are being ordered, recognize the signals and want to obey them. If the ordered community is complex and large, then the signals are often distorted or lost. Despite public propaganda, moral suasion and constant 'awareness campaigns', mere commands are not obeyed when the motivation to obey is absent. Then, coercion and punishments have to be relied on for motivation. Planned orders have then to be accompanied by the coercive exercise of force (Section 5.1). This reduces freedom, which in turn places additional cognitive requirements on the rulers. They have to monitor who fails to obey before they can punish him – not an easy task when numerous people interact and many make great efforts, using considerable resources to disguise and dissimulate their true behaviour, in short when principal-agent problems are rampant.

The limitations of hierarchical, made social orders can become critical when circumstances change and new solutions are required. Then, spontaneous experimentation and the decentralized, competitive search for solutions can have great advantages over the centralized interpretation of the signals and the design of centralized responses. Soviet-style central planning had very limited capacities to develop innovative solutions, as compared to decentralized market economies. Typically, the possibly most centrally-ordered and authoritarian state in human history, the mighty Inca empire, collapsed in the 1530s because their rigid command system, coupled with cognitive weaknesses at the centre, could not adapt creatively and quickly to the challenge by a small number of Spanish conquistadors and their unheard-of weapons. Similarly, other regimes that depended heavily on central ordering, from the Persian empire under Darius and Imperial China in the nineteenth and early twentieth centuries to the Soviet empire, ultimately failed because of the rigidities of central ordering and resulting entropy. Indeed, the rise and fall of entire civilizations has been explained by the problems of coordinating increasingly complex communities (Quigley, 1979/1961).

Often, the knowledge problem, which policy makers have when they want to prescribe specific actions, manifests itself in unintended, unforeseen side effects. The immediate impact of a policy intervention promotes the intended purpose, but – within a complex, open system – other effects may subsequently become dominant, so that the original intervention ultimately has perverse results. A good example to demonstrate this is legislation that tries to promote job security by making dismissals costly or impossible. This may prevent some people from being fired but, by making dismissal more costly, also erects a barrier to hiring new employees as employers can often not be sure about the duration of jobs. Another practical example of perverse side effects is rent control. Rent ceilings may originally have been imposed to protect renters. In times of cost increases, the side effect is invariably that the provision of rental accommodation becomes unprofitable. In addition, if it is fraught with legal compliance costs, less accommodation is provided over time. Housing becomes short and the renters as a whole lose out.

In certain situations, designed orders and coordination by directives can be an advantage. This is one reason for the existence of firms and government organizations, which are planned orders. Where the subject matter is not overly complex, it is often more effective for authorities to coordinate and direct all agents according to a preconceived plan so that a purposeful pattern of interaction emerges. Another circumstance where hierarchical orders make sense is the production of joint products. In these cases, producers often combine their resources more or less permanently in an organization. Where indivisible joint products are produced or exclusive private property cannot be established, the results cannot be distributed as a direct pay-off for the individual's action; tasks and results have to be allocated by command. After all, individuals can act within a spontaneous order, such as a market, only if they can expect to receive an exclusive, defined pay-off for their efforts directly and fairly immediately (for more on this see Chapter 7).

The spontaneous order of actions

Human limitations make it often advantageous to rely on spontaneous ordering and to cultivate the devices that facilitate it. To cite Hayek again: "Human intelligence is quite insufficient to comprehend all the details of the complex human society, and it is the inadequacy of our reason to arrange such an order in detail which forces us to be content with abstract rules" (Hayek, 1967b, p. 88). In other words, it becomes necessary to rely on coordination by the invisible hand that works through spontaneously obeyed rules. Adam

Smith had made the concept of social ordering by the forces of competition popular by inventing the term 'the invisible hand', showing how people were driven by self-interest to coordinate their actions to mutual benefit. In the market process, actions are ordered by profit-loss signals and the pursuit of selfishness, channelled by universal institutions. The system of rules tells market participants what they cannot do (rule of law laying down where harm is inflicted on others) and what they may want to do (system of prices that emerge in markets). This has the unintended side benefit that an order of actions emerges on which people can rely and which provides others with material benefits and new opportunities.

The spontaneous order of actions in the market process gives answers to the following questions:

(a) How are individuals to search for and procure knowledge that may be useful to their own individual purposes?
(b) How is this knowledge disseminated so that it may be useful to others?
(c) How are possible errors corrected in the light of feedback, so that the overall economic system is not destabilized? (Streit, 1998).

The market system does this spontaneously through the dual signals of legal limitations and price signals that emerge in competitive processes that expose people to incentives and controls. These signals convey information in the greatly simplified form of price variations. It makes participants take the risks of discovery procedures (Hayek, 1978b). In Chapter 2, we defined such a process of spontaneous competitive interaction as 'catallaxy'.

Dependence on rules of conduct

The spontaneous order of actions emerges when individuals respond to a system of rules governing their conduct. Market activities, for example, fall into a predictable, orderly pattern because all are subject to rules – protected property rights and the freedom of contract ensure that most market participants act in predictable ways. If the price goes up, suppliers will normally offer more quantity and buyers will normally reduce the quantities they demand. Buyers and sellers make complex decisions in response to such price signals, but – despite their freedom and the diversity of reasons why they respond – they can be expected to act in spontaneously coordinated ways. The market is not a chaotic free-for-all, as it is sometimes described by ignorant observers.

The rules that bring about a spontaneous order in the market economy must ensure that individuals are motivated to use their subjective knowledge to pursue their own purposes and are able to form reliable anticipations of how others will behave. In the market, this depends critically on whether participants are allowed to keep what they have earned (protected private property) and can be confident that others will keep their promises (enforcement of contracts). The institutions that ensure this are critical to the effective order of the market.

The advantages and disadvantages of the two kinds of ordering in dealing with complex tasks were illustrated in a telling way, when, in the late 1980s, there were two major earthquakes. One occurred in Leninakan in Armenia, then still a Soviet republic. It took numerous committee meetings in distant Moscow and elsewhere to identify and plan the reconstruction effort. Work had not got very far when the Soviet Union imploded.[1] A second earthquake shook San Francisco in California, and within hours glass suppliers as far afield as Chicago were loading trucks for the San Francisco market. Social critics may argue that the firms in Chicago acted out of selfishness, to make a fast buck. But were the results of presumably 'unselfish' planning in any way preferable from the viewpoint of the earthquake victims?

Some historic philosophical concepts of society

Preferences about how to order social and economic life have much to do with fundamental philosophies about society and the human condition, as well as the preference for individualism. There are two distinctly differing ways of perceiving individuals and their relation to overall social and economic life:

(a) One perception of society is that of an organic whole. The whole is seen as more than the sum of its individual parts, and the whole has purposes of its own. Society is perceived somehow as a huge organization – a collective entity to which all belong and in which all have to serve. It is up to the leaders, however chosen, to define what is in the interest of society and what each individual's duties towards society are. This basic worldview prevailed in many historic societies.

(b) An alternative perception of society, on which this book is based, differs fundamentally from the above organization model of society. It starts with a perception of human beings as self-interested, autonomous and equal individuals with limited cognitive powers and limited knowledge. Society is seen as a web of essentially voluntary interactions. In principle, all people are equal, but this is not a vision of atomistic individualism, since people cooperate within overlapping networks and organizations. They do so spontaneously by following shared institutions. Where collective action is needed, it is preferably inspired from the bottom up.

The central notion of the individual as autonomous and endowed with certain inalienable rights goes back to the Greek philosophers, such as Aristotle, and the Roman legal practice in Antiquity (Némo, 2006). Individualist perceptions of society are the result of a long discourse in the West about the individual and society. They gained renewed influence during the Renaissance, for example when merchants in different jurisdictions and of different social classes had to sort out conflicts on the basis of equality, rather than on the basis of prevailing feudal law, which allotted class-specific privileges and obligations to everyone.

Perceptions of society that see it as akin to a huge organization, in which the leaders order human interaction, were strong in the era of the absolutist states of Europe, when King Louis XIV of France, for example, had himself presented as the head of society, which in turn was represented as his body.[2] Most eighteenth century philosophers of the Enlightenment attacked this concept because they saw all people as equals before the law. However, Jean-Jacques Rousseau (1712–1778), who opposed individualism at both a conceptual and practical level, made the collectivist notion of society popular again. He popularized the concept of a General Will (*volonté générale*). It reflects some sort of a social consensus that is separate from, and overrides, what individuals want. Mature citizens, he wrote, should voluntarily subject themselves to a collective will. To the extent to which Rousseau's General Will can be understood as a system of institutions that make living and working together feasible, there is no problem. Where the interpretation of a General Will goes beyond that, it leads to dictatorship and wanton collectivism. Since Rousseau wrote, many a dictator has professed his belief in the general will (invariably as exercised by himself!) and has given society a vision, a mission and a destiny. Subsequent writers such as Auguste Comte (1798–1857), Georg Wilhelm Friedrich Hegel (1770–1831) and Karl Marx (1818–1883) depicted individual pursuits as the source of considerable social evil, simplified complex historic evolution and depicted predetermined historic patterns of grand societal developments (historicism).

The notion of a general will led Jacobin radicals in the French Revolution to stipulate the 'primacy of politics', namely that the leadership with its coordinated political programme should always be entitled to claim precedence over the diverse, petty pursuits of the citizens. This philosophy ended in a bloodbath. Nevertheless, the 'primacy of politics' has since been claimed not only by dictators, such as Lenin, Mussolini and Hitler, but in more recent times also by democratically elected leaders of Western nations, a sign – it would seem – of a growing contempt for individual freedom.

The most prominent example of the organizational concept of society in Western philosophy was Karl Marx's belief that societies will run through a preordained path of historic stages, until they end up in communism – a kind of paradise on earth where scarcity is suspended. Karl Marx thought in terms of 'iron laws of history' determining the dialectic movements of society (historic determinism; Popper, 2002/1957). In an interim stage of socialism, it was necessary to actively pursue the objectives of society by organizing individuals into collectives (organized mass action). The collective was to propel the course of history; it is legitimated as a body that exists separate from its members. In case of a conflict of interests, it has the right to override individual aspirations and to impose its superior objectives.

This world view led to the totalitarian form of Soviet and Maoist socialism, but is also mirrored in numerous social-democratic programmes around the world, which are based on the presumption that the right things only happen if they are mandated by government.[3]

The opposite, individualistic world view is based on the understanding that society lacks an identity of its own, which is separate from the individuals who constitute it, and that knowledge at the centre is always insufficient to coordinate complex, evolving systems. Social and economic life evolves along a path that is not known and cannot be predetermined by anyone. As individuals are capable of creativity, they can shape history. Hence it would be contradictory to assume anything like an iron law of history. Karl Popper, a foremost student of this matter, once remarked that attempts by leaders to create heaven on earth invariably created hell for all individuals (Popper, 2002/1957).

In the individualistic perception of society, the diversity among individuals and their characteristics is considered desirable, as diversity enriches the evolutionary potential. The same applies to the coordinative institutional system. The order of rules is seen to evolve in the light of experience to economize on the need for costly knowledge search.

The two kinds of ordering are related to two differing visions of the world and society. One's preference for one or the other hinges crucially on whether one acknowledges a constitutional knowledge problem, in particular on the part of the leaders.

KEY CONCEPTS

Order means that repetitive events or actions fit into a discernible pattern, which allows people to have confidence that the pattern of future actions, on which they may depend, can be predicted reasonably well. If the world is ordered, complexity, and hence the knowledge problem, is reduced and economic agents are better able to specialize and to innovate. Appropriate institutions serve to facilitate the emergence of order.

Someone, who plans a cohesive pattern of interaction and enforces the directives, may produce an order of actions. Alternatively, the various agents follow shared rules in a spontaneous manner. The former leads to an **organized** or **planned order**; the latter a **spontaneous order**. The planned order goes along with a measure of coercion; the spontaneous order comes with more freedom. As long as independent agents obey shared institutions more or less voluntarily, they are left the freedom to decide what to do. An example of spontaneous ordering is the market economy, where stealing and cheating are prohibited by institutions, but where participants are not directed, for example, to produce certain goods with certain technologies (as they are under a planned order).

We speak of an **order of rules** when the various institutions form an internally consistent set of institutions. The order of rules itself is often the result of evolution in the light of experience, but the visible, ordering hand of government can also influence it (codification of formerly internal institutions; constitutional or legal reforms).

Historicism (or **historic determinism**) is based on the perception of society as a closed system, in which developments follow predictable patterns, possibly towards a desirable end state. An example of a historicist theory was Karl Marx's historic materialism, which predicted a progression of society from feudalism, to capitalism, to socialism and to communism. Analysts (such as Karl Popper), who see society as an open system, contradict deterministic perceptions of society. They see that evolution is dependent essentially on the discovery of human knowledge, which is unpredictable.

Behavioural syndromes of hierarchical and spontaneous social order

The two types of ordering are tied to different value systems, mental attitudes and modes of behaviour, so that switching from a planned, hierarchical to an open, spontaneous order is not always easy. Experiences with each type of order also forms and reinforces a different syndrome of human behaviour. If you are fatalistic, passivity and fatalism will reinforce your attitude to life. If you are enterprising and keen on improving your lot, chances are that the experience will make you more enterprising and ambitious. When the members of a community are subject to a primarily hierarchical social order, they practice and learn different virtues as compared to those who act under a free, spontaneous order. These patterns become internalized and are turned into social norms, which others emulate. This will then reinforce the existing order. The patterns and attitudes become part of the society's shared culture and indeed its entire civilization (Mayhew, 1987; Kasper 2011b). The virtues that underpin hierarchical, closed orders prevail in societies that have little experience with open exchange and the rule of law. Here, the loyalty with the small group (the family, the clan, the village, the secret society) overrides the readiness to cooperate with strangers based on abstract, universal principles. When such communities are confronted with globalization and rapid technical change, only limited numbers will initially learn to be enterprising, and many will resent the challenges. It is only under persistent outside challenges that the shared culture becomes more entrepreneurial (Bauer and Sen, 2004).

A central element in defining a social order is openness. If members of groups believe – as French sociologist Claude Lévi Strauss once put it – that "the concept of humanity ceases at the borders of the tribe, of the linguistic group, sometimes even of the village", then different rules and norms apply, depending on whether basic perceptions are cosmopolitan and focused on universal human values, or whether they are tied to the tribal mentality of 'us and them'. Canadian social critic Jane Jacobs (1992) made an interesting attempt at listing virtues and behavioural symptoms typical of the two kinds of order (Table 6.1). She described the two sets of attitudes and virtues as 'The Guardian Moral Syndrome', typical of closed hierarchical orders, and 'The Commercial Moral Syndrome', typical of the open society. People who live primarily in hierarchical orders tend to focus on protecting their territory from strangers. People, whose primary experience is in trade or science, focus on curiosity and adapting to new, emerging circumstances.

Often, people who subscribe to the one syndrome attack the other as morally or culturally inferior. Thus, Jacobs notes the disdain for traders among guardian groups, such as the military, the bureaucrats and the aristocracy. Merchants and researchers – people who live by trading in goods and idea – are full of contempt for people who preach vengeance, are uncompromising and dwell on their honour. Similar systematic differences occur between people, who are nationalists and live in closed societies, and cosmopolitans, who think in terms of the open world. When communities are subjected to economic reforms, so that the fundamental institutional settings change, there is a need to change from one value syndrome to the other, but old sets of virtues often persist. This delays personal adjustment to a new order and causes difficulties in systems transformation. This is a core problem with the present-day spread of globalization and the spread of modern economic growth to hitherto backward economies.

The behavioural norms of the closed order can be observed, for example, among traditional East Asians, south Italians, or some Mid-Easterners who

Table 6.1 Behavioural symptoms typical of the two kinds of social order

Planned, closed order: 'The guardian moral syndrome'	
Shun trading	Exert prowess
Be obedient and disciplined	Adhere to tradition
Respect hierarchy	Be loyal
Take vengeance	Deceive for the sake of the task
Make rich use of leisure	Be ostentatious
Dispense largesse	Be exclusive
Show fortitude	Be fatalistic
Treasure honour	

Spontaneous, open order: 'The commercial moral syndrome'	
Shun force	Come to voluntary agreements
Be honest	Collaborate easily with aliens
Compete	Respect contracts
Use initiative and enterprise	Be open to inventiveness and novelty
Be efficient	Promote comfort and convenience
Dissent for the sake of the task	Invest for productive purposes
Be industrious	Be thrifty
Be optimistic	

Source: Jacobs (1992).

are loath to cooperate with the representatives of government authority and outsiders. These are deemed to belong to another (hostile) clan. It is automatically assumed that everyone pursues exclusively the interests of his or her own group. When government officials also behave as if they were representatives of a tribe – and not the defenders of universal values – it is extremely hard to break with the guardian syndrome and to spread the spontaneous, open order of rules, and with it the material benefits from a wider division of labour and knowledge (Klitgaard, 1995). The order of rules relies on the willingness and capability of people to distinguish between tribe and open society.

KEY CONCEPTS

The **guardian syndrome** covers a set of norms that proved to be essential for the survival of small tribes and for the defence of their domain: sharing, loyal obedience to authority and tradition, exclusivity and insistence on one's honour. This contrasts with the **commercial syndrome**, an alternative, inherently compatible set of virtues that make sense in an open exchange society: the rejection of force, openness of exchange and collaboration with strangers, inventiveness, honesty and thrift.

The micro society of the tribe can offer members considerable comfort (Hayek, 1976, pp. 133–135). The seeming security of the group is no doubt one of the attractions of living in a closed system. However, as the world evolves and requires coordination among people in more complex and changing circumstances, people have to learn to interact with strangers, live in the open society and acquire attitudes and virtues compatible with it. This frequently leads to what Karl Popper once called the 'strain of civilization' (Popper, 1945). It forces us to cope with insecurities of open-ended change and great complexity, as is now evident with progressing globalization. We then have to rely increasingly on abstract rules that are open to evolution, rather than on authorities and specific rules.

Many will ask whether the material gains and the freedoms of the open society are indeed worth the loss of security. This is a valid question. However, competing within the rule system of the open society also educates people in practicing social virtues such as honesty, parsimony and industry (Giersch, 1989). It was the hope of analysts as far back as the pre-industrial age that spreading commercial activity would control base passions and would ultimately enhance rule compliance and thereby support civil liberties (Hirschman, 1977, pp. 56–67). At least to some extent, the limited insecurity of the market order has led to the spread of order by rules, for example in Western Europe and the United States, among many professional groups worldwide and more recently in East Asia where a new middle class has emerged. This now gradually offers better assurance of civil liberties by more contestable elections and a more rule-bound legal system. As a consequence, more and more people on earth now feel increasingly at home in the open order. Persisting with the tribal, inward-looking mentality in the dynamic modern world may offer some comfort and security in the short run, but will eventually lead to inconsistencies, which could inflict unsettling, revolutionary adjustments. As of 2012, these potential conflicts can be observed in North Africa and the Middle East.

6.3   Perceptions of order influence public policy

Individualism and collectivism

There is a major divide in worldviews between individualism and collectivism:

(a)   As noted in earlier chapters, individualists see individual motivation as the foundation of all social action as well as the reference point in studying social phenomena. It is acknowledged that individual actions have side effects for others, which requires constraining rules. Individualists tend to prefer a system of rules which secures domains of freedom, and favours spontaneous coordination.

(b) Collectivists see society as a separate whole, which is more than the individuals that make it up at any point in time. They presume that it is possible to identify the true and overriding interests of a society and that some legitimate authority can be established to take care of these collective interests.

These two perceptions of society are normally coupled with some other basic preferences on how to conduct public policy. Although these have been noted at various points in the preceding text, it seems useful to restate them:

(a) Individualists prefer coordination by voluntary exchanges within a framework of rules, whereas collectivists are inclined to central ordering by planning and command. Individualists appreciate that people accept full responsibility for their actions, collectivists do not.

(b) Individualists normally prefer general, universal rules and, if possible, proscriptive rules and negative liberties. Preference is given to market processes and limits on collective action. Collectivists rely more heavily on prescriptions, directives and compulsion and subscribe to central planning.

(c) A third difference relates to perceptions of what a social system is – closed and static, or open-ended and dynamic? Individualists see the social system as in the grips of ceaseless, unpredictable evolutionary change. They accept that there is no pre-determined path of development. By contrast, collectivists see society often as a system that goes through predictable historic patterns, following iron laws of history (determinism, historicism).

Philosophical visions of society are also influenced by two fundamental attitudes among people, which have little to do with individualism and collectivism: egotism and altruism. Egotism gives priority to one's own interests, altruism also respects those of others. Many observers have wrongly identified individualism with egotism and have claimed the moral high ground for collectivism because it supposedly promotes the interests of others (Popper, 1945, pp. 100–123). It is by now evident that ruthless collective group egotism plays a big role in politics, in the form of discrimination by a group against outsiders ('us and them'). It is also quite normal for individualists to act in altruistic ways, helping others without expecting a reward in return.

Figure 6.4 Visions and attitudes

		Vision of society	
		Individualism	Collectivism
Attitude to fellow human beings	Egotistic	Self-seeking individualism	Group egotism (discrimination against outsiders)
	Altruistic	Altruistic individualism (individual charity, cosmopolitanism)	Group altruism (sharing; group solidarity)

The dichotomy between individualism and collectivism has not only been philosophical (Figure 6.4). It has been one of the major influences around the world in the twentieth century. Totalitarian collectivist movements of the socialist and the nationalist descriptions mobilized much political support and overturned existing societies, first the communists in Russia, then the fascists in Italy and Germany, later communists in Eastern Europe, China, Vietnam and Cambodia. The observation that collectivism requires coercion has been shown to be true as many tens of millions of people were killed and more incarcerated during the imposition of collectivist designs, and many more died in wars triggered by collectivist regimes last century. With the 'Arab spring', the individualist-collectivist dichotomy is likely to come into sharper focus also in North Africa and the Middle East. Interpretations of Islam vary between individualist and collectivist visions. Therefore, emerging civil movements and governments are likely to promote one or the other to advance their political causes.

Influential variants of collectivism reflect the longing for a model society that resembles a big family. Softer forms of collectivism are pursued with less coercion: the welfare states in the affluent countries and collectivist-nationalist regimes in many of the newly independent countries in the Third World. We shall look at the (in the long run not very attractive) track record of collectivist models in Chapter 13.

Individualism as a basic perception of society has, however, survived and, at the turn of the millennium, seems in the ascendancy in the world at large, not least because the material results of individual motivation and spontaneous ordering in the market yield materially superior results. As a consequence, newly affluent middle classes in emerging nations are now demanding individual, civil and economic rights, both as worthwhile ends in themselves and as means of maintaining and furthering their prosperity.

KEY CONCEPTS

Individualism is a view of society that anchors explanations of economic and social phenomena in individual motivation and behaviour. It is based on the insight that individuals have differing knowledge, preferences and purposes and that, in the final analysis, only individuals can decide and act.

Collectivism is a social theory, which is the diametric opposite of individualism. It takes the group, the collective, as a being in its own right, which is subject to (collective) purposes of its own. Indeed, its purposes should override individual purposes if necessary. Collectivism was once defined (by the great British constitutional jurist Albert V. Dicey, 1835–1922) as "govern-

ment for the good of the people by experts or officials who know, or think they know, what is good for the people better than any non-official person or than the mass of the people themselves".

Constructivism (also called **instrumentalism** or **social engineering**) denotes a habit of perceiving society and policy in terms of an organization, that is, as a cohesive hierarchy in which solutions are designed and implemented by the leaders. It is based on optimism about the feasibility of top-down problem solving and on the assumption that central actions do not lead to unforeseen side effects. It tends to be associated with static concepts of society.

Two styles of public policy

Obviously, these two perceptions of order imply fundamentally differing recommendations for the conduct of public policy. If one's basic worldview is grounded in collectivism and the organization model of society, one is likely to embrace comprehensive social goals, which leaders and members of society should follow, as well as a collective-hierarchical approach to ordering societal life. One is likely to accept authorities, which mandate and, if necessary, coerce individuals to fall in line with the planned order. Individuals who pursue their own interests in the face of social interest – as defined and interpreted by the rulers or elected governments and their agents – are depicted as egotistic or are even prosecuted. Their repression is readily accepted 'in the group's interest', 'in the national interest', or 'for reasons of state'. In societies, where the organization model of social order is widely accepted, the claim for the 'primacy of politics' is also readily accepted; vertical power distances tend to be great and horizontal ties between individuals weak.

In all Western democracies, the collectivist worldview and the interventionist instinct of parliamentarians and administrators (and the pursuit for political rents by organized interest groups) has led to a massive increase in 'regulatory density', which now ever so often complicates business and job creation. Figure 6.5 shows the volume of legislation handed down by

Figure 6.5 Legislation passed by the Commonwealth Parliament of Australia

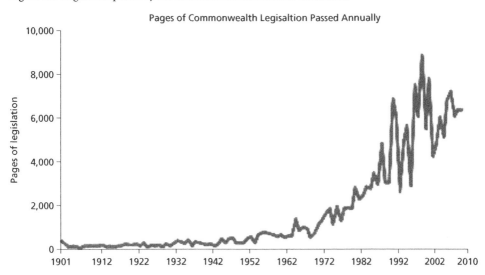

Pages of Commonwealth Legisaltion Passed Annually

Source: Institute of Public Affairs, Melbourne.

Australia's national parliament since Federation in 1901. Such a steep rise in legislative activism since 1960s is typical of most OECD countries. Yet, Australia is – by international comparison – still less heavily regulated than most other developed countries.[4]

Those who subscribe to the alternative individualistic perception of society tend to be rather sceptical of authoritarian top-down policies. Instead, they stress horizontal and voluntary coordination between free and equal individuals. Goals are set individually by the individuals themselves and vary from person to person. People's plans evolve and may of course clash with the aspirations of others. People with this worldview do not advocate a preference for anarchy, they focus on order-supporting institutions, including some institutions that are imposed externally and enforced formally by government.[5] Public policy is seen as the activity of agents whom the citizens have appointed collectively in order to foster an order in which individuals have the best-possible chances to attain what they aspire to. This basic philosophy gives preference to the rule of law over the rule of men (who are seen as self-interested and fallible). In essence, people are not expected to obey authorities, but to follow incentives derived from abstract rules. They cooperate with others by voluntary contract. Only where individuals break implicit and explicit agreements is it necessary for third parties, such as government agencies, to intervene. According to this perception of society, public policy is expected to concentrate on protecting the rules (protective government).

CH 6 – CASE ONE

Gruzino: an early example of planned order

Russia was traditionally a slovenly as well as a grotesquely inefficient country, and its reformist rulers have tended to pounce on the visible external signs of its shortcomings . . .

[The most prominent reformer of the early 19th century was general Alexis Alexandrovich Arakcheev who created a new, progressive order on his estate Gruzino.] Gruzino has a strong claim to be considered the first modern experiment in social engineering, an attempt to create the New Man, who, Rousseau had argued, could be born in the right conditions. The estate was 35 square kilometres and contained 2,000 'souls'. The General destroyed all the old wooden buildings and put up new model villages in brick and stone. He drained the muddy roads and paved them. He dug a lake, with an island in it, on which was a temple. He built belvederes and towers, each of which equipped with a clock . . . The clocks dictated [the workers'] work-, meal- and bedtimes . . .

The idea was to get all peasants to work, ten hours every day of the year except Sundays. Orders, dictated by the General personally, were issued regularly, numbered and dated. . . .In theory, Gruzino had some of the characteristics of a miniature welfare state. There was a hospital and a school. The General got regular health reports. But the inhabitants had even less control over their lives than ordinary serfs. In an effort to raise the birthrate, lists were compiled of nubile unmarried females and widows capable of childbearing, and pressure was put on them to find partners. But the General had to approve such unions . . .

[Running Gruzino depended on] the universal reliance on savage physical punishment . . . All floggings were recorded in an estate Punishment Ledger, and the General inspected the backs to see that chastisement had been thorough. Each peasant also carried, at all times, a personal punishment book, in which his or her offences were listed along with the sentence . . .

Source: Johnson (1991), pp. 291–293.

The two worldviews in history

A preference for spontaneous ordering, the concept of the rule of law, as opposed to the rule of men, has a long tradition in Western civilization, going back at least to Solon of Athens (ca. 640–561BC). The Greek philosopher Aristotle (384–322BC) wrote: "He who asks Law to rule is asking God and Intelligence and no others to rule; while he who asks for the rule of a human being is bringing in a wild beast; for human passions are like a wild beast and strong feelings lead astray the very best of men. In law you have the intellect without the passion" (cited after Walker, 1988, p. 93). We have already mentioned that the law of the Roman Republic knew the concept of the sovereign domain of the *persona* and the family, within which matters were sorted out without outside interference under the *patria potestas*, the personal discretion and control of the *pater familias*, the father of the family. He could control matters within his *dominium* – the family, the land, the assets he owned (Némo, 2006, pp. 17–27). Traditional Celtic and Germanic notions of free men later fused with the Greek and Roman traditions of individual freedom and helped to give rise to the European tradition of individual freedom that flourished from the Renaissance onwards (Kasper, 2011b).

In medieval Europe, the rules that allowed spontaneous ordering of free individuals were given clear expression in the *Magna Carta* of 1215 that still is a binding part of the constitution that shapes government in Anglo-Saxon countries. It has been reaffirmed, time and again, and survives to form part of the living constitutions of all common-law countries. The order of rules was also high on the agenda of the new American Republic. And it was an aspiration of the French Revolution, where the revolutionary demand for *égalité* was initially understood as equality of all, including the rulers, before the law and where *propriété* was the third motto besides *liberté*. 'Property' was only replaced during a later, more radical phase of the Revolution by the ill-defined concept of *fraternité*. In modern times, it is recognized that the order of rules requires not only the supremacy of the institutions, but also the formal acceptance of rules that safeguard open debate and adherence to due process in the administration of the law and other institutions (Walker, 1988, Chapters 1 and 2).

In the late eighteenth and the nineteenth centuries, the order of abstract rules was criticized by writers such as Hegel and Marx (as noted). They paved the way for major political efforts to construct social orders, ranging from totalitarian Leninist-socialist and national-socialist attempts to less coercive, social-democratic attempts at 'social engineering' in the democratic societies of Europe and Third World countries. Many anthropologists, psychologists and sociologists, who ignored the knowledge problem (such as Margaret Mead[6]) promoted these efforts because they saw human beings as a product of a culture, which could and should be reshaped into 'new men'. These twentieth century writers did much to promote an unjustified optimism that society as a whole could be organized along the lines of a coherent, designed order (Sowell, 1987; 2009).

The feasibility of collective ordering has also been the foundation of neoclassical welfare economics and its application to public policy. To begin with, economists closed the model by assuming perfect knowledge, at least on the part of the scientific observer. Thereby, it became possible to deduce what conditions needed to be met to obtain a social optimum in the allocation of given resources, with given technologies and known consumer preferences. Next, economists could ask what mechanism would produce the optimum that is already known in advance to the outside scientific observer. The answer was 'perfect competition', and the conditions to be met were those of general equilibrium. Under these assumptions, institutions are not needed to channel the choices of private decision makers. They were faced with equilibrium market-clearing prices, and adjustment to these prices is assumed to be the only rational response open to them. A computer can perform the task of maximization in this model of perfect competition. Entrepreneurial talent, alertness, and preparedness to incur transaction costs are then superfluous (see *Epilogue*).

In this simplistic model world, it was possible to identify a plethora of cases in which competition fails to bring about the so-called 'social optimum'. 'Market failures' abound. This, in turn, provides ample reasons for policy interventions by the high and knowledgeable. The policy maker was assumed to be able to correct market failures in perfect ways, for example by taxing and subsidizing, by regulating, cajoling and educating. Though this model is simplistic – despite its seeming formal sophistication – it was and still is in many quarters the prevalent mode of thinking about economic policy. The verdict that it is based on an illegitimate pretense of knowledge, however, applies to it all too convincingly. The model of welfare economics which comes inadvertently close to the view of a central planner, has little bearing on the real-world policy maker who has to deal with a complex and open market system (Streit, 1992).

Although the question of individualism versus collectivism has been argued here predominantly from the standpoint of Western history, we should note an important East Asian notion of ordering, which has been shaped by the basic rules of Confucian morality. There, predictability and coordination are achieved much more by personalized relationships than in the West. In Chinese society, for example, one relies more on personal relationships and loyalties based on familiarity and ongoing contacts, so that predictability is ensured among people in authority. Traditionally, it is not so much the rule of the impersonal law, but a rule of informal moral standards and networking among reliable persons that ensures order (*guanxi* in Chinese society; Redding, 1993, pp. 66–68). Accordingly, there is more reliance on personalized exchanges, which are governed by unwritten rules of interpersonal relationships to constrain arbitrary action. On the whole, interpersonal trust rests on rules about losing face and fears of losing repeat business.[7] The order that emerges under such institutions is largely spontaneous, but the rules of conduct are often less formal and more tied to people in authority (Habermann, in Radnitzky and Bouillon, (eds) 1995b, pp. 73–96). Like in the Western tradition, one can of course find numerous contradictory strands of thinking about authority and individualism in East Asia. Thus, the doctrine that the Emperor should have the power to rule only as long as prosperity reveals a 'Mandate of Heaven' is not a recipe for absolutist empowerment; and eminent Confucian thinker Mencius (*Meng Zi*, ca. 372-289BC) is frequently cited: "The people are to be valued most, the vitality of the state next, and the ruler least". He also taught: "Do not give in while facing power". This is hardly the voice of collectivist submission (Yu and Lee, (eds) 1995). Whether the Chinese style of coordination can, in the long run, produce equal or superior outcomes to the Western approach is as yet an open empirical question.

6.4   Rule systems as a central part of culture

Many of the informal institutions, which have evolved and are shared in a community, form part of system that is called 'culture'. Indeed, shared rules and values define a society's identity; they are essential to social behaviour, including economic behaviour (Casson, 1993).

Culture defined

The terms 'culture' and 'civilization' are used in many different ways. This is bound to lead to misunderstandings if the definitions are not clarified.[8] We prefer the classical definition of culture by English sociologist Edward Burnett Tylor (Tylor, 1883) who defined it as comprising "all capabilities and habits acquired by a man as a member of society". It indicates nicely the tension between the individual and the social group which culture bridges. It also focuses on the fact that culture hinges on learned institutions and the values that underpin them. Newborn babies have no culture. Culture always has normative content. Indeed, one might say that culture is all that is worth passing on to the next generation.

Culture in our preferred meaning consists of language (based on a rule system that governs the sounds and signs we make), ideas, values, internal and external institutions. In many definitions, it also covers the valued material fruit of the cultural rule system: the tools, the techniques, the works of art and architecture, the rituals and symbols that underpin the purely institutional side of culture. (In that wider sense, the term 'civilization' is often preferred, while other authors use 'culture' and 'civilization' interchangeably, Kasper 2011b.) Culture contains many internal institutions – mores, customs and conventions – that are acquired by practice and that are hard to spell out and transfer in a disembodied way to people who are not part of that culture. We may see culture as a largely implicit rule system that is underpinned by symbols and other visible reminders of its institutional content.

A shared cultural rule set underpins the division of labour, as it cuts the risks and costs of interaction. This is why fellow citizens, who share one's culture, are often given preference over strangers, for it is easier to interact with them. Those who have acquired the shared culture in their youth, often without reflecting on it in their youth, feel at home amongst others of their cultural community. From the standpoint of individuals, their own culture is, subjectively, superior to other cultures, because their familiarity with their own culture's institutions saves them costs. If people move to another culture, they will often at first be tempted to conclude that the other culture is inferior, because it does not produce for them the customary ease of interaction and foists additional transaction costs on them. In other words, it is subjectively true that everyone may claim to possess a superior culture. However, the cosmopolitan knows that cultures are rule systems whose value depends on what the individual has learnt. Alternative cultures can be learnt and function equally satisfactorily. Cosmopolitans recognize that others, too, will probably also prefer their own culture. What is alien is not necessarily bad or threatening. Once this is realized, cultural superiority, xenophobia and self-centred missionary zeal should evaporate. With luck, cosmopolitans even adopt and adapt cultural concepts from other cultures (Cowen, 2002). Within multicultural societies cross-fertilization sets in.

One can only compare the quality of cultural institutions by testing how they help people in practice to attain their shared fundamental values – such as freedom, peace or prosperity. One will then come to recognize also that not all cultures are equally functional in coordinating people or coping with change (Mayhew, 1987; Sowell, 1994, 1998; Kasper, 2011b). Cultural openness does not mean cultural relativism and the uncritical acceptance of all cultures as equally valuable.

The role of culture is paraphrased well in one of Sowell's books:

> Cultures are not museum pieces. They are the working machinery of everyday life. Unlike objects of aesthetic contemplation, working machinery is judged by how well it works, compared to the alternatives. The judgment that matters is not

the judgment of the observers and theorists, but the judgment implicit in millions of individual decisions to retain or abandon particular cultural practices; decisions made by those who personally benefit or who personally pay the price of inefficiency and obsolescence. That price is not always paid in money, but may range from inconvenience to death. (Sowell, 1998; p. iv)

The cultural rule set is not passed on from generation to generation by genetic inheritance. Rather, it consists of learnt attitudes, habits and rules, which are transmitted by differing methods in different civilizations. This places views on institutions into the centre of the education debate and casts education – both informal within family and close community and in formalized schooling – into a hotly contested arena. In earlier ages, cultural continuity was understood to be crucial to continuing prosperity, peace and other fundamental values. However, in the twentieth century alternative educational philosophies, which derived from psychology and growing general prosperity, took hold: Children were meant to discover the world freely, unhindered by authoritarian constraints. Indeed, educational disciplining was often depicted as a violation of freedom and a hindrance to the full unfolding of the personal individuality and creativity of the child. As a result, many in Western civilization grew up with little understanding or respect for tradition and social coordination by institutions. It is, as yet, premature to fully assess the comparative merits and costs of these shifts in culture. However, if contemporary institutional economics, as sketched in this book, is any guide, the adherence to rule-focused education, creativity, and tradition is crucial to future social order, as well as individual and collective achievement. The old adage 'from rags to riches and back to rags in three generations' highlighted the need for continuity and the passing-on of institutionally backed discipline. If this warning were ignored, it could amount to the rise and fall of civilizations, a fate which Western civilization has so far been able to avert.

Cultural change

Culture is not a monolith, but a web of (overlapping) sub-systems. An individual may belong to a village culture, share the worldwide cultural conventions of his profession and also feel deeply attached to the culture of a foreign country. Nor is culture – just as any single institution – immutable. Culture is indeed a slow-moving average of individual, time-tested ideas, which is torn between the 'conservative pole', the necessity to preserve the common basis for communication, and the 'experimental pole', the necessity to prevent rigidity and atrophy in the face of changing physical, technical, economic or social circumstances. It is important that cultures remain open to outside influences and maintain a capability to adjust. Globalization now destroys traditional cultural norms, but also spreads cultural products around the world (Cowen, 2002). If cultures do not adjust – as many historic precedents demonstrate – the rise of that particular civilization is followed by its decline and fall.

Cultures normally evolve slowly; many of its elements are path dependent. Yet, sometimes specific cultural traits change rapidly in the light of experience, either because new ideas are discovered within a community or, more frequently, come from the outside and are found to be superior. They are then imitated and gain critical mass so that they become new norms. New concepts may require systemic adaptations manifested in overall cultural change. Thus, the rulers of fourteenth to sixteenth century Europe discovered that merchants and manufacturers were able to migrate to jurisdictions where they found more rule-bound government and reliable institutions. This not only forced the rulers to abstain from arbitrary opportunism and to provide credible rules, but also rewarded internal cultural institutions, such as honesty, punctuality and thrift. The bourgeois society and capitalism emerged when external institutions and internal, cultural institutions were adapted and a new 'civic morality' spread (Weber 1927/1995; Jones, 2003/1981; Radnitzky, 1987; Giersch, 1996). Similarly, cultural change in East Asia accelerated in many, mainly Chinese, communities that were suddenly excluded from the traditional centre of their world and felt threatened by the Maoist revolution of 1949 (Redding, 1993; Jones et al., 1994). When forced openness and the urgent need to acquire Western technology and organization occurred, the once rather conservative, atrophying cultural system of China mutated into the 'cultural growth asset' of neo-Confucianism.[9] The changes in values and institutions were often marginal, shifting the emphasis from conservative to future- and learning-oriented interpretations of the general institutions (Section 13.2). As a result, East-Asian social mores have shifted in the direction of more individualism and a greater preference for improving the material human condition.

Despite ongoing adaptations in the era of globalization, there is a high degree of specificity and continuity in most major cultural systems. Consequently, there is no danger that one might mistake someone with Chinese or Japanese culture for a Frenchman or an American, because the bulk of the cultural system has great persistence even if certain elements shift. The prospect of a homogeneous world culture is not on the horizon. What is in prospect is rather an evolving competition between different cultural systems to see which assists people best to realize their self-chosen aspirations. This need not amount to pervasive clashes between civilizations, or to an interminable dominance of the Western model. It is more likely that 'multiple modernities' evolve, each with distinct cultural characteristics (Tu, 2000).

Cultural capital

Culture and civilization – the values and institutional system, as well as its more tangible elements – constitute an important part of a society's capital (Ostrom and Kahn, (eds) 2003). It has important consequences for the effectiveness or otherwise of how physical resources of labour, capital and nature are converted to serve peoples' wants and aspirations. When discussing the idea that culture has powerful economic effects on the economy, one has to be aware that most cultural institutions are implicit and are often embodied in organizations (Chapter 5). Indeed, cultural rules can often not be easily made explicit and culture cannot be easily learnt from books. The rules are often embodied in 'cultural goods' and organizations, which make certain cultural concepts effective (Weede, 1990, 1995; Kasper, 1994; 2011b; Giersch, 1996). Thus, the rule of law is a cultural concept. It requires complex organizational infrastructures to be effective: various types of tribunals, firms of lawyers with different professional specializations, agreed professional practices and conventions, and so on. Cultural systems can only be adopted effectively by outsiders – for example in order to promote economic growth in hitherto less developed countries – when the cultural rules are transferred and are learnt by association together with the organizational structures and the 'cultural hardware'. Cultural goods and rules tend to be much harder to transfer internationally than mere machines, requiring more learning of implicit skills and knowhow by consistent practice. At least temporarily, such learning may possibly lead to inconsistencies between indigenous and imported institutions. Nonetheless, it will be important for the effective performance of the machines that the complementary cultural habits are learnt, too (Klitgaard, 1995). This is the widespread experience over the past half-century with economic development: It requires hardware (capital) and software (productive, uncorrupted social habits) (Bauer, 2000; Bauer and Sen, 2004, Boettke et al., 2008).

As a matter of fact, the system of ideas, organizational rules and tangible assets that are often called culture ('the organizational culture of the ABC Company', 'the culture of capitalism', see Kreps, 1990) is particularly important to the production of sophisticated, modern services, such as running a stock exchange, a legal system or a complex distribution network. This is why efficient service production often cannot be easily transferred to other countries and cultures and why opening national markets to foreign service providers (banks, accountancy and legal firms, telecommunications and so on) is often resisted by the elites of less developed countries. Acquiring cultural goods, and making them work, always implies adaptations in one's own institutional system, and hence in the self-evaluation of oneself and one's community.

KEY CONCEPTS

Culture is defined here as shared values and a shared largely implicit rule system, as well as more tangible elements of social interaction in a community. Some of the rules may be explicit; many are implicit and informal; many are supported by symbols. Cultures tend to evolve in the light of experience, as some members of the community experiment and others try to conserve familiar, time-tested institutions.

The concept of **cultural capital** highlights the insight that certain cultural concepts, values and institutions can be of great importance to the material wellbeing of the group which shares them. Culture is an intangible productive asset, but – if rigidly adhered to in the face of change – traditional culture may also become a liability.

6.5 Social order and human values: the rule of law

It seems useful to conclude this chapter by casting a quick glance at how institutions can be shaped under the rule of law, so as to enhance the chances of freedom and internal peace (conflict avoidance). The 'rule of law' doctrine was developed primarily, but not exclusively, in Western Europe. It relates closely to the institutions of capitalism, which we shall discuss in the following chapter. The basic concept that underpins the rule of law is that political power can only be exercised on the basis and within the constraints of the law and that certain substantive and procedural institutions are needed to protect civic and economic liberties from arbitrary interventions by authorities.

The legal and constitutional doctrine of the rule of law embodies many of the key concepts of ordering social and economic life that we have developed in this chapter. This doctrine is particularly entrenched in the legal philosophy of the Anglo-Saxon countries, where it has a long tradition (see the excerpt from a House of Commons petition to King James I in 1610 at the top of this chapter). The 'Glorious Revolution' of 1688–89 in Great Britain enshrined basic legal controls of government power. At about the same time, John

Locke (1632–1704) gave a systematic philosophic explication of freedom under the law and tied this to the division of powers, an idea taken further by French philosopher Charles de Montesquieu (1689–1755). The rule of law is of course not exclusive to the Anglo-Saxon tradition. In the Roman-French tradition, the concept of legality reflects similar notions, as does the German concept of the 'law state' (*Rechtsstaat*), a doctrine of constitutionalism. In Chinese philosophy the tradition of legalism advocates similar ideas (Habermann, in Radnitzky and Bouillon (eds), 1995b, pp. 73–96).

The doctrine of the rule of law can best be described by a number of substantial institutions, which allow ordered human interaction to develop in known, certain ways and which keep the arbitrary, opportunistic rule of men at bay. The rules also contain certain procedural *meta* rules (Walker, 1988, pp. 23–42). The rule of law doctrine favours spontaneous ordering of actions with a view to giving individual liberty the best possible scope and to avoiding conflicts that diminish the liberty of some (Hayek, 1960; 1973; 1976; 1979a). It contains a number of principles:

(a) In the first instance, it is necessary to ensure that all citizens are protected from the arbitrary use of force by others. This would only lead to anarchy, the opposite of order under the law. To this end, the laws must be certain, general and non-discriminatory (equal), in short, universal. The principle of universality is violated when certain persons or organizations are formally or de facto held to be above the law, for example when breaches of contracts by trade unions are not sanctioned or when powerful figures get away with infringements of the law. Thus, the rule of law is based on certain stipulations of private law, which order the relationships among private citizens.

(b) A second element, which follows from the first, is that the rule of law must also apply to those entrusted with political power. The actions of politicians and officials must be open to scrutiny under the law. Exempting government officials from the law for *raisons d'état* is a breach of the rule of law. The same holds true when administrative actions are exempt from judicial review to establish whether officials obeyed the institutions, when high government officials cannot be sued by citizens, or when governments do not have to follow the same accounting rules that they impose on private businesses. In this respect, the rule of law implies certain stipulations of public law.

(c) Like all institutions, laws of course require obligatory sanctions. But rule-bound, impartial professionals must be in charge of administering these coercive sanctions. Violations must be adjudicated by an independent judiciary and impartial tribunals, which adhere to the rules of due process. Kangaroo courts, lynch justice by private citizens, the negation of a proper hearing of the evidence, and the neglect of standard procedures of proof are violations of the rule of law principle. In this respect, the rule of law requires certain procedural rules.

(d) A further substantive requirement of the rule of law doctrine relates to the interaction between internal and external institutions. The laws must be such that they do not, on the whole, clash with the community's internal institutions and its fundamental values, so that people are able and willing to obey the law. Where frequent infringements occur because people's fundamental values clash with the legislation, this is a sign that the rule of law is endangered. Mere adherence to the letter of the law (legal positivism) and to the formalities of due process, but violation of widely held fundamental values and ethical rules, does not establish the rule of law. Thus, the legal formalism in Nazi Germany with regard to the rights of Jewish citizens and in the Stalinist era with regard to dissidents clearly negated the rule of law. Likewise, if officials admit that certain actions violate natural rights, but nevertheless insist on enforcing the letter of laws or regulations, they are violating the spirit of the rule of law.

(e) Finally, it is necessary for the sustained rule of law in a community that the attitude of legality is cultivated and that the citizens, by and large, willingly subject themselves to the laws of the land, including in cases of conflict. Widespread lawlessness can make it difficult to protect individual freedom and avoid conflicts. Therefore, the rule of law requires a generally law-abiding civil society in which formal judicial sanctions are supplemented by spontaneous enforcement, such as social disapproval, shaming and exclusion.

The rule of law is a government-supported system of institutions intended to protect civil and economic liberties and to avoid conflicts:

- by protecting citizens from the arbitrary use of power by other citizens (in the sense of the quote from Cicero at the head of this chapter);
- by obliging agents with political power to find and enforce the law; and
- by binding agents with political power to the law in dealing with private citizens and acting within government.

These substantive elements, which jurisprudence has developed, relate directly to the fundamentals of institutional economics. They are essential to the proper functioning of the capitalist system.

KEY CONCEPTS

The **rule of law** is a legal and constitutional concept to protect individual freedom and social peace which stipulates:

- that the people and government authorities should be ruled by the law and obey it;
- that the laws should be such that people are, on the whole, able and willing to be guided by them, more specifically, that protection from private license and anarchy is guaranteed;
- that government is placed under the law;

- that the laws are certain, general and non-discriminatory (universal);
- that the laws are generally in harmony with social values and internal institutions;
- that the law is enforced by impartial, rule-bound coercion, and adjudicated by an independent judiciary and impartial tribunals which follow due process; and
- that the law and its practice encourage an attitude of legality throughout the community.

NOTES

1 In the 1990s, an American charity with links to the Mormon Church built a cement plant in Armenia to assist with reconstruction.

2 The vision of society as a whole that has its own 'personality' and objectives separate from and superior to the individual goes back to Plato (427-347BC), certain group-focused Judeao-Christian visions and the long tradition of corporatism in Europe. Similar notions of collective entities exist in Eastern societies, but there the notion of collective aims is more closely tied to the notion of what the ruler represents as a symbol of society as a whole.

3 Nationalism and national socialism also contended that nations have a collective destiny, which is above the individual. This has led to other variants of collectivism.

4 The international Fraser-Cato survey of economic freedom for example, rated the regulation of capital, labour and product markets in Australia as of 2008 with a relatively favourable 8.34 out of 10 (Gwartney and Lawson, passim, also see Sections 14.2 and 14.3).

5 There is a tradition of anarcho-capitalism that maintains that all economic life can and should be coordinated by private transactions (for example Rothbard, 1962). Classical liberals, including the authors of this book, believe that this is not possible, indeed that the demand for the complete abolition of all collective power diverts attention from the eternal, difficult task of limiting government to those areas where it has a comparative advantage (see Chapter 10). We consider anarchism an intellectually easy cop-out.

6 M. Mead enjoyed great international respect for her views that society could be reshaped. These views were based on superficial, if not fraudulent research in American Samoa. Her conclusions pretended that stress-free societies without repression of animal instincts were possible. It has since been proven in empirical research that Mead misread Samoan society, which is governed by strict codes of conduct, taboos and controls (Freeman, 1983).

7 Chinese ethics tends to focus on general duties in personal relationships. As the Confucian scholar and teacher Mencius (375-289BC) wrote: "ethics [dictates] . . . the principles that between father and son there is affection, between ruler and subject duty, between husband and wife distinction, between elder and junior priority, between friends faithfulness" (cited after Rozman, 1991, p. 58).

8 Culture is defined and used in the following different meanings:

- cultivation, ordered organic growth (main original Latin meaning, as in agricultura);
- a normatively better state or habit of mind ('cultured person', 'culture is what distinguishes your surgeon from your butcher');

- a high intellectual and moral state of social development (derived from the German Kultur which is better translated into English by the French-inspired word 'civilization'); and
- a body of artistic and intellectual work (as in Ministry of Culture) which is better designated by the words 'the arts'.

9 The great pioneer of exploring cultural institutions in economic growth, German sociologist-economist Max Weber who had framed the term 'Protestant work ethic', had concluded that Chinese culture was too locked into its 'pro-conservative pole' to allow economic growth (Weber, 1951). Now, commentators speak admiringly of 'the neo-Confucian economies' and attribute their success to cultural traits (see Kasper 1998, also Chapter 11).

Part II

Applications

7

The institutional foundations of capitalism

In this chapter, we will describe the essential elements of a capitalist system. It is based on property rights and the autonomy of individual property owners to make contracts. Here, we will concentrate on the definition and effects of property rights, leaving a discussion of how these rights are used to Chapter 8, which deals with markets and competition.

The capitalist system depends on the institutions that establish and secure exclusive private property rights, which can be used in voluntary exchanges based on contracts. Well-defined and protected property rights are essential to motivating people to undertake, of their own free accord, efforts that also benefit others, often people they do not know. This is not an abstract topic of interest only to big business or high finance. It affects everyone's daily life: how to save and invest one's money, whether one can employ one's labour and skills to the best advantage, and whether one can thrive with one's inspirations and resources. Property rights are not an abstract concept, but are of immediate relevance to everyone's daily life, as they shape job opportunities, consumer choices and everyone's incentives to learn. Property rights are thus of central importance to the life opportunities of ordinary citizens, in particular those not born with a silver spoon in their mouths.

Private property can only serve its function effectively if unauthorized persons can be excluded from the use of other people's property and if the benefits and the costs accrue exclusively to the owners of the property.

Where this is not possible, particular economic problems arise; political solutions may then sometimes be relied upon to determine property use (public goods, externalities). These political solutions have their own set of problems to be discussed later in the book.

What is required for a capitalist system to work therefore are institutions, which allow free contracts and establish clear claims and liabilities. If contracting is unfettered, people are able to get the price information they need to interact effectively and to exploit their knowledge and other assets properly. We shall see that particular problems arise with relational contracts, that is, open-ended agreements to cooperate over time in circumstances in which not all eventualities can be determined beforehand, such as employment contracts. Institutions are particularly important to make this type of contract work.

We conclude this chapter with a brief discussion of money, assets which serve as a means of payment and reduce transaction costs enormously. We show that the usefulness of money depends greatly on institutions that constrain its supply.

Let a merchant begin to sell his goods on the principle of brotherly love, and I do not give him even a month before his children will be returned to beggary.

French economist, Frédéric Bastiat (1848)

Without the accumulation of capital the arts could not progress, and it is chiefly through their power that the civilised races have extended.

Charles Darwin, *The Descent of Man* (1871)

[I]n the socialist system, everything depends on the wisdom, the talents, the gifts of those people who form the supreme authority. . . . But the knowledge which mankind has accumulated in its long history is not acquired by everyone; we have accumulated such an enormous amount of scientific and technological knowledge over the centuries that it is humanly impossible for one individual to know all these things. . . . In capitalist societies, technological progress and economic progress are gained through . . . people who have the gift to find new paths. . . . If a man has an idea, he will try to find a few people who are clever enough to realize the value of his idea. Some capitalists, who dare to look into the future, who realize the possible consequences of such an idea, will start to put it to work.

Ludwig von Mises, *Economic Policy* (1979)

The right to private ownership . . . is fundamental to the autonomy and development of the person. . . . The modern business economy has [as] its basis human freedom exercised in the economic field. . . . We acknowledge the legitimate role of a profit, this means that productive factors have been properly employed and corresponding human needs have been duly satisfied.

Pope John Paul II *Centesimus annus* (1991)

7.1   Capitalism: property rights and private autonomy

In this chapter and the next, we shall deal with capitalism, that is, the economic system that is based predominantly on private, autonomous property ownership and the spontaneous coordination by competition among individual property owners using their rights. Capitalism – a term originally coined by socialists to denigrate the rules for the individualistic economic game – is based on institutions that ensure respected and secure property rights and liberties of autonomous property use. Many of these institutions are the result of evolution (Berger, 1987).

We shall in the first instance deal here with a pure capitalist system. For didactic reasons, we postpone the discussion of collective ownership and political activities to produce and redistribute income and wealth to Chapter 10.

Private property rights

The great British lawyer William Blackston defined property rights in his classic eighteenth century *Commentaries of the Laws of England* as "that sole . . . dominion one man claims over the external things of the world . . . [It] consists in the free use, enjoyment and disposal . . . without any control . . . save the laws of the land".[1] In most contemporary societies, individuals or organizations enjoy such autonomous rights to own and use certain assets, as long as they do not interfere with the rights of others (private, several properties). In the case of individuals, those assets include their own bodies, skills and knowledge (right to life and right to work). John Locke called it 'self-ownership'. Individuals also have the right, widely respected and protected in society, to appropriate the fruit of their labour (except where there is slavery, see Engerman in Drobak and Nye, (eds) 1997, pp. 95–120).[2] Individuals and firms, as well as other organizations, thus have the right to enjoy the assets they own, to use them in ways they decide autonomously, to appropriate the returns from these uses and to dispose of their property as they see fit (Demsetz, 1964; 1967; Alchian and Demsetz, 1973; Alchian, 1987; Bethel, 1998, pp. 9–29). This gives people confidence that the benefits of property uses, which are valued by others, can be appropriated. In turn, this motivates property owners to maintain, discover and pursue property uses that their fellows want. Violations of property rights incur sanctions, which are foreshadowed by known institutional arrangements. Where these protections are deficient and where the private autonomy of property use is curtailed, property rights are less valuable. Less effort is then dedicated to offer what others value highly and to employ one's property to discover and provide even more highly valued goods and services.

We can therefore define property rights as a bundle of protected rights of individuals and organizations to hold, or dispose of, certain assets, for example by acquiring, using, mortgaging, lending and transferring assets, and to appropriate the benefits from these uses. This of course also covers negative returns – the cost of maintaining property and suffering possible losses from misjudged uses. Property thus entails responsibilities, as well as benefits.

The bundle of property rights is open-ended, which means that owners may discover new uses of certain rights of which they were previously unaware. Indeed, the long process of mankind's economic development can be seen as a chain of millions and millions of little discoveries what to do with property rights, including one's own labour and talents. The sum of it all is called economic growth. Thus, a landowner may one day discover that minerals can be extracted from his land, or he may discover the right to use the land for tourist purposes. Such discoveries are often made by different property owners, who then combine what is theirs to make new, mutually beneficial uses. For example, the rancher may discover in cooperation with a golf entrepreneur that part of the property so far used for grazing can be more profitably used as a golf course. Over recent years, we have discovered that the ownership of desktop computers enables us to use them for writing, calculating, storing text, sound and images, telecommunicating and much, much more. These millions of acts of discovery have added mightily to economic growth over the past few decades.

Property rights must not be confused with the physical items in one's possession. To put it in the words of American economist Irving Fisher (1867–1947): "A property right is a liberty or permit to enjoy benefits of wealth – in its broadest sense – while assuming the costs which those benefits entail . . . It will be observed that property rights, unlike wealth or benefits, are not physical objects nor events, but are abstract social relations. A property right is not a thing" (Fisher, 1922, p. 27).

Private property rights always establish a relationship between defined individuals and defined assets, which can be physical goods, ideas or people's own bodies. Property rights define who owns what useful assets and what owners can do with them in a specific society. Where these rights are well respected and protected, we speak of 'economic liberties'. It is important that the property rights relationship is universal in the sense defined in Section 5.5. Where property rights are fuzzy and uncertain, many advantageous property uses are put out of reach. For example, the ill-defined and ill-protected command over property in the former Soviet bloc and many present-day less-developed countries has led to great uncertainties and a correspondingly poor exploitation of physical and intellectual assets. The economy then stagnates. And the growing uncertainties of land ownership originating from Aboriginal land claims in Canada and Australia has begun to lead to less investment in, and use of, land than before, when the legal fiction of *terra nullius* underpinned secure land rights of those immigrants who had claimed the land.

US economic historian Robert Higgs makes the same point when he argues that one of the primary reasons for the depth and duration of the 1930s Great Depression in the US was 'regime uncertainty'. Private investment failed to recover from 1935 through 1940 because of a "pervasive uncertainty among investors about the security of their property rights in their capital and its prospective returns" (Higgs, 1997, p. 564). During the early period of the transition from socialism to capitalism in the former Soviet Union, a similar ambiguity over property rights plagued entrepreneurship and investment (Chapter 13). The Russian economy of the 1990s was supposedly a free market, yet foreign direct investment lagged. In fact, for most of those years, the country experienced capital flight and the domestic economy was characterized by bazaar-style consumer good markets, limited investment in the supply chain, and mafia-style rule enforcement. None of these were natural by-products of the transition, but rather a consequence of ill-defined and weakly enforced property rights, combined with the constant threat of predation by both public and private actors.

As David Hume (1740) argued long ago, the foundation of civil society and social cooperation is provided by the establishment of private property rights, the keeping of promises made in contracts, and the transfer of property by consent. In situations where there is an absence of, or ambiguity over, property, contract and consent, social order breaks down.

Property is an individual right, not a favour granted by some authority. Its free use should only be limited by the rights of others, in other words, one's property uses must not harm the rights of others. In a well-defined property rights system, the onus of proof that another has been harmed by a particular property use rests squarely on the party that claims to be aggrieved. What is deemed in any particular society as unjustified harm is defined by the rules of the land. In case of conflict, the aggrieved party may take property owners to courts that then adjudicate on the basis of the known rules. Justice demands proper judicial proof (not suspicions, hearsay or fears of possible future damages). Placing the onus of proof on claimants is important because proving the claim is an important material constraint on excessive limitations of free property uses (economic freedom). As we shall see, however, modern jurisdictions have often shifted the burden of proof, for example by governments decreeing that licenses are needed for specific uses of property. For example, land owners may be required to obtain government permits to develop what they own, which puts them into a position of 'harmful till proven innocent'. A proliferation of such interventions violates justice and erodes the content and usefulness of the capitalist system (de Jasay, 2002; pp. 149–151, 159–163 and. 291–295).

Under the rules of the capitalist economy, property owners are exposed to a dual set of signals: (i) positive signals from the market, which tell owners whether others appreciate their uses sufficiently for them to make a profit, and (ii) negative signals in the form of customary and legal institutions, which tell property owners which uses they must not make. If the institutional system is clear and universal and markets are permitted to function, property owners – despite ubiquitous cognitive limitations – will interact to do their best to meet people's demands by employing their available resources and exploring new ones (Seldon, 1990; 2004).

Intellectual property

Property rights can be attached not only to physical assets but also to identifiable bits of knowledge. As we saw in Chapter 1, modern economic growth depends greatly on improved technical and organizational knowledge and knowhow. People will produce and test knowledge, a risky undertaking, if they can expect to appropriate the gains. This means that institutional arrangements have to be found which allow the owners of valuable knowledge to reap material benefits from sharing it with others. One such device is patent protection. Government bodies evaluate the originality and merit of distinct bits of patentable knowledge and award patent rights, which allow the owners exclusive use of that knowledge for a defined period.[3] In certain circumstances, this may serve as an incentive to generate and test innovative knowledge, even though the patenting procedure costs resources.

Caution and much specific technical knowledge are needed to protect intellectual property, because excessive licensing and patenting creates monopoly positions that can hinder innovation (Section 8.2), especially if industry and licensing authorities collude. Therefore, the protection of 'knowledge capital' must always be of limited duration.

Self-ownership

Property ownership extends – as philosophers of the liberal tradition since John Locke have stressed – to the autonomous control of one's own body and skills. Thus, slavery is seen as a violation of the basic human right to self-ownership, a point that has of course long been accepted. But it also applies to the person's rights to do with his skills and efforts as he sees fit, as long as this causes no harm to others. This aspect has led in many countries to practical controversies over the fundamental right to work, that is, the freedom of any person to voluntarily enter into contracts to provide services to an employer at mutually agreed conditions. Many organizational arrangements by labour unions and governments, which, for example, stipulate minimum wages or make union membership a compulsory condition of employment in a particular plant or industry, are violations of this basic right.

The debate over the right to work has played an important role in the United States since the Roosevelt administration signed the Federal National Labor Relations Act (NLRA, also known as 'Wagner ACT') into law in 1935. On certain conditions, Section 8.3 of that act made union membership a condition of private-sector employment. By the end of the Second World War the majority of unionized workers were covered by such 'closed shop' regulations (Mix, 2011). Legislative revisions in 1947 brought little effective change. However, 22 State legislatures have protected a worker's right not to join a union (as a corollary of the right of association, which includes the right not to associate). In practice, this means that workers are not obliged to financially support unions who negotiate over pay and work conditions. A detailed 1990 study came to the conclusion that "employees are better off [in right-to-work States] and also have greater employment opportunities than those living in the states that have not adopted [right-to-work] legislation" (Bennett, 1990, p. 75). This conclusion is also borne out in more recent experience: in the 'right-to-work' States, industrial production and personal incomes have grown markedly faster over a survey period (1999-2009) than in the other States, and young adults in considerable numbers have migrated to 'right-to-work' States (Mix, 2011).

Capitalism

The capitalist system is nowadays the most prevalent economic system in the world, although hardly ever in its pure form. Owners decide to offer their property, or rights to certain uses of their property, at a certain quality, in certain amounts and at a certain price in the market (Bethel, 1998). They will hope to contract with buyers who decide whether to accept the offer and who will typically offer money in exchange. If buyers value what is on offer sufficiently to cover the price demanded by the suppliers, the suppliers will probably make a profit. They may then even be induced to expand the quantities offered in the future. If demand falls short, suppliers are disappointed and incur a loss. In this case, the signal of red ink will induce them to discontinue offering that particular good or service at the original conditions. In this way, buyers influence what is being produced and supplied over the longer run (consumer sovereignty).

Many institutions have evolved spontaneously to order and facilitate exchange relationships and to give business partners more confidence in what to expect. Institutions make exchanges of property rights possible and develop to make exchange transactions less costly and risky, allowing markets to become more effective. (These market processes of coordination of individual property owners will be considered in more detail in the following chapter.)

7.2   Essential characteristics of property rights

Excludability

The defining characteristic of private property rights is that owners have the right to exclude others from passive possession, as well as from active uses and benefits from using the property. They are also fully responsible for all the costs of property use. Excludability is the precondition for the autonomy of the owner and for incentive mechanisms through which private property rights work. Only when others can be excluded from fully sharing the benefits and costs can these benefits and costs be internalized, that is, have complete and direct impact on the expectations and decisions of the owners. Then, the valuations of others about the uses of property rights are signalled completely to the owner, who will then have the incentive to engage in property uses that others welcome, expressing their wishes through 'dollar votes'.

These signals and incentives are distorted when some of the benefits, or some of the costs, do not impact on the property owner. To illustrate this by a few examples:

- A landowner, who regularly loses part of the yields of his fields to theft, will not plant and cultivate his land as intensively as a landowner, whose yields are fully protected.
- Those who incur the costs of having themselves vaccinated create private benefits for themselves, but also external benefits in that they reduce the risk of contagion for others. More people would have themselves vaccinated if, somehow, the external beneficiaries could be made to pay those who take the vaccination.
- A factory owner who creates costs, which are only partly internalized (his expenses incurred for inputs), but which partly impact on external agents (for example, pollution of the environment) will decide to produce more than someone who has to bear the full costs, because he is forced to compensate the victims of pollution.

Excludability is thus important in ensuring that private property uses are steered to reflect what others want. The incentives work through the profit-loss signal. The provision of goods and services that are wanted by others are no more than a by-product of that incentive (Schumpeter, 1961/1908, p. 148; Berger, 1987).

Externalities arise when there are knowledge problems. It is sometimes too costly to measure all costs and benefits or even altogether impossible, so that costs and benefits do not impact directly on their originators. Thus, it is too costly to identify who benefits from a neighbour's vaccination and how much that benefit is valued by others. The costs of factory emissions on others may also be costly or impossible to measure and evaluate. If techniques of measurement improve – for example thanks to improved computer and communications technology – then excludability may become feasible and externalities can be converted into internalized benefits and costs (Coase, 1960).

When costs and benefits can, by and large, be internalized, property owners will thus be guided voluntarily by profits and losses expected from their bilateral contracts, competing with each other in doing so as a matter of individual choice. When major externalities exist, coordination can become much more complicated as multilateral agreements may have to be negotiated. The give and take is then less clear than in bilateral exchanges, and the incentives to act are often fuzzy.

In practice, excludability is often imperfect and externalities are widespread. Many external effects are simply tolerated and do not prejudice voluntary exchange activities. Often, there may be private settlements to deal with externalities, for example when my activity affects my neighbour and we agree that I compensate him. In other cases, externalities of private action are dealt with by government agencies, for example by regulations or transfers. In some cases, external effects go beyond national boundaries and may require inter-government action, for example when upstream industries along a river system in one country affect downstream users in another, as is, for example, the case along the river Rhine. Here, a Rhine Commission was established to settle by negotiated agreements what is permissible and what not. Other cases arise in environmental policy where external effects of certain activities have worldwide impact, for example the emission of gasses that may affect the global atmosphere. Here, global political agreements may have to be negotiated to address the externality problem, that is, a political agreement between a great variety of conflicting national interests has to be attempted.

In the 1930s, British neoclassical economist Arthur C. Pigou built on earlier theories, originally put forward by Alfred Marshall, to discuss externalities. Pigou argued for government interventions, taxing those property uses that were seen to cause external costs and subsidizing uses that caused external benefits, as well as compensating those who bore the impact of external costs. The political consequence was that an army of government officials should tax and subsidize – always on the assumption that they could know the costs and the benefits and prove them in court – to correct the failures of the pure property rights model. Pigou's concept was, however, rejected after 1960 when British economist (and 1991 Economics Nobel Prize winner) Ronald Coase demonstrated that taxes and subsidies were not necessary to remedy the problem of externalities. Those who caused external costs and those who were impacted by them could get together to bargain and exchange property rights under mutually beneficial agreements, as long as there were no transaction costs (Coase, 1960). Parties that caused external costs could also get together with parties that suffered them and exchange property rights by integrating into one firm. For example, a rancher, whose cattle trespass on neighbouring farmland and cause crop damage, might fuse his operations with the aggrieved farmer, thus internalizing the externalities. A consequence of Coase's insights is that there is much less need for the visible hand of government to intervene, an option which is often fraught with the risk of administrative failure. The 'Coase theorem' also affected the accepted theory of public goods (see below), for example the assertion that lighthouses needed to be provided by government because fees could not be collected from the owners of passing ships and could therefore not be operated for profit. Coase showed that, in reality, lighthouses were privately financed in Britain, as ship owners valued the security that lighthouses pro-vided and paid for them.

Coase's influential contribution on external costs was enriched more recently by American economist Harold Demsetz, who pointed out that the integra-tion of agents, who cause external costs with agents who suffer them, still causes costs, this time in the form of organization costs to run the bigger, more complicated venture. In other words, external costs are transformed, but there are still costs (Demsetz, 2003; McChesney, 2006).

Coase's main insight was not to stress the logic of the zero transaction costs world, but to clarify the basis for comparative institutional analysis. His cri-tique, like the one levelled by James Buchanan in his work *Cost and Choice* (1969), was to insist first and foremost on behavioural symmetry across institutional settings. Second, Coase pointed out that under the assumption of zero transaction costs – an assumption that Pigou had indeed made – the actors within the system could negotiate away any conflict. This makes many Pigovian remedies – that is, government interventions (subsidies, taxes, reg-ulations) – redundant. This of course led to Coase's famous 'theorem' that it does not matter what the initial distribution of rights was, as long as individu-als are free to negotiate away all externalities. But Coase also emphasized that if such negotiations were to break down due to transaction costs, then we also had to examine political solutions. In the face of transaction costs, political actors would not be able to discover the optimal tax or subsidy scheme to internalize externalities either. In short, in the presence of positive transaction costs, the Pigovian remedy is non-operational. An amazing example of how simple economic reasoning can explode a more elaborate theoretical system when pursued persistently and consistently to its logical conclusion, the Coase Theorem has arguably become the most influential concept in the field of 'law and economics' and comparative institutional analysis.

Of private, free, public and common property

We speak of private goods when all costs and benefits from their use accrue to private owners (full excludability). Decisions about resource uses can then be left, as we saw, to voluntary, bilateral interactions that are coordinated in markets.

When excludability as to some benefits or some costs cannot be ensured, particular economic problems arise. We then have to distinguish a number of different categories of property, depending on whether exclusion needs to be brought about and how such goods and services are provided.

One case is that the good in question is not scarce, that is, intending users need not rival with each other. We then speak of free goods (Figure 7.1). Free goods are provided by nature and may be claimed for the mere trouble of claiming them. Clean water was once a free good and still is in parts of the world. As more people live in an area, clean water gets scarce and its use has to be rationed by some economic device. Likewise, parking spaces were once free in city centres; anyone could claim a free spot. As demand increased, parking spaces became scarce and had to be rationed by price (incidentally a process, which made it rewarding to supply more parking spaces in garages, thus alleviating the scarcity). Fish stocks in the open sea have long been free goods, but many types of fish are now scarce. Exploitation rights are now assigned in many places by mutual agreements or by governments allotting fishing licenses. It is also possible for previously exclusively owned goods to become free goods. For example, the junk you throw out becomes a free good; and when someone claims it and treats it as an antique, it may become a valuable private good again. No economic problem exists with free goods, as scarcity and hence allocation problems play no role.

There are certain assets that can be accessed and used – at least within certain limits – without denying others access. We then speak of pure public goods (Figure 7.1). An example of such a public good is street lighting: if I walk home safely along an illuminated street, others can enjoy the same benefit. There

Figure 7.1 Forms of property

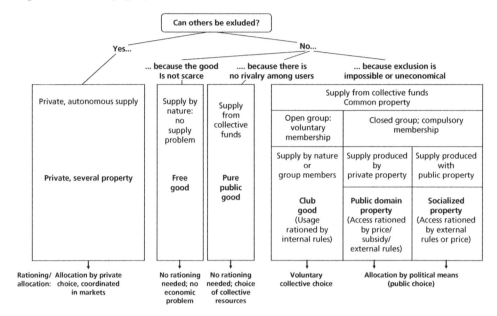

is no rivalry among users. Access by the public to the good (lighting) then causes no economic problems, but users will not be prepared to pay voluntarily. Whereas free goods are provided by nature or human generosity, street lighting is normally provided at some cost. Some kind of collective action is then needed to bankroll its provision. Such goods would not be supplied automatically because everyone will try to free ride and it would be impossible to collect a price for their supply. One solution is collective provision, financed by compulsory levies (taxes). There are also other ways of funding collective provision, for example, raising voluntary contributions and selling additional services (for example, street cleaning and roadside advertising).

Another reason why people cannot be excluded from the use of a property by having to pay a price may be that such rationing of access is impossible, rejected by the community or uneconomical. We then speak of common or collective goods. Access has to be regulated through some sort of political mechanism. We can distinguish between various types of common goods, depending on whether sharing in the costs of providing common property is voluntary or compulsory, how it is provided and how access is rationed (Figure 7.1).

Common goods may be provided jointly by an open group, open in the sense that one may belong voluntarily to the group or stay away (a club).

Sharing in the provision and use of such a common good is therefore voluntary. We then speak of 'club goods'. Non-members are excluded from access and use, but insiders can freely appropriate the benefits from club property. Where their use rivals that of other club members, because what one person uses is not available to others, the club has to ration use. This can be done effectively by internal institutions as long as the club is small and people meet sufficiently frequently and therefore exercise internal mutual control of property uses. When the number of club members multiplies, more formal rules may have to be instituted. Organization costs then rise. On the other hand, new technology, such as electronic cards, may facilitate measurement and allow more goods to be treated as club goods. An important historic example of club goods is the commons: everyone belonging to a tribe or village can collect timber or graze his privately owned animals in the forests and meadows that make up the commons. In some parts of the world, fields are the jointly owned property of the village. They are planted on a first come, first served basis by the members from the village community, but access is rationed by traditional internal institutions (Ostrom, 1990).

As of the early twenty-first century, the institutional conception of club goods is being revived as a more practicable alternative to the government provision of welfare services, which has been running into growing information and incentive problems, for example in health care and education (see below and Chapter 10).

Another category of property comes into existence when a closed group with compulsory membership, such as a nation, provides certain goods. Here, too, we can think of assets whose use is not subject to rivalry, so that we have pure public goods (for example, the defence of the nation against external aggression, which is funded by compulsory taxes and which benefits every citizen without diminishing the protection of all others). In other instances, rivalry for public goods exists, so that their use has to be rationed. This can be done in two ways (Figure 7.1):

(a) The goods or services may be produced by private owners, who are subject to competitive discipline and guided by the prices they get. However, access is facilitated by the political decision to provide cash or vouchers that are handed out to everyone or selected groups (example: school vouchers to buy private education services, access to public-domain hospitals after authorization by doctors or emergency services). Political decisions will have to determine the size of the access subsidy. We call these goods 'public domain goods' or 'public access goods'. Access is partially rationed by political choice. In these cases, the political redistribution of property rights is combined with the competitive discipline of private production and competition (Demsetz, 1970).

(b) Goods or services may also be produced by government-owned, administratively run enterprises. Rationing of access to the benefits of such socialized property is by external rules that are designed in political processes.

An example of a public-domain good would be a health-care service, from which no-one is excluded and to which certain classes of citizens are given subsidized access. But these services are supplied by private doctors and clinics. An example of socialized property is a hospital run by bureaucrats and owned by the government, with access rationed by external rules, directives and queuing. Experiences with privatization since the 1980s in many countries have demonstrated that it is often feasible to switch from socialized production to provision of public-domain goods, which are produced with private initiative and provided competitively (O'Leary, 1995; also Section 13.3). Since the 1980s, governments have often withdrawn from socialized production and concentrated on providing open access, for example in Sweden where the bureaucrat-run school system was partially converted to a voucher system with schools having to compete for the vouchers that are given to the parents of the pupils. And in Britain's ailing public hospital system, the creation of trust hospitals has brought great improvement. Local entrepreneurship (and voluntary labour) run hospitals that receive tax funding for health services provided and hygiene standards observed.

It has therefore to be noted that public ownership of the means of production is certainly not a precondition for redistributing access rights and providing social welfare. We must not equate public access with public ownership. For this reason, we caution against employing the confusing term 'public good', which can easily lead to equating public access with public ownership of the means of production and bureaucratic management.

A separate category is socialized property. It is owned by a large, closed group, but in reality controlled either by elected representatives or expert agents and its uses are authorized by politically appointed representatives. If political leaders do not wish to bear the opprobrium of visible rationing, socialized property may be made artificially abundant and funded by compulsory levies. For example, government may decide to make the results of basic research freely available to all comers, may provide art and entertainment to all who bother to enjoy it, or may dispense medical care without rationing. This makes it of course necessary to expand supply and funding by increasing compulsory taxation. Because political rationing is often not very effective, costs of such artificially created public-access goods tend to snowball, leading to unsustainable budget deficits. If the cost controls are also lax, then their provision will be doubly unsustainable over the long run (Cowen and Crampton, 2003).

The perception is widespread that socialized property is used to promote the common good – such as to defend us against external aggressors. The reality, however, frequently is drastically different: Political and bureaucratic elites with the monopoly to use legitimate force often use collectively owned assets for their own benefit and enjoyment. Principal-agent problems are rampant, although this is often disguised in modern democracies, for example when officials travel to conferences in pleasant places to conduct drawn-out international negotiations on trade or climate change. In earlier ages and in many developing countries, the pretense was and is done away with. Louis XIV of France had Versailles built unashamedly on the shoulders of overtaxed, impoverished peasants for the greater glory of France; political elites in present-day East Asia, the Middle East and Russia are accumulating untold wealth in the name of national greatness without making excuses and relying frequently on traditional attitudes dating from a feudal past. Socialized property must therefore not be equated with property used to the best benefit of the general public and the common good.

Although keeping the means of production in government hands tends to serve the particular interests of political elites, there are rational and tenable justifications for socialized production. They lie with a completely different argument: It may be necessary to control the providers of some specific goods and services directly through fiscal purse strings. This is, for example, the case with some 'violence professions'. It may be decided that the civilian authorities must control the military through direct, year-by-year fiscal resource allocations, even if competing mercenary forces might produce military protection at lower cost. After all, mercenary and other autonomous armies have a tradition of seizing power, as well as of inflicting collateral damage if they begin to compete violently with each other.

Changes in property status: nationalization and privatization

The property rights treatment of assets changes with time and technology. When few humans lived on earth, there was little scarcity of natural

Figure 7.2 Changes in property arrangements: selected cases

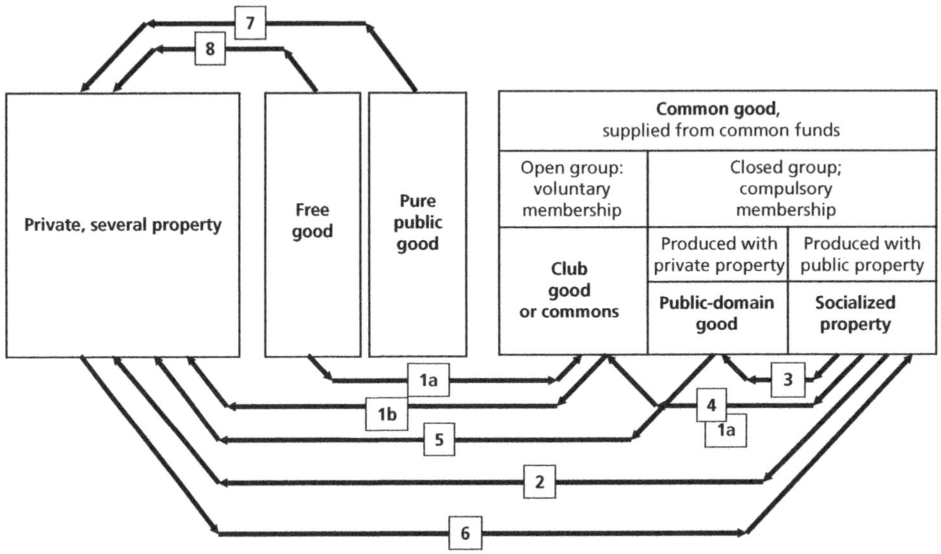

resources. This state of affairs is still remembered in the Bible as Paradise. When more people moved into an area, more resources became scarce and the institutional device of club goods was invented. Tribes excluded outsiders from the use of their land (case [1a] in Figure 7.2). As groups grew and informal rules began to fail in rationing property uses, the commons was subdivided and fenced off, turning commons into plots of private property. In post-medieval Britain and Spain this was called 'the fencing of the commons' (case [1b] in Figure 7.2). The invention of property rights is closely tied to the emergence of agriculture and herding (the 'neolithic revolution', Bethel, 1998). Indeed, people engaged only in ploughing and sowing, or building up herds of animals if they felt reasonably assured of being able to exclude others from their assets and keeping the fruit of their efforts.

Harold Demsetz (1967) argued that property rights emerge to ameliorate the conflicts that arise over competing claims to scarce resources. They limit access, assign responsibility and establish graduated penalties for violations. By doing this, property rights also provide high-powered incentives for individuals to behave cooperatively and to husband the property in their possession effectively. They thus become the foundation stone of civilization.

If socialized property does not function effectively, one may think of breaking up big groups, so that socialized property can be treated as club property and cheaper, less formal rationing devices become feasible. This has been happening in Britain in the afore-mentioned case of state-owned hospitals being turned into 'trust hospitals', run by local groups under a charter that ensures access. Sometimes, local clubs take over state-owned property, for example owning and running parklands or golf clubs (cases [3] and [4]). In similar ways, national health services can be handed to small communities and groups who operate them exclusively for the benefit of their members and ration or subsidize access. As the welfare state is becoming too cumbersome to manage and too onerous for taxpayers, common, socialized property is being converted into club goods or even private goods (privatization: cases [2] and [7]).

An important aspect of socialized property deals with 'state capitalism', an arrangement under which state-owned property is corporatized, often exposed to global competition and managed professionally, but remains under the ultimate control of either the government or a core of political power brokers, for example a political party. We will leave the discussion of state capitalism, which plays an important role in many emerging economies, to Chapters 13 and 14.

Privatization is likely to lead to different forms of managing and rationing the assets. By depoliticizing resource allocation and production, it has the advantage of making governance by elected politicians easier. The privatization of public-domain assets tends to be regretted by those who enjoyed below-cost, subsidized access to these goods, but economic allocation under private competition ultimately leads to a more effective provision with goods and services (at least as long as the public-sector monopoly is not simply replaced by a private one). Privatization also obviates cumbersome, often ineffectual and politically contentious administrative arrangements to ration access by citizens. Another reason for privatization may be that government-paid employees have organized themselves to control the activity (public-sector union monopolies), making it expensive and near-impossible for elected governments to provide effective, user-friendly goods and services (a case of agent opportunism by unionized bureaucrats). Public-domain goods may also be transferred into private ownership, in the hope of reducing either budgetary burdens or the political and economic costs of rationing access. Thus, food vouchers may be withdrawn, or certain classes of people may lose free transport entitlements (case [5] in Figure 7.2). We already saw that free goods can become private goods and vice versa and that pure public goods can become exclusive private ones, for example when private security agencies are replaced by public police protection (case [6]).

When private property rights are collectivized (case [6]), private, bilateral contracting is replaced by political choices. The problems of private choice are then replaced by the problems of public choice (Chapter 10). Conversely, socialized (nationalized) property may be transferred to private (several) ownership.

We have to conclude that the property categories discussed here are not cast in stone, but depend on choice and technology. Different societies will therefore shape the property rights and the attendant exclusion mechanisms in differing ways.

KEY CONCEPTS

Property rights were defined in Chapter 2 as the rights to exclude others from the use of an asset and the right to use, hire out or sell the asset to others. Property rights are thus a bundle of rights: to possess an asset and hold it, including maintaining it (passive use), to exchange it or to let others use certain aspects of it temporarily (active uses). The bundle is open-ended in the sense that owners may discover new uses, which they had not been aware of before. Property rights may be attached to physical assets, but also to intellectual property.

Excludability is the defining characteristic of property rights. It means that others can be excluded not only from the benefits of an asset, but also that the owners are exclusively responsible for the costs of asset uses, as well as the costs of ensuring exclusion.

Patents are rights that guarantee the exclusive exploitation of discreet bits of valuable knowledge. They are one way of establishing **intellectual property rights**.

Private property rights are held by individuals, private associations and firms. Where the costs and benefits of property use impact directly and exclusively on the owner, we speak of **private goods**. Where

externalities become important, special problems of economic coordination arise.

Externalities are benefits and costs of property use that do not impact on the property owner, either because monitoring is too costly (high transaction costs) or because it is altogether impossible.

Where exclusion of others from benefits is impossible or unnecessary, we speak of **common property**. Such a good may be shared in a small, voluntary group (**commons**, club property), from which outsiders are excluded, or in a large, inclusive group with compulsory membership (**socialized property**). In large groups with compulsory membership, it may often be necessary to ensure open access, in other words, to keep goods and services in the public domain. Open access to public-domain goods can be assured either by socialized production with means that are owned by a government body, or by institutions that guarantee certain access conditions to the public. This can be done by regulations or by endowing qualifying citizens with funds to gain access. The general public's access to privately produced **public-domain goods** tends to be through paying a price, with certain members of the

➡

←

public being endowed with cash subsidies or purpose-specific vouchers.

Free goods are assets in which no one has claimed property rights, because they are not scarce. There is no economic problem with free goods. The same applies to **pure public goods**, that is, goods and services for which intending users do not rival, once they have been provided (example: street lights can be enjoyed by you without diminishing their benefit to your fellows). Such public goods have to be financed from collective resources.

Capitalism is defined here as an institutional system in which the means of production are held predominantly as private property and in which voluntary private property uses are coordinated in the market place. Capitalism can only function if certain ground rules are enforced.

Socialism is an economic system in which most means of production are held collectively and controlled by the political leadership or its agents.

State capitalism is a system, in which a considerable share of production enterprises are either wholly or partly state owned, but in which the government keeps business at arms' length. Often, insider cliques in government gain control of these state-owned enterprises (SOEs). The management of these corporations may be competitively hired and may be subject to performance criteria, and many of the contemporary state-owned corporations (in China, the Middle East, India and Brazil) also operate internationally. The combination of government patronage and modern management enables such enterprises to expand rapidly, at least until they have reached the technological frontier and the usual disincentives of rent-seeking patronage have not left their mark.

Exclusion costs

Excluding others from using one's property without authorization causes the owner costs. Such unauthorized uses may for example be theft or squatting on land. To prevent this, people incur, for example, expenses for locks, fences, share registries, land titles, and information-protection systems in computers. We call these costs exclusion costs.

High exclusion costs lower the value of property. To a considerable extent, they depend on institutional arrangements, beginning with underlying standards of ethics that are shared in the community. If private property is respected spontaneously, private exclusion costs will be low and property values will be relatively high. If a community has invented a low-cost system of enforcing property rights, this will also boost property values. Thus, an effective land-titles registry and expedient courts that resolve contested property issues raise land values. Where property law is enforced by collective action (legislation, police, judiciary), a large part of the exclusion costs are borne collectively, which may have cost advantages for property owners, even though they pay taxes, as compared to a situation of individual protection (scale economies). We know that different institutional systems have great influence on exclusion costs and hence property values. It is not surprising that property owners, when they have the chance, shift their property to environments where it is well protected and hence highly valued. Nor does it surprise that they are prepared to contribute taxes to fund protective collective action.

Low exclusion costs have not been a normal feature of the human condition. In vast parts of the developing world, ordinary people enjoy little effective protection of their property (de Soto, 2001). They are frequently subject to rackets and excessive regulations; many experience the property risks of war and civil strife. Many are farming and dwelling on land as squatters with uncertain tenure, because government or other powerful authorities have failed to register land titles or do not enforce them for poor people (de Soto, 1993; 2001; Bauer and Sen, 2004). Slum dwellers in Third World cities suffer from high exclusion costs and uncertain tenure, which often traps them in poverty. Similar conditions – often underpinned by envy and anti-capitalist ideologies – persist in large parts of the former Soviet empire and in communist Asia (Chapter 13). Much could be done to reduce the costs of holding property and enhance the value of property in these countries by more effective institutions, including a more effective, less corrupt organizational back-up of these institutions (by the police and courts). When the exclusion costs are reduced, people find it more attractive to acquire and activate property, thereby helping themselves out of their poverty.

In war and internal civil strife, existing protections of private property may disintegrate. When property rights are ill defined and poorly protected by legal means in chaotic societies, people may try to define and protect them for themselves. This is the origin of protection rackets by the Mafia and self-help organizations, which take the law into their own hands (vigilantes). Thus, the conditions after the demise of the Soviet Union and existing corruption in China, Vietnam, India and Africa have shown that the institutions and their enforcement by the state are deficient. Self-organized groups who command the tools of violence set themselves up to offer 'private' property protection for a fee. Notwithstanding the propriety of this activity, it may provide a useful service to property owners. They may even value this service enough to pay protection money voluntarily. The danger of course is that the self-appointed 'violence professionals' use their means of coercion to extract high prices for the protection, or that rival gangs fight over the clientele of property owners, causing 'collateral damage' among innocents. In such a situation, collective, law-bound government can offer great reductions in exclusion cost to property owners (even if financed by property taxes).

Shared respect for private property may decline also when wealth distribution becomes extremely lop-sided and is widely perceived as unjust. It then becomes necessary for property owners to incur rising exclusion costs for locks, barbed wire, fences, security guards and insurance. Certain vulnerable forms of holding and using property – even if potentially very useful – may then be avoided altogether. However, if government tries to redistribute property by selective interventions, this may raise exclusion costs further. If, for example, renters of a property are accorded increasing rights by legislators (ceilings on rental prices, protection from eviction) at the expense of the property owner or the police and courts cease to persecute violations of property rights, the motivation to invest in housing property for renting to others will wane. The unintended side effect is that renters, who were meant to be protected, are worse off. Similar consequences must be expected when the penalties for failure to repay loans are not enforced: The credit system breaks down and scarce capital is less well utilized. Thus, credit and banking – other than on an interpersonal level – were long poorly protected in the Middle East, so that the large accumulations of capital needed for modern industry were hard to achieve. One can then observe deleterious consequences for economic growth. These consequences are often underrated because they materialize slowly, reflecting the typically slow adjustment of the internal institutions of society. Likewise, improvements in property protection may take time until the entire system of internal and external rules is adjusted and a more productive culture of property protection had emerged.

The divisibility and transferability of property rights

To work effectively, property rights also must be divisible. Large chunks of property can often be utilized effectively only if the rights to them can be divided. Frequently, various elements of property can be used most effectively by separate people and groups. Thus, people may value real estate most highly if institutional provisions allow some to own the property, others to use some of its benefits temporarily for a rental fee. For example – if we take a forested property – some may pay an entrance fee for recreational use, others may use the land for growing trees, or enjoy hunting animals. This divisibility allows the owners who hold title to the land to assign differentiated rights to hunt, go for walks and invest in tree growing, which greatly enhances the usefulness of the property. Important institutional innovations, for example, facilitated the foundation of modern stock companies with limited liability. It was made possible to divide the ownership of a large company into shares, which relatively small investors could buy, while the large stocks of capital needed for major industrial and infrastructural projects could be accumulated and liability for losses was limited to the shares owned.

As mentioned before, property embraces an open-ended bundle of rights that are created and divided by demand and human creativity. Divisibility allows people with different demands and knowledge to put a particular asset to the most highly valued uses that they can discover. Thanks to the institutions that establish such differentiated and divisible property rights, enterprising people without property of their own, who have creative ideas and the confidence that they could make good use of assets, can more easily attain access to the assets of others. In institutionally creative societies, new types of property rights emerge that may be traded separately from the right of outright possession. Divisibility thus promotes the benefits of specialization and knowledge search, whilst still upholding the owner's ultimate responsibilities of asset ownership.

Clearly, the gains from partitioning certain uses of property can only be reaped when the institutional arrangements are reliable enough to make this possible. Loans will only be made when assets are returned as and when agreed and debts are repaid as promised. When the institutional protection of property rights deteriorates – for example when credit is not repaid fully because of a poor payments morale, or governments impose 'haircuts' on lenders – gains from property use are lost and general living standards will drop.

Another aspect of property rights is that they should be disposable (or transferable). Where tradition or other institutions prohibit the disposal of property rights, for example through trade, they tie property to the one traditional owner and prevent others, who may value the property more highly because of their better knowledge and skills, from making better use of it. An interesting example to illustrate this came about when inalienable property rights to certain tracts of land were granted to groups of indigenous Americans and Australians. They were made inalienable because authorities wanted to protect the aboriginal owners from exploitation and wanted to prevent sale or rental at prices deemed by them as not advantageous to the owners. Such protection has, however, greatly reduced the value of the property to the aboriginal owners, who now resent this sort of state paternalism. Young, educated aboriginals may want to lease their land to mining companies or sell it, so that they can earn income and move to activities they find more suitable. The freezing of property transfers can also have deleterious consequences when governments make land inalienable for environmental reasons (national parks). It may be discovered subsequently that a greater variety of animal and plant species could be protected if some areas in national parks could be traded for other pieces of land with superior flora or fauna. After all, land resources are limited and opportunities for nature conservation change (Wills, 1997, pp. 29–47). The best-possible use of limited resources for nature conservation can therefore be enhanced by transferability, whereas inalienability – made with the best intentions and with limited knowledge at the time – may impede conservation.

KEY CONCEPTS

Exclusion costs are incurred when owners employ resources to exclude others from owning or using their property, for example, the cost of a lock, or of a computer program that requires a password before you can access a computer.

Divisibility means that property rights can be unbundled, mere passive ownership rights can be separated from rights to specific uses of an asset, for example the title to a lake being separated from the right to fish in the lake or the right to swim in it.

Transferability is a quality of property rights that refers to the change in ownership, for example through sale, inheritance or donation.

Inalienable property rights cannot be traded and used by others, and hence cannot be used to the fullest potential.

7.3 Using property rights: free contracts and transaction costs

Contracts: a deal is a deal

As we saw in the opening section of this chapter, property can be used by its owners when they exchange some or all of the rights to their asset. In the case of private property, this is done by entering into voluntary contracts, which establish a binding agreement, based on the consent of two parties;

(a) to pay an agreed price, and
(b) to hand over property rights as agreed.

Yet, even at the conclusion of complex negotiations, it is not always clear what the precise conditions of the contractual agreement are. It is therefore customary in many cultures to reiterate the agreed conditions and to mark the contract by symbolic gestures, for example a handshake or a formal ceremony to exchange signatures. It pays to invest in 'affirmation rituals' as part of the contract in particular when the contract establishes a durable relationship. With the lapse of time, contracting parties may be tempted to behave opportunistically, shirk duties or simply forget obligations. Cultural signals that reinforce contracts are aimed at making the mutual obligations more memorable, for example, the smoking of a pipe among North American Indians or the appearance before a *kadi* (judge) in the Middle East to affirm the contract. The appropriate institutional signals vary from civilization to civilization. What may bind a Chinese merchant may not seem sufficient to bind an American to a contract and vice versa. It is therefore a challenge for pioneers in inter-cultural contracting to find mutually binding signals and rituals.

In its simplest form, steps (a) and (b) occur simultaneously with the conclusion of the agreement (one-off contracts, simultaneous exchange, an example being a cash purchase at the market). But frequently time elapses between the conclusion of the contract and steps (a) and (b). Thus, it may be agreed that the purchased good will only be delivered some months in the future, or that payment by instalments will be made over many months ahead. When this is the case, contracts have to include provisions for credible commitments that the obligations will indeed be fulfilled. Sanctions have to be provided against opportunistic non-fulfilment, and provisions have to be made for sorting out subsequent misunderstandings or disagreements among the contracting parties. A typical example of this type of contract is a loan. One side obtains the use of a physical or financial asset, that is, the owners temporarily cede a property right, and the borrower makes a credible promise to return the asset or repay the borrowed funds as agreed. To make such promises credible, specially protected forms of contract may have to be entered, providing harsher enforcement than under common contract law, or the borrower has to provide securities, such as a house to be mortgaged, which the lender accepts as a 'hostage'. Often, intermediaries who have a reputation to lose (such as banks) join contracting parties as middlemen who offer more credible commitments (than the ultimate borrowers could offer) to ensure that the loans will be repaid. To make intermediaries like banks even more credible, they tend to adhere to transparent accounting rules and meet prudential requirements. These rules are often supervised by public authorities to add even more credibility.

Another type of contract is very frequent in contemporary economic life: an open-ended contract which establishes a more or less permanent contractual relationship that carries mutual obligations over time, but cannot regulate all eventualities that might emerge. These are called 'relational contracts'. A typical example of such an open-ended relational deal is an employment contract: provision of a wage and other emoluments in exchange for the delivery of a certain work performance.

In the face of uncertainty and given the costs of negotiating and concluding contracts, the contract can never enumerate and regulate all aspects of the deal that extends over a long period of time. Such contracts have to rely on universal, abstract institutions within which specific eventualities can be settled in reasonably predictable ways. Certain general legal principles, such as 'acting in good faith' or 'a deal is a deal' belong in this category of rules that enhance trust. In this context, we should recall that institutions are time-tested 'store houses of knowledge' which help intending contract partners to economize on the costs of contracting and contract fulfilment and which establish the trust needed to ensure low transaction costs.

Institutions help to convert specific aspects of contracts into standardized routines and thereby save on information and re-negotiation costs. This puts numerous additional opportunities to utilize property at the disposal of property owners. Just imagine if there were no rules and no enforcement mechanisms to ensure the punctual repayment of debts! A large part of possible economic interactions would not even be attempted, and living standards would drop.

KEY CONCEPTS

A **contract** is an agreement, namely the concurrence of two declarations of the will to exchange property rights. The property-owning party may wish to offer outright property ownership (sale or gift) or the right to possess and use property for a limited time (for example, to loan or hire out); the other party may have a demand for the property or a specific property use and typically offers an amount of money. In the case of an exchange, an agreement to sell may be based on a **one-off**, **simultaneous contract** or a **non-simultaneous contract**, that is, an agreement that provides for fulfilment of the contract at a subsequent point in time: physical possession may, for example, be passed over the following month, and payment may be by instalment over many months after the sale.

Non-simultaneous contracts involve **credit**. One party acquires a claim, the other a liability. In this case, particular problems of monitoring and enforcement arise. Institutional safeguards have to be found against opportunistic shirking of the contractual obligation to return the property.

Open-ended or **relational contracts** are agreements to perform certain services over an indeterminate period. Not all eventualities can be foreseen, let alone regulated by contract provisions. Relational contracts are very frequent in a complex modern economy where many economic relations are durable and repetitive.

Relational contracts confront the contracting parties with knowledge problems. They offer a reliable structure and confidence to both sides of the agreement. But they depend on institutions to economize on information costs and permitting flexibility if adjustments are necessary. Appropriate rules lay down procedures as to how unforeseen circumstances will be handled, so that transaction costs are limited and contract partners can have trust that the specifics of their future relationship will be sorted out satisfactorily in case of conflict.

Autonomy – economic liberties

High and rising standards of living require that people and firms are free to contract, in other words, they have the greatest possible autonomy to dispose of their property rights. This maxim is not fulfilled if social customs preclude certain contractual uses of property rights (for example: 'In our family, it is not acceptable for women to work for money!'; 'it is simply unacceptable that people take up loans, mortgaging the family farm!'), or if political controls deprive people of their economic autonomy (for example, by legislation that requires licenses for certain property uses). Private autonomy and the practice of disposing physical and intellectual property in exchange for money are thus institutional preconditions for free contracting.

Private autonomy is the freedom to use property without specific interference from other citizens or government authorities as long as others are not harmed. Autonomy is essential to give individuals (and private firms) the scope that allows them to explore the best uses of what they own, including their knowledge. The autonomy of property owners is of course constrained by universal rules; it is however violated when property owners are confronted with a plethora of limitations that may derive from private power (restrictive practices of market participants) or from collective action (for example, a proliferation of specific regulations on environmental, human health or income distribution grounds). Such interventions may be legitimized by political action, but they nevertheless reduce individual autonomy and increase the knowledge problem of property owners in that they increase their information and other transaction costs. When such limitations of private autonomy proliferate, they tend to become contradictory. Prosperity is then likely to suffer. Private autonomy is the projection of individualism into property law. In collectivist regimes where there is a great tendency to impose collective goals, private property – even when formally recognized – will be hollowed out. A great frequency and pervasiveness of prescriptive directives and regulations – together with the corruption of the rules – then eliminates private property in all but name, as well as responsibility and self-reliance.

Autonomy in using what one owns – including one's knowledge and own labour – amounts to what is sometimes described as 'economic freedom', a respected and central part of overall freedom. The economic liberties in the possession and use of private property give substance to civil and political liberties. Citizens of property are able to defend their rights, and can do so without prior reference for permission from others (Friedman, 1962). Paupers have few liberties.

Private and political restrictions of private autonomy

Private property rights lose some of their value when their use is curtailed by the actions of other citizens, for example, when a cartel excludes newcomers from offering their property in a market. Private restrictions of property uses have to do with the exercise of economic power that we discussed in Section 5.4. The institutions therefore should protect property rights beyond the merely formal protection of private property as such and safeguard autonomous property uses as far as is feasible. This includes external institutions, enforced by government, against restrictive practices such as cartels and monopolies which close markets to outsiders and newcomers (see Chapter 8).

In most modern democracies, the freedom of citizens to use and dispose of their assets, indeed to shape their own lives as they see fit, is severely constrained by government regulations. Even in their daily lives, citizens find that they are not permitted to make their own free arrangements for how to cope with the economic consequences of illness, how to tackle the risks of unemployment, how to school their children, on what conditions to work, how to rent out accommodation they own, what risks to incur as consumers, whom to employ and how to dissolve a labour contract, and so on. The principle of equality before the law is habitually violated, for example when employers are forced to comply with quotas on female employment or hiring people with disabilities. The growing interference of the visible hand of government has had the consequence that citizens have become habituated to restrictions and passively accept the progressive loss of the freedom of contract. In the process, many are resigned to progressive losses of civil liberties and are becoming subjects of the state, instead of being the self-assured citizen-principals. In other words, the consequences of the intensive regulation of daily life are not only material (less economic growth), but also affect the fundamental human right to freedom.

Turning again to the economic consequences of restrictions on the free use of property rights, it is worth observing that, in an open, dynamically changing world, positions of economic power rarely persist for long without political patronage. Even where one or a few powerful players have closed a market, they will sooner or later face actual or potential contests from other property owners. Nowadays, in the era of low transport and transaction costs, as well as rich information flows and transparency, most markets will sooner or later be contested by outsiders who offer more autonomous choices to the other side of the market. Most monopolies and cartels thus depend for their durability on the support of government (Friedman, 1991).

The more durable and far-reaching restrictions of private economic autonomy therefore originate in political action. Political powers are often used to
curtail the rights of property owners (their economic liberties). The primary
role of external institutions is to protect property rights, primarily through
proscriptive, universal rules. If the principle of universality is abandoned and
prescriptive, specific rules proliferate, governments are likely to discriminate between different property owners. Then, property users incur rapidly
rising transaction costs. It is not the use by government of prescriptive rules
(directives) per se that is the problem, but the frequency and density of
their use.

We will return to this problem in Chapter 8 when we discuss competition
and in Chapter 10 when we deal with collective action.

KEY CONCEPTS

Private autonomy means that the rights
of property owners are free from detailed
private and public limitations on how property is to be used, in other words, that economic liberties are safeguarded. Autonomy
is curtailed when other property owners
with power interfere with someone's property rights by arbitrary and discriminatory
action. An example is private action to
restrict trade, for example by excluding new
suppliers from selling in a market, forming
a supplier cartel. Autonomy is also curtailed
by government. When governments go
beyond protecting the equal property rights
of all and decree and enforce a great multiplicity of prescriptive directives, they erode
private autonomy – and with it the proper
functioning of the capitalist system.

Transaction costs

When property rights are used actively, that is, when they are exchanged
or combined with property rights in production factors owned by others,
coordination costs arise (compare Figure 5.1 in Chapter 5). When people
use their property rights by contracting in markets, these costs are called
'transaction costs'.[4] Before people know what they want and how they
might trade their property rights with others, they have to obtain much
information, often a costly and risky process in itself (Section 3.2). Next,
they have to negotiate and secure contracts. This creates further costs
(Section 5.6). Finally, contract execution has to be monitored and measured and, if necessary, adjudicated and enforced. This may again be costly.
The level of these transaction costs can be reduced by appropriate institutions, for example when standardized weights and measures are adopted or
imposed.

Information is costly. Much knowledge has to be acquired before a business transaction can even be contemplated: What goods and services are available? Who owns them? On what conditions are they offered for sale or loan? Can existing goods and services be adapted to new uses? Who could make the necessary variations? At what cost? What sort of persons are potential contract partners? Where can they be found? Can they be trusted to fulfil contractual obligations? What prices have to be paid? What other circumstances have to be known? Once all this information has been collected, it has to be evaluated. The entire information-search effort may end with the conclusion that, after all, the intended transaction promises insufficient material advantages. In short, the information paradox applies. As we saw, information search cannot be optimized because the value of information cannot be ascertained before it has been acquired and the cost has been incurred. The way in which people typically proceed is to expend effort on information gathering until they judge from their past experience to have acquired sufficient knowledge to risk a decision. At what point their experience tells them that they are able to decide can normally not be known beforehand. And once the information costs have been incurred, they are of course sunk costs (Streit and Wegner, 1992). The fact that one cannot assess the likelihood of the value of information before one has acquired it, makes information search a risky activity, which many people resent.

Information-search costs tend to be relatively low when it is possible to extrapolate from past experience or analogous cases. They are higher when new factor combinations are to be tried out (innovation). Then, costs have to be incurred to test whether products or processes are technically and commercially feasible. In all but the most favourable institutional settings, the necessary expenses on information search and other transaction costs may be prohibitive, so that innovations are often not even contemplated (see Chapter 8). This explains the experience of slow economic growth for most of human history (Chapter 1). More generally, private, bilateral exchanges are complicated where information costs are high.

Once economic agents have gathered the information they consider sufficient to conclude that a certain transaction will serve their purposes, a string of further costs have to be envisaged: the costs of negotiating, concluding, monitoring and enforcing the contract. It was this type of recurrent transaction cost that British economist Ronald Coase 'discovered' for economic theory when he tried to explain why firms exist. He concluded that the costs of sub-contracting certain inputs in markets can be reduced by entering into open-ended, semi-permanent hierarchical relations, in other words by combining resources in organizations such as firms (Coase, 1937/1952; Cheung,

1983; Demsetz, 1988). A more or less permanent organizational relation-ship, say of an employee with a firm, saves on the costs of hiring employees on a daily basis. A permanent share company saves on the costs of pooling capital and other resources for each venture. Modern share companies came into existence initially to finance a single voyage, say from Amsterdam to the Spice Islands. The profits were then distributed (if there were any) and the company was dissolved. Gradually, it was discovered that permanent share companies to fund long-distance trade reduced organization costs.

Transaction costs may be costly to measure and predict, as complex tech-nical properties, timing, guarantees of contract fulfilment and provisions regarding what happens in cases of non-fulfilment have to be monitored. Moreover, the agreed conditions have to be met to the satisfaction of both parties. If there is disagreement, possibly costly adjudication is required, as well as contract enforcement. Given these costs, it often makes sense to enter into firm, open-ended arrangements, such as in an employment contract, to regulate recurrent routine interactions. Such open-ended arrangements also create firms whose existence can only be explained by the existence of trans-action costs that are higher than the organization costs.

Some authors have called these recurrent, operations-related transaction costs, which Coase first highlighted in the 1930s, 'Coasean transaction costs'. They differ from the fixed costs of up-front information search.

KEY CONCEPTS

Transaction costs are incurred when property rights are exchanged in market transactions (based on contracts). In the first instance, transaction costs consist of information search costs (to find a sufficient number of exchange partners, their loca-tion, product design, quality, reliability and numerous other relevant aspects prior to making a decision – **fixed costs** of transac-tion), as well as costs of negotiating, con-cluding and monitoring the contract and the costs of possibly dealing with contract breaches (**recurrent costs** of transaction). The costs of information search and prepar-ing contracts are 'sunk' prior to deciding whether a transaction is worthwhile.

Externalities again – the costs of measurement and exclusion

Differences between the private costs and benefits and the societal costs and benefits (externalities) are frequently the consequence of transaction costs. If it is too expensive to measure and assign all consequences of private property uses to the owners, people are not able to negotiate a market price to compensate everyone for the all costs they cause, and to charge them for all the benefits. Common goods occur also when users cannot be readily excluded because of high costs of exclusion.

Improvements in measurement and information technology frequently eliminate externalities. Private production then becomes profitable even when public production was previously seen as the only way to come to grips with an insoluble externality problem. For example, roads have long been financed by taxation because road-usage costs were near-impossible to measure, attribute and collect, and it was near-impossible to exclude citizens from using the roads. Now, it is possible to rely on new electronic technology (transponders) to internalize the costs and benefits of certain types of road usage, so that private toll roads have become feasible and the building and operation of public-access roads by government is less appropriate. In many fields, the spread of computer networking and other amenities of the communications revolution is now shifting the dividing line between market and government organization in the direction of more coordination by markets and competitive outsourcing and away from collective action and reliance on socialized property (Barzel, 1982).

When private agents rival with each other in using common goods, they may also cause externalities among themselves. If, for example, more people use public open-access roads, they may contribute to congestion which impacts on them and others. In recent years, clean air has ceased to be a free good in many areas of urban and industrial concentration. Economists have therefore proposed the principle that the polluter pays, namely that those who cause emissions are rationed in their polluting activities either by price (setting caps on each producer's emissions and making them buy additional pollution rights if they so wish) or by direct quantitative regulation. This of course presupposes that sources of pollution can be measured and identified and that there are effective means of preventing potential polluters from contributing to the environmental problem. It also requires political judgments as to which users of environmental assets should have priority and whose emissions should be capped.

What has been said about rivalling demand and external costs, of course also applies *mutatis mutandis* to the case of external benefits. Where private agents used to provide amenities for others without getting paid (external benefit), new measurement technology can at times make it possible to reward these activities and hence to stimulate their production, for example by the technology that now allows private providers to charge for the use of TV signals.

Externalities arise in two types of cases:

(a) Private property owners are not fully compensated for the costs and benefits of their activities through private exchanges, because they consider the exclusion and transaction costs of their property uses as too high (Coase, 1960).

(b) Private operators use common property and lay political claims to their share of common property.

In case (b), we can speak of externalities in the narrow sense. They take the form of external costs when private uses of common property have negative consequences for others, for example when road users have to rival for road space and each user adds to traffic congestion. They take the form of external benefits when private users alleviate the rivalry for common property (external benefit), for example when private tree planting or private water conservation enhances the general environment.

In all these cases, better measurement technology and lower monitoring costs – mainly thanks to new electronic technology – can alleviate problems and facilitate a their resolution.

The IT revolution probably marks a change in a long-term trend. Because of high measurement and transaction costs, certain goods and services used to be provided collectively as a matter of course. This led to externalities in their use (such as road congestion). Cost controls in production were often lacking since government monopolies provided the goods and services collectively. Advances in technology now allow for the measurement and accounting of the use of many such goods, so that externalities disappear. As already mentioned, it is then possible to convert such goods from collective to private production and competitive provision (privatization). As a result, governments are able to devolve numerous activities (Chapter 14).

Private property, eminent domain and environmentalism

The pure capitalist system is not a free-for-all, but – as we saw – contains restrictive rules that protect others from possible harm from private property uses by others. We have also seen that there are instances of externalities which cannot be handled by private exchanges of property rights and which are most effectively and cheaply handled by political intervention – even taking into account that political intervention frequently produces unintended side effects, rent-seeking and problems of administrative ignorance (Chapter 10). In Anglo-Saxon legal jurisprudence, widely distributed, but important collective interests are recognized as valid grounds for governments seizing private property rights under the doctrine of 'eminent domain' (Epstein, 1985). Many other jurisdictions with constitutional protections of private property have similar legal constructs. Normally, the confiscation of property rights requires that the state offers 'just compensation'. The doctrine of 'eminent domain' was already spelled out by Dutch jurist Hugo Grotius in 1625 when he wrote in his famous opus *De iure belli et pacis:*

> the property of subjects is under the eminent domain of the state, so that the state or he who acts for it may use and even alienate and destroy such property, not only in the case of extreme necessity, in which even private persons have a right over the property of others, but for ends of public utility, to which ends those who founded civil society must be supposed to have intended that private ends should give way. But it is to be added that when this is done the state is bound to make good the loss to those who lose their property. (cited after Nowak and Rotunda, 2010, p. 263)

While the principle is easily declared, the details of applying the doctrine of eminent domain lead to often intractable and controversial problems (Epstein, 2007): How is the public interest defined? What are circumstances under which it should be permitted to prevail over private property rights? Is, say, the public interest in building a highway across someone's private land sufficient reason to seize that land? Is the interest of a local government in raising revenue from property taxes sufficient reason to seize privately owned houses, so that a shopping complex can be built? In practice, what is meant by 'just compensation' for a taking is controversial. It should be the market value of the property right, if such a value can be established, before expropriation was threatened. In practice, authorities may first declare that they will take a property, may threaten legal action and then seize the property at a greatly downgraded market value. In short, the doctrine of eminent domain and its practical interpretations by the courts of the land have the potential to erode the entire property rights system, and with it the institutional foundations of capitalism that has produced such enormous material and non-material benefits (Epstein, 1985; 2007).

Related conflicts, which are sometimes dealt with legally as an application of 'eminent domain', are arising increasingly from avid environmentalism. The conservation of a livable environment is a fundamental value (Section 4.4) and in so far enjoys broad political support. When political intervention leads to the confiscation of hitherto secure private property rights (and when this is done with insufficient compensation), environmentalism clashes not only with economic freedom, but freedom in general, as well as justice (Kasper 2007; Klaus, 2008). The practical conflict is exacerbated where adjudication is not conducted under the rules of the common law or other fundamental and familiar law codes, but is done instead by special environmental courts and rules of evidence that violate procedural justice (which is nowadays quite common). The conflicts are exacerbated even further when environmentalism becomes the transparent foil for promoting political primacy over economic life and when it is used to undermine or abolish capitalism. Different from traditional socialist attacks on private property ownership through outright nationalization, contemporary, environmentally motivated attacks proceed piecemeal, taking individual rights from someone's bundle of property rights, but leaving increasingly meaningless property titles in the hands of individuals.

Anti-capitalist sentiments are not only promoted by those who have to gain direct influence and income from shifting matters from private to public choice (Chapter 10), but also from intellectuals, who act as self-appointed arbiters in these matters. Intellectuals often subscribe to a simplified, top-down vision of society and the assumption that unanticipated side effects do not occur. They have little or no direct experience of commercial life and the concerns of 'ordinary people' and therefore promote collectivist causes over a wide range of public topics (Sowell, 2009). The media tend to sympathize, too, because media opinion makers perceive more of an influence when matters are dealt with collectively than when thousands make daily, humdrum decisions in markets. In the face of these trends, it seems important to reaffirm the benefits of a secure private property rights system.

7.4 Relational contracts, self-enforcement, and the judiciary

We already noted that specific problems of contract monitoring and enforcement arise when property rights are used in open-ended, relational contracts. One cannot simply assume that everybody will resist the temptation of acting opportunistically if they can get away with it. People are often forgetful, negligent and lazy, they shirk obligations or are inclined to cheat and lie, especially when dealing with strangers. Institutional constraints are then needed to combat these innate, base instincts and to induce people to behave more reliably and predictably. In the modern capitalist economy, many property uses are based on open-ended contractual relationships, which depend more than other contracts on self-enforcement mechanisms and reliable external enforcement (Axelrod, 1984; Benson, 1995).

Self-enforcing contracts

Confidence in contract fulfilment over time derives, in the first place, from the existence of self-enforcing mechanisms, which are based on internal institutions and do not require formal enforcement:

(a) Profitable business relations extend over a long time. This means that the contract parties have a reciprocal and automatic hold over each other. If one party breaks the contract, the other has the option of retaliating in some way or discontinuing the business relationship altogether. The threat of such tit-for-tat responses can be a powerful sanction. In the extreme and in small groups, it can take the form of exclusion of offending parties from all trade (ostracism). Tit-for-tat retaliation is effective when contract partners know that they depend on each other and can hold each other hostage. Then, they are less likely to shirk and will ensure a smooth execution of the contract. Over time, the experience of honesty, punctuality and reliability in trade may become an internalized habit – second nature. Experience shows such merchant virtues to be highly beneficial to both sides of the trade (Giersch, 1996).

(b) Another way for contract partners to make credible commitments is that they build up a reputation, which they can easily lose if they act opportunistically. Building up a good reputation may take a long time, but reputations are quickly lost. Suppliers invest in product and service quality and advertise their goods to earn a reputation, which is often costly. The reputation becomes part of the supplier's intangible capital. If customers turn to a reputed retailer, they know that part of the price they pay is for the confidence that a contract with such a supplier will be properly executed and possible disagreements will be settled expediently. They also know that they have a certain hold over the supplier, should they be disappointed, in that they can destroy the reputation of the supplier. In other words, they can – if necessary – hold the supplier hostage. Suppliers of course often set themselves up as hostages as part of their business strategy.

Modern technology has made repeat contacts and the spread of information easier, so that the reputations of opportunistic agents are now more at risk. However, reputation only works as an enforcement mechanism in communities in which information is communicated and some basic values are shared. What is necessary for the reputation mechanism to work is that the members of the community react to the news of opportunistic behaviour in roughly equal ways. If an opportunistic act – say fraud perpetrated on a rich man – is greeted by some in the community with approval and by others with condemnation, then the reputation mechanism fails. This is why a shared ethical and value system is an important foundation for the enforcement of many internal institutions and crucial to low transaction costs. After all, spontaneous enforcement of internal rules is cheaper than heavy reliance on external sanctions (litigation).

(c) Self-enforcement of non-simultaneous contracts can often be enhanced by the introduction of third parties (intermediaries). One way is to include a well-known third party as a guarantor. This role is, for example, played by banks that issue letters of credit and guarantee payment for product delivery.

(d) Enforcement is also assisted by prior agreement on an adjudicator. Adjudication means that an independent person or organization is asked to look into a conflict and to give a verdict, although this is not binding on either party. Thus, Chambers of Commerce may be designated in a contract to step in to adjudicate in the case of disputes over contract fulfilment. To enhance confidence in contract fulfilment further, contracts can even provide for the stronger form of compulsory arbitration, a provision that binds the disputing parties to accept the third party's verdict.

(e) Contract enforcement in certain trading environments may depend on a third party, who enters as a directly involved intermediary: the middleman or intermediary whom we mentioned in the preceding section. Middlemen conduct back-to-back transactions on their own account. Apart from helping with information search, they fulfil the important role of offering trust in contract fulfilment. They tend to be well known and well established in their line of business and have a reputation to lose. They thus offer themselves as 'hostages' to both sides of a deal, which constitutes a credible commitment. Middlemen can thus remedy general institutional deficiencies, for example when legal guarantees are underdeveloped and judicial law enforcement is corrupt or costly.

The credibility of middlemen can be strengthened even further, if they form an association that offers a collective guarantee for the performance of their members. Such group guarantees may derive from shared family or racial bonds (the Chinese, Jewish and Indian Marwari traders in various parts of the world), from formal professional associations (like the merchants of the Hanseatic League in northern Europe in the Middle Ages), or from mutual-insurance contracts among middlemen (which was, for example, part of the beginning of Lloyds' Insurance in London and which in many countries is still part of bank insurance). Individual middlemen, who fail to fulfil their obligations, face the penalty of ostracism: exclusion from the business network by the other middlemen who know them. If the sanction of ostracism is to work, the group has to be relatively small and mutually dependent on a network of ongoing transactions (Landa, 1994).[5]

These institutional provisions are internal to society. They work with effective sanctions that are not dependent on any government action. Most of today's trade, including world trade and international capital flows, depends on such more or less formal, but internal sanctions. Such internal institutions are effective, flexible and relatively cheap to operate. Societies that cultivate these mechanisms therefore enjoy competitive advantages over societies where self-enforcement is weak.

KEY CONCEPTS

Eminent domain is a legal doctrine under which political authorities may, under certain conditions, confiscate private property rights; in most civilized countries, the powers of government to take private property are strictly circumscribed and expropriated owners have to be justly compensated. Loose interpretations of eminent domain lead to an erosion of property rights and consequent losses in long-term dynamic efficiency.

Self-enforcing contracts provide for credible commitments. They rely on devices that ensure contract fulfilment without (costly) formal enforcement despite ever-present temptations to shirk contractual obligations. Some such devices are tit-for-tat, the creation of a reputation, the provision of a security (offering hostages) and reliance on an intermediary to make contractual commitments more credible.

Middlemen are persons or organizations that mediate between ultimate buyers and sellers. They have the functions of reducing information costs for end buyers and sellers and of enhancing trust. In this way, they trade in environments where impersonal institutions are deficient. They tend to vanish when institutions improve information flows and trust. Middlemen thus often help to remedy general institutional deficiencies, such as legal insecurity or high information costs.

An **adjudicator** or **mediator** is an independent person or organization that passes judgments on contested aspects of contract execution, but whose recommendations are not binding.

An **arbitrator** is an independent person or organization that passes judgments on contested aspects of contract execution, whose decision is binding for the two contracting parties. In some legal systems, the law allows appeals to public courts to challenge private arbitrators, in other systems people can contractually bind themselves to accept the verdict of private arbitrators as final.

Merchant (or bourgeois) virtues, such as honesty, punctuality, a high payments morale, reliability and flexibility in conflict, are internal institutions of capitalist society that enhance confidence in contract fulfilment and hence the efficient operation of the market economy. They constitute a valuable, intangible capital asset of a community.

External back-ups: the judiciary

In many cases, the self-enforcement of contracts is supplemented by external institutions (legislation and government regulations) which rely on public enforcement organizations: the judiciary, the police, inspectors, and prisons. Rulers and parliaments have tended to offer themselves as credible third parties to ensure contract fulfilment, as we saw in Section 5.3. They developed formal contract law and created specialist arbitrators (commercial courts), which often enjoy scale economies (North and Thomas, 1973; Rosenberg and Birdzell, 1986). External enforcement mechanisms may thus enhance the confidence of contract partners. They also may reduce the information and contract-negotiation costs of the trade by providing standardized conditions, for example a standard model contract for real-estate sales or work contracts. However, heavy reliance on external litigation can weaken the internal institutions, which tend to be cheaper and more flexible. Litigious societies – such as the United States – develop large and sophisticated networks of arbitration experts who have a self-interest in fostering disagreements and complicating conciliation. After all, they derive their incomes from it. This conflict plays an important part in the often-heard criticism of the heavy reliance on business lawyers and the cost that this creates to business in the United States, as compared with conditions in East Asian countries such as Japan, where heavy reliance on internal institutions and ready recourse to simple external institutions contains the costs of doing business. For the United States, it has been estimated that (in the 1980s) "each additional lawyer who is churned out by American law schools reduces the level of GDP by $2.5 million, a figure far greater than the present discounted value of that lawyer's earnings, substantial though they may be" (Magee et al., 1989, p. 17). Irrespective of the precise methodology in arriving at this estimate, it indicates the economy-wide transaction cost advantage of an institutional system that relies primarily on spontaneous self-enforcement.

7.5 The consequences of capitalism

On the early history of property rights

The creation of identifiable and protected property rights was the most important invention of the neolithic revolution, which probably began in the Middle East (northern Mesopotamia) about 12,000 years ago and soon thereafter in the Far East (northeast Thailand). At that time, agriculture (sowing and harvesting, rather than simply gathering wild seeds and tubers) and animal husbandry were invented. Humans turned from being opportunistic exploiters of nature to wealth creators using physical assets for production. It is not imaginable that these important technical revolutions could have taken place without the respect for and, if necessary, the protection of the exclusive use of land and animals by the owners. For all we know, property in Paleolithic hunter-gatherer societies was much more limited, if it existed at all. There is evidence that possessions were under constant challenge in those societies, much like animals possess an item of food until a stronger rival takes it away. The notion that 'good fences make good neighbours' was certainly not widely accepted before the neolithic revolution. Then, assets which had previously been under the vague collective control of a tribe (or the chiefs and elders in command) were assigned more clearly to individuals or family groups. Once people had control of their property and its benefits, they were better motivated to make use of their assets by toiling, labouring and experimenting with them, precisely because they could have confidence to appropriate the rewards of their efforts and their risk taking. Private property rights thus are one of the very foundations of civilization (Radnitzky, 1987; Bauer and Sen, 2004; Clark, 2007).

In subsequent ages, lawgivers refined and codified existing property rights (Benson, 1995). They often drew on already-existing internal institutions in society; they did not invent property laws. In this respect, the dictum applies that "law is older than legislation" (Hayek, 1973, p. 72). In the European tradition, it was above all the Romans who most clearly distinguished between mere possession of an asset and genuine ownership. They designed private law rules, which allowed owners to retain property titles while ceding possession and assigning certain rights of property use to others, for example by hiring or renting an asset (Némo, 2006). They also laid down legal rules which dealt with disputes over property use and obliged those who harmed others by their property uses to privately compensate them (torts). The Romans also regulated certain uses of property, which might conflict with the interest of others and put in place arbitration and adjudication mechanisms to settle conflicts in a predictable and non-violent manner. Thus, a clear basis of legal rules was created so that exclusive property rights could be divided and traded by private agreement and at low cost. Rome prospered and Roman law became the basis of Western civilization.

The emergence of capitalism

For most of human history, private property was of course not strictly respected. Thieves, as well as rulers and other groups with violence potential, tended to impose capricious levies on property-owning citizens or arbitrarily confiscated whatever assets they were able to grasp. This has often made it necessary for owners to hide their assets even if this complicated or even negated its use. After the Dark Ages in Europe, effective governments again began to protect private property more systematically. The rulers of the small, open European states, who acted opportunistically, were often confronted with an exodus of capital, propertied people and merchant-entrepreneurs to other, safer jurisdictions. Some jurisdictions began to enhance property rights protection and to encourage free markets in which property rights could be traded; they promoted contract enforcement through codifying the law and setting up effective tribunals. Taxation was made orderly and transparent. It was subjected to the law. Jurisdictions such as Venice, Florence, Genoa, later Portugal, Nuremberg, the Netherlands, and England gained from the influx of capital and enterprise, so that their trade and their revenues grew. Jurisdictions that gave property good institutional protection thus flourished, whereas states that did not became poorer. The success stories were imitated so that the protection of property rights by governments spread through much of Western Europe. The princes of course often resented the loss of power to mere merchants, but had little option but to respect private property rights (Weber, 1995/1927; Jones, 2003/1981; Rosenberg and Birdzell, 1986; also see Section 12.1). In the twentieth century, property rights protection had spread to many non-European economies.

CH 7 – CASE ONE

Max Weber on the conditions for the rise of capitalism

It seems appropriate to mention the conditions identified by German sociologist and economic historian Max Weber, for the emergence of modern capitalist business – and subsequently the industrial revolution, which capitalism built. Weber, a pioneer of the study of the rise of capitalism, stated that business enterprises had emerged as a specific type of economic organization when the following six conditions were fulfilled:

1. Physical resources could be appropriated by organizations that were recognized as separate legal entities (in other words: property rights of firms were respected and protected).
2. Firms were able to operate freely in markets (free entry, competition and free exit were safeguarded).
3. Organizations used proper accounting methods to support rational calculus as a guide to what it should and should not do (in other words, business leaders made rational calculations and genuine market prices made rational economic calculus possible).
4. The law and other institutions surrounding business firms became reliable and predictable (the rule of law, including commercial law, prevailed).

CH 7 – CASE ONE *(continued)*

5.	Labour was free, that is, people were free to appropriate the returns from their labour (sovereignty of the individual and free labour markets, that is, the end of slavery, indentured labour and bondage).

6.	Commercialization was possible (property rights became alienable, that is, it could be sold to others) and companies could be financed by raising capital through the issue of joint-stock shares (creation of a share market).

Only when the appropriate institutional framework surrounding the modern capitalist business firm is ensured, can business organizations operate effectively. Violations of alienable property rights, lawlessness and impediments to competition do not necessarily make it impossible to run capitalist businesses, but they undermine their effectiveness in generating innovation and aggregate growth.

Weber's (historic) analysis thus highlights the interdependence between the framework of institutional conditions and the performance of firms and entire economies (Weber, 1995/1927, pp. 275–278).

As mentioned in Chapter 2, the emergence of the rules that allowed the rise of capitalism was explained more recently by British-Australian economic historian Eric L. Jones, when he contrasted the industrial revolution in northwest Europe with the experience of China, by the year 800AD a technically well developed country, as well as other huge, but closed Asian economies. There, the rulers retained unchecked despotic and arbitrary powers to confiscate property, since capital owners and others in these huge empires were not able to emigrate to neighbouring jurisdictions. The experience of Christopher Columbus, who went from one court of Europe to another with his plan to sail west to India, could not have been replicated in China. As a matter of fact, the long-distance maritime ventures of Chinese admiral Cheng Ho, who had sailed as far as East Africa in the fifteenth century, simply stopped when the Imperial court issued an edict to discontinue all exploration!

The superior technology and organizational skills of the Chinese thus did not translate into a self-sustaining industrial revolution. China was a state ruled by a small elite which taxed the peasantry, treating it 'as its fowl and fish', that is, taking as much revenue as they pleased, or managed to extract arbitrary revenues without triggering too many peasant uprisings (Jones et al., 1994). The rulers could persist with an exploitative mentality; they were not induced to cultivate the common wealth. Only in periods when official confiscation was constrained and was subject to some rules, such as during the Sung dynasty (960-1279), did the Chinese economy flourish. The lack of order and confidence, and the practice of arbitrary official confiscation, therefore discouraged investment in industry and enterprise (Jones, 2003/1981). This historic comparison confirms that the institutional protection of private property and its uses is essential to triggering and sustaining economic growth.

The central importance of property rights was discovered by the philosopher-economists of the Scottish Enlightenment. In 1739, David Hume wrote in his *Treatise on Human Nature*: "Property must be stable and be fixed by general rules. Though in one instance the public be the sufferer, this momentary ill is amply compensated by the steady prosecution of the rule and by the peace and order which it establishes in society" (Hume, 1965/1786). Hume, Adam Smith and other writers of the Scottish Enlightenment understood that exclusivity is necessary to make the system work in the interest of the maximum number of people. They also focused on the basic economic freedoms of autonomous property use and castigated public monopolies and the political protection of private privilege. Reflecting these considerations, the US Constitution protected property explicitly against arbitrary confiscation. These protections were later emulated in many other constitutions around the world – at least the wording, though not necessarily the spirit.

Capitalism: community consequences of property rights

The historic experience has shown, time and again, that private property and autonomy have a number of distinct advantages that transcend the individual. Admittedly, property owners act in their self-interest, but they produce by those very actions side effects that benefit others. In the real world, economic systems are, of course, never pure, in that they are based exclusively on private property rights and private autonomy in disposing property. They do not work perfectly. But a solid case can be made that a system based largely on widely distributed property rights and the individual autonomy to use and dispose of them as the individual sees fit (economic freedom) tends to have a number of (unintended) beneficial consequences for the community.

Arguably the two most important consequences of a properly working capitalist system are that it helps to control individual actors, including those with power, and that it gives everyone incentives to make active use of property and knowledge – including by stimulating the creation and testing of valuable information, in short by leading to prosperity. Respect for, and protection of, property rights is beneficial in that it channels entrepreneurship, human energy, creativity and rivalry into constructive and peaceful directions. Wars or theft only divert enterprising spirits into zero- or negative-sum games, whereas the protection of private property rights facilitates numerous positive-sum games (Tullock, 1967; Baumol, 1990). These positive-sum games add up to overall economic growth and make it easier for people to realize their aspirations.

The central importance of a capitalist order for productivity was dramatically, though unintentionally demonstrated by the Russian Revolution of 1917. The centralized and still backward Russian economy had first been wrecked by a war that the Tsarist troops were losing and then by the Leninist *coup d'état*, after which private property was abolished, markets were prohibited and money done away with in a wave of run-away inflation. In its place, the Bolshevik leadership introduced 'War Communism', a system of forced labour and brutal confiscation of agricultural produce by the *Cheka*, the Soviet secret police (Malia, 1994 pp. 109–138). "[B]y 1921 the output of mines and factories had fallen to 21 percent of the 1913 level and ... agricultural production was down to about 38 percent of normal" (*idem*, p. 143). The total collapse of this ruleless economy forced the communists to introduce a partial market system and a new (New Economic Policy). It nevertheless replaced many market incentives for voluntary production by central control and sheer coercion, and led to never ending penury (Section 13.1).

As already noted, a second important consequence of private property rights is that they give material substance to individual freedom. When government agents show an inclination to limit individual freedom, protected private property serves as the most potent bulwark for individual freedom (Mises, 1994/1920; Friedman, 1962, chapter 1; Seldon, 1990, chapters 7 and 8). In societies, which are made up of 'citizens of property', the people strive to buttress their economic liberties by democratic and legal constraints on the rulers. As long as people are in control of their material resources, they enjoy considerable autonomy to proceed freely in civil and political affairs. The interaction between private property and freedom was evident in Europe and North America over the last two centuries and was well understood by the early protagonists of individual liberty. This connection has now become equally evident in a growing number of capitalist countries in East Asia where the rising middle class demands the rule of law and democracy, as well as economic liberties and economic autonomy (recent examples are the new democracies of South Korea, Taiwan, Thailand and Indonesia, with a number of neighbouring countries beginning to follow the same path, see Chapter 13; Scully, 1991, 1992; Gwartney and Lawson, *passim*).[6]

A third welcome community consequence of the institutions that guarantee private property is that owners are normally induced to economize on resources. People tend to conserve valuable assets if they own them and can appropriate the benefits for themselves and their heirs. When people own depleting assets, they control the rate of depletion and make the best long-term use of their scarce assets. The fundamental fact that ownership encourages careful stewardship was already known to the Greek philosopher Aristotle (384-322BC) who wrote: "What is common to many is taken least care of, for all men have greater regard for what is their own than what they possess in common with others" (cited in Gwartney, 1991, p. 67). Empirical studies that we already referred to have shown that – in modern mass societies – conservation of assets, including of natural resources, is greatly assisted by clearly defined property rights. In small, traditional communities, internal institutions that are applied informally often suffice to conserve commonly owned property, such as natural resources, at least as long as population pressures on existing resources are not high (Ostrom, 1990; 2005). But in big communities private property seems often better suited to nature conservation.

Wise stewardship of scarce natural resources can thus be promoted by permitting private owners to claim exclusive property rights to natural assets, where this is feasible. Successes in nature conservation through this procedure can be observed in numerous privately owned conservation areas in several continents. Depleting fish stocks, once they have been turned into the exclusive property of private owners, have, for example, increased because the owner could use the offspring as a return on what is now their property (Anderson, in Block, (ed.) 1990, pp. 147–150; Anderson and Leal, 1997; Wills, 1997; Anderson and McChesney, 2003). This point was for example demonstrated convincingly in Zimbabwe after property rights in (endangered) African elephants were assigned to local villagers. That led quickly to an end to poaching and a big increase in elephant numbers (see Box 7.2).

In many instances, conservation has a better chance when property rights in natural resources are made tradable, so that people who wish to make long-term investments in material resources can get access and have a better chance of reaping long-term material rewards (Gwartney, 1991).

CH 7 – CASE TWO

Property rights and nature conservation: African elephants

While elephant populations have declined throughout most of Africa, the conservation policies of some southern African countries have been . . . successful . . . In 1900, Zimbabwe's number of elephants was estimated approximately 5000. Today it is estimated to be 43,000.

Wildlife is a continual source of danger to rural populations . . . During certain months of the growing season, villagers have to spend valuable time protecting their crops against marauding wildlife. If a villager's maize field is destroyed by an elephant, he will not be compensated. If a family is unfortunate enough to experience such a disaster, it may well face starvation. Under such conditions, it is not surprising that poaching flourishes.

[I]n 1989, local Zimbabweans were [made] responsible for reporting poachers. [Institutional changes were introduced that gave] . . . local people . . . [the right to] manage the wildlife in their area . . . [The programme] gave landholders the responsibility for the conservation and use of wild animals on their lands. Some predicted that this would result in the widespread destruction of wild animals. Instead, the opposite has occurred.

The effects [of this institutional innovation] . . . were felt much more slowly on communal lands . . . [But in 1989], the Government gave the district councils . . . the right to manage their own resources. The main objective . . . is the strictly controlled use of wildlife to create income . . . [Now] local people are once again benefiting from their wildlife . . . They are receiving cash dividends from the proceeds of wildlife management and being compensated if their crops are damaged . . . Meat is distributed at cost price . . . The main source of income at present is from safari hunting . . . Before the ban [on ivory trade] ivory from the shoot was also sold by the communities.

[Local] support for the scheme is . . . strong . . . new skills and techniques acquired by locals enable them to carry out some of the more fundamental management tasks . . . the project now looks as if it may offer real long-term hope for the ecological and economic future of these communities.

Bradstock, A. 'Community is Key to Conservation', *Geographic Magazine* (Dec.) 1990, p. 17.

Private property promotes nature conservation by leaving the decisions to dispersed private actors. If private owners, for reasons of their own, decide to prefer short-term exploitation, this may inflict long-term (inter-temporal) external costs. Thus, monocultures or big concentrations of tourism development may well cause long-term damage which nature cannot regenerate and subsequent generations cannot repair. In these cases, public policy may have to step in, but this of course presupposes that policy makers know better – and have the motivation to attain outcomes which achieve (someone's) nature conservation goals better – than the decentralized judgments of different, self-interested resource owners.

The importance of private property in the conservation of nature has also been made clear by the track record of the socialist countries of Eastern Europe and East Asia. The politicians and bureaucrats entrusted with the stewardship of collectively owned natural resources obviously saw no direct incentive to conserve natural assets, but they could expect political and career rewards for resource depletion in order to meet production targets. Since the natural assets belonged to no-one in particular, no-one defended them against excessive exploitation.

A further important consequence of widely held private property is that it tends to enhance peace and social harmony by preventing or defusing material conflicts. When people have no property to lose, they engage more readily in confrontation and destructive conflict, whereas property-tied people risk much if they tolerate a chaotic society. When property is owned widely and the owners have acquired the habit of cultivating what is theirs by long-term maintenance, investment and learning, the majority has an interest in keeping the peace, internationally and internally. Popular notions that capitalists are warmongers may have some historic foundation in regimes where property was held by the few who hoped to gain from armaments or conquest. But it does not apply to nations where property rights are widely distributed (Gartzke in Gwartney and Lawson, 2005, pp. 29–44).

•••

Although the above-mentioned advantages of private property have been evident and capitalist production has been at the heart of the industrial revolution that eventually lifted most out of traditional poverty, capitalism has always been under attack. Both intellectuals who dislike the dynamic changes wrought by dispersed, self-interested creativity and leaders and commentators who believe in the superiority of central *ex ante* coordination (that is, by a plan that they have designed), tend to reject capitalism. Fact-based analysis has rarely informed the debate about the merits or otherwise of capitalism. Karl Marx became prominent in the nineteenth century with his prediction of the inevitable demise of capitalism. That prediction not only turned out to be somewhat premature, but most Marx-inspired designs of the socialist alternative of organizing economic life have since been thrown 'into the dustbin of history' (Section 13.1). This has, however, not stopped Marxist philosophers like Herbert Marcuse and collectivists like Peter Singer rejecting capitalism for the reason, among others, that it generates too much wealth and income in private hands and that it empowers individuals, including more recently producers in far-away places who benefit from globalization (Hessen, 2008).

In the final analysis, one's attitude to capitalism will be determined by whether one judges a rule system by its results in terms of the fundamental values discussed in Chapter 4, or whether one prefers collective community life and the power that collective controls bestow on political and intellectual elites.

What the long-running controversy of capitalism versus socialism makes clear is that institutional design is not value-free, but is inevitably enmeshed in passionate argument about values and the eternal debate about what constitutes the good society.

One must of course not conclude that dispersed private property is a panacea for all human problems, only that it draws on the knowledge and motivation of many people and can achieve community consequences that the majority of citizens find beneficial (Epstein, 2007).

CH 7 – CASE THREE

How secure is private property? An international comparison

Classical liberal lawyers and economists emphasized the crucial importance of private property rights being securely protected from private theft and illegitimate, arbitrary public taking or abridgement. This is now again realized, not least in poorer and less developed countries, as well as by internationally mobile capital owners and entrepreneurs. In response to these insights an international grouping of independent think tanks and research organizations has compiled estimates of how well private property in physical and intellectual assets is protected in 129 countries around the world (Jackson et al., 2011).

It is worth noting that, as of 2011, an average of the 20 per cent of nations where private property was best protected had a per-capita income of US$38,350, more than double the income level of the next quintile ($18,701), about four times in the third quintile ($9316),

---

CH 7 – CASE THREE *(continued)*

eight times on average in the fourth and fifth quintiles of countries ($5065) where individual property is least protected (average income in that group: $4785).

Uncertainty about property rights, for example, because politically opportunistic environmental regulations take individual rights away, is therefore a handicap to economic growth and a contribution to political tension.

We shall return to the evidence in Chapter 14.

7.6   Institutions, which secure the services of money and avert financial crises

Money and the division of labour

Money is a device that allows enormous savings of transaction costs. It is therefore of great importance to the division of labour and the functioning of the exchange economy. Money serves as a generally accepted means of exchange. It is also a unit in which assets, liabilities and transactions are measured and accounted for. And it can be used as a store of value (Brunner and Meltzer, 1971). These three basic functions of money are often tied to physical money symbols, which come in many different shapes and forms – cowry shells, bits of metal, pieces of paper, and a debit entry in a bank's accounts. However, money fulfils its functions only if its creation is constrained, so that the stability of its value in terms of a basket of goods is secured (controlled money supply). In the case of money symbols that were taken from nature to be monetized (outside money, such as gold), natural availability controls the supply. In the case of money, which is based on credit (inside money), the control of supply depends on institutional constraints on the provision of central-bank money (a form of outside money).

Economists have long realized how important the institutions that underpin the stability of money are to the proper functioning of economic life – indeed the study of money, and what it takes to make it function properly, was one of the earliest concerns of institutional economics. Inflation, caused by increases in money supply bigger than the volume of production, not only expropriates the holders of monetary assets, but also distorts capital and investment structures. For a while, it appears to enhance many lines of business, but – like heroin – inflation eventually is destructive of prosperity and security.

To explain the importance of money, we have to start by considering multiple, bilateral barter, that is, a system in which a person can trade items of property only if he can find exchange partners who want some of the specific assets, which he wishes to dispose of and is willing to exchange them for specific assets that he is offering. This creates an enormous information problem, as soon as the trading community covers more than a few and a very limited number of commodities. Most of the transactions that we carry out would be prohibitively expensive without money. Barter also causes storage costs. These costs reduce the gains from trade and therefore limit the division of labour. Clower, in his analysis of money (1969, p. 25), makes the point with a colourful example quoted from British economist Stanley Jevons (1835–1882). Obviously, a certain Mademoiselle Zélie, a celebrated nineteenth century singer from Paris, was on a worldwide tour when she entertained the Polynesian natives in the Society Islands with her arias, in exchange for which they gave her pigs, fowl, coconuts and fruit. As Mademoiselle could not consume the payment herself and found the information costs of identifying the demand for pigs, fowl and fruit in the local market overwhelming, she stored the proceeds from her concert, soon to discover that the animals had to be fed the fruit.

When a widely accepted intermediate means of exchange – money – is introduced into an erstwhile barter system, the information, storage and other transaction costs are greatly reduced. It is possible to shift from direct, bilateral exchanges to indirect exchanges through the intermediation of money. This economizes on transaction costs by splitting a direct, bilateral barter transaction into two separate transactions with money serving as an intermediate medium of exchange (indirect exchange). The potential for gains from the division of labour is greatly enhanced. If necessary, money can also serve as a temporary store of value (Brunner and Meltzer, 1971). In a world of perfect information with zero transaction costs, as assumed by orthodox neoclassical economics, there is no need for money. Everyone would know all possible barter opportunities. It is only the knowledge problem that makes money a useful, indeed a crucial institution in facilitating the division of labour. Likewise, the need for financial intermediation (by banks, insurance companies, money markets and the like) cannot be understood if we assume perfect knowledge.[7]

Price level stability

It is also essential that the value of money – in terms of a representative basket of goods and services – does not fluctuate unpredictably. If institutions are in place that create confident expectations of a stable value of money, business lenders can concentrate on producing and marketing their products, investing, innovating production methods and saving costs. They will then interpret movements in individual prices in factor and product markets as signals of changing scarcities and adjust their plans accordingly. They will, for example, trust that a factor price increase signals that they should economize on that particular production factor. A product price increase signals that buyers want more of a particular product, and that they should think about expanding supply. In other words, if institutions safeguard price-level stability, the 'radio traffic' of price signals sends clear messages. If, on the other hand, the ground rules fail to secure stable money and people experience erratic variations of the price level, then producers cannot know clearly what the price variations they are observing mean: Is a price increase just part of general inflation, or is there a new market opportunity? The radio traffic is – so to speak – overlaid by static. Communication and coordination become more difficult and less reliable. Producers get distracted from their core business and have to risk guesses about future inflation, a task for which they are ill prepared. They may divert scarce time and resources from their specialization in production into asset speculation. In the longer term, inflation therefore always undermines economic growth, destroys jobs and redistributes incomes and wealth from net savers to the (often well-connected and more affluent) net borrowers (Friedman and Friedman, 1980). Consequently, the end result of poor monetary institutions is a lesser provision of goods and services and therefore a poorer economic outcome for the community at large. Moreover, it can have serious consequences for security, social peace and stability.

Limitation of money supply

The most fundamental aspect of money, if it is to fulfil its functions effectively, is that its supply must be limited and seen to be limited and that money supply does not fluctuate unpredictably over time.[8] Only then will all members of the public readily accept effectively valueless money tokens in exchange for their work effort or their property rights. The only reason why money is accepted to settle contractual claims is that everyone assumes that everyone else will also accept it. When this assumption proves wrong in times of inflation, money is soon replaced or at least loses some of its effectiveness.

Outside money supply is – as already noted – limited when a material, which cannot be readily multiplied by human effort, is used as the money token. Thus, cowry shells were money in the remote mountains of Papua New Guinea, but of course not in seaside communities. Rare metals, such as gold and silver, were turned into money. Money can also be created inside a community, for example when members of society create credits that are monetized, that is, are accepted as highly liquid means to settle debts. This means that the users of these credits (inside money) have to trust that they can be turned into outside money at any time, for example physical gold or central-bank money. As long as creditors keep a reputation of converting these monetized credits into outside money, the credit chain holds. But such trust depends on institutions. If the issuers of paper (or fiat) money break the rules and supply excessive quantities of money ('quantitative easing'), the services of money as a unit of account, store of value and means of payment deteriorate and, in the extreme, disappear (see Box 7.4).

H 7 – CASE FOUR

The disappearance of the Cook Island dollar

The small South Pacific Island territory of Cook Islands (2006: 19,500 inhabitants), a self-governing democracy freely associated with New Zealand, issued its own currency, the Cook Island dollar at a par with the New Zealand dollar. However, in 1994 after a phase of profligate spending, the Cook Islands government appeared to be issuing excessive supplies of the currency to cover its budget deficits. The two locally operating commercial banks refused to accept Cook Island dollars as payments into savings accounts and for transfer overseas. Depositors had to produce New Zealand dollars to have their accounts credited and payments made.

The Cook Island currency disappeared promptly from circulation. The government slid into a budget crisis and near-bankruptcy, as soon as its deficits could no longer be covered by supplying its own money and foreign aid donors refused to bail them out.

Source: *The Australian*, 13 March 1996, p. 11

The disappearance of the Zimbawean Dollar

If there were an award for the world's worst economic policy, [Zimbabwe] might well have won it several times over the past decade. In particular, in 2008 and 2009, it experienced truly spectacular hyperinflation. Prices rose so fast that the central bank eventually printed 100 trillion-dollar notes for people to carry. The nation has since abandoned using its own currency.

Source: N.G. Mankiw, 'Four Nations, Four Lessons', *The New York Times*, 22 October 2011.

After the Mugabe regime of Zimbabwe confiscated farms owned by whites and repudiated its debts to the International Monetary Fund in the early 2000s, it printed money to finance its expenditures. Zimbabwe was to set a new world record in hyperinflation: Once a Zimbabwean dollar (ZWD) had been worth 1.59 US dollars. By November 2008, the ZWD had lost value by 89.7 sextillion (10^{21}) per cent. In December 2008, inflation accelerated

---

CH 7 – CASE FOUR *(continued)*

further with great speed to reach an unimaginable percentage rate (65 followed by 107 zeros).

The experience was preceded with the printing of ever-increasing quantities of Zimbabwean paper dollars to pay the salaries of the soldiers, policemen and bureaucrats that upheld President Mugabe's regime. Slashing three zeros from all banknotes and prices in 2006 and fixing certain prices in 2007, but persisting with the issue of more and more paper money by the Reserve Bank of Zimbabwe, made no difference to the dwindling of the value of Zimbabwean currency. Extreme shortages of basic food inflicted huge pain on the population and induced many to flee to neighbouring countries. By mid-2008, the printing presses were running out of paper and the Reserve Bank of Zimbabwe came up with a resource-saving innovation: it printed only one side of the new banknotes. At the same time, it announced plans to issue banknotes with a face value of Z$100 billion. Soon thereafter, it redenominated the currency by deleting ten zeros, so that a Z$100 billion note became a new Z$1 note. As underlying constraints on supplying money were not changed and the public had lost all confidence in the ZWD, the Reserve Bank had to issue new Z$100,000,000 banknotes and a few days thereafter Z$200,000,000 banknotes. The government tried to control inflation by limiting daily bank withdrawals to Z$500,000, that is, US¢25 per day.

In early 2009, some one thousand shops were licensed to transact business in foreign currency. Later the by now widespread practice of using foreign currencies (South African rand and US dollars) was made legal. By then, even street vendors refused to accept local currency, since counting the banknotes was becoming too cumbersome. In April 2009, the government suspended the use of its own currency, but did nothing to heal the economy, which was destroyed by hyperinflation.

Sources: Hanke, S.H. 'New Hyperinflation Index Puts Zimbabwe Inflation at 89.7 Sextillion Percent', http://www.cato.org/zimbabwe and Wikipedia http://en.wikiperdia.org/wiki/ Hyperinflation_in_Zimbabwe, accessed 9 February 2011).

Numerous rulers have found it advantageous to enter the business of supplying money and imbuing it with their authority. King Croesus of Lydia in Asia Minor (sixth century BC) is credited with having invented gold coins, pieces of metal certified by his stamp to be of standard quality and weight. This reduced the transaction costs of payments (better information by standardization). Like many other rulers, the Ming Emperors of China issued money. Their innovation during the Great War period (1368–98) was to imprint pieces of silk and paper with the unmistakable warning that "he who imitates the Emperor's money will be executed". Nowadays, governments have created central banks that issue money and are meant to control its supply lest its volume grows at an inflationary rate.

Political rulers (and anyone else who issues money) enjoy a profit, called seigniorage, that is, they reap material gains from turning a material of lesser value (copper, silk, paper and so on) into money tokens that people hold. This means that the issuers of money enjoy credit at zero interest cost. Seigniorage thus amounts to an incentive to issue more money. It is only the long-term consequence of a particular type of money being rejected that acts as a brake. Since the public cannot do without money, rejection is made much easier if the public can choose between alternative money assets to pay for exchanges, to store value and to use it as a general measuring rod. Where legislators prohibit the use of alternative moneys, they claim an influential monopoly and deprive the public of an important economic freedom. Competition among emitters – whether private or public – of money is an essential characteristic of a good monetary constitution. Whether money should be de-nationalized altogether to enhance the responsibility of central banks for the quality of the money they issue is largely an empirical question (Hayek, 1978a; Vaubel, 1985). It has, however, also to be realized that competition among moneys imposes transaction costs: users have to verify the quality of the assets (a big problem in the European Middle Ages, when the metal content of coins was often adulterated) and have to deal with changing rates of exchange between different monetary standards (again, European history illustrates the information costs of ceaseless changes in the gold-to-silver price ratio). In any event, competition among emitters of moneys is key to limiting excessive 'seigniorage harvesting' and the consequent decay of the currency, which then inflicts huge losses on the savers among the population.

The institutional constraints on the opportunistic expansion of government-made money supply have frequently been weak. Opportunistic kings and other agents of government diluted the gold and silver value of coins by adding cheaper metals to finance their expenditures more easily, and the first experiment with paper money by the Ming Emperors ended in destructive run-away inflation and subsequent economic and cultural decline.

It is therefore a great priority for public policy to create effective institutional constraints that prevent the inflationary expansion of money supply, in order to control obviously massive temptations to do otherwise. In the case of credit-based (inside) money, now the prevalent form of money around the world, there are essentially three institutional mechanisms:

(a) Those central banks, which are licensed to print money, are subjected to transparent rules and are made independent of the vote-seeking agents of government and parliamentarians who are naturally subject to the usual temptations of political opportunism. An outstanding example of this was the German central bank which – given earlier experiences with run-away inflation – was made independent of detailed government directives in the 1950s and which was committed by legislation to a policy of providing stable money. In another case, that of New Zealand, the central bank is subject to clear-cut general instructions. The *Reserve Bank of New Zealand Act* assigns only two roles to the central bank, namely; (i) to operate money supply so as to keep consumer price inflation within limits that are stipulated by periodic contracts between the government and the central-bank governor, and (ii) to supervise the commercial banks so that they comply with certain standards of prudential behaviour. Since the 1980s, many other governments around the world have made central banks independent of political directives from the government or the finance minister of the day.

(b) Those who issue money are subjected to open competition with other money issuers. If one central bank expands the quantity of its money too rapidly, alert investors will shift their portfolios out of this currency into others. Exchange-rate movements then discipline money suppliers who fail to stick to the rule of supplying stable money. In the case of competing central banks, the institutional framework to ensure competitive discipline consists of the free convertibility of the currency and freely floating exchange rates. Exchange-rate movements quickly signal the judgments of alert financial markets; this should have immediate controlling feedbacks into the conduct of the central bank.

(c) In reality, however, massive political influence is often brought to bear even on formally independent central banks. Moreover, supposedly independent central-bank boards are often staffed by handpicked supporters of the political elites. Adherence to price-level targets has often been haphazard, too. If in addition, the leading central banks coalesce into de facto cartels (for example, political associations, such as the G-20 Group of the world's leading economies), the self-correcting mechanisms described in paragraph (b) no longer work. Political initiatives to expand aggregate demand by monetary easing in a recession will then eventually lead to a concerted, excessive inflation of national money supplies.

Slogans such as 'quantitative easing' and 'recapitalizing the banks' are used to describe how central banks are directed to buy up untenable government debts. Eventually, the resulting expansion of money supply is bound to cause price-level inflation. Scarce resources are then misdirected, monetary assets are devalued, and capital structures are distorted to the detriment of long-run prosperity (Hayek, 2008/1933, Chapters I and II; 1935). Given these uncertainties about a stability-oriented monetary constitution and actual experiences since the onset of the 'global financial crisis' in 2008, public money creation by central banks may be supplemented or replaced either by a return to an external monetary standard, such as the gold standard, or by competing private banks supplying money assets – the denationalization of money, as Hayek called it (Hayek, 1978a).

Neither system is unproblematic. Gold is costly to mine and refine and its supply may fluctuate with new discoveries and technical changes in mining. Competing private moneys would impose considerable information costs for ordinary users of the means of payments: Which issuing organization qualifies for top rating? How do holders of specific moneys find out that issuing organizations remain financially solid? In which of many alternative private currencies should long-term credit contracts be written? European monetary history of the Middle Ages and after is replete with examples of fraud by competing banks and high costs of assessing the quality of competing private moneys. However, the risk of such occasional mishaps may be preferable to the cost of a concerted push by a cartel such as the G-20 central banks to inflate the way out of an unsustainable fiscal and monetary situation.

Which of the above three institutions is more effective in securing the services of stable money depends on the costs of monitoring differing moneys and shifting between different monetary assets, as well as the likelihood or otherwise of central banks adhering to given institutional constraints, even when put under political pressure.

KEY CONCEPTS

By enabling direct, bilateral exchange (barter) to be converted into indirect, multilateral exchanges, **money** saves information (transaction) costs and thereby allows huge gains from the division of labour to be realized, making many erstwhile impossible property uses rewarding. Money serves as a means of exchange (or payment), as a unit of account to express values of assets, liabilities and transactions, and as a store of value over time.

Money can only perform its functions if its supply is credibly limited. In the case of paper money this requires institutions that prevent the opportunistic expansion of money supply. In addition, money suppliers can be disciplined by competition. Such competition requires convertibility and flexible exchange rates.

We have to distinguish the functions of money from the token or symbol to which it is attached. **Money symbols** may consist of physical items, such as gold, cowry shells, or banknotes issued by a central bank with a monopoly to issue legal tender. These come from outside the private community (**outside money**) and liabilities of reputed organizations, like banks, which gain acceptance as currency (**inside money**).

➡

←

Monetary stability is important to **credit**, the loaning of property rights for a fee. Credit is transacted in **capital markets** between savers (people who plan to accumulate positive net monetary assets) and borrowers (who plan to accumulate negative net monetary assets, typically for the purpose of investment in capital goods). In these markets, **financial intermediaries** operate to convey information, for example by creating a reputation and offering a reputation of their own to give savers the confidence to part with their assets in exchange for the payment of interest as a user fee.

The **denationalization of money** is a process whereby corrupted national, central-bank moneys are replaced by liquid instruments (banknotes) issued as bank liabilities by private banks of good repute and high financial quality. Private moneys may spread when national central banks are no longer protected from political influences, operate as cartels and unduly inflate money supplies.

Rules versus authorities in controlling money supply

The supply of money by a central bank can be steered by rules or by trusted authorities (Simons, 1948/1936). A money-supply rule might stipulate that the money volume can only be expanded each year by the projected rate of real economic growth plus the rate of unavoidable or tolerable inflation. A central bank that consistently adheres to this rule would probably stabilize the expansion path of national monetary demand: At times when demand expansion exceeds the growth of money supply, market interest rates rise, which curbs the increases in the demand for money. At times of demand expansion slower than predetermined money supply growth, interest rates drop, which stimulates money demand. This is an automatic stabilizer. Simons and many other economists prefer such rule-bound behaviour to putting our trust in a discretionary central-bank authority, which judges circumstances from time to time and acts according to its forecasts and judgments (or the directives of political opportunists, see the Zimbabwe case above). Simons knew that authorities may commit forecasting errors and may be subject to political directives and opportunism, so that adherence to a rule seemed, on balance, preferable in the conduct of monetary policy. By contrast, economists who are in a habit of assuming 'perfect knowledge' tend to argue for discretionary monetary policy. In recent decades, the discussion of 'rules versus authorities' in controlling money supply has received great attention and many monetary authorities have adopted policies, which tie monetary expansion to the growth of the gross national product or some similar measure. Being made formally independent of political directives from the government makes this easier. Subsiding high inflation rates since the early 1980s are testimony to the fact that control of money supply is effective in controlling price levels.

It is clear that money has a pervasive influence over economic coordination and that the internal and external institutions that rule a society are intimately tied to the monetary system which a community maintains. The Austrian-American economist Joseph Schumpeter famously stated in a German, posthumously published work that "all of a nation's conditions pertain to the condition of its monetary system" (our translation) (Schumpeter 1970, *Das Wesen des Geldes*, Göttingen, Germany: Vandenhoeck & Ruprecht). Indeed, monetary theory has been one of the key sources of institutional economics, and the insight that a monetary system can be foisted upon a society without regard to its traditional, internal institutions and values is neglected only to the peril of that society and the people who try to manage the money (Section 11.5).

To sum up, money only fulfils its functions properly if its supply is subject to constraints, either physical or institutional constraints. Throughout history, these constraints have unfortunately often been respected more by violation rather than adherence.

NOTES

1 Cited after W. Samuels 'Property', in Hodgson et al. (1994), p. 180.
2 The doctrine of self-ownership played a major role in the abolition of slavery. In the early decades of the nineteenth century, a major public debate raged between free-marketeers and economists in Britain, led by John Stuart Mill, Charles Darwin and Thomas Huxley, who advocated the freeing of all slaves, and 'humanitarians', such as historian Thomas Carlyle, journalist-writer Charles Dickens and poet Alfred Tennyson, who held that slaves needed a 'beneficent whip' (Levy, 2002). The economists and free-marketeers held that the backwardness of Africans was due to poor customs and laws, certainly not nature and race.
3 Official protections for the exclusive exploitation of knowledge, such as patents, tend to be unwieldy and costly to obtain. To appropriate the gains from new ideas, innovators dedicate much effort to embodying knowledge in devices that inhibit imitation. For example, new knowledge is built into mechanical or electronic contraptions that imitators cannot easily construct. Or companies who own intellectual knowledge refuse to hand out licenses, which might enable imitation later on, and instead insist on producing with that knowledge in their own plants.
4 As we shall see in Chapter 9, similar coordination costs arise when people interact economically within organizations. We shall call these costs 'organization costs'.
5 The reader may ask why middlemen, who fulfil such an important function in filling institutional gaps and in wealth-creation, are so frequently despised and prosecuted (Sowell, 1994, pp. 46-59). Their cultural or ethnic peculiarities seem an insufficient explanation. Rather, many middlemen have created monopolies and enticed national government leaders into closing off markets on their behalf, often exchanging licenses for lucrative kickbacks. This does not always protect middlemen from subsequent persecution by those same government leaders. The way to reduce the cost of middlemen is to enhance the institutional infrastructure, fostering universal institutions of a relatively impersonal market order, which is accessible to all, thus reducing the relative advantages of middlemen.
6 This is not to say that only electoral democracy is capable of protecting private property and autonomy. Some autocratic rulers have given effective protection to economic freedoms, including security of property rights from confiscation. The case of colonial Hong Kong comes to mind where private property has

been well protected (under British law and in a wide-open economy), with all the growth benefits that follow from this. But without electoral control, such protection is normally fragile, in particular when the rulers have the power to close the national economy (tariff protection, controls on capital flows and migration).

7 Social critics of the financial industry tend to assume (implicitly) perfect knowledge, and then of course fail to understand the information function of money and financial intermediation between savers and investors.

8 Tokens of money should have other useful attributes, namely that they are portable, homogeneous, recognizable, divisible and indestructible (Clower, (ed.) 1969, pp. 12–14).

8

The dynamics of competition

The focus of this chapter is on capitalism in action. It is about economic competition, the dynamic processes of market interaction among buyers and sellers. And if we hope to understand the market process, we must study the economic forces at work within a market economy, that is, the processes and not the state of affairs after these forces have done their job. Economic competition is a dynamic process that induces rival sellers (as well as rival buyers) to incur costs in searching for and testing new knowledge. Buyers and sellers then enter contracts to exchange property rights with each other, setting prices, which inform others. It is the buying and abstaining from buying by consumers on the market that directs the process of production and the distribution methods of the sellers. Through the loss signal, competition among property owners also contains inevitable errors.

As long as buyers are alert and incur transaction costs to inform themselves, the economic rivalry among suppliers stimulates product and process innovation. We will highlight the role of the enterprising supplier and the role of institutions supporting pioneers who test innovative ideas in the hope of a profit. We will also show that political interventions in competitive processes undercut competitive rivalry and hence the need to incur the costs of innovation.

Finally, we move beyond competition in a single market and look at the intensity of competition in entire economic systems. We shall find that competing entrepreneurs in one industry often create the conditions for commercial success in others, so that clusters of competing entrepreneurs help each other to innovate and be profitable. Competitive economies enjoy considerable economic and non-economic advantages: property owners are, time and again, challenged to employ their assets and search for knowledge, so that power is controlled and economic progress is pursued. Competition also controls economic and political power and makes economies more flexible and hence more stable in the face of changing events. It will therefore be argued that economic competition deserves promotion and protection.

> The monopolizer engrosseth to himself what should be free for all men . . . the monopolist that taketh away a man's trade, taketh away his life . . . all monopolies concerning trade and traffique are against the liberty and freedom.
>
> British lawyer Sir Edward Coke (1552-1634), cited after Walker (1988, pp. 111–112)

> The very industriousness of commercial life . . . eats away at grinding drudgery. Commercial life creates novel and enterprising ways of evading it, not only on assembly lines and in mills but in homes, too, and on farms.
>
> Jane Jacobs, *Systems of Survival* (1992)

> Capitalism is by nature a form or method of economic change . . . [It] never . . . can be stationary . . . The fundamental impulse that sets and keeps the capitalist engine in motion comes from the new consumers' goods, the new methods of production or transportation, the markets, the new forms of industrial organisation that capitalist enterprise creates.
>
> Joseph A. Schumpeter, *Capitalism, Socialism and Democracy* (1947)

8.1 Competition: rivalry and choice

Competition as a discovery procedure

Owners exchange their private property rights by voluntary contracts to put them to active uses. Thus, an owner of financial funds may have to acquire capital goods, labour services, the services of knowledgeable, skilled experts and raw materials to start producing. What sorts of uses owners can envisage for their property of course depends on their knowledge, which is – as we saw in Chapter 3 – constitutionally limited: Individuals have 'sideways uncertainty' about what others are doing and 'forward uncertainty' about what will happen in the future. As circumstances change, the stock of knowledge, which they acquired in the past, depreciates. Acquiring new, more up-to-date knowledge is costly and risky, because people have only a limited capacity to collect information and digest it in order to create new knowledge through reflection. Moreover, the process is liable to errors: What people perceive may be wrong, they may wrongly extrapolate from their knowledge of the past, they may predict certain consequences of their actions that prove to be incorrect, and they may face unforeseen difficulties in implementing their decisions to use their physical assets, labour and knowledge.

This raises three questions that go to the core of economics and should inform the design of public policy, namely:

(a) How can constitutional ignorance be reduced?
(b) How can useful knowledge be dispersed?
(c) How can knowledge use be controlled to ensure that errors are not perpetuated and the system is not destabilized?

The main point we will make in this chapter is that the competitive use of property rights by individual buyers and sellers promises the best solutions to these problems that mankind has yet discovered. Competition among property rights owners certainly offers on the whole better solutions than central planning and the imposition of someone's plans by a visible hand.

Economic competition is a dynamic-evolutionary process of human inter-action in which people are motivated to pursue their self-interest, because they are able to internalize the costs and benefits of property use. In the process, they benefit others as a by-product of their pursuit of self-interest. This interaction takes place in markets, which are meeting grounds of the buyers and sellers of closely substitutable goods and services (Figure 8.1). The process of interaction and exchange, in which people discover and test new knowledge, is called *catallaxis*. Whereas neoclassical economics focuses on scarcity and economizing, *catallaxis* stresses the dynamic dis-covery procedures – how people discover new wants and new means to satisfy them. The dollar prices established on the market, as we will see, are aids to the human mind and enable individuals to cope with their ignor-ance by providing both informational signals and behavioural incentives. The most immediate task of money prices is to signal relative scarcities to economic actors and to economize on the information they must utilize to shape their behaviour and coordinate it with that of others in the market system.

Typically, in most markets there are fewer buyers than sellers. Intending sellers rival with each other to position themselves advantageously for poten-tial exchanges with the buyers and incur transaction costs to do so. Likewise, intending buyers vie with other buyers to be well-positioned for contracts with suppliers; they, too, incur costs to inform and position themselves so they can strike advantageous deals. The sellers will try to offer better substi-tutes to what other sellers are offering, and entrepreneurial buyers will try to gain a competitive position that enables them to attract a choice of offers from sellers. The buyers thus rival with each other to find knowledge about better substitutes and exchange partners, as do the sellers. The alternative is what has been described as 'nightcap competition', the cozy continuation of the way suppliers have always made and marketed their goods and buyers passively accepting what is on offer out of an aversion to incur information costs.

New information and new knowledge do not come cost-free to sellers and buyers. The intensity of rivalry among potential participants on either side of the market depends on their readiness to incur transaction costs, which – as we saw – have the insidious quality of having to be sunk without a known

Figure 8.1 The market: a meeting place

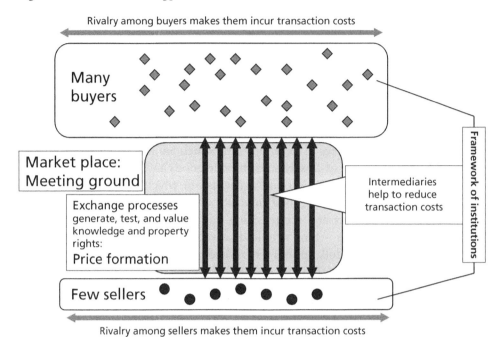

probability of a return.[1] The preparedness to incur information costs in turn will depend not only on the curiosity, creativity, boldness, acquisitive urge and readiness to incur risks on the part of the various competitors, but also on the institutions which shape their operations (Kirzner, 1973, 1997). If a community's institutions make information search relatively cheap and establish trust so that people can afford to cope with less explicit information, information search will be intense. On the other hand, if institutions are poor and fuzzy, so that information and transaction costs are high, buyers and sellers will not invest much in information search. They will, correspondingly, discover less useful knowledge and will in the aggregate probably achieve less economic growth. The cost of information is also determined by available technology. In this respect, huge advances have been made over the past generation. Thus, electronic technology has greatly reduced the costs of information search – think of commercial websites, eBay, live auctions on the Internet, critical product reviews, all this provided at home from sources around the world!

What matters here in particular is the capacity and preparedness to make surprising discoveries: finding knowledge of which the discoverer had no inkling prior to the discovery, and not just the capacity to explore for second-order information about matters of which people had some partial, prior knowledge (Section 3.1). Israel Kirzner, in a survey article of Austrian economics, put it well when he wrote:

> Without knowing what to look for, without deploying any deliberate search technique, the entrepreneur is at all times scanning the horizon, as it were, ready to make discoveries. Each such discovery will be accompanied by a sense of surprise (at one's earlier unaccountable ignorance). An entrepreneurial attitude is one which is always ready to be surprised, always ready to take the steps needed to profit by such surprises. The notion of discovery [is] . . . midway between that of the deliberately produced information in standard search theory, and that of sheer windfall gain generated by pure chance. (Kirzner, 1997, p. 72; 1992)

The knowledge search by alert and interested buyers is essential to the supply of innovative products in a market. Buyers have to invest time and effort to find out what is new and available. They have to vie with each other to find the special deals and the novelties. If potential buyers of computer software were to make do with what they have and did not search for new, improved programs, advances in software programming would soon slacken. Therefore, the keenness of the buyers – whether they devour the computer magazines or search the Internet for new programs – is essential to drive suppliers to invest in improvements of knowledge. This explains why innovative markets require a demanding clientele and why sophisticated, active demand is so essential to industrial success (Porter, 1990).

Readers who doubt that buyers compete should think of the intense knowledge search of homebuyers and their rivalry, for example at auctions. Or think of the competition among art buyers for rare pieces. Competitive knowledge search plays an important role in inter-industry trade. For example, the various car assembly firms invest much effort and finance to find the best and cheapest sources for the components they buy from subcontractors. They also conduct much costly technical research and quality testing to help potential suppliers to produce what they wish to buy. It has been rightly argued that France's and China's demanding restaurant clientele is one of the main reasons why the cuisine of these countries is excellent, whereas restaurants in (better unnamed) places where clients are rather indifferent, offer poor quality food.

When products have no near-substitutes, so that there is no rivalry on one side of the market, we speak of monopoly (single seller) or monopsony (single buyer). People who lack rivals have no incentive to incur information costs and the knowledge search flags. However, as economic life evolves ceaselessly, monopsonistic buyers and monopolistic sellers can never be sure that they will hold their position for long. They should remain in what Joseph A. Schumpeter called 'creative unease'. For example, buyers may sooner or later find new substitutes in other countries and import them. Or suppliers in another industry may invent close substitutes for what a monopolist had been offering. Thus, the railway monopolies of the nineteenth century, which to some contemporary observers seemed at the time to spell the end of competitive capitalism, had to discover that motor-cars and trucks emerged as new rivals. And the Swiss makers of mechanical chronometers had to discover in the late 1960s that cheap electronic watches did the same job. These cases illustrate that commercial monopolies are contestable. And this realization is what forces even single sellers, who enjoy temporary monopolies, to engage in knowledge search, just in case. Market power is thus often controlled by potential, and not only by actual rivalry.

These processes of rivalry on either side of the market are closely related to the exchanges between buyers and sellers *across* the market. In negotiations between buyers and sellers, conditions of contract are sorted out before the two sides conclude deals. This is a continual process in which people vote with their money on the basis of their diverse, changing, subjective knowledge, expressing their own preferences and valuations (Figure 8.1). Once a buyer or seller has acquired sufficient knowledge about products, exchange partners, qualities, and other conditions of exchange, and personally values what he has found out, he will select a contract partner to strike a deal. His personal knowledge about alternatives (substitutes) will be important in the negotiation, in particular about the price. The price communicates new knowledge to others, albeit in coded form, also expressing the valuations of other participants in the game. For many decisions, the coded price signal will be sufficient to convey all needed information; indeed more detailed knowledge about what is behind a price change might overtax people's cognitive capacities. Suppliers will often be content to know that a higher price is better, and buyers will prefer a lower price and act accordingly.

The rivalry on both sides of the market and the exchange process between the two sides of course take place all the time and simultaneously, in a ceaselessly evolving web of numerous concurrent actions and reactions. Competition has, therefore, to be understood as a dynamic process in which useful knowledge is sought, tested and validated, in which, so to speak, individuals dedicate resources to peering ahead into the fogs of ignorance. Competition does not operate without errors, but – as in all evolutionary processes – errors are corrected if necessary. In this way, the competitive process is a discovery procedure, but not one that will ever produce perfect knowledge, given the constitutional forward and sideways lack of knowledge. Rather, it reduces ignorance to levels that market participants can manage.

We should remind ourselves here of what was said in Chapter 3 about information search and decision making: Paradoxically, one can never assess rationally how much expense one should invest in information search. One can only incur information costs up to a certain point and make a decision when one's experience indicates that one probably knows enough to make that decision. One can try to arrive at a decision when ignorance is reduced to manageable levels (bounded rationality).

It should be evident that people only expend transaction costs on searching for knowledge to stay ahead of their rival suppliers (and buyers, as the case may be). People will welcome the rivalry on the opposite side of the market because that gives them more and better choices. Also note that buyers and sellers always have opposing interests in the competitive game.

The functions of competition

We can now return to the three questions raised earlier in this section:

(a) *Finding and testing useful knowledge*: A system of private property rights motivates people to search for rewarding uses of their assets. It allows them to keep the rewards, thereby inducing rivalry among suppliers (or competing buyers) who respond competitively by searching for new knowledge that may be useful to improve their position. In that way, competition is a process in which many are engaged all the time in costly and risky information search. It is not a comfortable situation for those involved but one that is good for freedom of choice of the other side of the market and for the wealth of nations! Where and how people search for knowledge will differ from individual to individual, depending on what subjective experience and inclination dictate. A great variety of search methods will be employed. The broad base of the search effort and the multiplicity of search methods promise more advances in useful knowledge than the alternatives, such as delegating only a few specialists to find new information. All this is good for prosperity, a fundamental value.

(b) *Dispersal of knowledge*: The second question relates to how tested, useful knowledge is made accessible to others. In a competitive economy, successes in the market place become known. Profitable suppliers attract imitators, and successful buyers will often be emulated by their neighbours. Moreover, the price signal spreads coded information about what the other side of the market wants and what one's rivals are prepared to offer. A price change can be recognized quickly and will trigger appropriate reactions by third parties to raise their property values. This spreads information quickly to interrelated markets. Thus, very few people needed to understand the full reasons for the petroleum shortages of 1974-75, the early 1980s or the 2010s, whether it was a war in the Middle East, rapidly growing transport demand, the exhaustion of oil wells, the OPEC oil cartel, or Arab revolutions. Whatever the complex, hard-to-decipher reasons, the oil price shot up. Drivers in far-away New York and London reduced their demand immediately and began to think about switching from gas guzzlers to petrol misers. Industries around the world adjusted their energy use patterns. But the price information ricocheted much further. In thousands of laboratories, people began to incur search costs to find oil-economizing technologies: more fuel-efficient engines, electronic controls, weight-saving, replacing oil with other energy sources, re-examining nuclear power options, and so on. The price impulse also rippled through to energy suppliers, spreading outwards like the waves from a stone you throw in a pond. The drilling of new oil and gas wells was speeded up; new technologies were tried out to extract oil from continental shelves and other difficult locations; new coal fields were opened; and research into coal liquefaction and shale-oil extraction was started. Refining methods were enhanced in hundreds of different locations. The oil crises were overcome thanks to a myriad of costly search efforts both on the supply and the demand side. The competitive system 'radioed' the necessary information through the simple, easily-perceived price signal and quickly dispersed the knowledge that oil was in short supply. The signal gave incentives to property owners who acted in their self-interest and did so with urgency, hoping to beat their rivals. No other system could have spread the knowledge as effectively and quickly as the price mechanism in competitive markets and no other system could have mobilized so much follow-up knowledge search. Again, this is favourable to prosperity.

(c) *Control of errors*: When people commit (unavoidable) errors in a competitive system, they will soon learn from the reactions of the other side of the market and from how they are beaten by their rivals. They will learn that they are not using their property rights to the best benefit of others and hence their own profit. In short, they incur the 'reprimand of red ink', a loss. In an institutional system that ensures private property rights, they are responsible for that loss and are therefore likely to correct their errors. If property is held collectively and decision makers are financed out of compulsory taxes, the agents can go on throwing good money after bad, arguing why they should persist ('voice'). When they are deserted by exchange partners in markets ('exit'), they have to make corrections quickly and search pragmatically for remedies. As a consequence, the competitive system has built-in, spontaneous self-controls. Errors usually remain limited and are not perpetuated because competitors, who know better, will exploit someone's error. This is not only good for prosperity, but also for social peace.

The system of knowledge search through competitive market processes has been given the name catallaxy, as we learnt earlier – the interaction between buyers and sellers to find out what ideas are useful. The system, and its knowledge-and-prosperity generating capacity, was well understood by the philosopher-economists of the eighteenth century Enlightenment, such as Adam Ferguson and Adam Smith. These thinkers also stressed the need for rules of the competitive game to ensure that competitive rivalry remained intense, that others were not unduly harmed and that property owners were challenged, time and again, to expose their assets to the challenges of competition. Protection from competition – for example monopolies, political privileges and tariffs – were seen by the founding fathers of economics as great impediments to the knowledge search-and-dissemination process and hence to progress.

In recent times, these well-known considerations have become the core of what is now called 'robust political economy' (Boettke and Leeson, 2004; Pennington, 2010) which amounts to acknowledging that markets are best suited to tackle ignorance and limited rationality and that public policy in majoritarian democracies can easily undercut the market system in attaining the above-listed benefits (Section 10.5).

Robust political economy highlights, yet again, that the essence of the competitive process, as set out here, was lost when economists made the assumption of perfect knowledge a hundred years later. This was done so that they could construct the elegant, simple, comparative-static models of neoclassical economics.[2] The phenomenon of competition, which deals with an evolutionary process of decentralized knowledge search, cannot be grasped by the static neoclassical analysis of supply and demand based on the assumption that all relevant knowledge is already known! The concepts of transaction costs, a consequence of ignorance, and institutions to economize on transaction costs, cannot be meaningfully analyzed unless we consider competition as a discovery procedure of knowledge which no one has (unknown unknowns, Section 3.1). Only when we see competition in the context of human ignorance and as part of a complex, evolving system can we comprehend what important functions it serves: to cite Hayek, competition is a "procedure for the discovery of such facts, as without resort to it, would not be known to anyone, at least would not be utilized" (Hayek, 1978b, p. 179, also Streit, 1993a). Making the economics profession again aware of its lacking realism, as we are trying to do in this book, should help to create a body of knowledge about simple, robust truths that the public and policy makers can understand.

Competition can therefore not be depicted by snapshots, for example by counting the number of competitors and saying that monopoly (one seller) or oligopoly (a few sellers) are inferior to atomistic competition (countless sellers) – as is so often done in textbooks and policy debates. Comparative-static economic models are as unsuited to capturing the essence of competition as the comparison between two still photos – the runners in the starting blocks and on the finishing line – can show the excitement of a race. It takes a film to depict the full drama of a race, or of any other sort of competition. Competing must be understood as a *verb* – an active process – and not as a *noun* – a state of affairs – as depicted in many textbooks. It is not a snapshot at a point of time, but a 'movie' that tells an unfolding story, which emerges in the very process in which it is being told.

The profit-loss mechanism – absolutely central to the functioning of the market economy – exerts a discipline on competitors, which is rarely popular with them. Politicians, government officials or the wider public do not necessarily support such an impersonal system of coordination and knowledge search. Indeed, many of competitors exploit potential reservations about markets to allot or seek political and material advantages (rent-seeking, see Section 10.5). By doing so, they undermine the single most important driver of prosperity known to man: efficiency, innovation and social harmony. One may summarize the role of the price system as relying on three P's – property, prices, and profit-loss – and of providing three essential I's: incentives, information and innovation.

KEY CONCEPTS

The **market** place is a meeting ground between people who want to buy and sell, offering or demanding property rights in exchange for other property rights. Typically, suppliers offer goods and services in exchange for money. Typically, people exchange goods and services indirectly through money, as opposed to direct exchange that occurs when people barter.

Competition is the evolutionary process of interaction between buyers and sellers in ➡

◄

markets: Buyers rival among themselves to obtain relevant knowledge where and what to buy, what new products to try out and how to get advantageous deals; sellers rival with other suppliers of close substitutes to place themselves in an advantageous position vis-à-vis potential buyers by exploring new knowledge on product variations and production processes, on organization, communication and selling methods, and on possible exchange partners. At the same time, exchange processes between buyers and sellers take place across the market. These convey important information – whether deals are profitable (and might be imitated) or whether losses are made, so that errors need to be corrected by search for alternatives. Actual and potential exchanges trigger the rivalry on either side of the market. The entire process of competition creates strong incentives to search for and test useful knowledge because the competitors risk their own private property and are responsible for their actions and their errors. The intensity of competition depends on the propensity of both sides of the market to incur transaction costs and the institutions that facilitate and protect competition.

The concept of **catallaxis** derives from the Greek *katallatein*, which originally means to exchange and thereby turn an enemy into a friend. It relates to voluntary mutual interaction and accommodation, as distinct from coercive imposition. Catallaxy evokes the image of processes in which new demands, new production methods and new products are discovered. This contrasts with 'economizing', which relates to the maximization of utility or profit with given demands, given production technologies and given resources. What matters to economic growth is society's catallactic capability. The concept was revived for modern economics by Ludwig von Mises (1949, chapter xiv). It has gained growing acceptance with the spread of evolutionary economics.

Monopoly is a situation in a market where there is one supplier only. Because a single supplier faces no rivalry from others who might offer buyers more advantageous substitutes, the monopolist does not have to incur transaction costs in the search for new knowledge and in offering better and cheaper products. However, many single suppliers have in reality to fear competitive challenges from potential substitutes, unless the market is closed by government intervention. As a consequence, they will perceive creative unease and behave competitively, that is, engage in information search against potential future rivals.

Dharma – the principle of non-competition – and economic development

The concept of competition can be explored further by reference to its opposite, non-competition, not being alert, not making an effort to gain advantage and knowledge. In traditional Hindu philosophy, non-competition is perceived as an ideal, *dharma*. The word derives from the Sanskrit word *dhar* – to bear, to accept – and is often translated as 'unquestioningly obeying custom, duty, making a virtue of a fatalistic acceptance of how things are'. The concept is often used to describe the submissive acceptance of their fate by the members of a caste into which they are born and the unquestioning acceptance of the knowledge of the forefathers. *Dharma* has to be contrasted with the attitude that 'I can make a difference; I can find salvation in improving life on earth', which is typical of Western and Far Eastern individualism. It is reinforced by an attitude of sceptical curiosity. People whose behaviour is ruled by the principle of *dharma* can of course be easily controlled, but they are also less likely to explore new ways and means to better their own condition and, with it, those of others. Competitive attitudes in economic life are necessary for catallactic or dynamic efficiency, the capability of people to discover and test ideas, to generate economic improvements (Pethig and Schlieper, 1987; Cordato in Boettke (ed.), 1994, pp. 131–136; Kirzner, *idem*, pp. 103–110).

Living with the principle of *dharma* may be more comfortable than being subject to the dictate of competition, as people unthinkingly follow established rules, whether this hurts them or not. One does not have to put up with the transaction costs of knowledge search. When established institutions regulate every detail of life, information search costs are indeed low. Power hierarchies remain intact. The disciples of *dharma* never query existing institutions, irrespective of their consequences. This is the hallmark of a conservative, unfree society and a stagnant economy. Economic development and a free society, in which conflicts are minimized, require occasional institutional innovations – the challenge and testing of old rules and their re-affirmation or adaptation in the light of new circumstances. Competition therefore depends not only on given rules that make human interaction predictable, but also on the adaptation of rules when circumstances merit this in the eyes of (most of) the participants.

Dharma-like behaviour has dominated economic conduct in many traditional societies. The notion, which became strong in Judaeo-Christian, Western civilization that humans ought to seek salvation by being productive and innovative in this world, rather than remain fatalistic and non-competitive, has spread only gradually to other civilizations. Once this basic attitude to life is accepted, it becomes important to economic development and capital accumulation. As the doyen of development economics, the late Lord Peter Bauer emphasized time and again, small-scale competitors, who are profitable, become medium-sized ones. If the competitive system remains in place (that is, parasitic rent-seeking is controlled) and if they remain alert and profitable, many medium-sized enterprises become large-scale, accumulating more and more physical and human capital. It is by the spirit of enterprise that many communities transition from subsistence to exchange and wealth (Bauer and

Sen, 2004). In the process, competition expands incomes and trade, wider markets enable more and better specialization and enhance the cooperation amongst more and more people. Thus, the competitive capitalist economy pulls itself out of the cycle of poverty. Adam Smith already recognized this when he wrote in his *Wealth of Nations* that the cooperation of a great multitude of specialized competitors is a powerful driver of economic progress.

Search goods – experience goods: who bears transaction costs?

Market institutions are often adjusted to reduce the buyers' transaction costs, including their information costs. Phillip Nelson (1970) pointed to an important dimension when he introduced the distinction between 'experience goods' and 'search goods'. The quality of some goods and services can be readily evaluated by inspection prior to a purchase, for example a dress on a rack or fruit in a produce market. Buyers can search for the quality they desire at low information costs (search goods). But in many instances, the quality of goods and services can only be established by the experience of using or consuming them (experience goods). Examples for such experience goods are tinned fruit, motor cars, tourist packages, and open-heart surgery – first you get it, then you find out! When product qualities are variable, buyers of experience goods often incur high information costs in assessing quality prior to the purchase.

Where buyers can easily search for the desired quality (and may even enjoy the experience of shopping around!), market conventions tend to leave the information search costs to the buyers (Barzel, 1982). However, in the case of experience goods suppliers often shoulder those costs. They find this useful (and incorporate their costs in their prices) to standardize the quality and give buyers credible commitments of quality, for example, through advertised brand names, setting up chains of outlets and franchising. One way for suppliers to signal the quality of the experience goods is to acquire a reputation for quality, a costly and time-consuming exercise that saves buyers much costly information search. Customers are therefore prepared to pay a premium price to save themselves from disappointing experiences. They can assume that it would be irrational for producers with a good reputation and for owners of known brands to sell rubbish, because this would become quickly known and destroy the competitive advantages of their good reputation. Many techniques aimed at cutting the information costs of buyers of experience goods amount to standardizing and averaging, even if buyers have subjective preferences for diverse product qualities. What might be an exciting tourist package for you may bore me to tears! Nonetheless, many intending travellers are loath to incur higher information costs by trying out alternative holiday offerings, instead opting for standardized packages.

Another way for suppliers to compete by reducing the transaction costs of the buyers of experience goods is to offer catalogues, free samples and other trial experiences. Thus, nightclubs may offer customers free entry for the first ten minutes, pay TV channels let you watch the first ten minutes of a movie before you have to pay, and computer software may be available free of charge for a trial period.

The costs of transacting business are sometimes shifted between sellers and buyers in response to changing competitive conditions. When the rivalry between sellers is intense, they incur a large share of the transaction costs to ensure that deals can be struck with buyers. When supplies become scarce, buyers shoulder a larger share of the transaction costs. Such a shift in market power from a buyers' to a sellers' market, which is reflected in who bears what share of the transaction costs, can, for example, be observed in hotel accommodation: In the low season, when hotels have a low occupancy rate, they advertise, drum up business by staging special events and offer free bottles of champagne. In the high season, customers have to ring around to find a hotel room and even accept being put on waiting lists. Similarly, the incidence of who has to bear the transaction costs may fluctuate over the business cycle. In a slack housing market, for example, sellers advertise and offer to pay the title-registration fees; when the market booms, intending buyers have to queue and ring around. Indeed, much of the profitability of boom times results from businesses saving on transaction costs and customers shouldering them because sellers' markets prevail.

It should be noted in this context that neoclassical economists – and the practitioners who follow them by assuming perfect knowledge – frequently castigate advertising as an abuse of the capitalist system and argue for controls of advertising expenditure. However, advertising makes sense if one starts with the realistic assumption of competition as a process of knowledge search and accepts that buyers often face considerable information costs, so that they welcome advertised information. Moreover, those who propose to control advertising (other than to ban fraudulent or deceptive advertising) imply that it is possible to centrally determine what information is objectively useful to buyers. They overlook completely that all perception and all knowledge acquisition is subjective.

Frequently, suppliers win the competition when they concentrate on lowering their and their customers' transaction costs, rather than their production costs, particularly in markets for services (see Box 8.1).

CH 8 – CASE ONE

An innovation to reduce transaction costs: micro loan banking

In less developed countries, many have useful knowledge of how to operate small local businesses more profitably, if only they had access to some capital and credit. However, the fixed costs of assessing credit risks and administering enforcement mechanisms in institutionally fuzzy environments severely restrict credit availability to small borrowers. Credit is therefore available only on a personal basis and often only to people with a large asset backing (personalized credit). Small, asset-poor borrowers can only go to money-lenders where they face forbiddingly high interest rates, because institutional deficiencies lead to high loan monitoring costs and costly enforcement in the case of default.

These problems have been tackled in an imaginative and effective way since 1983 by the *Grameen Bank* in Bangladesh. The bank was founded by a US-trained economist, Dr. Muhammad Yunus, who understood the institutional deficiencies and addressed them in the following way: Small operators and vendors could obtain small loans if their loan application was guaranteed by a circle of 5 to 10 others. This enabled the borrower to start or upgrade small businesses, for example to operate a cellular phone for rent in the village. When the first borrower from a borrowers' circle had duly repaid the loan, other members qualified for credit. The risk-assessment costs, as well the enforcement costs, are thus borne not by the bank, but by the borrowers' circle. Members act responsibly, because they have a keen self-interest in establishing their own credit-worthiness. If there is a default, the entire circle is in default and no longer creditworthy.

The organization of borrowers' circles also serves as an important information exchange and turns a one-off loan contract into an open-ended, ongoing game (offering 'hostages'). Borrowers learn how to keep accounts and what to do to repay on time. Thrift is thus learnt in a community-support setting. Many borrowers have subsequently become micro shareholders in *Grameen Bank*.

Grameen Bank has a low default rate, and most borrowers are women, an extraordinary circumstance in a Muslim country. By reducing the information, monitoring and enforcement costs through the formation of borrowers' circles, the Bank has been successful where less innovative enterprises have failed. It is the case of an enterprise that thrives through institutional innovation. The empowerment of the poor and of women was resented not only by reactionary local villagers, but has not been welcomed by the government of Bangladesh. Nevertheless, the model of micro-finance – both for-profit and not-for-profit – has since spread to numerous Third World countries and – despite relatively high costs for small loans – has made access to finance for micro-entrepreneurs much easier.

Sources: Fuglesang and Chandler (1987) and www.grameen-info.org/.

KEY CONCEPTS

Search goods are products whose (variable) quality the buyers can establish readily, at low information cost and prior to the purchase decision (example: fruit in a market). By contrast, the quality of **experience goods** can only be measured by acquiring and using up the product. To help buyers avoid high or insurmountable information costs, competing suppliers develop devices to give prior assurance (for example, brand names, reputed seller, samples, employment of middlemen).

Buyers' market conditions exist when sellers rival intensely with each other in searching for purchase opportunities and therefore hold a relatively weak bargaining position. This is reflected in the sellers incurring a large share of the transaction costs. **Sellers' markets** are markets in which the sellers hold a relatively strong position and do not have to shoulder a great deal of the transaction costs, because it is the buyers who are prepared to bear these costs to find a deal.

The shift from buyers' to sellers' market conditions can consequently have a great impact on the profitability of business.

Intermediation

Buyers and sellers can also reduce information problems, particularly in experience-goods markets, by trading through middlemen. Buyers tend to know them better than the original producers. Middlemen may also want to continue doing business with the buyers and therefore offer credible quality guarantees (Section 7.4). This is, for example, the case in the markets for real estate, second-hand cars, horses and tourist services where intermediary agents are common. The middlemen have experience in assessing product quality and enjoy scale economies in measuring it; they also have a reputation to lose if they pass on bad products. The one-time final buyer knows this and therefore trusts the middleman whose livelihood depends on his good reputation. Thus, we shop in a department store because we trust its image and because we buy many products there and avoid direct marketing from producers with whom we might deal only once.

The role of intermediation in saving transaction costs has in recent years also become evident in the new Internet trade. Intending buyers and sellers preferred the structure of rules developed by eBay instead of dealing with each other bilaterally. Rules were established on how prices can evolve and the credibility of sellers and buyers was soon assessed in systematic and transparent ways. To avoid credit card fraud, intermediaries like PayPal emerged who put their reputation on the line to guarantee that payments are made and the confidentiality of both partners' banking details is safeguarded.

Other devices of intermediation to save on transaction costs are franchising and the creation of brand names. In both cases, buyers of experience goods prefer to pay more in exchange for the services of a known intermediary – even if the actual product is made by someone unknown. They confide in the middleman's stamp of approval.

Middlemen thus help buyers and sellers to economize on their respective transaction costs. Their services of course cost resources, but their role in the community is only resented by people who make the unrealistic assumption of perfect knowledge.

In traditional societies, competition relies heavily on personalized trade and credit, personal ties with people with whom one has an ongoing economic relationship and who keep their contractual promises because they benefit from the ongoing relationship. Such personalized economic ties are reinforced by personal friendships, sometimes even by adoptions and marriages. However, as external institutions and third-party enforcement by government bodies improved, more and more open competition and exchanges among strangers became possible. This is now happening in those Third World countries that are enhancing the institutions of the market economy. One will deal not so much anymore only with whom one knows, but more and more according to what is offered. These shifts often imply deep cultural changes. If proper, transparent rules do not evolve or are fostered externally, the changes lead to frictions and resentment about development and progress.

As the division of labour develops to become more complex, there are new demands for intermediation, and new types of middlemen cater to those demands. An example is modern credit-card organizations, which allow buyers to acquire goods and services on credit without having to build up a reputation with the shop or to negotiate credit terms first. A second example is the enormous rise of financial intermediation in global financial markets. International payment transactions may appear quite impersonal to the outside observer, but in reality this extended market network is supported by much intermediation, which reduces risks and transaction costs. International payments depend on chains of intermediaries that have frequent contact and guarantee mutual contract fulfilment.

At closer inspection, a personalized microcosm of relationships thrives within the extended, supposedly anonymous order of competitive markets, as individual traders often deal with partners whom they know and trust and who will return a favour, if needed.

8.2 Competition from the suppliers' perspective

What has been said so far about competition and knowledge search applies to both sides of the market; supply and demand. To gain more specific insights on how the capitalist system works, we now turn to the rivalry among the suppliers of goods and services for the favours of buyers.

Price and non-price competition

Suppliers rival for the attention of potential buyers by employing a number of different means, namely:

(a) price variations (price competition);

(b) product innovation: the product may be improved in the hope of attracting more loyal and, they hope, price-insensitive buyers; to this end suppliers incur research and development costs;

(c) advertising (and the creation of brand names) for a particular product as a way for a supplier to position himself in the market, which causes transaction costs;

(d) sales organization: distribution channels are developed in the hope of beating the competition and attracting loyal buyers (for example new logistics networks, wholesale outlets, own retail shop fronts, mail order trade), again at a cost;

(e) financial assistance is extended to buyers, for example through credit or instalment payment;

(f) after-sales services – such as ongoing advice on product use, guarantees of speedy repairs and reliable spare parts supplies – can also serve to bind buyers to one specific supplier, because this cuts their information and other transaction costs when using the product; for technically complex or hard-to-use and hard-to-repair products and services, which are typical of many modern markets, after-sales service has become the most important tool of competition; the necessary arrangements on the part of sellers can be costly, but are made in the hope of beating other rivalling sellers; and

(g) sellers may also seek to gain advantage through lobbying for political restrictions of competition, which again costs resources, but may nonetheless be advantageous from the standpoint of the sellers.

Cases (a) to (f) constitute economic competition; suppliers perform useful services to attract voluntary buyers. In that category, we distinguish between price competition (case [a]) and non-price competition (cases [b] through [f], see Figure 8.2). In contrast to economic competition, lobbying in the political arena [case (g)] seeks interventions to compel or restrict buyers. In this case, suppliers collude with government agents to gain economic advantages by influencing the external institutions that govern their markets by introducing elements of compulsion or restriction, instead of rivalling for the favour of buyers. While economic competition leads to better performance from the standpoint of buyers and the general public, lobbying for political protection allows sellers to offer buyers lesser choices.[3] Political competition to obtain artificial rents therefore is not in the buyers' and the public's interest.

In most markets, there are a few suppliers who know each other and rival for the favour of large numbers of buyers. This is much more common than markets with numerous anonymous suppliers. In other words, oligopolistic competition is the norm, and atomistic competition is rare. Modern markets for industrial goods and services are, moreover, typified by experience goods, open-ended relational contracts and long-term demand-supply relationships between business partners who know each other, rather than one-off purchases amongst anonymous agents (as textbook models imply).

Each individual supplier usually has some understanding of the reactions of potential buyers to possible variations in their offer prices, as well as of the rivals' reactions to his price variations. From past experience, a supplier can often conjecture by how much the demand for his products is likely to drop were he to raise the price a little or vice versa. Given the transaction costs of searching for new suppliers, buyers will hardly react massively to small price variations. But the quantity a supplier can expect to sell varies by a disproportionately wide margin if the supplier introduces a large price variation. Buyer loyalty tends to be limited, after all. Each supplier therefore enjoys a market niche (a section of relatively price-inelastic demand, to put it in the terminology of economic theory). Each seller has, at any time, a mental image of the demand curve he faces which has a double kink in it (Blandy et al., 1985, pp. 47–60; Figure 8.2).

Rivalling suppliers typically operate in circumstances of limited knowledge, amidst complex, dynamic changes and face considerable fixed costs. Therefore, they prefer to operate within a market niche, where small price increases lead only to small quantity reductions of demand. Should unexpected costs increase and force suppliers to raise their prices, turnover does not drop much, so that (possibly high) fixed overhead costs do not have to be distributed over a much reduced sales volume. After all, this would drive up unit-costs and prices even further, leading to further expected losses of

Figure 8.2 Instruments of competitive action from the suppliers' perspective

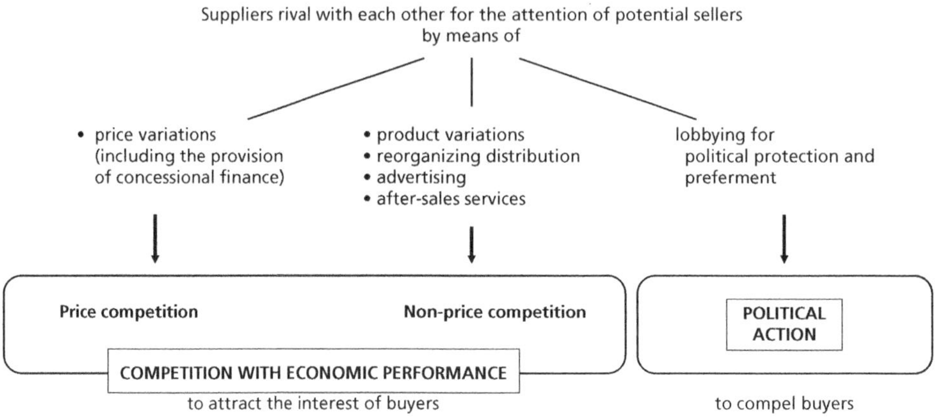

Suppliers rival with each other for the attention of potential sellers
by means of

• price variations (including the provision of concessional finance)	• product variations • reorganizing distribution • advertising • after-sales services	lobbying for political protection and preferment

Price competition	Non-price competition	POLITICAL ACTION

COMPETITION WITH ECONOMIC PERFORMANCE

to attract the interest of buyers   to compel buyers

sales. Suppliers therefore have a great incentive to widen and secure their market niche and to stay within it.

The market niche – the limited preference by buyers for a particular supplier – is cultivated by the tools of non-price competition (cases [b] to [f] above). Suppliers incur costs to gain such a position, and their rivals will employ the same tools to the best of their knowledge and ability to compress the first supplier's market niche. This leads to a continual tug of war and to considerable insecurity of each supplier about his market niche, instigating him to incur new transaction costs. If, for example, a car producer has gained a fairly secure market niche because of the introduction of a well-received new model (product innovation), his competitors will not rest until they can also offer improved models, even if that forces them to incur high R&D costs. This rivalry compresses the first supplier's market niche again (Figure 8.3). Competition thus is an ongoing process of rivalry, which exerts an unrelenting discipline, so that no one can rest on his laurels for long. Oligopolistic suppliers have to live with unease, which keeps them creative and makes them search for knowledge that enhances living standards. Although the supplier's search efforts are costly and often uncomfortable to them, valuable new productive knowledge is developed and the wealth of the community is enhanced. The results of non-price competition are thus of genuine value to buyers who may welcome product variations or reductions in their own transaction costs.

As long as buyers remain alert and are prepared to incur information costs of their own to find out what is on offer and what serves them best, competition promotes useful knowledge and quality. Competition may of course be seen by suppliers as an unwelcome cost and the cause of disappointing

Figure 8.3 A supplier's competitive position: a snapshot from a dynamic process

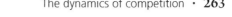

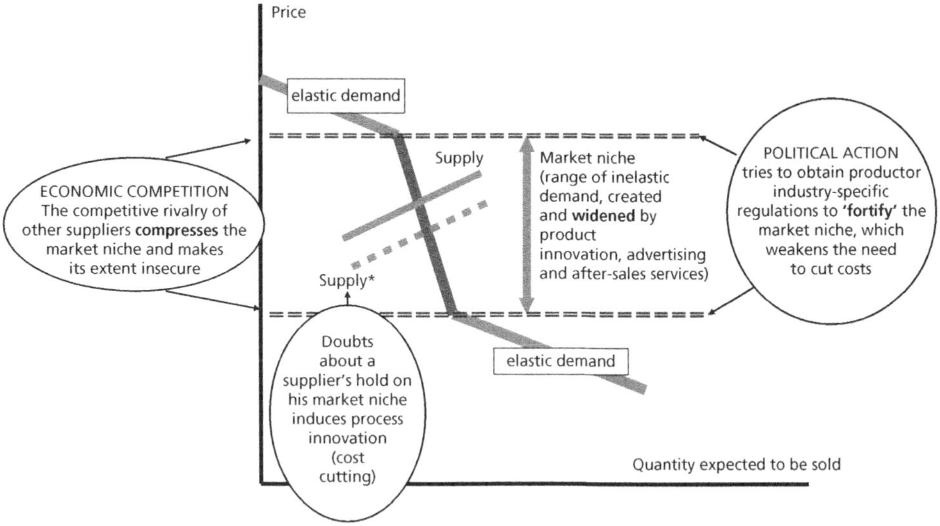

business results. Therefore it is understandable that they often try to organize themselves to reduce their rivalry. They may do so by private agreement (forming a cartel) or by obtaining political protection from competitive pressures (political rent-seeking). For time immemorial, this has occurred not only in product markets, but also in markets of production factors, such as labour (trade unions). Once political agents offer to intervene, buyers and many property owners lose out (Epstein et al., 2005; Epstein, 2007). They are not given as wide a choice as before. They may also be impeded from using the 'exit option' from the specific market by substituting other products, for example imported cars when domestic producers are handed tariff privileges at the car buyers' expense. Then, car sellers are under less pressure to improve their products and need not incur the transaction costs of advertising, after-sales services or reliable spare-part supply. As we shall see in greater detail shortly, rent seeking has profound deleterious consequences for innovation and general economic welfare.

It is, however, easy to exaggerate the notion that market competition is always unpopular. After all, many derive regular inspiration and stimulation from going to markets, fairs and auctions. It is also a historic fact that competitors and partners in market deals often become friends. As already mentioned, this was seen by the ancient Greeks, who used the verb *katallatein* not only to describe market exchanges that generated knowledge, but that also turned strangers into friends (see *Epilogue*).

Product and process innovation

The attempts of rivalling suppliers to improve their position drive them to improve their products to find better substitutes for what other competitors produce. Often, product innovation occurs by incremental, adaptive steps, but sometimes also by discontinuous improvements. These steps shape the evolution of an industry, for example how the fragile flying contraption of the Wright brothers developed into today's 'Dreamliner'. Buyers may value the new products sufficiently to justify the transaction costs which the innovating supplier has to incur. Then, the innovating pioneer earns a (probably temporary) 'pioneer profit' (Schumpeter, 1961/1908). Yet, business success also often eludes innovating pioneers; instead they incur losses. Probably the greater share of new products which are launched each year in affluent economies fails to make a profit, because they are not accepted sufficiently by the ultimate arbiters of product innovation, namely the buyers. They therefore ultimately decide what survives in the basket of goods and services on offer ('consumer sovereignty'). Buyers of course do not choose from an unlimited range of possibilities, only from what suppliers offer in the hope that it will be profitable. Rivalry and buyer choices thus interact to drive product innovation.

Competition also drives process innovation. Because the width and durability of their imagined market niche is never precisely known to suppliers and, in any event, is always open to challenges from rivals, suppliers face constant pressures to control their costs (Figure 8.3). They will try out new production processes, search for cheaper inputs or adjust their organizational arrangements. In short, they will engage in process innovation. Thus, insecurity about the bounds of buyer loyalty and the readiness of buyers to inform themselves of alternative offers of rivalling suppliers are essential to keeping producers in creative unease, forcing them to incur information costs about how to cut costs.

Unease about future sales and profits thus induces cost control, including the control of organization costs, which would otherwise be easily driven up by agent opportunism in big firms, as we saw in Section 3.4. Only the disciplining pressures of competition, which endanger the market niche, will mobilize the energies of managers and workers to perform on behalf of the owners of firms and to cut back unnecessary expenses. Without rivalry among suppliers and active buyers, it would be virtually impossible for firms to keep control of their costs.

Most innovations may affect one individual product or production process, or benefit a few other innovations. But some are *mega* innovations, which pave the way for numerous follow-up innovations. These innovations typically have a certain public-goods character, which means that they make many other, derivative innovations possible thanks to more or less free access to the 'foundation technology' (Romer, 1990). *Mega* innovations may also be organizational ones. Thus, the creation of the Hanseatic League among medieval trading cities – a public initiative – in northern and northeastern Europe created a secure framework for individual private merchants to introduce new products to new markets and get tradesmen to produce for a much wider market. It is not far-fetched to contend that great jurisprudential efforts that create expedient and trust-inspiring law codes are institutional *mega* inventions, which facilitate numerous useful follow-up innovations.

A more recent dramatic *mega* innovation is the Internet, which was initially financed by the US Department of Defense and made available to a wider public free of charge. Initially, this permitted cheap communications between computer owners in affluent countries, such as – in our case – three academics in three different continents joining together to write a book about *Institutional Economics*. Soon, images and sound could also be communicated. In poor countries, the most widely distributed computer, the mobile cellphone, was not only used, within a few years of the invention, for private and business communication, but also to gain weather and market information, to participate live in auctions, to transfer money balances, to learn English, to check codes on pharmaceuticals ensuring they were not fakes, to communicate political opinions and to organize public protests against arbitrary and corrupt governments. The social and economic effects have been nothing short of sensational in many less developed regions. In the authoritarian Arab countries, the effects of the Internet have been nothing short of revolutionary.

For the past 200 years the competitive market process has been powerful in ceaselessly driving process and product innovation forward, raising productivity, choice and living standards. It has been the major driving force in the evolution of useful knowledge and economic progress (Schumpeter, 1961; Clark, 1962; Hayek, 1978b; 1988). Let us note explicitly that the innovative performance of suppliers and economic growth are not automatic. Rather, this depends to a large measure on whether the buyers are willing and able to incur transaction costs, so that pioneer profits remain a temporary phenomenon.

KEY CONCEPTS

Rivalry among suppliers is conducted by means of price variation, as well as **non-price competition** (product differentiation, improving distribution channels, advertising and after-sales services). Apart from these forms of **economic competition**, competitors may form alliances (particular interest groups) to lobby for political interventions that 'protect' them from the need of having to rival with each other by economic means (**rent-seeking**).

A **market niche** is a conjecture in the mind of suppliers that they can expect small quantity responses to small price variations around the existing market price, but disproportionately large variations if the price is varied by a big margin. It reflects limited knowledge and transaction costs on the part of the buyers, and is reinforced by instruments of non-price rivalry amongst suppliers, as well as political interventions.

Innovation is the practical application of new knowledge through new combinations of property rights, for example to create a new product or implement a new (cost-saving) production process. Persons or teams who risk innovations and organize the many diverse resources and ideas necessary for an innovation are called economic **entrepreneurs**. Entrepreneurship assumes the risks of seeking to overcome existing constraints by new, untried combinations of property rights and the exploration and testing of new knowledge or hitherto existing knowledge from untapped sources.

Product innovation is carried out by producers who vary existing products or launch altogether new products as a means of securing a market niche, hoping to reap pioneer profits.

Process innovation is motivated by uncertainty about the extent of the market niche and the wish to lower production costs by implementing new production processes. Frequently in practice, product and process innovation are connected.

A **pioneer profit** is reaped by an innovator who meets with sufficient approval of buyers so that they pay prices that exceed the costs of supplying the novelty. Pioneer profits tends to be temporary, because successful innovations are either imitated by competitors or challenged by further innovations, which competing suppliers introduce to gain market share. This in turn tends to trigger efforts to implement further innovations in the hope of earning renewed, albeit again temporary pioneer profits, keeping the process of dynamic rivalry alive and driving the innovative search for, and use of, knowledge forward.

***Mega* innovations** consist of novel goods and services, often with partial public goods properties, that permit numerous other innovators to come to the fore and produce innovations of their own. Thus, the *mega* innovation of the Internet, initiated by the US Department of Defense, but made cheaply available to the world's public, has spawned an unimaginable wealth-creating innovative boom. Such innovations tend to give rise to long waves of economic growth and facilitate innovation clusters.

A partial view: scientific discovery, inventions, and technical innovations

The knowledge, which market participants search, may consist of technical knowledge that can be described explicitly and conveyed to others for their evaluation, an invention. Such technical knowledge may sometimes derive from a scientific discovery, the result of scientific research. When scientific discoveries are tested for their technical feasibility and are developed by engineers and applied scientists into laboratory models, we call this activity 'applied research and development'. The result is an invention (a discrete idea about how to use or manipulate nature). But inventions as such are not necessarily useful to the members of society. They also have to be tested for their organizational and commercial feasibility, that is, whether the inventions are sufficiently valued by buyers to be profitable. This is often a much more complex task than establishing mere technical feasibility. Whether a product or service will be commercially viable is the province of entrepreneurial judgment: Will the product be bought and at what price? Whether entrepreneurial hunches are indeed correct will then be tested in market competition (Harper, 1996).

Technical changes that move from scientific discovery to invention and on to innovation are described as the 'linear model of innovation'. Such a path was, for example, followed by nuclear energy and space satellites. However, relatively few innovations come about in this way. Much more frequently, innovations derive from the adaptive development of existing products and concepts, from responses to suggestions by clients, from capital replacement and from the imitation of successful rivals, that is, 'reverse engineering' which diffuses technology. Innovations are often adaptive and piecemeal. Frequently, we also observe important emergent innovations, which owe nothing to science, for example the innovation of the railway in the nineteenth century by George Stephenson, an untutored engineering tinkerer who lacked all theoretical knowledge of physics and mechanics. Like some other innovators with connections to the English mining industry, he mounted existing steam engines on carts and prevented the carts from sinking into the mud by placing them on iron rails, gradually improving the new engines (Johnson, 1991, pp. 580–583).

Knowledge which ensures high and advancing living standards in the capitalist system therefore often consists not of grand scientific or technical ideas, but of dispersed, petty knowhow about conditions that vary in space and time. If suppliers wish to produce something as commonplace as a quality pencil or a computer program, they need – apart from the discrete technical description of the product (the invention) – much practical commercial knowhow of how to obtain the raw materials and power supplies, where best to buy components of precisely what shape, quality and content, how to train the skills needed for production or where to hire skilled workers, how to organize the logistics of the distribution system, how to find out who can best assist with advertising to inform potential buyers, how to finance the cost of setting up production, where to acquire land or buildings, how to link the factory to transport and distribution systems, how to set up communications networks, how to set up marketing and after-sales services, and many more specific practicalities. The entrepreneurial task is to marshal all necessary knowhow to solve each of these many interlocking problems. Most of the necessary information is costly to get and has often to be found by time- and resource-consuming trial and error (Hayek, 1945; Rosenberg, 1988; Harper, 1996).

Innovating suppliers will be influenced in their knowledge search (i) by how well existing ground rules help them with finding and testing the new information, (ii) by the intensity of rivalry with other suppliers, and (iii) by the expected responses of potential buyers. Intensive competition tends to induce more innovation. Once market niches are perceived to be secure, the innovative drive is likely to lose momentum. Different institutional systems therefore differ enormously as to their innovative capacity. Although entrepreneurs are always present in a society, the institutions channel their energies either into innovative economic performance or into other, non-productive outlets for their energies, for example military, political or sport rivalry (Baumol, 1990). Entrepreneurial people sometimes even migrate to other institutional environments, which are more conducive to using their knowledge in economic competition. Thus, backward regions and, even more so, developing countries, often lose their brightest technical and economic innovators, because the institutional framework there does not give them the necessary business confidence, whereas developed market economies do.

KEY CONCEPTS

A **scientific discovery** is a new insight into how nature works. Sometimes, this gives rise to an **invention**, that is, a discrete addition to knowledge about how use can be made of nature in a technically feasible way. But only when an invention is commercially (economically) feasible will it be turned into an innovation. **Technical feasibility** is proven when the invention works under laboratory conditions. **Commercial feasibility** is tested in the market place where the receipts from buyers are assessed against the costs of the producers: Is the innovation profitable?

The progression from scientific discovery to an invention, the result of technical development, to an innovation, the result of a profit calculation by the producer is

➡

←

called the **linear model of innovation**. An example of this is the progression from the discovery of atom splitting, to the invention of the test reactor, to the innovation of nuclear energy generation. More important are other forms of innovation, particularly creative responses to feedback from the market and imitation of successful rivals.

The **diffusion of technology** occurs when technical processes and products are imitated in the hope for a better market position.

Entrepreneurs are people on the alert for opportunities, who overcome constraints to exploiting new knowledge. More specifically, the term relates to actors who go beyond the bounds of existing knowledge and combine production factors (property rights) in novel ways. Entrepreneurs have to find out whether they pioneer property uses that meet with the approval (in the form of 'cash votes') of sufficient numbers of buyers, so that they make a profit. They may also incur a loss, which conveys the knowledge that that particular property use does not find sufficient approval from the clients.

A panoramic view of technical and organizational progress

Technical change always requires organizational changes and adjustments throughout the economic system. Thus, a new product can only be marketed if necessary organizational dispositions for its production and distribution are made. What is necessary is not always known beforehand, indeed this may cause higher transaction costs than the technical side of the innovation. The demand for new products is not known beforehand because buyers do not know of the new product; they may not even be curious to find out about it. When, for example, the technical invention how to bond carbon particles to paper by light for photocopying was made, the major task was to induce potential buyers to discover that they had a demand for photocopying (Mueller, 1996).

If sellers and buyers in an economy are generally on the alert and prepared to incur transaction costs to discover new opportunities, the entire market system will be competitive. Indeed, the existence of some competitive operators generates the opportunities for other suppliers to compete successfully. This often enhances the competitive attitudes in yet other markets. A good example of how innovative, competitive enterprise led to 'virtuous circles' of economic progress was the railways boom of the nineteenth century. Enterprising mechanical engineers overcame obstacles of technical feasibility in building faster and more reliable steam engines, but they depended on – and created opportunities for – civil engineers who devised bridges and tunnels and laid the tracks. Both interacted with steel producers and bankers whose contributions were essential in revolutionizing transport. The steel producers could apply the then new technology of the Bessemer process to bulk steel making; and the bankers pioneered new financial instruments to benefit from the rise of a prosperous middle class eager to invest their capital. This induced the organizational innovation of the modern share company, as well as numerous further organizational changes in banking. In the mutual interaction of entrepreneurs in these diverse industries, a whole cluster of competing suppliers created technical and commercial opportunities for each other. Over time, this widened markets as transport costs fell and gave rise to numerous new activities in areas as far apart as new wheat production in the American Midwest, tourism in the Alps and the opening of Canada and Siberia to logging. Joseph A. Schumpeter, who analysed this phenomenon of development, spoke of the "swarm-like appearance of entrepreneurs [who create, by their competitive interaction] new possibilities more advantageous from the private economic standpoint" for each other (Schumpeter, 1961/1908, p. 214). A similar competitive process is currently taking place in clusters of computer-related industries: Because competing manufacturers have driven down the cost of microchips and enhanced their reliability and size, computer assemblers, software developers, telecommunications firms, teachers of computer skills, developers of knowledge, computer graphics artists, desktop publishers, email marketers and distance-education experts interact in a cluster of dynamic development. They all depend for their commercial success on the readiness of each part of the cluster to incur search costs and on innovative entrepreneurs in new fields. They also depend on avid buyers discovering their rapidly changing demands.

In a similar vein, competitive product markets depend on competition in factor markets for labour and capital. In turn, factor markets will only be competitive if the products, which capital and labour produce, are exposed to product-market competition. The economic effects of competition thus depend on the competitive interaction of all elements of the market system. It is very difficult for individual competitors to succeed when the institutions fail to discourage opportunism on the maxim of 'rip off and let rip off'. This highlights the importance of a consistent institution set that facilitates knowledge search and reduces the risks of opportunism among business partners and by government authorities.

The interactions of buyers and sellers in response to new ideas can often be time-consuming. Thus, the Crusaders of the European Middle Ages brought back – among many new ideas – the knowledge of Arabic numerals, including the concept of zero. This gradually enabled merchants to calculate assets, expenses and revenues more easily and facilitated double-entry book-keeping. This, in turn, helped with the emergence of big trading houses and the reorganization of European distance trade. It had manifold impacts on the division of labour. Of course, numerous other conditions were needed to favour this historic sequence of events, a complex web of changes in knowledge, physical capital and technical expertise.

It is also interesting to reflect on why the invention of powder in China led only to innovations of fireworks and rockets, whereas the Europeans, with their traditions of rivalry in war and commerce, soon used the original invention for guns and cannons, in mining and road construction, and to obtain more solid building materials – each initiative setting off further long-term chains of innovative effort.

8.3   Restrictions of economic competition

Private restrictions of competition

The free exercise of property rights, which leads to competition in the exchange process, can be inhibited by restrictive business practices of others who try to avoid or mitigate competitive pressures. Where economic agents wield economic or political power, they may use it to defend their market niche by artificial impediments. This strengthens their hand in contract negotiations and reduces the (cost-controlling) unease with which they would normally have to live. A case in point is the formation of a cartel, an agreement among sellers to supply only at uniform conditions of sale. At first glance, this could be seen as a legitimate use of the freedom of contract. But such a cartel agreement interferes with the freedom of the buyers. The sellers' cartel makes their freedom of choice between different sellers meaningless. As the freedom of choice and contract is a quality worth promoting and protecting, sellers have to be denied the freedom to cartelize by anti-trust rules.

It is essential to growth, freedom and the control of power that private restrictions of competition are suppressed. Private business practices that hinder competition can be the result of horizontal and vertical concentrations of businesses – buying up former rivals (mergers) or integrating suppliers or buyers into the same business organization. The empirical evidence shows that merged organizations are frequently hampered by a progressive rise of their internal organization costs, that internal rule coordination becomes increasingly difficult and that the adaptive capacity of *mega* firms is reduced by internal bureaucratization. This can be explained by principal-agent problems in big organizations, which are not subject to sufficient competitive discipline. Seeing matters from this point of view, one could make a case that it is up to those who have merged to internalize all benefits and costs of such action. Nonetheless, there may be cases worth investigating officially whether a particular takeover infringes the freedom of other property users to contract freely. But such an investigation always poses serious knowledge problems, as well as creating problems of legal definition: What is the size of a merger that will come under prior or subsequent investigation relative to the entire market?

As mentioned, private restrictions of competition can also result from agreements of firms to cooperate informally instead of competing (collusion) and from the readiness of powerful firms to defeat rivals by underselling them until they are squeezed out of the business, to the coercive or fraudulent treatment of rivals or contract partners. In such situations, competition may need to be protected, in the first instance by rules that sanction impermissible force and fraud. Institutions should be framed to establish what private restrictions of competition are not allowed and what actions require the intervention of an arbiter because they represent a misuse of market power. In many countries, the rules are laid down in trade-practices and anti-trust legislation. They require supervision of undue market power by specialist competition agencies. However, such official supervision often fails to produce the desired results because these agencies are easily captured by the supervised firms and because those in charge of such agencies suffer from intractable knowledge problems, as well as the policy handicaps inherent in enforcing specific outcomes (for a thorough assessment of competition policy, see Armentano (1991), also McChesney in Henderson, 2008, pp. 11–14). The alternatives to surveillance of competition by authorities are simple rules that proscribe private restrictions of competition combined with sanctions. Possible infringements of the rules of free competition, which are not ruled out by proscriptions, are then left to the controlling discipline of open markets, that is, to potential competition. This, of course, requires that governments abstain from all actions to artificially close markets or favour incumbent competitors.

A case where there is no rivalry, which has long played a role in the economic literature, is 'natural monopoly', that is, a situation where someone holds all property rights to a unique asset, one with no close substitutes. However, such cases are extremely rare, because potential rivals of the monopolist will seek to find close substitutes. Rivals will invest heavily in substitutes if a natural monopolist reaps high returns. Experience shows that few natural monopolies have ever been durable, unless protected by a political authority (Friedman, 1991). One reason is that monopolies normally occur in a defined geographic area, so that high profits attract out-of-area competitors. With the secular decline in transport and communication costs, such out-of-area rivals have become increasingly common.

Political restrictions of competition

Frequently, the free use of private property rights is restricted by political interventions. As we saw earlier in this chapter, suppliers or organized supplier interests try to obtain political interventions that soften the competitive pressures on them and secure their market niches more permanently than can be done by purely economic competition. This enables them to save information costs and therefore is worth the expenses to obtain political favours (rent-seeking). Political agents respond – often willingly out of agent opportunism or poor understanding of economics – by regulating markets and restricting market access. Some of these interventions may be justifiable in that they enhance the knowledge-creating capacity of competition, for example when government stipulates standardized weights and measures. However, in most instances, regulations simply exclude or hinder potential rivals, increase the compliance costs of market participants and limit the freedom of contract. Specific rules, which stipulate certain outcomes may, in isolation, not be a problem, but their proliferation quickly over-taxes most entrepreneurs' cognitive capacity, so that this hinders the use of knowledge.

To suppliers, government restrictions of competitive action are often welcome substitutes for private restrictions (Stigler, 1971). Supplier lobbies and government agents all too often disguise their rent seeking as promoting some worthy health or safety purpose or serve as a means of redistributing incomes. Government interventions in the complex, open market system, however, tend to have unforeseen and unwelcome consequences, simply because the intervening authorities cannot foresee all consequences. We only need to recall the example of price ceilings for house rentals and asymmetric contract conditions that are intended to benefit low-income renters, which – sooner or later – inhibit house building and then work to the disadvantage of renters, especially those on low incomes.

A typical and frequent case for a market intervention to benefit some suppliers is the tariff. The short-term impact of a new tariff is to raise the price of competing imported goods, thus easing the competitive pressure on domestic producers of import substitutes. This reallocates property rights from the many dispersed and unorganized buyers, as well as foreigners, to the few organized domestic producers. Tariffs are often being justified with the argument that producer profitability, once enhanced by import substitution, raises domestic investment and therefore enhance employment and incomes in domestic industry, or that they buy time for ailing industries to adjust, helping to conserve jobs. The worldwide evidence of import substitution, however, supports the conclusion that these advantages are, at best, temporary. Over the long run, tariff protection only creates an industrial, politicized rentier class and eases the competitive pressures to innovate, so that protected 'infant industries' end up as high-cost, un-enterprising senescent industries (Papageorgiou et al., 1991; Bhagwati, 2002).

In electoral democracies, rent-seeking producers are able to appeal to politicians who themselves have to compete for re-election, party finance or promotion (and who are often imbued with a 'guardian instinct'). Rivalling suppliers thus develop a strong demand for political efforts to fortify their market niches (see Box 8.2). When agents of government issue licenses to producers or impose tariffs to exclude new rivals from entering the market, this assists in converting active economic rivalry among suppliers into cartels or monopolies.

Parliamentarians, bureaucrats and other political agents have strong incentives to supply favours that protect client producer groups. By legislating, regulating or passing judicial judgments to reduce the intensity of rivalry among suppliers in a market, political powerbrokers can prove their own importance to the few suppliers and their workers in an industry, each of whom may gain a solid advantage. Political entrepreneurs, who seek rewards from redistributing property rights by recourse to political power, therefore respond willingly to demand for political favours because patronage increases their influence (Stigler, 1971a). Few political leaders are therefore wedded to a strategy of 'no favours all around' that is, a policy of non-discrimination between particular firms or industries.

Intervening government officials and parliamentarians may share in the profits that they allocate to regulated industries (through collecting license fees; contributions to party funds; political support or lucrative positions for retired bureaucrats and politicians, or through outright corruption).

Interventions that tamper with competition typically affect each of thousands of buyers in the same market only by a small margin, so that a political intervention may go unnoticed or – if noticed – is not worth the expense and effort of lobbying against. It is rational for buyers to remain ignorant and not to engage in political action to counter particular supplier lobbies and the political favouritism of political elites. This is why interventions in competitive processes tend to be supplier-biased and disadvantage the many ill-organized buyers.

The capitalist market economy therefore needs institutional constraints of political favouritism. The constraints should be placed on suppliers, who have strong incentives to escape the relentless economic-competitive bind, as well as on political agents, who benefit electorally or materially from their meddling (Olson, 1965; Buchanan and Tullock, 1962; Tullock, 1967; Stigler, 1971a; Buchanan *et al.*, 1980; Tollison, 1982; Mueller, 2003).

Another form of political intervention in the free private dispositions of property rights is judicial activism. In some countries, judges, whose traditional function has been to protect citizens under a transparent, cohesive system of law, have become activist creators of new interpretations of the law aimed at obtaining specific outcomes, often on behalf of organized interest groups. Given a constructivist bent in legal training and an absence of checks – such as election to office or the discipline of having to raise the finance for implementing the outcomes of one's decisions – judges have, in many countries, arrogated to themselves the role of hampering free competition by remaking the law. The courts then become preferred battlegrounds for circumventing economic competition and for benefiting from political competition. In these circumstances, it is particularly important that the principles of competition and protected private property rights are given a protected, high legal status.

When those in control of a country's external institutional framework are siding with the interests of the influential few, they divert the pursuit of market niches by entrepreneurs from active, productive economic rivalry and innovation into political action (Figure 8.2). The political elites then act against the interests of the citizen-principals whose agents they are. Once the rules fail to prevent political and bureaucratic operators from intervening, the commitment to knowledge search wanes and the pace of innovation slackens. Cost controls in business are then likely to become lax. Economic growth slows down, and we can speak of 'economic sclerosis'.

It is therefore important for the growth of useful knowledge – as well as the equity of opportunity – that firm rules are in place which force parliamentarians, bureaucrats and judges to support a constitutional principle of competition. Protecting the rules of competition must therefore be one of the core tasks of public policy.

Of course, in a free country, property owners cannot be forced to risk their assets to explore new uses and new knowledge. Economic freedom also implies that affluent people refuse to compete. However, they must not be protected by political and administrative means from the consequence of that refusal, namely from their assets losing value or even becoming value-less. When certain skills became redundant due to technical change, political entrepreneurs were tempted to prevent this by intervening on behalf of groups with superseded skills. In European history, rioting hand-weavers were sometimes given political protection against machine-weaving to the detriment of the buyers of textiles, international competition and economic growth. A remarkable case of resistance to technical progress, which amounted to a massive anti-competitive move by the political elites, is recorded in Korean history. Among numerous legal, technical and agricultural reforms, the modernizing King Sejong the Great (1397-1450) fostered the development of a phonetic alphabet (*hangul*), which replaced the cumbersome and for Korean inappropriate Chinese writing system, to promote the education of the people. However, after Sejong's death, the officials and the aristocracy again suppressed the writing reform in favour of the hard-to-learn Chinese system to prevent general literacy and keep their privileged position. Only in the late nineteenth century was the information-cost saving *hangul* system re-introduced, giving North and South Korea a writing system that can be quickly learnt and is much more efficient than, for example, the confounded system which the Japanese still use to write their language. Korea's writing reform of the late nineteenth century is an outstanding example of institutional change that has been highly productive in economic, cultural and civic terms.

CH 8 – CASE TWO

Rent seeking – illustrated by two historic cases

I

In his *Useful Information for Engineers* (1860), William Fairbairn, one of the best-known engineering pioneers of the Industrial Revolution in England, wrote about his youth when the Engineer Mechanics Union objected to his legal entitlement to enter his chosen trade:

> When I first entered London, a young man from the country had no chance whatever of success in consequence of trade unions and guilds. I had no difficulty in finding employment, but before I could begin work, I had to run the gauntlet of the trade societies. [After having tried in vain to be accepted as a member of the union], I was ultimately declared illegitimate and sent to seek my fortune elsewhere. [There were three competing unions] to exclude all those who could not assert

CH 8 – CASE TWO *(continued)*

their claims to work in London and other corporate towns. Laws of a most arbitrary character were enforced, and they were governed by cliques of self-appointed officers, who never failed to take care of their own interests.

Fairbairn was forced to move and seek work with the Dublin inventors of a revolutionary nail-making machine: "The Dublin iron-manufacture was ruined . . . not through any local disadvantages, but solely by the prohibitory regulations enforced by the workmen of the Trade Unions" (cited after Johnson, 1991, p. 574).

II

An early case where initial privileges granted to an organized group led to growing rent-seeking, including by violent means, occurred in the United Kingdom after the Napoleonic Wars:

Trade unions, which had long existed in Britain, were given special privileges through several Acts of Parliament in 1824. Prior to this legislation, the urging of workers to strike had been punishable under the conspiracy provisions of the Common Law and specific statute laws. Now, unions were legalized and awarded a privilege – the right to break contracts – denied to anyone else . . . The two bills went through Parliament almost without debate, the general assumption being that they would help to produce industrial peace.

Never was an illusion more ill founded. The consequence of lifting legal penalties produced the first real wave of organized strikes . . . [In 1825], there were strikes among the spinners and weavers of Scotland, among the textile workers of Lancashire and among the colliers in . . . the coal fields . . . [A strike] . . . halted London seagoing traffic – something which had never happened before in the port's existence, which went back to Roman times . . .

Moreover, some of the most destructive and frightening aspects of modern trade unionism at its worst made their instant appearance . . . There were widespread demands for the introduction of the closed or union shop; for restrictions on entry, especially for apprentices, and the introduction of new machinery; for the dismissal of unpopular (efficient) foremen; and for limitations of every kind on recruitment of new labour. In short, most unions immediately produced long shopping lists of requirements, each of which tended to lower productivity, raise manufacturers' costs or restrict the employer's right to run his business. All were backed by the threat of strikes.

What was particularly alarming were the harsh and often brutal efforts by union leaders and militants to compel their fellow workmen, whether they liked it or not, to back these demands. New union rules, now lawful, not only enforced a wide range of restrictive practices but introduced entry fees, forced levies on wages, and inter-union action, or what are now called secondary boycotts . . . The new activity of 'picketing', often violent, began outside workplaces . . . There was a good deal of terrorism, . . . a union passed a sentence of death on four men . . ., one of whom was actually murdered.

(Johnson, 1991, pp. 868–869)

8.4   The competitive system

The benefits of a competitive economy

It is useful to look beyond competition in individual markets and to review the wider, societal benefits of competition in the use of property rights.

Intense competitiveness throughout an economic system has a number of important benefits for the community at large:

(a) As we now know, intensive rivalry encourages the incurring of information costs and fosters the discovery of valued knowledge and hence overall economic growth.

Competitive economies therefore tend to cope flexibly and promptly with the need for structural change in response to inevitable shifts in demand, technical opportunities, resource supplies, income levels and other circumstances. Competitive economies respond to changed conditions, including the ready responsiveness of the owners of production factors to changes in relative prices, that is, a high degree of factor mobility. Market rivals continually explore variations to what they have been doing so far, and exchange partners ceaselessly select what they prefer. What succeeds, expands, what fails to find favour is discontinued or varied, so that errors are corrected.

The resulting structural changes may mean that some skills are no longer needed, capital loses value and old technology becomes worthless. Some market participants are forced to adjust their expectations downward. However, competitive, flexible economies also offer resource owners new opportunities. And if economic growth is fast, the winners will exceed the losers. If, for example, labour markets are competitive, a high share of the labour force will be employed. In competitive economies, individual workers who lose their jobs have a better chance of soon finding new employment. By contrast, uncompetitive economies with rigid prices and little factor mobility tend to grow slowly, so that people who have lost their jobs are permanently out of work. When more suffer from structural adjustments, this inspires more widespread resistance to structural change, setting off a vicious circle.

(b) Another important benefit of intense competitiveness is that economic power is controlled. Monopolies and market niches are temporary and limited in scope, so that property rights are not overly concentrated in a few hands.

Competition challenges property owners, time and again, to validate their assets by using them and search for new ways to test whether their assets are still valued by the other side of the market (revealed preferences). As rivals strive to discover new alternatives to attract contracts from the other side of the market, old property rights may lose their market value – what Joseph Schumpeter aptly called 'creative destruction' – but other items of property may rise in value. The game is evolutionary and no social and economic positions are sacrosanct. For better or worse, competition exposes everyone to ceaseless challenges.

(c) Another benefit of a competitive society is income distribution. In competitive economic systems, income distribution is always in flux. The pioneer profits of property owners and the incomes of workers wax and wane, as market fortunes change. When one, by contrast, observes fairly durable differences in incomes and wealth in advanced economies, this has normally much to do with political intervention and anti-competitive regulations (Friedman, 1962, pp. 119–132). For instance, restrictions in the labour market and controls of house rentals often cement unintended inequalities, which public redistribution policies subsequently try to mitigate. It is worth noting in this context that several of the most competitive new industrial societies of East Asia, such as Taiwan, also have a fairly even income distribution, although none of them have implemented redistributive welfare policies (Riedel, 1988, pp. 18–21).

(d) On a wider societal level, economic competition ensures that industrial power brokers will be cautious in using their wealth to buy undue political influence. As long as economic competition is lively and widespread, 'monopoly capitalism' is kept at bay. Ordinary citizens thus have a better chance of escaping the consequences of attempted political discrimination and rent seeking (Friedman, 1962, pp. 119–132).

(e) A further consequence of a competitive economy is that agents on both sides of the market are offered numerous choices with whom to contract. They are able to exit from previous contractual binds and situations where they feel exploited by powerful counterparts. This not only controls power, but also promotes freedom at large, for private autonomy becomes effective when people are free to choose.

(f) On a closely related plain, inevitable conflicts between buyers and sellers are defused when the 'exit option' exists. Conflicts in competitive economies tend to be handled in decentralized, anonymous ways.

People accept changed market prices and adjust. By contrast, conflicts are often allowed to build up in non-competitive systems, which then leads to a confrontational recourse to the political 'voice option'. Conflicts are then emotionalized and politicized by political entrepreneurs, who hope to rally conflicting parties behind their cause. Seen in this light, economic competition tends to serve social peace and stability by pulverizing and de-emotionalizing unavoidable economic and social conflicts.

(g) Last but not least, competitive economies also tend to absorb exogenous shocks better. Business cycles are smoothed by spontaneous, flexible price and quantity responses. If monetary policies are conducted in a stable, predictable manner, they are met with stabilizing responses in competitive systems, whereas economic systems that are dominated by rigid monopolies and oligopolies may require major doses of discretionary counter-cyclical policy to correct boom-bust cycles, which is problematic. Where wages and work practices are rigid, cyclical demand fluctuations are reflected in big fluctuations of profits and employment. This is likely to set off further, destabilizing fluctuations in investments. Flexible wages and competitive work practices in labour markets, by contrast, act as buffers that avert cumulative instability. Some may argue that labour should not act as a shock absorber. However, one may also ask whether greater overall job security and the stability of employment levels are not more valuable to the workers than a constant wage. These considerations apply more generally: Competitive markets are conducive to spontaneous self-stabilization and hence economic security; in other words, a competitive economy is more robust.

The autonomous, competitive use of property rights – a constitutional principle

These advantages of the competitive use of property rights – of what one might call the constitution of capitalism – are easily undermined by economically harmful political action that is driven by populist political rivalry. Secure private property rights and free contracting should therefore be considered principles with a high moral and constitutional status. In the general interest, they should be made into overriding, universal institutions which govern the making and implementation of lower-level rules and which cannot be overturned by simple court judgments, simple parliamentary majorities or mere administrative actions to suit specific interests. If the basic institutions of a competitive economy enjoy the high legal protection of constitutional rules, this establishes trust in a self-controlling, self-organizing economic system in which policy interventions need to be used sparingly and ordinary citizens can thrive.

In Chapter 10, we will return to this idea when discussing the style and content of public policy. First, however, it seems necessary to turn to economic organizations, such as business firms.

NOTES

1 This conception of the competitive process owes much to what has been termed 'German market process theory' (for a survey see Streit and Wegner, 1992; Kerber, in Boettke, 1994, pp. 500–507; Kasper, in Henderson, 2008, pp. 73–76).

2 For a discussion of different approaches to model the competitive process, see Addleson, 'Competition', in Boettke, (ed.) 1994, pp. 96–102, and Kirzner, 1973; 1985.

3 It should be noted in passing that most neoclassical textbooks ignore non-price competition although it is much more important in most markets for complex products and services. Focusing exclusively on price competition in standard textbook analysis is only possible because of the assumption of zero transaction costs (see *Epilogue*). In this unrealistic case, the supplier's offer price equals the price that the buyer pays and there is one equilibrium market-clearing price that has a direct bearing on the suppliers' cost curves and the buyers' indifference curves.

9

Economic organizations

The reader will become familiar with the possibly surprising insight that teams, firms and other economic organizations are created primarily to save on the costs and risks of frequent market transactions. To economize on such costs, people commit production factors in more or less enduring, cooperative, purpose-oriented arrangements, called firms.

What matters in deciding whether a firm should perform an operation in-house, keeping it under its direct organizational control, or sub-contract in the market is the ratio between (i) the organization costs of the coordinating processes within the company and (ii) the transaction costs of buying the necessary inputs in markets. Where markets function poorly and hence are costly to use – or do not function at all, as was the case in the socialist countries – there is a tendency to integrate as many activities as possible within the organization. In market economies, advances in computing, communications and institutional design over recent decades have led to growing specialization, devolution, sub-contracting and networking through markets.

Particular institutional problems arise within organizations, as people cooperate on the basis of open-ended, incompletely defined relational agreements. The owners of specific assets, such as large chunks of capital, may sometimes fear being 'held up' by the owners of complementary production factors, for example the suppliers of vital material inputs or skilled labour.

Many modern organizations, such as joint-stock companies, are managed by agents (company directors), rather than the owners of the capital, the principals. This gives rise to principal-agent problems, the risk that the managing agents may not act in the principals' interest. The problem is addressed by internal rules of corporate governance, external laws and regulations and – most importantly – competitive markets for products, capital and managers, which surround corporations in a functioning capitalist economy. We shall also see that different forms of private economic organization – for example clubs, mutual societies, family companies, and stock companies – have a differing likelihood of performing effectively in their principals' interest, because different incentive structures and sanctions apply.

A leader is best when people barely know that he exists . . .
A good leader talks little.
When his work is done, his aim fulfilled, they will all say: We did this ourselves.

Lao Zi (Laotse), *Dao de ching*, sixth century BC

Right is the proverb which says: More skills are required to make a successful businessman than are required to make a good lawyer.

Luca Pacioli (1445-1517), inventor of double-entry book-keeping (1494)

The directors of . . . companies . . ., being managers rather of other people's money than their own, it cannot well be expected that they should watch over it with the same anxious vigilance with which partners in a private copartnery frequently watch over their own . . . Negligence and profusion, therefore, must always prevail, more or less, in the management of the affairs of such a company.

Adam Smith, *The Wealth of Nations* (1931), p. 229

We have witnessed in modern business the submergence of the individual within the organization, and yet the increase to an extraordinary degree of the power of the individual, of the individual who happens to control the organization.

Woodrow Wilson, 31 August 1910

To some extent every organization must rely also on rules and not only on specific commands . . . it is possible to make use of knowledge which nobody possesses as a whole, . . . [An] organization will determine by commands only the function to be performed by each member, the purposes to be achieved, and certain general aspects of the methods to be employed, and will leave the detail to be decided by the individuals on the basis of their respective knowledge and skills.

Friedrich Hayek (1973), *Rules and Order*

9.1   Economic organizations: definition and purposes

Up to this point, the reader may have gained the impression that we focus excessively on individuals pursuing their economic and other interests and that they do so independently by competing, each on his own, in the market place. But, of course, individuals often cooperate in organizations and submit property rights they own to the control of a leader, or leaders, of organizations on a more or less permanent basis. As a matter of fact, organizations often provide humans who are 'social animals' with the stimulus of their fellows' company. Organizations – whether family enterprises or large corporations – provide individuals with a social framework, in which they can thrive and validate their thoughts and actions by working alongside others.

Much of the division of labour to produce what we need to survive has therefore always taken place in reasonably durable organizational relationships, such as the family group, the tribe, cooperative ventures, business partnerships or work teams. In all of these, productive activities and rewards are coordinated at least partly by leader(s) who command and control from the top down. The spontaneous form of coordinating the division of labour – through market exchanges – certainly seems a more recent innovation in the long history of humankind, as compared with the hierarchical organization of economic life in hunting packs and cooperation within families and tribes. Only when technology and the number of participants in the division of labour reached considerable complexity, were property rights defined and market exchanges invented to complement organizational forms of human coordination. There was then a need for what Hayek called an 'extended order' under the universal rule of law. As we have seen, this permitted a much more complex division of labour and higher living standards than was possible within self-sufficient organizations. But this does not mean that organized coordination is not highly effective in many circumstances, or that competitors in markets should not at times become part of organized teams. Common sense (and game theory) show that organized cooperation is frequently of mutual advantage in coordinating people, indeed that it often yields more desirable results for participants than rivalry (Axelrod, 1984; North, 1990, pp. 12–16; section 5.1).

A definition of organizations

We define organizations as more or less durable, planned arrangements to pool productive resources (property rights) in order to pursue one or several shared purposes. These resources are coordinated within some kind of hierarchical order by a mix of institutions and commands. Performance is monitored and controlled to ensure that it meets set goals. Organizations are based on sets of rules, a constitution which derives either from voluntary contracts or political authority (Vanberg, 1992). Examples of private voluntary organizations are cooperatives, mutual trusts, clubs and business firms. An example for the creation of an organization by political authority is an administrative body. In this chapter, we shall deal only with private economic organizations, which are based on voluntary contractual commitments, leaving political organizations to the following chapter.

In most communities, organizations are entitled to act as independent legal units (corporate actors); they may sign contracts on their own behalf (firms from *firma*, Latin for signature). Organizations normally cover complex internal interactions that cannot be spelled out and negotiated completely, in other words they are based on relational contracts.

The mere juxtaposition of resources, where the property owners retain completely autonomous rights of disposition and are not subject to any directives, does not constitute an organization, even if all resource owners share a common interest. Thus, the gathering of spectators at a football match, who share the purpose of being entertained, does not make an organization. Only when economic agents pool some of their resources and abandon part of their rights to use these resources independently, do they form an organization, which then becomes a 'collective actor' (Coleman, 1990). This would, for example, be the case when certain spectators form a club, promise to pay membership fees and subject themselves to shared rules that are monitored by a committee of the club.

Economic organizations serve the purpose of mobilizing and exploiting resources for a material purpose. Organizations allow individual collaborators to combine the production factors in which they have property rights and to operate them conjointly in an ordered, predictable setting. Organizations create an environment in which individuals are able to interact closely and enduringly with others and economize on information and coordination costs. The other members of the organization and the hierarchical order in which individuals are placed are familiar to them, as are many of the organization's internal rules and routines. Part of the task of organizational leadership is to save on information requirements by designing and realizing a plan and informing the various collaborators of their role in it, as well as fostering implicit and explicit institutions which guide the members of the organization.

As long as organized teams are exposed to external competition, which forces them to adjust to outside changes and challenges, the organized order is unlikely to rigidify and become an obstacle to the exploitation of new opportunities (Section 8.1). One may therefore see economic organizations as social arrangements, which facilitate information flows, serve the acquisition, testing and exploitation of knowledge and satisfy aspirations for social stimulation, interaction and material gain.

KEY CONCEPTS

Organizations were defined in Chapter 2 as purposive and reasonably durable arrangements of productive resources, which are coordinated to some extent in a hierarchical order by a leader (or leaders). Typically, the relations, benefits and obligations are incompletely defined.

Economic organizations may, for example, be business firms that have chosen profitability as their objective and that operate between input and output markets, requiring voluntary cooperation under contracts with people who do not belong to the organization.

Political organizations are created by political will and may then be able to compel others to interact with them.

Economic organizations take diverse forms. The probably best known example is the incorporated firm, which nowadays is a fairly durable arrangement to pursue an open-ended purpose, such as making a profit. But temporary economic organizations are also quite common. For example, they may be set up for the sole purpose of building a bridge or developing a piece of land; they are disbanded after the completion of the project. Other forms of open-ended voluntary economic organization are family firms, trade associations, clubs, cooperatives, trade unions, trusts, and mutual community organizations. What they have in common is that they bundle some resources with the aim of pursuing a shared purpose and give themselves some constitutional structure, for example statutes fixing the duties of the chairman and secretary.

The defining questions for any economic organization are: Who keeps residual profits or bears possible losses? How are profits and losses distributed if more than one partner shares ownership of the organization? Follow-up questions are: Who controls the organization's operations, both short- and long-term, and how do owners control the managers, if ownership and management are separated?

A great variety of legal forms have been developed to address the problems of voluntary economic associations. Owner-managed firms and partnerships may provide for total, unlimited liability of the owners. Alternatively, liability for contractual obligations may be limited by statute to the organization's capital (limited liability company). Some economic organizations may be not-for-profit, dispersing possible surpluses through reduced prices, additional services, or higher rewards to the production factors they employ. Other organizations may pool limited property of a great many partners in pursuit of a shared financial aim, such as insurance against certain risks or joint saving and investment (mutual societies, *kongxi* societies in Chinese communities, trusts). Yet others not only pool capital and land, but also the rights to the owners' labour, knowledge and skills in order to pursue a specific purpose (cooperatives). Some organizations are set up under traditional and private law, others are heavily regulated under specific statute laws, have to be licensed and are formally supervised by government authorities.

Transaction costs and organizations

A producer may buy all inputs he needs in the market place. Additional help could conceivably be hired in the labour market every day, all capital could be borrowed on a periodic basis, each quantity of input could be bought separately, and all items of output could be offered and sold in the open market. But – as Ronald Coase famously discovered in the 1930s (1952/1937) – such a way of marshalling productive resources would involve extremely high transaction costs. Relying exclusively on one-off contracts would create enormous information costs; in each instance, new contracts would have to be negotiated, monitored and enforced. This is why repetitive production is normally coordinated within organizations called firms. They combine the key resources more or less permanently by entering into relational contracts and operate in pursuit of a shared purpose (or purposes). Such more or less permanent arrangements, which create 'durable coalitions of property rights', may reduce the freedom of individuals to dispose of their property rights at any one point in time. However, because the commitments to the organization reduce coordination costs, they enhance the value of the property rights.[1] The desire for complete independence and freedom from all commitments therefore tends to come at a price in terms of effectiveness in attaining one's goals and one's income (Milgrom and Roberts, 1976; Williamson, 1987, 1988).

Asset specificity

Oliver Williamson (1985) drew attention to a related aspect for the existence of firms: owners of capital, knowledge and other resources are often obliged by technical circumstances to commit their resources irreversibly and for a long time to specific forms (asset specificity). The owners of financial capital thus commit their assets to specific capital goods – just as putty is 'committed' to a fixed form when it is baked into clay objects. The owners of a company who have invested their capital in buildings and specific equipment cannot readily switch out of those investments. They also acquire valuable specific knowledge, which they can use only if they remain in specific operations (human capital specificity). These investments will only pay the expected returns if the specific assets can be operated undisturbed over a long period. However, the owners of complementary resources, such as skilled labour, may want to exploit the inflexibility of the capital owners and holders of specific knowledge by 'holding up' operations and extorting higher pay. This is a case of people having and exploiting power because their counterparts have no scope for substitution or evasion (exit, see Section 5.4). When such power constellations are prevalent and are not ruled out credibly by internal and external institutions, there is a motive for binding the owners of complementary resources into the organization. In many cases, this may even be the precondition for a specific investment. Thus, capital owners may only invest in an aluminium smelter or a steel plant, if they can secure input flows by obtaining direct organizational control over the sources of power and ores. In such cases, the motive for combining property rights in an organization is risk-avoidance, in other words the wish to reduce uncertainty and economize on information costs by creating a more credible, organized order.

The need to deal with asset specificity is predicated on three interlocking conditions: (i) people have limited information, limited aspirations, and consequently act with bounded rationality, (ii) people are opportunistic, unless prevented by institutions, and (iii) some hold assets of pronounced specificity (Williamson, 1985). In these conditions, the usual gaps in relational contracts may be exploited by opportunistic individuals at the expense of the owners of the specific assets, who do not have rewarding alternatives by changing the uses of their assets.

The test of whether these assumptions apply depends also on wider social circumstances and traditions. Frequently, opportunism is controlled by external institutions (the law) and internal institutions of the community at large (morals, customs). In many communities, people take a long-term view and do not play opportunistic end games. They understand that their prosperity depends on mutual, ongoing and rule-bound interaction, as well as on trust and good faith (Flew in Radnitzky, 1997, pp. 107–124). Neither is it clear whether the leaders of organizations can always anticipate the future costs and benefits of buying inputs in markets as compared to tying supplies of inputs by including the supplier within the organization. The ever-present knowledge problem complicates such an assessment, as the ratio between transaction and organization costs keeps changing due to technical and institutional evolution.

Conclusions from the Williamson model for the conduct of public policy – namely that vertical integration should be tolerated in the interest of overall efficiency – therefore seem based on frequently untested assumptions, not least the notion that the overall effects of alternative arrangements can ever be known.[2]

KEY CONCEPTS

The **putty-clay concept of capital formation** refers to the fact that people save monetary assets (often called capital), which can be invested in numerous alternative forms of hardware. Like putty, monetary assets are fungible. But the act of investment into real capital goods locks capital into a fixed form (so to speak sets it in clay). The costs of converting out of specific capital investments are often high, so that capital owners become vulnerable to the exercise of power by the owners of ➡

←

complementary and supposedly more fungible production factors.

Asset specificity is a condition of a productive asset – such as an item of capital equipment or a body of specialized knowledge – which does not allow it to be switched to alternative uses. The proprietors of specific assets cannot exit and are therefore open to abuses of power, namely the hold-up of their operations by the owner's complementary production factors. Thus, aircraft owners depend on pilots to make a profit and may be forced by a pilot strike to concede increased salary payments. This explains why owners of specific assets have a keen interest in binding complementary inputs providers in organizations (or in obtaining strong institutional controls).

Hierarchy and leadership

The definition of an organization invariably contains the constitutional element of having a unifying purpose or set of purposes (goals). The goals may be set autonomously by the leaders or arise from consultation and participative decision making among members of the organization. In this respect, organizational coordination always differs from the coordination of independent agents in the market place. In markets, no goals are set *ex ante* for participants and from the outside. Instead, people are self-motivated and coordinated by evolutionary processes of trial and error.

The definition of private economic organizations also contains the element of durability over time – property rights to capital, labour, knowhow and land are durably pooled (Vanberg, 1992). The early joint-stock companies of early modern Europe were set up for one venture of limited duration by merchants who pooled capital and, maybe, their own knowledge and labour. Rights to complementary resources were bought in the market. For example, ships were leased, sailors were hired and trade goods were acquired. Like time-limited ventures in real-estate development nowadays, they entered into incompletely defined contracts with the purpose of exploiting a specific trading opportunity, such as bringing a shipload of spices back from the East. After the voyage, the partners shared the profits (or losses) as agreed in the company's constitution and then dissolved the share company. Many of the early share companies thus lasted only for the duration of a specific venture. Nowadays, most economic organizations are of course intended to be permanent.

The concept of organization also contains the notion of coordinated action under a plan that assigns specific tasks. This requires some decision about who has ultimate powers to plan, command and control at least some aspects of activities. This implies some kind of hierarchy. The hierarchical aspect may be pronounced (strong subordination, complex multi-level organization) or weak (much self-responsibility of team members, flat organization). In any case, not all aspects of an organization's activity can be planned and commanded, so that rules have an important part in organization-internal coordination. When discussing organizations, one therefore should again distinguish between directives (or instructions, commands, prescriptions) that order affairs by assigning specific tasks, targets and functions to agents, and general rules of conduct that assist spontaneous ordering (Vanberg, 1992, pp. 244–245; also Section 5.1). The pooling of resources under common control has to be based on a constitution (a set of general rules how to proceed and how to change rules) to bind the individual resource owners who form the organization (*idem*, pp. 239–241).

General rules invite collaborators to make independent judgments and take the initiative, whereas prescriptions are based on authority and subordination. The organization-internal rules are normally bound by the constitution of the organization and steer the use of pooled resources and the distribution of the joint product between the various owners. When rules do not bind the leaders in charge of organizations, there is scope for arbitrary decisions. If not exercised with care, this may destroy order in the minds of the members of the organization and undermine their productivity and loyalty.

Whether the hierarchical command elements in a business organization are pronounced or weak has great impact on its performance and flexibility (see Section 9.3 below). Heavy reliance on hierarchical commands may stress cohesion and tight coordination, but often conflicts with limits of knowledge on the part of the leaders and of cognitive limits on the part of the subordinates. Command structures often require costly control, measurement and monitoring. Heavy reliance on command may also undermine the motivation and creativity of the collaborators. These problems tend to weigh more heavily in a complex, changeable world, so that de-emphasizing hierarchy and command in the mix of the means of internal ordering frequently confers competitive advantages. Business leaders who have to manage rapid change, often discover that control is more effective when exercised through broad, universal rules that give collaborators and sub-teams only general guidelines and leave them much scope to make decisions. This requires trust that the collaborators will further the company's shared purpose. Modern firms therefore often emphasize training in judgmental skills and try to motivate collaborators by imbuing them with the 'business culture', that is, the general goals and rules of the organization (Kreps, 1990). They promote flat hierarchies, teamwork and performance-derived rewards for successful internal competition. This style of management is nowadays often seen as more appropriate than hierarchy, pyramid-climbing, obedience to commands and reliance on tight, detailed controls (Cyert and March, 1992).

Firms tend to be structured, coordinated and led by the owners of the production factor, which happens to be the bottleneck to growth. The owners of bottleneck factors tend to design the organization, coopt rights to other resources and control the use of all production factors. What constitutes a bottleneck factor to economic growth has of course varied with time and circumstance. If security of life, limb and property is the bottleneck to economic growth, economic organizations tend to be led by the providers of security. This was frequently the case under feudalism in Europe, when knights controlled economic activity, and now is still the case in parts of the Third World. Once community-wide institutions safeguard security of life and property, as was done after the Middle Ages in Europe, capital tends to become the bottleneck to growth, so that the capital owners typically controlled businesses. They hired the other resources (capitalism). In industries where labour is the bottleneck to the expansion of business – be it because labour is scarce or because artificial constraints limit labour supply – labour representatives typically control economic organizations (worker co-determination).

Recently, the owners of scarce knowledge have begun to run new ventures. They borrow capital and hire labour. For example, some gifted fashion and computer-software designers have created their own businesses; and some famous stars are running film ventures and theatres. Where deficient institutions make market access the bottleneck to business expansion, it is typically the operators with market access, for example, people who are able to obtain licenses through political connections, who organize businesses.[3]

KEY CONCEPTS

Authority is the right and the power to enforce obedience, that is, to compel subordinates to follow instructions. Authority may be comprehensive (and allow arbitrary decisions at the top) or may be limited by institutions to specific circumstances (rule-bound behaviour).

   Directives are detailed, prescriptive instructions for concrete actions. Directives

leave no scope for free, self-responsible decisions. Directives tend to downplay trust in subordinates and their judgment and require much knowledge from those who direct.

   A **pooling of property rights** to resources occurs when market transaction costs are expected to be higher than the organization costs to combine production factors.

9.2 Organization costs, relational contracts, and hold-up risks

When people are coordinated within organizations this creates organization costs, just as coordination in markets causes transaction costs (Sections 5.6 and 7.3). As mentioned, organization costs may often be less than the transaction costs for coordinating similar activities through markets because organizations impose a more clear-cut order on the various agents. Since many intra-organizational transactions are repetitive routines, organization also offers the opportunity to reap scale economies.

In principle, business organizers incur fixed (and, once incurred, sunk) costs of finding information when they plan and set up an organization, as well as recurrent costs when they run the organization: communicating with collaborators, (re)negotiating assignments and deals, monitoring the performance of the various agents, and sanctioning under-performing members of the organization.

Organization costs and leadership

The art of leadership of an organization has much to do with keeping internal organization costs low, in particular with (i) gaining correct information on all aspects of the organization's activities, and (ii) making that information compatible. It also has a lot to do with avoiding conflicts and disagreements amongst collaborators and sorting out possible conflicts. An understanding of shared objectives and, as mentioned, outside competitive pressures can greatly facilitate the leadership task. If leaders stick to transparent rules in their own actions and abstain from arbitrary decisions, they will build up a reputation of trustworthiness amongst their staff who will then identify their leader with a predictable internal order. This becomes a valuable capital asset that saves organization costs (Milgrom and Roberts, 1992, pp. 89–99).

Trust is especially valuable when routine operations are disrupted because the organization has to undergo some structural change. Then, it is doubly important that all those who are to be coordinated have an understanding of the shared strategic purpose (the overriding goals) which goes beyond tactical specifics. Napoleon referred to this aspect of leadership when he demanded that every soldier should "carry a marshal's baton in his knapsack".

The mix of reliance on directives and universal rules has great impact on the costs of running organizations. What mix is possible depends, however, on the quality of the team and on the task at hand. The better educated, trained and motivated the various collaborators are, the more will they share rules that serve to create a competitive advantage over organizations that rely heavily on case-by-case commands. The comparative advantage of a style of management that emphasizes rule-coordination, also increases with the complexity of the productive tasks. For example, mass production of a standard industrial product on the assembly line may well be coordinated most cheaply by relying on a fixed plan, on commands and close supervision. This style of management became known as *Taylorism*, named after the American engineer who became probably the world's first modern management guru, Frederick Winslow Taylor (1856-1915). By contrast, piecework, service provision and quick changes in markets require complex, changeable responses by motivated, skilled staff who act responsibly within firm-internal rule sets. When products and services have to be tailor-made, reliance on commands and close monitoring would only erode the motivation of collaborators to perform spontaneously and share information with the top. In organizations that rely heavily on rule-coordination, it may sometimes even pay to give members of the team scope to commit errors or risk their own experiments, because that could well unearth useful new information. The comments in the preceding chapter about rule-protected domains of freedom and innovation in markets also apply to internal information usage in organizations. As the share of the service industries in the economy grows, rule coordination is becoming more and more important in management.

The knowledge problem is thus a central challenge for all organizations. The art of leadership has much to do with handling this problem. If there was perfect knowledge, there would indeed be little need for management. This is one of the reasons why management teaching and business administration courses have turned away from teaching neoclassical economics, assuming perfect knowledge. If that assumption were true, most managers would be virtually superfluous! (Dahmén et al., 1994).

Much coordination of production factors can be done either *ex ante*, in other words before any action takes place, or *ex post*, that is, in the light of market experiences. Business firms rely partly on *ex ante* planning, but should be ready to make corrections in light of feedback from the market, that is, undertake *ex post* coordination with their customers and with what their competitors are doing.

Vertical integration and out-sourcing

Business leaders also have to evaluate regularly what to coordinate as an integral part of the organization and what should be left to sub-contracting. A general rule is to compare the expected transaction costs and risks in markets with the expected organization costs. This ratio is a function, amongst others, of the quality of market institutions, available technology and organizational skills. Where market institutions are poor and create high transaction costs, for example because of poor regulation, legislation and law enforcement, one can observe a tendency to integrate many activities within organizations. A high degree of vertical integration is, for example, typical of dysfunctional markets for inputs where genuine prices are not formed, so that much valuable information is never communicated. By contrast, well-functioning market economies give rise to numerous specialized sub-contractors to whom producers can delegate specific tasks, not least in information gathering. Thus, the financial industry has developed specialized sub-contractors who serve the big savings and investment banks. Independent specialists may deal with foreign-exchange risks, overnight money, forward markets, options, hedging, insurance, legal issues and many other such capital-market tasks. Another example is building contractors who rely on specialist suppliers to sell them electricity and water, advise on statics, waste treatment, colour schemes and building security, amongst others. Building contractors may even sub-contract earthworks, bricklaying and landscaping. Because mobile phones have made such transactions easier and more reliable, subcontracting and just-in-time delivery have been on the rise.

The relative costs of organizing and contracting are greatly affected by technology and taxation. For a considerable time, the spread of mainframe computers favoured big organizations. In the 1960s and 1970s, computers came as big, indivisible packages that could handle large volumes of standardized information, so that big corporations and big government had competitive advantages. This created an incentive to integrate more and more activities into big organizations. But from the late 1970s onwards, technology changed to decentralized, flexible computing power, user-friendly software and low-cost, user-friendly, even wireless communications equipment. This gave small operators the tools to better exploit their decentralized, highly specialized knowhow and skills. Contracting out frequently became the cheaper option, as distributed computer networks lowered transaction costs and cheaper telecommunications allowed frequent, intensive communications between a client and the providers of inputs. It is no coincidence that this has given rise to numerous new market niches and increased out-sourcing and networking. Thus, the car industry has increasingly used sub-contractors to develop and produce specialized components and concentrated on design, the final assembly of the components and marketing. Computer links now permit just-in-time delivery and intense sharing of technical expertise among independent businesses (networking, productive alliances). Entirely new markets emerged to support big organizations with inputs and specialized information. This also gave rise to the enormous growth of logistics through parcel delivery services and computer trade in inputs. Concentration on the core business became the slogan in business management. This was often accompanied by flatter, less complex, less hierarchical internal management structures and a trend towards encouraging firm-internal competition amongst fairly autonomous teams. In government organizations, that same shift in the cost ratio has favoured out-sourcing and privatization (Drucker, 1993; Naisbitt, 1994; Bickenbach and Soltwedel, 1995; Siebert, (ed.) 1995). Big business, big unions, big government have often shrunk to specialize on core tasks of design and quality control.

The shift to more reliance on market coordination puts a premium on reliable institutions and low transaction costs. These form social capital that can make an economy internationally more competitive, whilst economies with fuzzy, costly institutional environments are at an increasing disadvantage. The increased interest in institutional economics, to which we referred in Chapter 1, has much to do with this shift, as does the need to reduce transaction costs by appropriate public policies and fostering appropriate business ethics in developed and developing countries alike (Chapter 14 and *Epilogue*).

Explicit and implicit relational contracts

One-off contracts are relatively less important in modern complex economies than open-ended or relational contracts. Cost-ratios change over time, so that it is impossible to completely cover all contingencies by explicit stipulations in such contracts. Relational contracts therefore often contain implicit understandings of give and take and of implicit sanctions. Implicit internal contracts establish institutions that make up the company culture or the team spirit, they keep internal information and coordination costs low and guarantee scope for independent decision making for those who act within this rule structure. This is important for motivation and creativity, for shifting the organization from mere set-goal compliance and satisficing ('Don't ask me, I only work here!') to creative-entrepreneurial behaviour. Hierarchical controls may conflict with reliance on implicit relational contracts – control maniacs destroy motivation! Explicit and implicit relational contracts establish a measure of predictability and contain clauses that deal in a universal, non-specific way with contingencies (for example, an agreement to refer matters to an independent arbitrator in case of conflict). Ongoing relations depend heavily on institutions that establish a measure of confidence for both sides of the agreement.

Relational contracts between the owners of property rights in different production factors make the owners and their assets part of the organization. The bond is reinforced by sanctions for deficient or incomplete fulfilment of promises in relational contracts. These may consist of pre-agreed firm-internal penalties (for example exclusion from profit sharing, payment of penalties for late performance, non-promotion, or loss of influence over management decisions), as well as exclusion from the organization and hence from future benefits, or sanctions under external law.

KEY CONCEPTS

Organization costs are the resource costs of planning, establishing and running an organization. They include fixed, sunk costs of information search and design, and variable costs of operating organizations. The latter contain the costs of monitoring the performance of collaborators according to their contractual obligations, the notification of shortcomings and adjudication of intra-organizational conflicts, and, if necessary, the enforcement of agreed performance standards.

Implicit relational contracts are mutual understandings of give-and-take between the members of an organization or a team. They cover open-ended internal institutional arrangements that guide many of the vertical exchange relationships between the owners, the leaders and the collaborators in an organization, as well as some of the horizontal exchanges between collaborators and teams.

9.3 Ownership and control: the principal-agent problem in business

The defining criterion in any economic organization derives from the answer to the following question: Who gets the profit, once all contractually-agreed expenses have been deducted from the receipts, and who bears the risk of losses? Those to whom this applies are the principals. The question then is: Do the risk-bearing principals have effective and direct control over the organization and the details of its operation? This is the central issue of corporate governance in any organization. It arises whenever the principals of the organization do not manage all activities themselves, and in particular in joint-stock companies where the owners have delegated the control of daily business to executive managers who act as their agents. The manager-agents are of course much closer to the action and normally much better informed about what goes on than the principals.

Agent opportunism

When agents are better informed than the principals, there is a danger that the agents may act opportunistically in their own self-interest, neglecting the interests of the principals (Section 3.4). They may try to shirk risks and hide behind cumbersome committees instead of taking decisions, preferring the quiet life, despite the fact that taking risks and deciding expediently would probably enhance the profits earned by the principals. They may create unnecessary subordinate positions to justify promotion to a supervisory position. They may enjoy high on-the-job consumption (use of business facilities and company property for one's own personal ends; splendid offices, prestigious company premises, frequent enjoyable conferences and unnecessary business trips; excessive investment in equipment which is subsequently underutilized; acquisition of information and skills on the job that one then can market elsewhere; preparation of reports that no one reads; frequent staff lunches, and the like). They may vote themselves high salaries and bonuses, irrespective of whether the company is profitable or has to dismiss workers. They may tolerate avoidable costs although these expenses do nothing to promote the firm's ultimate purposes. And they may readily settle for higher wage claims and accept costly settlements in court cases, because fighting a strike or defending a court challenge is uncomfortable and risky to management. They may also readily comply with government directives that hurt the principals' interests, as was, for example, the case when major European banks 'voluntarily' wrote off massive claims on the bankrupt government of Greece in 2012 (called a 'haircut'), to the detriment of the principals (bank shareholders, old-age pensioners and small savers). A frequent manifestation of agent opportunism is satisficing, adjusting performance standards to disappointing past outcomes, rather than pursuing excellence to attain set goals or risking creative-entrepreneurial actions to overcome obstacles (Section 3.4).

Some forms of agent opportunism are against the law (for example, fraud), other forms may only violate general ethical standards, such as violations of honesty and punctuality. In all cases, agent opportunism may be difficult and costly for the owners to detect and prove.

The principal-agent problem can arise from the moment the owners hire others. Even owner-managers have the problem of monitoring the performance of their employees and enforcing their compliance with the firm's objectives. It is therefore a focal task of management to prevent or contain such opportunism, by obtaining sufficient information about the performance of collaborators and by providing appropriate incentives and mixes of command and organization-internal rules (for a good survey of the principal-agent problem in business see Arrow, 1985).

The principal-agent problem has been analysed in particular detail for joint-stock companies where the control of day-to-day operations – indeed even of major strategic choices – is left to the managers. The principals, the shareholders, are not directly involved in the running of the business. The executive managers are closely involved so that they may be tempted to act in their own interest to the detriment of the shareholders' interests (Berle and Means, 1932). For example, the managers of a joint-stock company may arrange business so that they run low risks of being fired or enjoy high salaries and bonuses. At the same time, they may tolerate low profits, which presumably runs against the principals' interests. The separation of ownership and control thus has the potential of creating high information and organization costs. The problem is compounded by the fact that shareholders – and in particular small investors – have insufficient incentives to incur the high information cost to find out whether managers act responsibly and in their interest.

Is the principal-agent problem the Achilles heel of capitalism?

Some analysts who observed the growth and spread of the modern corporation considered the principal-agent problem the Achilles heel of capitalism, predicting increasingly poor usage of capital by risk-shirking managers and growing resistance to cost controls, which would benefit the principals, but may hurt some of the agents (Berle and Means, 1932). Some observers concluded that only strong legal and regulatory interventions in corporate governance could overcome the principal-agent problem (Galbraith, 1967). Others saw insurmountable knowledge and enforcement problems for the public corporate-watchdog agencies (Demsetz, 1982, 1983, 1989/1982). These latter observers also feared that the judgment of managers on risk-taking would suffer when corporate governance is heavily regimented, since many management decisions are, by their very nature, beyond analysis by lawyers, bureaucrats and others who are the wiser only with hindsight. Given the knowledge problem, there are real dangers of regulatory failure in the close supervision of corporate governance.

These issues re-emerged in the wake of the 'global financial crisis' starting in 2008 with regard to big financial businesses. Managers had frequently awarded themselves high salaries and bonuses, which were not tied to performance, but had – in the opinion of investors and political elites – failed to properly assess the risks of a recession to the values of companies. This led to losses in share portfolios and consequently calls for tighter regulation of the finance industry in affluent countries. However, the eternal problem of regulatory oversight is present here, too. Will the regulators predict the future better than the managers of financial firms? Will they be captured by the managers, whom they are supposed to regulate? How will they prove that their predictions are more valid than those of market insiders? Will regulatory powers be abused for political ends? The tendency of policy makers is to rely on budget formulae, rules and mathematical models, but creativity in inventing new financial instruments and design to get around official regulations makes this a dubious proposition. And critics still fear that risk-taking management will become less enterprising to the detriment of well-functioning capital markets and hence long-term growth.

Judging by past performance, management-run corporations in the advanced capitalist countries have not performed systematically worse than owner-managed firms, so that the principal-agent problem in corporate governance is obviously less severe than originally thought or than utopian critics of capitalism assume. Indeed, experience has shown that there are powerful checks on the agent opportunism of corporate managers (Jensen and Meckling, 1976, especially pp. 308–309; Jensen and Ruback, 1983; Jensen, 1983):

(a) Modern business organizations have designed a number of effective company-internal institutions to contain manager opportunism and created incentives for managers to act in the owners' interest: regular internal and external audits to ensure transparency and accountability, imposition of budget controls, shareholder meetings and auditing committees that work on behalf of the shareholders, incentive pay, part-remuneration of managers in company stock that they cannot sell immediately, and job tenure dependent on performance. These devices create what has been called 'bonding costs' (Jensen and Ruback, 1983, p. 325). They are arguably less than the costs incurred when managers are poor and self-seeking.

(b) Competitive capital markets tend to evaluate the performance of share companies regularly. Freely traded shares allow owners to exit or enter at low cost, so that share price movements reflect these evaluations almost daily. Moreover, experts in financial institutions assess management teams professionally as a client service to shareholders, in particular when companies try to raise new finance. This tends to uncover manager opportunism sooner or later.

(c) New, specialized information markets, professional analysts acting for large and small investors, and the business press also reduce the principals' monitoring costs, as long as corporations are held by law to report regularly and completely on the business (accountability).

(d) Markets for managers and management teams are competitive. Manager-agents who have earned a reputation for honest, effective management are promoted and paid higher salaries. These markets, too, are supported by specialist information markets and agencies, for example the corporate head-hunting agencies.

(e) Markets for the corporate control of going businesses exist in most capitalist economies: When incumbent management teams obviously perform below market standards, new owners may come in with (friendly or hostile) takeover bids and merger proposals. They then sack poor management and install new management teams who are expected to be more effective. Managers may also attempt buy-outs to realign control and ownership. Takeover battles can of course be costly, but they enhance ownership control and reduce potential losses due to self-seeking management.[4]

(f) Product markets also reflect the performance of managing agents. As long as product markets are not monopolized, management teams that act opportunistically will sooner or later lose market share. This will signal the opportunism of the managers. Product-market competition complements the competition in the markets for capital and managers, ensuring that the interests of the principals are safeguarded.

None of these control mechanisms are completely failsafe. It lies in the dynamic character of capitalist enterprise that occasional mishaps occur. It is then tempting to apply hindsight and second-guess what happened. This may be part of constructive learning processes, an integral part of the competitive market order. However, it is not justified to deduce from such mishaps that the entire system is misconceived and needs to be overturned. One always has to guard against utopian critique and consider whether any alternatives could have performed better. Comparisons of overall performance with regard to the fundamental aspirations discussed in Chapter 4, suggest that capitalist enterprise is – to vary Churchill's famous dictum – the least imperfect system for overcoming scarcity yet invented.

Competition and the rules, which ensure transparent information, enhance shareholder control simply by serving as a potential threat to and discipline of opportunistically inclined manager-agents. The unrelenting pressure of rivalry for market share (discussed in Chapter 8) thus empowers the shareholders of companies and reduces their monitoring costs. Costly direct controls and sanctions of opportunistic managers then need to be implemented only sparingly. The principal-agent problems in joint-stock companies tend to become virulent only when managers obtain political protection against the various challenges to their position, for example when parliaments legislate to impede takeover bids or prohibit foreign investment.

In the economics literature, the consequences of the principals' knowledge problem about the actions of opportunistic agents have sometimes been discussed under the label of X-inefficiency. Leibenstein (1966) contended that firms, which had market power and were not exposed to vigorous competition, tended to operate not as effectively in pursuit of their principals' objectives and tended not to innovate as much as firms that were exposed to active market rivalry. The extensive work on X-inefficiency thus underpins the general message from this section – namely that competitive (product and factor) markets surrounding a firm ensure that the principals' interests in stock companies are pursued, rather than the opportunistic goals of the agents. Competitive markets are thus in the interest of the capital owners, even if not necessarily in the interest of company managers and workers.

Profits and multiple bottom lines

In recent decades, social activists and political operators have promoted the notion that big firms should be made responsible not only to shareholders for profitability, but also to the wider public for promoting certain social-welfare goals and environmental conservation – the 'triple bottom line'. Assigning more than one goal (profitability), and indeed non-quantified goals, to the top managers of firms is bound to test their cognitive capacity and to downgrade the coordinative power of the market (Henderson, 2001). Company executives may often yield to political pressures and subscribe to non-profit objectives as a way of enhancing the public reputation of the firm. To the extent that companies pursue voluntary policies, which reduce profitability, but are accepted by the capital owners, this seems acceptable, even commendable, for example that hiring policies are varied to give certain social groups opportunities (hiring members of minority groups, promoting women or donating to charities). However, activist single-issue groups and populist politicians nowadays often demand coercive interventions. Where this is the case, such interventions amount to the taking of private property rights from the shareowners, normally without compensation, which diminishes the coordinative efficiency of the capitalist free-market order. Managers often collude with demands for social and environmental responsibility at the expense of profitability because this makes their jobs easier – it is a form of agent opportunism which is best tackled by supporting greater competitiveness.

KEY CONCEPTS

The **principal-agent problem**, which was defined in Section 3.4, is seen by some to be particularly pronounced in **joint-stock companies** where managers control the business operations, and shareholding principals are often far removed from business activities. Experience has shown that competition exercises strong spontaneous checks on manager opportunism: share markets constantly evaluate company performance, markets for managers reward managers who act in the interest of the principals with higher salaries, and takeover bids exert control over opportunistic managers.

On-the-job consumption is prevalent in business organizations that enjoy market power and are shielded from vigorous competition in a market niche (see Chapter 8). On-the-job consumption – like other aspects of the principal-agent problem – is curbed by exposure to intense competition. It also occurs in the management of government agencies (Chapter 10).

X-inefficiency describes the phenomenon of weakened cost controls, reduced risk taking and on-the-job consumption that can be found in corporations which have fairly secure market niches and are not exposed to competition in product and factor markets.

The **triple bottom line** is devised by political outsiders and single-issue groups to foist social-welfare and environmental objectives on profit-maximizing companies. It reflects the notion that everyone is a stakeholder in business and that the interests of the shareholders, who own the company, ought to be downgraded. It is a contribution to making the capitalist market order less effective.

Organizational design: styles of management

Experience in businesses shows that a very effective way of structuring economic cooperation has been competition among organized teams (profit centres, enterprises within enterprises, intrapreneurship). Teams are bound by implicit, relational contracts between the leaders and the team members that require the delivery (and trust in the delivery) of certain mutually agreed performances, for example a salary for performing agreed work duties. Within the team, information and coordination costs can be kept low because team interaction is intensive and repetitive. Individual team members can be confident of a certain, ordered division of labour and are informed of the knowledge and skills of other team members. They follow a team leader who coordinates activities.

The regime within which the members of a business team operate with confidence is always a mix of top-down, designed order and bottom-up, spontaneous order. The traditional approach of scientific management (Taylorism) was to rely heavily on the top-down (command) end of the spectrum, whereas the flexible pursuit of changing opportunities by creative, internally entrepreneurial firms requires a management style much closer to the bottom-up (rule-coordinated) end of the spectrum. When surrounded by competitive markets, teams and firms are disciplined by competitive outside challenges. Outside competition enhances the leader's coordinative influence (he can point to a common enemy!), as it is based on the understanding that 'we are all sitting in the same boat'. External competitive challenges ensure that infighting and insubordination are quickly sorted out and information feedbacks work well.

Organizational design can differentiate in many ways between top-down command and participative management to cope with different types of tasks (Table 9.1). Thus, a company's big strategy may be driven by a cohesive, designed plan, whereas tactical decisions in implementing the strategy may be left to decentralized initiatives within certain general rules. Organizations may need more coordinated, top-down management when they find themselves in a crisis, whereas more participative management, which fosters evolutionary creativity, may be appropriate for times of steady business.

Which approach to organizational design is appropriate depends on the framework in which the organization operates and the quality of the workers. When industrial mass production was developed to cater for stable markets with the help of standardized production technologies and many workers were unskilled in industrial work, scientific management was developed to address these handicaps. It relied on good planning and effective control. In a steady state, this approach to organization can reap scale economies and achieve reliable product standards even with low-skilled workers, as the production process is broken up into many small, repetitive steps. This model was, for example, perfected at the Ford motor company's assembly lines. However, markets have become more changeable and specialized in recent decades. Many outputs no longer consist of standard mass products, but are demanded and sold in flexible, customized job lots. In particular, many services are tailor-made. Each job is customized and sometimes even designed in close interaction with the customer. In such markets, perpetual adjustment and innovation are required (Vickery and Wurzburg, 1996). In these conditions, there is great advantage in participative management, which gives collaborators or sub-teams much scope for

Table 9.1 Organizational behaviour: scientific versus participative management

	Scientific management (Taylorism)	Participative management
Main area of application	Industrial mass production; control of standardized product quality; scale economies	Market-oriented job lots; service industries; flexible, spontaneous adjustment; made-to-measure production; economies of scope
Organizational design	Multi-stage hierarchy; separate specialized steps in production process; big firms (vertical and horizontal integration of activities)	Flat structures; teams; stress on creativity; integrated processes and functions; concentration on the core business; inter-firm networking; subcontracting; joint development by groups of firms
Mode of operation and control	Hierarchical control, vertical communication; top-down quality control; penalties for under-performance ('sticks')	Scope for decision making and self-control of quality; reliance on self-motivation and spontaneous horizontal communication, backed by incentives ('carrots') and sanctions ('sticks')
Main motivational principle	Command and control, design of detailed work plan; authority based on position, avoidance of penalties by subordinates	Incentives through implicit contracts; shared general goals; penalties for gross malfunction/opportunism and differentiated pay incentives for goal attainment; multi-skilling
Focus of leaders	Good planning; close supervision; ensure obedience and compliance	Consultation of all staff; shared enterprise culture; training to enhance the productive and creative potential and the responsiveness to new information of all staff
Ideal conditions	Stable, predictable environment, low skills and low motivation of workers, mass production	Variable, diverse markets; highly skilled and motivated collaborators; complex production processes

decision making and mobilizing their creative-entrepreneurial potential. This approach to organizational behaviour is certainly suited to emphasizing creative rationality on the part of all members of the organization (Sections 3.2–3.3).

Business organizations that want to compete successfully in dynamically changing, highly specialized markets will focus on the demands of their diverse customers, rather than the internal requirements of rigid production processes. They will stress performance by the whole team over individual performance and will create incentives for performance rather than reward mere attendance or effort. This requires organization-internal rules that cope with divisions of interest. It also requires the defeat of inward-looking attitudes, which only lead to the monopolization of information.

Such a style of participative management fosters organization-wide cooperation. Reliance on team support is of course likely to cost networking time, but it saves on control and monitoring costs, such as paperwork, internal reporting, long hierarchical decision channels and enforcement of commands. It will also economize on the information cost of the leaders of the firm. If one of the key problems of leadership is to obtain and digest the necessary information, then the leaders have to be ready to listen and, at times, be prepared to withhold criticism and sanctions. Above all, trust in subordinates is needed to let them carry out their own experiments and act on their own knowledge and judgment. The need for information and coordination can be reduced by encouraging subordinates to take a degree of proprietary interest in their own team or operation, for example by materially rewarding performance at the team level (salary premiums for measured success, see Box 9.1) and by encouraging inter-team competition. It also helps when agents are kept in jobs long enough to identify with them.

CH 9 – CASE ONE

A case of participative management

In June 1996, the American clothing manufacturer and distributor Levi Strauss & Co promised to distribute $750 million in bonuses among all its 75,000 employees worldwide on condition that the company met a sales-growth target of 2.1 per cent per annum to the year 2001.

This 'global success sharing plan' was based on the company's avowed opinion that 'motivated employees are our source of innovation and competitive advantage'. The plan had the

---

CH 9 – CASE ONE *(continued)*

characteristic of a simple-to-understand, general target and shunned detailed prescriptions and controls, relying instead on implicit, open-ended understandings (institutions) between employer and employees. The incentive scheme relied on the creativity and cooperation of workers and work teams to come up with creative solutions of their own that promote the company's overall sales objective, and it made the bonus payments clearly conditional on measured performance.

Source: Press reports (June) 1996.

Management style and societal institutions

The style of management and the preferred type of organizational behaviour depend not only on the diversity and dynamism of individual markets in which firms compete, but also on the wider institutional framework of the society in which they operate. Thus, participative management, which is based on trust, is less likely to succeed if the internal institutions of society do not encourage honesty. Similarly, the regulation of wages and salaries (as has been proposed for the finance industry) may make it impossible to offer the material incentives that motivate collaborators to align their own purposes with those of their firm. Legislation or juridical interpretations of the law may also make it difficult for supervisors to discriminate between those collaborators who perform well and those who do not. Under non-discrimination laws, it may not be possible to uphold such managerial judgments in court. This indicates that labour market deregulation and the confinement of governments to protecting individual liberties is an essential precondition for successful participative human resource management and that it should be made part of a robust policy design. A similar complementarity between the wider institutional context and the internal constitution of organizations also exists with regard to internal sanctions for breaches of implicit contract conditions and the responsiveness of collaborators to incentives. These complementarities between organization-internal management and a society's cultural and legal institutions explain why multinationals often have to make adjustments to their organizational behaviour when they move to new locations in other cultures and why institutional reforms to enhance a country's competitiveness require time to pay off fully: Business cultures react only slowly to new societal institutions. As we shall see in Chapter 13, this was evident after the demise of communism, when work habits adjusted only gradually. When the entire institutional environment changes, business leaders have to rethink their philosophy of leadership and workers have to adjust their routines and practices to remain or become successful.

There are also important differences between civilizations and nations. It is no coincidence that participative styles of management have been greatly inspired by Japanese and other East Asian experiences. In these neo-Confucian societies, much depends on informal, implicit institutions that encourage self-control of opportunistic instincts. Thus, team competition and non-prescriptive management were able to draw on general cultural characteristics, whereas societies with strongly individualistic, self-seeking attitudes, such as those of Latin America or the Middle East, probably require more reliance on top-down control and stronger sanctions for agent opportunism. When management analysts now speak of a 'global competition of workplace cultures', they normally refer to the ease or difficulty with which flexible, low-cost organizational designs can be implemented in different civilizations, as well as the ease or difficulty in motivating collaborators to loyally support a business' purpose.

KEY CONCEPTS

Organizational behaviour refers to the vertical and horizontal interaction of the members of an organization and the institutions, which structure that interaction. It is an important part of leadership of an organization to ensure that agents, who are bound to pursue their own purposes, act in the interest of the organization's self-set goals, for example by designing incentive pay structures, stipulating performance, skill development and pay in explicit contractual terms, fostering informal institutions and shared values.

Scientific management was the term applied to the teachings of F.W. Taylor who developed the principles of how industrial work processes should be planned, controlled and broken up, so as to obtain standard quality and economies of scale. These methods led to a many-layered man-agement hierarchy, complex approval and monitoring processes ('control mania'), but also were successful in attaining set objectives. They are suited to the world of 'end-means rationality' (Section 3.2).

Participative management describes a style of organizational behaviour that is fairly decentralized and not very prescriptive, leaving scope for decentralized decision making by collaborators and sub-teams. It relies on incentives within a network of often implicit, open-ended contracts and on the cultivation of the creative-entrepreneurial potential of collaborators. This style of management is better suited to a competitive, dynamically changing environment, as well as tailor-made job-lot production to cater to specialized market niches. It is suited to promote an entrepreneurial motivation.

Business organization and profitability

How well the principal-agent problem is controlled under various organizational arrangements, has great impact on the returns on the invested capital. The question has been asked whether various types of business organization – owner-managed firms, partnerships, cooperatives, mutuals and share companies – are equally effective in making use of capital, controlling costs and making a profit. Or do differing internal management mechanisms produce systematically differing results? This is an empirical question. However, what we know about human nature and institutions would suggest that the rules, which coordinate the internal dealings of an organization, are of great relevance to performance and the achievement of the organization's purposes.

Owner-managed firms, partnerships, cooperatives, mutual societies, trusts and non-profit organizations may have some advantages over large corporations: The owners enjoy easier direct information exchanges and easier monitoring of agent performance, and they can spontaneously enforce directives and agreed rules because they are on the ground. This will lower internal organization costs. If the boss is present and is familiar with the daily business, collaborators and appointed managers may be reluctant to act opportunistically. This explains the strength and resilience of many family firms and small and medium-sized businesses.

We noted above that the exit option for share capital owners – the ease of selling their shares if they are displeased with the management – is an important lever to control manager opportunism and cost levels. Partnerships, mutual societies and trusts are less open in the sense that new capital owners can join in or disassociate themselves from the venture, than is the case with public joint-stock companies. Here, exit and entry through share transactions on the stock exchange are done at low transaction cost. The resulting openness of joint-stock companies therefore promptly signals manager performance. This suggests that the managers of joint-stock companies face stronger incentives to support the principals' stated objectives than economic organizations whose capital cannot be so easily traded. In small firms, direct internal information flows may be sufficient to control the principal-agent problem, but if organizations grow in size and complexity, one would expect a growing knowledge problem on the part of the principals and greater opportunities for self-seeking agents. Then, indirect signals through the share and other markets need to be relied upon to keep a check on the manager-agent opportunism. Based on this logic, one would expect particular principal-agent problems in non-profit organizations where surpluses are left in the organization until profits are dispersed by one means or another. The incentives to effectively control costs are then correspondingly weak.

Available empirical evidence indeed shows that this is correct. Small companies can be run effectively, when few owners directly supervise the manager(s). If enterprises grow and more owners join, it becomes difficult to form a joint view amongst the various owners, nor may each individual owner have a sufficient personal stake to incur the considerable costs of constantly monitoring the managers, so that they are often able to 'hijack' organizations. At least for the United States, the evidence indicates that joint-stock companies attain better results in comparable activities than mutual societies or non-profit organizations. In particular, the evidence suggests that managers of joint-stock companies are, on balance, inclined to take more profitable investment decisions (Fama and Jensen, 1985). The gradual conversion of many family enterprises, partnerships, trusts and mutual societies which have grown in size into listed share companies also suggests that the indirect evaluation through the open markets give owner-principals advantages. Openness (owners buying and selling shares in companies) thus tends to enhance company performance and serve innovation.

•••

To conclude, we may say that teams and organizations, which combine goal-setting and coordinative directives from above and rule-guided coordination within which there are competitive checks from without, are best placed to tackle ever-present knowledge problems. Besides, rules that give collaborators spheres of autonomy and self-responsibility pay off as they motivate people to give their best. A welcome by-product of a participative, rule-based management style is, incidentally, that working life, which takes up the larger part of many peoples' waking hours, contributes more to fulfilment and satisfaction.

We may conclude by saying that the general insights from institutional economics shed much light also on organization science and helps organizations to better exploit available and new knowledge, as well as other resources.

NOTES

1 The obverse question why markets exist can be answered with reference to the increasing complexity of the coordination task as organizations grow. The exponential rise in organization costs draws a line to the growth of organizations and brings markets into play.

2 We owe these points to an article by Daniel Kiwit (1994).

3 Since the right to organize business confers material and non-material benefits, the owners of different production factors tend to engage in collective, political action to shape the external institutions that enhance their chances to set up organizations or hamper the opportunities of the owners of rivalling production factors to do so. Such collective action may of course undermine overall economic growth and, with it, the chance for all production factors to earn high returns.

4 Takeovers may not always enhance knowledge. Where takeover merchants engage in the sheer 'conquest of territory', for example by highly leveraged buy-outs which saddle companies with high debts, they may promote a management culture that lives by the virtues of tribal conquest and not the virtues of the commercial-innovative culture, as described in Chapter 6. Managers of taken-over firms may then concentrate on more takeovers and on liquidating bundles of assets, rather than competition by performance in serving demand. Such a shift will, however, sooner or later run its course. Companies that adhere exclusively to the tribal conquest strategy will frequently go bankrupt and leave unpaid 'junk bond' debts in their wake, as was the case, for example, in the United States takeover flurry during the 1980s.

10

Collective action: public policy

Apart from a protective role (as mentioned in Chapters 5 and 7), governments also assume productive and redistributive functions. In advanced economies, productive and redistributive functions have been expanded over time, raising the government share in the national product almost inexorably. In fact, US economist James Buchanan argued in 1975 that there is a theoretical and empirical puzzle, which modern political economy must confront if the goal is to maintain a constitutionally limited government under the rule of law: How to empower the protective and productive state without unleashing the unconstrained redistributive state? The 'churning state', which confiscates and redistributes incomes and wealth, negates the allocative role of prices and destroys the capitalist order. It is the outcome of rent-seeking and is evident in intractable fiscal crises that currently plague Europe in particular. The same consequences of unfettered redistribution are now also played out in the United States, not only at the level of some States, but also manifested in the mounting Federal deficits.

Particular problems arise when decisions are made collectively, as compared to a situation in which private property rights are disposed on the basis of voluntary, bilateral contracts. We shall discuss systematic reasons why outcomes of collective action are often less likely than free market solutions to satisfy individual aspirations.

It is in the nature of collective action that principal-agent problems are prevalent. Political agents (rulers, parliamentarians, administrators) often pursue their own purposes at the expense of the average citizen, who is after all the principal in public choices. In government, competition is normally absent. Because of this, political agents do not face the same constraints that agents in business do. Where possible, it therefore often pays to reduce the functions of government by corporatizing, deregulating and privatizing. Where this is not feasible, attempts can be made to control political agents by other means; constitutional rules, hierarchical controls, the separation of powers and periodic electoral control (democracy) for example. Yet, such controls constrain government agents only imperfectly. To be more effective in promoting the interests of the citizen-principal, these controls have to be complemented, wherever possible, by openness to competition with other governments and by openly accessible information about the government's actions (openness to international trade and payments, free press, transparency, accountability, whistle-blowing).

Policy makers who wish to cultivate the

self-organizing properties of the market system should be cautious when interfering with private property rights and specific economic processes and outcomes (robust political economy). Policy makers will then also be better protected from being pursued by particular rent-seeking interests.

This chapter ends with a brief discussion of the attributes of economic and political constitutions, which support discovery and information search and keep property rights open to the ceaseless challenges of competition, thereby safeguarding freedom and prosperity.

A country is not a company.

Title of a public lecture by R. Epstein (2004 in Auckland, New Zealand)

The state is a potential resource or threat to every industry in the society. With its power, to take or give money, the state can and does selectively help or hurt a vast number of industries.

G. Stigler (1971), p. 3

The objective of the Constitution was to define the islands of government powers within the ocean of individual rights.

W.A. Niskanen, in Gwartney and Wagner (1988)

The government is not a cow that is fed in Heaven and can be milked on Earth.

L. Erhard, West German Minister of Economics (1957)

Economic activity, especially the activity of the market economy, cannot be conducted in an institutional, juridical and political vacuum. On the contrary it presupposes sure guarantees of individual freedom and private property, as well as a stable currency and efficient public services. Hence the principal task of the state is to guarantee this security, so that those who work and produce can enjoy the fruits of their labours and thus feel encouraged to work efficiently and honestly.

Pope John Paul II, *Centesimus annus* (1991)

In autocratic countries . . . the most influential people devote a disproportionate amount of energy to . . . rent-seeking. In liberal democracies, ordinary folk are better defended. Elections force politicians to take the public's wishes into account every few years . . . Competitive markets force business leaders to heed their customers' demands all the time.

The Economist, 'Special Report', 22 January 2011, p. 20.

This chapter deals with collective action and public policy, that is, collective economic choices and the political coordination of entire communities. Such action has to rely often on top-down directives and legitimated coercion. The authority for this is derived from a political mandate, which gives authorized persons defined powers to coerce all those who live or operate in a jurisdiction. This authority may be derived from the transcendental ('by the grace of God', 'the Mandate of Heaven'), inheritance, conquest, or one-off or periodic elections under a constitution. Public authority normally needs to be legitimated by the support of private citizens who assess whether it generally assists them in the pursuit of their fundamental objectives and self-set goals. Public choices should normally do so in ways that are predictable and commensurate to the cognitive and coordinative limitations of the citizens.

Political authority places a coercive bind on individuals that differs fundamentally from the power of the leadership of private organizations. In private business, individuals' actions are based on voluntary contracts; members can exit relatively easily if perceived advantages dwindle and disadvantages increase. Under political authority, individuals normally lack the power to exit and therefore have to rely on voice to influence political choices. When overarching laws are in the hands of local communities (federalism), as opposed to the national level, individuals are better able to exit; they can then exert at least a degree of influence over policy choices, 'voting with their feet'.

10.1 Public versus private choice

The complexities of public choice

When we discussed the various forms of property in Chapter 7, we identified certain types of property whose uses cannot be made exclusive, that is, whose costs and benefits cannot be internalized so that private competitors are unable to allocate these assets through voluntary, bilateral contracts. They are:

(a) free goods, where no rationing and hence no economic choices are needed;
(b) pure public goods, where demand does not need to be rationed, as no rivalry among users occurs, but where the supply has to be decided by collective choice, as their provision costs resources;
(c) common property, in particular in groups with compulsory membership (public-domain property and socialized property).

Categories (b) and (c) require collective choices, determined by some sort of centralized political process. We noted briefly in Section 7.2 that this created difficulties in allocation and knowledge search as compared to private choices. We now have to elaborate this point (Table 10.1):

Table 10.1 Private versus public choices

	Private Choice	Public Choice
Exchange	reciprocity in direct give and take	multilateral; fuzzy, indirect give and take
Incentives	meritocratic (and some luck)	egalitarian
Shirking	monitored; curbed by institutions and contracts	shirking of contributions; over-claiming of hand-outs
Coordination mechanism	voluntary, spontaneous	coercive
Meeting of wants	diversity: choice, creativity, 'chaos', duplication	uniformity 'unity of purpose' ('one size fits all')
Principal-agent	agents are controlled by competition; markets economize on the need to know	agents have scope to pursue pervasive rent-seeking; 'rational ignorance'
Monitoring/enforcement	mostly spontaneous, sometimes uncomfortable	costly; limited; cumbersome
Innovative potential	markets generate knowledge by *catallaxis*	political influence often employed to resist change
Main mode of the game	positive-sum rivalry	zero-sum redistribution BUT: • greater role for agents and elites; • more influence of intellectuals; • politics is more visible; • 'sells newspapers'.

(a) When others cannot be excluded from certain property uses, more than two contracting parties have to agree. Since collective decisions involve more participants with their own changing opportunity costs and diverse purposes, clear-cut decisions are harder to achieve. The transaction costs of decision making tend to be higher in public decision making than in private, bilateral choice.

(b) As individual preferences have to be amalgamated and averaged, collective decisions are unlikely to match the usual diversity of individual aspirations as well as diverse private choices. 'One size fits all' expresses this phenomenon. The experiences after the end of comprehensive collectivism in the formerly centrally planned economies and the repressive controls of public behaviour and thought in some Muslim countries show how much people appreciate the choice of their own diverse clothing, hairstyles, careers, cars and lifestyles. Likewise, laws mandating medical insurance companies to provide coverage for a plethora of services ranging from in vitro fertilization to end-of-life counselling are a prime example of the problems and price hikes associated with 'one size fits all policies'. Individuals, who are extremely unlikely to contract certain diseases, resent being forced to pay for services they do not even need. This makes socialized health provision costly and wasteful.

(c) Give and take are clearly related in reciprocal and equivalent private exchanges; the decision makers have complete material feedback from their decisions. By contrast, collective choice involves multilateral give and take; the benefits are normally indirect and non-mutual; decision makers get no immediate feedback. The collective choice of a community may, for example, be to build a bypass road around their town. This affects taxpayers who have to fund the construction costs and the inhabitants differentially. Some will discover that they benefit from less traffic noise, others that their businesses lose customers. Because it is a 'package deal' and the costs and benefits are diffused and non-equivalent, the decision on a bypass road has to be forced on the community by appropriate rules once the relevant policy makers have made a decision. Otherwise, people would be tempted to opt out of paying the taxes and free ride on the benefits. Where costs and benefits are not equivalent – as is the case in private, self-responsible decisions – there are unavoidable 'moral hazard' problems, dangers of a 'tragedy of the commons' and high monitoring and enforcement costs (Sections 3.4, 5.3 and 7.3).

(d) A further problem of public choice relates to what Kenneth Arrow called 'the impossibility theorem' in an analysis that earned him the 1972 Nobel Prize in Economics (Arrow, 1951). He showed that a mix of individual preferences cannot be aggregated by a voting procedure in ways that ensure that the choice which individuals prefer will also be made by the collective. Inconsistencies arise, which prevent the aggregation of individual preferences without contradiction and conflict. The 'collective will' can only be expressed imperfectly, as compared to the method of decentralized, diverse individual 'dollar votes' in the marketplace.

(e) Except in very small groups, public choices have to be made by representatives. They may be self-appointed, selected or elected. They amalgamate individual preferences to arrive at feasible decisions. Public choices by representatives require three basic arrangements:

- Rules and procedures for collective voting have to be agreed. For example, a rule might demand unanimity (which normally imposes very high negotiation costs), a two-thirds or a 51 per cent majority.

The rules and procedures also have to lay down how votes are taken and what matters the representatives are empowered to decide.

- Because there is no direct reciprocity between give and take, as in the bilateral exchange of private property, the 'give' has to be determined by political choice, for example by setting the conditions and rates of compulsory taxation. Incentives are considerable for individuals to reduce their contributions (by free riding and claiming benefits), so that monitoring and enforcement become necessary. Hence, agency costs have to be incurred. In smaller collectives (local government, clubs), participants may be still able to perceive a measure of correspondence between 'give' (tax) and 'take' (benefit from collective action). Then, the agency costs may be relatively small. Elinor Ostrom notes that individuals rely more on self-monitoring at the community level, which allows monitoring to be a 'natural by-product' of the designed rules in order to minimize costs and ensure their effectiveness (Ostrom 1990; p. 96). But in big collectives, such as nations, and in collectives where individuals feel powerless and disenfranchised, solidarity is weak. Monitoring and enforcement costs then soar.
- A third arrangement has to lay down how collectively generated benefits are distributed, on what criteria citizens can access common-property goods for which they rival with each other. This requires political power and leads to principal-agent problems of its own.

(f) As we saw in earlier chapters, the use of political power creates pervasive principal-agent problems: How can the citizen-principals ensure that their agents, once appointed, indeed do their bidding? The problems multiply, as we shall see shortly, when the political landscape is populated by party organizations, organized interest groups with diverse, often single-issue, objectives and self-seeking bureaucracies, who pursue ends of their own. A related problem of collective choice arises in multi-stage majoritarian decision making: If general decisions are made on bundles of collective choices, such as reflected in party programmes, and specific decisions are made by particularly concerned persons within the elected party or committee, it is possible that only 51 per cent of 51 per cent (that is, 26 per cent) of the votes of the principals determine the outcomes. Indeed, a single, forceful operator can sway relevant committees. If governments subsequently adopt those decisions, ordinary citizens are left disenfranchised. Constellations exist, where even small minorities with a keen interest in a particular public choice make the decision. In that case, avid, well-organized minorities exploit the majority.

(g) In complex matters of public policy, the information costs of citizens – if they wanted to be aware of all public choices – are extremely high. Most will prefer to remain 'rationally ignorant'. If the citizens wanted to give their individual preferences political weight, they would have to incur high organization costs, often for modest gain. It is therefore often rational for principals to remain passive and tolerate collective choices that disadvantage them to some degree (Downs, 1957a; 1957b; Gwartney and Wagner, 1988). Whilst 'rational ignorance' is understandable, it nevertheless contributes to an erosion of solidarity with the group and with politics. It fosters a feeling of disenfranchisement and insecurity, in particular when a large share of decisions on property uses are subject to collective choice and traditional rules of private property and self-responsibility are eroded. Then, reforms that seek to de-collectivize economic decisions (privatization, devolution or conversion of socialized property into club goods, see Section 7.2) can be a way of enhancing spontaneous community cohesion, voluntary rule adherence and confidence.

This is why many analysts, who are aware of the costs of information search and coordination, of unintended consequences and a tendency towards political rent-seeking (as discussed in previous chapters), tend to prefer private choices to the reliance on collective choices that are now customary in most mature economies (Table10.1). This is why they advocate privatization, wherever this is feasible, and why many critics have reservations about the merits of majoritarian democracy (Pennington, 2010).

The relentless expansion of the sphere of public choice

The demand for small and limited government, which many citizens share with liberal economists, is rarely met. Instead the size of governments making public choices and repressing the sphere of private choices appears to grow relentlessly. Over time, the size of government and the share of the nation's resources that government agents command have grown enormously. Government spending as a percentage of the gross domestic product in what are now the big five industrialized economies – USA, Japan, Germany, France and the United Kingdom – used to average about 10 per cent in 1870 (Tanzi and Schuknecht, 1995). This average rose to about 25 per cent in the mid-1930s and is almost double today, averaging about 45 per cent. In 2010, the share of government expenditure in overall demand was 54 per cent in the European Union and nearly 45 per cent in the United States, but only about 30 per cent on average in the East Asian manufacturing countries. In China and Vietnam, the fast growth of private enterprise has reduced the public-sector share to less than 40 per cent (Section 13.2) and some post-communist East European regimes have managed to greatly reduce the relative importance of public choices. Overall, however, the worldwide trend has been towards bigger government (Radnitzky-Bouillon, 1996). Where the sway of collective decision-making had been cut back, for example in post-war Germany and Japan, it was before long pushed up again.

Because of the relentless push for bigger government (and attempts to pump up aggregate demand by fiscal expansionism), the 2010s witnessed a huge increase in gross government debt in the mature economies (from 75 per cent of GDP in 2000 to 108 per cent in 2011), whereas the developing countries on aggregate reduced the debt burden on future generations (from 50 per cent to 35 per cent respectively – sources: International Monetary Fund; *The Economist*, 11/2/2012, p. 68).

British economist Anthony de Jasay paraphrased Rousseau when he lamented "man is born with a desire for minimal government and everywhere he keeps creating maximal ones" (de Jasay in Bouillon and Radnitzky, 1993, p. 74). The unremitting expansion of the public sphere has a lot to do with confusion over who is the principal in political action and who is the servant: the citizens, the elected politicians, the public 'servants'? During much of human history since the neolithic revolution, the rulers 'owned' the citizens or at least arrogated for themselves the right to treat them as their underlings. Rulers and public administrators have often used war or fear of war to keep the populace under their control and make them pay for collective purposes. For example, war with France enabled the British government in 1799 to pioneer a modest income tax – as a temporary (!) measure.[1] More recently, government departments have been fomenting fears about the environment and even the long-term livability of planet Earth to expand their influence.

Over the past two generations, the statistical evidence points to proliferating socialized welfare as the main cause (Section 10.4). In electoral democracies, political parties often rival for the vote by promising to provide more and more 'free' goods and services through government; voters have long welcomed such offers. Since each average voter's interest in an additional government programme is negligible and political operators and well-organized groups push for additional spending programmes (asymmetry of motivations), it is likely that political decisions in majoritarian democracies favour more spending, rather than deny demands for 'social justice'. Given the voters' rational ignorance, political and bureaucratic entrepreneurs can find more and more 'public interests' on which to spend taxes and through which to promote their careers.

As a result, more and more economic decisions have become politicized and bureaucratized. It has only been since the late twentieth century that Western democratic governments have met with resolute taxpayer resistance and unmanageable problems of growing public indebtedness that signs emerge that the secular shift to ever bigger government is resisted by the wider public. Another factor that may set limits on big government is the international competition with emerging economies that are less debt-addicted and more inclined to favour private decision making. It is now increasingly realized that the free citizens have become clients of the state and that the public servants are acting as the masters (Radnitzky and Bouillon, 1996).

Arrogant, distant top civil servants (those who take command) also affect the productivity of lower-level front-line staff (for example doctors, nurses and teachers). This often leads to disenchantment and low productivity in government entities, as self-control by those who deliver the services is replaced by paperwork and formal supervision (the motivational consequences of such a management style were drawn in Sections 9.2 and 9.3). Among the citizenry, it creates a feeling that the democratic ideal – 'government by the people, through the people, for the people' – has been subverted and that the people are back 'on the road to serfdom', serving as mere servants of bureaucratic masters.

Austrian-American economist Joseph A. Schumpeter, who thought deeply about these trends, concluded that sheer utility maximization and the asymmetries of electoral democracy would lead to ever-bigger spheres of collective action. Only 'private fortresses of bourgeois business', based on secure property rights, would stem the tide (Schumpeter, 1947, p. 151), and Anthony de Jasay, who worried about the same trend, concluded that only deep-seated beliefs and taboos (*metis*) could prevent the relentless advance of collective choice (de Jasay, op. cit., pp. 93–96).

Democracy, political parties, bureaucracies and interest groups

Much of what is said in this book about public policy is implicitly related to representative, majoritarian democracy, that is, the version of collective decision making that controls agents by periodic elections, the division of powers and the rule of law. Modern democracy is based on the recognition of certain inalienable, basic rights of individuals, which override other rules (Section 6.1), and on the ultimate sovereignty of the people in temporarily empowering collective representatives.

In its traditional version, the modern model of democracy was first developed in the Netherlands and England, in a long process in which the parliament defended the 'people's law' against the ruler. The process culminated in England during the Glorious Revolution of 1688 when the Bill of Rights was affirmed. The original English model of democracy did not incorporate certain important elements one observes in modern public-choice processes: namely political parties that bind elected members to a collective programme, bureaucracies that have the expertise and hard-to-get information to dominate complex choices, and organized and well-funded interest groups. These elements nowadays have a major influence on public choices, often to the disadvantage of the individual citizen. From the standpoint of an individualistic worldview, these conditions often augment the influence of small, well-organized collectivist elites. This often makes reliance on private choices in markets more advantageous for the average citizen than the degree of public choice that has become customary (Mises, 1944; Sowell, 2009).

Elected political agents in most democracies are now concentrated into a few political parties that engage in political competition for the periodic vote. Given the voters' high information costs, parties will offer simplified, summary programmes. Where there are two parties or blocks of parties, they rival for the median voter, that is, the swing voter. The bulk of the voters, who are committed to one party or the other or who shy away from incurring the costs of making fresh voting decisions time and again, can easily be neglected. As a consequence, most political programmes focus not on the bulk of the electorate, but only on decisive minorities who may pursue single issues. This distorts political action to the detriment of the silent majority.

The political interest is to get re-elected and gain the majority in parliament and the dominance over the administration. Political parties demand group solidarity and are able to enforce it by influencing candidate selection or re-election, as well as by expulsion of renegades. Moreover, the running of political parties nowadays requires massive funds to cover agency costs and advertising. This and the re-election motive often lead to collective decisions which disadvantage most citizens.

The problem is aggravated by well-organized interest groups, which typically represent concentrated supplier interests and are free to organize under the freedom of association, a basic right. As we saw in Sections 8.1-8.2, suppliers often try to fortify their market niches against costly rivalry with competitors by seeking political restrictions of competition by lobbying. The advantage of obtaining political interventions tends to be massive for the few suppliers, whereas the disadvantages to buyers are thinly spread and hence not worth the high fixed costs of counter-lobbying. A related problem in modern democracies is the proliferation of single-issue 'non-government organizations' (NGOs), which are in reality financed by governments. Social and environmental lobbies thus argue for transfer payments to the causes they represent and which are in the interest of bureaucracies that subsidize those NGOs.

Bureaucracy-NGO complexes thus represent another type of rent-seeker lobby. Politicians and bureaucrats often find it convenient to be lobbied by such organizations, as this makes it easier for them to widen their influence by taking property rights from individuals and thereby enhancing their own power. Nowadays, however, such unholy alliances between political decision makers and lobby groups are constrained by the progressive spread of information over the Internet. The Internet has also made it cheaper and easier for ordinary citizens sceptical of collective power to organize counter-lobbies (Mises, 1944; Tullock, 1967; Buchanan et al., (eds) 1980; Gwartney and Wagner, 1988).

Nonetheless, privileged producer groups still find it advantageous to invest a share of their potential gains from a political intervention into lobbying and bribing political parties and bureaucracies, as well as into re-educating the public into thinking that certain interventions are in the national interest. Thus, the farmers' lobbies in the United States and the European Union have a vested interest in ensuring the passage of farm subsidies. Indeed, lobbies often succeed in winning the support of public opinion for specific interventions, even if they harm the majority of citizens. Thus, the interplay of supplier lobbies, NGOs and political parties has decisive influence over public choices and continually creates new political motives to interfere even more with private property rights (Hayek, 1979a, pp. 17–50). The scope of what is decided in an economy by the second-best mechanism of public choice – with its potential for arbitrary decisions and rule erosion – has thus been expanded, and the scope of private choice has been correspondingly reduced.

It needs to be said that the public-choice bias in modern jurisdictions is exacerbated by self-seeking bureaucracies, a group that was not part of the historic model of democratic government. Public officials often have a massive self-interest in regulating markets, over-shadowing or replacing free private choices by public choices. They create specific institutions that confer power on them. The observation that someone's transaction costs are normally someone else's income applies. This leads to the bureaucratic distortion of the institutional system and an unnecessary displacement of internal institutions by external ones. This expands government budgets, burdens citizens and future generations with more taxation or public debt.

Bureaucracies often enjoy information advantages, so that they can often not be effectively controlled by elected politicians, who may be loath to incur the information costs to know what is really going on in government departments. There is a tendency, given the complexity of modern economic life, for parliaments to create no more than a framework of enabling legislation, which allows bureaucratic experts to write the specific rules and regulations. Where the tendency to delegate regulatory authority is strong (as in the European Union), detailed rules proliferate and are changed frequently. The domain of free private choice is then correspondingly curbed. The deluge of black-letter legislation and ordinances in all advanced countries, most of which are initiated by self-centred bureaucracies, is testimony to this tendency (Bernholz, 1982).

As parties, lobby groups and bureaucratic interests are not part of the original model of democracy, they are rarely mentioned explicitly in constitutions and are even more rarely constrained by explicit rules of collective action.[2] Below, we shall elaborate on how political competition in a world with political parties, as well as industry, social and bureaucratic lobbies might work. But first, we have to turn to the basic functions of government: protection, provision of public goods and redistribution of incomes and wealth.

KEY CONCEPTS

Public choice relates to decisions on the uses of property rights, which are not made by individuals and firms. Whereas individuals are aware that they have to shoulder the full costs and enjoy the full benefits when they enter into contracts over uses of their property, decisions that involve a multiplicity of people agreeing on the choice are normally less well informed. Most individuals are then also less well placed to influence the decisions. Public choices have, however, to be made where costs and benefits cannot be fully internalized (where externalities exist). But they are often extended to areas that can be left to private choice. Because public choice involves no reciprocal give and take, but only non-mutual benefits, it can easily lead to free riding, moral hazard, the tragedy of the commons and agent opportunism. In any event, public choice therefore requires coercion.

Voters and market participants find it often not worth their while to incur the information costs necessary for better informed public decisions: **rational ignorance**. In many instances, they know that the gains from acting on additional information are nil or negligible. Rational ignorance is, for example, part of the constellation that facilitates rent seeking by organized supplier groups, but dissuades the many disorganized and only marginally affected buyers from engaging in lobbying against political rent creation.

The **median voter** in electoral democracies describes the median or swing voters, whom two contending political parties need in order to gain a 51 per cent majority and, with that, dominance of the legislature and frequently also the executive.

10.2 The functions of government

The protective function

When discussing external institutions in Chapter 5, we said that protecting and enforcing the institutions of society was one of the major functions of government. The protective function of government is to facilitate order and to give individuals and private firms and associations confidence to make their coordinative tasks easier in the face of ignorance ('order policy'; Eucken, 1992/1940; Streit, 1987; 1993b). We also saw that the protective task may at times require the use of legitimate force (courts, police, gaol, military) to prevent free-riding and agent opportunism and to enforce the rules if necessary.

KEY CONCEPTS

Government is an organization (top-down, hierarchical order), which pursues certain collective aims and is politically authorized, within certain rules, to exercise power over its jurisdiction.

The **functions of governments** typically are (i) to protect the freedoms of the citizens, (ii) to produce public goods, and (iii) to redistribute property rights. To carry out these functions, governments incur agency costs and have to raise taxes to administer and finance material resources to meet these costs.

The protection of order and the rule of law by collective action have a long tradition. Its origins go probably back more than 10,000 years, at least to when permanently settled villages, towns and cities in the Neolithic age came under some kind of leadership. Kings, high priests and judges emerged in these communities to adjudicate disputes and to enshrine principles according to which disputes amongst members of the community would be resolved or avoided (external institutions). The role of a third-party adjudicator was at first given to respected and experienced elders or priests, but later formal, constitutional arrangements were put in place to set up rulers (Benson, 1995). The concepts of collective action, political power and government were thus born. Certain actions were undertaken collectively on behalf of the community and certain officials and organizations were accorded authority and coercive powers over ordinary citizens and citizen associations. Constitutional arrangements determined the fundamentals of collective decisions of how to appoint representatives and allocate the costs and the benefits of these public choices.

The most obvious protective function of government is to prevent citizens from coercion by others. It has been argued that the takeover of the protective function by government amounts to a kind of (hypothetical) 'disarmament treaty' amongst all citizens (Buchanan, 1975; 1978). Anarchy is extremely costly (as was the case in the European Dark Ages and still is the case in underdeveloped parts of the world today). Then, coercion is only confined by the 'violence potential' of other parties. Every citizen has to defend his property against others, which inflicts high exclusion and enforcement costs on everyone. Anarchy, if defined as lawlessness (as opposed to merely lack of a central monopoly supplier of law and order) therefore prevents much beneficial division of labour and hinders prosperity. This is not to ignore the fact that self-regulating systems have throughout history demonstrated that communities are able to produce a very high degree of social order (see, for example, Ostrom 1990, Ostrom and Kahn, (eds) 2003), but the complete absence of government-made law and rules would prevent many gains from social cooperation and internal rule making. It is therefore expedient to employ an agent who is given the task of preserving the peace and enforcing just rules. To be effective, the agent must be given powers to coerce.

At the same time, it has to be ensured that this agent – the government – does not use the powers illegitimately against the citizens. James Madison, one of the Founding Fathers of the US Constitution famously remarked: "[W]hat is government itself but the greatest of all reflections on human nature? If men were angels, no government would be necessary. If angels were to govern men, neither external nor internal controls on government would be necessary" (*Federalist* 51). The creation of coercive, protective government has thus led to an intractable dilemma. Our efforts to curb private predation have given rise to the very possibility of predation by agents with public powers. Government agents have the potential to become the by far more destructive predatory agent. Therefore, the effort to establish a working political system must from the start be combined with constraints on political power. As David Hume argued long ago, when designing the institutions of governance we must assume that all men are knaves. Human knavery comes in the form of arrogance and opportunism, and with Adam Smith's 'man of systems', who is happy in his own conceit. He must be checked by constitutional constraints. Statesmen must not be permitted to use their position of power to lie, cheat and steal to enrich themselves at the expense of those they are supposedly serving. In other words, it is the role of constitutionally limited government to protect spheres of individual freedom (Hayek, 1960). The necessary creation of political power thus creates an inevitable dilemma with which every society in every age has to cope. To simply assume that communities can do without any political power, as anarchists do, is an easy and cheap way to shirk addressing one of the fundamental and most critical questions of social science. Every community and every generation has instead to be eternally vigilant in watching over the agents of government and in confining them to the minimum of necessary tasks.

How can government keep the peace and protect justice and freedom? The answer lies primarily with institutions. It is necessary to establish and enforce a system of rules that apply to all citizens equally (rule of law) and that prevent them from pursuing their purposes by force, deception or other forms of thuggery. Protection is thus closely related to the preservation of individual freedom. Without such institutional constraints, liberty would become license, and order chaos. In modern states, many of the rules that governments are asked to enforce under its protective function are formally laid down in constitutions, as well as in penal and civil codes. In addition, protection also refers to the prevention of external threats, namely the defence of present and future freedom (security) against outside coercion.

The limits of protection

A considerable part of the protective function of government is implemented through regulations, for example to protect health and safety. Such regulations are often economically justified because they address externalities. Thus, the untrammelled use of a private asset by an industry may endanger the safety of workers. One way to protect them is to regulate the uses of industrial assets and prescribe safety rules. A purpose of public health regulation is to reduce people's information and other transaction costs. Therefore, one presumes that a government-certified pharmaceutical can be taken safely within stipulated limits – without the need to undertake one's own research into the consequences of taking that medication. Or, a rule that limits driving speeds in certain locations prevents costly 'discovery procedures', that is, accidents. However, the ultimate regulatory purpose must always be kept in mind, namely that the institutions serve the citizen. In many countries, this is hardly the case. Numerous health, safety and environmental regulations have been adopted that do not stand this test. Their proliferation raises transaction costs and undermines the coordination and control function of competitive markets. For example, regulations forbidding individuals to give legal advice or pharmacists to prescribe medicine for simple, everyday symptoms are prevalent in the United States and other affluent countries, although possible harm to ordinary citizens cannot be demonstrated. The problem is not the existence of specific interventions as such, but their high incidence and frequency (regulatory density). Therefore, each such regulation needs to be assessed as to the likely costs and benefits on the overall system (Epstein, 1995; 2007).

The costs of regulations, including the compliance costs that have to be borne by the citizens (see below), need always to be taken into account when deciding whether governments should engage in regulating to protect citizens from certain risks. The attitude that no cost is too high to protect certain purposes – such as human lives, the health of children, or national grandeur – may often be popular, but the average citizen has to bear the opportunity cost of the regulation. Therefore, the long-term costs and the long-term benefits have to be assessed rationally.

The total-system costs of regulation are frequently overlooked when private self-constraint and commercial discipline are replaced by collective regulations – at least if the compliance costs are widely distributed and thus not immediately evident. When it comes to health, safety or environmental protection, parliaments have often decreed regulations that impose exorbitant compliance and other costs. They do so typically in response to pressures from single-issue groups whose members do not bear the costs of regulation. One has to ask, for example, whether US safety regulations that cost $168 million in order to save *one* life when benzene waste standards were tightened in 1990 makes sense. Or are $920 million per one life saved justified, when new drinking water standards were decreed in 1991, let alone the cost for saving an additional life in listing hazardous wastes from wood preservation in 1990 of no less than $5,700,000 million per one life saved? (Breyer, 1995; Viscusi, 1993; for an illustrative example, see Box 10.1).

These examples illustrate that governments and sections of the voting public opt for costly ways to ensure 'security' at the expense of intervening with the coordination and control capacity of the market, which is, however, crucial to prosperity. When the costs are ignored, alternatives to public intervention are not even considered and the interest of the average citizen is neglected. If the prevention of one premature death costs billions of dollars, it is likely that these resources, if used in another way – for example by producing dialysis equipment – could have saved or extended numerous lives. If parliaments and bureaucracies yield to tunnel vision on safety and the environment, they allow the costs of protective regulations to snowball. This then curtails the citizens' freedom to experiment and decide for themselves. The result is a loss of freedom, poor economic growth, ultimately greater risks to human lives and safety and a spreading feeling of being disenfranchised and unjustly treated (Epstein et al., 2005).

CH 10 – CASE ONE

Protecting Canadians from Camembert and Roquefort cheese

Health Canada, in all its collective wisdom recently proposed an amendment to the Food and Drug Regulations that would have prohibited the production and sale of raw cheeses. This amendment would have outlawed about 90 varieties of raw-milk cheeses, including Camembert and Roquefort. The proposed regulation appeared to be based on links between unpasteurized cheeses with outbreaks of listeria, salmonella and *E.coli*.

The regulators at Health Canada obviously wanted to create a safer world. Since 1971, 14 outbreaks of disease believed to have been caused by the consumption of raw-milk cheeses were reported *world-wide* [emphasis in original]. These outbreaks resulted in 57 deaths.

What Health Canada regulators set out to do was, by and large, more destructive than useful. They appeared to have very little regard for the practical consequences of the proposed amendment . . . Given the relatively low level of risk associated with non-pasteurized cheese and the extremely low level of risk in Canada, eliminating a whole industry seems a rather drastic course of action . . . Regulating the minimal risks raises the cost of the things we buy. In this case . . . it would have destroyed a new and thriving industry and the livelihood of many. Legislation such as this suggests that Canadians are incapable of understanding and assessing risks. Indeed, it seems that the government has taken upon itself to act as a parent.

Source: K. Morrison and L. Miljan (1996), 'Cheese, Politics, and Human Health: How the Media Failed to Critique Recent Government Policy', *On Balance*, vol. **9**, no. 5 (May), cited after *Fraser Forum*, September 1996, p. 38.

Note: Public resistance ensured that the recommendation by a scientific panel was not enacted.

The proliferation of specific protective regulations overburdens the cognitive capacities of economic agents and undermines the order which private decision makers need to compete with confidence. Proliferating health and safety regulations are often also used merely for the purpose of asserting political or bureaucratic control (the primacy of politics). In view of this, regulations need to be simplified and streamlined if government is to be effective again in its protective function. However, the regulators (both those who create the regulations and the bureaucrats that enforce them) of course have a self-interest in complex regulations.

While such legislation is perceived to advance the common good and protect the average citizen, many such regulations are actually driven by small, special interest groups who benefit from the regulation at the expense of the wider public, as already noted above. For example, the US Supreme Court, in *Lochner v. New York*, dealt with a regulation by New York that prohibited bakers from working over 60 hours a week with the justification that it 'protects the worker'. The regulation was struck down because it only benefited special interest groups who competed with immigrant bakers who desired to work longer hours.

The protective function of government has been increasingly supplemented by two other functions: provision of public goods, and redistribution of opportunities, income, and wealth through the visible hand of government.[3] These activities have greatly driven up the agency costs of government, which have to be funded by taxes, fees or borrowing.

The productive function

A case can be made for government provision of access to certain goods (Section 7.2). Where private owners would have to tolerate free-riding by others who do not contribute to the cost of procurement and maintenance, there is a prima facie argument for public provision and funding by compulsory taxation. A classic example of such a natural public good is defence against outside aggression: If one member of society were to provide a defence force, all his fellow citizens would automatically get the benefit of protection. The larger the gap between the costs and the benefits that can be exclusively appropriated, the smaller is the incentive for private producers to procure such a good. As we saw, the possibility of free-riding – the impossibility of exclusion – prevents the emergence of a market for such goods. These goods would be under-supplied. Pure public goods are extreme cases where provision by government has marked positive external benefits (Cowen and Crampton, 2003).

As we saw in Chapter 7, new technology may make it possible to capture and internalize the external benefits and measure hitherto external costs, for example by new electronic devices that measure and exclude property uses. Therefore, what is a public good, and what not, is subject to change.

A general case for the provision of common goods thus exists. However, this gives rise to the same problems just discussed in connection with protective government. Governments may respond mainly to the preferences of specific, organized groups when deciding what goods to provide and how to spread the costs among the citizenry. Consequently, problems of hidden redistribution easily arise. They can be contained to some extent by fiscal decentralization (competitive federalism, see Section 12.5). Then, some citizens and capital owners are able to move to the jurisdiction which comes closest to providing the mix of public goods and other locational qualities that they desire. This is so because the mobility of taxpayers and production factors among jurisdictions (openness) exerts some control on governments eager to redistribute costs and benefits in the provision and financing of public goods.

External rules and government directives can of course be implemented to ration the access to non-excludable goods that face rivalling demand. Whether they are produced and managed with collectively owned means of production and managed under administrative procedures or by private competitors is a separate consideration. What matters is the *provision* of goods and services from public resources. It certainly is not necessary for public access to goods and services that they are *produced* with socialized property (Section 7.2). However, for a number of reasons, governments often choose to organize and fund production by employing publicly-owned property:

(a) Where large indivisibilities are presumed to transcend the financial capacity and organizational capability of individual firms or where sizeable scale economies are perceived to exist, the rulers have often taken it upon themselves to mandate the design of work, its financing and implementation. This was frequently so in the case of large-scale irrigation and drainage works in early Egypt or China, but has also been the case throughout history in the provision of infrastructures. The same rationale has been relied on more recently to turn initial space exploration into a government activity. In this context, it is often argued that large-scale ventures constitute natural monopolies and that it is desirable for such monopolies to come under direct political control. In reality, however, such monopolies have frequently come into existence because government authorities erected barriers to competition or failed to reduce the transaction costs of competing (Friedman, 1991). Once these operations are turned into government-owned monopolies, they tend to become high-cost. Nowadays, however, large and internationally open capital markets are able to finance even the biggest of ventures, as long as adequate user-fees can be charged (excludability). With improved measurement technology, the case for many of the traditional public monopolies has now fallen by the wayside.

(b) One reason for producing certain services by public monopoly is that this gives more direct control to political authorities. Thus, the non-violent control of violence professionals, such as the police and military forces, as well as law courts, is a valid argument for public ownership of the relevant resources. The costs of competition among these professionals would, after all, be excessive (for example, collateral damage when private mercenaries fight for control). Therefore these services are provided in most countries by publicly controlled and government-run monopoly enterprises. The financial purse strings are then seen as essential. Control problems of course also exist when these services are produced by public monopolies (police corruption, military coups, corrupt tribunals). Nonetheless, organizational command and direct financial controls by the political authorities are considered preferable.

(c) Governments have often claimed exclusive production rights to certain types of mining and trade as convenient sources of revenue (for example, salt or alcohol monopolies). When promising, new technologies seem profitable, governments often claim monopoly rights and take over the ownership of these activities (for example, public ownership of rail and telegraph systems when these technologies were new and highly lucrative more than a century ago). Likewise, many governments have nationalized the oil and gas industry as a means of getting easy access to revenue. In these cases, other arguments for public production are usually also adduced, but the interest in monopoly revenue no doubt plays the key role.[4]

(d) State-operated production is often a politically convenient mechanism to facilitate redistribution (see below).

Providing access to public domain goods

Where these considerations are not dominant (such as in education, communication and health), these goods can be produced by private competitors and public funds can be used to acquire and make them accessible to the public (public-access or public-domain goods). In such cases, the government may act as a quality controller, but not the producer.

This requires elaboration on a number of aspects:

(a) The question of how access to public domain goods and services is funded, needs to be kept apart from the question of whether these goods and services should be produced with government-owned (socialized) means of production.[5] If it seems politically desirable to provide citizens with certain government-funded goods and services, private production and subsidized access will often be less costly and offer citizens better choices. The argument that public production saves on transaction costs and eliminates the duplication of competitive private suppliers, which one often hears, assumes however prior knowledge of outcomes and overlooks the potential of competition to uncover process and product innovations. In any event, public production is always fraught with long-term dangers of unchecked agent opportunism and a diminished likelihood of innovation (see following section).

(b) The issue of public ownership and control should also be considered separately from the issue of public monopolies. Even where government organizations engage in productive activities, there may be a case for competition among different agencies (for example, between different publicly-owned, but corporatized power plants, hospitals, universities and communications networks) and for competition with private suppliers (for example letting private schools, telephone companies, trains, buses or airlines compete with public-sector providers of the same services). Thanks to the drop in measurement and communications costs, there are now few natural monopolies where competition is not technically feasible. Few existing monopolies survive for long unless backed by political intervention.

(c) A third important issue in the socialized production of public goods is accountability, that is, full and transparent information about all costs of, and returns from, the use of public property, as well as the subjection of government-owned producers to firm budget constraints (Mises, 1944). Accountability is enhanced when public production ventures are corporatized, that is, their activities are administratively separated from the budget that covers the general government business. It is not always politically easy to enforce hard budget constraints and withhold budget subsidies from loss-making public enterprises. However, if competitive pressures and the accountability of public office holders are weak, public servants are bound to become self-serving (high salaries, overstaffing, lax cost controls, excessive on-the-job consumption). Where lax practices have become entrenched, moves to control the private appropriation of public property tend to be fiercely resisted, as the widespread public-servant demonstrations against cost cutting in heavily indebted European countries demonstrate. This has become evident after numerous privatization projects around the world revealed that massive productivity reserves existed (Chapters 13 and 14).

(d) Production by government agencies creates 'political firms'. Such firms enjoy not only economic power in markets, often even monopoly power, but state ownership also gives them direct economic influence in markets, and direct political over policy making (de Alessi, 1980;

1982). Since no interested individuals have a direct claim to the residual profit of public-sector operations (nor are directly liable for the losses) and ownership rights cannot normally be transferred (except by privatization), it is likely that 'political firms' will not be as closely monitored by the principals, that is, elected politicians and auditors, as private businesses are. After all, monitoring is costly. The managers of public enterprises are therefore exposed to incentive structures at variance from those applying to the leaders of private firms (Chapter 9). For example, it is not uncommon that one finds that the monitoring of leave applications in public operations costs two or three times as much administration time as in private industry, or that the management of a comparable volume of billing costs five times as much, because the pace of work is slower and higher-cost employees carry the work out than employees in private industry. Indeed, monitoring can be particularly expensive when opaque, public-sector accounting practices apply or when public-enterprise accounts are not publicized because the operations of political firms are kept secret (defence, intelligence agencies). In any event, the outputs of publicly owned firms are often difficult to measure.

De Alessi reviewed much evidence from private and public production of comparable goods and services. This confirmed that political firms indeed have a poorer economic performance than their private counterparts (de Alessi, 1980). The higher costs of carrying out and monitoring tasks under public-sector conditions may, for example, be the consequence of the need for more intensive supervision and lesser reliance on self-responsibility. When the relentless discipline imposed by genuinely competitive markets is lacking, the discipline of political and administrative controls often proves comparatively weak and costly, and public-sector unions sideline the appointed administrative managers. Frequently, these matters are decided by unelected, tenured bureaucrats, and not even the elected politicians.

Reforming socialized production

The principles of for-profit business accounting should be applied to public production ventures to provide quality information about them, which allows elected leaders to check. This means that not only recurrent outlays and revenues (in the budget) should be estimated and made public, but also that the impact of each such activity on the government's assets and liabilities is accounted for (accrual accounting). Each year, the activities of public-sector corporations should be reviewed in independently audited public-sector balance sheets, so that the effects on the government's net wealth is made transparent. Few governments around the world, however, produce this information, even though they demand it of private corporations.[6] Public-sector production sometimes seems advantageous for the sole reason that not all costs and revenues are taken into account and are clearly separated from general government business. This allows hidden subsidies. An advantage of transparent and full accounting by publicly owned businesses is that they are then shielded to some degree from day-to-day political intervention, which tends to disrupt production planning and opens the door for political rent-seeking.

Reforms can alleviate the problems inherent in public production. For example, socialized production can be devolved to competing lower-level governments, which would turn socialized property almost into a kind of club goods (Buchanan, 1965; Demsetz, 1970; Foldvary, 1994, pp. 62–78; 86-112). Production in the hands of competing low-level governments can enhance feedback about what goods and services better meet the desires of the community. Of course, public production can also be privatized with assurances that access to the goods and services is guaranteed by government.

In addition, procedures in government-owned enterprises can be reformed to match the best practice in private firms. Modern management techniques of motivation and monitoring help to extract efficiency dividends for the taxpayer. To this end, the managers have to be given clear, quantified output targets by their political masters and have to be allowed to choose by what methods the targets are met and how the necessary inputs are acquired. Such a responsibility system will only work when public-sector managers remain at arm's length from government, have limited tenure and are paid for their performance – an arrangement that differs fundamentally from the traditional public-service approach with life-long tenure. Where such reforms are not feasible, the production of goods and services should be taken out of the public sector and privatized, so that the disciplines of competitive private business apply.

Private-public partnerships and chartered associations

Given pervasive problems with agent opportunism in public ventures, numerous governments have, since the 1990s, experimented with Private-Public Partnerships (PPPs), that is, arrangements by which traditional tasks of government are partially shared with private enterprises. Sometimes, the design and construction of projects is entrusted to private enterprise, but the running is retained under government control. Thus, public roads in many countries are built by competing private contractors, but then managed and repaired by public entities. Alternatively, government bodies design and construct, but entrust the operation to periodically competing private operators. An example is the running of public prisons by private security firms, who have to compete for the renewal of management contracts every five years. Sometimes, private investors are given a franchise to operate new projects for a limited time to recoup their costs, as is the case when roadways or rail links are built by private firms and are allowed to charge tolls for usage. The underlying assumption in all these cases is that, in specific operations, private enterprise can attain better productivity and other objectives than a purely public operation could.

Empirical studies, for example by the United Kingdom's Audit Office, have shown that on the whole, PPPs had markedly lower cost over-runs during construction and fewer delays in the completion of projects. This is plausible as private operations tend to reward performance and on-time delivery, whereas such incentives tend to be much weaker in the public sector where the political motivation often is to throw good (tax) money after bad investments to defend political reputations. In long-lasting public monopolies that employ specific assets, key operating agents tend to capture and exploit positions of influence (as discussed in Chapter 9 under the heading of asset specificity), which then raises the costs and limits the benefits and convenience to the public.

The advantages of governments employing private firms to deliver productive functions of government require that clashes in management culture between a private, for-profit orientation and a tax-funded, for-election orientation and rent-seeking incentives are addressed. There will always be a tendency to privatize the profits, but socialize costs and risks, maybe in non-transparent ways and certainly at the expense of the wider public. This happens, for example, when public roads are closed or narrowed to channel more traffic onto private toll roads as part of a PPP contract. There is also a tendency amongst political and bureaucratic agents to prevent the failure of PPPs, thus removing the important incentive of 'red ink' and bankruptcy from the private part of such operations. If projects cannot be allowed to fail at all cost and are therefore subsidized, there is little point in engaging private cooperation.

The rapid increase in PPPs is ultimately due to the fact that governments have reached limits in their capacity to raise taxes, borrow and manage projects. Political agents, who still resist the conclusion that the reach of the public sector should be pegged back, try to extend their influence further by fostering PPPs. Seen in this context, it must in each case be examined whether a clear-cut privatization, coupled if necessary with some ambit regulation, is not the more honest and straightforward solution.

When problems associated with public-sector production are widespread, communities may turn to local clubs and similar organizations to provide certain public-access goods. In many affluent Western countries, citizens now realize that central governments cannot provide the welfare services that parliamentarians have promised, indeed that promising more welfare services is electorally dangerous. Governments are therefore encouraging local initiatives to set up club-like organizations, which are open to voluntary local membership, to initiate and operate health, education and other welfare services. For example, local groups may take over and run schools under a charter that commits them to deliver an agreed curriculum in return for tax subsidies, or set up charter (or trust) hospitals. Here, the incentive structure is not mainly informed by profits, but by direct local community feedback, and the inputs are not acquired solely from the market, but draw on volunteer contributions of labour, skills and finance. Traditions of volunteering and honesty greatly help to make such charitable activities successful. In these cases, governments are confined to providing the financial means of general access and supervising quality standards. Where dependency on big government has prevailed, such charter or trust operations can do much to cultivate a constructive community spirit and to demonstrate that, in practice, there is much scope for solutions between exclusive reliance on big government and profit-seeking private enterprise.

We shall return to these issues in Chapters 13 and 14 when we discuss privatization, the transformation of socialist economies and the reform of mixed economies.

KEY CONCEPTS

Common property was defined in Chapter 7. These goods are, as we saw, institutionally deficient in that many of the benefits and costs cannot be exclusively internalized (captured), since third parties cannot be excluded from using such goods. Where demand needs to be rationed, provision and control may be enhanced through the transfer to clubs (or local governments), through subsidized access to privately-produced, public-domain goods or socialized property.

Public provision refers to the government's administrative arrangements that make goods and services available to citizens or certain classes of citizens, either through public funding (cash hand-outs, tax remission), purpose-bound vouchers (food, education and health-care vouchers), or *in specie* distribution (the distribution of blankets after a catastrophe). Public provision does not necessitate **public production** of these goods and services in publicly owned and run enterprises. Public access neither requires nor justifies public ownership or monopoly.

Political firms are publicly owned and managed production agencies. They

➡

◀

tend to have access to subsidies out of tax revenue, and hence face softer budget constraints than private companies that can go broke more easily. The managers of political firms also tend to capture the politicians and bureaucrats who are meant to control them. They can often exert indirect influence on those governments that shape the rules governing them.

Accountability relates to standards of reporting the costs and benefits of actions to the principals of an organization, normally both the recurrent flows (income and loss statement; budget) and the effects on the value of their stocks of assets and liabilities (balance sheet). Accountability also implies that breaches of stipulated standards meet with sanctions, that is, agents are held accountable and not given subsidies out of general budgets (no **soft and fuzzy budget constraints**).

Accrual accounting is the practice of deducting recurrent expenses from the net capital position and adding benefits (receipts) to that position by constructing a balance sheet of assets and liabilities. It reveals the debt and asset position, including unfunded contingencies from new political initiatives. This method furnishes quality information to political decision makers and the electorate. Nowadays, most national governments can only guess whether they operate with net liabilities (are broke) or own net capital assets, and whether new initiatives will enhance or prejudice the nation's public wealth.

Privatization is an act of transferring publicly-owned property rights to private owners (opposite of socialization or nationalization), whereas **corporatization** refers to acts of reorganizing publicly-owned assets and organizations so that they con-

stitute an entity separate from the general core business of government. The leaders of corporatized, publicly-owned organizations should be made clearly accountable to their political masters and the electorate and should have to face clear-cut budget constraints without recourse to budget subsidies.

Private-public partnerships (PPPs) are operations, in which competing private firms cooperate with government entities in either the financing and setting-up or managing of public-domain projects. Such divisions of labour may often have advantages, but they require careful and binding contractual rules to ensure that private (often monopolistic) operators face the incentives to perform and that political and bureaucratic agents do not obtain rents to the detriment of the wider public.

Charter (or trust) enterprises are initiatives that (normally local) clubs set up and operate as community ventures with public access. These ventures receive public funding in exchange for adhering to a charter. Thus, in a growing number of countries, schools are run under such charters by local groups with parents receiving voucher funding that they can allocate to the charter schools of their choice. Likewise, trust hospitals are managed by (better informed) representatives of local communities under a charter that ensures service delivery meeting quality standards with public funding. Such community ventures tend to have advantages over centralized welfare delivery, in that the management is better informed about local conditions and can mobilize voluntary contributions, apart from cultivating a community spirit.

The redistribution of property rights

A third function of government in most countries is redistribution of income and wealth: the confiscation of the property of some and the reallocation of that property to others. This is based on concepts of social justice (Tullock, 1983). In Europe, the rulers have long relied on public taxation to assist 'the waifs and widows', and public organizations – such as communal poor houses – have long been attending to the basic needs of the destitute. Based on this tradition, social reformers, such as the Fabian socialists in Britain and the former British colonies, the social democrats in Continental Europe and a strand of the Democratic Party in the United States, have claimed the moral high ground. Similar notions of 'social justice' influence policy in the Muslim world and Buddhist countries. In the process, security and justice have been equated to the conservation of certain social and economic positions in the face of change and to ensuring a measure of outcome equality in the distribution of incomes and wealth (Sections 4.2 and 6.3). The advocates of redistribution by government also base their case on optimism about the practical feasibility of political redistribution programmes, disregarding problems of cognition, rational ignorance, moral hazard, and self-interest of political agents. On the basis of such popular philosophies, governments have served as insurers of last resort against the risks of life – a role that is typically left to the family in other civilizations, for example in large parts of East Asia.

Redistribution can be attempted by two categories of policy instrument:

(a) One is to attenuate or even neutralize the outcomes of the competitive game by using the government's coercive right to tax and hand-out transfer payments.

(b) The other is to alter how markets function by directly intervening with the competitive game that is founded on private property rights by influencing the accumulation of financial, physical and human capital, and by interfering with the freedom to conclude contracts (Figure 10.1).

The distribution of property rights amongst people is the outcome of past market processes and a measure of random luck. No visible hand does the distributing; the outcome results from millions of dispersed individual decisions (Hayek, 1986/1978). To change this pattern, governments rely on their coercive power to raise taxes and make transfers, which are decided politically. For example, a progressive income tax does not treat all dollars earned equally (as a flat tax would), instead it takes the size of the income flow of the property

Figure 10.1 Instruments of redistributive intervention

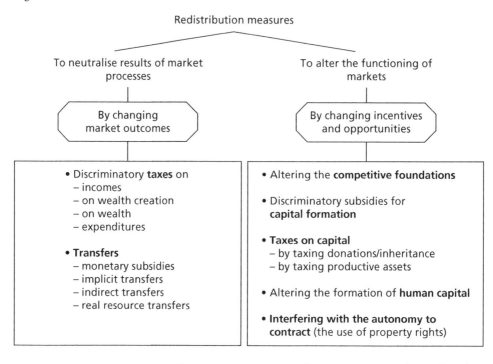

Redistribution measures

To neutralise results of market processes

To alter the functioning of markets

By changing market outcomes

By changing incentives and opportunities

- Discriminatory **taxes** on
  - incomes
  - on wealth creation
  - on wealth
  - expenditures

- **Transfers**
  - monetary subsidies
  - implicit transfers
  - indirect transfers
  - real resource transfers

- Altering the **competitive foundations**

- Discriminatory subsidies for **capital formation**

- **Taxes on capital**
  - by taxing donations/inheritance
  - by taxing productive assets

- Altering the formation of **human capital**

- **Interfering with the autonomy to contract** (the use of property rights)

owner into account. Some taxes are imposed on some types of spending, but others are exempt. Transfers may consist of outright cash payments, but may also include real resource transfers, such as food hand-outs, free accommodation or vouchers for services. Similarly, administrations and parliaments may decide to provide more government-made infrastructures to regions where average income is low or where critical votes can be garnered.

The second category of redistribution instruments aims at altering the starting opportunities before people engage in competitive uses of their property rights in markets (Figure 10.1). These include measures to assist certain groups with the formation of physical or human capital. Government may fund access to education, considering education as a public-domain good (as discussed in Sections 7.2 and 10.1). The intention is to redistribute the chances of young citizens in competing more evenly in the labour market. Opportunities to compete may also be altered by direct interventions in the private autonomy to contract. Other instances of redistributive intervention are regulations that prohibit employers dismissing workers despite their non-performance or landlords evicting tenants who have consistently failed to pay their rents. By such interventions, legislators not only create asymmetric privileges, but also destroy incentives to supply jobs and rental accommodation. Indeed, rent control appears to be one of the most effective ways presently known to destroy a city, second only to bombardment.

Another example of the second type of redistribution policy is tariff protection, a topic touched on in Chapter 8. Foreign producers and domestic buyers see the value of their property diminished by a government-provided tariff obstacle to selling freely across national borders, whereas domestic producers see the value of their property increased because they may sell at a higher price. Such redistributive interventions have unintended, long-term consequences for the supply of the regulated product; they also hamper innovation. The short- and long-run consequences of such redistribution policies are hard to know. Redistribution is always complicated by unexpected and unwanted side effects. For this reason alone, it seems preferable for redistribution policy to rely on the more transparent means of taxing and transferring through the budget: a method that is subject to more explicit parliamentary and public control than direct administrative interventions in markets.

Redistribution always implies acts by the visible hand of government to take private property rights away from some and allot them to others. Redistribution always interferes with the protective function of government, which covers the protection of private property rights. Whatever the motives for political actions to redistribute private rights, one should be aware that the accumulation of such interventions – rising regulatory density in the economy – disturb the signalling mechanism of free market prices and the important social quality of self-responsibility. It also leads to a widespread claims mentality and a culture of victimhood, which often leads to learnt helplessness and cultural malaise. How much redistribution is attempted in a society is of course for the voters to decide. Here, we can only point to unintended consequences of such policies that are commonly observed and discuss ideas that may help to contain the unintended side effects of pervasive redistribution by government. We shall return to the consequences of massive redistribution policies when we discuss the failures of the social democratic experiment in Section 10.4 below.

KEY CONCEPTS

Fabian socialism and **social democracy** split from totalitarian socialism, which aimed at the violent overthrow of the 'bourgeois order' and the expropriation of the means of production in the late nineteenth century. In perpetuating pre-Marxist philosophical traditions, social democrats were for most of the twentieth

➡

---

century suspicious of private property and advocated the gradual and piecemeal nationalization of property rights in land, housing and a great variety of industrial assets, as well as banking and other important services. They also advocate 'corrective intervention' in the market, so that people may attain more equal incomes. They nationalized the provision and production of health and education services, as well as old-age care and some housing provision, and more generally try to replace the private provision of welfare by public welfare.

Social democrats tend to have great faith in the capability of political leaders and administrative processes in bringing about outcomes to meet politically pre-determined goals (optimism about feasibility of collective programmes).

Takings and just compensation

In Chapter 7, we discussed the takings of property rights by governments under the doctrine of 'eminent domain' or similar problematic juridical constructs. How can the protection of private property be reconciled with claims on private property by the state? Clear rules are always needed, especially in countries where single-issue groups and governments collude to pursue policies that are at odds with a well-functioning free-market order. Various jurisdictions and legal traditions have shaped rules that tie takings to 'just compensation'. These are, first, that takings are only justifiable if harm from the exercise of individual property rights has been proven – not alleged or merely feared. In particular, the notion that harm to the environment has to be treated preemptively on the basis of a 'precautionary principle' overlooks that policy should proceed with precaution all around: about future prosperity, job security, peace and all other such aspirations. Claiming the 'precautionary principle' for environmental conservation alone amounts to a demand for the political empowerment for groups that pursue only one objective to the possible detriment of all others. Because the assessment of environmental risks is also of necessity highly subjective, the adoption of an environmental precautionary principle advances the (arbitrary) rule of men at the expense of the rule of law.

In cases where individuals claim being harmed by a property use, the burden of proof within the laws of the land falls upon them. Where governments claim harm on behalf of the wider public, the burden of proof should rest on their shoulders. Legislation to reverse the burden of proof – "harmful till proven innocent" – should be seen as an attack on the property rights order. Once harm is proven, three tests have to be conducted:

(a) Does the proposed taking of existing private property rights promote stated and accepted policy objectives?

(b)   Will, to the best of expert judgment, the expected benefits of the intervention exceed the expected costs?

(c)   Are the expropriated owners compensated on just terms, that is, to the
equivalent of proper free-market values?

Only if all three questions are answered in the affirmative is a proposed confiscation compatible with the maxims of a well-functioning capitalist order.
If confiscation happens without these conditions being fulfilled, it is a case of
neo-socialist expropriation and an attack on one of the pillars of long-term
prosperity and modern civilization.

As governments in mature economies are facing increasing taxpayer resistance (for example from the 'Tea Party movement' in the United States),
elected governments rely increasingly on regulations that abridge and confiscate private property without due compensation. They do so to win or
keep the support of single-issue lobbies. The gradual erosion of the capitalist
order in Western democracies is the reason why concerned observers are
now calling for 'regulatory impact statements' that address the above three
tests in a transparent manner prior to any political interventions (Epstein,
1985; Epstein et al., 2005; Epstein, 2007). In some jurisdictions, legislators
are proceeding to safeguard the property-rights regime by demanding a regulatory constitution, such as has been the case in New Zealand since 2011.
In many others, the security of private property rights is still assumed and the
long-term effects of its erosion are ignored.

Agency costs: tax and administration

In order to fulfil their functions, government agents incur agency costs that
are normally paid by the compulsory levying of taxes. Taxation and the
administration of public moneys in turn cause further agency costs.

The organization of the administrative business of government and its
funding is the subject of fiscal studies. Although institutional economics can
offer numerous applications to the running of political organizations, most
of that discussion remains outside the framework of this book. However,
we should note that institutions may have a major impact (i) on the size of
government, and (ii) on how high the agency costs are for attaining a given
set of government objectives.

The size of government, and with it the agency and tax costs, can be reduced
if socialized property is turned into club goods – devolving tasks of government to small, self-organizing and self-monitoring groups. Moreover,

socialized property can be privatized and public-domain services can be sub-contracted with access provided from public funds to separate production from access provision. Thus, a substantial part of the erstwhile government school system in Sweden and some American States has now been entrusted to charter schools, that is, schools founded and run by community organ-izations that compete for school vouchers. Similarly, the non-government trust hospitals in the United Kingdom and Spain have taken over health care services that were previously provided within a unitary (bureaucratized and ailing) national health system. Such shifts make the government's busi-ness more feasible because its agents can then concentrate on the planning, directing, monitoring and correcting of its core activities.

The core functions of government

In order to decide the proper functions of government, there must be some regard to fundamental value judgments. These have played a major role in the public debate about the size and reform of government in recent years. One such normative answer was given by Milton Friedman:

> A government which maintained law and order, defined property rights, served as a means whereby we could modify property rights and other rules of the economic game, adjudicated disputes about the interpretation of rules, enforced contracts, promoted competition, provided a monetary framework, engaged in activities to counter technical monopolies and to overcome neighborhood effects widely regarded as sufficiently important to justify government intervention, and which supplemented private charity and the private family in protecting the irresponsible, whether madman or child – such a government would clearly have important func-tions to perform. The consistent liberal is not an anarchist. (Friedman, 1962; p. 34)

A similar position was adopted by the reformist former New Zealand Treasurer, Ruth Richardson (see Box 10.2) in which she argued for a reduc-tion of the functions of government to a core. This is premised on a perception of government that sees the citizens as the principals. Some of their elected agents form the board of directors (the cabinet), which lays down general guidelines and clearly spells out objectives, against which the performance of bureaucrat-managers and their government departments are measured. Clear and simple targets, as well as performance-based pay coupled with limited tenure for the top managers create incentives to perform and control agent opportunism in public administration. The elected directors (minis-ters) should not get involved in the technical management of how govern-ment services are produced or how the necessary inputs are acquired. This is the task of the expert managers, the heads of government departments and their assistants. Over time, contracts with the top managers of government business may stipulate an efficiency dividend.

CH 10 – CASE TWO

Small government in action

Excerpts from an interview with Ruth Richardson, reformer and former New Zealand finance minister:

> We should start with asking the fundamental question: what should the state do? We should 'de-invent' government in many areas. The state definitively has a role in protecting the rule of law; in addition a minimal role in ensuring income sufficiency as discussed. It must be funded to that extent. . . . The state's role is to establish the rules, to be the steward who ensures that citizens get quality, and to fund pupil or patient choice. If you ask the people they still think that the state should be the referee as well as the player! We know the state is bankrupt as a business operator, but most still think it can produce quality health and education services! . . . By reducing the role of the state, government spending will automatically shrink. Governments should not produce, for they cannot create wealth. They can only protect a climate in which private citizens can assess freely what enhances their wealth. . . .Regulation has to be general and light-handed. Governments should for example come in only as referees where a market becomes uncontestable. The state has a legitimate role to blow the whistle when monopolies undermine competition.

[Reform] is about doing away with political privileges for organized groups. When you redesign taxation, you begin by thinking afresh about the role of government and therefore the expenditure demands that taxpayers can legitimately be expected to fund. Next you make sure that you get the most efficient way of obtaining the desired results from collective action. You organize the business of public administration by creating incentives to be as effective as possible. The citizens have every right to ask that the administration is run competently and efficiently. Modern management methods need to be applied to financial and human resource management. Ministers should contract for the production of specified outputs and leave the chief executives of the government departments the responsibility for organizing the inputs and production processes, as they see fit. Over time, the politicians should extract an efficiency dividend. In New Zealand, this performance-based management approach has yielded enormous fiscal savings, income tax reductions and freedom from foreign debt.

Once one knows what has to be funded from taxes, one must ensure that this is done with the least distorting tax system one can design. People must chase market opportunities and must not be diverted from solid business reasons by artificial tax reasons. Therefore, the tax system must be broad-based with low rates of tax. I would probably favour a mix of income and value-added tax – a flat 15 per cent income tax, 20 per cent maximum, with a negative income tax at the low end, and a comprehensive 10 per cent value-added tax. If tax rates go higher, they become distortive.

CH 10 – CASE TWO *(continued)*

A broad-based, low-rate tax regime would induce governments and households to save; it would lower the cost of capital. We would gain much voluntary compliance and an enormous saving on transaction costs. . . . Such an intelligent tax regime would – in the interest of fairness and credibility – have to be coupled with strong sanctions and draconian penalties for tax cheats. There is no scope for forging and forgetting – just as it is false, self-defeating generosity to forgive violence or offences against the laws of ethics and crime.

Source: W. Kasper (1996b), pp. 25–31.

International benchmarking can assist with meeting the stipulated targets. Changing the rule set can thus create incentives to reduce the agency costs of government.

Once the functions of government are spelled out and the best production method of public services has been identified, one can estimate the costs. Then, the politically elected board of directors can decide how the public expenditures to meet those costs are funded, taking into account time-tested principles of financial prudence and inter-generational justice. It is important that all elected politicians have access to proper financial information, including the government's balance sheet. Simple, broad-based taxes would impose low compliance and monitoring costs and free the energies of taxpayers from tax minimization to pursue their genuine economic objectives. Such a tax regime would also keep the agency costs of tax collection relatively low.

Historically, the agency costs of a purely protective state were small in times of peace, namely about one tenth of a community's income. As we saw, modern states make massively bigger claims on private production and incomes, because they subsidize public-sector production and, above all, redistribute incomes and wealth (potentially without limits). In the process, the number of government employees has increased enormously and with it the agency costs. Frequently, a growing government sector has become a purpose of government, for example when government is expanded in the hope of ensuring more jobs or when agents expect better career promotion opportunities if they supervise more subordinates.

Compliance costs

Collective action not only imposes resource costs, which citizens bear by paying tax and other compulsory levies, but also compliance costs. These are the resource expenses that private citizens and organizations have to incur when they obey government laws and regulations (external institutions). For example, taxpayers have to keep records they otherwise would not, fill in paperwork for the government, conduct their activities in ways different from what they would otherwise, and so on. They may have to desist from certain activities and engage in others involuntarily, sometimes at great cost. Citizens and businesses are often obliged to hire staff to cope with the paperwork. In most countries, government has given rise to an entire 'compliance industry' of tax agents, government-relations experts, lawyers and lobby groups.

The costs of complying with government demands vary considerably between jurisdictions. Often, administrative practices and – gradually grown – legislative and regulatory systems can be streamlined without much loss in regulatory purpose. Certain health or safety outcomes can be achieved in various ways, some with massive savings in compliance costs (Chapter 14). National tax systems also impose compliance costs. For example, income and corporate tax regimes that contain numerous exemptions and stipulations for the purpose of redistribution tend to be more costly to comply with (in terms of paperwork, use of specialist tax consultants and litigation) than exemption-free, low income-tax regimes or low, general indirect taxes (see Box 10.2 above). Compliance costs are also driven up by frequent changes in the administrative instructions intended to fine-tune or re-engineer legislation and regulations. Finally, it should be noted that many compliance costs are fixed costs, so that small and medium-sized enterprises face higher cost obstacles than large corporations, which can better afford to run specialist legal and government-relations departments. Compliance costs are therefore an obstacle to competition, job creation and innovation by small start-up firms.

KEY CONCEPTS

Redistribution is a process inspired by notions of social justice. It is based on the ability of political powers to reallocate property rights from some to other citizens and organizations, either by taxing and subsidizing, or by intervening in the free play of market forces, that is, by rental controls that lower the value of houses to owners and enhance the position of renters, or food price controls that enrich consumers and make agriculturalists poorer. Redistribution by the visible hand of government interferes with private property rights, and therefore often conflicts with the protective function of government.

When redistributive measures intervene in specific market processes or aim at specific outcomes, the consequences are typically underrated. Markets work through self-coordination by exchange and ➡

⬅

self-control by competition. These spontaneous, ordering forces in the complex economic system are disturbed or even incapacitated by specific policy manipulations that produce unintended side effects, which, in turn, frequently necessitate further interventions.

Compliance costs are incurred by private citizens and firms who have to obey mandatory collective action. For example, taxpayers have to prepare cumbersome paperwork or firms have to monitor and report certain activities (for example, providing employment statistics). The design of government administration and legislation has great impact on the level of compliance costs. Constant re-engineering and fine-tuning of administrative rules violates the institutional principle of universality and drives up these costs.

10.3   A liberal model of public policy: order policy

Order policy versus process intervention

Three red threads that run through this book underpin the maxim that the central function of public policy should be to support and enhance social and economic order ('order policy'). They are:

(a)   People's cognitive abilities are limited, so that an order, which allows them to uncover recognizable patterns, enhances the division of labour and hence living standards. It also gives people known spheres of freedom.

(b)   Freedom of individual action (autonomy) is a precondition for competition, the most powerful discovery procedure and the most effective control device known to man.

(c)   It is normal for people to have asymmetric information and to yield to temptations to act opportunistically (principal-agent problem). This makes it necessary to establish binding commitments and to enforce the rules.

If public policy is guided by a commitment to fostering order, individual freedoms are likely to be more secure and economic coordination will be more effective. Discrimination and rent-seeking are more likely to be kept at bay. Such a style of policy focuses on cultivating the institutions and their coordinative capacity. The approach is to emphasize the need for competition and secure property rights and to de-emphasize policies aimed at directly influencing specific processes and outcomes. In other words, policy must work to ensure that competition is protected from capture by special interest groups. A style of public policy that relies on arbitrary ad hoc decisions can easily run into problems of cognitive overload, both amongst those subjected to it and amongst government agents. It also leads to conflicts among different policy measures and different parts of government. The likely consequences of a result-oriented, instrumentalist style of policy are apathy amongst the public and confusion and mal-coordination in public administration.

This basic philosophy was first advocated in a consistent and detailed manner by the German *ordo* liberal school. Economists and lawyers at the University of Freiburg, most notably Walter Eucken and Franz Böhm, analysed the dire failures of democracy in the Weimar Republic, which gave rise to totalitarian National Socialism. Writing in the 1930s to 1950s, they concluded that majoritarian electoral democracy had failed to foster a non-discriminatory, sufficiently competitive order. Instead, organized pressure groups and the politicians that did their bidding had engaged in pervasive opportunistic rent seeking. The *ordo* liberals – similar to those who are now calling for a 'robust political economy' – went back to the basic tenets of the Scottish Enlightenment, which recognizes that the protection of private property rights, the freedom of contract and the rule of law are essential to the functioning of a capitalist economy. The Freiburg circle of lawyers and economists focused on the essential control and incentive functions of a competitive system, but added further considerations to the basic principles of the Scottish Enlightenment so as to adjust the liberal policy design to the modern age, multi-party democracy and pervasive rent seeking. They acknowledged that concentrations of industrial and union power were a fact of life, that modern electoral democracy with universal suffrage created major temptations for selective political interventions and that organized pressure groups had great influence on parliaments and public administrations. They became known as the 'Freiburg School' or the 'German *ordo* liberals'[7] (Vanberg, 1988; Kasper and Streit, 1993).

The fundamental advice to public policy makers was to distinguish between (i) making the protective function the focus of government, particularly by fostering and setting institutions that are conducive to a competitive economic order, and (ii) constrain intervening in specific economic and social processes (Eucken 1992/1940). The former – so the *ordo* liberals asserted – was to have precedence over the latter. Government should concentrate on using its coercive powers to promote and defend competition as a public good. The freedom of contract, the *ordo* liberals concluded, does not encompass a freedom to form cartels and close markets to new contestants. Such contracts abridge the freedom of others, including the freedom of choice of buyers. They also found that public policy interventions often introduce disturbances that destabilize expectations and hence are counter-productive. The hold of public policy over the external institutions should therefore be steady. Political activism in pursuit of specific outcomes was condemned as disorienting and destabilizing.

The *ordo* liberals' reservations about intervening in economic processes led them to be critical of the conscious discretionary policy, advocated in the 1940s and 1950s by the Keynesians, of using budgetary and monetary policies to counter cyclical swings in aggregate demand. Instead, they preferred stable institutions, competitive markets and steady public policies to enhance the inherent, spontaneous self-stabilization of the system. They feared that pump priming and the manipulation of aggregate demand would gradually erode market signals and change patterns of private behaviour. In that respect, they anticipated the criticism of the 'rational expectations school' of the 1980s, but placed it in the wide methodological context of market conformity.

Market conformity

The focal concern of the *ordo* liberals was with competition – not so much in single markets, but throughout the entire market system. Competitive systems deserved to be defended and shored up, they taught, because they have essential knowledge-generating and controlling functions, which alternative collective systems cannot match in a modern complex economy. They therefore stipulated that all measures of public policy should be 'market conform', which is to say, policy should not undermine the pervasive role of competition. Each measure of policy, as well as the overall design of collective action, should be evaluated as to whether it affected competitiveness. Thus, redistributive measures of the sort discussed in Sections 10.4 and 10.5 below found little favour with the *ordo* liberals, unless they enhanced the starting positions of competitors in ways that do not distort market signals.

The constitutive principles of *ordo* policy

The basic principles that constitute the essence of *ordo* policy are:

- private property rights;
- freedom of contract;
- liability for one's commitments and actions;
- open markets (freedom of entry and exit);
- monetary stability (inflation-free money); and
- steadiness of economic policy.

These principles should be given overriding, constitutional status and made the guiding stars of public policy, the *ordo* liberals said. These principles constitute a strong, consistent support of the free-market order that permits the unfolding of effective coordination, the use of knowledge by creative entrepreneurship and the control of economic power (Sections 8.1 and 8.4). If public policy is guided by these simple constitutive principles, this does not foster untrammelled laissez-faire, but protects individual rights and effective cooperation within a knowledge-saving institutional framework. This type of policy also binds the rulers to follow the principle of 'no favours all around'.

An important insight of the *ordo* approach, which Walter Eucken stressed, is that these principles should apply in equal measure to all interdependent markets (Kasper and Streit, 1993). If the sub-order of institutions in the labour market, for example, is incompatible with the sub-order in product markets, this is likely to cause costly contradictions, such as distorted relative prices. Regulated labour markets alongside freely competitive product markets would, for example, make some production unprofitable and destroy jobs. Such incompatibilities would sooner or later require the deregulation of labour markets or the suppression of untrammelled competition in product markets. The compatibility of sub-orders is also important in areas that border on economic life. Thus, an incentive-destroying social welfare system or a corrupt legal order that erodes property rights tend to clash with a competitive economic order. Only a compatible mosaic of sub-orders is stable and efficient. This fundamental insight relates to the plea for a cohesive order of rules, which we discussed in Chapter 6.

Adhering to such a style of public policy of course precludes legislative and regulatory activism. It also requires tolerance of some outcomes that certain groups of society may dislike. Above all, it requires great caution with redistributive policies and counsels that observed unequal outcomes in income and wealth are best analysed and addressed in the context of ongoing evolution. Relatively poor individuals may, however, need assistance with gaining better starting chances, rather than being given unconditional hand-outs.

Alas, the hope of the *ordo* liberals that the mere commitment to 'order policy' protects governments in the heat of political battles and public controversies from readily yielding to rent-seeking pressure groups and from being held responsible for everything, has not been borne out by post-war German history (Giersch et al., 1992). Mere commitment to the above catalogue of guiding principles did not protect West German parliaments and bureaucrats from the errors of activist macroeconomic stabilization policy and favouritism for well-organized interest groups, when governments were facing elections.

The politico-economic processes, which were later described by the public-choice school, proved too powerful. Established interest groups could not be fended off by simply tying the hands of politicians to *ordo* principles.

The members of the Freiburg School anticipated the public-choice economists to some extent in diagnosing rent-seeking and political favouritism as the influences that undermine the proper functioning of the capitalist system. Beyond stating the general principles, the Freiburg School had little advice to offer by way of practical antidotes for what is nowadays called the 'institutional sclerosis of the market system' in parliamentary democracies (Streit, 1992; Kasper and Streit, 1993; Pennington, 2010). The critical observer half a century later has to admit that substantive reforms to block the rent-seeking drive from within are still not unlikely. What incentives there are nowadays to reform seem to derive primarily from the pressures of institutional competition among different jurisdictions (Chapter 12).

Ordo policy and coordination

Assuming for the moment that the hands of opportunistic politicians and bureaucrats could be effectively tied, *ordo* policy could make communities more governable and the job of governance more feasible in real-world conditions of limited knowledge. Adherence to a relatively simple set of principles could help the agents of government to resist temptations to promise lobbies a plethora of specific outcomes, which in reality are far beyond their capability to deliver. It would also facilitate coordination in collective action. By sticking to these principles, the various government departments would remain reasonably coordinated, so that one department does not have to correct, or compensate for, unintended side effects created by the actions of other departments (inter-agency coordination). *Ordo* liberal principles also assist in keeping policies consistent over time, thus fostering a predictable pattern of policy (inter-temporal coordination). Beyond that, adherence to these few guiding principles – instead of frequent interventions in specific processes – would, before long, lead private decision makers to predict the rules of the policy game and induce them to react more predictably (private-public coordination). Policy, by being more predictable, then becomes more credible and more effective.

As noted, order policy requires policy makers to be blind to the specific outcomes of rule-guided behaviour. Adhering to a policy of supporting the known institutional system and desisting from 'outcome engineering' will, of course, sometimes be unpopular. Policy makers who then place the specific outcome over and above the maintenance of the rule, trigger hard-to-foresee side effects and undermine the general, easy-to-perceive institutional system. They raise the coordination costs. Process intervention, for example in the form of knee-jerk legislation in response to undesirable singular events, may earn short-term popular acclaim, but this violates the non-discrimination rule and, over the longer run, destroys confidence. Order policy therefore demands political backbone and a good understanding of how human interaction is coordinated over the long term. This probably exceeds what politicians in electoral democracies (and other systems) are able and willing to deliver.

Economists and other social scientists with a preference for individual liberty and economic growth have advocated a design of public policy which places the cultivation of a simple, easy-to-understand order of actions and order of rules for many years. In recent years, they have more explicitly acknowledged the evident practical temptations for policy makers and populist electorates in majoritarian democracies. They now argue again for concentrating on simplifying the fundamental rules of private property protection and the rules that govern free competition (robust political economy, Pennington, 2010; Boettke, 2012).

Although the *ordo* principles and the postulates of the robust political economy school clearly spell out the proper rules for successful, growth-enhancing governance, success is dependent on a practical question: Are these rules embraced by the public and policy makers alike, and *how are* these rules implemented? External institutions are only effective if they are backed by the internal institutions and values of the community. Imposed institutions with no regard to the local culture and social norms are destined to fail. The development of rules requires the local knowledge, practices and customs of communities and ongoing interactions of individuals to reinforce these arrangements. As Boettke and Coyne explain, "formal institutions must be based on the metis of the people acting within them. If metis fails to align with the formal institutions, then they will fail to sustain and be effective" (Boettke and Coyne, 2006; p. 55).

KEY CONCEPTS

Ordo policy focuses on the internal and external institutions and their organizational back-up as a framework for economic processes with the intent of facilitating the emergence of order in the minds of the citizens. It places the maintenance of a clearly understood, transparent system of policy rules above interventions in specific ➡

←

economic processes. The maintenance of competition is seen as a public good whose promotion and preservation has priority over and above providing stabilization of economic activity over time or the redistribution of incomes.

The **constitutive principles** of *ordo* policy are:

- private property;
- freedom of contract;
- liability for one's commitment and actions;
- open markets (freedom of entry and exit);
- monetary stability (inflation-free money);
- steadiness of economic policy.

If imbued with constitutional quality, these principles can serve to coordinate government activity between agencies and over time and to create private expectations that make their attainment easier and the pursuit of rent-seeking harder.

The **compatibility of sub-orders** is a feature of policy design that pays attention to the interdependence of institutional frameworks governing inter-dependent markets. This requires not only that product and factor markets are subject to similar freedoms to compete, but also that social, economic and legal policies are compatible. An institutional system that consists of compatible sub-orders of rules is effective in the sense that the various institutions mutually support each other and can be more easily deciphered.

When we speak of the **coordination of policy**, we have to think of making public policy actions compatible (i) amongst various departments of government, (ii) over time, and (iii) between the public policy makers and the private individuals, organizations and associations who are subjected to public policy.

10.4 Failures of the social democratic experiment

The consequences of redistribution

It has long been argued in economics and public policy that market processes fail to produce a distribution of incomes and wealth that correspond to certain normative conceptions. This has given rise to the social democratic argument that the visible hand of government should intervene to correct the market, ensuring a distribution of property rights different from that which the competitive process generates. Powerful private and public interests, of course, distort real-world income and wealth distribution by restrictions of market rivalry. This normally leads to further concentrations of power. The choice then is to enhance the competitive process or to intervene politically to redistribute. Most electoral democracies have, most of the time, gone the interventionist route, but have in the process often entrenched power positions and undermined the intensity of competition. This was also true when the design of *ordo* liberalism was practiced in post-war West Germany; over time, interventions to redistribute property rights (the *social* market economy) destroyed the political commitment to protect the competitive order (Giersch et al., 1992). Under the pressures of electoral politics, organized interest groups and powerful bureaucracies, the commitment to protecting the constitution of capitalism crumbled.

As of the early twenty-first century, the commitment in many Western parliaments to engage in redistribution policy by numerous corrective interventions has come under growing scrutiny, as such interventions have made market systems dysfunctional – the coordinative capacity of the system and incentives to bear risks and produce have been eroded. Redistribution has also led to budget deficits and a crisis of governance in many mature democracies.

Since politicians can derive political advantage from redistributing incomes and wealth, there are great incentives (as we have seen) to expand the redistributive function of government. The opportunistic rivalry among competing political parties for the popular vote, combined with entrenched popular and interest-group pressures, have added more and more to the redistributive function. In Western 'welfare democracies' (as represented by social democrat and interventionist conservative political parties in Europe and by left-liberal movements in America), redistribution has grown enormously in importance since the middle of the twentieth century, causing considerable problems for public policy:

(a) Most political redistribution programmes have not worked. Even where redistribution policies have been massive, poverty and income inequalities persist or even increase.

(b) Public provision to cope with more and more individual contingencies has led to widespread 'moral hazard' among welfare recipients and an entrenched claims mentality. Individuals and families no longer feel obligated to make sufficient provisions of their own for sickness, accident and old age. Nor do they any longer avoid risks to their health or security. However, collective risk provision is, invariably, less well tailored to diverse individual requirements, since knowledge of details at the centre is inevitably limited. Instead, risk coverage is provided for the average consumer according to the motto 'one size fits all!' The shift to socialized provision therefore leads to a poorer coverage of individual risks. At the same time, people learn to rely on claiming handouts and blame their misfortunes on insufficient hand-outs, rather than relying on their own effort and seeking fault with themselves if they have insufficient means. The growing transfers through taxation and subsidy have consequently not produced the promised results in terms of eradicating poverty and achieving a more even distribution of economic opportunity.

(c) In the long term, the socialization of charity has reduced solidarity with the poor and hence voluntary giving (Streit, 1984; Olasky, 1992). Voluntary giving, combined with some personal supervision and advice to the indigent recipient, has been replaced increasingly by an impersonal, compulsory tax-subsidy apparatus. Affluent people conclude that they already pay enough tax and that anonymous welfare recipients receive sufficient support. Therefore less is given to voluntary charitable organizations. In a historical analysis of the rise of the modern welfare state in the United States, Marvin Olasky documents the decline in voluntary contributions after the sudden hike in government takeover of social welfare. "Individual giving as a proportion of personal income dropped 13% between 1960 and 1976 . . . the proportion of philanthropic giving devoted to social welfare declined from 15% to 6%" (Olasky 1992; p. 189). Debates in the 1960s pushed for an increase in government welfare. By 1980, the US poverty rate was in fact 13 per cent, despite billions of dollars having been pumped into welfare programmes over close to 20 years. Moreover, charitable organizations often neglect the difficult business of genuine fund-raising from private citizens and concentrate instead on lobbying for a part of the tax cake. They then become little more than extensions of the public welfare machinery.

(d) Redistribution policy is based on the (false) premise that inequality is injustice (Flew, 1989; de Jasay, 1985; 2002). This assertion serves to politicize and emotionalize economic life. What used to be the outcome of anonymous market processes, which one simply had to accept, has now become the political responsibility of government. The consequence is much public posturing and lobbying, whereas before one tried to address problems of poverty by self-help, increased resourcefulness and effort. In the shift from self-responsibility to reliance on government agencies, social harmony is lost. There is group polarization between recipients of welfare and preferential programmes and those who have to fund the cost, which endangers social harmony (heightened tension, mob violence and so on, Sowell, 1990, p. 174). Related to this is another impact of the welfare state on the constitutional control of state powers: Many objectives of welfare policy cannot be achieved by universal laws – instead they require open-ended legislation and the delegation of powers to public welfare bureaucracies. As a consequence, a growing part of the administration escapes parliamentary and judicial scrutiny (Ratnapala, 1990, pp. 8–18). This can easily pave the way to what Hayek called "the miscarriage of the democratic ideal" that is, the weakening of the principle that government should be subjected to the constitution (Hayek, 1979a, pp. 98–104).

(e) The inter-generational effects of public redistribution have changed individual habits and long-term life plans, so that many young citizens now behave in a manner to minimize the risks and costs of tax confiscation and maximize the chances of obtaining welfare services. This became evident in Sweden, which was converted into a collective 'people's home' (*folkshjem*) where shirking by the younger generation has become widespread (Karlson, 1995; Lindbeck, 1995; however, Sweden has more recently embarked on welfare reforms, see Section 14.7). As a result, the tax base from which public welfare can be funded grows only slowly.

(f) The public provision of welfare has favoured the emergence of public-sector monopolies in the production of health, old-age and other services. The consequence is less choice, a lack of competitive cost control, an appropriation of rents by organized groups of service providers (unionized health workers), and fading stimuli to experiment and innovate. Generally, industries with rapid technological progress produce cheaper and cheaper goods. Yet, in the health industry, where technical progress is fast but public monopolies dominate, costs keep going up relentlessly. The reason is that bureaucratic procedures encourage pointless administration to proliferate and real production and problem-solving to wither, as well as demotivating front-line staff.

(g) Where redistributive interventions (and consequently tax and regulatory burdens) are massive, black markets develop. People, who find that the visible hand inflicts injustices and inefficiencies on them and deprives them of their freedom, opt out of the law and into a domain of lesser security where their transactions depend solely on internal institutions and self-enforcement. Often this works, but it may also give rise to black markets, thuggery and crime and outcomes that are inferior to those obtained under securely protected property rights (Streit, 1984).

(h) The demand for social justice is the mirror image of genuine freedom. The *freedom to* claim resources costs *freedom from* interference. Pervasive social welfare underpins the notion that there are 'freedoms to claim something', such as funds that protect you from penury and ill health, which is a limitless, utopian agenda. Parliaments in electoral democracies are therefore subject to an endless creep of claims for more collective action. They are increasingly liable to disappoint the electorate, apart from curtailing personal liberties, which poses a danger to democracy.

(i) It is often claimed that political redistribution takes from the rich and gives to the deserving poor. In reality, this is often not the case. The politically powerful and the well-organized use their influence to have governments take property from individuals and groups with little or no power. The empirical evidence in countries with strong redistribution policies is that benefits have gone disproportionately to the more fortunate, not the poor (Sowell, 1990, p. 174). A good example of this is that the beneficiaries of US cotton subsidies – about 20,000 cotton farmers – are each on average making a high income of close to $125,000 a year. In electoral democracies, this process has spread particularly in circumstances where the property rights of the majority can be diminished by small, almost imperceptible margins to confer sizable benefits to the well-organized. All members of the majority face high (fixed) information and transaction costs if they wanted to change a political intervention, whereas the few recipients of substantial, concentrated intervention benefits have solid material motives to organize and lobby for more such redistribution. This constellation is particularly prevalent in markets where a few suppliers (with an interest in high prices) face countless buyers (with an interest in low prices and good quality). As a consequence, public redistribution policy tends to be governed by a supplier bias, in particular if conditions have been undisturbed for a long time, so that vested interests and political alliances have had the time to become entrenched (Olson, 1982).

(j) The unrelenting growth of welfare provision has, in many nations, created the popular impression that the public servants, who plan and organize these goods and services, are the masters (principals), and the citizens – as well as elected politicians – merely their servants.

(k) Preferential policies that are introduced as temporary measures, not only persist, but are expanded for political reasons, even if they turn out to be economic failures.

(l) In electoral democracies, parliaments and governments tend to rival for the vote of the median voter, that is, the middle class. Many public welfare hand-outs are therefore aimed at winning the electoral support of the middle class, which in turn forms the biggest class of taxpayers. What may be intended as redistribution thus is in reality what Anthony de Jasay aptly called 'churning', giving and taking from the same people (de Jasay, 1985). Churning of course creates considerable agency costs (but from the angle of the churners, good careers and nice incomes).

(m) Growing redistribution by government has run into serious macro-economic problems: fiscal deficits, unmanageable public indebtedness, often also destabilizing foreign debts, erosion of private saving, taxpayer revolts and the undermining of the country's international competitive position. Although numerous factors are driving up the share of public spending at the expense of private spending in the mature economies, 'vote buying' by new welfare promises is central to the slide into unsustainable deficits. In Western Europe and America, no one seems to talk about budget surpluses in boom times; the discussion is only about reducing perpetual deficits. As of 2012, none of the ten major economies in the world is expected by the International Monetary Fund to run a surplus; some welfare states are expected to run even very large budget deficits (USA, 7.8 per cent of GDP, France, 4.7 per cent, and Britain, 7.6 per cent). Serious expert observers with a long-term orientation believe that the mounting fiscal imbalances could even endanger the eminent political and economic position of the West and endanger the viability of Western civilization (Hayek, 1988; Ferguson, 2011). Taxpayer resistance to increased taxation for the purpose of bankrolling welfare programmes mounts and public debt limits endanger the financial stability of the mature welfare states. As of the early 2010s, the European debt-financed redistributive states appear to have slid into an intractable crisis. Further loans to finance public deficits can only be had at exorbitant and unsustainable interest costs. As British Prime Minister Margaret Thatcher used to observe: "Pretty soon, you run out of other people's money." The global financial crisis since 2008 has made clear that fundamental policy adjustments are eventually unavoidable. They then of course inflict adjustment burdens on individuals who had trusted in the permanence of public welfare provision.

(n) A more fundamental problem caused by the social-democratic welfare state is that (as briefly noted above) it is in direct conflict with the rule of law and the protective function of government. If the central function of government is to protect individual freedom and hence private property without discrimination between citizens, then this clashes with the reallocation of private property by public intervention. Redistribution undermines market signals, so that the redistributive state makes it impossible for people to internalize all the gains from using their property, labour and knowledge. The constitution of capitalism then becomes fuzzy and the market order is undermined. The likely consequences are less individual effort, risk-taking and innovation. In addition, many perceive a sense of injustice if their earnings are taken away by public fiat. Spreading disaffection with the political process may sooner or later outweigh gains in communal loyalty and support for the government. Cynicism and falling support for the democratic system can then undermine the legitimacy of political authority, the stability of the regime, and long-term trust in a reliable order.

(o) Another fundamental problem with redistribution policy derives from the static vision of society, on which such policies are based. Economists who take the complexity and openness of the economic system seriously are aware that the observed income distribution among groups or individuals at any point in time is only a snapshot from the 'film of social life', so to speak. In reality, there are ongoing dynamic changes in relative positions of wealth and incomes, as well as in the size of the cake. Kirzner derided what he called 'the given-pie framework for distribution of economic justice' in the context of discussing the negative effects of redistribution policies on the entrepreneurial discovery potential (Kirzner, 1997, p. 75). Income and wealth distribution is rarely static for long. People who are relatively poor this year may be affluent a decade down the track, and hugely profitable corporations may have disappeared in a generation from now (only few of today's 'Fortune 500' companies existed back in 1950!). It is also natural in an economy with private old-age provision that young people are relatively poor and people on the threshold of retirement relatively asset-rich. Should redistribution policy intervene to make old and young people more equal? Who would bear the consequences? Should redistribution policy intervene on behalf of those who are momentarily relatively poor, and thereby undermine their incentives to enhance their economic position by personal effort?

(p) The combination of slow productivity growth, an eroded tax base and a greater preparedness to claim welfare has led to severe fiscal deficits in virtually all welfare democracies. In Western Europe, governments are now spending on average more than half of the gross domestic product, (marginal) income tax rates are high, but governments nevertheless keep accumulating deficits. Governments face mounting public debts also in the United States. Faced with slower or even negative population growth and the progressive aging of the population (changes partly influenced by past redistribution policies), public policy makers are compelled to respond by tightening or rescinding promised welfare provisions, for example the postponement of the retirement age. Such unforeseen changes in the lives of people, who had banked on enduring generous public welfare, lead to deep resentments and mounting distrust in democracy. Many now feel insecure despite 'social security'. As of the 2010s, the fiscal cut-backs of welfare services has led to growing street demonstrations by 'beneficiaries' of tax-funded pensions, recipients of lower than expected pensions and retrenched civil servants. The social democratic promise to ease social tensions by copious welfare has led to the unintended consequence of raising social unrest.

(q) Redistribution policies also undermine opportunities and motivations for individuals to earn an honest living, as more and more citizens are made dependent on the state. The destruction of self-responsibility hampers community engagement and devastates civil societies. For example, many of the problems in the Soviet Union and its successor states have rightly been attributed to the communist regime's parasitic mentality, which caused the "loss of individual responsibility . . .and destroyed civil society and crippled economic life" (Boettke 1994, p. 440). A properly functioning, autonomous civil society is essential to an effective liberal regime. After all, a liberal social and political society is not of human design, but an unplanned phenomenon carried by free associations of self-organized, self-regulated citizens (see *Epilogue*). The evolution of a vibrant civil society is a precondition and reinforcement of the institutions of a liberal economy. Without a culture of individual responsibility, communities are unable to create a culture of collaboration, association, and responsibility, the basis of all prosperous communities.

These many difficulties and contradictions have taken time to become virulent – and economists have been slow to diagnose that welfarism is based on a comparative-static world view based on *ceteris paribus* assumptions, whereas evolutionary reality reveals the many unintended, deleterious side effects. This became increasingly evident, as the welfare state was expanded further and further from the 1970s onwards. As of the beginning of the twenty-first century, this points to the conclusion that the social democratic welfare state is not sustainable.

Despite the evidence, there will always be voters in the affluent democratic welfare states who favour a degree of political redistribution. Voters expect governments to alleviate cases of poverty and extreme bad luck (for example after a natural calamity). Observers who are critical of the size of the welfare state and recognize the dangers to liberty and justice from the growing redistributive function of government may nevertheless see government as a last line of defence against poverty, once self-responsibility and voluntary private assistance have been exhausted (Green, 1996). In the final analysis, social policy has to be analysed in terms of overall personal wellbeing, not solely what is in one's purse. Pervasive welfare deprives people of freedom to take control of their lives; they are often alienated by policies that treat them as inert creatures, which an anonymous state provides with socially engineered satisfactions. (Richardson, 1995, p. 207).

Income redistribution and competitiveness

Proponents of the welfare state often remark that "the rich are getting richer and the poor are getting poorer". If this were true, would this be *despite* the growing redistributive efforts of government or *because* of them? The question seems justified as one observes that property rights are frequently redistributed from the unorganized poor to the better organized and well-to-do. If governments intervened less in markets, established positions of wealth and power would be more readily challenged and pioneer profits would be dispersed more quickly (Section 8.4). It is also likely that free labour markets provide for high employment, arguably the best welfare policy. When general access to education and similar measures that ensure the equality of starting opportunities are combined with a comprehensive competitive order, vertical mobility is enhanced and gross income inequalities are then unlikely to survive.

The evidence supports this point of view. Competition is a common feature of many of the new industrial countries of East Asia, which pursue very limited, if any, public welfare policies. Responsibility for material welfare is one's own concern and resides primarily with the family, which explains high savings rates and small government budgets. Yet, despite – or shall we say, because of – the lack of public welfare policy, measured income and wealth differences are surprisingly low, certainly lower than in most OECD countries (Riedel, 1988, pp. 18–21; Fields, 1984). Indeed, fast-growing, competitive Taiwan had a most even income distribution, with Singapore, South Korea and Hong Kong not far behind (Riedel, p. 20). In the dynamic societies of East Asia, the poor frequently do not belong to a 'class' of poor people for long, but move instead to higher income echelons.

As the international competition between mature and emergent industrial countries is becoming more intense, pervasive welfarism will have a major impact on the international competitiveness between them. The competition is not only for product markets, but also to attract capital, high skills, technical knowledge and firms (Chapter 11) and the deadweight of massive redistribution will be a decisive handicap.

In the light of what has been said, one may ask why public welfare provision in Western democracies has been expanded to the extent observed. The answer probably has a lot to do with the mistaken application of the small-group model of tribal solidarity to large industrial societies (Section 6.2). It also probably has a lot to do with mistaken conclusions from the historic experience of the 1930s Depression, when a massive drop in aggregate demand and employment, accompanied by a politically engineered disruption of the international division of labour, created pockets of poverty and gave rise to demands that government should give the people a new deal.

10.5   Political action and rent seeking

Principal-agent opportunism in government

The problems of collective action are not caused primarily by the knowledge problem per se and unwarranted optimism about the feasibility of collective action alone. Throughout history, another critical problem with political power has been that the agents of government – whether hereditary rulers, elected parliamentarians, ministers, or appointed officials – have been tempted to act in their own self-interest. In other words, the principal-agent problem applies pervasively to political and administrative organizations, as insider agents (bureaucrats, politicians) are much better informed than their principals, the outsider citizens. However, different from competitive businesses, where agent-managers are disciplined by market competition, the principal-agent problem in government lacks such automatic checks. This makes for a greater imbalance in information and, consequently, greater opportunities for agent opportunism (Buchanan and Tullock, 1962; Tullock, 1963; Tollison, 1982; Radnitzky and Bouillon, 1996).

The principal-agent problem surfaces at all levels of collective action. It frequently arises from the collusion between organized interest groups and government agencies. There is a political market for interventions and discriminatory variations to the universal institutions of government: Producers often seek regulation of their industry to mitigate the ceaseless rigours of competition (Section 8.2). On the supply side of the political market for interventions, the politicians, bureaucrats and judges cater to this demand by rent-creation. This has benefits for politicians and bureaucrats; they gain influence with powerful groups, as well as political and material support, whether for the party or personally for the interventionist (Stigler, 1971; 1975). Political interventions normally also confer the satisfaction of being a guardian and living by the guardian virtues of caring for one's fellows (Section 6.2).

The alliance between rent-creators and rent-seekers, which creates 'welfare for commerce and industry', but acts against the interest of the general public of citizen-principals, can be documented for all epochs and nations and is found at all levels of collective action. Thus, Queen Elizabeth I of England, Louis IV of France and other mercantilist monarchs granted well-connected traders monopoly rights to trade with certain parts of the world, for example India and America. In exchange, they shared the monopoly gains in the form of funds for the nation's and their personal treasuries. More recently, protection from international competition through tariffs and quotas has created rents for domestic agriculture, industry and banks, as well as kick-backs for protectionist governments. Governments in new industrializing countries of the nineteenth century (for example Germany) and in our age, have given multinational and local businesses political preferences that initially may have spurred development, but before long led to high transaction costs, destabilizing politicization and civic discontent with 'crony capitalism' (Chapter 14). In this way, the institutional emphasis is shifted from a commercial positive-sum mentality to the mentality of redistributive political guardianship and economic stagnation (Thurow, 1980).

CH 10 – CASE THREE

Mega bankruptcies, rent creation and the health of the capitalist system

A well-functioning market mechanism is essential not only to economic outcomes, such as efficiency, innovation and economic growth, but also to maintaining trust in government and to social harmony. Even people who have no understanding of the effects of genuine market competition develop a sense of injustice when they observe how well established businesses obtain government favours. People, who accept that huge profits are justified to successful innovators, such as the entrepreneurial leaders of well-known computer and software giants, instinctively resent profits and high salaries obtained by companies that owe their returns to government protection and subsidy.

This has become evident, yet again, during the global economic slowdown that began in the early 2000s. When US energy giant Enron announced soaring sales and profits in April 2001 and its top 140 executives were paid average salaries of US$5.3 million each, the company was the toast of town and observers lauded its superb management. Seven months later, Enron sued for bankruptcy, amidst accusations of fraud, misleading accounting, greed and political favouritism, it became clear that most of the company's debts had been hidden through complex financial maneuvering. Soon, US$1.2 billion of shareholder equity was wiped out and many small investors lost their funds providing for old-age. Painful as it was the company was eventually wiped out, The profit-loss mechanism had not worked as effectively as economic theory assumes and stipulates, but eventually 'creative destruction' occurred, of course not winning popular support for capitalism.

The outcome differed fundamentally in the wake of the global financial crisis that began in 2007. Many banks and other financial firms that were closely networked around the world had assumed huge risks on the strength of recent fast economic growth and confident government

CH 10 – CASE THREE *(continued)*

assurances that the good times were here to stay. Instead of permitting market-conforming 'creative destruction' by losses, most governments assumed that many of the loss-making organizations were too big to fail. Politicians were afraid of voter backlash from shareholders, whose savings would have been wiped out, and therefore interfered with the profit-loss mechanism by either bailing banks out or nationalizing them altogether. A case in point was the giant Bank of Scotland in the United Kingdom, whose collapse was prevented by political intervention. Political elites acted out of similar considerations in almost all Western democracies, when they re-discovered the (mistaken) theories of Keynesianism, inflating public spending and money supplies under labels such as 'monetary easing' and 'assisting bank liquidity'. Such policy measures were also motivated by mounting concerns over excessive, untenable, highly risky debts of governments, which had engaged in even less honest and transparent accounting than the likes of Enron, that were held by banks. Once considerations of political convenience and social justice induce governments to override the profit-loss mechanism, it of course fails.

The longer-term result is that popular support for capitalism erodes. The call for more regulation tends to be eagerly followed by political elites and economic freedom is diminished, eroding the power of free markets further. Public opinion swings behind activists, who point to huge salaries of executives, who have led companies to ruin, but nevertheless help themselves to part of the hand-outs that governments have made available. The end result is that anti-capitalist mass movements (such as 'Occupy Wall Street') support politicians who propose to undermine the institutions of capitalism and that markets are increasingly prevented from doing their coordination job. The developments of the late 2000s thus demonstrate, yet again, that public policy has to ensure the proper functioning of markets. History is full of dire illustrations of what happens over the longer term if they fail.

Modern parliamentary democracies are dominated by voting alliances, which are frequently beholden to interest groups. Parliamentary majorities hand out privileges to their client groups. Indeed, majorities are often formed for the very purpose of awarding political privileges to specific interest groups. The phenomenon is called 'log rolling' in the United States. It follows a strict political rationale, namely that parliamentarians want to be re-elected and have to raise funds for that purpose. To achieve their objective, they have to buy off organized pressure groups, which will give them political and financial support. And this can only be achieved by agreeing with other politicians who represent and want to favour other pressure groups. Log rolling alliances have become a way of life in many parliaments – but also of course to widespread disillusionment with democracy and cynicism about the political process. In the extreme, this may lead to the refusal of the wider public to defend democracy when attacked by totalitarian enemies. The Weimar Republic in Germany in the 1920s and early 1930s was dominated by ruthless representatives of special interest groups and unfortunately was not defended by the people when the totalitarian onslaught came (Kasper and Streit, 1993; Giersch et al., 1992).

Where government agents are involved in rent creation, they redistribute income and life opportunities. They also politicize and emotionalize public life. The example of successful rent-seeking coalitions induces emulation by other groups. Once the general presumption that everyone has to compete in the market (as opposed to competing for political favours) is given up, capital owners and organized labour coalesce to demand political privileges for more and more industries. Favoured industries then easily become prey to organized labour. With the passage of time, innovation and productivity improvements fall behind, so that protected industries become unprofitable. Eventually, they clamour for even more protection. Officials respond by raising the intensity of their interventions to avert political criticism and to safeguard their own political and material gains. Good money is then thrown after bad. The spiral of interventionism eventually destroys the spontaneous forces of market-driven initiatives and progress.

KEY CONCEPTS

Rent creation is a political activity by parliamentarians and bureaucrats to allocate 'rents', that is incomes that are not obtained by competitive effort in the market. They derive from political privilege to private supporters or organized groups of supporters of political elites. Typically, political intervention redistributes property rights from the unorganized many to the organized few who are then able to share their rents with the intervening agents of government. It is the mirror image of rent-seeking, already defined in section 8.3.

Vested interest groups are politically active associations of agents who have a shared interest in obtaining political interventions that favour their income position and give them influence over political decision making.

The **political market** is a process in which vested interests (often of producers) demand political interventions to redistribute property rights in their favour and in which agents of government supply interventions to give preferment to vested interests. According to this simplistic analogy with economic markets, the demand side tends to pay a price in the form of outright bribes and political support to the suppliers of market interventions (parliamentarians, politicians, bureaucrats, judges).

10.6 Controlling the political agents: authority, rules, openness

Over the centuries, a large number of policy devices have been proposed to control the intractable problem of agent opportunism in public choice and to enhance the chances that public policy supports – as best it can – the aspirations of citizens (de Jasay, in Radnitzky and Bouillon, 1996, pp. 73–97). Some of these control devices are:

(a) The highest government leaders are made the guardians of sustainable, non-discriminatory institutions. This of course requires that the leader – the king, the president – is informed of the actions of her or his subordinates and that the provisions of administrative law are obeyed and enforced. The chances of leaders ensuring non-corrupt public choices are enhanced if the wider citizenry are also imbued with high moral convictions. In modern mass society, this is a rather naïve assumption since the rulers have cognitive limits, too. Bureaucrats can be expected to collude in covering up corrupt breaches of proper administrative principles, and judges sometimes collude with the executive power. Indeed, the ruler's authority by itself has proved a fallible safeguard of citizen interests (Streit, 1984). Many observers since Confucius and Plato have therefore suggested that future rulers should be imbued with the highest moral standards, so that these would later be applied to their oversight of the administration and the enforcement of the external institutions. Relying on education of course poses the problem of who is to do the educating – and in whose interest – against the temptations of power.

(b) The device of a constitution, which subjects the rulers, elected politicians and officials to general, constraining rules, became popular in modern times in Europe, and now increasingly worldwide. One important constitutional device – which was made popular by French philosopher Charles de Montesquieu (1689-1755) and was subsequently enshrined in the American Constitution – is to separate the powers of government between the legislature (rule making), the executive (rule-bound implementation) and the judiciary (adjudication in conflicts) and to lay down a system of checks and balances over the holders of these three types of authority (for one Swiss example of how this worked effectively in practice, see Box 10.4). However, the principle of the separation of powers is frequently undermined, for example when judges de facto make the law or when the executive creates rules by decree and regulation (Ratnapala, 1990; Chapter 6).

The division of powers is undermined in particular in those many democracies where the parliamentary majority also forms the executive, as is, for example, the case in the modern Westminster system. 51 per cent of the seats, which may at times be obtained even on the basis of a minority of the votes, confer temporary powers to legislate as well as to execute policy. Then, effective controls on the exercise of power are weakened and the legislative process becomes deformed by the dominance of the executive and the bureaucracy (Hayek, 1979a; Bernholz, 1982; Pennington, 2010). This easily creates an atmosphere in which arbitrary uses of powers go unchecked and the political competition for votes leads to a growing redistribution of property rights.

CH 10 – CASE FOUR

A Swiss case study of how to control the agents of government

Swiss democracy is based on a division of powers in ways that often seem to the outsider fuzzy and clannish. However, the system is given a backbone by the instrument of citizen-initiated referenda (that is, not the politician-initiated referendum typical of many other countries). One hundred thousand voters are, for example, able to initiate a referendum to alter Switzerland's written Federal Constitution.

A referendum was used after the emergency of the Second World War, when the government was reluctant to cede its plenary powers obtained during the war. A small group of French Swiss agitated for a quick and complete return to direct democracy by the insertion of a clause in the Constitution, which guarantees that the Federal government cannot abuse its emergency powers. A popular vote on 11 September 1949 liquidated the central government's wartime powers, whereas many other democracies were permanently settled with some authoritarian legacies of the war. Typically, Swiss referenda have thrown out government initiatives and countermanded administrative projects.

One telling episode of effective citizen control, which served, yet again, to caution the Swiss Federal parliamentarians, ministers, and the bureaucracy that the Sovereign, namely the Swiss people, will not tolerate misleading information and overspending occurred in the wake of the purchase of new jet fighter planes for the military in the early 1960s. The episode became known as the Mirage affair. The military High Command proposed to buy French-made Mirage jets. Cabinet and the two chambers of parliament duly approved the expense of sfr870 million. Cost overruns (and possibly the initial underestimation of the costs) made it necessary to ask parliament to raise the authorization to sfr1350 million (a 55 per cent increase). This led to the threat of a citizen initiative to ditch the entire project. Various public inquiries revealed that bureaucrats had believed they would later be able to mobilize support for supplementation and that the military had demanded numerous costly upgrades in the aero-

CH 10 – CASE FOUR *(continued)*

plane's technical specifications. Essentially, a different plane was being bought from the one originally authorized by parliament. Cost controls had been lax, leaders were kept partly in the dark, and the Military Department proceeded despite being well aware of the unauthorized cost increases. Had this process not been stopped, the total-systems expense would have risen further, to some sfr2000 million, more than double the original expense. In the face of popular threat of a citizen referendum, it was decided to nearly halve the number of jet fighters that the military were permitted to acquire (from 100 to 57 planes) and to put a strict ceiling of sfr1750 million on the entire project.

The mere threat of a recourse to a citizen-initiated referendum thus induced parliamentarians to assert their control over administrative spending. The considerable powers of Cabinet and government departments were reined in. Under the pressure of people power, the Swiss parliament reasserted its right to directly control the administration. It seems hard to imagine such decisive action to control government on behalf of the people, if the ultimate backstop of a citizen-initiated referendum had not been available.

Source: After W. Martin-P. Béguin (1980), *Histoire de la Suisse*, pp. 350–353.

(c) Another form of dividing the powers to make public choices, which has served many affluent and stable nations well, is the division of the powers between several autonomous levels of government, say local, State and national governments (federalism). When much collective action is devolved to the local level, information and control of government by the principals, the citizens, is easier. Then, local and State government agencies also have to compete with each other. They will do so by searching for different administrative solutions and discover relevant administrative knowledge (Section 12.3). In addition, central and State governments can control each other, as long as each has independent taxing powers (fiscal equivalence). In her empirical work, Elinor Ostrom confirmed this when she concluded that "a political system that has multiple centers of power at differing scales provides more opportunity for citizens and their officials to innovate . . .[these systems] are more likely than monocentric systems to provide incentives to self-organized, self-corrective institutional change" (cited after Aligica and Boettke 2009, p. 23).

(d) Many nations also try to control agent opportunism in legislatures by dividing legislative powers in a bi-cameral system; in federations this is normally attempted by matching a directly elected first chamber of parliament with a controlling second chamber that represents regional interests. However, second chambers have come to be dominated by party discipline and bloc voting along party lines, just as first chambers have, so that this offers only weak controls of political opportunism.

(e) In the face of failures to effectively check the concentration of political powers, proposals have been made to devise further constitutional checks against the opportunistic behaviour of temporary parliamentary majorities. One such proposal is to establish a separate chamber responsible only for setting the framework rules, as against passing enabling ('purpose') legislation. Hayek proposed a model constitution with a Legislative Assembly, whose task it would be to pass laws that legitimize the collective coercion of citizens, and a Governing Assembly, whose task would be to execute the general laws adopted by the Legislative Assembly (Hayek, 1960; 1979a, pp. 147–165 and 177–179). He advocated the election of mature age persons to the Legislative Assembly by age cohorts and only one time but for long terms of, say, 15 years, so as to ensure representation independent, as far as possible, of party discipline and narrow sectarian interests. The decisions of the Legislative Assembly could be scrutinized by high courts. The Governing Assembly would appoint the executive and determine how public goods are supplied and financed. This arrangement might give teeth to the basic principle that elected parliaments are there to serve the average citizen and not organized group interests. In the past, elected parliaments had been the protectors of citizens' rights against the rulers, for example in eighteenth century England or in Switzerland. It seems, however, doubtful whether rent-creating party machines can nowadays be prevented from dominating all chambers of parliament, however constituted.

(f) The growing complexity of public policy makes it increasingly difficult for the concerned citizen to remain informed of government actions (rational ignorance) – a fundamental precondition for controlling agent opportunism in government. Governments have therefore sometimes been obliged by parliament to provide better and systematic information, for example sticking to agreed, transparent standards of accountability, annual budget plans and regular reviews, reporting to elected parliaments, and scrutiny of the accounts by an independent expert agency, such as an auditor-general. An independent press and review of government activities by expert scrutineers, such as academic researchers, credit-rating agencies or international agencies, further enhance accountability and control political opportunism in office.

(g) Another constitutional control of agent opportunism in government is the periodic exposure of at least some government agents to review by the electorate, be it the leaders of the administration (democracy) or other officials in the executive and judiciary (election of city officials and judges). This certainly makes the leadership of government contestable. But whether this controls agent opportunism between election dates depends on correct information and citizen engagement.

(h) In many constitutional settings, electoral contests between political parties have become periodic 'auctions' of discriminatory, redistributive measures that appeal to median voters. Observers therefore advocate constitutional rules that constrain political opportunism and limit the sovereignty of elected parliaments to engage in discriminatory intervention (Hayek, 1960; Buchanan, 1987, 1991; Brennan and Buchanan, 1985/1980; 1985; McKenzie, 1984). The rules that may be imposed on governments can relate to the procedure and the results of parliamentary collective choices. Examples of procedural constraints are the prescription of big majorities, or even unanimity, when raising taxes or public expenditures, so that taxpayers are protected. A good example of effective hand-binding of parliament was instituted in Australia, when a controversial federal value-added tax was implemented: The tax rate of 10 per cent can only be varied with the unanimous consent of all State governments as well as the federal one (by contrast, value-added tax rates have been raised opportunistically, time and again, by most European parliaments). Certain revenues may also be tied to specific expenditure purposes (equivalence) and automatic sunset clauses may be imposed on collective actions. Rules that prescribe results of collective action may demand a balanced budget or ceilings for the government's debt. It is also possible to limit the growth rate of the budget or the level of certain spending programmes. Thus, higher-level rules may lay down maximum tax rates, as was done by 'Proposition 13' in California in 1978 when State property tax was formally limited to 1 per cent of the property value. Another such result-oriented constraint would be an institution that forces governments to correct income tax collection for inflation or to tie public expenditures to absolute or relative maxima, such as a certain percentage of the national income.

(i) A related procedural constraint to control executive powers are term limits, which make it harder for elected representatives being captured by lobby groups to form rent-creating coalitions, and to avert the sterility of life-long careers in politics.

KEY CONCEPTS

The **control of political opportunism** has to rely on a multiplicity of devices, such as the moral education of leaders and the public, constitutional constraints, such as the division of powers and citizen-initiated referenda, safeguarding free information ➡

flows, the practice of accountability, electoral democracy, a general commitment to high standards in public life and openness of jurisdictions to competition with other jurisdictions.

The **separation of powers** is a constitutional device first made popular by French philosopher Charles Montesquieu (1689–1755). It demands the separation of the legislature, the executive and the judiciary as a means of dispersing and controlling political powers and making rent-creation less likely.

Citizen-initiated referenda allow the citizenry to overrule public choices, which they do not like. They differ from politician-initiated referenda, which are common in many countries, in that the initiative for a vote on a particular measure comes from the people and their associations, and not from the top down.

(j)   Yet, another control device is the citizen-initiated referendum, whereby the principals are given a tool to vary or throw out government initiatives they do not like (see Box 10.4 above). Most democracies, however, have only politician-initiated referenda.

(k)   One device to control opportunistic agents of government, which is preferred in some North American jurisdictions, is the recall (or impeachment) of elected representatives: If an elected parliamentarian, judge or administrator behaves in ways unacceptable to the vast majority of the citizens, they have the right to recall that person through a renewed vote at any time during the tenure of office. Such a procedure is of course costly and will therefore be rarely used. But the mere possibility of a recall may act to moderate agent opportunism. It may also induce the electorate to incur the information costs necessary for good government. Related to a general recall provision is the possibility of indictment of officials by courts or committees if specific misdemeanors are proven.

(l)   Affluence and education give teeth to citizen control. Effective controls of government powers benefit from a reasonably advanced level of education, which makes citizens economically and politically literate, and a level of affluence, which enables citizens to bear the information and monitoring costs needed for decent democratic government. This is one justification for secure private property rights. Citizens of property have the material means to stand up to the arbitrary rule of the powerful. Non-corrupt public choice has been facilitated by the rise of a broad middle class, citizens of property who have a stake in a stable and growing economy, as European countries demonstrated in the nineteenth and early twentieth centuries and newly affluent countries in East Asia, the Middle East and elsewhere have demonstrated more recently. Autocrats tend to initiate economic development to find legitimacy and increase national power. An unintended side effect is that, a generation later, a new middle class demands and obtains economic freedom first and civic and political freedom later (Chapter 14). In this context, it should be noted that the freedoms of speech and association are important conditions because they allow like-minded citizens to organize in order to control officials. While general political and social conditions are reasonably favourable to the control of government agents in the affluent democracies of the West, this often still remains an unfulfilled aspiration elsewhere. Poorly educated paupers can be easily dominated by regimes which suppress free associations and an independent electorate.

(m) Nowadays, the arguably most powerful control of agent opportunism in government is the openness of jurisdictions to international trade and factor flows (globalization). History has taught us the importance of openness. The exit challenge to exploitative political power brokers by relocation of production capacities and emigration has become stronger, as the transaction costs of gaining information about far-away places and moving there have declined. Freer information flows over the Internet are now making direct inter-jurisdictional comparisons easier. Where government agents are self-seeking, demand high taxes and bribes and offer poor services and poor infrastructures, the economy and the revenue base are nowadays likely to shrink. The threat of becoming the mayor of a ghost town or the leader of a state with capital flight is bound to give a strong feedback to opportunistic officials, similar to the effective control of agent opportunism of the managers of competing joint-stock companies (Section 9.3). Over the long term, the new openness will therefore constrain the principal-agent problem in government and empower ordinary citizens (a point to which we shall return in Chapter 11 and Section 12.3).

(n) Some jurisdictions have enacted mechanisms to protect whistleblowers, that is, informed insiders in governments who publicize corrupt abuses of power. This has raised difficult questions about what constitutes loyalty to the employer and the team, where the boundaries of loyalty to the team lie, as against loyalty to the citizens at large, and what sanctions should apply to opportunistic whistleblowing, for example by disaffected officials who seek revenge. In the age of decentralized Internet communication, the practical problems with insiders 'going outside' have multiplied, but – on the whole – transparency and constraints on corrupt rent-creation have been enhanced.

A number of these proposals have been tried out in various jurisdictions, but it is necessary to note that merely implementing constitutional changes will be ineffective in ensuring success. Constitutional reforms must emerge from within societies and accord with their internal institutions – the social norms, customs and other informal rules or what the literature sometimes calls the *metis* in a society (Boettke et al., 2008; Ostrom, 2005). Identifying the constitutional arrangements to restrict agent opportunism in public choice by analysing institutions of good governance is important, but a crucial aspect in the effectiveness of these rules is that they must be carried by the community. Otherwise, they amount to no more than social engineering. We have learnt from experiences with reforms in the former Soviet orbit and the Third World, that the societal pre-conditions for non-corrupt governance are frequently lacking, which then frustrates the reforms of the external rules of governance (Chapters 13 and 14).

We have to conclude that no single device is effective enough by itself to control the agent opportunism in government. At times, several of the above devices will be needed to contain the problem, and even that may sometimes fail to protect the citizens from the deleterious consequences of political opportunism. Like a mother's job, the defence of the citizens' freedom and the rule of law is never quite done.

10.7 Political and economic constitutions

The principles and institutions discussed here are high-order, universal constraints on officials, which are aimed at checking the uses and abuses of political power. They are intended to limit collective authority, safeguard individual domains of liberty and constrain agent opportunism and rent seeking. In other words, these principles and institutions are designed to limit political powers to discriminate outside the constraints laid down by the law. They have often been elevated to form part of political and economic constitutions, that is, overriding principles that will be upheld even in the face of evolutionary change.

Constitutions contain such high-level institutions that cannot be changed as easily as lower-level rules and that therefore give a framework of continuity and predictability to the inevitable adjustments of lower-level institutions, as we saw in Section 6.1. Constitutions – whether written down or not – contain affirmations of basic inalienable rights that must not be negated by lower-level rules or the use of force by other private citizens or government officials. Individualist constitutions include the protection of private property because it lends essential material substance to individual autonomy.

Figure 10.2 Constitutionalism: a web of mutually supporting institutional systems

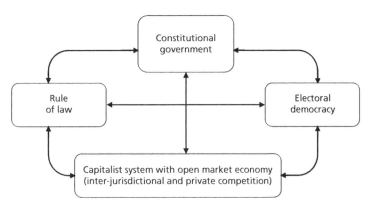

The constitutions of individualist communities also assert the sovereignty of the citizens in selecting their representatives to make public choices Constitutions also contain provisions on the division of powers, although these may nowadays often be rather illusory.

Constitutionalism that binds those in charge of collective action to certain constraints depends for its effectiveness on the electorate and its internal institutions and values, as well as the prevalence of the rule of law and the openness of the economy and the society to outside competition between jurisdictions and economic agents (Figure 10.2). These conditions form a web of mutually supportive sub-orders that underpin individual liberties.

Constitutional economics: choice among rules

One may in this context ask: What are the economic consequences of alternative sets of constitutional rules? Which constitutional rules serve individuals in coordinating their own, self-chosen economic pursuits, given everybody's limited knowledge? Specifically, which constitutional conditions serve best to ensure competition and innovation? The first question falls in the category of positive economics (positive constitutional economics). The other questions belong to normative constitutional economics. Over recent decades, the focus on constitutional economics has moved attention from the issue of choice *within given* rules to choice *between* alternative rules (Buchanan, 1991; Voigt, 1997).

As we saw earlier, the constitution of a capitalist market economy requires the protection of private property rights and the autonomy to freely enter contracts (to determine what individuals and firms may do), as well as formal equality before the law (to prevent what individuals and firms cannot do lest they harm others). This implies the protection of private autonomy and full responsibility for everyone's contractual obligations, as well as the freedom of information, speech, occupation, association and movement.

In this context we should recall that 'constitution' is defined here as a set of fundamental, high-level principles and recognized precedents according to which a community or an organization is governed and according to which existing lower-level rules may be altered (Section 6.1). Constitutional rules should be universal (general, open-ended), abstract (not case-specific) and reasonably predictable.

On contractarianism

The concept of a constitution derived from the concept of an assumed collective will has been attacked by public choice theorists (Buchanan and Tullock, 1962; Buchanan, 1975, 1978, 1987, 1991; McKenzie, 1984; Gwartney and Wagner, (eds) 1988). These authors have also drawn attention to the likelihood and danger of opportunism by self-seeking officials, including in electoral democracies. The public choice school began by perceiving society as unstructured – an anarchic world, in which individuals live in a state of 'war of all against all'. It saw a constitution as a general contract to enhance life conditions for all, a notion first made popular by British philosopher Thomas Hobbes (1588-1679). Public choice theory took up Swedish economist Knut Wicksell's (1851-1926) notion that a constitutional contract requires unanimous acceptance to ensure that no members of society are worse off. At least hypothetically, a consensus of this kind should be conceivable with regard to specific constitutional rules. The contractarian school of constitutional economics, which pursues this line of argument, perceives the members of society as being in a prisoners' dilemma, which can be ended by a contract of all with all which leads to the 'disarmament' of harmful opportunism. The constitutional contract then gives government a protective function.

The contractarian concept of the constitution is, however, at variance with historic reality. Communities did not originally live in anarchy, but developed internal institutions and organizational support structures long before formal government ever came into existence (Benson, 1990; Ostrom and Kahn, (eds) 2003). Contractarianism also implies that some observers, who design the constitutional rules, somehow have superior knowledge about which constitutional rules are optimal. The contractarian model of constitutional economics may also be criticized on the grounds that even the highest-ranked agents of government may have a self-interest in breaking constitutional rules. Such breaches would require regress to an even higher authority than the leaders of the national government to enforce compliance, infinite regress. But such an authority does not exist. Ultimately the critique of collectively based constitutions by the public-choice school is based on a utilitarian consideration: Do constitutional arrangements enable private citizens to attain their purposes better?

An alternative critique of collectivist constitutions comes from Hayek, who considered the protection of individual liberty as the ultimate function and normative test of a constitution (Hayek, 1960). His position is based on an evolutionary worldview and a high priority for civil and economic liberties. He advocates a constitution of liberty based on constitutionally bound behaviour. This approach does not require the fiction of a prior, unanimous contract.

Given the fundamental logical problems with the contractarian concept of a constitution, an alternative school of thought has emerged from the Hayekian position. It sees a constitution as a bundle of pre-existing conventions. Constitutions do not exist to solve prisoners' dilemmas of anarchy among isolationist individuals. They cannot be reconstructed as a contract among the many. Rather, it makes more sense to perceive humans as social animals who develop social ties from birth. Many of these ties are standardized and consolidated into internal institutions. This, and shared fundamental values, then form the foundation for higher-level institutions, including constitutional rules. Culture thus precedes constitutions. Admittedly, constitutions need not necessarily be based on shared values and the principles put forward in this book. But constitutions do not require explicit, or at least tacit, agreement by millions of individual citizens. Indeed, they function when imposed by a minority, as was for example the case in colonial Hong Kong. A further indication that the contractarian theory of the constitution is misguided derives from the fact that many constitutional provisions lack the explicit, formal sanctions typical of contracts; instead, they rely on spontaneous compliance (self-enforcement).

Is hand-tying possible?

From a functional viewpoint, the main purpose of political and economic constitutions is to tie the hands of policy makers when, in the heat of battle, they are tempted to abandon the principles of a free society. Constitutional provisions are then made to rule out arbitrary rent seeking and disorder-creating decisions in the conduct of day-to-day policy. Certain constitutional provisions – such as the independence of the central bank, or a balanced-budget rule – can serve to prevent short-sighted and costly political opportunism, in ways similar to the tying of Ulysses to the mast of his ship in Homers *Odyssey*, lest he be lured by the Sirens. However, many democrats are of the view that the parliamentary majority of the day is absolutely sovereign and should not be subjected to any constraints, an interpretation that is commonly accepted by politicians in Westminster-style democracies: absolute power rests with the elected parliament. Those who reject hand-tying of legislatures open the way for the parliamentary majorities of the day to pass erratic and inconsistent legislation, which undermines good order and trust. Only when one understands the importance of order will one favour safeguards against the opportunism of parliamentary majorities.

Rigid hand-tying, if successful, creates problems when conditions change and rule adjustments are necessary. To alleviate this problem, rules governing the method of how rules may be changed can be laid down, and constitutional amendments can be made dependent on prescribed majorities.

A more fundamental problem with hand-tying is that constitutional provisions are very difficult to enforce if those in government violate them. After all, they control political power, enjoy enormous financial resources and the monopoly over the use of legitimate force. When parliaments and governments are bent on breaking constitutional constraints, the constitution may only serve as a reference point for castigating parliamentary or governmental opportunism. One therefore has to conclude that constitutions on their own are only a weak bulwark against political attacks on individual liberties.

Available empirical evidence with prominent attempts to hand-tie political and bureaucratic agents does not enhance one's optimism about the effectiveness of such measures. Thus, the Maastricht Treaty and subsequent European Union agreements even made provisions of penalties for public overspending and exceeding debt ceilings by those sovereign countries, which entered the monetary union of the Euro (Streit and Mussler, 1994; Kasper, 2011c). These proved wholly ineffectual when powerful governments, such as France and Germany, openly flouted the rules. Renewed attempts, as of 2012, to institute similar rules on debt ceilings and deficits in national European budgets may well suffer a similar fate. It should be remembered that a large number of developed-country governments that were subject to constitutional limits on public spending, promptly cast these strictures aside to embark on a spree of Keynesian demand expansion, as soon as private demand plummeted in the wake of the 2007-08 global financial crisis.

KEY CONCEPTS

A **constitution** is a set of high-level institutions, which circumscribe what lower-level institutions may or may not stipulate, determine who governs and which *meta* rules apply to form general principles for the shaping and adjustment of the more specific, lower-level external institutions.

The analysis of the economic consequences of different types of constitutions is the subject of the new discipline of **constitutional economics**. Whereas we normally study human **choices within given institutions**, constitutional economics is concerned with alternative rule sets and **choices between rule sets**.

As in public-choice theory (the economic analysis of political choices), from which it derives, the basic premise of constitutional economics is that only individuals act and do so in their own interest; classes or groups of people cannot act. The constitutional-economics approach therefore is focused on the rules that channel individual choices and appeal to individual values.

We speak of **positive constitutional economics** when we analyse the emergence of constitutions and the observed or hypothesized outcomes of alternative rules, and of **normative constitutional economics** when the quest is for the rule sets that enable the members of the community to achieve certain purposes better and more effectively.

Contractarianism is based on the fiction that a society's constitution is derived from – or may be hypothetically conceived as – a social contract of all, on the assumption that the pre-constitutional state is anarchy where all are in the bind of opportunistic, selfish behaviour.

Hand-tying relates to constitutional arrangements and agreements which are intended to preclude short-sighted, opportunistic choices by agents with political power. An example would be a constitutional stipulation that obliges governments not to raise budget expenditures by more than 3 per cent each year, or the formal promise by parliament to forego their right to change certain laws.

Formal constitutional provisions can, at best, serve as a limited constraint in controlling agent opportunism in public policy. Constitutional provisions need to be supplemented by the other institutional devices, discussed earlier in this chapter (free press, accountability, federalism, openness to trade and factor flows, and so on). The control of political power in the interest of the freedom and prosperity of the citizen-principals is bound to remain a never-ending and a challenging task in any community. This is an evolutionary problem, not one that can be solved once and for all by some 'magic bullet'. Freedom-supporting government is, and will remain, a never ending task.

The dual pretense of knowledge and feasibility

Many government interventions are still being justified with the argument that they rectify market failure. This argument is based on the comparison between complex, imperfect reality and perfect competition – a utopia that does not exist. The comparison is therefore invalid. Harold Demsetz aptly labelled this as the 'nirvana approach' to public policy (Demsetz, 1969, p. 160). The model of perfect competition has little bearing on the evolutionary market processes that one observes in reality. Above all, it ignores the knowledge problem and the role of institutions in tackling it. Instead, critics simply assume that government knows best and that government agents are benevolent. As explained earlier in this chapter, government does have an important role to play, but in discussing public policy one also has to allow for the fact that officials simply do not know and hence the possibility of government failure. It cannot be automatically assumed that collective action is driven by high-minded altruism. Nor can it be assumed that costly solutions, which private agents have evaluated and rejected, will be less costly when implemented by the government. The only effect of subjecting knotty problems to public choice may be that this frees us from the burden of rationally calculating all resource costs and benefits. The cumulative, long-term neglect of proper cost-benefit calculations, however, undermines the material and non-material aspirations of the people.

Public policies always have unintended, unforeseen side effects. Once side effects appear, corrections may be implemented, but these amount to further interventions, which produce yet more side effects. Modern mass societies are so complex and evolve so unpredictably that only relatively general and simple government programmes can be comprehended by those in charge (the minister and his top advisors). Complex intervention programmes get invariably enmeshed in unpredictable contradictions. Coordinating the policies of different government agencies to achieve official goals then becomes a task that no one can fully understand or carry out. Public policies are often also ineffectual because the citizens fail to pay perfect attention.

Analysts who ignore the knowledge problem are often overly optimistic about what discretionary collective interventions can achieve. They advocate or engineer elaborate government programmes to achieve specific aims.

They believe that an increasingly complex community needs to be ordered by increasingly complex legislation and regulation, and then are bewildered if disorder, confusion and apathy result. By contrast, the analyst who is aware of the knowledge problem, who knows of the dangers of cognitive overload and understands the function of universal, abstract institutions in ordering complex situations, will advocate modest government and stress the need for officials to always be mindful of the need for order. He will advocate simple rules for our complex world (Epstein, 1995; Pennington, 2010). He will beware of ambitious public guardians who pretend to have knowledge, which they cannot have, and of unwarranted optimism about what is feasible.

NOTES

1 The Chinese Empire had periodic episodes of income taxation (normally with a rate of 10%) since the Han dynasty, which was possible because Chinese professionals had more accurate and complete accounts of their affairs, and hence their incomes, than their European contemporaries did.

2 Some constitutions make explicit mention of political parties (for example that of the Federal Republic of Germany), thus raising their status further relative to the individual citizen-voter.

3 It has also been argued that the maintenance of stability over time of specific indicators, in specific markets or the overall national economy, is also a function of government. However, lags in cognition, difficulties in reacting promptly and political conflicts about stabilizing interventions have made this a controversial assignment for governments. In any case, the single-most important aspect of stabilization, namely the provision of stable money, can be subsumed under the protective function.

4 Sources of easy revenues, which are often beyond the scrutiny of elected parliaments, tend over the long run to open the way for appropriation of these revenues by organized groups, such as the employees of public enterprises. Instead of contributing to general revenue, the proceeds from public production are frequently used to fund high salaries, sinecures for officials, overstaffing and high on-the-job consumption (opportunistic rent-seeking by agents of government). These abuses are now reasons why public opinion in many countries favours the privatization of government-owned enterprises (Chapters 13 and 14).

5 In the public-finance literature the provision of access to certain goods and services is often equated to the in-house production of these goods and services in the public sector. This has led to the term 'productive function of government'. We have reluctantly retained this term in this book to remain consistent with other authors (for example, Buchanan, 1975). 'Public provision function' might be a more appropriate term.

6 A newly elected Australian government appointed an independent commission to audit its assets and liabilities. To the government's discomfiture, it was shown that successive governments had been in the business of massive value destruction. Liabilities exceeded assets by more than half a year's revenues and uncovered liabilities added a further quarter of revenues to this. Any private business with such a balance sheet would long have been declared bankrupt (Kasper, 2011a).

7 *Ordo* is the Latin word to describe that state of society in which free Roman men could feel free and prosper.

   Eucken – like other German *ordo* liberals – used the word 'Ordnung' (order) throughout his writings whenever he argued for *ordo* policy. However, the translator of one of Eucken's books, T.W. Hutchinson, avoided the word 'order' and misleadingly used the word 'system'. It has less of a normative connotation and fails to convey the full meaning of order as used in this book, Eucken's second seminal book on *ordo* policy (*Grundsätze der Wirtschaftspolitik* – Foundations of Economic Policy, first published 1952). Though often reprinted in German, it apparently still awaits a translation into English.

11

The international dimension

This chapter looks at problems peculiar to international exchanges: trade between different jurisdictions governed by different institution sets and the movement of capital, knowhow and firms across national borders. Such exchanges have to deal with a particular risk, namely that contractual obligations of defaulting contract partners in foreign jurisdictions are treated differently from what is familiar and can sometimes not be readily enforced. Various institutional and organizational arrangements have been developed by the international business community to tackle these commercial problems. International trade and finance are thus based on effective and complex institutions, which fall outside the umbrella of national rule systems.

Openness gives the subjects of national jurisdictions an exit option; they can trade and invest abroad. This weakens the power of national governments and local elites, who may perceive openness and globalization as an affront. Powerful national interest groups, who clamour for protection from international competitors, often also induce governments to interfere with international trade, capital flows, migration and technological exchanges. This reduces international competition, diminishes the institutional underpinnings of a non-discriminatory order based on private property and abridges the property rights of foreigners and nationals. Such interventions then often become a source of international conflict. It is therefore useful to constrain the scope for opportunistic national interventions in international exchanges. This is, for example, done under the World Trade Organization (WTO) and OECD codes on foreign investment. Such elements of international law differ from transnational authorities, which some now wish to create, in that transnational authorities (for example, the International Criminal Court, or the European Commission) can coerce sovereign national governments.

Finally, we shall discuss the international monetary order from an institutional angle. It has changed over the past century from the gold standard to fixed parities and then to more or less flexible exchange rates, except where monetary unions, such as in the Eurozone, were established. We shall also discuss the rules that allow international merchants and financiers to cope with the existence of different currencies and differing national monetary policies.

If a foreign country can supply us with a commodity cheaper than we ourselves can make it, better buy it off them with some part of the produce of our own industry. In the home trade, . . . [the merchant] can know better the character and situation of the persons whom he trusts, and if he should happen to be deceived, he knows better the laws of the country from which he must seek redress.

Adam Smith, *The Wealth of Nations* (1776)

To the Honorable Members of the Chamber of Deputies:
Gentlemen: We are suffering from the ruinous competition of a foreign rival who apparently works under conditions far superior to our own for the production of light that he is flooding the domestic market with it at an incredibly low price. From the moment he appears, our sales cease, all the consumers turn to him, and a branch of French industry whose ramifications are innumerable is all at once reduced to complete stagnation. This rival, which is none other than the sun, is waging war on us.

We ask you to be so good as to pass a law requiring the closing of all windows . . . and outside shutters through which the sun is wont to enter houses to the detriment of the fair industries with which, we are proud to say, we have endowed the country.

Frédéric Bastiat, 'Letter from the Manufacturers of Candles, Tapers, Lanterns, . . . and Generally Everything Connected with Lighting', *Le Libre Échange* (1846)

11.1 The growing significance of the international dimension

Engines of growth

International trade, investment and payments have outgrown world output in most decades. Exchanges of the mature economies with the economies that used to be at the fringe of the world economy have intensified even more. Thus, world output (at current prices) went up more than 5.8 times between 1980 and 2010, but direct international investments into the emerging and less-developed counties expanded nearly 44 times and private financial flows into these countries 24 times (source: IMF, *World Outlook Database, passim*). In many rich and poor countries, international trade and direct investments have been the most important conduits for transferring new, useful knowledge to local producers and buyers. Many of the concepts and ideas that make high living standards possible can be learnt most easily by observing what works well in other places. This applies both to imported products and services and to technical and organizational methods and institutions that foreign subsidiaries and immigrants practice. Of course, the transfer of such knowledge to new locations and cultures also requires some adaptation and learning on the part of the trader and foreign investor. As such, international economic relations have feedbacks into the institutions of origin countries.

The process of intensifying international exchanges of goods and services and the growing international migration of production factors is now called globalization. Its ramifications are reaching most of the world population in one way or another. Never in the history of mankind have so many people gained access to modern and changing forms of production, exchange and consumption, and never have more fellow human beings escaped dire poverty. The widening of markets across national borders is a corollary of the unprecedented acceleration of global economic growth, to which we referred in Section 1.2. All this would not be imaginable without the unprecedented development of an institutional framework that facilitates border-crossing transactions. Advances in these institutions – coupled with technical progress in communications, transport and travel (which lower 'space-bridging costs') – have been powerful engines of economic growth and have increased the relative importance of the international dimension of national economic activity. This has also had great impact on the capacity or otherwise of national policies to affect developments at home. Where the exit option is available, the political power over economic life is limited and freedom is enhanced. When economic and social networks go beyond national borders, the nation state loses a considerable part of its clout. The new openness therefore has had feedback into the evolution of internal and external national institutions of most nations (Chapter 12).

The drop in exit costs

Since the 1960s, the competition among distant locations and national jurisdictions to attract mobile production factors, such as capital, technology and enterprise, has greatly intensified. In part this is due to advances in technology. In the second half of the twentieth century, containerization, roll-on/roll-off ships, pipelines, jumbo jets and speedy parcel delivery systems have saved transport costs in innovative ways. But advances in transport technology pale compared to revolutionary advances in communications (the transportation of ideas). The fax, satellite communication, fibre-optic cables, computing and data compression, the Internet, email, microwave transmission, and widely distributed portable video cameras and video phones have brought down the costs of long-distance communication by phenomenal margins. People are now better informed about living and working conditions in distant places and civilizations. The monopoly of big governments, big banks and big media is now challenged by distributed and personalized networking technology (such as Facebook and Twitter).

There have been secular declines in the costs of international bulk shipping and port handling (–0.9 per cent per annum from 1950 to 2000) and passenger air travel (–2.6 per cent); the costs of inter-continental telephone and similar communications fell even faster (1950-2000: across the Atlantic by an astounding 8 per cent every year), thanks to the steep decline in information-processing costs and the re-organization of the communications business on a competitive footing.

Moreover, the producers and traders in the core countries of the world trading system (OECD countries and industrialized East Asia) can now rely on established, fairly standardized trading practices, shared procedures of insurance and conflict resolution and a body of globally oriented executives who share a common set of customs and business practices. The risk of disruption of trade and foreign investment by war and blatant anti-foreigner discrimination among OECD and the new industrial countries has dwindled compared to what was historically normal. Nevertheless, the costs of doing business internationally differ greatly from country to country due to differences in values, the traditional culture of internal institutions and government policies. International factor mobility has become very responsive to margins of potential returns on investments in different locations. This has led to worldwide specialization and the intensification of trade in intermediate goods, many of which are shipped from one branch of the same multinational corporation to another. For example, cotton fibres grown in Australia are crudely processed in China, then chemically treated in Japan, spun and dyed in Thailand, woven in the United States and tailored into garments in Vietnam – all this for the German market! Nowadays, no motorcar is made up from components produced in one single country, as a quick glance under the hood of your vehicle will reveal. The value-adding chain of modern industrial production spans across many locations and nations. With the progressive division of labour, local and national institutions are becoming a key cost factor which determines what is produced where. This is not surprising because coordination costs nowadays vary greatly between one nation and another and because they often account for half of all costs.

The ease of international communication has created an altogether new phenomenon, namely the long-distance trade in services, which could previously only be produced near the buyers. More and more services are now internationally tradable. This has great impact because services are now the dominant sector in the world economy, accounting for some two-thirds of world production. Up to the 1980s, few activities involving organization, planning, controlling, administering, advising, servicing, logistics, quality control, teaching and designing were traded internationally. But as of the 2010s, bookings for American customers on US airlines may be done overnight by a clerk in Ireland, letters dictated in New York are typed in Jamaica and remitted back online, the daily accounts of New Zealand firms are processed online in Manila, and sections of Singapore's major daily newspaper are written and edited in Sydney. When criminal interference by the Chinese Triads and rising cost levels created problems for the Hong Kong betting industry, it simply relocated the settling of bets to Australia. ATMs and Internet connections give individuals a choice of banking overseas and of insuring their life, health and cars off-shore.[1] And authors who jointly write a textbook can critique and edit each other's contributions in cyberspace between Australia, the United States and Germany.

Globalization has widened markets, thereby spreading productive knowledge and reaping economies of scale and scope. As people have access to wider choices, they are better able to realize their individual aspirations and can discover new wants and means to meet them. The widening of markets beyond national borders has been a key factor in the accelerated rise of prosperity in the world over the past generation.

Locational choice

The number of potential locations for production has therefore multiplied for many types of enterprise, in particular for plants of multinational companies. Some 70 per cent of world trade in the 2010s is between subsidiaries of the same multinational corporation or has a multinational corporation as one of the two contract partners. Different production processes in the same value-adding chain are thus located in different places depending on the countries that promise the highest expected profit. The expected profit from production is defined as the difference between the expected selling price and the (weighted) sum of expected unit-costs of production, transporting and distribution, multiplied by the expected volume of sales:

$$\text{Profit} = (\text{price} - \text{unit costs}) \times \text{sales};$$

$$= \left(\text{price} - \frac{\Sigma \text{ factor prices} \times \text{w}}{\Sigma \text{ factor productivities} \times \text{w}}\right) \times \text{sales}$$

where w designates the weights of the various production inputs.[2]

This definition may look simple, but – even for one given location – it is often extremely difficult to collect and assess all relevant knowledge about changing prices, the many input markets, production techniques, logistics and distribution networks, the costs of using available public-domain infrastructures, the laws, regulations and customs that affect production, productivity and products, labour, investment and commercial transactions, the political risks and many other aspects which determine long-term profit expectations.

The information and entrepreneurial assessment problems multiply when different locations in different countries are evaluated and compared, particularly when little empirical experience is available with regard to the new industry locations. Locational innovation therefore requires real entrepreneurial talent. The attractiveness of different locations to mobile production factors – capital, technical knowledge, high expertise, and bundles of these factors that are organized in firms – is thus shaped by expectations of the relative movement of all factors affecting profitability: the costs of input materials and production, as well as transaction, organization and compliance costs.

Despite the enormous difficulties of assessing these complex and changing data, businesses are now making international locational choices all the time. What critically determines the levels of unit costs in a specific location are the owners and managers of the internationally immobile production factors. These are typically labour (unions), government administrations and land owners. Because of high shares of transaction costs, location-specific institutions (work practices and external institution) are nowadays often decisive for the competitiveness and attractiveness to mobile production factors of competing locations (Kasper, 1994; 1998).

KEY CONCEPTS

Profitability measures a business organization's expected excess of receipts over expenses, often expressed as a percentage of a business' capital. When the difference is negative, the firm expects a loss. Per unit of sales, profitability is the difference between the sales price and the unit-costs of production and distribution, including the transaction and compliance costs.

The **attractiveness** of a location relates to the expected profitability of specific economic activities in that location as compared to alternative locations. Different footloose activities are attracted to different locations, because the profitability conditions vary between production activities. Attractiveness is greatly influenced by the availability and cost of factor supplies, as well as the institutions that facilitate or hinder the combination of production factors.

Institutions and international attractiveness

If a location loses its cost competitiveness, the plants of nowadays internationally mobile companies tend to move elsewhere. We therefore now observe a frequent form of innovation, locational innovation. It has become easier because many firms now have direct experience of conditions in different nations and cultures and much manufacturing is now lightweight and footloose. It can be easily relocated and its products can be easily transported to distant markets. Many production units can also be quickly moved elsewhere; sometimes they can even be packed into only a few containers!

In the production of most sophisticated modern services – such as banking, insurance, accounting, planning and logistics – the quality of human capital and institutions (including taxation) is of much greater importance than even in manufacturing or agriculture, and the costs of liaising with the demand are even lower. Many services are tailored to specific customer requirements and change all the time, so that there is a premium on an institutional environment that facilitates quick innovative responses and low-cost coordination.

The tax rules and compliance with government regulations, as well as the quality of government-provided services and infrastructures matter greatly to the attractiveness of a specific jurisdiction for service providers. Financial intermediaries, for example, depend crucially on staff who share cultural traditions of honesty, reliability and caution, in addition to the external institutions of financial regulation, fiduciary oversight and accountability. What also matters greatly is credible, unbiased law enforcement. Jurisdictions that offer business-friendly customs, work habits, conventions, laws and regulations and that facilitate lower transaction costs and a reliable competitive order, attract international producers who cater to global markets (Kasper, 1994). Major financial centres have flourished where these conditions are favourable, but have been readily relocated when new taxes and regulations were imposed. Jurisdictions that fail to provide the right 'institutional infrastructure' experience an increasing emigration of service industries such as banking, architectural planning, research and development, entertainment, accounting and legal advice, production planning and logistics services, and so on.

CH 11 – CASE ONE

Factors that shape international attractiveness

The owners of those production factors that are in a position to move among locations and nations tend to assess the costs of the immobile or less mobile production factors in making their locational choices. Nowadays, capital, technical and organizational knowledge, high skills, and bundles of these factors – called firms – as well as bulk raw materials tend to be internationally mobile. Labour, land, electricity and other local service suppliers, as well as legal, political and administrative systems tend to be the immobile inputs, whose costs and qualities determine the international attractiveness or otherwise of a location or nation. Institutions in turn determine the capacity of the owners of the various factors to interact in creating economic growth. They are therefore important in determining the relative transaction costs of production and innovation.

Against this background, various research organizations and business consultancies measure international competitiveness and attractiveness, for example the Swiss-based *World Economic Forum*, in whose 1996 annual report Harvard economists Jeffrey Sachs and Andrew Warner wrote:

> [I]nternational competitiveness means the ability of a nation's economy to make rapid and sustained gains in living standards . . .The Competitiveness Index attempts to summarize in a single quantitative index the structural characteristics of an economy . . . that are likely to determine the economy's prospects for medium-term growth . . .One of the key assumptions of this study is that certain kinds of structural characteristics can be measured with standard published data, while other kinds . . .are better measured by opinion surveys. . . . The survey data come from 2000 business executives in the 49 countries considered in this report.

In the end eight clusters of characteristics are settled upon:
- openness of the economy to international trade and finance;
- role of the government budget and regulation;
- development of financial markets;
- quality of infrastructure;
- quality of technology;
- quality of business management;
- labor market flexibility;
- quality of judicial and political institutions.

Judicial and political institutions measure, however, imperfectly, the extent to which legal and political systems provide for low 'transaction costs' in writing and defending contracts and in protecting property rights. The expectation is that an honest and efficient judiciary and a political system that respects private property rights, are important factors in producing economic growth in complex, market-based economies. . .

CH 11 – CASE ONE *(continued)*

Differences in economic growth attributed to differences in competitiveness are sizeable. According to the slope of the line linking competitiveness and growth, the difference in medium-term growth due to differences in competitiveness between the most and the least competitive countries in the sample, is on the order of 8.1 percentage points per year. . .

Does the index help to explain cross-country patterns of economic growth? The answer is a resounding yes: competitiveness matters. . .The bottom line on competitiveness is that national economic policies make a profound difference to economic growth in the medium term. Open markets, lean government spending, low tax rates, flexible labor markets, an effective judiciary and stable political system, all contribute. . .

Infrastructure, management and technology also contribute, though measurement is much harder and effects are much more elusive. These basic facts are becoming increasingly appreciated: indeed, they are helping to orient market reforms. . .the quest for national competitiveness can be an important stimulus for much needed policy reforms in many economies around the world.

Source: World Economic Forum, 1996, pp. 8–13.

On the supply of, and demand for, protectionism

Free international trade and factor flows are often blamed for the need to make uncomfortable adjustments and the loss of previous socio-economic positions. Globalization therefore often triggers defensive moves by political elites to handicap untrammelled international economic competition. Political entrepreneurs can hope to gain influence and political advantage by discriminating against foreign suppliers and investors, who do not have the vote. Domestic buyers, who would benefit from unhindered international trade competition, often remain rationally ignorant about the effect of such unequal treatment imposed on them, because their gains would be small and diffuse.

The point can be illustrated by the example of a tariff to protect domestic car manufacturers. Let us assume a medium-sized country with, say, five local car assemblers and a tariff that raises the price of the average car by, say, $3000. If one assumes that the price rise does not reduce the volume of 750,000 domestically produced cars sold each year, the intervention benefit (rent) to every national car producer is ($3000 x 750,000)/ 5 = $450 million per annum on average.[3] On top of this, some buyers will switch demand from imported to domestically produced cars. The gain from a tariff to suppliers is therefore massive. They can afford to bribe politicians and the media. By contrast, each car owner may buy a new car only every eight years (in particular when tariffs make cars artificially expensive), so that each buyer's disadvantage inflicted by the car tariff is:

$$(\$3,000: 8) = \$375 \text{ per annum.}$$

Instead of forming a car buyers' lobby organization to fight this discrimination, it is probably rational for car owners to swallow the disadvantage and concentrate on recouping the political redistribution loss in markets where they have supplier power, for example by joining a union to extract higher wages.

It is understandable, given the high costs of organizing a lobby group, that car producers have a high capacity to invest some of the rents from the tariff into political lobbying for the perpetuation or further increase of the car tariff. The usual asymmetry in markets (Section 8.1) thus plays into the hands of political entrepreneurs who wish to discriminate against foreign competitors and transfer property rights from the poor, poorly organized citizens to rich, well-organized vested interests. Similar political motives for redistributing property rights sometimes come to bear when foreign producers (multinationals) wish to set up production facilities in a country and politicians try to lure them by guaranteeing them a protected domestic market (Coughlin et al., 1988; Streit and Voigt, 1993, pp. 54–58).

The political economy of protection and similar interventions in international economic relations is straightforward. Supplier interest groups lobby for protection, and political parties are willing to grant it as it will improve their chances of getting re-elected. Opposition parties, too, are willing to take up pleas for protection because they are also trying to win support to become elected. Potential domestic interest groups who might lobby for free trade (for example consumers, producers that use imported inputs, exporters who bear the burden of costly inputs, wholesalers and retailers that rely heavily on imported goods) tend to have more difficulty in rallying support.

The net result of these asymmetries is that the political economy is subject to a pronounced 'supplier bias', that is, a tendency for politicians and bureaucrats, as well as the media, to favour suppliers of goods and services at the expense of the many potential buyers. Once a government intervention has set up a vested interest group, that group will work to perpetuate, or even intensify, the intervention.

The preparedness of politicians to supply protection to an industry is determined by the shared values of a society (for example popular views on cosmopolitanism versus nationalism, or preferences for security and welfare redistribution versus freedom), the prevailing institutional arrangements (for example whether officials have great discretionary powers or are bound by legal principles that protect private autonomy), and economic circumstances (such as unemployment or import penetration). It also depends on the perceptions of politicians about the potential costs of breaking the free-trade rule, such as fear of foreign retaliation and formal proceedings under WTO rules. Internationally agreed institutions bind governments to some extent not to provide opportunistic protection measures. They can play a role in stemming protectionism, at least in the case of smaller economies (Odell, 1990; Sally, 2008). The binding power of WTO rules is, however, weakened by a confusing proliferation of escape clauses, for example preferences for developing countries and exemptions for agricultural goods and services. As with institutional hand-tying in other areas of politics, formal trade rules have only limited power, in particular in the case of big countries.

The challenge of openness

International trade and factor flows exert pressures, as we said, that challenge established political power constellations. Ambitious power brokers therefore often have the incentive to keep the economy closed. In an open environment, political rents from the discriminatory reallocation of property rights are harder to obtain, as globally mobile investors are frequently not part of established national 'old-boy networks' and entrenched political cliques. They often realize that political favours can be costly for them in the long run, as political entrepreneurs extract corrupt returns for political favours granted. Therefore, experienced, internationally mobile investors can nowadays no longer be easily attracted by specific protective measures and hand-outs. Instead, they normally prefer a clear set of abstract, universal rules that preclude political favouritism and treat nationals and outsiders equally (Giersch, 1993). An additional change, which has been increasing the challenge of openness in recent decades, is the rapid spread of the Internet and the ease with which decentralized, uncensored information now flows. Knowledge about secret political deals that give preferences to domestic producers or well-connected foreign firms (crony capitalism) is becoming quickly and fully public, also to those who are adversely affected by such political favouritism. The technical capability of governments to suppress information flows over the Internet is nowadays limited. This has repeatedly been evident, for example, when the Chinese or the Vietnamese governments tried to close down Internet connections or during the 2011 fall of the Mubarak autocracy in Egypt. After a day or two, when officials attempted to shut down the Internet, spontaneous private cooperation began to resurrect the Net (see Box 11.2). The Internet has of course also greatly reduced the costs of organizing lobbies that counter corrupt political dealings and, combined with cheap mobile telephony, it now enables people even in remote places to access internationally available information and organize business associations across borders.

CH 11 – CASE TWO

China: political control and the new international mobility of information

Excerpts from a press agency report:

> Unnerved Chinese leaders. . . are scrambling to defend against a threat they can't and don't understand – the Internet.

> Seven months after it was allowed into the country, the Internet is looming as the most unwieldy and revolutionary threat yet to the Communist government's obsessive control over information.

> It is estimated that more than 100,000 people in China – mostly the so-called intelligentsia – already have access to uncensored news from around the world on the Internet. In turn, grassroots information the Government wants kept in China is leaking out. While the Internet is still seen as essential in China's modernisation, leaders right up to Premier Li and President Jiang are on alert and moving to patch up dangers they see the system posing against stability.

> [A] new State Council committee is understood to have demanded that all registered Internet subscribers re-register and sign a pledge not to engage in destabilizing activities. Future subscribers would have to sign the same pledge. But this is one battle against freedom of information nobody expects the Government to win.

> Efforts to restrict capacity can easily be circumvented, and while material transmitted on the Net can be monitored, it cannot be stopped.

CH 11 – CASE TWO *(continued)*

The ramifications of the Internet on China's future cannot be underestimated. . .

[A] Western source says: "The Government really doesn't understand the Net. Li Peng and Jiang Zemin are always talking about it with foreign businessmen, asking questions about how to control it. . . In terms of a totalitarian regime keeping tight control, they have something to worry about."

The Internet won't create a consciousness, but it may, in the end, exacerbate it . . . The conflicting argument is that if this regime doesn't succeed economically – and the country can't modernise without the Internet – they're also doomed. In that sense, the Government is damned if it does and damned if it doesn't. There's no effective way to censor the Net. That's why it's known as the final blow in over-running national boundaries.

In the course of 1996, it was reported that the Chinese government authorized the acquisition of Internet connections by private citizens, but ensured that all international traffic went through two government-controlled gateways, which filtered out certain communications. It was also reported that back-alley shops were selling devices that allow Chinese Internet subscribers to bypass the gateways and plug directly into the Hong Kong network.

Source: AAP Report (29 January 1996) and subsequent press reports.

•••

Since the above report was written, the rapid spread of the Internet has converted the quantitative change of information flows into a qualitative one. The number of Internet users in China, which was estimated to be 100,000 in 1996, stands at an estimated 420 million as of 2011, more than in the United States, giving the PRC an Internet penetration rate of 32 per cent of the population (that is, more than the world average of 28.7 per cent, though still far behind the average rates of around 75 per cent in the developed countries).

Source: www.international.worldstats.com accessed 21 February 2011.

11.2 The institutional framework of international exchanges

The peculiarities of crossing borders: bridging gaps in space and between institutional systems

When people trade products, this normally entails transport costs, because producers and customers operate in different locations. In addition, they of course incur transaction costs. When production factors are moved to new locations, mobility costs have to be borne, too. These costs are low in the case of financial capital as it travels through electronic channels. Bulky, physical capital goods cost more to move. Applying knowledge in different locations causes greatly varying costs (relative to the market value of that knowledge), and the relocation of people tends to cause considerable expenses. The costs of transport and factor mobility, which we might call 'space-bridging costs', of course occur in interregional as well as in international transactions. Taken by themselves, trade and factor movements do not create a systematic difference between border-crossing and interregional transactions (Kasper, 2008b).

However, a new type of cost and risk arises when trade and factor flows cross national borders. The two contracting parties do then not transact under the umbrella of a shared institutional framework. National rule enforcement ends at the border, which means international contracts come with specific risks. If one party defaults on delivering on a contractual promise, the process of coercing the defaulting party or obtaining redress for damages is less straightforward than when both parties reside in the same jurisdiction. Sometimes, extraterritorial parties have diminished rights or there are even no rights at all under the customs and laws of specific countries (discrimination against foreigners).

Differing customs, conventions, work and business practices, design standards, laws and regulations cause specific international institution-bridging costs. Foreign governments may also act in unpredictable ways, causing sovereign risks. In extreme cases, there may be international enforcement failure. We can thus conclude that international transactions often take place under greater uncertainty and higher transaction costs.

KEY CONCEPTS

Space-bridging costs arise whenever an economic transaction is between contract partners who are in two different locations. They may consist of *transport costs* to shift physical products, *communications costs* to move information, and *mobility costs* to move production factors, for example when people migrate, a factory is moved to a different place or financial capital is transferred.

International institution-bridging costs arise when the institutions of different countries differ, so that people who trade or move production factors between different countries incur costs and risks that do not arise within the same nation. In particular, transaction costs and risks rise when contractual obligations have to be enforced in foreign countries.

➡

The risk of **international enforcement failure** arises when private contracting parties have no or lesser access to the enforcement mechanisms in foreign countries, or are ignorant of what enforcement mechanisms are available to them. It may be extraordinarily costly to seek tort damages or enforce contract fulfilment in another country, because internal norms differ or because the judiciary, police and informal enforcement mechanisms behave differently from those with whom one is familiar at home.

If we take an international trade contract as an example, higher information costs need to be incurred to identify contract partners. Product specifications may vary from the standards in the home market, as do essential attributes of potential foreign contract partners. Thus, their creditworthiness, solvency and payment morale may differ from the standards with which one is familiar. However, it is not necessarily always true nowadays that international transactions are more difficult and costly than national ones. Traders in New York may have lower transaction costs if they buy or sell in London than if they trade with someone in Wichita. Moreover, the communications revolution and intensification of distance trade have allowed important transaction costs to be slashed.

When production factors move across national borders, additional costs also arise. But again, this does not always mean that the costs of international mobility are higher than in the case of national relocation. For example, academics in China may have more information and share more cultural traits with their professional colleagues in America than with Chinese villagers, so that they may find it less costly to move internationally than within the country. Moving is thus often less costly within a professional network than outside it. Private networks often cut across national borders. Borders therefore constitute less clear-cut lines of division than a summary analysis might suggest. Nonetheless, one has to recognize that peculiar cost categories occur when trade and investment cross national borders.

One cost that frequently arises in international transactions relates to different languages, causing translation costs and possible misunderstandings. Inter-language communication involves not only vocabulary and grammar, but a host of cultural concepts and habits that may differ between nations and civilizations. To the extent that trading communities develop a shared lingua franca, they reduce the translation costs. This was, for example, the case with Greek and Latin in Antiquity, 'trader doggerel' in the Middle Ages in Europe, Arabic throughout the Middle East, 'bazaar Malay' in southeast Asia, and English on a global scale today. Sometimes, specific groups whose members reside in different countries share the same language, ethnicity and culture, such as Jews in Europe or certain Chinese communities in the Far East, which gives them a cost advantage that they exploit by becoming middlemen. Countries that are net recipients of immigrants, such as the United States and Australia, tend to benefit from immigrant middlemen, who act as bridge-building traders to foreign places and markets. Likewise, the big cities of China now are home to large communities of foreign professionals, who act as important transmitters of knowledge and knowhow from the wealthy West.

Additional transaction costs may arise in international contract negotiations because the tacit institutions differ between countries and cultures; differences may need to be made explicit and dealt with during contract negotiations. The internal and external institutions in different countries may be incompatible and require additional contract clauses to override the differences. It may take much specific and hard-to-learn knowhow to cope with these aspects of international business.

Arguably the thorniest problems peculiar to international transactions arise with the enforcement of contracts, both in trade and investment. A defaulting party cannot be coerced with recourse to the shared national jurisdiction operating under the same law. The judiciary or the police, even if their services are readily available to citizens of foreign countries, may operate under quite different rules and administrative practices, as people who trade, work or invest in developing countries will readily attest!

Another cost peculiar to international transactions arises from the existence of different currencies. Receipts or expenditures have to be converted in the foreign exchange market, which is not cost-free. Traders and investors also incur foreign-exchange risks, as deferred payments may eventually be converted at a rate of exchange different from the expected one. These problems and possible institutional solutions are discussed in Section 11.5 below.

Institutions that facilitate international transactions

Since there may be additional transaction costs in border-crossing trade and factor flows, one may ask why international trade has been growing so fast and why international investment and migration are booming. Indeed, how do people manage without overarching, transnational enforcement agencies based on external government powers (Curzon-Price, 1997)? One explanation could be that international trade and finance respond to higher profit incentives than those available in national transactions, possibly because relative factor prices differ more or because international trade, investment and migration exploit profitable transfers of knowledge (Sowell, 1996). As international trade and investment grow, extraordinary pioneer profit margins are, however, whittled away, so that profitability is not systematically higher than in domestic exchanges.

The answers to the puzzle lie with institutional economics: A rich variety of individual arrangements has been developed spontaneously to economize on the peculiar costs of international trade and factor movements. International exchanges do not occur in a vacuum, but within a sophisticated spontaneous order (Curzon-Price, 1997; Streit, 1996). These institutions allow people to risk their fortunes in dealings with partners in far-distant countries, whom they have never met. Transactions are frequently done even without written contracts and are simply based on trust in the informal institutions of a particular professional network and with enforcement mechanisms that owe nothing to government back-ups.

International private law

One approach to dealing with the uncertainties and enforcement problems of extra-territoriality is to take recourse to international private law, that is, laws created in specific jurisdictions to deal with international transactions. It contains legal principles that determine which state's private law is to be applied in specific circumstances. As such, the law of a specific country is chosen to reduce the scope for collision between conflicting legal norms and to reduce conflicts where they arise. Considerable uncertainties remain: How will national tribunals interpret certain rules? Will tribunals be able to cope with foreign laws, or reinterpret foreign law in the light of domestic judicial traditions? At times, related matters may be interpreted on the basis of either domestic or foreign norms. Moreover, what if foreign private laws collide with overriding domestic legal principles? Then, the national interest in public order may be taken to justify decisions that override foreign laws or rulings under international private law.

Despite these fundamental difficulties, a uniform code governing international commodity transactions was ratified under United Nations auspices in 1969 in Vienna. By and large, it codified existing trading customs.

The Vienna Convention on the Law of Treaties is now recognized in some 40 jurisdictions. Nonetheless, the application of the Vienna Convention does not necessarily create the certainty of effective institutions because it depends on national courts that operate within differing judicial traditions. Outcomes of court cases are far from predictable. US economist Peter Leeson has shown for the New York Convention on the recognition of foreign arbitral decisions, which also formalized trading rules across countries, that it had much less impact on international trade than many assumed (Leeson, 2008).

Contracting parties sometimes also agree on accepting the norms of a third country, so as not to give one party an asymmetric advantage over the other, but this of course increases the information costs for both contracting parties and may lead to 'forum shopping' by the more powerful party.

We thus have to conclude that international private law does not create legal certainty and often even increases transaction costs. It is therefore not surprising that very few trade conflicts are litigated by official courts on the basis of international private law.

The new *lex mercatoria*

The alternative to the formal, official judiciary processes on the basis of external rules is private arbitration on the basis of evolving internal rules, many of which may well be formalized. This is, indeed, how most disagreements over international trade contracts are adjudicated and settled. Some 90 per cent of all international transactions provide for a form of private arbitration, where necessary. And about 90 per cent of decisions by arbitrators are accepted voluntarily and without further recourse to public courts (Streit and Mangels, 1996, p. 24). The institution set on which this is based has become known as the 'new *lex mercatoria*', a term that echoes the legal principles that European international traders developed in the Middle Ages and thereafter to facilitate their business (Law Merchant). The Medieval Law Merchant was based on certain legal principles, such as equality before the law, which was a path-breaking deviation from the Feudal class-law prevailing at the time. It covered certain trading customs that were adjudicated by arbitrators who were part of the merchant profession. It was internal law, though at times formalized, but enforced without recourse to officials with public power.[4] The Law Merchant continued to be effective because it was closely connected to professional values and internal institutions, namely the trading habits, the customs and the traditions of the community. As so often, this experience demonstrated yet again that culture matters (Boettke, 1994; Cowen, 2002; Pejovich, 2003; Boettke et al., 2008).

The contemporary Law Merchant is likewise a set of internal, formal or informal, institutions (Section 5.2). They consist in the first place of trading customs that are generally recognized by all participants in a given branch of trade and are generally obeyed. Some of these customs bind the contracting parties tacitly. Some have been codified to enhance transparency, as for example the New York Convention on Arbitral Awards and the Washington Convention on Investment Disputes. Many of these conventions apply to specific activities to suit highly specialized circumstances. Some conventions have come about with the cooperation of national governments, and some have indeed obligated national governments to adapt domestic legislation to the conditions created by such new Law Merchant conventions (Benson, 1998a, 1998b, documents how the cooperative pursuit of wealth produced internal institutions, which owed nothing to governments).

The internal institutions that underpin international transactions also consist of standardized contracts, standard contract clauses and general conditions of business. These greatly reduce the costs of contract negotiation and monitoring. Examples are standardized letters of credit in international trade and standardized insurance coverage for certain transactions which are provided by international chambers of commerce. International traders in machinery and equipment often agree to standardized and highly elaborate conditions concerning the delivery and installation of the equipment to save on contract negotiation costs and to cover possible conflicts during the execution of such contracts.

Another type of transaction cost-saving institution deals with international trade clauses that apply to contracts across a wide variety of specialized trades, the so-called International Commercial Terms (Incoterms). These rules have been codified by international chambers of commerce to stipulate each contracting party's rights and obligations, for example 'free on board' (f.o.b.) and 'cost, insurance and freight' (c.i.f.). These terms are now used worldwide and across all industries. They simplify contracting and contract monitoring. Likewise, certain general legal principles are typically assumed to apply to international contracts, such as the '*clausula rebus sic stantibus*' (an escape clause under narrowly defined, exceptional circumstances) and an understanding of the principle of 'common honesty and decency' in reporting information to contract partners. These principles constitute a kind of general institutional safety net for people who normally operate in much more explicit national legal and cultural traditions and who cannot negotiate complete contracts to regulate all eventualities.

International arbitration

These internal institutions confine the scope for opportunistic action by international merchants and financiers. Where conflicts about specific actions or rule interpretations arise, most international operators appeal to non-government arbitration tribunals. This practice demonstrates a number of interesting institutional principles.

Specific arbitrators may be agreed on beforehand in the contract. Where this has not been stipulated, the parties may appeal to arbitrators by subsequent agreement. Arbitration tribunals are normally private and are run by chambers of commerce, for example in Zurich, London, Stockholm and Paris. These organizations typically make their arbitration rules known and then provide arbitration and related administrative services. They give formal backbone to trading customs, clarify the internal institutions of international trade and create confidence for contracting parties that venture outside the umbrella of national institutions.

Private arbitrators tend to be known for their expertise in specific branches of trade and investment. They earn the trust of contracting parties by their specialist knowledge, and they have to compete with other arbitrators who offer similar services. When contracting parties agree on a certain arbitrator, they will have expediency and the quality of his arbitration services in mind.

The arbitrators apply their own rules (different from government courts under international private law who apply laws made by others). They of course have a keen interest in keeping their services predictable and simple. If they fail, they lose their reputation and their business. Arbitrators have to earn a reputation for expediting matters and keeping procedures simple. They normally apply prevailing trade customs and legal principles – the law created by the private merchants and financiers themselves. Negotiations are confidential and pursue settlements that minimize possible damage to the reputations of the clients. Arbitrators tend to work towards preserving the commercial connection and facilitating the trade. Since international arbitration nowadays is big business, national governments have abstained from interfering for fear of upsetting the business.

Compliance with arbitration judgments

The decisions of arbitrators tend to be adhered to in 90 per cent of cases, as mentioned. Why is this so? The answer lies with the mechanisms of enforcement of internal institutions discussed in Sections 5.2 and 7.3: Contracting parties in an international trade deal, who appeal to a national court to overturn the outcome of private arbitration, face uncertainty about the final outcome, long delays, considerable litigation costs and the risk that their reputation will be damaged by publicity. If a government court were to award damages, the litigant would still face uncertainties about how the other party, resident outside his own jurisdiction, can be forced to pay.

The incentives to accept the judgment of private arbitrators and to expedite the business are therefore considerable. Moreover, since arbitrators tend to be specialized in specific industries and have an interest in remaining in business, they will shape judgments that are acceptable to the parties. Even if a specific arbitration decision is not welcome, most traders will recognize their long-term interest in the security of the rules. After all, they frequently are engaged in an open-ended sequence of deals that are to their reciprocal advantage. Cooperative behaviour therefore pays. Where there are one-off deals (end games), traders may make mutual commitments (offer hostages) that guarantee an honest and proper execution of the contract. In all of this, they will think of their reputations, fearing that – in their specialized branch of trade – they may in future be seen by others as a less desirable contract partner. At the time of rapid and intense international communication by fax and email, reputations can, after all, be quickly destroyed.

It is important to note in this context that modern international trade is typically not conducted among anonymous partners and in one-off deals. Business partners are bound up in more or less durable networks, although they always have the exit option. Networks of traders with highly specific knowledge and shared business practices conduct trade in the technically and organizationally complex areas of international exchange. Much of the relevant information could never be completely written down in contracts, and the open-ended nature of contracts forces people to rely on institutions. Thus, reputation, trust and other self-enforcing institutional mechanisms are crucial to saving on knowledge-gathering costs and thus beating the competition.

KEY CONCEPTS

Law Merchant (or **Custom of Merchants**, Latin: *lex mercatoria*) emerged in Europe in the twelfth to fifteenth centuries as a body of unwritten laws that were implemented by merchants for merchants to avoid local rulers and official courts. Its purpose was to establish known rules that facilitated the exchange of commodities and credit across the borders of different jurisdictions and reduced transaction costs. The Custom of Merchants introduced the concept of all being equal before the law. It ruled over groups who moved between jurisdictions and was central to establishing individual economic liberties that took precedence even over the dictates of the rulers.

The *new lex mercatoria* is a system of internal institutions that govern international trade and payments and contain self-enforcing mechanisms, apart from relying on private arbitration. The customs of international merchants and financiers are sometimes codified and formalized. They tend to be specific to particular industries or branches of trade. In many areas, merchant law replaces national and international private law, because it operates more expediently, flexibly and – in the final analysis – with lower transaction costs.

International intermediaries

Specialist international trading organizations may also become active middlemen who undertake back-to-back deals on their own account, cutting the costs of contract negotiation and monitoring and reducing perceived default risks. Trading partners often prefer to rely on middlemen because this makes negotiations easier and the fulfilment of trans-border contracts more secure. It also frees them from the uncertainties and costs of having to rely on national judiciaries. Sometimes, international trading houses, banks and government agencies are also involved in two-way trade, so that they present themselves as even more credible hostages or guarantors of contract execution (Chapter 7). Examples are trade-credit guarantees by government agencies and the minority participation by well-known companies in international ventures. Joint ventures of partners from two countries reduce the perceived risks of enforcement failure abroad. On similar grounds, multinational companies are nowadays often able to reduce their transaction costs by being established in various countries. They are credible trade partners because their international reputation is at stake. They have overcome part of the problem of extra-territoriality by internalizing business within their own network of subsidiaries.

It is no coincidence that international trade has frequently been taken over by middlemen networks when shared institutions are lacking. Networks of middlemen then have the advantage of lower transaction and enforcement costs, as we saw in Chapter 7. Such international networks become even more credible when the middlemen are bound by specific cultural and family ties that set them apart from the wider communities, in which they trade or give loans: the Jews throughout medieval Europe, German merchants in early modern Eastern Europe, ethnic groups like the Marwari from India, specific Chinese ethnic groups in East Asia and elsewhere (Sowell, 1994, pp. 46–59; Landa, 1994). These groups are often not confined to trade, but become dominant foreign investors. This was notably the case with Germans in post-medieval Eastern Europe and Chinese more recently in southeast Asia.

The understanding that relational trade and investment contracts with foreigners may involve steep enforcement risks and therefore depend on personal trust in shared internal institutions is particularly well developed in the overseas Chinese community, probably because of long and painful experience. It is virtually impossible for strangers to strike a quick major business deal with a Chinese family enterprise. Before this can be done, one has to establish and nurture a loyal personal relationship, often on the basis of non-commercial interchanges (Ch'ng, 1993). The oft-repeated story about Hong Kong shipping magnate, Y.K. Pao, is symptomatic: At their first business meeting, Aristotle Onassis, the Greek shipping tycoon, dispensed with all preliminaries to discuss a joint business strategy. He was rejected out of hand. Although the proposal was potentially rewarding, it was dismissed because deeply ingrained Chinese custom dictated that one simply does not enter into such deals with strangers, especially not from foreign cultures (op. cit., p. 47).

To sum up: international trade and finance are carried out in a social context of shared internal institutions that offer reasonably clear, transparent rules which are understood as stable and reasonably enforceable. Diverse trading associations may codify trade practices and give them a sufficient degree of certainty. Traders then have a choice of rule systems. This induces competition among rule setters and arbitrators. Autonomously evolved law (trade customs) thus not only keeps government-made law and external judiciary processes at bay, but often replaces them, because this is cheaper and works more expeditiously.

Trade and investment among business people in different nations thus operate within well-developed frameworks of internal institutions, which the traders and investors have created for themselves. Normally, personal contacts, reputations and the threat of exclusion play an important role in supporting the trade. International business is therefore in reality a far cry from the notion of anonymous, impersonal contracting that is frequently implied in traditional textbooks on international trade and finance.

CH 11 – CASE THREE

International business must bridge cultural gaps

Differences in internal and external institutions require international businessmen to adapt their modus operandi. This is probably nowhere more true than between Westerners, who have grown up with a tradition of impartial, universal rules and the rule of law, and the Chinese who have operated under deficient or non-existent general institutions and corrupt legal and court systems. They have learnt to rely on long-lasting personal relationships as the essential institutional foundation for contract enforcement.

This point is made evident in the following excerpts from an article in *The Economist*:

> many foreign firms have failed to grasp what networking in Asia is really about. Most western multinationals setting up in Asia have formed some sort of joint venture or alliance with a local firm – principally as a way of acquiring local influence and knowledge. . . The most common complaint of western businessmen throughout the region is that local partners often turn out to have an agenda of their own. Usually the local partner is less interested in building up brands or expanding market share than in extracting short-term profits in order to invest in new . . . ventures.

> Western and eastern firms have a different approach towards relationships . . . western firms . . . first . . . decide which businesses or projects it is interested in, and then seeks to cultivate the necessary connections. Asian companies believe that the relationships come first, and that investment opportunities flow from them . . . This philosophy has deep roots . . . local firms were established by migrant Chinese . . . they built up networks in which extended families and clans did business only with one another in order to reduce risk . . . This web of connections, or *guanxi*, still sits at the heart of most overseas-Chinese groups . . . Rather than move towards this system, most western firms seem to shrink ever further away from it. Sometimes they . . . associate networking with bribery . . . the current trend for moving executives every three or four years may tie in well with ideas about being a 'multicultural multinational'. But it means that business relationships are institutional rather than personal . . .

> [One leading western businessman] argues that western firms should treat networking in Asia as a form of protection. It will take years until Asian markets become as transparent as those in the West; years too until the necessary rules and regulations are written and enforced. In the meantime guanxi is often the safest or only form of commercial security . . .

> In the long term, business methods in Asia will probably come to resemble more closely those in the West. Already some of Asia's sprawling conglomerates are reaching the limits of the ability of their founding families to manage them.

Source: *The Economist*, 29 March 1997, pp. 73–74.

Financial intermediation

An extreme, well-nigh awe-inspiring, case of spontaneous rule compliance can be found in international currency markets. Participants in global currency markets have developed sophisticated, yet expedient arrangements to allow international buyers and sellers to transact huge volumes of business at high speed and virtually without any written documentation (although the online trade, which has developed since the 1990s, is now electronically recorded). It all happens with low transaction costs and a minimal number of mishaps. The *daily* turnover in global currency markets in 2010 was estimated at a staggering US$4 trillion, growing rapidly (Bank of International Settlements, *Triannual Survey 2010*). Among other things, these sophisticated markets allow international businessmen to cover their exchange-rate risks, for example by engaging in currency futures markets. The markets generate valuable information as they rotate non-stop around the globe. They cover tens of thousands of independent participants who never meet personally, but only deal with each other over the telephone and online.

International currency markets function smoothly without a central authority that enforces rules or might punish defaulters. Instead, the currency traders have developed a spontaneous, highly effective institutional infrastructure. It has adopted rapidly changing technologies and has expanded with great speed since the major currencies were floated in the late 1960s and early 1970s. The institutions of international currency exchange have been strong enough to withstand major oil shocks, wars, uprisings, political convulsions, recessions, government defaults and the demise of totalitarian socialism – all without a major panic or breakdown in the market network. Occasionally, governments have intervened with the goal of preventing sudden exchange-rate movements or, in the case of China, to prevent an appreciation that the authorities deemed too fast. But such interventions have normally proven destabilizing, rather than building confidence.

How can the 'miracle' of global currency markets happen on a daily basis? The key institutional enforcement is the sanction of ostracism (exclusion). If a currency trader violates the unwritten rules of the trade, for example refuses to fulfil a contract or fails to bear his share of a loss incurred due to a misunderstanding, he or she will soon find that no-one accepts their offers. Reputation is essential; repeated opportunism destroys reputations and entails virtual exclusion. Informal information networks around the globe are nowadays incredibly efficient, and sanctions can be very swift. This is essential to allow currency traders to transact their risky business at low margins, to rely on punctual delivery from business partners in far-away countries, and to do so without costly legal documentation.

Hegemons and extra-territoriality

In some cases, international commerce and finance have benefited from cost- and risk-reducing government involvement. When hegemonic powers established themselves, they often used their supremacy to enforce certain institutions in business dealings beyond their borders. This is why empires were often perceived as good for trade and prosperity. The *Pax Romana* spread beyond the vast borders of the Roman empire and projected certain Roman institutions to regions where traders from the empire engaged with outsiders. The *Pax Mongolica*, after the conquests of Chinggis Khan (1155(?)–1227) whose empire soon crumbled, was strong enough to back up institutions that made the Silk Road trade between China and the Far West possible for two centuries. The Aztecs projected their power far beyond their borders in present-day Mexico to back certain informal mercantile institutions. And the *Pax Britannica* and the *Pax Americana* gave institutional infrastructures to trade and investment far beyond their immediate sphere of military influence. Although the wealth-creating benefits to the general public of secure, shared institutions were normally enormous, the opening-up of closed national markets by such regimes was often unpopular among local elites because the imperial power challenged their established power structures.

Indian-American economist Deepak Lal highlighted the importance of free-trade, free-investment institutions for wealth-creating integration and the role which a dominant hegemonic power can play in the establishment and enforcement of such rules. He showed that Britain, because it was free-market oriented, set up the *Pax Britannica* in the nineteenth and early twentieth century, which instituted a liberal international order. It facilitated competition and innovation, including the rise of new competitors. The *Pax Americana*, which was founded on American preferences for political and economic freedom, extended and reinforced what Lal called the Liberal International Economic Order (Lal, 2004). Newcomers to the integrated international market place, such as the small East Asian 'tiger economies', later China and India, have not only prospered, but also created important growth markets for old industrial producers (Sections 14.2-14.4). This process created and enforced rules for unhindered payments, free trade and secure foreign investment. It has been at the heart of the unprecedented global growth experience since the middle of the twentieth century (Chapter 1). Lal stresses the role of the liberal hegemon in this, casting doubts on the alternative of a transnational authority, like the UN, or a club of national governments.

Finally, something needs to be said about institutional arrangements that facilitate the international movement of production factors. The fixed costs of such relocations are often high and have to be sunk before one can find out whether relocation has been a worthwhile undertaking. In other words, living or working in another country is an 'experience good', as defined in Section 7.1. The information problems are considerable when one deals with a border-crossing business relationship that may last many years into the future. To overcome these peculiar costs, host governments have long granted immigrants and foreign investors cost-saving privileges. German merchants and craftsmen were granted special privileges, including the right to run their own law courts, if they settled in Norway as far back as the twelfth century. Later, East European rulers extended similar privileges to attract German and Dutch knowhow and people: extra-territoriality, guarantees of protection of their own customs and practices, tax-exempt status, and grants of free land. Similar devices were employed in medieval China to induce northern people to migrate south (Rozman, 1991, pp. 68–83) and by the Ottoman Sultans to attract Jewish and Western knowhow and capital to Istanbul after the Moors were ousted from Iberia.

From there it is only a short step to present-day efforts at attracting foreign capital and enterprise to new industrial countries in the face of the handicap of ignorance and high mobility costs across an 'international institutional discontinuity'. For example, the provision of free industrial land and infrastructures, tax exemptions, pioneer status, free-trade zones and free enterprise zones (which reduce information and compliance costs in institutionally deficient countries), and official participation in joint ventures are used to compensate for such fixed transaction costs. Such measures have been employed widely in East Asia since 1960 (Chapter 14) when initial information costs about producing in the Far East were high. The privileges were reduced as the pioneers in the new industrial locations demonstrated how well the previously unknown institutional framework of East Asia worked and as internal and external institutions were enhanced in response to the demands of mobile capital and enterprise (Section 14.4). Once the new industrial countries had established a reputation for being attractive locations, Asian governments and workers were able to demand higher taxes and wages. In a similar vein, many southern-hemisphere governments, such as those of Australia and Argentina, long assisted migrants by subsidizing their transport and settlement costs. Once international migrants could observe the demonstrated success of previous migrants in the new countries, the subsidy was reduced or abolished. Settlement gradually also became more convenient for new migrants. The adjustment costs to becoming productive in the new country dropped thanks to institutional modifications in these immigrant societies, which reduced the institutional gap that migrants had to overcome. The same now holds true with illegal international migration into the affluent countries. As early immigrants have established 'beach heads' and their own networks in the new host countries, newcomers face lower information costs of relocating. This in turn now accelerates migration flows, despite more determined government efforts to stem illegal migration.

Not an institutional vacuum

Diverse historic evidence shows that the sphere of private international transactions, which is essentially government-free, has been far from an institutional vacuum. Time and again, people, who wanted to trade, invest or resettle beyond the borders of their own jurisdiction, went about developing a great variety of institutional arrangements and networks that made international transactions less risky and more profitable. It is worth noting that the solutions that evolved were frequently not dissimilar to those internal institutions that one can observe in national economic life in areas where governments are reluctant to intervene.

11.3 Policy issues: international economic order

Trade policy: discrimination and the most-favoured nation clause

Governments and other political agents often intervene in international economic relations for the same reasons that motivate domestic interventions: Initially, it is promised that interventions will enhance transparency, open access to international trade and finance, limit free-riding, and make the institutions more credible. But, sooner or later, government interventions in international trade and payments also close markets in response to organized domestic lobby groups and to protect the government's own position from competition with administrations in foreign jurisdictions. Frequently, interventions to reduce the openness of a national economy are the corollary of domestic redistribution policy.

Mercantilism in post-medieval Europe had much to do with the fact that rulers could gain revenue by licensing and protecting selected merchant groups. Thus, Queen Elizabeth I gave the East India Company an exclusive license to trade with India and took a royal share in the resulting monopoly rents. The Dutch United East India Company (VOIC) opened most of what is now Indonesia under a similar deal, and the Hudson Bay Company did the same in Canada. The granting and protection of international trading monopolies was not an exclusive European invention; the Japanese government licensed a few of their traders to deal with the Portuguese and the Dutch, and the Chinese Emperor licensed a limited number of *hongs* in Guangzhou to trade exclusively with Westerners. In these latter cases, isolationism was probably a primary motive, though the cut in the trading profits that went into government coffers was not unwelcome.

As we saw in Section 11.1, instances of rent-seeking and rent-creation in foreign trade and investment are frequent. Domestic suppliers, whose interests are concentrated and can be easily organized, seek an intervention against international competition. The rulers oblige, receiving fees, undercover payments, influence and protection from those who compete internationally. This allows political transfers of property rights that are not possible in an open economy and enhances the domestic influence of the political operators. In closed economies, a culture of redistribution and interventionism can reinforce itself and increasingly entrench uncompetitive practices. Once such a state of affairs is reached, capital flight or the emigration of citizens is seen as an affront to the rulers and their 'crony' groups. The fundamental fact that free trade and a high degree of factor mobility are important conditions for a better division of labour and for the diffusion, discovery and use of productive knowledge around the globe, is then easily lost sight of.

The World Trade Organization

The agents of government find themselves frequently in a conflict between interests in free international exchanges and particular national interests. A case can then be made for fostering a free international economic order through multilateral agreements that ban protectionism and political opportunism in discriminating against outsiders. In other words, there is a case for an international truce in the discrimination against foreigners. Inter-government agreements are intended to promote growth opportunities and overcome a government's reluctance to liberalize its trade unilaterally. Such a multilateral agreement was adopted among Western governments in the late 1940s when they signed the General Agreement on Tariffs and Trade (GATT), which has now been converted into the wider World Trade Organization (WTO). The central institution of the GATT/ WTO is the most-favoured nation clause (MFN). It stipulates that a trading concession – in the sense of removing government-made obstacles to trade – granted to one country must be extended to all others in the club. In other words, it enshrines the principle of non-discrimination in international trade. Since the 1960s, a growing number of governments have also agreed to treat foreign and national investors equally. Certain risk-reducing conventions that protect foreign investors have also been put in place, for example under OECD auspices. However, a planned, all-embracing Multilateral Agreement on Investment (MAI) fell prey to national opportunism and lobbying.

When they negotiate international treaties to open up, governments stake their international reputation and act as middlemen (Streit and Voigt, 1993). Commitments to free international exchanges often become more credible when governments enter the game of multilateral give and take. Such inter-government commitments are of course not enforceable outside a government's own jurisdiction, since there is no regress to a higher-level enforcer. At best, the WTO can find out about rule violations and admonish compliance. Also, there are sanctions of collective international moral suasion and collective retaliation (trade bans on violators). The narrow limits to such extraterritorial sanctions for rule breaches have become evident, time and again. In the case of the WTO, at least the big players have often been able to flout the agreed rules with impunity. Free-trade rules work only if the big players want free trade and if the national public supports it, as was the case under the *Pax Americana* from 1945 to the late twentieth century. But frequently, influential domestic political alliances between industry lobbies, political parties, and government bureaucracies are able to subvert commitments to free trade. In these circumstances, the formal international trading orders as well as formal treaty commitments not to discriminate against foreign traders and investors are only a weak institution against interventionist governments, at least nowadays.[5]

Further frustrations with liberalizing international trade in goods and services arose during the Uruguay Round of the WTO, when implementation of agreed rules became patchy, and then during the subsequent Doha Round, which ended in a long-lasting stalemate (Sally, 2008; Sally and Sen, 2011). The entire post-1945 history of diplomatic negotiations was based on the assumption that liberalizing government somehow grant foreigners costly trade and other 'concessions', disregarding the fact that the interests of importers and ordinary citizens in cheap imports are overlooked in this way of thinking. Because unanimity or large majorities are needed for liberalization, obstinate protectionists, such as the European Union on agricultural trade and many emergent economies on the free trade in services, were able hold the world community to ransom and frustrate progress.

As trade liberalization advanced during the second half of the twentieth century, it also became evident that reluctant free traders often countered the removal of border interventions with in-country discrimination against foreign suppliers and investors. Health and safety regulations can always be adduced (or invented) to handicap importers or direct foreign investors (Sally, 2008). Likewise, importers can be hampered in setting up distribution networks and providing after-sales services. Local borrowing by foreign firms has also been controlled, for example by government tests of whether loans to them are in the national interest. In short, whether trade and capital-flow liberalization has the assumed wealth effects depends greatly on the degree of economic freedom in the liberalizing country. An entrenched culture of nationalist preferment and dense regulation can subvert agreed liberalization measures. The benefits of bilateral trade agreements are then of very limited value. Here we encounter the role of *metis* again: Rather un-free economies and societies frustrate border liberalization by erecting in-country protectionism.

The resulting frustrations in nations with relatively free economic orders have disillusioned many about the merits of multilateral and bilateral agreements to liberalize border-crossing exchanges. They have given rise to an alternative way of proceeding towards more liberalization, namely that willing parties that have relatively free economies should enter bilateral and multilateral free trade agreements, forget about reluctant governments and deprive them of their 'hold-up power'. Nations with relatively free domestic economies can readily enter 'coalitions of willing free traders'. This is a second-best solution because progress in trade and investment rules is not universal. However, the abandonment of the cumbersome and frustrating WTO process has had the tactical negotiation advantage that the veto of the unwilling no longer counts, as the willing liberalize because it is in their interest.

Since the failure of the Doha Round of WTO negotiations, the United States, Australia, New Zealand, Chile, Singapore and other economically free nations have embarked on a free-trade alliance of the willing, the Asia-Pacific Partnership. It is based on a shared interest in open international exchanges and it will only accept members to this club that abstain from the WTO-style 'concession game' asking for exemptions and hard-fought concessions.

Economic integration: free trade areas, customs unions and economic blocs

Travel, trade, transport, communications and finance increasingly transcend the borders of nation states. Border-crossing transactions are weaving national or regional markets more closely together: This is 'economic integration from below', which is driven by the spontaneous action of autonomous private agents (Kasper, 1970; Streit and Mussler, 1994; Streit, 1998). Part of this type of integration is the gradual emergence of transaction cost-saving internal institutions that facilitate border-crossing exchanges, as described above. Integration can, however, also be driven from above by the adoption of shared external rules and policies based on government-to-government agreements and detailed top-down directives.

When several jurisdictions join in a free-trade area, they agree to remove all artificial barriers to trade across their joint borders from above (removal of tariffs and quotas) and trust that private traders will bring about market integration from below, that is, voluntary integration by autonomous private decision makers. Nations in free-trade areas retain their individual border controls vis-à-vis third countries, for example their individual tariff regimes. If tariffs with outside third countries differ greatly, traders will export from that part of the free-trade area that meet the lowest trade barriers and import from third countries across low-tariff borders. As this diverts international trade (and reduces customs revenue), governments may introduce secondary regulations, for example imposing local-content rules. This means that free international trade has to originate where the bulk of the product or service has been produced. The monitoring and enforcement costs of such arrangements are considerable.

One way to obviate these problems is to create a customs union: a multi-jurisdiction alliance with a common set of external trade regulations, in particular a common external tariff, with free trade within the union. When customs unions are internally tied together through intensive trade links, inter-jurisdictional competition tends to become intense, as entrepreneurs make locational choices on the basis of competitiveness factors, including government and cultural institutions, wage differentials, land prices and proximity to markets (see Section 11.1 above). Government agents who find themselves exposed to such competitive pressures, as well as established private operators, then often argue for economic union, which is a customs union in which all production factors, such as labour and capital, can move about freely. An example is the European Union, which began in 1957 among six member States. In the early years, integration from above and below was, by and large, complementary. The EEC treaty provided for an unimpeded flow of trade and production factors within the Community and banned national distortions of competition, whether by private or public action. The integration from above, as contained in the treaty rules, paved the way for the integration in the markets below. However, some of the EU treaty rules of 1957 implied quite a different kind of integration from above. For example, rules were introduced to establish a Common Agricultural Policy that were highly specific, prescriptive and interventionist. Over time, the European Commission obtained further scope for such interventions, so that integration from above relied on a multiplicity of specific, prescriptive interventions rather than on paving the way for competition (Streit and Mussler, 1994).

When economic ties between countries are close, international cooperation may also extend into areas beyond trade and finance. National governments may agree to fix certain rules concerning economic competition and enforce them in their own territories, or they may follow social-welfare, environmental and income redistribution policies that are laid down by union-wide agreements. In some instances, such cooperation is justified by genuine externalities, for example when environmental externalities of certain activities fall outside the countries where these activities take place. In many other instances, integration relies on top-down directives that reduce competition in product and factor markets, as has become increasingly the case within the European Union ('harmonization'). Such integration from above then amounts to the formation of a cartel of national governments and the disenfranchisement of the electorate.[6] When national governments are no longer allowed to compete with each other in providing rivalling administrative solutions, nation states become increasingly constrained in their autonomy. International cooperation among governments gives way to coercive transnational authorities and national sovereignty is lost (Fonte, 2011).

The feedback from the increasingly open economy that empowers private autonomy in trade and the location of economic activities on the development of external institutions can be powerful, as we saw repeatedly when we touched on the emergence of the institutions of capitalism in the small, open states of Europe. In the following chapter, we shall discuss the evolution of institutions over time, in which the international dimension is playing a central role.

KEY CONCEPTS

The **most favoured nations** (MFN) **clause** is the embodiment in international trade agreements of the principle of non-discrimination. It says that a freedom granted by government to the nationals of one foreign country must be automatically

➡

←

extended to the nationals of all countries that participate in such an international agreement. In other words, governments forego the right to discriminate among foreigners from different countries who are part of the club. The best-known enshrinement of the MFN clause is in the General Agreement on Tariffs and Trade (GATT).

Economic integration relates to intensified interaction between market participants in different local or national markets. We speak of 'economic integration from below' when inter-regional or international exchanges intensify as a result of growing trade and investment; this normally goes along with the development of internal institutions that facilitate these exchanges. By contrast, 'integration from above' relates to the setting or changing of external institutions through political processes. An example where this procedure now dominates is the European Union, which has, since the late 1950s, developed external institutions that remove barriers to trade and factor movements within the Union, creating rule sets which are shared throughout the EU area, but that increasingly prescribe a certain conduct for the citizens of all member countries.

A **free-trade area** covers a multiplicity of jurisdictions between which obstacles to border-crossing trade are abolished; the various jurisdictions may retain differential trade obstacles vis-à-vis third countries. A **customs union** is a free-trade area with a common external set of trade obstacles, for example a common tariff. An **economic union** embraces a customs union, but also allows free factor movements throughout, as well as imposing harmonized economic policies on the participating countries. Compliance with these central impositions, at least by the big participants, cannot be readily enforced.

International cooperation takes place between sovereign governments who agree to obey certain rules. We speak of **transnational interaction** when an authority with coercive powers directs formerly sovereign national governments to implement certain policies.

Since the end of the Cold War, the traditional international order of sovereign nation states interacting (mostly) on the basis of international law has been altered by the introduction of a growing number of transnational authorities and top-down directives to national governments. Under UN auspices in particular, sovereign governments have concluded treaties and conventions that cede national sovereignty to transnational bodies and oblige them to implement rules and programmes decided in transnational fora. This interferes with democracy in sovereign, free nations. One example has been the Kyoto Treaty that obliges affluent member states to control greenhouse gas emissions and imposes penalties for non-compliance. Another is the transfer of national sovereignty from democratically elected parliaments and administrations of EU countries to the (unelected) Commission in Brussels. A growing part of new legislation and regulation in EU member states is now not assessed and decided by democratic deliberation in the various countries, but is simply handed down from Brussels. The intent is a growing uniformity of the external rules across the diverse European Union, but the side effect is the waxing discontent of the citizens who feel disenfranchised. Thus, national action is increasingly replaced by governance through supranational and transnational bodies (Fonte, 2011). As political decision making is further removed from the citizens under such schemes for global governance, power is shifted further from the citizens to political elites and pressure groups and the advantages of diversity and are lost (compare Section 12.5). Astute observers fear a diminution of democracy and a loss of hitherto creative diversity (*idem*).

Transnational rule making now even occurs without the consent of elected national governments. Thus, the European Commission has arrogated to itself the right to tax carbon emissions of air traffic across continents outside Europe, pretending it has extraterritorial rights to do so. Such developments are most problematic because they lead to international conflicts. Besides, national policies are anchored in distinct national identities, whereas transnational policy making has no such democratic and cultural foundation. There is no European identity and there are no UN citizens. Readers, who believe that the nation state is an outdated model and no longer has foundations in people's identity and internal institutions, should ask people in an airport lounge who they are. The answers will invariably be: "I am American", "I am a Frenchman", "I am from China" – no one will say "I am a European", or "I am a cosmopolitan".

11.4 International monetary arrangements

Gold standard, political money standard, flexible exchange rates and monetary unions

One peculiarity of international, in contradistinction to inter-regional transactions is that the two contract partners calculate their gains in different currencies. This leads to conversion costs (which are nowadays minor) and exchange-rate risks. Monetary assets and profits are typically valued in the national currency, which is underpinned by the monetary policies of state central banks and finance ministries. Consequently, international monetary transactions are of concern to government agencies. There are certain rule sets under which national authorities conduct their international monetary policies, which establish an international monetary order. The rules may, for example, establish a gold standard or the presently prevailing system of more or less flexible exchange rates. These rules have pervasive impacts on the conduct of national monetary policy.

The gold standard, which prevailed among many European countries in the late nineteenth century, laid down the following rules of the game: Each national currency that participated in it was defined in terms of a certain quantity of fine gold. This fixed the exchange rate between national banknotes and gold, and therefore also between the various national currencies. The gold link was considered irrevocable, although repeated breaches occurred, even before the system had to be abandoned at the onset of the Great War. Central banks undertook to convert national banknotes into gold at the fixed rate (free convertibility). National central banks, which lost public trust and were therefore asked by the public to convert their banknotes into gold, were forced to contract the money volume, as people withdrew gold and possibly shipped it abroad. When the money volume shrank, factor and product prices were expected to drop. This would make the producers internationally more competitive again, boosting exports and enabling domestic producers to compete better with imports. The gold redeemed from the central bank would probably be transferred to a more trusted central bank of another country, triggering an expansion of that country's money supply and a rise in its price level. This, it was assumed, would impact on the external balance and contribute automatically to correcting international imbalances and price-level divergences. It was assumed that prices would respond flexibly to changes in the national money volume, so that recessions and unemployment would at worst be only temporary. If prices are sticky, then deeper recessions and more unemployment will occur (Lutz, 1963/1935).

In this system of rules, central banks and governments had little sovereign control over the national money volume, let along domestic price levels (and possibly employment levels). The rules of the game thus essentially deprived governments of an influence over the macro economy.

The advantage of the gold standard was that the exchange rates between two currencies were fixed and predictable. International currency conversion was cheap and easy – an important consideration in the era before computers and telephones. Another advantage was that the 'gold mechanism' effectively tied the hands of governments that wanted to pursue inflationary policies.

A variation on the gold standard is the currency board regime: Here, domestic financial discipline (limitations on money supply and controls of bank lending practices) is enforced by an institutional arrangement under which the central bank credibly commits itself to redeem local currency for a foreign currency at a fixed rate of exchange, and to supply local money only in exchange for foreign currency at a fixed rate. This means that the central bank cannot expand credit, for example extending it to the local government, and that local monetary conditions have to stay more or less in line with those in the country with the reference currency, for example the US dollar. Flexibility of demand management is given up under those rules to obtain credibility for the local means of payment. Smaller economies have opted for such an institutional arrangement, for example Brunei since 1967, Hong Kong after 1983 (although the monetary authority has attempted some independent monetary manipulation), and more recently transition economies with no tradition of domestic money-supply control, such as Estonia. In Argentina, a country with a history of hyperinflation and unmanageable public sector deficits, the Menem government in the 1990s introduced the *Peso Convertible* at a fixed exchange rate to 1 US$, obligating the central bank to match the US dollars in the currency reserves with the national Peso money volume. However, the Argentine parliament and State and local governments did not play by fixed-exchange rate rules. A strong trade union movement exerted wage pressures and Argentine price levels rose exorbitantly. As a consequence, the government of Argentina incurred more and more debt. Eventually, the fixed Peso-dollar link had to be abandoned during a major economic crisis in 2001. A huge devaluation and major losses of savings by the middle class inevitably followed, and foreign holders of (high-interest) Argentinian government bonds suffered a massive 'haircut', that is, were paid minimal amounts for their Argentinian bonds. Since its bankruptcy, the Buenos Aires government, which did not honour its debt obligations, has found it hard to raise new credit. This case seems typical of the modern era: it appears that, nowadays, governments and organized labour are loath to play by the rules of fixed exchange rates.

In the eyes of those who expect governments to influence price levels and employment, a system of rigid exchange rates deprives national governments of the opportunity to influence national money supply to cope with changing circumstances and contingencies. This is why hand-tying of domestic money-supply policy by the gold standard promptly broke down at the outset of the First World War. After failed attempts to resurrect the gold standard in the 1920s, the great depression after 1929 heralded the definitive abandonment of the gold standard. A successor regime – namely the Bretton Woods system – was set up in 1944 to fix parities among national currencies. In certain circumstances, national governments were allowed parity changes. The institutions governing this system worked in the 1950s and early 1960s, as long as international capital flows were limited and were strictly controlled. As currencies became fully convertible and national monetary policies diverged in the late 1960s/early 1970s, the Bretton Woods rules had to be abandoned amid repeated international financial crises. It was patently clear that national governments chose to give national monetary sovereignty (and expedience) precedence over fixed exchange rates.

The Bretton Woods system was replaced by new institutions: the free formation of the price of a currency (in terms of others) in response to supply and demand in the market of that currency. The floating exchange-rate system gave national monetary authorities the sovereignty to inflate and deflate, but governments had to cope with the highly visible depreciation or appreciation of the currency, as well as the trade and employment consequences of currency fluctuations. These new institutions eliminated the contradiction between a fixed exchange rate and independence in monetary conduct, giving national governments and central banks control over, but also responsibility for, the price level. Monetary authorities that pursued the objective of stable money were no longer challenged by inflationary capital inflows and the pull of external prices (imported inflation), and monetary authorities that pursued lax policies soon felt the feedback of a depreciating currency value on domestic inflation. Overall, the effect of the change to floating exchange rates has been that unforeseen crises were less disruptive and that most national authorities pursued a less inflationary course. Since the move towards flexible exchange rates, it has been found repeatedly that monetary authorities who want to return, for whatever reasons, to fixed or predetermined exchange rates, introduce an institutional incompatibility. Sooner or later, they are forced to again abandon their attempts to fix currency rates.

Optimal currency areas and monetary unions

There are advantages in creating as big a currency area as possible, because traders, travellers and investors, who operate outside their own currency area, face the risk of unexpected exchange-rate changes and transaction costs for exchanging money. On the other hand, a community's shared monetary system is intimately tied not only to the external institutions (such as fiscal and regulatory behaviour, tax codes, the legal system and bank policies), but also to the internal institutions (such as work and payment practices, mutual trust, honesty and other bourgeois virtues), as Joseph A. Schumpeter emphasized long ago (Schumpeter, 1991/1970; Lutz, 1935/1963). This is so because, over time, the international competitiveness of an area is shaped by the cost prices (for example, wage rates and energy tariffs) relative to the corresponding factor productivities (for example, labour productivity and energy efficiency); in other words unit costs. If institutional conditions make for sustained divergences in unit-cost trends, which are greatly influenced by the institutions, then producers in one region may become increasingly uncompetitive, so that it is necessary for capital flows to compensate the disequilibrium if the common currency is to be maintained.

Capital flows may consist of voluntary private capital or tax-based, public capital. Private investors may move to uncompetitive locations in the expectation that they can exploit cost differentials (for example, lower wages) or that matters will change. Solidarity between regions may underpin a public transfer union for long periods, as has for example been the case since 1990 within reunited Germany. Whatever the case, these factors militate against extending the currency area to vastly differing institutional cultures (the importance of *metis*, again). All this makes what should be considered the optimal currency area a difficult, dynamic guessing game (Giersch (ed.) 1971; Kasper, 1970; 2011c).

These considerations have been, and are, playing a crucial role in the evolution of the biggest currency area of modern times: the creation of the Euro across (as of early 2012) 17 disparate nations and cultures.[7] The question from the outset was whether the gradual integration of markets and market behaviour should precede the formation of a currency union, or whether European integration could be pushed by the imposition of a common currency. If left to institutional evolution, gradual market integration could be expected to lead to stable exchange rates, even if the various currencies were not formally fixed vis-à-vis each other. This was evident in the unchanged exchange rate, for example, of the German Deutschmark and the Dutch guilder, while less fiscally disciplined nations with less productivity-oriented behaviour had to depreciate periodically to restore balance-of-payments equilibrium and not disrupt the integration of trade and investments.

Yet, the creation of a single, common currency was a political project of social engineering, imposing the same money in 2002 on Europeans from Lisbon to Helsinki, from Hamburg to Athens. Politicians and bureaucrats realized that this would require adherence to common fiscal rules (stipulated in the Maastricht Treaty of 1992), but national parliaments and cabinets soon disregarded the rules. The initial gains from imposing a common currency came in the form of lower transaction costs (no more conversion of national currencies and no exchange-rate risks). However, these were soon overshadowed by emerging imbalances in intra-EU payments due to divergent cost trends and incompatible institution sets. The tension between fixed parities and divergent national macroeconomic policies had of course not vanished with the introduction of the common currency, despite the fact that certain official rules were adopted to tie the hands of governments and unions to prevent inflationary policies. Europe-wide solidarity and capital flows were unable to bridge the widening gaps, so that borrowers in relatively less competitive areas – in particular local, regional and national governments – had to pay rising interest rates to attract buyers to their bonds. Keynesian concepts of deficit finance and a preference for ever-more-perfect government-funded social welfare aggravated the imbalances (Section 10.2). Over time, the fiscal as well as other restraints imposed by the creditors and EU officials on less competitive national areas showed that national sovereignty was lost. This was unpopular.

The only possible solution for retaining a single currency in these circumstances would be the automatic sharing of every nation's new debts by creating a 'Euro bond' and an automatic transfer union (Eurozone-wide bail-out pact). What medium-term incentives such a solution would have can be readily understood if one looks at the incentives within an extended family, in which everyone may borrow and all conjointly guarantee repayment.

A comparison between the political imposition of the Euro and the emergence of the US dollar offers valuable insights into how sustainable institutional systems can be created. In the newly independent American ex-colonies, a currency was used that was derived from the Mexican silver dollar. After the War of Independence, many States had stifling debts. In 1789, US Treasurer Alexander Hamilton therefore argued that the United States government must assume a considerable share of the individual States' debts and finance repayment by new federal taxes (Brueghel Institute, 2012). The political union was thus promptly followed by an, albeit limited, fiscal union. States with solid finances resented that the new US government should rescue deficit States, and many objected to the fact that speculators who had bought heavily discounted State debts should be rewarded with solid, federally guaranteed bonds. Nevertheless, Hamilton saw this as the price for liberty and financial stability of the new Union. The US did not become a 'bail-out union', indeed by 1840 an explicit no bail-out rule was formalized and several improvident States went bankrupt. A central bank, the Federal Reserve Bank, was only set up in 1913 as a lender of last resort, which made it possible in the 1930s for the Roosevelt government to embark on massive spending. While many States are now bound to balanced-budget standards, Federal US public debts have risen inexorably since.

In contrast to the US, the common currency in Euroland was politically imposed and a quasi-fiscal union was attempted before a political union. Increasingly, bail-out conditions for member states with untenable budget deficits and ailing banks are negotiated. As there is no central political power and as fundamental values and attitudes vary greatly across Europe, disparate fiscal and debt policies have persisted. This is likely to continue, given the great European diversity of mores and worldviews and deeply entrenched linguistic and cultural differences, which impede the complete integration from below that the new American nation achieved.

The Euro story has, yet again, demonstrated an important fact that we have emphasized throughout this book: the success or otherwise of such externally imposed institutions depends critically on the internal institutions and that society's particular *metis*.

Competing moneys

The flexibility of exchange rates makes it evident that national currencies are in competition with each other. National authorities cannot act with unconstrained monetary arbitrariness, for depreciating monetary assets are soon jettisoned.[8] In the extreme, poorly managed moneys simply disappear (see the stories of the Cook Island and the Zimbabwean dollars in Chapter 7). Thus, international monetary authorities are subjected to the assessment by investors and traders in currency markets. They have to conduct themselves in ways that attract and maintain demand for their assets. If, for example, a government engages in fiscal stimulus and pumps up money supply before an election, the foreign exchange rate will immediately drop, drive up import prices and generally demonstrate that such public opportunism is unwarranted. This is a powerful, though of course not always welcome constraint on opportunistic national monetary and fiscal conduct.

It has been argued that the replacement of official central bank money by the private production of competing monetized assets (private banknotes of high quality) deprives opportunistic governments of the capacity to cause inflation. The competition amongst private providers of monetized assets would provide the public with competing money (Hayek, 1976). Competition would discipline the private producers of moneys, among which private actors could choose. The ground rules would ensure that stable moneys (in terms of a basket of products) would gain wide acceptance by the public. Inflationary moneys would not be held in portfolios and would ultimately disappear. This would lead to a competition among issuing banks, the producers of monetary assets, to supply quality assets, as it was done in Europe in earlier ages. A problem with such a system is that it imposes relatively high information and other transaction costs on the public. Holders of different types of money would have to inform themselves all the time whether their assets are safe and recipients of payments might incur high information costs about the qualities of alternative means of payment.

This goes back to a point made in Section 7.6, namely that money, to be useful, depends on credible institutions. The relevant rules may be designed and imposed from above, as national monetary authorities now do, or money may be provided competitively and the requisite rules evolve in the process of competition between various monetary assets. What is preferable is an empirical question, namely where the public's information costs are lowest and where surreptitious redistribution by inflation is best controlled. In practice, government-made money and the spontaneously created, competing private moneys need not be mutually exclusive. A particular government-designed currency nowadays has no monopoly in the eyes of the citizens, given the free convertibility into other currencies. National central banks have to provide reasonably stable moneys lest private and public holders of foreign currency abandon their money as a store of value. Neither are inflationary currencies used in invoicing contracts or paying debts. Thus, many payments in inflationary countries such as Russia or Vietnam are made in US dollars; and savings may be stored under mattresses. Citizens nowadays therefore have choices as to what moneys serve them best as a means of payment, store of value and unit of account. What matters most to the interest of the citizens is the rule of free convertibility, which gives them a choice and destroys the monopoly of the central bank, empowers them and constrains the issuers of money, whether they are public or private.

KEY CONCEPTS

The **gold standard** is a set of rules that is based on the definition of each currency in terms of a fixed quantity of gold. This institution established fixed exchange rates between various national currencies and subjected national central banks and national governments to the rule that they had to defend the gold parity even at the expense of pursuing national price-level stability and employment.

The **exchange rate** is a price ratio of the value of one currency in terms of another. When you read that the Euro exchange rate of the US dollar is $0.80, this means that one US$ is exchanged for €0.80.

➡

> ←
>
> A system of **flexible exchange rates** is a regime in which the price of a national currency is determined by the interplay of supply of that currency (by exporters and foreigners who want to bring foreign capital in) and demand (by importers and people who want to export capital). Flexible exchange rates allow national monetary and general economic policies that differ from one jurisdiction to the other (monetary sovereignty). However, exchange-rate movements signal important information to policy makers and the public and tend to have powerful 'educational feedback' into monetary policy making. Insofar as they constrain the monetary sovereignty of national authorities.
>
> A single monetary system has to be based on shared external and internal institutions. Where these differ and diverge, flexibility of exchange rates is needed to avert costly direct interventions in the free exchange of goods, capital, enterprises and people. If a common currency (**monetary union**) is foisted onto disparate regions and nations, with different fundamental values, work and saving habits and fiscal rules, growing imbalances and limited political solidarity has to be expected. This will lead to political tensions and risks disintegration.
>
> The theoretical concept of an **optimal currency area** is based on the notion that a bigger area reduces the transaction costs of exchanging money and the risks of unexpected exchange-rate changes, but it normally ignores the dynamic effect of persistently differing institutions and hence diverging productivity trends. What is optimal is therefore not a static concept, but a dynamic, hard-to-predict one.

11.5 International migration and cultural integration

Over recent decades, the number of persons who migrate across national borders and between different civilizations – whether temporary or permanent, whether legal or illegal – has increased exponentially. This is a part of globalization, which not only amounts to cross-border flows of the production factor of labour, but which directly affects societies and their cultures (Sowell, 1996). Anyone with a basic understanding of institutions will realize that the international transfer of people differs in important respects from the transfer of goods and services or capital. People come with fundamental human rights and also embody values and human capital. This means that additions of 'foreigners' exert an influence on a community's institutional system, in particular the fundamental values and its internal institutions. Not all come culturally equipped to equal measure for material success in the new host countries (Sowell, 1996; 1998). Like openness to trade, such additions can have worthwhile evolutionary consequences for the host country. Old concepts and rules are tested and possibly challenged by the newcomers. This may enhance evolution. Thus, cultural influences from the outside, such as foreign cuisines, ways of expressing oneself and habits of working and trading, may do much to overcome cognitive barriers and enhance learning, both among the citizenry and the political agents of the host country. This enhances a community's adaptive capacity (see Section 12.4 below). However, the issue is one of quantities and qualities: If large numbers of immigrants join the host country, the community's familiar institutional capital may be eroded and the host-country population may resent the outside challenges. This may then easily cause xenophobia and damage internal peace (Kasper, 2002). Communities acknowledge instinctively that their traditional institutions constitute valuable, productive capital and therefore demand border protection from illegal mass immigration. It is a difficult empirical matter to establish where the long-term benefits of enhanced cognitive capacity are surpassed by the long-term costs of institutional disintegration. This cost-benefit equation is influenced by a plethora of hard-to-measure factors, such as the cultural proximity between the immigrants and the host population, their migrants' willingness to integrate with the host civilization, and the cultural rigidity or otherwise of the host population. The problems are more likely to become acute when the immigrants hail from rigid cultural settings and refuse to integrate, despite the fact that they left materially underperforming or failing cultural regimes. Political elites both among the immigrants and the hosts may then exploit the problems by fostering enduring institutional differences in values and institutions (multicultural policy). The problems are more manageable if incumbents and immigrants are aware of the challenges, de-emphasize cultural peculiarities and embrace integration, and if policies are based on shared fundamental aspirations, such as freedom, justice, peace and prosperity.

11.6 Strengthening the open economic order

Political groups are likely to strike back when the 'affront of openness' undermines their power. They may justify border controls by arguing that poorer countries engage in 'social dumping', undercutting domestic wage levels or operating with lower levels of tax. In a similar vein, they may try to obtain protection on the grounds that foreign competitors are not burdened with environmental imposts that they have to bear, and therefore that they require trade protection for their high domestic standards of environmental protection (environmental dumping). These arguments are now evident in the debate in the mature industrial economies about their de-industrialization. Domestic industries migrate to low-wage locations, creating structural unemployment levels in the mature high-cost economies. Controls of capital outflows are then demanded to restore high domestic employment, irrespective of the cost of labour. This amounts to an intent to defend political power and old socio-economic positions. The same problem is evident when environmentalists demand trade protection to prevent that capital, enterprises and jobs from 'vote with their feet', namely moving to locations that are less heavily regulated to achieve environmental objectives. This has favoured demands for a global imposition of emission controls by industry, transport and households, which would of course greatly reduce property rights and attack the economic freedom on which high modern living standards and progress are based. More generally, particular interest groups who discover that they are losing clout in the open economy, appeal to popular feelings of nationalism to contain the affront of openness. As of the early 2010s, however, the closure of national markets is rarely feasible. Technology has changed, and capital owners and enterprises are internationally mobile. This is why those who wish to avoid being disciplined by openness are now increasingly resorting to economic bloc formation. The European Union, a North American Free Trade Area, and efforts to create an East Asian Economic Caucus promise political operators at least a degree of political primacy over economic life.

The battle for openness is not fought in a static world. The transport-cost and communications revolution is moving on. It is making it harder to organize and keep together protectionist coalitions: In the era of the Internet, it is now virtually impossible to stop the free flow of capital and ideas between the citizens of different countries. Technical progress gives the essentially open international economic order a chance of survival.

Sovereign nations cannot coerce each other to fulfil international treaty obligations (short of the use of military force). It may therefore pay to enhance the self-fulfilling qualities of treaties that keep national economies open. To this end, Jan Tumlir, the long-time chief economist of the GATT, proposed to enhance economic openness by introducing self-executing treaty provisions. He argued for giving citizens, who lost property rights when protectionism was imposed, actionable legal rights against governments who violate openness and the principle of non-discrimination against foreigners (Tumlir, 1979, pp. 71–83; Banks and Tumlir, 1986). Under this proposal, private citizens and foreigners would be given the legal right to take government agencies to court in private tort actions, should new border controls diminish their property rights. This rule would certainly give teeth to the principle of equality between nationals and foreigners. The concept is applied within the European Union in certain circumstances, however not vis-à-vis third-country governments. It fits well with an era in which technological developments increasingly militate against the concept of national boundaries and strengthen cosmopolitan concepts and modes of behaviour.

In the next chapter, we turn to a very important reason why the battle for openness is important, namely that international competition augments the evolutionary potential for enhancing national rule systems.

NOTES

1 Some services are of course unlikely to ever become footloose (think of haircuts) and will continue to be produced where the demand is located.

2 The weights *w* reflect the importance of the various cost factors. These differ between the various economic activities, so that different locations are of different attractiveness to specific economic activities.

3 If the assumption that higher prices do not reduce the volume of sales is dropped, one can expect lesser sales, higher unit costs of production and hence lesser rents accruing to car manufacturers. However, this does not alter the basic logic of the argument.

4 Many conventions and rules to facilitate international trade and investment evolved even prior to the emergence of modern nation states in Europe (*lex mercatorum* or Law Merchant) and in the Islamic world (Pirenne, 1969; Rosenberg and Birdzell, 1986). The privately developed Law Merchant first established the legal principle of contracts between equals and equality before the law, with everyone having legal autonomy. It was the traders, and not the rulers or the legal philosophers who first established this important principle (Jacobs, 1992, pp. 38–40). The *lex mercatoria* was the result of human action, and not designed by anyone.

5 We write 'nowadays' because the option of military compulsion (gun-boat diplomacy, military incursion after trade violations or the confiscation of foreign owned assets) is ruled out.

6 Admittedly, there is a European parliament made up of elected deputies from member states, but this body has so far little influence over actual policies and no right to overrule the European Commission's rulings. Low voter participation in European elections regularly shows that the general public hold little store in the European parliament.

7 The Euro is also used by currency boards of some smaller European countries and a few African nations, which have pegged their currencies to it.

8 In reality, the issue is complicated by variable nominal interest rates and expectations about future rate movements.

12

The evolution of institutions

So far, we have considered institutions as given. Indeed, we worked on the assumption that institutions are better known and hence more effective in making human behaviour more predictable when they remain stable. But circumstances change, so that existing rules may have to be adapted as well.

We begin with some historic reminiscences to illustrate how and why institutions have changed over the long term and how collectivist and individualist philosophies have influenced the evolution of rule systems. We then observe how the internal institutions and the underlying values of a community evolve – not haphazardly, but normally along a path of gradual evolution within a system of *meta* rules that give change a measure of predictability and continuity (path dependency).

By contrast, the external institutions (set up through legislation, regulation, judicial rulings) are changed by political action, sometimes abruptly. In other instances, political action may rigidify institutions and then produce social sclerosis. Nor are the external rules always changed in the direction of greater freedom and easier wealth creation for individuals, although openness has favoured the adaptation of external institutions in that direction.

Since the mid-twentieth century, intensified international trade and worldwide factor mobility have enhanced openness (globalization) and made institutional reforms necessary. As never before, national cultures and external institutions are now exposed to competition with other cultures and institutional systems. Appropriate rule systems can form important competitive assets in attracting producers, traders and investors. Institutional competition can also take place at sub-national levels within federations when local communities and state governments rival with each other to attract investors by shaping business-friendly institutions.

Finally, we discuss the role of the constitutional principle of freedom in shaping the framework for institutional evolution. Freedom helps individuals to realize their aspirations and to discover what others want. It also hampers the political interplay of parties and pressure groups that rigidify institutions and hold up the timely evolution of the rule system.

Παντα ρει – all is in flow.

Antique Greek proverb

It is an error to imagine that evolution signifies a constant tendency to perfection. That process undoubtedly involves a constant remodelling of the organism in adaptation to new conditions; but it depends on the nature of those conditions whether the direction of those modifications shall be upward or downward.

T.H. Huxley, *The Struggle for Existence in Human Society* (1888)

Capitalists have the tendency to move towards those countries in which there is plenty of labor available and in which labor is reasonable. And by the fact that they bring capital into these countries, they bring about a trend toward higher wages.

Ludwig von Mises, *Economic Policy* (1979)

Institutions gain much of their normative power over individual behaviour from their immutability (stickiness). But when circumstances change, immutable rules may create harm and require adjustment. After all, a given institution is not an end in itself, as conservatives sometimes assert. It is only a means to pursuing fundamental values, such as freedom, security, prosperity and peace. We therefore have to explore how and why institutions change, and how predictability (order) can be safeguarded in the process.

12.1 Historic reminiscences – the long view on institutional change

The 'European miracle'

Habsburg Emperor Charles V (1500–1558), whose court bragged that the sun never set in his empire, once complained bitterly that the Jewish bankers and merchants, who had been advancing him money but were now fleeing from the Inquisition, were by this very act "pointing the crossbows at the very heart of my power". Two and a half centuries later, German poet-playwright and historian Friedrich Schiller, who was at the time considering the offer of a chair in history at the University of Jena, wrote to a friend about the university: "The governance of the Academy, because it is divided among the four Dukes of Saxony, makes this a fairly free and safe republic, in which suppression is not easy. The professors in Jena are almost independent people and need not worry about any of the Princes" (written in 1781, our translation). He referred to the fact that the university came under the joint rule of four independent princes and expected that their rivalry would ensure sufficient protection of his academic freedom.

These two apparently unrelated snippets from European history neatly bracket the great historic transition to modernity, from the medieval system of feudal rule to the emergence of values and institutions that made the industrial revolution possible. The two historic references also highlight the interrelations of political power and the inter-jurisdictional mobility of capital and gifted, enterprising people in the evolution of the institutions of capitalism.

The fundamental influence on Western Europe's social history was its geographic diversity, which favoured the emergence of small states with independent rulers, but states that played by shared underlying rules of a common civilization (Bernholz et al., (eds) 1998; Kasper, 2011b). The rulers rivalled with each other not only through war, but increasingly also through inter-jurisdictional competition to attract productive capital and skilled, knowledgeable people. One may conclude with German sociologist Erich Weede, that "European disunity has been our good luck" (Weede, 1996, p. 6). The small size and openness of the European economies, which made inter-jurisdictional factor mobility possible, created the conditions for an evolutionary process that acted in two ways:

(a) Faced with inter-jurisdictional differences in rule systems, some of the owners of capital, knowledge and enterprises decided to move to those locations where the immobile production factors – land, unskilled people, the institutional infrastructure and government administrations – promised them a good and secure rate of return, as well as security and freedom to work and live. In some cases, the primary motive was the search for religious freedom. Thus, religious repression in the Spanish Habsburg Empire, and later in France, caused Jews and Huguenots to move to domains where they enjoyed better guarantees of their religious, civil and economic liberties. In other cases, the main motive was the pursuit of economic gain. Some rulers had an interest in enhancing the tax base of their realm, thus noble lords from Norway to Bohemia and Hungary attracted settlers by guaranteeing them freedom and sometimes cheap land. Small states could not obtain sufficient revenue from taxing the peasants and the land, so that they had to rely on long-distance trade. They began to offer credible guarantees of economic and civil liberties to attract merchants and manufacturers (Jones 2003/1981; Findlay, 1992). The cultural values and the internal institutions of the various West European societies also differed (Casson, 1993). Some places, where 'commercial secondary virtues' were cultivated, offered locational advantages. Thus, a new respect for wealth creators and bourgeois leaders in the Netherlands did much to advance the local economy (McCloskey, 2010). The experience soon showed that the guarantee of property rights and individual autonomy, as well as rule-bound government, did much to attract valuable mobile resources. Civil and economic freedom also mobilized domestic economic entrepreneurship. Instead of being drawn into costly political rivalry at court, gifted people in jurisdictions with these freedoms increasingly turned to economic entrepreneurship in trade, finance and production. They often combined their property, knowledge and labour with newly attracted immigrants and incoming capital. Economic growth in enterprise-friendly jurisdictions – such as Venice, Genoa, Florence, Antwerp, Nuremberg, the Netherlands, England and Prussia – demonstrated the material rewards for rule-bound behaviour of the rulers, whereas absolutist, arbitrary monarchies that ruled over larger, more closed areas – such as Spain, Russia and Austria – began to lag behind in economic development (Weber, 1995/1927; Jones 2003/1981; Giersch, 1993). Economic entrepreneurs voted with their feet; they exited and engaged in 'locational innovation'. This caused divergences in productivity trends, innovative activity, living standards and the economic base for political power.

(b) This mobility also challenged the political system to respond and enter into political competition with other jurisdictions. Political rivalry thus set in motion processes of institutional evolution. Faced with the exit option of mobile capital and skilled people, the rulers felt constrained from taking opportunistic, arbitrary action (the control function of exit) and learnt that it paid to foster secure property rights, individual autonomy and unlicensed investment, as well as liberties in general. The rulers' purpose was of course to retain and augment their power, but the unintended by-product was that they were educated to act on behalf of the individual citizen. At the same time, the resident population learnt to adopt values, habits and customs conducive to trade and innovation. The feedback from material success or failure thus set off learning processes that reshaped the internal and external institutions. Merchants cultivated civic virtues – such as punctuality, honesty and urbane manners – and the political regime was eventually converted from feudal and, later, absolutist reign to constitutional monarchies and electoral democracies. In this long-term process, the rulers lost powers to control private pursuits, some administrations remodelled themselves into support organizations for economic development, individualism emerged, and modern capitalism became possible.

When Emperor Charles lived, the rulers of Western Europe were perceived as ruling by the grace of God, with great powers, though in theory bound by notions of Christian morality and natural law. Two and a half centuries later, when Friedrich Schiller wrote, governments were increasingly considered as subject to the forces of inter-jurisdictional competition, which limited their absolute powers. At least the leading spirits of the times expected them to respect inviolable individual spheres of freedom and other human rights.

By Schiller's time at the end of the eighteenth century, the understanding and the practice of the institutions essential to the spontaneous order of capitalism and economic growth were most advanced in Britain. There, the writers of the Scottish Enlightenment (Section 2.2, *Epilogue*) had highlighted the necessary institutional conditions for a market order after the Glorious Revolution of 1688 and its aftermath had brought growing formal recognition of individual autonomy and property rights. As we saw in the preceding Chapter, Adam Smith had a good understanding of inter-jurisdictional competition.

An offshoot of these developments in Western Europe were the Declaration of Independence (1776) and the Constitution (1787) of the newly formed United States. The people who framed these influential documents were aware of the power of the exit option, since many Americans had left England no so long ago in pursuit of greater freedom and of material opportunities. The Constitution was shaped in an explicit debate about institutions that support the pursuit of happiness. The US Constitution, with its clear statement of the legal-constitutional rules of a free society, has become an inspiration and a model for subsequent reformers in numerous countries around the world, in the first instance and – for only a brief, passing historic moment – the French Human Rights Declaration of 1789, which proposed to guarantee the citizens "Liberty, Equality (before the law) and Property". Alas, the radicalization of the French revolution soon abandoned these individualistic aspirations and spoke of '*liberté, égalité, fraternité*', the latter a woolly concept.

From individualism to collective design – from open to closed systems

The concepts of rule-bound, limited government and inalienable basic individual rights captured the people's imagination, when Schiller wrote shortly after the American and shortly before the French revolution. As his letters indicate, it was understood that inter-government rivalry was an effective way of guaranteeing these institutions. In the eighteenth century, many West European intellectuals discussed the institutions, so crucial to freedom and prosperity. Some also accepted that institutional systems could be shaped by conscious design, as the French revolution was soon to demonstrate.

Admittedly, philosophers ever since Plato (427-347BC) had speculated about utopian visions of an ideal society and its governance. But they never bothered about designing or describing in detail how such a society might actually work. The institutions were never discussed in any realistic detail. The notion of a concerted, active change in a nation's constitutional design was a novel development in the late eighteenth century. In the following century, philosophers – such as Georg Friedrich Wilhelm Hegel (1770-1838), Claude Henri de Saint Simon (1760-1825), and Karl Marx (1818-1883) – tried to design entire, collectivist ideologies of the nationalist or socialist *genre* to overturn the inherited, spontaneously-grown social order. But, again, they failed to think through the institutional details, if they bothered at all to address such mundane practicalities. They were also unaware that an infrastructure of traditional values and internal institutions (*metis*) made revolutionary change virtually impossible. When collectivist conceptions were put into practice in the twentieth century, first in the Russian Revolution (1917-1923), then by Fascist-nationalist attempts at redesigning society in Italy, Germany and, after the Second World War, in many less developed countries, the practical problems of institutional design to coordinate complex economic systems turned out to be overwhelming. It is no coincidence that these regimes tried to reduce the complexity of the economic coordination task, for example by closing the economy to international trade and investment and by reducing the number of goods that were to be produced.

Inevitably, the revolutionary overthrow of evolved institutional systems and their replacement with consciously designed rule systems is disruptive (for the catastrophic material consequences of the Russian revolution, see Section 13.1). When the inherited order is smashed up abruptly, people are disoriented; coordination of their activities becomes difficult or even ceases. In the totalitarian revolutions of the twentieth century, many internal institutions were replaced by designed, external institutions. The most spectacular experiment was arguably the Russian Revolution. The revolutionaries faced the difficult task of having to invent new institutional mechanisms to coordinate economic life, having decided to abolish private property and money, Karl Marx's writings offered them no practical guidance. In the early 1990s, the system that Lenin's Bolshevik revolutionaries had put in place 70 years earlier was again overturned, again confronting Russian society with an institutional *tabula rasa* (Section 13.1).

Collectivist orders were also designed and imposed by the fascist regimes of the 1930s and 1940s. Many of the internal institutions of civil society were suppressed by external rules to be implemented by government-controlled organizations. Although these attempts failed during the Second World War, they subsequently inspired imitators in the Third World, from Argentina to India and Indonesia, where leaders sought to engineer change by designing national ideologies and imposing a new order of their own making. To make this easier, they preached autarky and closed the economy to international trade and investment in the name of nationalism. Even many development economists of the time (as well as most international organizations) supported this approach to development (Chapter 14). As Peter Bauer critically commented in 1957, the orthodoxy of development economics relied on central planning of local markets and large influxes of official foreign aid into developing countries (Bauer, 1957). A milder form of closure was the UN-promoted fashion during the 1950s to 1980s of import substitution among the leaders of many developing countries. This sort of closure to international trade and investment suited the leaders of many developing countries who tried to revolutionize society and the economy after independence in the 1950s to 1970s.

Return to the open order

The disappointing experiences with scientifically developed rule systems, which were designed on the basis of collectivist ideologies to repress many of the traditional internal institutions and organizations of civil society, led to a better understanding of the merits of capitalism. This paved the way for renewed openness in coordinating modern economies and facilitating institutional evolution to keep pace with ongoing changes (Bauer, 2000; Bauer and Sen, 2004; Boettke et al., 2008). The new insights also focused attention on the need for interplay of internal and external institutions in maintaining a functioning socio-economic order in the face of ongoing technical, demographic, social and economic changes. Indeed, modern Austrian economics and philosophy gained great impetus from the debate of economists with the protagonists of central planning (Hayek, 1937; 1940; 1944; Mises, 1936/1922; 1994/1920; 1945; 1949; 1978); and modern philosophers such as Karl Popper were inspired in their study of individualism and collectivism by actual experiences with totalitarian collectivism and closed regimes.

The worldwide experiences with economic growth in open, market-coordinated economies since the 1960s have again demonstrated the advantages of individual autonomy, secure private property rights and the coordinative power of competitive markets, with governments concentrating on protecting that order and being cautious with discriminatory process interventions (Sections 14.4-14.5). Regimes that kept their economies closed to international trade and factor movements tended to grow more slowly. The closed economies were of course less exposed to challenges to reform their institutional set-up and gained less experience in adapting traditional institutions and self-controlling political opportunism. Nonetheless, the economic success of neighbouring countries, who had created favourable conditions to attract capital, enterprise and knowledge and who demonstrated the benefits of regulatory reform, often exerted a powerful influence on the thinking in backward nations. Demonstrated success with economic growth thus enhanced the chances of institutional reforms in laggard countries in the neighbourhood. A telling example is an episode in Malaysia in the 1970s and early 1980s, when the Malay-dominated government embarked on a major income redistribution scheme to promote the poorer Malays at the expense of the more affluent Chinese-Malaysians and foreign investors, whose autonomy and property rights the government curbed. Private investment soon stalled despite big oil-and-gas financed public spending, whereas neighbouring economies with less discriminatory regimes continued to prosper. This brought about a pragmatic reorientation of Malaysian economic policies. Discriminatory controls were mitigated or undone. Public participation in industry was cut back. Infrastructures were privatized. The Malaysian economy then resumed rapid growth (subsequently, the Mahathir administration again resumed interventionism and fostered crony capitalism). Similar cases of neighbourhood demonstration effects have spread economic liberalization to other parts of the Third World, even to communist China and later to communist, until then stagnating Vietnam. In these officially still communist countries now well over half of all output is produced by private enterprise. Similar outside influences worked on some quasi-feudal regimes in Latin America, where oligarchies ruled until major economic difficulties of the 1980s and 1990s, although some later relapsed into nationalist-feudalist denial. As a result of such inter-jurisdictional competition, reforms to move the external institutions in the direction of capitalism became a world-wide phenomenon (Scobie and Lim, 1992; Sachs and Warner, 1995; Gwartney and Lawson, *passim*). We shall return to this topic in Chapters 13 and 14.

Globalization: changing the political game

By the beginning of the twenty-first century, globalization had brought a fundamental change to the political-institutional game plan of most nations (Chapter 11). By now, smaller cost differentials suffice to trigger locational arbitrage by private agents. More and more businesses are aware of conditions in different countries and are ready to move internationally, so that the responses to institutional changes and the feedbacks into national policies have become more immediate. Inter-jurisdictional differences are therefore less likely to persist. Institutions, which influence business transaction costs whose share in total costs is growing, are now subject to institutional competition amongst nations. However, the 'global financial crisis' (starting in 2007) and concerns about global warming have encouraged the political elites of many countries to reassert themselves and reclaim the 'primacy of politics'. This has produced new interventions with individual autonomy and private property rights; and it poses a new danger to economic freedom (Section 14.2). The conflict between national political control and globalization is likely to become sharper.

Globalization is of course often resented by those who are used to unquestioned political power and political preferment. In countries that are losing competitive position and are facing a net outflow of mobile capital, people and enterprises, this is perceived as an affront and a reason to doubt the merits of economic openness. Powerbrokers then argue that employment needs to be defended against cheap foreign competitors and that globalization lowers the chances for holding on to highly-skilled jobs (de-skilling). Defensive rhetoric then serves to postpone actions to address the challenges of openness. In the European Union, for example, agriculture is protected to the detriment of European consumers and non-European producers. Efficient export-oriented agricultural producers in the Third World, who would benefit from free trade in foodstuffs and fibres, are ignored. This protectionism encourages Third World governments to maintain their own tariffs and quotas on imported manufactures and to prevent foreign investment in service industries. The futile Doha Round of trade liberalization has demonstrated to what extent rent-seekers and rent-creators are still prepared to impede foreign competition and flout the principle of non-discrimination. However, if history is any guide, the likelihood of an outside challenge to domestic institutions will increase, as will the likelihood of disruptive, less evolutionary institutional adjustments (Giersch, 1993, pp. 121–134).

Despite such political resistance, globalization has – in recent decades and on the whole – been a major force in driving the evolution of national institutions in the direction of less political interference (Section 14.3). Civic, political and economic freedom has been improved by creative entrepreneurs in politics, government administrations and industry associations, who have emulated growth-promoting rules elsewhere. A big factor has probably also been the memory of the 1930s, when spreading political interference was the key to deepening the 1930s recession into the Great Depression, then extending it and, ultimately, leading to the calamity of global war. This gave rise to the principle of non-discrimination amongst nations, enshrined in the 'most-favoured nation clause' (MFN clause) in the General Agreement on Tariffs and Trade (GATT) and now in the World Trade Organization (WTO) (Section 11.3).

It was equally important that, soon after the Second World War, economic success in the wake of liberalization under the auspices of the Organisation for European Economic Cooperation (OEEC) encouraged reformers to abandon discriminatory policies. An important role was played by the US Marshall Plan, because it obliged the victors and the vanquished of post-war Western Europe to gradually introduce free trade under the auspices of the newly founded OEEC. The moves towards free trade and a freer flow of people and capital, which the OEEC (later OECD) spearheaded, as well as the adoption of market-conforming policies became the major factors in averting collectivist policies in post-war Europe.[1] Since then, the option of easier exit has done much to improve the economic and other institutions and to benefit freedom and prosperity, not only in the developed West, but also around the world.

New media, in particular the Internet, have greatly increased the flow of information and thus opened national cultures and jurisdictions further. Usual cognitive limits to learning about alternative conditions and institutions are thereby more easily overcome. The literature discusses the role of media and the Internet as mechanisms to either change or reinforce existing institutional structures. US researchers Christopher Coyne and Peter Leeson have, for example, documented the effect of the traditional and the new media in helping to change the institutional structures in Poland. After decades of government control of the media and constrained free speech, an underground press emerged in the 1970s, which communicated the truth. Its popularity sparked an entire media network and eventually helped to foster institutional change from within. Coyne and Leeson explain that the media "created common knowledge around alternative ideas and communicated planned and actual acts of dissent. For example, the underground media played an important role in coordinating worker strikes orchestrated by the Solidarity dissident movement" (Coyne and Leeson 2009, p. 11).

12.2 Internal institutions: evolution within cultural values and *meta* rules

Spontaneous self-organization: internal institutions

The internal institutions of society evolve in the light of chance and experience within certain higher-level rules, which ensure a degree of inter-temporal consistency and continuity (*metis*): What works well for individuals and organizations is adopted and emulated by others, what does not is discontinued. This is a process of pragmatic, decentralized trial and error as people try to cope with their ignorance about the many side effects on complex social interaction when the rules are changed (Parker and Stacey, 1995). The process of experimentation, selection and adjustment is informed by the knowledge, wisdom and rationality of the many, as far as this can be called 'rational', given the inescapable limits of human knowledge. Internal institutions, such as conventions, work habits and customs, have an automatic problem-solving, coordinative capability even if the specific circumstance might suggest otherwise: People stick unthinkingly to the rules and others rely on this fact. Only if experience shows repeatedly that the old customs and conventions yield poor results and cause people to miss opportunities, will the pressure of expediency induce people to adapt their internal institutions.

In Section 5.2 we touched briefly on the process of how internal institutions evolve by innovation and variation, by acceptance and rejection (selection), with some gaining critical mass, so that they become accepted new community standards with normative effect. This evolutionary and pragmatic view of institutions differs from the conservative stance that invariably defends the known, old rules for their own sake.[2]

Acceptance or rejection of internal institutions is normally informal, as they are not *rigidly* enforced (soft institutions). Consequently, internal institutions offer scope for further experimentation and evolutionary change. In certain circumstances some players will violate established customs and conventions. They accept the risk of sanctions because they feel that breaking the rule nonetheless confers advantages. In case they are proven wrong, they will soon return to rule compliance; in case they are right, others will sooner or later also see an advantage and imitate the new pattern of behaviour. If sufficient numbers emulate this, a critical mass will develop so that eventually a new internal institution becomes established.

Decentralized experimentation with tentative breaches of established internal institutions form a large part of cultural evolution. Thus, internal rules defining what constitutes acceptable behaviour are occasionally violated, either in word or deed. For example, someone found it too pompous to end letters with the formula 'your obedient servant' and replaced it by 'yours sincerely', and someone else changed the greeting 'good morning' to 'hi'. This may have attracted the conservative response of (slight) social disapproval, but then the new convention spread (Bush, 1987).[3]

Another example of evolutionary change of the internal rules has been observed in the new industrial countries of East Asia (Hofstede and Bond, 1988). In the bitter post-war conditions and the new world-competitive atmosphere of the 1950s and 1960s, the population began to emphasize future-oriented values and de-emphasize the traditional Confucian rules of hierarchical submission. This proved to be widely advantageous. The East Asian market economies were increasingly exposed to world-market influences, which ensured that some who broke the traditional rules were materially successful. Gradually, the accepted internal institutions changed across the board, at a time when most people were desperate for material success. This process often created personal conflict, some confusion and mal-coordination, though much less than the pervasive disruptions of the social order during the communist revolutions in China and Vietnam, which were brutally enforced from above in the name of modernization. In the final analysis, the capitalist East-Asian societies adjusted their internal rule systems and turned their modified (neo-Confucian) rules into an asset in international competitiveness (Section 14.4).

Thus, institutional evolution is propelled by those 'million little mutinies' and the evaluation of these little mutinies by numerous other people. In the process, much considered wisdom is incorporated into the institutional system.

Inertia: path dependency

Normally, a community's shared fundamental value system and its *meta* rules are reasonably stable. This stickiness makes for steady institutional evolution and path dependency. After all, new institutions impose learning and adjustment costs and may lead to mal-coordination in the transition phase, which is the conservative argument for sticking with tradition. New rules therefore often fail to obtain the critical mass of voluntary followers to make them sufficiently accepted throughout the community. The acceptance of new rules is often also hindered by fears that these innovations may clash with other rules. Traditional rule systems contain many complementarities, which have grown out of long experience and which make for cohesive networks. People have adjusted their complex interactions to make the best use of the prevailing rules. The dictum that 'old rules are good rules' has considerable weight, as widespread, quasi-automatic rule compliance reduces coordination costs. Consequently, there is path dependency in institutional change, also because institutional systems rest to a considerable measure on fundamental cultural values (Boettke, 2001; Boettke et al., 2008). Evolutionary adjustments, rather than convulsive, revolutionary shifts, are the norm. This is essential for the continuing, information-economizing function of institutions.

In situations, where communities fail to attain their fundamental values by big margins, because the rule system is totally out of sync with new conditions (as in post-war East Asia), fairly rapid institutional change may occur, once the old rules are widely recognized as the cause of poor performance. The disruptions of wars and the PRC's threats of invasion in smaller East-Asian countries created conditions in which a critical mass for new rule interpretations was quickly reached. The new export orientation and the information revolution ensured that adherence to new rules produced palpable material success in these societies (Tu, 1996). Yet, despite the pervasive cultural revolution in the new industrial countries of East Asia, it is amazing how continuous the adherence to traditional values and rules has nevertheless been. No one would confuse present-day Taiwanese or Hong Kong society with European or American society despite shared technologies and the same trappings of the global consumer society. What is evolving is a multiplicity of 'modernities' (Eisenstadt, 2000; Tu, 2000). In many instances, the lower-level norms were adjusted, but within a framework of time-tested higher-level rules and values. Where totalitarian attempts at changing the rule system by external intervention were made, as in the People's Republic of China, Vietnam and Cambodia, the results were extremely painful for the population, until many of the old rules were eventually re-instituted (Sections 13.2 and 14.4). These countries then followed a more predictable path which would have flabbergasted the earlier revolutionaries.

Institutional evolution

The emergence of internal institutions and their evolutionary changes are driven by dispersed, entrepreneurial discoveries. Because the sanctions are often soft, as we said, some people gamble readily on experimenting with moving outside the accepted rules. They may hope that they will be able to explain their violations to those affected and to obtain acceptance or at least toleration for their experiments. Thus, sons and daughters of a certain age tend to violate the family's institutions, for example regarding obedience to parental authority. The young may explain to parents why they broke a certain rule and may be met with empathy and understanding. But such experimentation is of course not conflict-free. However, the conflicts tend to be sorted out at the decentralized, personal level.

How internal institutions are adapted also often makes the difference between successful and failing multicultural societies. Where – as is the case in the United States, Canada and Australia – the implicit knowledge and the embodied rules of various immigrant cultures merge or are adjusted to form a new, more or less shared institution set, creative cultural cross-fertilization is triggered and new knowledge is put to constructive use. But where the host society rigidly defends pre-existing implicit institutions and where immigrant groups persevere obstinately with their own traditional institutions (think of Muslim groups in Europe), integration is difficult and costly social conflicts arise (Sowell, 1994, 1996, 1998).

Which challenges to internal rules are readily accepted or widely rejected, depends in part on how experimental variations relate to people's fundamental values (their *metis*). We saw in Chapter 4 that these values inform the institutions and are overriding priorities in deciding which institutional arrangements are adopted. As these values are deeply held, they underpin continuity and cohesiveness in the evolution of internal institutions. Communities that share a high degree of clear and common understanding of fundamental values manage a more predictable, orderly evolution of their institutions than societies whose members share few values. Shared values thus serve as a filter and as the cohesive cement for the evolving internal rules of society (Bush, 1987; Gerken, (ed.) 1995).

Some internal *meta* rules: tolerance, humour and free speech

Given the importance of cultural change to the continued wellbeing of a community that is faced with changing circumstances, the decentralized processes of testing and re-evaluating customs and habits deserve protection. Informal internal *meta* rules that enhance the evolutionary capacity of internal rule systems are important here, for example a measure of tolerance of individual experimentation, the rule that conflicts can be eased by a sense of humour, a friendly disposition towards strangers, and a commitment to free speech. Societies, which are too narrow-minded to tolerate experimentation and are doctrinaire in rejecting any deviations from established internal rules, tend to lose out when material or technical conditions change. As Hayek (1944 [2007], p. 245) noted, "Conservatism, though a necessary element in any stable society, is not a social programme; in its paternalistic, nationalistic, and power-adoring tendencies it is often closer to socialism than true liberalism". The static nature of conservatism prevents innovations and change both in markets and cultural settings.

When conflicts arise and internal institutions fail to handle them, the practice of a humorous escape may serve as a safety valve; it is a way of economizing on interpersonal transaction costs. Another *meta* rule in an evolving system of internal institutions, which can reduce conflict and transaction costs, is the rule that one should depersonalize the argument, play the ball and not the man. In a society, in which factual debate typically overrules *ad hominem* vilification, there is more likelihood of peaceful, problem-oriented evolution than in a society where personal slurs are applauded.

Societies, in which the free expression of one's ideas is considered a punishable crime, forego the rather cost-free exploration of alternatives by discourse. Open discourse – including the expression of outrageous deviant opinions – is a useful part of how communities cope with change. An open discussion of alternative solutions costs fewer resources than either trial and error by implementing, maybe later rejecting institutions, or by settling simmering conflicts by force and repression. Free discussion and the virtue of listening to dissidents is a means of keeping the process of cultural evolution open to all members of the community and hence open to all available experience, knowledge and wisdom. The institution of free speech fits in with the 'commercial entrepreneurial syndrome', discussed in Section 5.5, as it is a major engine of non-violent institutional evolution. It deserves to be protected.

12.3 Changing the external institutions: political entrepreneurship

Political action – rigidity, convulsion and orderly adjustment

External institutions are designed and enforced by political authorities from the top down on the basis of constitutions. Changes in the external institutions therefore require political action. External rule changes depend on collective decisions, which are more difficult to bring about than gradual, organic voluntary decisions, as noted in Section 10.1. External rules may therefore sometimes be rather rigid, even in the face of changed circumstances. When they are made, the adjustments occur sometimes in convulsive steps. They are inevitably caught in a fundamental conflict between the maxim of predictability embodied in existing institutions and the need to cope flexibly with changing circumstances, including changing internal institutions. This may lead to inconsistencies in the rule system. The conflict is exacerbated by the fact that changes in external institutions often affect the distribution of incomes and economic opportunities. It touches on the very foundations of institutional arrangements. After all, institutions are like good wine: They improve with age, at least for some time! But sometimes they have to be changed, even if this disrupts the smooth coordination of human actions.

When external institutions are adapted to address changed circumstances, this is normally more disruptive, as this may clash with political opportunism. Unfortunately, modern mass democracies with changing coalitions of political parties, organized interest groups and a commitment to social welfare generate much opportunistic, often ephemeral legislation that caters to organized interests. This often creates conflicts with the internal rule system. In other cases, political opportunism may produce institutional rigidity and sclerosis, as vested interests defend the existing rules against adjustment, even if this would be advantageous for the community as a whole. Indeed, external institutions can become so rigid that they prejudice material progress and frustrate other fundamental human aspirations. Numerous historic experiences bear witness to this: The Byzantine Empire, for example, was unable to adjust its institutions of governance to rise to the Turkish challenge. The China of the Ming and Ching dynasties rigidified its external institutions in the face of growing outside challenges. The many autocracies of North Africa and the Middle East clung to rigid controls that hindered economic enterprise and job creation for a generation or more, until revolutionary uprisings in 2011 broke out. The same applies to big corporations and associations, such as the Pan American airline or the British coalminers' union during the 1980s; they rigidly adhered to time-tested rules which had gone beyond their use-by date and eventually went out of business. Big businesses which suffer from the ossification of the rules that govern them may have the means to resist reforms, but free market competition eventually sends them into bankruptcy.

If powerbrokers are able to resist necessary reforms of external institutions, they eventually cause material decline and conflict. In other instances, outside challenges trigger timely reforms of the external institutions and help to rejuvenate a jurisdiction's institutional capital. This has been a major consequence of globalization, as discussed.

Overcoming external institutional constraints

Various agents are part of the processes by which external institutions are adjusted:

(a) Business firms, led by entrepreneurs or teams of enterprising individuals, and persons normally pursuing their self-set objectives within given and accepted constraints, be they of a technical, economic, or institutional nature. The normal mode of behaviour is to pursue self-set objectives within these constraints to the maximum (end-means rationality), another is to adjust one's objectives in the light of past experience (adaptive, bounded rationality), even if existing constraints have disadvantages. The constraints are nevertheless accepted, as altering them is perceived to be too costly, if not impossible.

(b) Another course of action is to tackle the constraints head-on to overcome them in creative, entrepreneurial ways. Once constraints are recognized as a hindrance, entrepreneurial creativity may lead to overcoming them. Firms may organize cheaper or new factor supplies, save costs through process innovation, streamline the organization, innovate products, or move to a new, more competitive location. In all these cases, the creative effort aims at innovation in the sense of a 'new factor combination' as defined by Joseph Schumpeter (Schumpeter, 1961/1908). The same entrepreneurial creativity may also be directed against costly institutional constraints, once these are recognized as obstacles to success. Individuals and firms may, on occasion, refuse to accept existing institutions, challenge them head-on, either in court or by disobedience, even risking punishment. Technical innovations may sometimes require such institutional innovations. For example, new forms of production, transport, communication and consumption may necessitate adjustments in the definition of property rights or in business and work practices. Thus, the railway construction boom of the nineteenth century not only ushered in many technical changes, but also new institutions governing share and bond markets (Rosenberg and Birdzell, 1986; Gerken, (ed.) 1995).

So far, the process is essentially identical for internal and external institutions.

(c) When external institutions are to be altered, individuals and firms have to become involved in political processes by raising their 'voice'. They may try to exert direct influence on policy makers, but this is relatively rare in modern mass societies, because the fixed costs of such action are high. For many citizens, it remains rational to ignore or tolerate existing external institutions. However, where the costs imposed by existing external institutions are sufficient to be perceived as important, people may organize themselves to make their political voice heard. In most modern societies, political constitutions are meant to facilitate orderly external rule changes by offering formal channels of change, such as legal challenges and parliamentary votes. If political operators recognize the signals and interpret them correctly, the laws are changed by elected legislatures within the general, higher-level constitutional framework and are subject to possible judicial review. In many countries, the judiciary has become another agency for changing the rules, if judges interpret the law in innovative ways.

(d) The mechanisms for changing the external institutions are populated by political agents, who of course pursue their own objectives and who are subject to the usual cognitive limitations (Downs, 1957a; 1957b; Bernholz, 1966; Buchanan et al., 1980). The political entrepreneurs, who set out to break with the established rules, may be politicians, bureaucrats and leaders of private associations and clubs, such as industry organizations, trade unions and other special-interest lobbies. They promise to reform existing external institutions in exchange for political support, payments and other rewards. They act as middlemen, who have insider knowledge of the political process, of personalities and of relevant organizations. Such political entrepreneurs drive a large part of the process of public policy in modern states. They of course act out of their personal interest when they propose to reform or conserve certain external rules, reflecting their own personal aspirations. The thrust of their actions may often go in the direction of more reliance on collective mechanisms and less towards empowering the spontaneous self-organization of civil society. In parliamentary democracies, political entrepreneurs will try to convince others and seek allies in exchange for support for other political deals (political trade-offs, log rolling).

Private acceptance and legitimacy

Not all innovations to the external rule system are in the interest of private citizens. It is, for example, possible that political operators get it wrong and institute rules which later turn out to damage wealth creation. Political motivations ever so often lead to rule changes that complicate the effective economic coordination by private businesses and individuals. If the system is open and the various political agents are on the alert for growth opportunities, errors will be corrected and obstacles to economic growth removed proactively, that is, before outside challenges force renewed rule changes. However, this is often not the case.

If the proposed change of an external rule is to be adopted in a parliamentary democracy, the change has in the first place to be privately accepted by sufficient numbers of people and private organizations, either because they expect benefits from it or they tolerate the change as the negative impacts are imperceptible. The acceptance of a rule does, by itself, of course not guarantee that this rule is conducive to economic growth. Thus, tariff protection may be retained with popular consent, if it is perceived to confer benefits on a sufficient number of members of the community and its negative impacts are imperceptible. This happens when the beneficiaries of protection (the capital owners and the workers in protected industries) are well organized and united and those disadvantaged by the consequences of protection remain rationally ignorant. The tariff will then stay in place. Rent seeking and the impairment of the catallactic capability of the economy continue. If reforms in the external rules are wanted, the citizens and firms have first to see the merits of reform and accept the necessary changes.

If external institutions are to be changed to enhance the capacity of market participants to generate prosperity, they have to become more universal, that is, less discriminatory. As we saw when discussing rent seeking in Chapter 8, political operators are often motivated to create rents, rather than to reform the external institutions to curb rent seeking.

As information about the potential for economic growth is nowadays easily spread around the globe, a poor economic track record will probably induce political entrepreneurs, sooner or later, to again seek political advantage in reforming the external institutions. Political entrepreneurs, possibly of a new generation or from a new political grouping, will then see a chance to gain political support by promoting reforms that break the cycle of stagnation and institutional rigidity. They may even seek to forge political majorities for comprehensive constitutional change. Entrenched interest groups and self-seeking parliamentarians and bureaucrats, who trust they can rely on a disinterested public, may nevertheless repeatedly defeat such reform initiatives. This then reinforces the sclerosis and relative economic decline. Resistance to reform may trigger widespread cynicism, if not political and sectarian conflict, which undermines prosperity further and then hinders the evolution of rules that ensure non-discrimination and openness.

Sooner or later, communities with political recalcitrance and a poor economic performance will be confronted by another type of agent of institutional change: outside challengers, leaders of foreign polities who have the potential to intervene politically or militarily to take advantage of the apparent economic weakness of the community in question. They may threaten or actually use force to have their way. One possibility then is that the outside challenger imposes new external institutions. Examples are the take-over of a country by a colonial power and the imposition of the victors' will after a lost war. This was the case in Germany or Japan after the Second World War, when the establishment of a democracy and a market economy was in the vital interest of the United States, once the Cold War began. Such outside intervention simply disbands the entrenched rent-seeking coalitions (Olson, 1982, pp. 76–80; 130–131; Bush, 1987; Olson, 1993; Lal, 2004). Another possibility is for the outside challenger to become an active player in the internal political process, initiating reforms, but adhering to existing constitutional arrangements. This is, for example, the case when international bodies such as the International Monetary Fund, the World Bank and the Brussels EU authorities intervene in debtor countries, when foreign agricultural exporters lobby the European Union to abandon its agricultural protectionism, or when governments direct pressure on other governments to reduce trade barriers. Such outside challenges (or even threats thereof) depend to a considerable extent on a country's already existing openness to foreign trade, ideas and factor flows. The more open an economy, the more likely it is that the government and interest groups have to yield to such outside pressures.

12.4 Outside challenges: institutional competition

Inertia and change

The evolution of internal and external institutions is driven not only by passive responses to international trade and factor flows. They may also proactively reform the institutions to enhance competitiveness in international trade and attractiveness to internationally mobile production factors. Globalization and especially the information technology revolution have made 'institutional (or systems) competition' more visible and more intense. Institutional conditions now influence cost levels to such an extent that they are important elements in international competition. Consequently, government officials increasingly realize that they are competing directly with officials in other countries.

Although globalization is now giving real bite to international institutional competition, the concept is not new. Unsurprisingly, Adam Smith already referred to the basic interplay between mobile and immobile production factors and the evolutionary effect of factor mobility in his *Wealth of Nations* in 1776, when he wrote about expected reactions to differences in the taxation of capital:

> land is a subject which cannot be removed; whereas stock easily may . . . The proprietor of stock is properly a citizen of the world, and is not necessarily attached to any particular country. He would be apt to abandon the country in which he was exposed to vexatious inquisition, in order to be assessed to a burdensome tax, and would remove his stock to some other country where he could either carry on his business, or enjoy his fortune more at ease. By removing his stock, he would put an end to all the industry, which it had maintained in the country which he left. Stock cultivates land; stock employs labour. A tax which tended to drive away stock from any particular country, would so far tend to dry up every source of revenue, both to the sovereign and to the society. Not only the profit of the stock, but the rent of the land, and the wages of labour, would necessarily be more or less diminished by its removal (Smith, 1976/1776, vol. 2, pp. 330–331).

One of the first social scientists last century to describe the relevance of institutional evolution was Max Weber (1978/1921; 1995/1927).[4] More recently these same issues have been analysed by Douglass North (North and Thomas, 1973, 1977; North 1981, 1993), Eric Jones (2003/1981; 1988; 1994), Nathan Rosenberg and L.E. Birdzell (1986), Richard Roll and John Talbott (2003), among others. They showed that openness to international factor flows has two combined effects:

(i)   Poor institutions lead to a poor trade performance and outflows of mobile capital and firms.
(ii)   These phenomena trigger corrective political action to reform the external institutions (as well as changing cultural norms and internal institutions).

For this to happen, political elites must recognize the link between institutional quality and economic performance.

Openness can thus be a powerful antidote to political rent seeking. An instructive historic case was the opening up of Japan by the American naval intervention in 1854, which led to the overturn of the hidebound *shogunate* in 1867 and paved the way for modernization in the 'Meiji Revival'. The institutional transformation was not without conflict, although many internal institutions of Japanese society offered those Velcro surfaces on which the capitalist regime could bond (Powelson, 1994). Nonetheless, the reformed capitalist institutions were far from deeply entrenched. In the 1930s and early 1940s, the Japanese fell prey to aggressive power groups, who preached economic isolationism. Renewed American intervention after 1945 opened Japan up a second time, which again triggered pervasive institutional reforms, as well as unexpected prosperity.

Openness has, however, not been a one-way street in history. Lower transport, communications and transaction costs have served as a powerful incentive to incur information costs about alternative rule systems, and place a premium on universal rules such as a straightforward private property system.[5]

Globalization and growing openness notwithstanding, prosperity-promoting reforms of economic institutions are often held up or overturned by entrenched political and economic elites, which Italian economist-sociologist Vilfredo Pareto termed the 'Iron Law of Oligarchy' (Pareto 2009/1901, also Acemoğlu and Robinson, 2008, pp. 19–23, Acemoğlu and Robinson, 2012). Entrenched socio-economic groups often persist with rent seeking, closing off international influences and suppressing reform-ist groups. This is particularly frequent where educational standards are poor and civil society has no tradition of autonomy. One only has to look at post-colonial Africa, the fluctuating reform record in Latin America and the backsliding on economic freedom in post-communist states (Chapters 13 and 14). Institutional evolution thus is rarely linear and not necessarily in the direction of more economic growth. The dictum that 'freedom requires eternal vigilance' may be extended to saying that 'economic freedom and openness require knowledge, eternal alertness and vigilance'.

The reform of external economic and political institutions normally depends on the presence of reform-supporting internal institutions. US economists Daren Acemoğlu and James Robinson have speculated that previously thinly populated settler countries with a moderate climate favoured growth-enhancing economic reforms (for example Acemoğlu and Robinson, 2008) without sufficiently acknowledging the obvious fact that institutional and economic development in immigration countries, such as the United States, Canada, Australia and New Zealand, owes almost everything to the imported British institution set, which lent itself to evolution (Kasper, 2011a). It is not surprising that countries, where the share of European immigrants in the population is small and the legal system is prescriptive and interventionist, post-colonial external institutions often deteriorated under the influence of tribalism, rent seeking and corruption.

Figure 12.1 summarizes the interactions of economic and political processes when institutional systems are exposed to international competition. As it is now easier for traders and the owners of mobile production factors to opt out and move into more favourable institutional systems, the public and policy makers are more and more likely to take alternative institutional conditions in different countries into account when they initiate reform policies. Thus, corporate tax rates are now being set less and less with a view to maximize the national tax intake or to redistribute income, and more and more in response to capital outflows to low-tax environments.

When owners relocate their internationally mobile factors across borders, they inevitably make a choice between institutional systems. This choice may even motivate them, as they expect differences in profitability to result from differences in the institutions of other countries. This makes it necessary for them to recognize and properly interpret the effects of differing institu-tions, a task that is now made easier by numerous expert consultants and the advertising of good institutional systems by governments keen on attracting mobile firms and capital. Institutional choice has thus become an option in

Figure 12.1 Institutional competition: basic interactions of economic and political processes

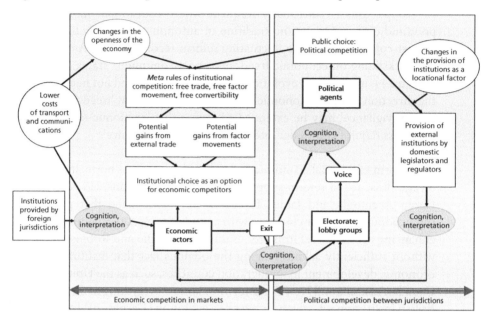

economic competition. Increasingly, economic agents therefore make locational choices, individually exercising the exit option.

Economic exits send signals to those engaged in the political process, either the wider electorate and organized interest groups or directly the political agents. It is, however, not certain that these signals are always properly recognized and correctly interpreted. Political agents in sclerotic jurisdictions, who have no experience of responding entrepreneurially to change and who are self-centred, may have neither the ability to adjust nor indeed the will to read the signals. Nor may vested interest groups and the electorate at large recognize the need for change (Figure 12.1). Their vote (voice) will only have effect if a sufficiently large group is convinced. Voting may or may not favour institutional adjustment, depending on how vocal rent-seeking groups influence voters and whether a tribal guardian mentality prevails. As noted above, parliamentarians and bureaucrats in alliance with rent-seeking lobbies are therefore often able to entrench discriminatory external rules, obstruct openness and hinder the evolution of competition-supporting rules. In most countries and for most of the time, this has indeed been the normal state of affairs in governance. Spreading freedom and the impacts of globalization are, for most nations, still a novel experience, made only over the past one or two generations (Gwartney and Lawson, *passim*). It is therefore not surprising that tribal xenophobic instincts often still dominate political life in the face of economic exit options.

Resistance to outside change may even lead to political lobbying on the international stage against inter-jurisdictional competition. Thus, the European Union appears to be promoting costly climate-change policies to hinder the competitiveness of emerging industrial countries. The trend towards transnational world government (Section 11.3) seems a political attempt to outflank the globalization of markets and the resulting empowerment of mobile businesses and individuals.

Only when majorities of voters support reforms despite interest-group resistance, or when organized groups discover merit in openness, will institutional reform begin. If it does, governments begin to compete with other governments. Thus, the health and safety regulators in one jurisdiction, for example, discover that they directly compete with their counterparts in others (inter-jurisdictional competition). Much therefore depends on the capacity of government officials and the public to recognize the importance of the exit signals and to draw from them the conclusions that they must implement reforms, which constitute an attractive locational factor. They must face up to pressure group resistance and their own inward-looking, atavistic-tribalist instincts.

We will put further substance to the complex interactions depicted in Figure 12.1 when we discuss the transformation of economic systems and the institutional reform of mixed economies in Chapters 13 and 14.

KEY CONCEPTS

Institutional competition (or 'systems competition') is a term that highlights the importance of internal and external rule sets to national cost levels and hence international competitiveness and attractiveness. Globalization – greater information flows, intensified trade and greater factor mobility – now causes more immediate and clearer feedback to those in high-cost institutional systems. This often overcomes cognitive limits on the part of politicians and the public about the need to reform those systems.

Political entrepreneurs are people and agencies who seek political advantage from implementing or hindering institutional change. Political entrepreneurs are often 'Young Turks' who see that existing institutions and power structures prevent them from gaining political influence and who therefore enroll support to gain more voice for a platform of institutional reform.

Institutional competition: economic, industrial and political-administrative creativity

Institutional competition mobilizes discovery and creative responses in several areas of human pursuit:

(a) Technical and organizational changes and the opening of national economies to the world have made it possible for competitors to engage in international locational innovation, mobilizing technical, organizational and economic creativity.

(b) The mobility of factors and freer trade in goods and services exerts a disciplining control on local institutions, both the internal practices and conventions, and the shaping and implementation of external institutions, as discussed. This contributes to control opportunistic political agents and triggers the search for better institutional arrangements. Over time, openness thus delivers feedback into the evolution of internal and external institutions, stimulating ongoing discoveries:

- It promotes entrepreneurship in industry associations and other groups of civil society who work to discover and test improved business standards, work practices, enforcement procedures and the like to expedite productivity growth.
- It alerts political-administrative and judicial operators that they should expedite productivity growth and enhance competitiveness.

American economist Paul Krugman attacked the notion that nations compete, because countries do not compete with each other as corporations do (Krugman, 2007). True. However, like other neoclassical economists, who habitually ignore institutions and transaction costs, Krugman was blind to the supply of a collectively produced production factor, namely institutional capital. Governments do compete with each other in setting tax rates, regulating business and fostering the expedient enforcement of the rules. Most of the economic reforms of recent decades have been driven by such competition among governments and communities for internationally mobile capital and enterprise (Kasper, 1994).

CH 12 – CASE ONE

Cutting a clearing in the regulatory jungle: charter cities

Although there are numerous historic precedents, a novel organizational concept has in recent years been promoted by US economist Paul Romer: the creation of 'charter cities' with growth-friendly institutions. One inspiration for the concept comes from the Renaissance-era trading cities of Europe, for example Venice in Italy or Nuremberg, Lübeck and other cities free from local feudal overlordship in Germany (Section 12.1). These cities were essentially

CH 12 – CASE ONE *(continued)*

governed by merchant oligarchies, who gave themselves their own rules to facilitate wealth creation. Another inspiration is the experience of many buoyant export-processing (or free-enterprise) zones in East Asia and elsewhere. Here, most of the cumbersome, wealth-destroying external institutions – including on foreign trade and investment, as well as restrictive labour laws – were suspended. So to speak, this was a way of cutting a clearing in a dense regulatory and custom-encrusted institutional jungle and making a new beginning with expedient rules, which allowed economic growth to sprout (usually with a dose of corruption and political rent-creation). In addition, host governments normally made cheap land available, often with convenient infrastructures in place (also see Box 14.1 in Section 14.4).

Particularly powerful examples have been the Special Economic Zones (SEZ) of China. Local governments (under the umbrella of provincial and the national governments) provided business- and development-friends institutions, (relatively) reliable public administration and new transport infrastructures. The most notable SEZ, Shenzhen at the end of the subway line from Hong Kong, was founded with the encouragement of Chinese reformist leader Deng Xiaoping in 1979 on land with a few farm and fishing hamlets. By 1982, already 350,000 inhabitants were engaged in labour-intensive manufacturing; by 2010, over 10 million people generated advanced technology and service products, enjoying individual freedoms rare elsewhere in the PRC. They had a per-capita income of US$14,615, that is, an income level comparable to Mexico or Chile.

The free-trade areas and SEZs have been laboratories in institutional reform and schools in which foreign investors and local administrators and workers learn to cooperate effectively. Their success convinced not only political leaders to reform traditional rules, but also the wider population to embrace a creative mentality and collaborative culture. In many instances, the rules that were tested there have been extended over wider and wider areas of the national territory.

The basic concept of a charter city is (i) for a host country to excise a piece of land from its national territory and free it from most of its detailed legislation and regulations, (ii) to create an autonomous board of governor-managers who shape and reliably enforce new and stable rules, and (iii) to attract outside investors who benefit from this institution set to create wealth. The governors and managers can be national figures, as in the case of China's SEZs, or may be foreign experts or organizations.

Source: http://www.chartercities.org/concept/, accessed 24 November 2011.

12.5 Competitive federalism

Trade and factor mobility within countries

Within a nation, federal-state constitutions can be designed to capture some of the advantages of inter-jurisdictional competition. Federalism is a way to distribute political power, encourage mutual control and exploit the rivalry among (State and local) governments in the interest of discovering new, useful administrative solutions and offering firms and individuals a diversity of institutional environments.

If people and producers have the opportunity to move between States, the State legislators and administrators are compelled to compete. The exit option gives them feedback from the citizen-principal.[6] When public policy is less concentrated in the hands of the centralized government, there is a better chance that rent seeking, pressure groups and agent opportunism can be controlled.

Subsidiarity

From the viewpoint of citizens and firms there is advantage in the principle of subsidiarity, the concept that each political task should always be assigned to the lowest-possible level of government, indeed that governments should only get involved when individuals cannot fend for themselves. Numerous tasks of governance can thus be decentralized and carried out by competing authorities. Competing State and local governments may, for example, raise their own finance, regulate the provision of public welfare, maintain local infrastructures and deliver the bulk of education and health services. In certain cases, there are of course advantages in centralizing government tasks, for example when common institutions, such as uniform commercial codes and road rules allow savings in transaction costs, or when there are advantages of scale and scope, such as in military defence. Because institutional evolution and the discovery of new administrative solutions can benefit from experiments by competing States or local governments, the normative principle of subsidiarity should be turned into a high-level constitutional principle. Exemptions should be made only when they can be explicitly justified.

Proponents of centralized government frequently object to subsidiarity with the argument that a strong central authority is necessary to secure national cohesion and unity by promoting equal income and employment opportunities and equal outcomes across the various regions and provinces. They also say that central government must guarantee the uniform provision with public goods to all citizens, irrespective of where they live and what politicians they have voted into office. However, the worldwide record of equalizing regional policy is hardly more convincing than the record of social welfare equalization (Section 10.4). It, too, weakens spontaneous, self-correcting responses to regional income differentials. Ailing regions that have easy access to central government aid may refuse to offer lower wage levels, which would attract new investors, or resist putting their fiscal affairs in good order. Besides, the uniform, centralized provision of public goods may go against differing regional preferences and priorities. Because public policy makers are more remote from the citizens, centralization also fosters agent opportunism in government, as well as moral hazard on the part of the voting public. Federal diversity in policy making allows voter choices. The style of governance can then make a difference to the provision of public goods. In this case, the citizens will take more interest in cultivating local and regional economic development.

To give content and substance to the principle of subsidiarity, competitive federal systems should adopt four general institutional devices (Bish, 1987; Kasper, 1995, 1996a):

(a) Federations should adhere to the rule of origin, which stipulates that products that are produced legally in one part of the federation are automatically legal for sale throughout. In other words, discrimination between different locations of production is ruled out.

(b) Federal constitutions should assign the various tasks of governance exclusively to one particular level of government. They should rule out overlap and the duplication of tasks, as this only confuses voters about who is to be held responsible for delivering the service. Exclusivity reduces the scope for shirking by politicians and administrators.

(c) Federations should stick to the principle of fiscal equivalence, banning vertical transfers of public funds and forcing each administration to finance the tasks for which it is responsible or which it has chosen to tackle, with the taxes, fees and debts, which it raises itself. This limits redistributive transfers and imposes fiscal responsibility on the various competing administrations.

(d) The constitution should oblige States to abstain from 'subsidy wars', that is, offering producers tax reductions and subsidies to attract them. This is best done with the stipulation of a most-favoured State clause: If a State government offers a privilege to one producer, it is automatically obliged to make that same offer to all other interested producers. (This is analogous to the most-favoured nation clause in the WTO agreement.)

Competitive federalism

One may call such a system 'competitive federalism'. It allows the (mobile) 'clients' of government administrations (who are stationary operators) to vote with their feet. Such federalism inevitably operates with some friction and creates some resource costs – as all competitive systems do. However, it is likely that State and local rivalry will generate outcomes that citizens find superior to those provided by the one centralized administration. Competitive federalism empowers the citizens and fosters those innovations in public policy that the citizens really want. It is no more than an application of the power-controlling devices of competition to governments. Under competition, they incur information and transaction costs so as to attract mobile citizens and investors. The evolutionary feedback from political-administrative entrepreneurship at local and State levels is also likely to strengthen the international competitiveness and attractiveness of the entire nation. Seen in this light, it seems no coincidence that many of the prospering democracies of long standing have federal constitutions (Switzerland, USA, Canada, Australia amongst others) and that regional communities in many other countries have been trying to affirm their collective identities by devolution of government functions (for example in Spain, Britain, South Africa, Russia, and the People's Republic of China). Channelling regional identity into constructive administrative-institutional rivalry seems preferable to smothering such initiatives by centralization, risking political confrontations amongst regions (Bish, 1987).

KEY CONCEPTS

The **principle of subsidiarity** stipulates that a task should always be carried out at the lowest-possible level: Only if individuals cannot manage a task, should local government get involved; and only if local governments cannot cope, should State or provincial authorities take over a task of governance. National governments should only undertake governance tasks if State-level authorities cannot cope. The principle is violated by a needless central-ization of tasks. Subsidiarity in governance needs to be given substance by the rule of origin (which rules out impediments to free trade throughout the nation), the exclusive assignment of tasks to specific levels of government (which avoids duplication), and fiscal equivalence (which makes each government responsible for financing its own tasks). It also is necessary to prevent 'subsidy wars' between rivalling governments.

12.6 The constitution of freedom as a framework for evolution

Our analysis of institutional evolution highlights, again, a point made repeatedly in this book: Institutions evolve to meet what people demand, as long as individuals have the freedom of choice. Where economic liberties are curtailed, established groups will use their power to entrench institutions that serve their particular interests. Powerful interest groups invariably strive to curtail equality before the law and individual liberty to shore up their particular positions. In this, they are often successful for considerable periods of time. When a system that is dominated by powerful groups is opened to spontaneous or forced outside challenges, institutional systems come under reform pressure. Much then depends on whether the freedom of action is guaranteed, so that all individuals are free to express their preferences.

This highlights how essential it is to make an overriding commitment to freedom in controlling power concentrations and hold-ups by politically well-connected groups (Gwartney and Wagner, (eds) 1988). Where freedom is made a high constitutional principle, individuals can experiment with alternatives, can by their example inspire others to emulate them and may generate a critical mass of followers to establish new institutions. In the case of external institutions, which require political processes for institutional change, a constitutional commitment to freedom is the foundation for marshalling the political will for institutional change if that change is widely desired.

The combination of tightly organized political parties and organized interest groups, including bureaucratic interests, makes it harder for individual aspirations and outsiders to challenge existing rule systems that curb individual liberties. In modern democracies, it is particularly important for the evolutionary potential of the system to protect the freedom of exit (free international trade, migration, information exchange and capital flows) and freedoms of speech, association, information, and so on as guarantees against ever-present tendencies towards institutional sclerosis and rigidification.

Because freedom is key to the evolutionary capacity, it should be enshrined in an overriding constitutional principle that has high protection.

NOTES

1 The Marshall Plan injected foreign-aid money into post-war Europe, but it has long been recognized that the injection of capital and US dollar liquidity, on its own, was not overly important to the economic resurgence of Western Europe, as the record shows: Recipients of relatively large portions of US largesse (the United Kingdom, Sweden and Greece) did rather less well than countries like Germany that often liberalized unilaterally (for example, Sohmen, 1959; Cowen, 1988). What mattered were new rules of the game of economic interaction in Western Europe.

2 In the last chapter of his *Constitution of Liberty*, entitled 'Why I am not a Conservative', Hayek showed that a clear dividing line runs between conservatives and liberals (or libertarians in American diction). Liberals always ask what is better. Sometimes, they find that new institutions serve human interests better, whereas conservatives always defend the old institutions and are fond of established authorities (Hayek, 1960).

3 Cultural evolution, of course, goes beyond the institutional system. Cultural content is subject to ongoing evolutionary processes of innovation, imitation, selection and rejection. Examples are how Ludwig van Beethoven or Gustav Mahler, or the impressionist painters of France breached the cultural conventions of the day and were initially rejected by a hostile public, yet eventually set new cultural standards.

In a similar vein, the economics profession has adopted the shared conventions that have been labelled the 'neoclassical paradigm'. This has facilitated interaction amongst professional economists.

When alternative conventions, which – for example – demand the explicit consideration of institutions and reject the tacit assumption of perfect knowledge, are being tried out, the established schools of thought and the adherents of the conventional paradigm are challenged. Their reactions may be inspired by a habitual conservative refusal to contemplate new conventions, which are perceived as unwelcome complications that only hinder coordination and the exchange of ideas among scholars. The intellectual challenge to the established paradigm may also induce attempts to defend acquired intellectual capital against potential depreciation. Hence, protagonists of the neoclassical paradigm may resist change, for example by rejecting publication of unconventional articles in journals or vetoing the career promotion of deviants. Changes in economic thinking are gradually promoted by attempts to integrate plausible parts of the alternative institutional-economics paradigm into the dominant school of thought, building hybrid models (Furubotn, 1994). If these turn out to be inherently inconsistent or fail to explain important real-world phenomena, further incentives to reconsider the mainstream paradigm will be felt. Only in the light of experience will the many participants in economic discourse evaluate, in gradual and decentralized ways, whether the change of widespread conventional assumptions is acceptable and useful.

4   Long before Weber focused on institutional evolution, British analysts wrote about it. Scottish philosopher-historian Adam Ferguson (1723-1816), with his *Essay on the History of Civil Society* (1767), and English historian Edward Gibbon (1737-1794), who wrote the celebrated *Rise and Fall of the Roman Empire*, deserve to be remembered as pioneers in the analysis of institutional evolution.

5   Openness to international challenges is not the only competition sclerotic institutions face: people may opt out of the shared external institutions, if they find them disadvantageous, and operate black markets. The shadow economy depends on internal rules and its spread can be interpreted as a competition between official formal and spontaneous informal rules.

6   In many countries, whether federal or otherwise, the free mobility of goods and production factors throughout the national territory is not guaranteed, for example because there are internal border controls or because regulations hinder inter-regional trade. Such countries forego important gains from the division of labour, both comparative-static specialization gains and dynamic gains from more intense competition among suppliers and regulators.

13

Socialism versus capitalism – system transformations

Whereas the primary intent of Chapters 2 to 12 was to make deductions from a small number of assumptions to gain insights into human nature and action, we shall now look at actual experiences in different institutional economic regimes: Do historic facts confirm our insights? Or do they have to be modified?

The Russian revolution of 1917 produced the first major empirical challenge to Austrian institutional economics. Austrian economists promptly asserted that the abolition of private property made rational allocation and resource mobilization impossible. Gradually, the Soviet command economy ossified, producing poor innovation and slowing economic growth, apart from permitting little individual freedom and low life satisfaction. Eventually, it collapsed throughout the Soviet empire, as Austrian economists had expected all along. The collapse presented the nations involved with the major challenge of comprehensive system transformation: How to invent and implement the institutions of market capitalism and democracy, and how to

ensure that the internal institutions could be affirmed and adjusted to modern times and external institutions reformed?

Nearly a generation since the demise of the command economy, most East European nations have managed to adapt the internal and external institutions sufficiently to embark on a process of economic catch-up, but they still remain behind the more advanced West European nations. The successor states of the Soviet Union have been less successful with political and economic reforms and often seem to relapse into authoritarianism.

In the People's Republic of China, the Soviet economic model was pragmatically abandoned when it proved unsuccessful. Since the late 1970s, the ideological drive of the Mao era was replaced by the pursuit of economic growth, while the Communist Party retains the political monopoly and persists with selective state capitalism. The resulting inconsistency of orders between a relatively free, open and competitive economy and a political monopoly poses new and, as yet unresolved, problems.

The distinguishing feature of communism is . . . the abolition of bourgeois property . . . modern bourgeois property is the final and most complete expression of the system of producing and appropriating products that is based on class antagonism, on the exploitation of the many by the few . . . The Communists . . . openly declare that their ends can be attained only by the forcible overthrow of all existing social conditions.

> Karl Marx and Friedrich Engels, *The Communist Manifesto* (1872)

It is the worst in us, which is being systematically activated and enlarged – egotism, hypocrisy, indifference, cowardice, fear, resignation, and the desire to escape every personal responsibility.

> Václav Havel (1936-2011) in a 1975 letter to Czechoslovakia's communist president at the time

They pretend to pay us, we pretend to work!

> Warsaw Cabaret, describing the socialist system in the 1980s

Eliminating the secret police is not enough . . . The only path to freedom is through a program of genuine economic transformation: transition to the market and private property, price liberalisation and monetary reform.

> Lescek Balcerowicz, Polish Finance Minister in late 1989

13.1 The Soviet experiment and its demise in retrospect

In late 1917, a small group of professional revolutionaries, the Bolsheviks, seized power in the young Russian republic. Their aim was to abolish private property, markets and money in order to introduce socialism. Among intellectuals around the world, the radical Soviet experiment attracted widespread curiosity and sympathy. How would the theories of Karl Marx (1818-1883) and Friedrich Engels (1820-1895), who had not bothered to elaborate any practical details of their grand vision of historic evolution, be translated into reality? The Bolsheviks promptly imposed a coercive Party-State from above, pretending it was in the name of the peasants and workers. To entrench themselves, they had to wage civil war on the peasants and workers. Immediately after Vladimir Lenin, Leon Trotzky, Joseph Stalin and their fellow revolutionaries had won political control, they were confronted with numerous unanticipated practical problems, which offer insights into institutional economics. Increasingly brutal uses of coercion were required to solve the eternal economic problem (that is, allocating scarce resources and discovering and mobilizing new resources), once the age-old coordination mechanism of secure private property and market competition had been abolished. The conflict between incentive-destroying coercion and revisionist easing to obtain economic advances could never be resolved during the entire 70-year Soviet experiment (Boettke, 1990; 1993).

The Soviet command economy

Key aspects of Soviet political-economic history are quickly sketched: Since the 1890s, the autocratic Tsarist regime in backward Russia had engaged in some constitutional and economic liberalization and had made considerable advances in industrialization. During the war with Germany and Austria–Hungary (1914-17), Russia went from defeat to defeat. After severe food shortages broke out in Russian cities, a 'progressive' bloc led by socialist intellectuals overthrew Tsar Nicholas in February 1917 (Malia, 1994, pp. 83–98). The Russian tradition of uncompromising political maximalism and violence contributed to further instability, until a small, hitherto little-known group of communist radicals and soldiers seized power in a *coup d'état*, which was styled later as the 'Great Proletarian October Revolution'.[1] The Bolsheviks garnered popular support by promising to end the war and to break up big estates owned by the government and the nobility in order to distribute the land to the peasants. While the purpose of the new Soviet regime was to introduce and spread socialism, the new regime proved a disaster in economic development. The period from 1918 to 1921, known as war communism, was the closest the Bolshevik's came to adopting the full Marxian vision. They abolished private property and markets. It had devastating results. By 1921, the output of mines and factories had plummeted to a mere 21 per cent of the pre-war level, and agricultural production was down to 38 per cent (Malia, 1994; p. 143; Boettke, 1993; Nove, 1993; Ofer in Myers, (ed.) 1996). Unemployment in the cities soared. Russia, long the world's leading exporter of grain, was gripped by famine. Peasants, who were not offered market prices, fed grain to their pigs and cattle, and then ate those, although Party commissars roamed the countryside to confiscate stocks of foodstuffs and animals and punish the peasantry. The pre-war economic order had been destroyed without any viable alternative economic institutions to replace them.

After four disastrous years of civil war, Red Terror and economic near-collapse of the Soviet Russian economy, the Communist Party adopted a 'New Economic Policy'. It now tolerated some private ownership in land (80 per cent remained nationalized), permitted some markets and kept the money economy alive. By 1927, agricultural production had recovered to 80 per cent of pre-war levels and industrial production to 75 per cent (Malia, 1994, p. 163; also Boettke, 1993; Gregory, 2004). However, hardly any new investments were made and obsolete plants could hardly be repaired. The socialist system was simply incapable of communicating demands and potential supplies. Incentives to work and supply were weak, unless brute coercion was applied. Moreover, the political leadership was frequently ignorant about what supplies ought to be mobilized by the government's coercion.

CH 13 – CASE ONE

On the Mises-Lange debate

In 1920, shortly after the Soviet revolution, the Austrian liberal economist Ludwig von Mises (1881–1973) published an article in which he showed that rational cost-benefit evaluations – and hence the efficient allocation of resources – were logically impossible under socialism (Mises, 1994; German original 1920). Originally he directed his criticism against the theories of German socialist economists, but his argument was soon seen as relevant to the socialist practice in Soviet Russia (Mises 1936; German original 1922).

Mises made the point that prices reflect manifold, evolving demands and supplies, so that profits and losses steer people's economic decisions. Under socialism, individuals could not engage in economic calculation. True money prices can only be found by trial and error in competitive markets, but the socialist suppression of markets makes this impossible. This is also true, he wrote, of the many intermediate goods that one industry buys from another. At best, a socialist economy can repeat in successive periods what was done before, but innovations and new opportunities cannot be incorporated into such a system (Mises, 1994/1920; 1945; Winiecki, 1988). How can central planning bureaucrats know what new processes and products to adopt? What old processes and products to abandon? Expressing everything in terms of the quantity of labour needed for production (as stipulated by Karl Marx) not only ignores the great variety of labour skills, but also overlooks the inputs of natural resources and capital into production. "There is only groping in the dark. Socialism is the abolition of the rational economy", he said. In other words, with the impossibility of economic calculation the end goal of an advanced material economy was also impossible to achieve under collective ownership of capital and central planning.

Mises' argument concentrated solely on the knowledge problem in economics. He had demonstrated the impossibility of a socialist system to perform rational economic calculation without even needing to mention the other, very real, problems that such a system creates. One such systemic problem deals with the incentives to act entrepreneurially and risk innovations. When decision makers are no longer allowed to appropriate the profits of successful innovations, because private property is suppressed, who would risk making innovations? Mises predicted in 1920: "What is happening under the rule of Lenin and Trotsky is merely destruction and annihilation".

•••

Before the First World War, mathematical economists, such as Enrico Barone and Vilfredo Pareto, had made certain assumptions about production technologies and consumer preferences and developed mathematical models to show that a central ministry of production could rationally allocate resources in the absence of money, private property and markets. Optimal allocation could be realized *ex ante*, that is, before production and exchange activities commenced (Pareto optimality). In the 1930s, Polish communist economist Oskar Lange (1904–1965) refined this approach to 'prove' that central planners could reflect the

CH 13 – CASE ONE *(continued)*

consumers' preferences even when all means of production were collectively owned. He and fellow socialists advocated a 'scientific trial and error' method of optimization, in which surpluses would be eliminated by price reductions and shortages by price increases. After criticism from Friedrich Hayek, Lange advocated the retention of private property in farms, commerce and small production businesses, but later, having returned to post-war communist Poland, Lange reverted to praising the Stalinist orthodoxy (Lange and Taylor, 1964/1939).

The *zeitgeist* of the 1930s to1960s era was one that supported Lange and the other market socialists, even some of Hayek's own students, including Abba Lerner (1944). Central planning was seen not only as necessary but also as the only course for reason and science.

The Austrian economists, however, kept disagreeing with Lange's assertions about the feasibility of central planning and emphasized the importance of individual freedom and the need for individuals with their diverse and ever-changing preferences to make their own choices (Vaughn in Boettke, (ed.) 1994, pp. 478–484). Thus, Mises wrote in a 1945 essay (pp. 44–49):

> As the self-styled 'progressives' see things, the alternative is: 'automatic forces' or 'conscious planning'. It is obvious, they go on saying, that to rely on automatic processes is sheer stupidity. No reasonable man can seriously recommend doing nothing and letting things go without interference through purposive action. A plan . . . is incomparably superior to the absence of planning . . . [However], the alternative is not: plan or no plan. The question is: whose planning? Should each member of society plan for himself or should paternal government alone plan for all? . . . Laissez faire . . . means: let individuals choose how they want to cooperate in the social division of labor and let them determine what the entrepreneurs should produce . . . and do not force the common man to yield to a dictator.

> •••

Reading the Mises-Lange controversy in hindsight, one is forced to draw two conclusions: (i) Mises' (and Hayek's) predictions and conclusions were fully borne out by the Soviet and other socialist experiments. (ii) The two sides of the argument persisted for so long, because Lange and other central planners made narrow assumptions – such as average consumer preferences and aggregate production possibilities – to construct their models, brushing aside Mises' and Hayek's assertion that there always is a constitutional 'knowledge problem' (Winiecki, 1988; Boettke-Leeson, 2004; also see Chapter 14).

In 1928, Stalin – Lenin's successor – launched a Five-Year Plan to push rapid industrialization, again abolishing profit, competition and private capital. Inspired by Germany's wartime mobilization under a central plan, Stalin worked with an expanding planning bureaucracy and relied on new oppressive controls. It was hoped that the new system of centrally planned coordination would do away with the waste of competition, the irrationality of decentralized plans by numerous producers and the unequal incentives of capitalism. This appealed to many intellectuals in the West, who had long shared a dream of a better world and of shaping a 'new man': "[The tradition of collectivist-rationalist philosophy] held with an almost religious fervor that the rational, scientific ordering of human affairs could produce a new society and a new man. It was not an accident that [French mathematician-philosopher and nobleman Nicolas de] Condorcet predicted the 'absolute perfectability of the human race', or that [French socialist philosopher and duke Henri de] Saint-Simon called his technocratic doctrine the 'New Christianity'" (Malia, 1994, p. 186).

From at the least the late 1920s on the Party and the *apparachiks* became the principals and the workers and the general population the subjects. Stalin's *nomenklatura* system allowed Party members and leading technical experts to seek and obtain huge rents, having freed them from all need to compete (Anderson and Boettke, 1997). The average worker and *kolkhoz* farmer, by contrast, lived a life of hard work and deprivation. The peasants, who had been given land in 1917 to win their support, were now again expropriated and forced to labour in *kolkhozes* (collective farms). They went on slaughtering their cattle and draught horses to eat them and prevent confiscation (Malia, 1994, p. 197). Party commissars everywhere supervised technical experts, since the experts were not deemed politically reliable. The command economy had to be made credible by a long series of show trials and deportations to labour camps (*gulag*). Fear spread to higher echelons of society, as Stalin's purges reached more and more people, including some in the highest ranks of the Party. This did much to lay the basis for the later difficulties in reforming the Russian economy (Anderson and Boettke, 1993; 1997).

Economic coordination under Stalin's central planning brought rapid advances in the quantity of capital investment and industrial output, but there was hardly any process or product innovation. The economy had to function without (price-profit) incentives and therefore without the necessary voluntary cooperation. Instead of the socialist promise of greater freedom and equality, the population was stratified into serfs and *nomenklatura* (the Party's planners and enforcers), controlled by a tight system of secret police, deportations and executions. Social and economic conflicts resulted in a major famine that claimed between six and eleven million lives in 1932-33. Agreed post-Soviet estimates speak of some 20 million political killings, that is, well over 15 per cent of the Russian population (Courtois et al., 1999).

The German attack on the Soviet Union during the Second World War (in 1941) initially led many Russians to expect betterment. The racist brutality of the National Socialists against the civil population and Russian prisoners of war of course soon provoked patriotic fervour and lined the population up behind Stalin. During the war, the centralized Soviet system proved well geared to mobilization at the expense of everything else. At the same time, the Soviet Union, till then a diplomatic pariah amongst nations, became a respected ally of the Western democracies. After an arduous and costly fight, the Soviet Union acquired an empire from the Elbe to North Korea and became one of the two superpowers.

The pattern of swings between hard, repressive socialism and episodes of soft reformism that had been evident since 1917 were now repeated: Khrushchev's de-Stalinization was accompanied by the promotion of economic development to meet consumer needs. After Khrushchev's sacking in 1964, a collective leadership under Brezhnev again tightened the controls and pursued the spread of communist world revolution. However, from the 1970s onward it became increasingly evident (except to Western socialists) that the central planning system was incapable of providing incentives to work and innovate and allocate resources rationally (except to give high priority to military and space projects). Whereas heavy investment and the multiplication of the standardized industrial plants had produced a respectable growth of average per capita income of 3.4 per cent per annum under Khrushchev, this figure fell to 0.9 per cent per annum by the early 1980s and was nearly zero in the late 1980s (according to a post-Soviet analysis of growth data – www.answers.com/topic/soviet economic growth, accessed 7 March 2011). The centrally planned command economy proved incapable of supplying some of the most fundamental consumer goods, such as blue jeans, which the young in the East Bloc saw on television and in magazines from the West. The system was simply incapable of innovation and offering a diversity of products and consumer choices. It could never have produced the rich, evolving variety of consumer software, an iPad or the variety of motorcars from which people in free market economies can choose. In the final analysis, socialism was defeated not by armaments or high diplomacy, but by consumer market competition and the economic choices for the people. The system seemed caught on a treadmill of reform, without being able to escape its history (Anderson and Boettke, 1993, 1997).

The deepening Soviet economic crisis led the new General Secretary of the Party, Mikhail Gorbachev, to shift again from Brezhnev's controls to reforms. He tried to dislodge the entrenched *priviligentsia* (*perestroika*) by doing away with the secrecy of earlier decades and abolishing the censorship of opinions that diverged from the official Party line (*glasnost*). Gorbachev's attack on his own Party was accompanied by an opening-up to the world and political détente with the West, in order to save unaffordable military expenditures. Gorbachev shed light on the important point that the choice of institutional economic systems is not merely a matter of economic allocation, but also a profound moral issue (Boettke, 1993; Cox, (ed.) 1999).

Between 1989 and 1991, the Soviet empire was quickly dismantled, and the old planning system under the dictatorship of the Communist Party jettisoned. Russia and the other Soviet Union's successor states, as well as the newly sovereign nations of Eastern Europe, were faced with the daunting task of inventing and quickly implementing alternative rule systems (Kukathas et al., 1991; Boyko et al., 1997).

It seems that very few observers, and certainly not the specialized Sovietologists, had predicted the sudden (and rather non-violent) implosion of the Soviet system. Indeed, it is impossible to predict such political revolutions, because people in repressive regimes will often dissimulate their true feelings and aspirations, when communicating in the public domain (Kuran, 1997). With hindsight, observers attributed this ignorance to the fact that the 'Kremlin experts' concentrated on the small detail, rather than the big theory of social evolution, 'on the footnotes over the text'. Political analysts, who specialized in communist economies, were also informed by standard, comparative-static economics, rather than a theory of institutional evolution (Anot in Cox, 1999, p. 220). At least some of the classical liberal Austrian economists, such as von Mises and Hayek, who had maintained all along that the centrally planned command economy was not viable over the long term, had understood the underlying incompatibilities of the Soviet system, but they had been overlooked or dismissed as irrelevant. In the final analysis, it was the incapacity of the regime to exploit new information and come to grips with changing circumstances (Shane, 1994).

One remarkable aspect of more than two generations of Soviet central planning and command and control has been the tenacious persistence of human nature. Despite fierce repression, public propaganda campaigns and political incentives, most inhabitants of the Soviet Union clung to traditional universal human nature: They reacted to material incentives (and disincentives) and cultivated private networks to encourage each other and enhance their chances of survival. The 'new socialist man' (and woman) remained a figment of official propaganda, while traditional values of a small-group, tribal variety were often passed on from one generation to the next. Indeed, under the onslaught of revolutionary social engineering, most Russians conserved old traditions, but probably missed out on the normal evolutionary changes, which people tend to derive from the experience of competing individually and self-reliantly in evolving markets. Whilst traditional internal institutions (and adherence of many to Orthodox Christianity) proved amazingly durable, generations of socialist planning and disincentives also prevented the evolution of a bourgeois society of independent, self-reliant citizens and a visceral understanding of the commercial moral syndrome (Boettke, 1993).

After Gorbachev dismantled the Soviet regime and its defective institution set, no alternative set of internal and external rules was readily available. The Yeltsin era that followed took Russia to democracy and facilitated free markets and privatization (Boyko et al., 1997). However, this was done top-down, *nomenklatura* style, and occurred in an institutional vacuum. Inflation snowballed, driving pensioners and others on fixed money incomes into abject poverty. The sudden changes disoriented most and caused deep-seated insecurity. Many collectively owned assets were 'spontaneously privatized', that is, appropriated by influential powerbrokers. Production plummeted, and the hope was disappointed that the new capital owners would resolutely compete with each other, so that a new order of competitive, disciplining rules would emerge before long. Instead, the new oligarchs tried to use their wealth to buy political influence.

Since Russia's public saw these developments widely as grossly unjust, the Yeltsin era (1991-1999) was followed by a more statist regime under Presidents Putin and Medvedev. The new leadership and the ruling elite hailed mostly from the erstwhile secret service, the KGB. They exploited popular insecurity to create a more authoritarian democracy and seize many important assets. High energy prices favoured oil- and gas-rich Russia for a decade, and the powerful ruling elites entrenched a strong rent-seeking culture, coupled with a new post-Soviet nationalism. A market economy may now work on the edges, but the dominant economic model is that of a corrupt, power-based monopoly-political complex (Gregory, 2008, also see 'state capitalism' below). The lesson is that a competitive order hardly evolves spontaneously and without an understanding of its long-term benefits for general welfare and overall political and economic stability. Russian history since 1989 demonstrates the importance of the intellectual and moral foundations of the capitalist civilization, as well as the persistence of earlier mental and institutional models (*metis*).

Essentials of transformation to free-market capitalism

Anyone aware of the fundamentals of institutional economics will realize that transplanting an economic system – in this case capitalism, onto a society without entrenched individualistic values and habits – is, if not illusive, at least extremely difficult. Genuine institutional changes take much time. Numerous interactive changes have to be instituted, ideally at the same time. This is a monumental task that no single mind is ever able to comprehend and master completely. It comes inevitably with at least temporary costs in terms of losses of jobs and living standards (Klaus, 1991; 1997; Naishul, 1993; Siebert, (ed.) 1993; Anderson and Boettke, 1993; 1997; Wagener, ed., 1994; Eggertsson, 1998).

The proper transformation of the former command economies had to be guided by only one, well-founded objective: establishing the basic conditions of a capitalist and democratic order for citizens, business firms and government authorities (Table 13.1). In this process, the reform initiative had to be carried predominantly by the citizens, because reforms imposed from above were always likely to serve the entrenched government *apparat*, as the history of failed Soviet reform attempts from Lenin to Gorbachev demonstrated (Cox, ed. 1999; Boettke, 2001; Boettke and Leeson, 2004; Boettke et al., 2008). However, fundamental values and basic attitudes to life and society can rarely change without delay. This held true especially in the former Soviet Union, where long behavioural traditions were dominated by the tribal, guardian syndrome, where two generations had known nothing but socialism and where the majority had never fully embraced the rationalism and individualism of the Western Enlightenment (Némo, 2006, pp. 103–104).

Let us list the essential steps of transition from socialism to capitalism:

(a) Private citizens have to claim their civil, economic and political liberties, including the rights to sell their own labour and skills freely, to own property, to associate, seek information, speak out and to move about freely. The resumption of free contracts and secure property ownership implies that the responsibility for material and spiritual wellbeing is fully reprivatized. Private responsibility also means that at least the young generations have to provide for their own retirement, as well as their health and the education of their children.

(b) The people have to realize that they are the principals of collective action, and the politicians and bureaucrats only their agents. Producer and trading organizations, which previously had to obey the directives of central-plan bureaucrats, have to be made fully autonomous and self-responsible, which includes a threat of bankruptcy. To this effect, firms need to be turned into independent legal entities, which enjoy the freedom to contract, but bear full liability for their contractual obligations. Business owners and managers must re-learn how to make risky

Table 13.1 Checklist of essentials for transformation from a socialist to a capitalist market economy

Area of reform	Institutional goals	Organizational support
Private citizens	Civil, economic and political liberties; establishing private responsibility	Civil and economic law; private property and autonomy; civil courts and policy subject to the rule of law
Firms	As above; full autonomy in decision-making; freedom of contract; liability for contractual commitments; bankruptcy	Corporatization; privatization; commercial code; expedient courts; standards of accounting; capital markets, labour markets; banking legislation and prudential supervision
Governments	Protection of the rule of law (rule-bound, limited constitutional government); control of agent opportunism; subsidiarity	Definition of the essential tasks of government in a constitution; reduction in the size of government; phasing out subsidies; administrative law; budget reform and a system of effective tax collection; assistance with (soft and hard) infrastructures, privatization; independent central bank with the task of pursuing monetary stability; devolution of tasks to local and regional governments; independent judiciary
	Redistribution	Measures to establish equity of opportunity; minimal social safety net; provision of access, but not necessarily production of public services
	Macroeconomic policy	Balanced budget; accounting of all public-sector liabilities and assets; independent central bank with commitment to price-level stability
	Opening the economy	Freedom of movement; liberalization of trade and capital flows; currency convertibility; flexible exchange rate; membership of international organizations that cultivate the rules of open international interactions

decisions under clear budget constraints. This requires government back-up by company law and a commercial code, as well as the administrative and judiciary organization and knowhow to implement and enforce these laws. Judges and commercial lawyers have to be trained. A streamlined, simple and clearly enforced regulatory regime and the strict control of corruption in business and government are core requirements.

(c) The role of government has to be re-thought *ab ovo*. The agents of government must be made to realize that the maxim for the government's existence is not some notion of national grandeur or the implementation of some presumed 'iron laws of history', but only service to the principals, that is, the citizens. The principle of rule-bound, constitutional and limited government needs to be recognized in theory and entrenched in practice. Strong institutional controls and accountability are required to control historically entrenched preferences for agent opportunism and opportunities for corruption. The rule of law has to be imposed on all government agents. As long as government agencies are permitted to act on the assumption that they do not have to pay their bills or are above the law, a core requirement of system transformation is missing. Given regional and sectarian tensions in many, formerly centralized communist countries, multi-level government with a strong commitment to subsidiarity and competitive federalism confers distinct advantages (Section 12.5).

Transformation requires a resolute commitment to the protective function of government, not least to draw a line under the socialist past, when citizens' freedoms and the institutions of civil society were poorly protected. In addition, there is arguably a residual role for a redistributive function. Elder citizens, who contributed during their working lives to the collective economic effort, were hindered in accumulating private savings for old age. They therefore depend on government for old-age support and other essential services. One may even acknowledge that they acquired some property claim to the socialized capital stock. A minimal social safety net may also have to be created to ensure political stability and minimum standards of equity of outcomes, at least for the very young, the old and the ill, even if this conflicts with formal justice, freedom and incentives (Section 10.1). However, there is merit in setting clear signals for the younger generation by establishing a system of low taxation, but with responsibility for private provision for old age, health care and education of the children. Nothing would be more likely to foster new attitudes to work, life and responsibility, which are the essential bedrock of a healthy capitalist society.

(d) Given the powerful influence of international competition and factor mobility, the transformation process and the imposition of strict budget constraints requires the discipline of openness. The freedom to travel abroad, to inform oneself of how people operate elsewhere and to trade internationally helps to convey much-needed practical knowledge to people who hitherto had lived in a closed, ill-informed world. Likewise, international investment and payments have to be liberalized to open the opportunities of a better international division of labour, to transfer productive and business knowhow, and to exert competitive stimuli. All currency controls have to be abolished, so that the exchange rate can reflect world-market prices. Domestic markets will then be informed by world-market prices.

Pathways to capitalism

The transformation checklist in Table 13.1 has probably been implemented fastest and most consistently in Poland, where, from late 1989, Solidarity's Deputy Prime Minister Lescek Balcerowicz led an expert commission to design a comprehensive 'shock therapy' to overcome the heritage of 45 years of communist rule (http://wikipedia.org/wiki/Balcerowicz_Plan, accessed 20 April 2011). While the drastic reforms brought some initial losses of real income and exposed the decrepitude of state-owned industry and 'on-the-job-unemployment', the medium-term results in terms of economic growth were better in Poland than elsewhere. Gross domestic product (at purchasing power parities in US$) grew by 6.6 per cent during the immediate transition period of 1990 to 1996. This is impressive when compared to drops by 16.1 per cent in Hungary and 1.9 per cent in the Czech Republic, and the massive production losses in the Russian Federation (–42 per cent) and Ukraine (–59 per cent). In most other post-communist countries, the transition years were also marked by drops in statistically measured per capita incomes. After the initial shock, however, Poland and Polish voters embarked on a course of reform that was erratic, so that the country still falls short of enjoying a genuine and completely free capitalist constitution (Table 13.2).

In almost all post-communist countries, the new democratically elected governments had to implement transformation policies against popular resentment, not only from the previous *priviligentsia*, but the wider public that was not used to hard work and self-responsibility (Boettke, 2001). The transformation era highlighted that change also depended on deep-seated moral attitudes and that a viable capitalist order has to be anchored also in people's values and attitudes (Naishul, 1993; Boettke et al, 2008).

The system transformation showed that the basic values and internal institutions of society take time to develop, which makes it doubly important that the external rules are clear, simple and consistent. As a result of inconsistencies between internal and external institutions, reforms typically proceeded in an erratic fashion. This disoriented private coordination, hampered

Table 13.2 Economic freedom ratings in selected European countries, 2009

Country	Summary Index out of 10 (2009)	Rank out of 141 countries (2009)	Transition years (1998 GDP as % of 1989 GDP-PPP)	2010 GDP per capita (US$ at PPP)
Switzerland	8.03	4	135	41,950
United Kingdom	7.71	8	148	35,059
Slovakia	7.56	13	99	22,196
Hungary	7.52	15	95	18,841
Germany	7.45	21	124	36,081
Lithuania	7.40	24	n.a.	17,235
France	7.16	42	143	33,910
Czech Republic	7.13	46	95	24,950
Romania	7.08	48	76	11,895
Poland	7.00	53	116	18,981
Italy	6.90	=70	140	29,480
Slovenia	6.78	74	104	27,899
Russia	6.55	81	55	15,612
Serbia	6.44	91	n.a.	10,252
Ukraine	5.70	125	46	6,698

Sources: Gwartney et al. (2011), pp. 8–13; UN; OECD; IMF.

private initiative and harmed the development of appropriate social attitudes. Over the generation since the fall of communism, however, most
Eastern European economies have become genuine electoral democracies
with open, mainly private economies and a decent measure of economic
freedom. Two decades after the demise of communist central planning and
economic liberalization at differing speed, some East European countries are
now ranking even ahead of the increasingly regulated, old European Union
economies (Table 13.2).

One institutionally interesting transformation device was launched in
Czechoslovakia, later the Czech Republic, by Czech economist Václav
Klaus: voucher privatization. Since communist governments had no idea of
what they owned and what their assets were worth, Klaus proposed that
each adult citizen should be issued with a given amount of vouchers for a
nominal price. This 'quasi money' could then be used to bid at auctions for
real assets, such as apartments and privatized small-scale and large-scale businesses. Auction bids could also be supplemented by hard cash, for example
foreign-currency loans that some Czechs were able to obtain. The procedure
was a quick and transparent way of transferring real property into private
hands and launching a capitalist economy. It turned three quarters of Czech

adults into shareholders, either in individual businesses or in privatization funds, which pooled vouchers for bids for assets (for example big industrial companies).

The voucher device to quickly transfer collective assets to individual private owners was also employed in Russia, Slovenia and some other countries in the 1990s (Klaus, 1991; Boyko et al., 1994; 1997), and later also in non-European countries, such as Chile.

The experience seems to show that – like everything else in institutional affairs – fundamental honesty, transparency and justice in administration are crucial to the success. The new private owners of shares and businesses were of course inexperienced. Many incurred losses. In Russia, for example, mafia bosses (former apparatchiks and KGB agents) managed to appropriate huge industrial and other assets, but the inclination to compete subsequently through investment and innovation was often weak. In Russia, fraudulent seizure of collectively owned assets (jocularly termed 'spontaneous privat-ization') was allowed to occur across a broad range of industries, reinforcing popular perceptions that capitalism is a system of theft, a view long spread by official propaganda. This, together with a long tradition of mystic authoritar-ianism in Russia, led to a popular and politically exploited backlash. It gave rise to a more nationalistic-collectivist economic constitution, numerous state-controlled enterprises and less press freedom than what has now been instituted further west (Klaus, 1997).

KEY CONCEPTS

Socialism is a system of economic institu-tions in which nearly all property rights to the means of production are held by agen-cies of the state. Government agents at the central, provincial or local levels determine how property rights (including labour) are used and allocated. To facilitate the top-down control over how the means of pro-duction are used, many internal institutions of civil society were replaced by externally designed, intrusive and predominantly pre-scriptive institutions. As well, *ex ante* central planning was substituted for the spontane-ous *ex post* coordination in markets.

Communism was a utopian state of affairs, which Karl Marx and other commu-nists imagined for a future when the state would wither away and no property rights in the means of production would be assigned to anyone. It was assumed that society would become so productive and affluent that it would be possible for all to consume according to their needs and work according to their capacity and inclination. By this defi-nition there has never been – and never will be – a communist country, but only socialist regimes that call themselves communist.

The **central plan** is a central compilation

←

of production plans for individual products and groups of products. It sets obligatory output targets (quotas) for selected types of products, production units and industries. The various production plans and resource uses are made compatible with each other *ex ante*, that is, they are coordinated before the production period begins. In the Soviet Union, central plans were drawn up on a four- or five-year cycle, supplemented by more specific annual or quarterly plans, which were often also regionally disaggregated. The main coordination task lay in the hands of the Central Plan Office.

Civil society consists of the individuals and the free associations and organizations that individuals form, as well as the internal institutions which govern their interaction. It is that part of society that is autonomous, that is, not directed by the political power of government. Totalitarian regimes have tried to replace these pluralist civil networks by external institutions and organizations under direct government control. Part of the recovery from socialism is the renewed cultivation of civil society. In democratic Western societies, too, governments often try to subsidize and influence parts of civil society, often through (government-supported) 'non-government organizations' (NGOs), which pursue single issues.

Transformation means to be completely changed or change from one state or regime to another. In the present context, the term relates to the comprehensive change of institutions, from predominantly collective ownership of productive resources and control of their use by government or party agents, to predominantly private ownership and use according to the decentralized decisions of individuals and independent private groups.

Privatization is the assignment of previously collective property rights to specific private owners. This can be done through a number of different mechanisms:

- Restitution of specific property titles to previous private owners, in some cases after possibly complicated and drawn-out processes of proving previous legal title; where specific restitution is found too costly in terms of transaction costs, previous owners may receive monetary compensation which they may then use to buy property titles;
- Outright sale to domestic and foreign buyers, either to a new individual owner or a newly formed group of share-owners;
- Exchange of specific property titles for vouchers that were previously distributed to citizens (**voucher privatization**);
- Donation of collective property to current managers, workers or other classes of people, for example, assigning a property title to apartments and houses to those who happen to live in them; and
- Theft of collective property by people with influence and the power to do so (spontaneous privatization), possibly as a consequence of managers, workers or squatters beginning to behave as if the property was their own and eventually obtaining legal title to the property.

As of 2012, most formerly communist countries in central and Eastern Europe have narrowed the income gap with the affluent, but slow-growing Western European welfare states and attained productivity standards and living standards comparable to emergent middle-income nations elsewhere.

Income levels, however, still remain markedly below those in the West (see right-hand column in Table 13.2). Time lost during decades of coercive socialism is hard to make good. In a number of cases, ratings of East European economic freedom now surpass those in the old industrial countries of Europe, a circumstance that promises further economic catch-up (see the next chapter). Where the economic and political institutions have been transformed to approximate those of the West, the losses after the demise of central planning were only a temporary price to pay for enhancing long-term growth prospects and allowing the people to reclaim their freedom.

We may conclude that the major economic experiments of the twentieth century – first the suppression of capitalism, then the transformation back to a relatively free, open economy – confirms that institutional change is gradual and complex. It also confirms what has been deduced from basic assumptions about human economic behaviour, made in Chapters 1 to 12. It also illustrates that rent seeking and restrictions on the free use of property in labour, ideas and capital (where they still persist) keep inflicting pain in terms of poverty and civil tension.

13.2   The evolution of socialism in China

After two generations of disastrous wars and social instability in China, there was a communist revolution in 1949. It led the People's Republic of China to adopt the strict Soviet-style planning model. When it became apparent in the late 1950s that this system failed to perform, the Chinese leadership pragmatically jettisoned it. Mao Zedong then instigated continuous revolution during the 1960s and early 1970s in order to prevent opportunistic agents in the Communist Party and the government to seek rents and entrench their power, so that he would be able to stay in control himself. Mao aspired to create a new, selfless man, who would be motivated solely by solidarity with the community. However, the continual upsetting of any semblance of order had dire consequences for living standards, personal security and freedom (see Box 13.2).

CH 13 – CASE TWO

The rule of men: an insider's view

"I thought of China as one huge family and believed we needed a head. Chairman Mao was the chief" (p. 127). "It was not until the Great Leap Forward, when millions of Chinese began dying during the famine, that I became aware of how much Mao resembled the ruthless

CH 13 – CASE TWO *(continued)*

emperors he so admired. Mao knew that people were dying by the millions. He did not care" (p. 125). "The individual was merely a tiny cog in a large and complex machine. If the cog performed its functions well, it could be of use to the machine. At the slightest complaint, the smallest deviation from the norm, the cog could be thrown aside" (p. 65).

"The country's scientists and intellectuals had never recovered [from the purges of 1957] . . . A pall of depression continued to hang over the intellectual community. Even those who had not suffered direct political persecution existed in a perpetual state of fear, afraid to speak out . . . [they were] forced to attend so many political meetings that their capacity to work had suffered" (p. 389).

"After sixteen years of revolution, it seemed to me that China had not progressed at all. The standard of living was terrible. The government was cruel. Life for the disenfranchised was harsh. However bad life may have been under the Guomindang, hard work and good luck had always brought rewards. Poor people with talent had a chance to rise to the top . . . Change for the better was always a hope" (p. 429).

"As the Cultural Revolution turned first against this enemy and then against that, as the Communist party was decimated . . . the people of China became fed up, disgusted. They were coming to see the political campaigns for what they really were – naked high-level power struggles" (p. 578).

"I write this book . . . for everyone who cherishes freedom. I want it to serve as a reminder of the terrible consequences of Mao's dictatorship and of how good and talented people living under his regime were forced to violate their consciences and sacrifice their ideals in order to survive" (p. 638).

Source: Excerpts from: Li Zhisui (1994), *The Private Life of Chairman Mao*, London: Arrow Books.
During Mao Zedong's last 22 years, Dr. Li served as his personal physician. He wrote this autobiographic book after moving to the USA in 1988.

Mao's successors embarked on 'market socialism' in the late 1970s. Workers and plant managers were given rights over how profits would be used, but they invariably voted for high pay and on-the-job consumption to the detriment of reinvestment in the capital stock and innovation. Unlike in the capitalist system, where the capital owners champion the long-term viability of the capital stock and the firm, workers and directors in state-owned and self-managed Chinese factories were motivated to appropriate the profits for their own personal enjoyment. In addition, numerous private companies began to flourish. The new, pragmatic leader Deng Xiaoping is reported to have remarked at the time that he did not care whether the cat was red (collectively owned) or black (privately owned), as long as it caught the mice! This result-oriented mindset led to major reforms, which gave indus-trial companies the right to self-manage their affairs and pay taxes, but keep the surplus (Qian and Weingast, 1995). This incentive structure mobilized considerable entrepreneurship throughout China's agriculture, industry and commerce (see Box 13.3).

CH 13 – CASE THREE

China's second revolution: institutional reform

From a press article about the legacy of Deng Xiaoping:

[During the Deng era, 1978–92] China's per-capita income . . . roughly quadrupled . . . the benefits were spread widely throughout the population . . . China stabilized internally . . . and achieved rapid technological advance . . .

In the mid-1970s, Chinese people could not choose their own haircuts, their own clothes, or their own jobs. They were watched every minute through neighbourhood associations. They went to endless political education classes and were grilled ceaselessly on their political beliefs . . .

Today, the people of China choose their colorful clothes and stylish haircuts. They increasingly move around the country and change jobs according to their own wishes. They hear not just their leaders' opinions, but also those of foreigners – through the radio, the TV, and direct contact with foreigners . . . The Chinese of today have diverse opinions, which they express vigorously, including personal opinions highly critical of the government . . .

In the 1990s, the Chinese government has acknowledged the right of the people to sue the govern-ment and the Party. However . . . inadequate the implementation . . . the emergence of a right to sue the government in formerly totalitarian China . . . is a milestone in the global development of human rights . . . recent years have seen . . . limitations on the rights of police to hold prisoners indefinitely without charge, of limitations on the Ministry of Justice's control over lawyers, and on respect for the concept of the rule of law . . . And China now has roughly four million competitively elected local officials . . .

As trade, tourism and television opened the country, people's minds were liberated. As China's economy changed from one where 100% of the working people were employed by the gov-ernment to one where fewer than 20% were, the government lost one of its principal levers of totalitarian control . . . As business reached . . . [large] scale . . . businesses demanded the assur-ance of institutionalized law. As the regime sought scientific progress . . . [It] had to acknow-ledge the legitimacy of open debate in a large number of areas . . . China . . . sent . . . its . . . elite students [overseas] . . . no totalitarian thought controls could possibly survive that decision.

CH 13 – CASE THREE *(continued)*

Determined to achieve his economic goals [Deng] . . . reluctantly conceded unintended freedoms in area after area.

Source: William H. Overholt, 'One Man's Legacy for One Billion', *The Asian Wall Street Journal*, 26 February 1997.

The biggest de facto privatization of collectively held property ever attempted in human history occurred in the late 1970s and early 1980s, when the Chinese authorities de-collectivized agriculture, doing away with the People's Communes, which so many Western fellow travellers had admired. The land and capital in Chinese agriculture, which had been confiscated in the 1950s, had been eventually aggregated into huge 'People's Communes' under Mao. Tens, if not hundreds of thousands of rural workers were coordinated under a command structure and instructed by a Party leader and manager what to plant, when to plant and harvest, and how to carry out all the other minute details of their daily work. In the second half of the 1950s, orders were issued by Beijing Centre to accelerate rice production and build up rural industries (the Great Leap Forward). The Party also set targets for China to overtake Britain in iron and steel production. Small-scale furnaces were set up in backyards all over China. Frequently, knives and iron bedsteads were melted down to produce new metal to meet production targets. The metal was then made into new knives and iron bedsteads! To fuel the exercise, large tracts of the country were deforested. The Great Leap Forward created great confusion and mal-coordination. It resulted in a massive famine costing the lives of some 30 million Chinese (Becker, 1996). This experiment in 'social engineering' repeated and even surpassed Stalin's forced collectivization. In the early 1960s, Chinese agriculture recovered, but the 'Cultural Revolution' soon disrupted food production and distribution again. It was another top-down political campaign, which massively disrupted production, exchange and people's daily lives, apart from intimidating the population.

By the late 1970s, after Mao's death, there were food riots in the western inland province of Sichuan (then some 100 million inhabitants). Provincial party leaders knew no solution other than to disband the People's Communes and allot specific land rights to the farmers. Families were not given outright legal property titles, but there was a firm understanding that household units (families) could till the allocated land in the future, by and large as they saw fit, could pass the land on to their children or sell it. Farmers were permitted to sell their produce freely in private markets, once officially claimed plan quotas, a tax, were delivered to the government.

The results of the Sichuan reform were immediate and spectacular. Food supplies went up by 50 per cent within two years and a much greater variety of fresh food became available (Kasper, 1981). For example, farmers now found it rewarding again to harvest and transport peaches to urban markets, whereas they had previously fed the fruit to pigs or distilled brandy for their own consumption. The plan had not set a target for peaches, for central planners cannot handle perishable products that ripen at unpredictable times. Self-management was also extended to a few selected industrial firms, where productivity, quality and worker satisfaction soon soared (*idem*).

The positive results of the Sichuan reforms soon spread the new institutional concepts to some 500 million peasants throughout China, as well as to growing parts of manufacturing industry and services. The People's Commune system faded quickly away. The biggest ever system transformation went without great problems and ushered in decades of rising rural living standards.[2] There have been no famines since.

By the late 1980s, China had a fairly liberalized economy, where private individuals and firms undertook the allocational decisions concerning about 60 per cent of all goods and services (a bigger share than, for example, in West Germany). The economy was opened increasingly to the world market, but Party commissars and officials often kept trying to extract rents (bribes) from producers. What remains of the State industry sector often incurs heavy losses, was allowed to wither away selectively, but in the new century received renewed attention and access to funding from the Party and the government. Other parts of the economy were corporatized, which has subjected the residual state sector to the institutional disciplines of de facto capitalism, separating ownership from management (state capitalism).

Workers and pensioners of former state-owned enterprises experienced marked drops in living standards as compared to those who worked in private enterprises. In 1997, the Party – under a new principle 'seizing the large and releasing the small' – decided to sell off or close numerous small, loss-making state-owned enterprises and to concentrate on retaining only about one thousand large ones in socialized ownership (International Monetary Fund, 1997, pp. 119–127; Jefferson and Rawski, 1995). This sent out signals that a growing part of the economy would be subject to market forces and stricter budget constraints.

Between 2000 and 2009, the relative importance of state-owned enterprises has trended further downward, from about half of all sales to less than 30 per cent. The number of private businesses has been estimated by one informed source to have risen by a staggering 30 per cent per annum, and this excludes the burgeoning small-business sector.[3] Of the 43 million companies in China, 93 per cent are now private; other insider estimates put the GDP contribution of firms that are majority-owned by private investors to gross domestic product at between 66 and 70 per cent (*The Economist*, 12 March 2011, p. 72).

As of the early 2010s, the state's role in the economy has thus been greatly scaled back, with the dynamic non-state sector now generating more than two thirds of the national product. The economy is in many respects open to international trade and foreign investment (although there remains much beyond-the-border discrimination, Section 11.3), and macroeconomic management has been passed to some extent to an increasingly less government-dependent central bank. In many of the new industrial areas, government influence over small businesses is small and free markets rule, based on sometimes fuzzy internal institutions (Ferguson, 2011, p. 284). The People's Republic of China is now even rated surprisingly well when it comes to the protection of private property rights, in particular in physical property. An authoritative international survey of property rights protection places China in the middle range of 129 countries, about on a par with India, Latvia, Turkey or Thailand (Jackson et al., 2011, p. 28). The rate of private home ownership in China is now close to 80 per cent, higher than in Britain, the United States or Switzerland (*The Economist*, 5 March 2011, 'Special Report on Property', p. 5), and private savings are high because most have to provide for their own health care and old age. The problems of the welfare state have so far been avoided.

All this is of course not to say that the institutions, under which most Chinese work and live, are equivalent of what is the norm in, say, the Anglo-Saxon countries, but China's state capitalism is an unimaginable qualitative leap away from the former socialist system. Despite the remarkable institutional changes, the Chinese economy still contains many spheres that are not guided by the 'invisible hand', at least not predominantly so. The one-party state tightened its influence over the economy in the 2010s, retaining majority ownership of big 'national champions', which normally receive preferential access to credit and official patronage (*The Economist*, 21 January 2012, Special Report on 'State Capitalism').

As in other fast-growing, emerging economies – and in earlier decades in Japan, South Korea or Taiwan (Section 14.4) – it is still relatively easy for bureaucrats in China to 'pick winners', imitating what has been successful elsewhere and then undercutting established competitors abroad. With sufficient capital, it is also easy to buy leading-edge technology and knowhow, often by taking over entire, more advanced companies in other countries. When governments remove administrative obstacles, such champions are in a position to add mightily to modernization and economic growth, in particular in infrastructures (such as rail and telecom networks) and key industries (such as steel and motor vehicles).

However, the history of state capitalism and economic analysis (as referred to in Section 7.2) suggest caution in concluding that China's state capitalism will beat traditional competitive market capitalism over the long term. The – once widely admired – strategy of Japan's Ministry of International Trade and Industry (MITI) found it impossible to 'pick industrial winners', once Japan's industry had reached technological frontiers, indeed even before MITI often 'picked losers' (OECD, 1983; Kasper, 1994)[4]. Likewise, many of the government-favoured South Korean *chaebol* came to grief and were found to have a corrupting influence over Korea's young democracy, as the theory of economic competition suggests (Section 8.4). The discipline of genuine market competition and the 'signal of red ink' have always proven to be the most effective incentives to innovate on a sustained and broad front.

The universal human characteristics that shape risk-taking, competition and rent-seeking (as discussed in Chapters 7 to 10 above) have not been overcome by East-Asian 'state capitalism', as practiced from Singapore to Beijing, despite a cultural disposition to collective coordination. In reality, the core of China's dynamic state-owned sector has become a tool of the monopoly political party, or rather its leadership. However, the managers, who are formally the Party's agents, often are also able to educate their supervisors and ultimate owners, in part because industry managers and supervising bureaucrats often change places. It is, however, relevant to note that, between 2001 and 2009, China's state-owned companies managed a negative average real rate of return of 1.47 per cent despite low-cost inputs of land and capital (*The Economist*, op. cit., p. 14). Moreover, the preferential access of state-owned corporations has made it harder for genuinely private enterprises in China to expand and innovate, and the pulling power of job security and favourable employment conditions in public-sector firms is diverting talented, skilled people away from private enterprises. As a result, a new-class elite has benefited, but the vast majority of Chinese workers has been left somewhat behind. This is reflected in widening and politically precarious income and wealth differences.

Chicanery and corrupt treatment of private firms persist, much of it springing from the power monopoly of the Party and a highly politicized legal system. The necessary shift from the rule of men to the rule of law is not easy and is not even half complete. But civil mores, based on a long tradition of Confucian values (and, to a limited extent, the present-day spread of Christianity), free labour markets, relatively small government and growing international competition are exerting institutional disciplines, within which traditional Chinese entrepreneurial traditions can unfold. As incomes rise and services become more important, there will be an unremitting and growing requirement to reduce transaction costs by institutional reforms, as in most other new industrial countries (Section 14.6). In how far these can be achieved under the political monopoly of the Party remains an open and problematic question.

To date, China's institutional changes have gone along with an unprecedented wave of economic growth that now reaches into the remotest villages. Although the statistics are not always reliable, it is safe to say that real gross domestic product has increased about ten-fold from 1979 to 2010 (yielding an average growth rate in real per capita incomes of some 6.5 per cent). Improved institutions have not only mobilized much capital investment, but have also substantially contributed to the improved productivity of capital, labour and skills (International Monetary Fund, 1997, p. 123).

China's rapid economic ascendancy is unprecedented in human history, which only underlines the crucial importance of appropriate institutions to economic growth (Section 1.3). The leadership of the Communist Party was no doubt largely ignorant of the institutions best suited to fostering economic growth, but once Maoist ideology was replaced by pragmatism, at least one influential Party faction set out to learn. One way was to study the apparent successes of the capitalist system elsewhere in East Asia, to analyse the fast economic growth in China's privatized (or corporatized state-owned) industries and to set up special free-enterprise zones in coastal China. In these Special Economic Zones, the Chinese leadership conducted pragmatic experiments with different, non-communist institutions, allowing private property, stock markets, and freedom from *dirigiste* regulation of factor and product markets. The stunning industrialization successes of these areas encouraged the spread of economic freedom to the rest of the nation (see Box 12.1 in Section 12.4).

Despite the odds and on balance, inter-jurisdictional rivalry has – as elsewhere – fostered more growth-promoting institutions (Section 12.3 and following Chapter).

Escaping socialist central planning: the Russian and the Chinese way

In both major socialist command economies, it became apparent that collective central planning was poorly equipped to deal with imperfect and changeable information, which was its Archilles heel (Boettke and Leeson, 2004). Liberal, decentralized planning and *ex post* coordination in markets is an infinitely more robust institutional system to gather and exploit useful knowledge. When the two major communist command regimes extricated themselves from central planning, they did so in remarkably differing ways: The People's Republic of China implemented fewer *de jure* changes, and the Communist Party is still in control. But de facto the policy changes have been major and the material outcomes amazing. By contrast, Russian governments implemented fundamental *de jure* changes, but the de facto changes have been less thorough. In other words, the Russian escape from the command economy relied on changing the external institutions, whereas the Chinese relied more on adapting long-standing internal institutions, while leaving the architecture, though not the spirit and substance, of the external institutions in place.

This raises the important question: why? While a definitive answer still seems elusive, it is tempting to speculate that the deeply ingrained value system of Chinese civilization, the attitudes to work and community relations, and the skills of the Chinese favoured a pragmatic and constructive de facto reorientation. An old saying goes: "The Emperor stops at the village gate", which means that, in Chinese understanding, external institutions can only go so far and that one has to make one's own pragmatic arrangements in one's own immediate community. The self-reliance of Chinese clans and families has provided essential support and social cohesion, whatever external institutions were put in place by government. The long tradition that the Emperor is far away and individuals must cooperate reasonably to make things happen stood the Chinese in good stead. Marxism was an alien import, which tried to change this, but with little lasting effect. By contrast, a long tradition of Feudalism and three generations of communist rule in Russia combined with an Orthodox Christian tradition that did not seek salvation in self-reliant, individual effort, but rather sees it as a mystical result of divine grace (Némo, 2006, p. 103). Authoritarian Marxism could link up with long cultural traditions of hierarchy and repression (Pejovich, 2003). Moreover, the rulers of

China have had for millennia to demonstrate that they have the 'Mandate of Heaven' by ensuring the prosperity of the people. Dynasties fell when discord and poverty spread. Party leaders are aware of it when they propagate the slogan: 'China has to become rich before it becomes old'. Most rulers in Russia's history have, by contrast, not been notably impressed by the thought that they might be responsible for the welfare of the masses. As so often in institutional evolution, it has been the culture that ultimately mattered most (*metis* again).

NOTES

1 Was it a revolution at all? While the February overthrow of the Tsarist regime deserves this label, the communist take-over of power in October arguably does not. Was it proletarian? Only very few workers took part. In essence, it was a coup by radical intellectuals and professional revolutionaries, supported by disaffected soldiers of the Petrograd garrison. Indeed, it was arguably not even an October revolution, as it happened in November according to our Gregorian calendar.

2 The income position of Chinese peasants improved partly because they were able to sell output privately at high prices in free markets, while continuing to obtain many inputs (such as fertilizers and electricity) at regulated, low prices.

3 This rapid expansion of the number of new firms is in line with the worldwide observation that the 'birthrate' of enterprises is closely correlated with real economic growth, whereas the winding down of companies – the 'death rate' – appears to be a fairly regular and steady phenomenon.

4 MITI officials famously told the Sony corporation in the early 1960s that transistors had no future and the Honda motorcycle company that the car market was already overcrowded, so that Honda should stay away. The big, well-known Japanese companies owe little of their innovative and marketing successes to the bureaucracy.

14

Economic freedom and development

This chapter, like the preceding one, has an empirical, inductive orientation: Is economic freedom important to economic growth and the quality of life both in developing and mature developed economies, as first asserted in Chapter 1? We will show how the hard-to-assess quality of economic freedom is estimated and what insights can be induced from actual experiences with economic freedom and reforms to promote it.

In less developed countries, the failure of central planning and *dirigiste* policies to attain rapid economic development demonstrated how absolutely harmful political interference with secure private property, competitive markets and the rule of law has been to lifting people out of poverty. Foreign aid to governments of less developed countries often runs counter to the beneficial effects of openness on institutional evolution, because it bankrolls established rent-seeking elites and discourages democracy.

More generally, *dirigiste* top-down development policies often only entrenched crony capitalism, including in fast-growing East-Asian export economies. As long as new industrial locations offer low-cost local production factors (land, labour and government services, often thanks to tax exemptions), internationally mobile production factors (capital, enterprise and technical knowledge) are attracted. However, over time economic growth raises land rents, wages and tax revenue – after all, the purpose of growth – and transaction costs rise. Further development then depends on economic reforms that reduce transaction costs.

In the mature, affluent economies, the democratic, redistributive welfare state led, from the 1970s onwards, to social disaffection and economic slowdown. This had much to do with a loss of competitiveness vis-à-vis the new industrial countries (globalization). Since the 1980s, slow growth and the new international competition have triggered some (Austrian-inspired) economic reforms in the affluent economies, as some new industrial countries also adopted more market-conform development strategies. Policy makers around the world were often obliged to become subservient to international market pressures. However, as of the 2010s, fears of climate change (and a global financial crisis starting after 2007) have enabled political elites in many countries to reclaim a 'primacy of politics', which causes renewed concerns about the future of secure property rights, free and open markets and the rule of simple and just laws, in other words about the robustness of economies to handle new challenges.

It is wrong to see the existing state as an all-knowing, all-powerful guardian of all economic activity. But it is also incorrect to accept the existing state, which is corrupted by interest groups, as irreversibly given . . . Without a competitive order, no government will be able to act, and without such a government there will be no competitive order.

Walter Eucken, *Grundsätze der Wirtschaftspolitik* (1952) – our translation

The most dangerous time for bad government is when it starts to reform itself.

Alexis de Toqueville commenting on the last French king, Louis XVI

The greatest concern of a government should be to get the people gradually used to make do without it.

Alexis de Tocqueville, *Carnets de voyage* (1831) – our translation

Today we resort to more and more administrative controls and receive less and less in exchange . . . there is an enormous and welcome political opportunity for any political party which understands that, by doing less, government will achieve more.

Richard Epstein, *Simple Rules for a Complex World* (1995)

Today's debate about global warming is essentially a debate about freedom. The environmentalists would like to mastermind each and every possible (and impossible) aspect of our lives.

Vaclav Klaus, *Blue Planet in Green Shackles* (2008)

14.1   Some growth comparisons

During the fourth quarter of the twentieth century, institutions that favoured economic freedom were enhanced in many places around the world, sometimes through revolutionary system transformations, as after the demise of totalitarian socialism in most of the former Soviet empire, sometimes by more gradual reforms in mature and emerging countries alike.

Fundamental differences in economic constitutions developed during the twentieth century due to ideology and the support of self-interested elites that benefited from an interventionist rule set. As we realize in hindsight, the reforms were often inspired by the pragmatic, utilitarian insight that economic freedom is good for economic growth. While some reformers saw liberty as a worthwhile aspiration in its own right, international political rivalry and the pursuit of economic growth to support it were clearly the main motivations for more competitive habits and the reform of poor regulations and freedom-hampering legislation.

During the last quarter of the twentieth century, political leaders and public opinion could not help but become aware of some basic facts about growth and economic freedom, which may best be illustrated with a few international comparisons:

(a) Germans in the (western) Federal Republic and in the (east bloc) Democratic Republic started from about the same (low) income level after the war. By the fall of the Berlin Wall in 1989, West Germans had reached one of the world's highest income levels by fostering a liberal order, private property, competition, constitutional government, economic stability and an open economy. After 40 years under a collectivist planning system with state ownership of industry, agriculture and services, the average productivity and income of East Germans were probably only 40 per cent of those of their Western compatriots.

(b) By 1975, a big difference was evident between increasingly market-oriented Taiwan and Maoist China. Although the Taiwanese started from a somewhat higher base in the early 1950s, within one generation their measured living standards were some 4.5 to 8 times higher than average living standards in the People's Republic. Free-trading Hong Kong citizens reached developed-country status within 45 years from the mid-1950s. By 1975, average living standards in Hong Kong were probably some eight times those of Mao's China, despite a big influx of destitute refugees and a total lack of natural resources.

(c) As of 1994, the 36 million overseas Chinese were producing about as much as the one thousand million Chinese operating under the gradually liberalizing institutions of the People's Republic (Tanzer, 1994, pp. 144–145).

(d) On all available indications, South Koreans, who started from a poorer industry base than the communist North and had to rebuild their totally war-ravaged country in the 1950s, were by the late 1990s at least ten times better off materially than their compatriots living under totalitarian socialism (*The Economist*, 22 February 1997, p. 33). The same floods that led to years of famine in the North were immediately tackled by South Korean farm owners and had no lasting impact. As of 2009, the average income of North Koreans was estimated by the CIA at US$1800, and that of South Koreans at US$30,000 (source: http://en.wikipedia.org/wiki/List_of_countries_by_GDP_(PPP)_ per_capita, accessed 25 January 2012).

(e) Two decades after the end of the Vietnam War, communist Vietnam was still among the poorest nations on earth, whereas neighbouring Thailand and Malaysia – with similar resource endowments and living standards in the 1930s, but open, pretty capitalist market economies – had affluent, fast-growing economies. By the mid-1990s, measured material living standards there appeared to be some 20 times those of socialist Vietnam.

(f) Towards the end of the century, market-oriented, though tribal and corrupt, Kenya had a per capita income roughly double that of neighbouring Tanzania, a preferred recipient of foreign aid and the poster child of 'African socialism'.

Such comparisons of course indicate only rough orders of magnitude. However, they show that the international rivalry for economic growth was lost resoundingly by socialist, centrally-planned regimes. The differences in track record went beyond mere income growth. Access for average citizens to education, health and old age support was poorer under socialism. The destruction of environmental amenities frequently far exceeded anything that democratic, capitalist societies would have tolerated. Repressive supervision and the intimidation of average citizens and dissidents were often pervasive. Top-down coercion in collectivist regimes also encouraged indifference, subservience, shirking, duplicity and careerism, as well as ruthless rent-seeking by elites. The freedom of speech, information, travel, career choice and association were frequently denied to ordinary citizens for the sake of maintaining a command economy and upholding the privileges of the leading elites of the regime.

These failures explain the speed with which the socialist order and central planning collapsed in most countries, once matters began to unravel in the late 1980s. These failures also explain why economic reforms advanced freedom in the capitalist economies.

14.2 Economic freedom and the consequences

The transformation of the former Soviet bloc economies and the gradual, though imperfect liberalization of the Chinese economy were part of a worldwide move towards greater economic freedom and an acceleration of average global economic growth. While there were exceptions to this, the big picture – outlined in Figure 14.1 – reflects the growing realization among policy makers and the wider public that the institutions which support economic freedom do matter.

Economists, such as American Milton Friedman (1912–2006), argued that public opinion and policy makers could be more easily convinced of the merits of a free market economy with secure property rights, if these institutional qualities could be somehow quantified and depicted for different countries. This led to an initiative of the Fraser Institute in Canada and the Cato Institute in the US to cooperate with a growing number of think tanks around the world to construct annual economic freedom indexes. The work is done under the intellectual leadership of James Gwartney and Robert Lawson (Gwartney and Lawson, *passim*; Lawson, 2008).[1] The researchers are drawing on a wide range of statistical data (such as the share of government consumption in national product, tariff rates and rates of inflation) and results of surveys of business leaders with international experience (such as assessments of the intensity of international financial competition) to construct an index, which summarizes the conditions in product and factor markets (for labour and capital), as well as fundamental public policies as to the security of private property rights and the freedom of their use.[2] The index now covers more than ten dozen countries with widely differing economic regimes, ranging from Hong Kong and Singapore to un-free economies, such as Syria, Algeria, Ethiopia, Venezuela and Zimbabwe.

Figure 14.1 shows that economic freedom in the world improved from the 1970s to the 1990s, coinciding with the rapid globalization and accelerating economic growth in many parts of the world, but that progress stalled since the early 2000s. The Figure also shows that major economies went through a period of deteriorating economic freedom in the wake of the first oil crisis and global recession in the 1970s, but that the prosperous 1980s and 1990s were marked by improvements. This broad impression is reaffirmed if one looks at the many countries reported in the 'Economic Freedom of the World Index' (Gwartney et al., 2011). The two rivalling, free-trading city states of Hong Kong and Singapore (in Figure 14.1, we show the unweighted average of the two) have consistently been rated as most free, and the United States had long been the benchmark for other affluent economies to follow. But that changed after the end of superpower rivalry with the Soviet Union and, since 2000, with the 'compassionate conservatism' of the Bush administration, increased interventionism by the Obama administration and growing US government deficits. A marked difference was also made during the Thatcher years in the United Kingdom, a move that was echoed in other Anglo-Saxon countries, such as New Zealand and Australia (not shown in Figure 14.1). Finally, the figure draws attention to the remarkable advances of economic freedom in China since the death of Mao Zedong, in India and Brazil since the mid-1980s and Russia since 1995, though these jurisdictions are still falling far short of the freedom standards of the West, as represented here by Britain and the USA.

Figure 14.1 Economic freedom in selected countries

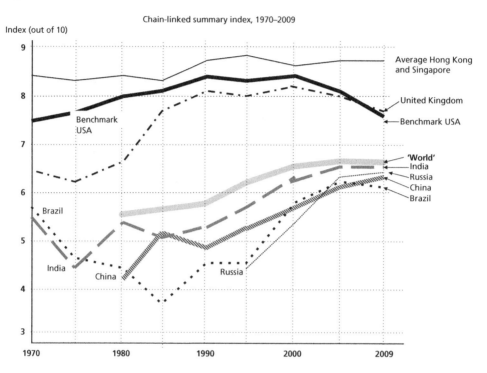

Chain-linked summary index, 1970–2009

Economic freedom: prosperity, wealth and happiness

Analyses of economic freedom across countries and over time show that a higher degree of economic freedom (as expressed by the Fraser-Cato index) is associated with:

- higher levels of real income (in 2008, the average of the freest quartile of countries enjoyed real per-capita incomes (PPP) some 8.5 times those of the least free quartile);
- better rates of economic growth in the freest economies (Figure 14.2).

More economic freedom also goes along with:

- marked rises in the *absolute* income levels of the poorest 10 per cent when economic freedom improves (although the *relative* income share of the poorest 10 per cent seems unaffected by income levels and standards of economic freedom);
- a difference in life expectancy of about 20 years between people in

Figure 14.2 Economic freedom and living standards

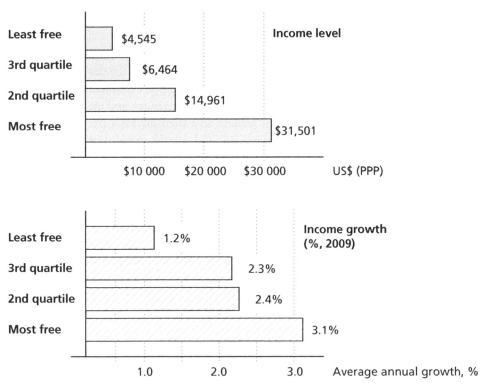

Gross domestic product per inhabitant at purchasing
power parity (PPP), 2009, by quartiles of 141 countries

Income level

Least free	$4,545
3rd quartile	$6,464
2nd quartile	$14,961
Most free	$31,501

$10 000 $20 000 $30 000   US$ (PPP)

Income growth
(%, 2009)

Least free	1.2%
3rd quartile	2.3%
2nd quartile	2.4%
Most free	3.1%

1.0   2.0   3.0   Average annual growth, %

Source: Gwartney et al. (2011), p. 17.

the freest and least free quartiles of economies, which may well be
considered the ultimate cost of the repression of economic freedom;

- a better attainment of political and civil liberties, reminding us of the
  assertion by Milton Friedman and others that economic freedom is often
  the lodestar of overall freedom (Friedman, 1962);
- a lesser likelihood of military conflicts and violence between nations that
  have realized a high level of economic freedom (Gartzke, 2005; Weede,
  2011), while civil war, organized crime and civic violence have been
  identified as causes of persistent poverty and widening gaps in living
  standards (World Bank, 2011); and
- on average, economic freedom comes with higher ratings on life satisfaction, which adds some empirical substance to the assertion that greater
  freedom and self-responsibility enhance 'happiness' (Gwartney and
  Lawson, *passim* (2010), pp. 17–19; also see Easterbrook, 2003).

These are not only statements of positive economics, but appropriately also shed normative light on institutional economics.

14.3 Economic freedom and development

Top-down development strategies

After attaining independence from colonial rule, many of the developing countries embarked on centrally designed and mandated economic development strategies. Most were inspired by constructivist visions and attempted social engineering. The new political leaders and their advisors frequently opted for modernization strategies that depended greatly on political guidance and collective action. They were coordinated by centrally mandated development plans, which set national targets. Often, attempts were made to replace fuzzy, internal institutions and existing cultural traditions by designed external institutions. Often, the imported laws, regulations and ideologies clashed with traditional internal institutions. The clash led to contradictions and a diminution of the traditional economic order (Bates, 1990; Aligica and Boudreaux, 2007). Often, centrally designed schemes failed to function as expected, because the administrative apparatus to implement them was lacking and the new external institutions were not supported by values and the internal institutions of traditional communities. Where attempted, the enforcement of central schemes was costly. The problems of development proved too complex and intricate to be comprehensible to anyone at the centre. As a result, private incentives to modernize were destroyed and knowledgeable elites in established private businesses were suppressed. The political elites in many developing countries acted on the arrogant pretence of knowledge, treating their nations as if they were simple organizations. This had a destructive effect on economic welfare and other fundamental aspirations.

The constructivist impulse, based on the notion that an elite knows best what it takes to trigger economic development, was often combined with increases in the ownership of socialized assets, either because property inherited from colonial times was transferred into government ownership or because new factories and infrastructures were set up as government-owned (and often foreign aid assisted) enterprises.

The need to couple economic development with the development of a rule system that facilitates a modern division of labour and the effective signalling of emerging opportunities and scarcities was not fully appreciated by foreign advisors and international bureaucrats either. Reflecting the prevailing neoclassical economic mindset, the fraternity of development advisors neglected the institutional dimension. At best, economists began to argue for the opening up of national economies and for macroeconomic stability from the 1960s onwards (for example, Krueger, 1994; 1997; Riedel, 1988).

In the 1950s and early 1960s, central development plans were typically drawn up to promote industrialization. The growth of government-owned enterprises was promoted by artificial means, such as import protection, national quotas and tax holidays. Information about supply and demand conditions in the outside world was often suppressed by public export monopolies and import tariffs and quotas. Import licensing and tariffs were intended to generate high profits for privileged domestic producers, often 'political firms'. But a side effect of import substitution was that rent-seeking politicians, business administrators, bureaucratic supervisors and organized labour were soon able to appropriate the profits. The owners of capital enjoyed preferment and farmers and workers saw their economic opportunities curbed. Piecemeal interventionism piled unintended consequences on various industries, as was revealed by the chaos in 'effective rates of protection', when such rates could be calculated (Abramovitz, 1979; Krueger, 1997). Comparative advantages and the knowledge transfer by international trade were grossly neglected as production costs were driven up. Political patronage allowed firms to shirk innovation and cost control. Constructivist drives for development frequently went along also with massive, but ineffectual public spending and large budget deficits. Resulting high levels of public and foreign debt often fed into an inflationary expansion of the money supply.

The development strategies from the 1950s to 1970s, as described in this thumbnail sketch, were of course far from uniform. Latin American countries started with higher levels of development, but also more deeply entrenched interest groups, such as big landholders and the military. These groups often seized the central political controls to appropriate rents. Little was done to foster the rule of law and protect the universal institutions of a genuinely competitive order, even where these had previously existed. Instead, politics was seen as the instrument for seeking gain from redistributive discrimination (Bauer, 1957; Kilby, (ed.) 1971; Bauer and Sen, 2004; Borner et al., 1992; Aligica and Boettke, 2009). Inflation tended to advantage rich, well-connected borrowers with good access to credit and disadvantaged the poor, who often were even unable to obtain title to what they owned and therefore were not creditworthy (de Soto, 1990; 2001). In South Asia and many African countries, development also depended on socialist five-year plans and heavy interventions. In many respects, the East Asian developing countries were the exceptions in the 1960s and 1970s, when they increasingly deviated from the predominant fashions in development economics and embarked on export orientation and the attraction of direct foreign investment.

More market-driven versus more planned development

Some regimes in the amorphous Third World relied on more constructivist development strategies and state ownership of the means of production than others. In the meantime, the evidence shows that more market-reliant economic regimes attained faster economic growth and less inflation, as well as a more even income distribution than the more interventionist-constructivist countries (World Bank, 1993, 1995; Gwartney and Lawson, *passim*). While many factors influence actual growth rates and statistical measurements have shortcomings, the following salient differences cannot be explained without reference to systematic institutional differences. Here are some telling examples:

- India's political leadership tried for a long time after independence in 1948 to imitate the Soviet model of development. Under Nehru, they adopted elaborate and detailed trade controls and central planning of industry and finance. In the 1960s, its *dirigiste* style of economic development was reinforced with experiments in direct state ownership of industry. Pakistan by contrast pursued a less interventionist strategy, indeed freed up markets and prices. India's real growth rate in the 1960s was 3 per cent per annum, little above the population growth rate, whereas Pakistan managed growth between 5 and 6 per cent per annum. India's inflation averaged in that period 5.5 per cent annually, whereas Pakistan's somewhat freer markets averaged an inflation rate of around 2 per cent. (Since then, the liberalization of the Indian economy has reversed the picture.)
- In East Africa, Kenya adopted a less interventionist set of institutions, whereas neighbouring Tanzania engaged in pervasive socialist development and imposed intrusive trade controls. Kenya's economic growth per capita in the 1970s averaged 2.4 per cent, more than double Tanzania's 1.1 per cent. By the turn of the millennium, the average Kenyan had a real per capita income about double that of the average Tanzanian. During the final quarter of the twentieth century, per capita incomes in Kenya had grown very slowly (0.45 per cent per annum), but Tanzanian ones had shrunk (−0.24 per cent per annum) (Maddison, 2001).
- In West Africa, Ghana originally implemented socialist-*dirigiste* concepts, suppressing markets and private enterprise, whereas neighbouring Ivory Coast (*Côte d'Ivoire*) relied more on markets, openness and private enterprise. In the 1970s, Ghanaians suffered a 2.6 per cent annual decline in living standards, whereas the citizens of Ivory Coast managed a 1.5 per cent increase annually in their per capita incomes. Growing *dirigisme* in

both countries, however, led to declining living standards over the entire final quarter of the century, in line with many other parts of poorly governed, aid-dependent Africa. In the erstwhile 'Pearl of West Africa', Ivory Coast, one-party rule, military coups and ethnic politics diminished economic freedom even by low African standards, whereas Ghana has liberalized its economy to some extent, so that real per-capita incomes in Ghana as of 2010 were 40-50 per cent higher than in Ivory Coast.

- In Asia, the former British colony of Sri Lanka shifted in the 1960s to central price fixing, investment controls and reliance on socialist capital formation, whereas similarly endowed Malaya (later Malaysia) pursued an open trade policy and relied for investment predominantly on markets. It overcame a communist emergency, not least thanks to the rule of law that gave the poor access to economic opportunities, education and modern health care. The growth rate in per capita income averaged about 4.5 per cent (1960-75), coupled with minimal inflation. By contrast, Sri Lanka's economic interventions became more and more detailed. As a consequence, per capita incomes grew by about 2 per cent in real terms (1960-75) and then decelerated. Racial discrimination and resultant tensions exploded out into a protracted and bloody civil war; despite mandated price controls, inflation steadily accelerated.[3]

The list of such country comparisons could be extended without affecting our general conclusion, namely that reliance on the institutions that secure private property, private autonomy and openness went along with faster growth. One may of course ask whether these differences in economic performance are due to market institutions causing faster growth, or whether only fast-growing countries can afford economic freedom. The economic theories developed in this book should leave little doubt that the causation runs mainly from the institutional regime to economic performance.

Admittedly, the above comparisons rely in the first instance on indirect evidence, inferring the growth consequences of a market orientation, which are brought about by differences in institutional frameworks. Direct microeconomic evidence of the impact of institutions on the growth rates in developing countries is still scarce and hardly systematic. However, studies such as de Soto's (1990; 2001) analysis of the informal economy of Peru drew attention to the central importance of secure property titles for development. Similarly, some cross-country evidence also shows how specific institutional arrangements can help or hinder economic development (Graham and Seldon, 1990; Borner et al., 1992; Brunetti et al., 1997; Aligica and Boettke, 2009; Boettke et al., 2008).

Institutional awareness is now also penetrating the policy advice of international organizations. Economic reforms since the 1980s have been strongly influenced by what has been dubbed the 'Washington consensus' namely monetary stabilization, structural adjustment and trade liberalization (Graham and Seldon, 1990; Edwards, 1995, pp. 58–70; World Bank, 1993, World Bank, *passim*). It was increasingly pointed out that the control of budgets and money supplies, financial development, deregulation of domestic trade, privatization and the move to a lean state requires thorough institutional reform (Aligica and Boudreaux, 2007). Yet, all too often economic advisors assumed that institutional change would somehow be managed through specific, concrete policy proposals. And those proposals themselves were all too often based on neoclassical micro- and macro-economics (see *Epilogue*). Only gradually have international organizations begun to consider that the problems of institutional change have to be solved first and that a good understanding of sociology, law and economics should take precedence over econometric modelling (for example, Klitgaard, 1995; Aligica and Boudreaux, 2007; Boettke et al., 2008; Acemoğlu and Robinson, 2012).

KEY CONCEPTS

Development plans are drawn up by bureaucracies and governments to predetermine economic and industrial structures over four, five or twenty years into the future and to identify the need for certain political actions to ensure that the planned developments will happen.

Where such plans are used as indicative, broad-brush exercises to identify needs for long-term infrastructure investments or to assist in consistent public budget forecasts, they may fulfil a useful information and coordination role. Where they are made obligatory and are seen as a replacement of coordination by markets, they tend to run into the typical difficulties of central planning of complex, dynamic development.

Import substitution is a policy of protecting domestic producers (local capital owners and workers) from international competition, normally by import tariffs and import quotas. The primary intent is to secure markets for initially non-world-competitive local producers in the hope that they will learn how to produce effectively. It is also intended to create investment, jobs and tax revenue at the expense of foreigners. Import substitution redistributes incomes and wealth from buyers, who now have to pay higher prices, to domestic producers and governments. In the process, import substitution also encourages rent-seeking by the domestic workers and capital owners in the protected industries. By making market niches durable, it reduces competitive stimuli to control costs and to innovate. Over the long term, import substitution therefore has hampered economic development.

Foreign aid, institutional rigidity and corruption

The economic rationale for transferring capital and other resources from affluent to poorer countries (as gifts or long-term loans) was that the productivity of capital and other resources in countries with few of these assets would be much higher than in the affluent, capital-rich parts of the world. It was also felt that solidarity should be applied worldwide – and not just to 'thy neighbours', as the Bible once advised. It was soon discovered that transferring mere capital goods was not a recipe for economic advances; the aid recipients had to be taught complementary skills. Yet, the reality of development aid to poor countries showed that the crucial conditions to make aid and imported machinery work productively were proper internal and external institutions in the recipient societies. Institutional defects were serious obstacles to modernization (Bauer, 1957; 2000; Bauer and Sen, 2004). The doyen of development economics, British economist Lord Peter Bauer, famously criticized official foreign aid as a "transfer from poor people in rich countries to rich elites in poor countries" (Bauer, 1957).

Time and again, rich-country governments and international organizations have laid down official plan targets for making transfers to the tune of certain percentages of donor countries' incomes. The United Nations, which failed in its original two missions, namely ensuring world peace and human rights, has over the recent decade pushed 'millennium goals', attaining a set of planned benchmarks with the help of massively increased foreign aid. This flies in the face of past experience. Thus, an estimated US$1000 billion were transferred to Africa alone between 1955 and 2005, and during the first decade of the new millennium, African regimes have received some US$80 billion annually in aid. Yet, with few exceptions, African living standards have fallen over the second half of the twentieth century (source: http://news. bbc.co.uk/go/pr/fr/-/1/hi/sci/tech/4209956.stm).

US economist William Easterly has attacked such summary global plans as utopian and foreign aid as ultimately self-defeating (Easterly, 2006). Economics Nobel Laureate Amartya Sen has made the same points (Sen, 1999). The knowledge problem, which is a fundamental reality for Austrian institutional economics, has ever so often been assumed away by development planners, but it surfaces regularly, not least because societal norms and the internal and external institutions in poor countries are deficient.

There have also been periodic actions to 'forgive' bad (un-repayable) government debts of underdeveloped countries. Forgiving debt destroys the long-term creditworthiness of intending borrowers in poor countries.

International capital markets, which depend on trust and rule enforcement, have thus been repeatedly undermined to the detriment also of honest Third World borrowers. In other words, as so often, good deeds have had unexpected, deleterious side effects.

It is now increasingly acknowledged that massive foreign aid created a related dilemma: Massive transfers from the affluent West (and to some extent the socialist 'Second World') to the Third World have hampered institutional development. Economists, who are aware of the central importance of institutional change to development (a school now sometimes dubbed 'The New Development Economics') have shown how often political elites and the wider population in previously poor countries have been forced to rethink traditional institutions and to change growth-inhibiting habits and laws because neighbours and rivals did better (Section 12.3). The role of free-market Singapore and Hong Kong in inspiring economic reforms and openness throughout Southeast Asia and the role of Hong Kong, Taiwan and South Korea in inspiring liberalization in the People's Republic of China come to mind. As so often in history, economic trauma overcomes cognitive barriers and triggers economic reforms (Sections 12.2–12.3). Foreign aid easily undermines this process. Corrupt institutions in poor countries, which are a blight on social stability and economic growth, need not be reformed, as long as the material consequences of corruption are neutralized by donations. "Foreign aid . . . tends to facilitate corruption. Because simply disbursing aid to kleptocratic regimes has debased the institutions essential for economic growth and has entrenched corrupt elites. Ruling *priviligentsias* frequently draw on nationalist and socialist sentiments to defend their privileges and to combat openness and transparency. Anti-globalisers now lend them support" (Kasper, 2006, p. 1). The effects of foreign aid on institutional evolution are thus comparable to the deleterious consequences of socialized welfare (Section 10.4). Aid creates disincentives to learn self-reliance and to enforce a universal rule system. Aid-funded reluctance to reform goes a long way to explaining the persistent backwardness of poor countries. Many young observers in poor, autocratically ruled countries have highlighted the fact that official aid has hampered the development of individual freedom and democracy.

It is no coincidence that the biggest recipients of foreign aid are among the most corrupt nations, for example Afghanistan, East Timor, the Congo, Papua New Guinea and Nigeria (Kasper, op. cit.). This is why some aid donors have tried to make foreign aid conditional on certain reforms, but such controls are denigrated as 'colonial'. In any event, it is near-impossible to enforce them, since aid agencies in Western capitals suffer from a knowledge problem, as well as agent opportunism: their jobs depend on aid flows.

Massive foreign aid has had another unintended consequence: If large parts of a government's budget are financed by foreign aid, the rulers have no incentive to seek political support from the local population. This is good neither for democracy nor the design of development policies. It has, for example, been shown how aid-financed public health bureaucracies set up costly capital-city clinics, yet highly paid doctors there are delivering few services to the general public, and few cost-benefit analyses are ever applied to health budgets. Lord Peter Bauer put it well: "To give money to the rulers on the basis of poverty of their subjects directly rewards policies for impoverishment" (Bauer, 2000; pp. 45–46).

Institutional economists and critical non-government observers from poor countries have concluded that the poor, the workers in these countries and frustrated exporters bear the brunt of the dual burden of aid and graft. In a growing number of poor countries, public agitation against official foreign aid has grown, and public pressure on the rulers to control corruption in high places has been mounting. Institutional reforms are now increasingly seen as the path out of poverty. In many parts, the fundamental problem of economic development is now understood as an issue of cultivating freedom and building the institutional foundations of trust (Sen, 1999).

KEY CONCEPTS

Foreign aid is the transfer of capital and other resources, typically from more affluent to poorer countries. Official foreign aid is the transfer of funds that have been 'collected by taxes from the poor in rich countries to the rich in poor countries', as Lord Peter Bauer used to put it. It tends to have the unexpected side effect that it frees ruling elites from doing the will of the electorate (weakens or avoids democracy) and enables them to pursue opportunistic rent-seeking. This institutional nexus goes a long way to explain for example why massive aid has not been successful in raising most Africans out of poverty.

Conditional foreign aid ties the disbursement of future aid transfers to previously agreed targets. It meets with objections of aid recipients and tends to overtax the capacity and will of donors to enforce the conditions (knowledge problem).

Reforms and tradition

Liberalization and a shift to universal institutions – both the external rules and, above all, the internal mores of society – are never easy, least in traditional, closed societies with a history of economic stagnation. After all, the institutions of capitalism emerged in the West only after a protracted process of trial and error (many errors, indeed!). Even in the nations with the institutions most supportive of competitive enterprise, the battle for economic freedom is never quite won. It also holds true that an important part of any nation's institutional capital consists of its traditional internal institutions, ranging from deeply ingrained attitudes towards social hierarchy, material wealth, peace and justice to individualism, habits of work, trading and innovation. The basic outlook on life varies greatly amongst different civilizations. Some cultures see the world as stationary (or locked into a repetitive cycle), so that it is a virtue to be fatalistic; others see the human fate in this world as something that can and should be improved (eschatological worldview, Kasper, 2011b; also Jones, 1995).

Observers of cultural change have sometimes concluded that only the complete transfer of the time-tested institutional structure of the West can support truly competitive modern industries and services. Others accept that external and internal institutions are based on deep cultural foundations, *metis* (Boettke et al., 2008). They make for path dependency, even if external technical and social changes come to bear on a society. On the basis of this view of institutional infrastructures, they have concluded that 'alternative modernities' will emerge (Kasper, 2011b). In particular the rapid modernization of East Asia now supports this conclusion, as adapted traditions are blending with technical and organizational modernization to yield the 'neo-Confucian growth model' (Section 12.2; Tu, 2000). The implication is that people from different cultures need not surrender their identity, as long as they show flexibility and pragmatism in making necessary cultural changes. This conclusion does not derive from cultural relativism. As we are arguing throughout this book, not all institutions, cultures and civilizations are of equal value when it comes to enabling the majority of people to pursue and attain their fundamental aspirations (Sowell, 1991; 1994; 1996; Casson, 1993; Jones, 1995). Yet, it seems likely that the twenty-first century will witness a renewed competition of institutional systems to realize the fundamental universal values that we discussed in Chapter 4.

14.4 East Asia: institutions and modernization

Contemporary thinking about cultural and economic development has been greatly influenced by the rapid economic development in East Asia. Economic growth took off first in a few small poor countries, which were cut off from the traditional focus of their civilization by the Communist revolution in China and which felt threatened. Later, sustained growth took off in one province of China after another.

In 1950, the share of East Asians, 28 per cent of the world's population, in global production and income (PPP) was a mere 14 per cent; midway through the first decade of the twenty-first century, their slice of the income cake was 24 per cent and rising. Did this singular economic advance have much to do with institutions and economic freedom? Some doubt this, since most countries in East Asia were ruled by autocrats in the early post-war period, and many of these countries, including China, still are not democratic.

The Second World War and the Chinese communist revolution had led to cataclysmic turmoil and extreme poverty in most of East Asia. However, the 1950s fashions of top-down development policy, in particular top-down planning, coercive birth controls and import substitution, were not emulated widely or for long in East Asia. The exceptions were most notably the Asian communist countries, as well as Sukarno's Indonesia, South Vietnam and the Philippines. The governments of the other, typically resource-poor, densely populated countries in East Asia decided instead to rely mainly on export orientation and, more importantly, on attracting foreign capital and enterprise (Kasper, 1994; 1998; World Bank, 1993). Given the threat to national security, economic prosperity was seen as the real source of strength in defending against communist aggression and internal subversion. The road to prosperity was sought in openness, which required respect for life and property by government, indeed the active protection of the property rights of international investors. Without these conditions, essential development assets would not be attracted. As governments in the Asia-Pacific region learnt how to deal with the owners of mobile resources, they began to undertake legal and regulatory reforms and enhanced their protective role. For example, foreign exchange and capital markets were gradually liberalized, the prudential supervision of banks was enhanced and industrial and building codes were clarified in one country after the other. While one could cite numerous exceptions and lapses in enforcement, the general trend in government activity has been to strengthen and clarify the universal rules necessary to underpin the extended order of the market. It is also worth noting that economic liberalization and the new prosperity brought demands for democracy from the new middle class, which soon changed the political institutions. In the more advanced Asian economies, it now matters less *whom* you know but *what* you know than was the case a generation ago. In this context it is also worth recalling that the survey of economic liberties, which we quoted in Section 14.1, ranks many of the countries in the Asia-Pacific region highly.

The fundamental decision in favour of openness to global markets – a generation before 'globalization' became a byword – had several gradual, but important institutional consequences:

(a) Knowledge from the outside world became more freely available and impacted directly and pervasively. World market prices, as well as direct feedback from sophisticated buyers, informed and guided much of the development effort.

(b) Policy makers were soon exposed to the learning process that we described in Section 12.4: They frequently went all out to attract capital, highly skilled people and enterprises from abroad, and they did so in pragmatic-evolutionary ways (see Box 12.1 on 'Free-Trade Zones'). Political leaders enhanced the attractiveness of their countries by fostering low-cost supplies of local labour, land and government services, as well as by facilitating higher productivity. In the process, they developed reasonably consistent and reliably enforced institutions, almost as a by-product. Complex, discriminatory political preferments were considered with scepticism, whereas 'getting the fundamentals right' proved a good and easy-to-manage way of attracting foreign investors and avoiding unintended side effects.[4]

There were of course exceptions to this general pattern, most notably in strongly nationalist, constructivist South Korea during the 1960s and 1970s, and of course the crass, xenophobic phase of communist development in the People's Republic of China prior to 1979 (Section 13.2) and in Vietnam. However, South Korea adopted democracy and curbed the influence of big, government-favoured corporations (*chaebol*). In China, and later Vietnam, the export-oriented, rule-focused 'Tiger model' inspired opening-up strategies, which have produced welcome economic results. This was true of China after Mao Zedong's death in 1975 and of unified Vietnam, belatedly from the late 1980s. Domestic lobby groups found it hard to organize themselves in these wide-open, competitive economies, even where these lobbies were based on ideological foundations and organizational structures, such as Communist Party membership. Most governments relied on a respectful, yet arms-length approach to private business interests, which emulated the Confucian teacher-pupil relationship and helped to keep the rules fairly universal (Kasper, 1994). Nevertheless, massive rents were created and shared by government officials, although on the whole, such practices are seen to be prejudicial to international competitiveness and growth (Mauro, 1995; Kasper, 1998).

(c) Different from less open economies in other parts of the Third World, the governments of the export-oriented East Asian countries aimed monetary and fiscal policies at safeguarding stability and international competitiveness (World Bank, 1993).

(d) Partly for reasons of tradition and partly because international competitiveness was a high priority, East-Asian governments did not engage in much redistribution through the tax-welfare mechanism. Rather, they concentrated on getting the basic rules right for promoting growth and competition. As already noted, this yielded a decent degree of income equality. Governments (except in the communist countries) fostered those external institutions that complemented the traditional internal institutions, instead of trying to replace them. Awareness of culture as a potential institutional asset was widespread. In addition, governments of the capitalist, export-oriented economies built up some production enterprises, but normally to modernize transport and communications infrastructures, whereas manufacturing was left much more to private enterprise than in South Asia or Latin America.

(e) Fast export-driven economic growth ensured that expanding busi-nesses had sooner or later to compete for qualified workers. This is, for example, reflected in the fact that economies with rising export shares in national production averaged a real-wage growth of 3 per cent per annum from 1970 to 1990, whereas inward-looking economies (with falling export/GNP ratios) averaged a decline of real wages (World Bank, 1995). This supports the contention that competitive markets are conducive to spreading the fruit of economic growth around. They cer-tainly do so more effectively than constructivist redistribution policies.

(f) As the East-Asian economies developed, many governments discov-ered that well-run, cheap infrastructure services were an important factor in international competitiveness. Governments also discovered that they had only limited administrative capabilities to run complex modern infrastructures, such as telecommunications, ports and urban transport systems. Since the 1980s, many existing public production ventures have been corporatized or privatized, and private competition of public-sector firms is encouraged. Motorways are often private roads; telecommunication is open to competition and is largely privately owned throughout the region; new infrastructure investments are fre-quently financed by private consortia. Even communist China now has numerous fee-paying, privately operated motorways. Governments laid the legislative and regulatory basis for the provision of public domain goods, but did not build up socialized property, relying on private ini-tiative instead. With respect to the productive function of government, East-Asian countries leap-frogged ahead of most old industrial coun-tries, with institutions that ensure competitive supply, quality control and open access of the public.

When modern development first took off in East Asia, political leaders initially involved themselves directly in fostering new industries. Like in Mercantilist

Europe 200 years ago, it often mattered whom you knew if you wanted to gain access to trade, mineral leases, credit and other resources. Personalized exchange and credit thus mattered a lot in the early phase of development. The universal economic institutions were poorly developed and enforced, so that only personal connections guaranteed contract fulfilment. Frequently, middlemen served the purposes of transmitting information and of lowering transaction costs, an important function in a less developed and rapidly changing economy. Had modernization depended solely on markets, some transaction costs might have been forbiddingly high, constituting a barrier to economic take-off.

As the East Asian economies modernized, economic interaction has become more complex and more closely integrated with the rapidly changing, competitive global economy. Limits to what can be achieved by personalized exchange and credit and without the institutions that ensure property rights and private autonomy have become obvious in the 1990s. Thus, big world-market oriented factories typically needed finance that went beyond the capcity of personalized credit. Nor could complex technologies be handled by the institutional mechanisms of personalized exchange, which had proven effective for developing initial, simpler trade and processing. The need for the impersonal, open institutions of the extended market order became obvious. Further economic development now requires that the institutional apparatus of capitalism – the extended order of markets and the rule of law – are fully developed and improved further. A key part of development policy in the more advanced, middle-income parts of East Asia now is now to lend support to more reliable institutions and enforcement (Kasper, 1994; 1998).

The need for a more consistent enforcement of the institutions on which a market order is based became obvious in 1997 when a currency and credit crisis hit East Asians after a decade of unprecedented growth and in the wake of credit expansion and rapid cost increases. The 'affront of openness' was now acutely felt by long-established political power elites, when global markets signalled – once again – that economic and political institutions had to be reformed or enforced better to enhance international competitiveness.

Openness and cultural change

The East-Asian experience since the 1960s of having to compete in world markets and setting up modern economic structures within little more than a generation has of course had profound and lasting effects on the internal institutions of East Asian communities. Civic virtues such as hard work, frugality, punctuality, honesty, reliability and an open-minded attitude towards strangers – which often exist in traditional cultures – were sharpened by the experience of economic competition, and have gained more weight (Section 12.2). As the economies became more complex and more 'experience goods' were produced, East-Asian manufacturers quickly discovered the importance of a good reputation, learning to supply good quality and to reliably fulfill their contractual obligations. They developed brand names, having initially competed only on price. They also learnt habits of searching systematically for innovations. They learnt to keep transaction costs low, although gradual institutional decay in some countries (see below) was to hamper these efforts. The new preferences appear to be more readily acquired by engaging in concrete activities, such as manufacturing, mining and agriculture, than in sophisticated services, such as finance or logistics, which rely on more abstract and complex institutional systems (Kasper, 1998). Nonetheless, centres, such as Singapore and Hong Kong, have cultivated the requisite institutions and consequently managed to expand service production rapidly.

The increasingly open, market-reliant societies of East Asia now rank high in economic liberties,[5] whereas the institutional uncertainty in the one-party states, such as Vietnam, Cambodia and China, often poses a serious obstacle to major, long-term investments. The structures of governance are often unclear, with overlapping authorities (Party, local, regional, provincial and central governments) engaged in decreeing laws and regulations, often with the aim of extracting legal, as well as corrupt, levies. Investors, who are prepared to pay off officials to secure a semblance of security for their operations, went to the 'institutionally vague and fuzzy' economies on the grounds of very low factor costs, market potential and hopes for institutional improvement. For the time being, they reap competitive advantages of cheap labour and land. Nonetheless, many international investors remain weary of political 'hold-up risks' and are withholding long-term investments. China, which currently still ranks a poor 82nd out of 141 countries on fundamental economic liberties (Gwartney and Lawson, *passim* (2010), p. 7), has begun to ensure some better-defined economic institutions (Section 13.2). The need for proper commercial and company laws, and their consistent enforcement, is increasingly recognized, lest the economy gets locked into a 'middle-income trap' due to the combination of rising production costs with high transaction costs.

In developing countries, the discipline imposed by inter-jurisdictional factor mobility is of course often considered an affront to national sovereignty. It is resented by established political leaders, as became clear, yet again, in the wake of the 1997 financial crisis in East Asia. Some try to use xenophobic sentiment to shore up their political positions and depict rent-seeking policies as in the national interest. Others stress the superiority of autocratic policies in obtaining economic progress as compared to the ways of supposedly decadent Western democracies. A degree of personal autocracy has certainly been a part of the East-Asian development equation (World Bank, 1993; Kasper, 1994; 1998), but in open economies autocratic rule is tempered by the feedback from trade and capital flows, as long as the autocrats are prepared to put economic prosperity first.

As the middle class has grown, new economic entrepreneurs want more open access to domestic and world markets. A young generation, who have grown up without the extreme penury experienced by their parents' generation, demand political, as well as universal economic and civil liberties. The new, educated middle class in South Korea, Taiwan, Thailand, Singapore, Hong Kong and Indonesia favours greater political liberties both as a quality of life and a means of shoring up their economic life opportunities. Many of the young are less tolerant of political and bureaucratic autocracy for the sake of economic advancement than their parents were. The rapid integration into global information networks has added to this tendency.

14.5 The spread of reforms

Elsewhere in the Third World, liberalization and privatization have also gained momentum since the 1990s (Scully, 1992; O'Leary, 1995; Alston et al., 1996; Gwartney and Lawson, *passim*). The worldwide tendency has, on the whole, been towards institutions that protect the autonomous use of private property rights and the free exploration and exchange of knowledge, many reversals in this trend notwithstanding. There is, however, nothing automatic about the drift towards more liberal political and economic institutions, despite the openness of the global communications era. As the institutional arrangements of a community have a habit of changing only slowly, except in traumatic circumstances, there is resistance to changing religious and other beliefs, for example in the Muslim orbit. There, it seems the same conflicts between religiously backed tradition and modernization is now played out as in post-medieval Europe (see Box 14.1). As readers of this book will by now understand, the mere reform of external institutions will not make much of a difference if the internal institutions and belief systems remain rigid. This lesson of history had to be learnt in many episodes, for example in Tsarist Russia where top-down reformers, such as Peter the Great (1682–1725) and Alexander I (1801–1825), met with the stolid resistance of the populace. Up to the beginning of the twentieth century, northwest European countries and Japan were the exceptions, developing institutions that diffused power and facilitated economic growth (Powelson, 1994, pp. 327–341; Némo, 2006). The signs for sustained growth now are looking hopeful elsewhere, but whether appropriate, free rule sets will be firmly entrenched, cannot yet be asserted with any confidence. We have not yet reached 'the end of history'. The search for an order-creating economic constitution will be decisive whether the large parts of humanity will succeed in attaining a materially more satisfactory and freer life. For many, it will be a matter of survival (Hayek, 1988).

CH 14 – CASE ONE

Institutional modernization in the Islamic orbit

Food and fuel price increases in early 2011 triggered a spreading civic uprising in North African and Mid-eastern nations ('Arab Awakening'). In these countries, powerful author-itarian elites had long ruled, often by oppression, so that economic freedom and development had lagged behind other parts of the world (compare West Asia with East Asia in Figure 1.1).

Admittedly, not all traditional civilizations and cultural value systems make it equally easy for a community to modernize and embark on sustained economic development (Sowell, 1994). Around the turn of the millennium, many observers noted the poor growth perform-ance and the growing internal tensions across the core of the Islamic world, from Casablanca to Islamabad (United Nations Development Program, 2002; Kasper 2005b). These facts had much to do with cultural and religious factors, such as religious reservations to adapta-tions of the (God-given) law, to individual property rights and to the equality of all before the law (Bethell, 1998, pp. 225–242). The Koran and the *hadith* explicitly recognize differences between masters and slaves, men and women, believers and non-believers. In the region, many communities are imbued with tribal traditions of intolerance and xenophobia (compare the juxtaposition of the tribal and the commercial syndrome in Section 6.2 and Table 6.1). Traditions of polygamy, under which all property is divided among many sons, and prohibi-tions of paying interest on loans have also been seen as a hindrance to the accumulation of capital, which is necessary to finance large-scale modern industries (Kuran, 2011). Other observers noted traditions in education that favour slavish rote learning, but discourage crea-tive, independent thought. The separation of church and state – which West Europeans and Americans embraced in modern times, though only after long, painful conflicts – is directly contradicted by most interpretations of Islamic doctrine and sharia law.

Some of these modernization-impeding traditions have only developed over time; early Islam, and later early Ottoman rule, were innovative, intellectually open and enterprising. The economies of the Middle East and North Africa were ahead of Western Europe a thousand years ago and even at the time of the Crusades. Only in more recent times have they become resistant to innovation and lagging behind the West scientifically and materially. US-Turkish economist Timur Kuran, who recently investigated the causes of this divergence (Kuran, 2009; 2011), showed that Islamic legal institutions became a drag on economic development, mitigating against the accumulation of sizable amounts of capital. Trust in commercial and credit transactions remained confined to personal networks, to the detriment of the impersonal cooperation with strangers. Rampant

CH 14 – CASE ONE *(continued)*

corruption, at best some sham democratic controls over the rule of strongmen, and weak civil societies have made it comparatively hard to embrace modernity in economic affairs and political governance. In many Mid-eastern nations, the availability of relatively easy 'petro dollars' has made it less urgent to modernize, whereas resource-poor East Asians simply had to adapt their internal and external institutions to prosper. As of the early twenty-first century, however, comparatively high birthrates are making modernization and job creation increasingly urgent. The overdue Islamic renaissance seems, however, out of reach without fundamental institutional changes.

Globalization and attractiveness to industry

Since the 1960s, globalization has spread modern industry and high incomes progressively outside the OECD countries, especially to East Asia. In the initial phase of globalization, producers of labour-intensive manufactures – textiles, garments, footwear, and later consumer electronics – in mature economies moved some of their production to new locations. They did so in reaction to wage-cost pressures and increasingly onerous government regulations, which inflated labour-unit costs in their home countries (Kasper, 1998; 2008a). In the new host locations, they admittedly often had to cope with imponderable internal institutions and the complicated administration of external rules, hence high transaction costs. Perceived risks were often also higher. These handicaps were eased where host-country governments granted credible commitments and offered tax exemptions to new foreign investors. For example, governments set up special industrial zones, in which cumbersome external institutions were suspended (see Box 12.1). There, the workforce was able to learn productive work habits and multinational managers gained experience with working in new cultural environments. Low costs of local production factors (wages, land rentals, tax costs) helped to overcome the initial handicaps in terms of high transaction costs, transport cost back to the rich-country markets and local skill shortages.

In societies with a cultural predisposition to reliable work and learning, the interaction between internationally mobile foreign investors and local production factors soon bore fruit. Factor productivities rose fast, so that unit costs of production fell even when wages and tax rates rose (unit costs are the ratio between the factor cost per unit of production and the productivity of that factor, see Section 11.1). When competitive, internationally mobile firms (bundles of capital, technical knowledge and organization skills with market access) were assessing alternative locations, they looked at total costs, the costs of production and transporting inputs and outputs, as well as transaction costs (Section 11.1). In the case of labour-intensive products, with which the new global spread of industry typically began, wage cost advantages were decisive. As East-Asian wages increased in the 1970s and 1980s, unit labour costs still dropped because the workforce and multinational managers rapidly learnt productive industrial skills.

Public administrations in the host countries learnt how to handle the new export industries (better external institutions and expedient administration). Development approvals were often streamlined ('one-stop shops' for interested foreign investors), intrusive industry controls were relaxed and establishment costs were cut, for example by the provision of efficient local infrastructures. East-Asian governments also concentrated on cutting international transport and communication costs (new ports, new airports, rapid development of telecommunications). The very success of export-oriented industrialization did away with post-colonial, nationalistic sentiments, as well as ideologies of import substitution. Industrialization thus soon spread out from the original 'Tigers' of Hong Kong, Korea, Taiwan and Singapore to new locations, such as Malaysia, Thailand and Indonesia. Before long, export-oriented industry even began to spread to post-Mao China (Section 13.2).

Crony capitalism and the middle-income trap

The dynamic interplay of institutional development and industrialization did, however, not stop there. As export-oriented industries became more diverse and broad-based, East Asia's political leaders and the wider public began to take rapid growth for granted. Local wage incomes and tax collection went up, which is after all the primary purpose of economic development. Higher incomes also fuelled local demand and hence boosted certain costs. Ambitious politicians and administrators came in on the act with new regulations to secure greater shares of the booming income for themselves and their local supporters. In the light of economic success, the external institutions of governance were often modified to redistribute income opportunities to locals. Expatriates had to be replaced by locals; directorships had to be manned by locals; the use of local inputs was made compulsory; and rates of tax were raised. In addition, many regulations were imposed to provide opportunities for illegal 'political and bureaucratic takings', in other words corruption. Such profit-nabbing impositions, which often arose from deep-seated cultural values at odds with modern capitalism, had no immediate impact on the growth of export industries as long as productivity advanced rapidly. But the scope for further fast productivity improvements got gradually exhausted. As export-oriented industries diversified, became more sophisticated and entered into a greater division of labour with domestic producers, the share of transaction costs also rose, so that the business exposure to new costly regulations went up. As new generations of politicians and officials, who had little understanding of the role of institutions, became more avid to share in the new wealth, export firms had to bear not only rising transaction and bribery costs, but also had to cope with growing compliance costs. The resulting loss of competitiveness of new industrial locations occurred at a time when new locational competitors – one Chinese province after the other – entered the fray, offering much lower wage and land costs. This led the emerging economies of the first generation into a 'middle-income trap', a phase in which previous growth rates of exports and incomes cannot be sustained and in which social and political discontent spreads.

In this situation, policy makers were faced with a stark choice: timely institutional reforms to increase trust and reduce the costs of transacting business, or depriving local workers and landowners of the potential for further income growth. Established political elites, buoyed in their confidence by past success, often suffered from cognitive limitations and ignored the need for institutional reforms (Section 12.4, also revisit Figure 12.1). As a consequence, local workers and input suppliers had to forego potential income gains to keep export-oriented multinationals from migrating elsewhere.

A new class of 'cronies' also became entrenched. They displayed great wealth, while the many felt deprived of opportunities for income growth. 'Crony capitalism' is thus becoming a dead alley in many East Asian locations. In Latin America and the Middle East, many economies have been caught in the 'middle-income trap' all along. Everywhere, the 'middle-income trap' is now recognized as an intractable problem. It highlights the need to become more aware of the need for institutional innovation, even where it conflicts with long-held traditions and deep-rooted values. How difficult it is to escape from this trap by embarking on incisive market-oriented reforms is demonstrated worldwide. Yet some nations, such as Turkey in the early 2000s, have managed to free their economies and resume dynamic growth, as have some advanced high-income countries (following Section).

14.6 Microeconomic (institutional) reform in mature economies

In the early post-war era, West Germans embarked on comprehensive economic liberalization and a return to constitutional democratic governance. Against all odds, they escaped, within a few years, not only the ravages of war and dire poverty, but, even more importantly, the psychological traumas of total defeat, regaining self-confidence and a spirit of enterprise (see Box 14.2). Although parliamentary opportunism gradually eroded the free economic order to some extent, the German microeconomic reforms were an early and successful modern example of what can be achieved in mature democracies, and how it can be done. A generation afterwards, a wave of evolutionary economic reforms swept through many affluent countries, which is now associated with the Reagan administration in the United States and the Thatcher government in the United Kingdom. These were political attempts to reverse the erosion of economic constitutions in the 1960s and 1970s, when opportunistic politicians had expanded tax-funded welfare, and Keynesian stabilization policies had relentlessly expanded the size of governments, increased public debts and produced inflation. Ever denser regulation of labour and product markets had rigidified the supply apparatus of most mature economies and given vested interests increasing power over political choices. When two waves of oil price increases hit home in the early 1970s and early 1980s and capital and industrial enterprise began to relocate to new industrial countries, a generation of political entrepreneurs found public support for reforms. International competition (and the revival of Austrian institutional economics) were crucial in overcoming the usual cognitive limits of policy makers to trigger these institutional reforms (Section 12.4).

CH 14 – CASE TWO

Germany: from comprehensive institutional reform to creeping sclerosis

1. The economic 'non-miracle'

In 1945, at the end of the Second World War, Germany was drastically reduced in size and divided in four military occupation zones. The economy was at a nadir. The Western Allies helped German liberals to impose a capitalist constitution on the western zones. They soon gave responsibility to political protagonists of private property rights and competition, who were inspired by the teachings of the 'Freiburg School' (Section 10.3). In 1948, the western occupation zones became the Federal Republic of Germany under a constitution which safeguarded basic civil and political liberties and ensured property rights, the freedom of contract, as well as limiting government and making it accountable. The Russian zone became a separate unitary communist state with Soviet-style central planning and collectivization (it was to collapse in 1989–90).

In the West, the Economics Minister of the first Federal government, Ludwig Erhard, made use of favourable political circumstances and, with skill and luck, quickly implemented

CH 14 – CASE TWO *(continued)*

market-oriented reforms (Erhard, 1960). Monetary reform wiped out the inflated paper values of assets and liabilities left behind by the inflationary policies of the Nazi regime. An independent central bank was set up to supply stable money, since many Germans feared a repetition of the destructive, painful consequences of run-away inflation that had occurred in the wake of the First World War in 1919–1921. Much emphasis was placed on fostering the basic institutions of protected private property rights and free competition in markets (reinforced by energetic anti-trust legislation). There was little macroeconomic policy along the lines of the then fashionable Keynesian school. Instead, the government created a stable framework of universal rules to give people confidence after the cataclysmic experiences of the war (Giersch et al., 1992; Kasper and Streit, 1993).

During the 1950s and early 1960s, the Federal Republic was a leader in liberalizing international trade and payments, often proceeding unilaterally. It also took the lead in promoting European integration. Capital formation and saving were promoted by preferential tax treatment. In the late 1950s, the government privatized some publicly owned enterprises, giving small-scale and often first-time share owners priority (popular capitalism).

At the same time, the unemployed, war veterans and the aged were guaranteed certain minimal incomes. The mix of fostering the institutions of capitalism with a measure of tax-funded social welfare was labelled the 'social market economy'.

The results of this programme were impressive. Between 1950 and 1960, real output more than doubled (average growth of 8.8 per cent per annum over the decade). Total employment went from 20 to 25 million. The number of unemployed fell from 1.9 million to 300,000 despite a massive influx of prisoners of war and refugees from the east. Labour productivity rose by an average of 5.7 per cent per annum and income per worker by 4.9 per cent per annum (see table below). Inflation remained very low, and the currency had to be revalued in the early 1960s. West Germany led OECD countries in making its currency freely convertible.

Foreign journalists and economists, who were at the time under the spell of Keynesianism and had a habit of overlooking institutions, dubbed the quick emergence of the war-torn economy the 'German economic miracle' – and miracles do not have to be explained. The post-war German economic track record does, however, not look like a miracle to informed observers. Rather, it was the result of simple, transparent and reasonably stable institutions, limited government and a central bank policy committed to the pursuit of price-level stability (*ordo* policy).

II. From growth to sclerosis

The economic momentum of the 1950s and early 1960s did not last. In part, this was to be expected, as the economy gradually reached full employment and industry caught up with international technical standards. But to a considerable extent, the slowdown between the mid-1960s and the 1990s (see adjoining table) had much to do with institutional rigidification. Parliament soon became again a forum for privilege distribution, as industries and groups organized themselves into rent-seeking coalitions (Olson, 1982). Political commit-

CH 14 – CASE TWO *(continued)*

	Productivity:growth of income per person employed *(% p.a. at constant prices)*	Income: growth of total income *(% p.a.)*	Socialized sector: government share in full-capacity GNP *selected years, % share*	
1950–60	4.9	8.2	1955:	30.3
1960–73	4.1	4.4	1965:	37.2
1973–80	2.2	2.2	1977;	47.2
1980–95	0.9	1.7	1987:	45.3
1995	–	–	1995:	57.6[a]

Notes:
1950–1989, West Germany; from 1990, all of Germany.
[a] All of Germany, including the one-off effect due to the take-over of eastern Germany.

ments to a social market economy opened the door for the growing redistribution of property rights, often to the electorally strong middle class and well-organized vested interests. As the redistributive function of government was expanded, parliamentarians and administrators became increasingly involved with outcome-oriented, specific interventions. Taxes and the regulatory burdens on producers were raised. Attention to a competitive legal-institutional order was soon lost sight of.

The decay of the rule system led to what has been called sclerosis, and weakened Germany's international competitive position. As well-meaning parliamentarians were piling new legal obligations on employers (more and more health, safety and environmental directives), they drove up the on-costs of job creation and constrained enterprise. The location Germany lost its attractiveness to foreign and German investors; capital and enterprises moved out.

Thanks to the high levels of affluence and the embedding of the German economy in the regulated European Union, the gradual loss of international competitiveness could be ignored for some time. Learning and political-institutional innovation could be delayed. The major challenge of taking over the failing former communist East after 1989 raised the share of public spending on the national product to 57.6 per cent by 1995 (source: OECD). Economic freedom was rated a modest 25th out of 115 countries (Gwartney and Lawson, 1997, pp. 98–99) and 24th out of 141 countries in 2008 (Gwartney and Lawson, *passim* (2010), p. 7).

Labour-market reforms and other supply-side policies around the turn of the 21st century, combined with a weaker Euro exchange rate, restored some international competitiveness, although costly energy policies, high social welfare costs and the continuing ageing partly undercut this trend. Despite the fact that Germany is again considered the industrial powerhouse of the European Union, the outmigration of industrial jobs to emerging industrial countries outside Europe nevertheless continues.

Sources: Erhard (1960); Kasper and Streit (1993); Giersch et al. (1992), and German Council of Economic Advisors, Annual Reports (passim).

Among other mature economies, the specifics of institutional reform and the zeal for reform differed, given the differences in national systems and the entrenchment of rent-seeking interest groups. Yet, a number of fundamental parallels emerged during the 1980s and 1990s:

(a) Government-owned agencies, which produce goods and services, were subjected to more scrutiny and were often privatized. Where it was decided to retain property in government ownership, companies were often at least corporatized and made more accountable, exposed to some private competition and sometimes subjected to detailed comparisons with world-best practice (benchmarking). Private mail delivery agencies are, for example, now allowed to erode public postal monopolies and public transport and communications monopolies have to face new competition (new airlines, private trains on public tracks, privatized toll roads, private broadcasters, a diversity of competing telephone and electricity distributors). Technical changes have also helped to erode public monopolies, for example in communications or power supply. In many instances, publicly owned enterprises were set aside from the general budget and given clear-cut corporate objectives. Admittedly, it remains to be seen whether firm budget constraints and the protection from day-to-day political interference will be upheld in the face of producer lobbying. The belief that some service providers are deemed too important to fail has not helped to expose some big privatized agencies to 'the market discipline of red ink'.

(b) The redistributive function of government and the welfare state have also come under renewed scrutiny. It is now widely understood in Western democracies that direct interventions in markets in pursuit of political and social goals have often failed to deliver (Section 10.4). Indeed, interpersonal wealth and income differences have often been exacerbated by policy interventions (for example in labour and housing markets), penalizing the poor and assisting the wealthy. Moral concerns and budgetary burdens of pervasive welfare provision have also driven attempts at welfare reform, although they have often been stymied by electoral resistance. As globally mobile enterprises gained political influence and made good on threats to relocate, new political entrepreneurs saw careers in deregulation and streamlining the remaining welfare programmes, not least to cope with the steep rises in future provisions for retirement. Some reformers have also streamlined regulations to cut the transaction and compliance costs of business.

(c) The redistributive use of taxes and subsidies came in for much criticism in virtually all mature industrial democracies, as individual behaviour to work and save gradually adapted to the expansion of public welfare and as ageing populations placed additional pressures on welfare budgets. Public welfare provision has been increasingly seen as an impediment to international competitiveness, although political action in response to these insights has varied greatly from country to country. This has become evident in the huge and disparate currency area of the Eurozone, a political creation, where differences in social-welfare regimes, government size and industrial productivity have made it necessary to convert the original monetary union into an uncertain transfer union.

(d) In a number of developed countries, the protective function of government was again being emphasized both by the political right and the left (see Section 10.5).

(e) In addition, technical changes have made it possible for many individual skilled workers to set up their own businesses, at least in countries where regulations and taxation make this easy. As big industry and big trade unions were in relative decline and the service sector became more important, many countries witnessed the rise of a new class of small entrepreneur. Microeconomic reforms and new, cheap computer and communication technology enabled many to start their own enterprises, working as sub-contractors in construction, personal services or transport. This class of worker became a political force for the further reform of external institutions.

In old welfare democracies with dominant socialized sectors, ranging from Sweden to Australia, a generation of reformers in the 1980s and 1990s did much to reaffirm a constitution of economic liberty (see Box 14.3). Remarkably, they managed to do so without social disruption and with the beneficial results that classical liberals and subscribers to institutional economics would expect, not least that these nations now have a more robust system to cope with recessions and world-market fluctuations.

CH 14 – CASE THREE

Two episodes of institutional reform

(a) **Sweden scales back the welfare state**
The Swedish economy was for most of the last century the model of an affluent, semi-socialist welfare state, in which cradle-to-grave social security was coupled with macroeconomic stabilization along Keynesian lines. Thanks to a skilled workforce, good resource endowment, neutrality during the Second World War (and huge profits from selling arms and materials to

CH 14 – CASE THREE (continued)

both sides in the conflict) and free trade in manufactures, Sweden was relatively affluent in 1950. In contrast to most other European welfare states at the time, Sweden never socialized private banks or major manufacturing industries.

From the 1930s, the country had been ruled almost without interruption by social democratic governments committed to ever more complete welfare provision. This boosted the public sector and produced decent, though not overwhelming economic growth (1950–75: 3.1 per cent per annum in per capita incomes; 1975–98: a mere 1.2 per cent per annum; Maddison, 2001). By the mid-1990s, the Swedish economy was rated among the least free non-communist European countries (1995: equal 42nd of 115 countries, Gwartney and Lawson, *passim*). Work habits gradually responded to the availability of easy welfare and job creation reflected tax levels, which had been driven up over time, as well as pervasive regulations. By 1979, the marginal income tax rate was raised to 87 per cent.

From the 1980s, it became evident that Swedish manufacturers were unable to compete despite new subsidies, for example to the senescent shipbuilding industry. Public deficits were becoming unsustainable. Financial market deregulation made it obvious that successive, inflation-boosting expansion programmes could no longer disguise deep structural problems. In the late 1980s, the Social Democrat government, relying on non-partisan experts, began a reform process, cutting some taxes. Marginal income tax rates were reduced to 50 per cent and capital taxes to a flat rate of 30 per cent. Yet, the Swedish economy continued to be haunted by industrial conflicts, as well as a lack of new jobs and start-ups, given interventionist labour-market regulations. Taxes on firms and capital were still confiscatory by international comparison.

In the early 1990s, when GDP contracted in three consecutive years, a centre-right government was elected. It started to implement an ambitious reform programme with wide-ranging deregulation and privatizations. The Social Democrats, when re-elected, paid lip service to social equality and security, but continued these reforms. Sickness and pension payments were curbed and savings for old age were put on a defined contribution basis (that is, people were obliged to save for their retirement). Social security was made less generous and was to be automatically balanced. Moreover, inheritance and gift taxes were abolished and numerous government-owned enterprises were sold off. In 2006, and again in 2010, right-of-centre governments were returned, who continued liberalization. Wealth tax was abolished; social welfare benefits were pruned, the health system was reformed and eligibility for the dole was tightened. All this happened without street protests and civil unrest.

Since the early 1990s, the reforms led the broad electorate to realize that everyone paid for additional government services, not just a few 'rich'. The government also pegged back the burdens of public debt, from 76 per cent of GDP in the 1980s to 36 per cent in 2010. Nevertheless, Swedish tax levels are still high by international comparison, and labour and housing markets are still heavily regulated. As a result, Sweden has not climbed up much in the league tables of economic freedom, because many other competitors also embarked on reforms. Nevertheless, the Swedish economy, which is not tied down by membership in the Eurozone, has bounced back from the global recession of 2008–09 to real growth rate of about 5 per cent in 2010 to 2012.

CH 14 – CASE THREE *(continued)*

One remarkable reform, which seems popular with the citizens, though not teachers' unions, has been the adoption of school vouchers. Since the 1990s, Swedish parents have been receiving vouchers that they can use to pay schools of their choice for their children. By 2010, more than 15 per cent of elementary and more than half of all high-school pupils attended private charter schools. This exposes public schools to quality competition. All this has contributed, it is reported, to a growing popular consensus that the semi-socialist welfare state was a costly and non-sustainable social experiment and that a more market-oriented public policy will in future underpin Swedish prosperity.

Sources: Bergh, 2011; Karlson, 1995 and Karlson, forthcoming.

(b) Australia embraces comprehensive reforms

Like Sweden, Australia in the 1970s was a mature welfare state with a strong commitment to Keynesian deficit spending. Unlike Sweden, there was a long tradition of unconditional industry protection, but also a well-endowed and innovative agricultural and mining sector that had to bear much of the discriminatory cost burdens of tariff protection. Also unlike Sweden, some flexibility in the ossifying economy was injected by substantial additions of young, skilled immigrants.

By the late 1970s, a widely recognized 'industrial malaise' and social confrontation led to near-stagnation of this over-regulated mature economy, which found itself on the frontline of competing with a rapidly growing and more self-assured East Asia. Influential opinion leaders advocated comprehensive liberalization, beginning with pre-announced, across-the-board tariff cuts. Reform advocates were able to appeal to a substratum of liberal British colonial traditions and traditional values of individual self-reliance, which had turned this young, under-populated nation into one of the richest and best-run democracies during the nineteenth century.

In 1983, a newly elected social democratic (Labor) government devalued the Australian dollar, then floated it and liberalized capital markets, including by opening them to international competitors. Soon, the government embarked on a policy of general, gradual tariff cuts, reducing the effective rate of industry protection from some 35 per cent in the early 1970s to about 5 per cent in the mid-1990s.[6] This did much to inject competition into product markets and keep inflation under control. The strategy had the tacit support of the conservative opposition.

The Australian Labor government's reform agenda, however, excluded a deregulation of labour markets and the control of public expenditure from the reform agenda. The lop-sided reform agenda, which violated the institutional principle of across-the-board consistency among sub-orders, led to persistent unemployment, low wage and productivity growth and persistent public deficits. Yet, Australia's economic freedom ratings improved gradually and persistently, taking the country into the top dozen of free economies (Gwartney and Lawson, *passim*).

After the Labor administration was succeeded by a conservative federal government in 1996, an energetic control of public spending and tax reforms allowed federal debt to be

---

CH 14 – CASE THREE *(continued)*

gradually repaid. The central bank became fully independent and committed to a price-level target; labour markets were slowly and tortuously deregulated and some welfare reforms were implemented. During consecutive conservative administrations, economic freedom ratings climbed further, but then stalled. As of 2008, Australia was listed in the top eight on that score (Gwartney and Lawson, *passim* (2010), p. 7) and was one of the few OECD countries that escaped the global financial crisis.

Thanks to a flexible supply-side and a highly skilled primary sector, the country is a major exporter of energy resources and energy-intensive products, as well as of metal ores, fibres and food, mainly to booming East Asia. The reforms not only helped to stimulate economic growth and job creation, but have inspired a sense of can-do optimism, which has had a positive signalling effect on political leaders and the wider public. The new self-confidence became an important evolutionary factor, which helped the institutional reforms along.

Narrowly elected Labor governments in 2007 and 2010, however, re-regulated labour markets and drew on climate concerns in order to tax and regulate energy markets. Because this would imperil one of Australia's strongest comparative and competitive advantages, attempts to claim the primacy of policy through the climate debate are – as of the time of writing – fiercely resisted.

Source: Kasper (2011a).

The policy conclusion from reform experiences in developed countries is that governments are able to wind back regulations and reform the institutions of capitalism. Many reform proposals have of course not been popular with welfare recipients and politically favoured groups, but political entrepreneurs have demonstrated that it is possible to obtain majority consent if they come prepared with a clear and consistent strategy and show political leadership in educating the electorate and desist from opportunistic political point-scoring. Cooperation across the traditional political spectrum and the open pursuit of a comprehensive reform agenda has paid medium-term dividends. It has also been important that reforming countries have a more or less flexible exchange rate, which gives political elites and the public cybernetic feedback when the old institutions can no longer be sustained.

On a more general level, economic liberalization in democratic societies has depended on the interaction of three overlapping types of agents. A first group typically consists of analysts, who interpret undesirable developments caused by government interventions and educate others, helping them to overcome their cognitive barriers (compare Figure 12.1). Frequently, these analysts are assisted by openness (globalization, flexible exchange rates), both in discovering the causes of undesirable developments and the reform opportunities and in getting economic actors to accept the diagnosis. A second group consists of strategic thinkers, who translate the concept of reform into a feasible plan for political action. Some of these strategists are political leaders, others rise above the humdrum of industry, commerce and finance and promote the general idea that deregulation and privatization can enhance economic and wider social outcomes. In democracies, the political strategists may be assisted by public opinion, but may also have been hampered by publicity campaigns against change. In many places, party finance from political interest groups has also played a crucial role. All too frequently, organized interest groups with stakes in retaining profitable interventions have had more fund-raising power than reform-minded groups. The asymmetry in public choices, discussed earlier, has frequently exerted a reactionary, anti-liberalization bias in policy making. It is worth noting in this context that, in Australia and Sweden, more collectively oriented, social democratic parties have become economic liberalizers, even against the immediate interests of major client groups. A third group have been the actual reformers, who get involved in the tactics of political wheeling and dealing, overcome interest-group pressures and make legislation and administrative changes feasible. In electoral democracies, these political entrepreneurs often come to the fore after elections, having obtained a mandate for reform, typically after the negative side effects of the political programme of previous incumbents had become overwhelming.

These three groups of course overlap and communicate with each other to realize structural institutional changes. In the process, general ideologies are often relied upon to make specific political proposals plausible, but skillful political entrepreneurs also often manage to reshape the political landscape.

14.7 Western civilization and the 'primacy of politics'

In Section 6.4, we touched on culture and civilization, a topic that transcends mere institutional economics, but is of great relevance to it (Quigley, 1979/1961; Némo, 2006; Boettke et al., 2008; Kasper, 2011b; Ferguson, 2011). It is also possible to conclude that it is the invisible institutions that matter most to a civilized quality of life.

Are civilizations subject to cyclical rise and decline?

The literature on institutions has been informed by historic studies of the rise and fall of civilizations, as well as comparisons between different civilizations. Two core questions have been: What was it that made the West economically and politically so successful and dominant in the world over the past half millennium? What is the likelihood of a decline of the West, given the frequent pattern of rise and fall of civilizations and the present-day industrial and political ascendancy of competing non-Western societies?

Most answers to the first question focus, as mentioned, on institutions, not least the core economic ones. It is widely recognized that the West gained crucial strengths (i) from the gradual enhancement of private property rights, free competition, which eroded inherited privileges, and equality of all before the law, and (ii) from a sceptical, critical scientific approach to explaining and mastering nature. These two 'pillars of Western modernity' enabled progress in industry, transport, medicine and numerous other fields. The institutions of economic freedom defined in reliable ways what individuals were legitimately able to do (freedom to use one's property and knowledge) and what they must not do (rule of law). Thanks to this two-pronged order, flourishing scientific knowledge could be translated by entrepreneurs into innovations, not only in major breakthroughs, but more importantly also by gradual, sustained evolution. This spread wealth to more and more countries, eventually also beyond Western Europe and North America (Taverne, 2005; Ridley, 2010; Ferguson, 2011). Often it proved easier for non-Western newcomers to adopt the material fruit and the technical ideas of the West – the 'hardware of civilization' – than the underlying invisible factors, that is, the institutional 'software'.

Historians and philosophers from Polybius (ca. 200-118BC) and Edward Gibbon (1737-1794) to contemporary writers have highlighted the cyclical nature of civilizations, with the rise and decay of favourable institutions being the harbingers of the rise and fall of civilizations and political entities. Many have considered cyclicality an almost inevitable 'law of history'. However, Western civilization has so far been different. It grew from Greek, Roman and Judeo-Christian roots and was synthesized into the complex modern system of Western civilization, first in medieval and Renaissance Europe and then in the more secular Enlightenment during the eighteenth and early nineteenth centuries (Némo, 2006). Thanks to its preference for individual freedom and the equality of all before the law, it has managed to rejuvenate itself after repeated crises (Quigley, 1979/1961). Obviously, the life of cultural entities differs from human life, which – alas – has an inevitable finality. As we saw in the chapter on institutional evolution, human societies are capable of learning and applying the lessons rationally to reshape both the internal and the external institutions, among other things. Mechanistic views of long-term history, as for example those of Karl Marx, have time and again been falsified by evolutionary learning and innovation (Schumpeter, 1947; 1961/1908; Howitt, 2006). Innovations are, however, not automatic, they require enterprise and freedom to re-form the rules of human interaction. Obstacles to change, often fiercely upheld by powerful socio-economic groups who defend outdated positions, can frustrate or prevent the evolutionary changes necessary to ensure that the rules again fit changed circumstances. Institutional rigidity has led ever so often to the downfall of previous empires and civilizations. Those who fear that the end of 'the West' is nigh imply that the capacity for institutional change in present-day Western democracies and capitalist economies is limited. They imply above all that commitments to political, civil and economic freedom are now weak.

Observers, who are adopting this pessimistic view (for example Ferguson, 2011, pp. 295–325), tend to point to widespread rent seeking, concerns about destructive fiscal and financial imbalances and renewed political claims of a 'primacy of politics' over private, social and economic life. The concept of a primacy of politics, which was first stipulated during the French Revolution by the Jacobin radicals, has since been embraced not only by totalitarian rulers from Hitler to Mao, but at the beginning of the new millennium also by Western democratic leaders.

One reason adduced by doomsayers is the spectacular material rise of long-stagnant China, which is now certainly offering Western producers and powerbrokers new and vigorous competition. Other parts of the world are now also in the process of closing the gap with the West, mainly because they – at long last – are mastering not only the 'hardware' of modern technology, but also embrace some of the essential, underlying 'institutional software' (Ridley, 2010, Kasper, 2011b).[7] Is such cultural imitation not a sign of Western success and a harbinger of a constructive stimulus to international competition to find the best institutions? Can the inhabitants of the West not see the new competition (as well as new affluent markets for their knowhow and products) as a reason to engage in the creative destruction of inappropriate institutions which will lower their transaction costs and reinvigorate enterprise? To date, the defining feature of Western civilization, individual freedom, has given Westerners the capacity to overcome repeated crises and avert rigidification of the sort that led to the decline of earlier civilizations (Quigley 1979/1961).

Because humans are capable of rational learning and institutions can be reformed, it seems rational to remain optimistic. In this context it also matters that a feeling of optimism and confidence in society has the important signalling function of inspiring appropriate reform action. Contagious optimism is not only a key to explaining why, in certain places and at certain times, entre-preneurs appear 'as if in swarms' (Schumpeter, 1961/1908, pp. 212–215), but also why optimistic leaders and population groups embrace reforms, which then become self-fulfilling by evolutionary win-win dynamics.

As to the question whether other civilizations must emulate the precise economic and political make-up of the West, as Euro-centric researchers and consultants often claim, the evidence to date indicates that the Western model is not the only feasible one to produce modernity. While the Anglo-Saxon rule set has been very successful, variants of the Western model have produced progress and proven adaptable to different 'cultural sub-soils'. The West has flourished not only under Protestant, but also Catholic capitalism, not only under common law, but also Roman law.

As of the beginning of the twenty-first century, an alternative Chinese model of modernization is producing breathtaking material advances. Arguably the most important insight, which the East-Asian ascendancy has so far taught us, is that different people from different races and civilizations are capable of achieving high economic growth and a better quality of life for everyone, without necessarily following precisely the Western path to modernity (Tu, 2000). The obstacles to modern economic growth and a peaceful, just society are certainly not racial, that is, embedded in traits which people cannot change. They are institutional, that is, they can be reshaped in the light of experience. East-Asian modernization now certainly draws on cultural trad-itions different from those of the West. In view of the important role of *metis*, it may, however, be relevant that both the Chinese-Confucian and the Western-Christian value and rule systems are derived from long histories of intellectual and moral refinement and a long experience with civil strife as well as phases of peaceful, constructive interaction, having grown in densely populated areas with highly specialized economies.

Globalization has made learning from successes and failures more likely and urgent, as the 'Arab awakening' has now shown. New cases of economic modernization are now emerging in many different civilizations. They show invariably that the fundamentals of economic (and political) freedom are indispensable conditions of sustained modernization. F.A. Hayek's dictum holds that "no advanced civilisation has yet developed without a govern-ment which saw its chief aim in the protection of private property" (Hayek, 1988, p. 32). But Hayek followed this observation with the warning that "again and again the further evolution and growth to which this gave rise was halted by strong government" (*idem*), in our terminology, opportunistic rent seeking. As long as the essential conditions are secured, second-order institutions can be combined with them into differing variants of modern-ization, so that different flourishing civilizations emerge. The Japanese have, for example, in many respects upheld their distinct Japanese culture whilst successfully embracing modern science, industry and commerce. They have remained Japanese. Likewise, it is likely that a rich cultural 'gene pool' of dis-tinct modernities will be created, even if everyone adopts modern technol-ogy and medicine and everyone's popular culture absorbs some influences from Hollywood, Bollywood or Kung-fu (Cowen, 2002). Seen in this light, optimism about mankind's future seems justified.

A robust economy for possible climate change

Is it naïve to subscribe to optimism about mankind's and the West's future after a century during which human numbers multiplied from 1650 million (in 1900) to some 6100 million (in 2000), putting pressure on the world's natural resources? To date, economic freedom and technical progress have not only ensured that average global living standards and food supplies rose spectacularly, but also that most of the essential natural resources have become cheaper (Simon, 1995). More and more people are enjoying the experience of improved living standards whilst working fewer and fewer hours. Many live longer and healthier lives than earlier generations. The prediction by English economist Robert Malthus (1766–1834) that food and resource shortages would inevitably confine human numbers to the edge of starvation and dire poverty, may have fitted the past, but has been patently wrong as to the future (Hayek, 1988, pp. 120–134; Kasper, 2005a; Ridley, 2010).

Nevertheless, an influential school of pessimists is now pointing, often with religious fervour, to cases of local environmental devastation and periodic bouts of food- and oil-price inflation to resurrect the Malthusian view of humanity's fate (Bennett, 2012). This tendency has received a new impulse from the assertion by scientists and politicians that growing carbon use to power economic progress and spreading comfort will before long lead to catastrophic global warming. This is not the place to address the natural science of climate change or the impact of human activity on the ever-changing, complex phenomenon of the world's climate, although doubts about the science remain (Carter, 2010). What is, however, rel-evant from the perspective of institutional economics is this: Ecologists, who rightly caution against human interference with nature because they fear deleterious side effects, are demanding interference in the equally complex web of economic life. Institutional economics suggests, however, that it is foolhardy to undermine a robust system of property rights and competition by those proposed massive new policy interventions. Besides, many of the policy proposals now on the table strongly smack of rent seeking by established political and commercial interests, at least in the developed countries and in international organizations. Should global warming eventuate, a heavily regulated economy would prove fragile. Distorted market signals would hamper creative entrepreneurial responses of the sort witnessed during the oil crises of the last century and would inflict much pain. A free-market order, by contrast, promises to facilitate the numerous innovative reactions to climate contingencies, costly as they may sometimes be, wherever and whenever they arise. (Kasper, 2005a; 2007; Klaus, 2008; Robinson, (ed.) 2008). Alas, it would not be the first time in history that Jeremiahs, who intervene to avert danger, end up fulfilling their prophecies.

Globalization has over recent decades forced political elites and societies to adjust long-established institutions, as described in Chapter 12. In short, globalization has demonstrated to political elites that their power and scope for sovereign action are increasingly limited – and this at a time when global power balances and patterns of economic life are shifting dramatically (for example, relocation of global manufacturing and wealth creation to East Asia and other emerging economies; China's political ascendancy; growing fiscal and financial imbalances; greater transparency about political machinations, including in the restive and institutionally hitherto rigid Muslim regions; terrorism; and the possibility to organize dissent over the Internet; possible oil shortages; Ferguson, 2011). Who could in this situation deny that climate fear offers itself to established elites as a good instrument with which to regain the primacy of politics?

The conflict between the new political goal of temperature mitigation and economic, civil and political freedom is real. The institutional economist is aware of the value-laden conflicts between fundamental human values, which underlie the climate debate. Positive institutional economics points to a major conflict between freedom (and its welcome consequences) and the costs of conserving the global environment. If public policy is to choose between these two fundamental values, policy makers have to address difficult and risky cost-benefit considerations. They cannot shirk this task by asserting that de-carbonization policies will boost employment, incomes and individual freedom. The creation of 'Green jobs' is uncertain and expensive, while de-carbonization already imposes big and widely distributed costs at the expense of jobs, living standards and freedom. Ultimately, national governments and international organizations will of course have to leave it to the democratic choices of electorates, how much freedom should be sacrificed and what climate risks should be acceptable. The observation that freedom normally has a strong positive correlation with other fundamental human values, at least over the medium and long term (Section 4.4), also should play a role in this respect. Nor should we lose sight of the important lesson of history that the twin pillars of Western civilization – critical, objective science and the promotion of economic freedom and democracy – have served human welfare better than any alternative approach to public policy and private endeavour. Ultimately, free and hence innovative economies are better equipped to tackle new challenges, including possible rises in global temperatures.

Reaffirming a constitution of capitalism?

Not all old industrial countries have embarked on comprehensive institutional reforms. Nor are all underdeveloped and now rapidly developing countries paying sufficient heed to the need of cultivating universal institutions. In the post-war period, the reforms in Germany and Japan were the exceptions to the then-prevailing worldwide trend away from free-market capitalism. After the swing of the *zeitgeist* in the late 1970s towards lesser controls, political entrepreneurs embarked on piecemeal reforms, but in the wake of the global financial crisis of 2008-09, many reforms were swiftly undone again. The results of (government-made) fiscal and financial imbalances encouraged many political leaders and organizations to call for re-regulation, curbing economic liberties. Climate fears have added to a political roll-back of the economic reforms in the mature, affluent countries.

Therefore, liberal observers, who fear for individual liberties, have called for the formal, constitutional entrenchment of the reforms. They wish to lay down rules of overarching constitutional quality, which prevent future opportunism on the part of parliamentary majorities, judges and administrators.

Many written constitutions, like those of the US and Germany, of course already contain explicit protections of private property. Yet, in practice the free use of property rights is increasingly being interfered with. High courts are normally not equipped to understand the importance of protected economic freedom. They cannot cope with the complex economic issues and the political trade-offs involved.

In the ultimate analysis it is the role of the citizens to defend their freedom. The ongoing defence of economic freedom needs to be inspired by attitudes similar to those reported after a meeting of the French finance minister, Jean-Baptiste Colbert (1619–1683) with the merchant Thomas LeGendre. When Colbert benevolently inquired what the government might do for LeGendre's business, he exclaimed: *"Laissez-nous faire!* – just leave us alone!".

The reader of this book will in future no doubt have the opportunity to test the veracity of the dictum that 'the price of freedom is eternal vigilance' and that fostering the right institutions is like a mother's job – never quite done.

NOTES

1 The data and other materials from the 'Economic Freedom of the World' project can be found at www.freetheworld.com.

2 Competing indexes of economic freedom, prepared with different methodologies are being compiled, most notably by the Heritage Foundation in Washington, DC. The overall results from their estimates are in line with the index of economic freedom that is being prepared by the coalition of think tanks, led by the Fraser Institute in Vancouver, BC, and the Cato Institute in Washington, DC, which we are citing throughout the text.

3 There were racial riots in Malaysia in 1969, but this remained a one-off event, as people of different races interacted by and large under the institutions of free markets, which are 'racially blind'. By contrast, *dirigiste* economic policies in Sri Lanka were given a racial edge, so that racial problems blew up in durable, open conflict. This comparison highlights the important insight that individual cooperation in dispersed markets tends to erode racial differences and prejudices, whereas centralized political action often exploits these differences and aggravates them (Rabushka, 1974).

4 There were exceptions to this rule, for example in Malaysia, where political discrimination favoured poorer Malays in education, employment and wealth accumulation at the expense of more educated and more well-to-do Chinese and foreigners. In many respects, this policy led to the socialization of industries (the government acting 'on behalf of' Malay citizens) and a pervasive culture of rent-seeking. In 2010, Malaysia was ranked 56th (out of 178 counties) on perceptions of corruption by *Transparency International*, an international organization concerned with corruption. See http://www.transparency.org/policy_research/surveys_indices/cpi/2010/results.

   Many other East Asian countries limit the ownership of real estate by foreign nationals, license direct foreign investment and demand the preferred employment of local citizens.

5 As of 2008, Hong Kong (1st), Singapore (2nd), Taiwan (22nd), Japan (24th) ranked among the top quarter of the 142 countries evaluated for economic freedom (Gwartney and Lawson, *passim* (2010), p. 7). China is ranked 82nd.

6 The effective rate of protection takes account not only of the tariff rate on an industry's output, which raises profitability, but also estimates the cost-boosting consequences of that industry's inputs, which reduces it.

7 It took a long time to diagnose the essential cause of material backwardness as ultimately the consequence of bothersome institutions and not of, for example, ingrained racial characteristics. Institutions can be learnt and adapted, racial characteristics cannot.

Epilogue

Institutional versus neoclassical economics

> I forecast that the twenty-first century will show a continuing expansion of catal-
> laxy . . . [I]nnovation and order will become more and more bottom-up; work will
> become more and more specialised, leisure more and more diversified . . . This
> catallaxy will not go smoothly, or without resistance . . . It will be hard to snuff [it]
> out, because it is such an evolutionary, bottom-up phenomenon.
>
> Matt Ridley (2010), pp. 355–358

The vision of economic analysis presented in this book owes much to classical liberalism and the institutional-evolutionary economics of the 'Austrian School'. As of the early twenty-first century, liberal institutional economics is again increasingly contesting the field against the alternative paradigms of 'neoclassical economics', which, in many parts, has been the established orthodoxy. Neoclassical economics has long been criticized by 'Austrian economists' as based on unrealistic assumptions and as too simplistic for the analysis of complex, dynamic reality and preparing policy advice. Greater realism in coping with a growing world economy is one reason why the institutional economics approach has gained growing influence over public policy in many developing countries, in the post-Soviet states and in those mature economies where leaders, such as America's Ronald Reagan and Britain's Margaret Thatcher, advocated reform.

The 'Austrian School', founded by academic teachers in late nineteenth century Vienna – Carl Menger (1840–1921), Friedrich von Wieser (1851–1926) and Eugen von Böhm-Bawerk (1851–1914) – was refined by philosopher-economists such as Ludwig von Mises, Friedrich August Hayek and – to some extent – Joseph A. Schumpeter.

This intellectual tradition has always been at variance with 'neoclassical economics' as practiced in the majority of British, Scandinavian and American university departments. This latter tradition goes back to nineteenth century economists such as Vilfredo Pareto and Enrico Barone, who developed simplified mathematical models, and economists at Cambridge University, most notably Alfred Marshall (1842–1924) and John Maynard Keynes (1883–1946), who derived models which became the mainstream orthodoxy in twentieth century economics teaching, research and policy making. Most post-war economists in the United States fell into line. Increasingly, the language of neoclassical economics was mathematics and econometrics, giving the models both a certain cohesion and a scientific mystique. The assumption of *ceteris paribus* – all other things remaining equal – helped 'economist kings' to prepare confident, clear-cut policy prescriptions; and policy makers could remain untroubled by risks of unforeseen consequences. Economists became increasingly experts on economic modelling, and not on the realities of economic life. The neoclassical approach also frequently introduced a bias towards short-termism and activist policy interventions, which in turn made neoclassical economists popular with policy makers. The neoclassical orthodoxy underpins a completely different vision of society and policy from the individualistic one of the Austrians, but serves 'self-anointed elites' well (Sowell, 1987; 2009; Boettke, 2012).

As made clear throughout this book, the neoclassical paradigm, and by extension much of present-day econometrics, is built on unrealistic assumptions about human motivation and knowledge. In order to model the real world, mainstream economists normally assume explicitly or implicitly (i) that all people are driven exclusively by maximization of utility or profit, and (ii) that economic agents, or at least theorizing observers, have 'perfect knowledge'.

The *Methodenstreit* between Austrian and neoclassical economics

People with practical life experience in business, law, engineering and psychology, as well as historians and general observers, are astounded when they discover that standard textbook economics is built on assumptions that many find patently absurd (Kasper 2010; Boettke 2012):

- 'Perfect knowledge' of everyone's preferences, as well as of all available skills, technologies and other resources, has led to the construct of a *homunculus oeconomicus* who knows all these things. By contrast, real people rarely know most of these matters. They struggle to reduce their ignorance and incur great costs to do so. Buyers and sellers have to discover by risky, entrepreneurial search processes what is feasible and what satisfactions might be found. The main thrust of economic pursuits in the real world is to gain more useful knowledge. Consequently, Economics

1.01 courses attribute only a minor, if any role to entrepreneurs, risks, transaction costs, innovation and profits. Most textbooks define these core concepts unsatisfactorily.

- Economic agents are depicted as reacting passively to given conditions, only maximizing their utility or their profits. This passive-static model of atomistic behaviour rightly strikes non-economists as a poor reflection of the world, in which the motivation is often not maximization under known conditions, but satisficing or active entrepreneurial drive (Section 3.2). In reality, maximization of ends by given means is impossible, because people's diverse, subjective preferences vary greatly over time and from person to person. Business practitioners know that the average consumer with a stable set of indifference curves and the representative firm with a standard production function are figments of the textbook writers' imaginations that have little semblance to real-world households and producers and traders.

- Neoclassical orthodoxy focuses implausibly on 'equilibrium' – a state of affairs where everyone's expectations are mutually compatible and no further change takes place. It speaks of a 'Golden Age', when no further economic growth occurs – stagnation as a 'Golden' ideal? Business leaders and technologists, who are continually on the lookout for new opportunities, are bemused.

- Neoclassical (and Marxist) economics contains – inscribed in its DNA, so to speak – the assumption of diminishing returns. This assumption may have been a realistic reflection of the era of stagnant agricultural knowledge. Contemporary reality is, however, one of ongoing and pervasive innovation. Few production functions stand still in our time, when computer programs are updated almost weekly, when professionals are engaged in life-long learning and new products appear in showrooms with every new season. In reality, new industries ever so often reap economies of scope and scale and succeed in attaining increasing returns by learning.

- Neoclassical textbook models that are built on the assumption of zero transaction costs have little appeal for professionals in the now dominant service industries. Their very job is to control and reduce these costs. Lawyers, bankers, accountants and consultants – one might call them 'transaction cost engineers' – find little use for economic theories that assume transaction costs to be zero, so that no room is left in neoclassical models for their contribution to material wellbeing.

- The *ceteris paribus* assumption of the textbook model – that the rest of the world stands still – implies that the economy is akin to inert matter, rather than a real living, dynamic organism. In reality, economics has much more in common with the life sciences than with, for example, celestial physics. Biologists and environmentalists have taught us about complex evolving systems. They warn us to heed the unforeseen consequences of interference with nature. Many who now understand that the web of economic life is equally complex, now realize that *ceteris paribus* economics educates policy makers to remain blind to the deleterious longer-term consequences of their actions.

● Orthodox textbooks also work with the unrealistic concept of the 'benevolent dictator', the all-knowing, all-powerful ruler who pursues the national interest. Men with practical life experience are rarely able to make that assumption. This is why public choice economics has been so readily accepted around the world over recent decades. The obvious reality is that politicians, bureaucrats, influential business leaders and organized lobbies act in their self-interest, often ruthlessly so.

Of course, all theorizing about the natural world and society requires the scientist to make abstracting assumptions. However, abstractions made 'for simplicity's sake' are not legitimate when they eliminate conditions that are constitutional to the problem at hand. When coping with scarcity, which is after all the core problem of economics, it is never permissible to assume the knowledge problem away (Section 3.1; Boettke, 2012).

In most neoclassical econometric models, actors are assumed to maximize or optimize target variables – such as income, profit or leisure – simultaneously, so that the modeller can then derive a static 'equilibrium'. The modeller can then 'disturb' the system by introducing a policy intervention, for example an increase in a tax rate, and derive a new equilibrium. The comparison of these two static states of the world then demonstrates the overall effects of the tax increase. Some constants in these models are derived from statistics, often with the refined conjuring tricks from the econometricians' tool kit, others are 'calibrated' – in other words are simply made up! Complicated mathematical transformations of the assumptions, prejudices and data inputs tend to disguise for the layman that models only show what has been initially fed in. A leading macro-economic econometrician recently explained why dynamic stochastic equilibrium models had failed to predict the global financial crisis of 2008-09 by saying that the failure did not reflect on the capacity of such models to do useful econometric modelling. The factors which caused the crisis had simply not been included in the models. What use are such models then to clients in business, finance and politics? If the assumptions are wrong, then the adage applies: 'Garbage in, garbage out!'

Many a time, model assumptions are also 'fine-tuned backwards' beginning with the desired conclusions that a modeller or a client expects, for example that a higher tax rate or a new tariff have desired or acceptable effects, or what carbon dioxide taxes and subsidies are politically acceptable to obtain a certain margin of global warming a century hence. Such models amount to mere speculation, but distract attention from observing the real world. They also serve to conjure up certainties, where in reality ignorance and uncertainties prevail. By disguising this fundamental fact, neoclassical econometrics has become the handmaiden for interventionist policies.

The *Methodenstreit* between oikos and katallaxis

These criticisms of mainstream economics are not new. Austrian economist Carl Menger made them back in 1871 when he published his ground-breaking book *Principles of Economics* (Menger, 1981/1871; also 1985/1883). Menger and his colleagues and successors saw economics as a dynamic process of complex, subjectively decided human actions, as competing entrepreneurs find, apply and correct dispersed knowledge. Menger originally attacked the static mathematical models of Léon Walras and Vilfredo Pareto, which were built on assumptions of known, fairly constant ends and means. From the 1930s onwards, "the 'Austrian School' . . . [again stressed] the subjective nature of economic values [and] . . . produced a new paradigm . . . Yet, [it was overshadowed by] . . . 'macro-economics', which seeks causal connections between hypothetically measurable entities of statistical aggregates. These may sometimes . . . indicate some *vague* probabilities, but they certainly do not explain the processes involved in generating them" (Hayek, 1988, p. 98).

Austrian economists have thus never ceased to dispute the neoclassical modelling assumptions. This has led to repeated waves of *Methodenstreit* (to use the German word for dispute over the right method to analyse economic phenomena; Huerta de Soto, 1998; Bostaph in Boettke, 1994; pp. 459–464; Kirzner, (ed.) 1994). They persistently criticized the concept of *oikos*, the mere rationing of scarcity, and commended instead the concept of *katallaxis*, ongoing discovery, typically in market processes (O'Driscoll and Rizzo, 1985). Most of the time, these criticisms were brushed aside by academic teachers, professional economic societies, journal editors and policy advisors. The neoclassical approach gained added momentum when Keynesian macroeconomics suggested that recessions could be avoided by appropriate interventions to steer aggregate demand. Keynesian concepts were eagerly taken up by activists in finance ministries, central banks and international organizations. In the 1950s and 1960s, the economics profession styled itself as benevolent controllers of the nation's economic fate, as the neoclassical orthodoxy became overwhelmingly dominant in the Anglo-Saxon and

Scandinavian countries. Where public policy was informed by the Austrian worldview, such as in post-war West Germany or in the 'Asian tiger economies' after the 1960s, the evident growth successes were characterized by the mainstream as 'miracles' (for example, World Bank, 1993). And miracles *ipso facto* defy explanation.

Matters began to change after the oil crisis of the early 1970s when Keynesian demand stimulation produced *both* accelerating inflation *and* rising unemployment (Dean, 1981; Hutchison, 1981; Burton et al., 1986). More and more observers also realized that property rights and free markets mattered more than was acknowledged by the neoclassical mainstream. The consequence of political interventions, which cumulatively constrained economic freedom, was a growing and troublesome sclerosis of the economy and society.

Partly as a consequence of these sobering experiences, evolutionary (Austrian) ideas made a remarkable comeback during the 1980s and 1990s (Chapter 1). Many of the hitherto little-read books by leading classical liberal economists were republished or drawn upon in new presentations of Austrian economics by a new generation of analysts (McKenzie and Tullock, 1975; Dolan, ed., 1976; Moss, 1976; O'Driscoll, 1977; O'Driscoll and Rizzo, 1985; Doti and Lee, (eds) 1991; Rockwell, (ed.) 1988; Howitt, 2006). Continental European authors, such as Carl von Menger and Walter Eucken, were translated for the first time into English. While established university departments showed little interest in this brand of economics, think tanks with a classical-liberal or libertarian orientation were founded or reinvigorated in many countries, ranging from Britain (Institute of Economic Affairs; founded in 1955) to the North America (Cato Institute, 1977; Heritage Foundation, 1973; Fraser Institute, 1974) and Australia (Institute of Public Affairs, 1943; Centre for Independent Studies, 1976). Since then, think tanks have become influential in the policy dialogue of dozens of countries.

The fundamental ideas of 'Austrian economists' – such as Hayek, Mises, Bauer and their colleagues in the *Mont Pèlerin Society*, an international academy – also helped a new generation of political entrepreneurs, ranging from Britain's Margaret Thatcher and America's Ronald Reagan to reformers in Australia and New Zealand, to reshape the public discourse about political economy. The (often autocratic) political leaders of the poor East-Asian countries, too, began to subscribe to notions of economic evolution and open international competition. They rejected central planning and import substitution, then the prevailing fashions in development economics. Recommendations for import substitution and planning were built on comparative-static neoclassical and Marxian thinking, but were contradicted by Austrian institutional economists. Gradually, many men of the real world abandoned the definition of economics as *oikos*-style rationing, because its policy recommendations proved fragile in a world of accelerating, dynamic changes. Instead, business and policy-making elites subscribed to the optimistic and confident understanding that reformed institutions should be fostered to support competition, discovery and growth.

A number of essentially neoclassical economists have since tried to incorporate institutions in one form or another into their theories, for example by including dummy variables to represent the quality of private property rights or the indexes about the degree of corruption in their regression analyses. Others make allowances for transaction costs, yet still depict the market by intersecting supply and demand curves, where the same 'market clearing price' applies to sellers and buyers. These attempts have led to inconsistencies in models and sometimes confusing policy advice.

In recent years, the message that institutions matter to economic development has spread in the mainstream of economics and policy making, for example when European leaders began to realize that the creation of a monetary union (using the Euro) required thorough adjustments in fiscal institutions and public policy or when researchers for the World Bank stressed the "main determinant of differences in prosperity across countries are differences in economic institutions" (Acemoğlu and Robinson, 2008, p. v). In our opinion, this marks some progress. However, much of the new mainstream emphasis has been on external, that is politically determined and enforced, institutions, while most observers remain blind to the often decisive and hard-to-adapt internal institutions of society. Thus, Acemoğlu and Robinson write in their analysis of institutional change and development: "economic institutions are collective choices that are the outcome of a political process. The economic institutions of a society depend on the nature of political institutions" (*idem*). This ignores that a society's important internal institutions are normally not shaped by collective action and that they normally are much more decisive (see Chapter 5).

A conclusion reached two decades ago still holds: Institutional economists of the Austrian variety have to convince others through the quality of their work that their paradigm is useful and that the spread of the discipline comes with great promise (Boettke, 1994, pp. 601–615). The task is not yet done.

Why has the neoclassical orthodoxy remained influential?

Meanwhile one needs to ask why the change in the style of economic policy and the institutional approach among influential policy and business advisors has not yet been fully reflected in the journals, the academic teaching and the analyses of research institutes and international organizations of the economics profession. The explanations for this inertia are obvious (Kasper, 2010, pp. 16–19):

- 'Simplifying' assumptions make it easy to build models and derive aesthetically pleasing results. This creates the impression that new knowledge is produced, whereas in reality modelling assumptions and imperfect knowledge have only been transformed in ways that may impress the layman and client. The illusion of certainty that models offer, may give comfort to people, who are nonetheless still confronted with the need to take risky decisions.
- Easily available statistics of some aggregates and averages have facilitated neoclassical model building. When not enough variables are known to mathematically solve a system of equations, econometric tricks, such as the insertion of 'dummy variables', help to create the illusion that economists have knowledge, which in reality no one can have.
- Generations of economists have invested great effort into acquiring their theoretical and econometric skills. They are understandably loath to write off their human capital. While they increasingly only write for each other, rather than the wider public, mutual 'publication and citation cartels' fortify the conservative position.
- Neoclassical models are easy to teach. Students with no real-life experience normally enjoy the ready-made insights from neoclassical micro- and macro-economic models. Whereas an understanding of Austrian economics demands at least some fundamental knowledge of economic history, sociology, law and psychology, relevant insights from these disciplines are made superfluous by the mathematically convenient assumptions of neoclassical economics.
- Neoclassical abstraction has allowed economists to pretend that theirs is a 'scientific discipline' akin to what natural scientists can offer to engineers, architects and industrialists. The more probabilistic, open-ended conception of Austrian economics is less appealing to the energetic policy maker; and the laissez-faire approach that explains changes by millions of diverse individual decisions is less appealing to political men of action.

The global financial crisis and recession of 2008-09 has again demonstrated how eagerly intervention-prone politicians embrace Keynesian concepts that encourage them to act, whatever the longer-term consequences (higher public debt, rising interest burdens, inflation necessitating painful restrictions later on; persistent structural weaknesses; public cynicism). Publicists and political activists also prefer a kind of economics that allows them to criticize or laud distinct actions by influential actors, rather than to accept the outcomes of thousands of decisions by anonymous market participants. Many also derive influence over public opinion by preaching the 'law of diminishing returns' to derive pessimism about the future and thereby gain popular support for corrective interventions. By contrast, the realistic worldview that innovative enterprise has widened mankind's material possibilities, which justifies optimism, is less appealing to the political elites (Berger, 1987; Sowell, 1987; Ridley, 2010). This critical, almost cynical conclusion about the role of modeling to top-down policy was, for example, expressed in a 2010 discussion of climate modeling: "plausible futures using computer models . . . are sufficient to undergird just about any view of the future that one prefers . . . the 'projective' models [are] . . . conflated . . . with what politicians really want . . . that is precise forecasts of the future" (Prins et al., 2010).

Consequences for teaching and policy advice

Our major motivation for writing an introductory book that brings the diverse insights of institutional and evolutionary economics together in a systematic, teachable form has been to address all those who are disillusioned with mainstream neoclassical economics (Kasper, 2010; Boettke, 2012). It is no secret that numerous business schools, engineering courses, law schools and faculties of sociology, history and politics have abandoned introductory Economics 1.01 as a course requirement. A body of theory, which leaves little room for entrepreneurial exploration, for technical innovation and the legal support of institutions, simply has no appeal to academic faculties that teach business, engineering and jurisprudence. However, these disciplines are poorly served by not taking on board the insights of a brand of economics, which focuses on dispersed, evolving knowledge search and the institutions that can help or hinder economic evolution. Therefore, many law schools have found it necessary to develop programmes of law and economics and to teach about property rights and competition in ways that occupy common ground with institutional economics. Long-term history and civilization studies have been both important contributors to institutional-evolutionary economics and beneficiaries of the Austrian worldview.

While faculties of economics and established economics journals in the old industrial countries of the West have been slow to switch to institutional economics, the same does not apply to universities and colleges in the developing countries. The challenges of economic development and the reality of growth-impeding corruption have induced many academic teachers and media analysts in these countries to embrace a wider, more realistic 'Austrian' and public-choice worldview. In those cultures, in which evolution is instinctively understood and Western concepts of ideal, static end-states have little popular appeal, one can now observe a natural acceptance with institutional economics. Thus, the moral teachings of Confucius, which are now being officially revived in China, are more congenial to the morality embedded in institutional economics than to the static, instrumentalist approach of the economic orthodoxy.

The debate over the most appropriate methodology to tackle complex economic reality is nevertheless likely to continue, because many economists and econometricians defend their neoclassical intellectual capital and because intervention-prone politicians and media commentators prefer models that reserve a big role for them. This is also becoming evident in the resolute reliance of climate politics on computer models, despite the fact that growing numbers of economists and natural scientists are weary of the econometric art.

Policy makers are of course rarely driven by philosophical advice from their staff or discussions of ideas of the sort that underlie the institutional-economics paradigm. But they tend to pay great heed to what is successful elsewhere. The free-trading approach and the enterprise-friendly institutional settings of policy in the East Asian 'tiger economies' were decisive influences on the reforms in neighbouring countries, even big ones with an interventionist tradition, such as Indonesia, China, Vietnam and India. Education about the importance of institutional quality can then help to make politicians, bureaucrats and industrialists receptive to policy constellations that are derived from the institutional-evolutionary worldview. Textbooks like this one, and teachers who use them, can then make a valuable contribution to the real fate of people and communities.

There is one further benefit for teachers and students who embrace the Austrian institutional conception of economics: Whereas the thrust of neoclassical theory hinges on fears of scarcity, earning it the label of 'dismal science', our approach is conducive to optimism about the possibility of individual achievement and a decent society, in which individuals can pursue their own happiness as they see fit. After all, improvements in the human condition have been the experience of most, though – alas – not all people on Earth over the past two generations. In any case, optimism is a valuable evolutionary signal that inspires others; it is contagious. Teachers, who teach modes of thinking that leave room for hope and optimism, will therefore find their work more rewarding, for they are fostering positive life attitudes.

Appendix

I, Pencil

by Leonard E. Read, Foundation for Economic Education*

I am a lead pencil – the ordinary wooden pencil familiar to all boys and girls and adults who can read and write. (My official name is "Mongol 482". My many ingredients are assembled, fabricated and finished by Eberhard Faber Pencil Company, Wilkes-Barre, Pennsylvania.)

Writing is both by vocation and my avocation; that's all I do.

You may wonder why I should write a genealogy. Well, to begin with, my story is interesting. And, next, I am a mystery – more so than a tree or a sunset or even a flash of lightning. But, sadly, I am taken for granted by those who use me, as if I were a mere incident and without background. This supercilious attitude relegates me to the level of the commonplace. This is a species of the grievous error in which mankind cannot too long persist without peril. For, as a wise man, G.K. Chesterton, observed, "We are perishing for want of wonder, not for want of wonders."

I, Pencil, simple though I appear to be, merit your wonder and awe, a claim I shall attempt to prove. In fact, if you can understand me – no, that's too much to ask of anyone – if you can become aware of the miraculousness that I symbolize, you can help save the freedom mankind is so unhappily losing. I have a profound lesson to teach. And I can teach this lesson better than can an automobile or an aeroplane or a mechanical dishwasher because – well, because I am seemingly so simple.

Simple? Yet, not a single person on the face of this earth knows how to make me. This sounds fantastic, doesn't it? Especially when you realize that there are about one and one-half billion of my kind produced in the US each year.

---

* First published in 1958. Reprinted with the kind permission of the *Foundation for Economic Education* in New York, who own the copyright.

Pick me up and look me over. What do you see? Not much meets the eye – there's some wood, lacquer, the printed labeling, graphite lead, a bit of metal, and an eraser.

Innumerable antecedents
Just as you cannot trace your family tree back very far, so is it impossible for me to name and explain all my antecedents. But I would like to suggest enough of them to impress upon you the richness and complexity of my background.

My family tree begins with what in fact is a tree, a cedar of straight grain that grows in Northern California and Oregon. Now contemplate all the saws and trucks and rope and the countless other gear used in harvesting and carting the cedar logs to the railroad siding. Think of all the persons and the numberless skills that went into their fabrication: the mining of ore, the making of steel and its refinement into saws, axes, motors; the growing of hemp and bringing it through all the stages to heavy and strong rope; the logging camps with their beds and mess halls, the cookery and the raising of all the foods. Why, untold thousands of persons had a hand in every cup of coffee the loggers drink!

The logs are shipped to a mill in San Leandro, California. Can you imagine the individuals who make flat cars and rails and railroad engines and who construct and install the communication systems incidental thereto? These legions are among my antecedents.

Consider the millwork in San Leandro. The cedar logs are cut into small, pencil-length slats less than one-fourth of an inch in thickness. These are kiln-dried and then tinted for the same reason women put rouge on their faces. People prefer that I look pretty, not a pallid white. The slats are waxed and kiln-dried again. How many skills went into the making of the tint and kilns, into supplying the heat, the light and power, the belts, motors, and all the other things a mill requires? Are sweepers in the mill among my ancestors? Yes, and also included are the men who poured the concrete for the dam of a Pacific Gas & Electric Company hydroplant which supplies the mill's power. And don't overlook the ancestors present and distant who have a hand in transporting sixty carloads of slats across the nation from California to Wilkes-Barre.

Complicated machinery
Once in the pencil factory – $4,000,000 in machinery and building, all capital accumulated by thrifty and saving parents of mine – each slat is given eight

grooves by a complex machine, after which another machine lays leads in every other slat, applies glue, and places another slat atop – a lead sandwich, so to speak. Seven brothers and I are mechanically carved from this "wood-clinched" sandwich.

My "lead" itself – it contains no lead at all – is complex. The graphite is mined in Ceylon. Consider the miners and those who make their many tools and the makers of the paper sacks in which the graphite is shipped and those who make the string that ties the sacks and those who put them aboard ships and those who make the ships. Even the lighthouse keepers along the way assisted in my birth – and the harbor pilots.

The graphite is mixed with clay from Mississippi in which ammonium hydroxide is used in the refining process. Then wetting agents are added such as sulfonated tallow – animal fats chemically reacted with sulfuric acid. After passing through numerous machines, the mixture finally appears as endless extrusions – as from a sausage grinder – cut to size, dried, and baked for several hours at 1850 degrees Fahrenheit. To increase their strength and smoothness the leads are then treated with a hot mixture which includes candililla wax from Mexico, paraffin wax and hydrogenated natural fats.

My cedar receives six coats of lacquer. Do you know all of the ingredients of lacquer? Who would think that the growers of castor beans and the refiners of castor oils are a part of it? They are. Why, even the processes by which the lacquer is made a beautiful yellow involves the skills of more persons than one can enumerate!

Observe the labeling. That's a film formed by applying heat to carbon black mixed with resins. How do you make resins and what, pray, is carbon black?

My bit of metal – the ferrule – is brass. Think of all the persons who mine zinc and copper and those who have the skills to make shiny sheet brass from these products of nature. Those black rings on my ferrule are black nickel. What is black nickel and how is it applied? The complete story of why the centre of my ferrule has no black nickel on it would take pages to explain.

Then there's my crowning glory, inelegantly referred to in the trade as "the plug", the part man uses to erase the errors he makes with me. An ingredient called "factice" is what does the erasing. It is a rubber-like product made by reacting rape seed oil from the Dutch East Indies with sulfur chloride. Rubber, contrary to the common notion, is only for binding purposes. Then, too, there are numerous vulcanizing and accelerating agents. The pumice comes from Italy; and the pigment which gives "the plug" its colour is cadmium sulfide.

Vast web of knowhow
Does anyone wish to challenge my earlier assertion that no single person on the face of this earth knows how to make me?

Actually, millions of human beings have had a hand in my creation, no one of whom even knows more than a very few of the others. Now, you may say that I go too far in relating the picker of a coffee berry in far-off Brazil and food growers elsewhere to my creation; that this is an extreme position. I shall stand by my claim. There isn't a single person in all these millions, including the president of the pencil company, who contributes more than a tiny, infinitesimal bit of knowhow. From the standpoint of knowhow the only difference between the miner of graphite in Ceylon and the logger in Oregon is in the type of knowhow. Neither the miner nor the logger can be dispensed with, any more than the chemist at the factory or the worker in the oil field – paraffin being a by-product of petroleum.

Here is an astounding fact: Neither the worker in the oil field nor the chemist nor the digger of graphite or clay nor anyone who mans or makes the ships or trains or trucks nor the one who runs the machine that does the knurling on my bit of metal nor the president of the company performs his singular task because he wants *me*. Each one wants me less, perhaps, than does a child in the first grade. Indeed, there are some among this vast multitude who never saw a pencil nor would they know how to use one. Their motivation is other than me. Perhaps it is something like this: Each of these millions sees that he can thus exchange his tiny knowhow for the goods and services he needs or wants. I may or may not be among these items.

No human master-mind
There is a fact still more astounding: The absence of a master-mind, of anyone dictating or forcibly directing these countless actions that bring me into being. No trace of such a person can be found. Instead, we find the Scottish economist and moral philosopher Adam Smith's famous "Invisible Hand" at work in the marketplace. This is the mystery to which I earlier referred.

It has been said that "only God can make a tree". Why do we agree with this? Isn't it because we realize that we ourselves could not make one? Indeed, can we even describe a tree? We cannot, except in superficial terms. We can say, for instance, that a certain molecular configuration manifests itself as a tree. But what mind is there among men that could even record, let alone direct, the constant change of molecules that transpire in the life span of a tree? Such a feat is utterly unthinkable!

I, Pencil, am a complex combination of miracles; a tree, zinc, copper, graphite, and so on. But to these miracles which manifest themselves in Nature an even more extraordinary miracle has been added: the configuration of creative human energies – millions of tiny bits of knowhow configurating naturally and spontaneously in response to human necessity and desire and in the absence of any human master-minding! Since only God can make a tree, I insist that only God could make me. Man can no more direct millions of bits of knowhow so as to bring a pencil into being than he can put molecules together to create a tree.

That's what I meant when I wrote earlier, "If you can become aware of the miraculousness which I symbolize, you can help save the freedom mankind is so unhappily losing". For, if one is aware that these bits of knowhow will naturally, yes, automatically, arrange themselves into creative and productive patterns in response to human necessity and demand – that is, in the absence of governmental or any other coercive master-minding – then one will possess an absolutely essential ingredient for freedom: a faith in free men. Freedom is impossible without this faith.

Once government has had a monopoly on a creative activity – the delivery of the mail, for instance – most individuals will believe that the mail could not be efficiently delivered by men acting freely. And here is the reason: Each one acknowledges that he himself doesn't know how to do all the things involved in mail delivery. He also recognizes that no other individual could. These assumptions are correct. No individual possesses enough knowhow to perform a nation's mail delivery any more than any individual possesses enough knowhow to make a pencil. In the absence of a faith in free men – unaware that millions of tiny kinds of knowhow would naturally and miraculously form and cooperate to satisfy this necessity – the individual cannot help but reach the erroneous conclusion that the mail can be delivered only by governmental master-minding.

Testimony galore
If I, Pencil, were the only item that could offer testimony on what men can accomplish when free to try, then those with little faith would have a fair case. However, there is testimony galore; it's all about us on every hand. Mail delivery is exceedingly simple when compared, for instance, to the making of an automobile or a calculating machine or a grain combine or a milling machine, or to tens of thousands of other things.

Delivery? Why, in this age where men have been left free to try, they deliver the human voice around the world in less than one second; they deliver an event visually and in motion to any person's home when it is happening; they deliver 150 passengers from Seattle to Baltimore in less than four hours; they deliver gas from Texas to one's range or furnace in New York at unbelievably low rates and without subsidy; they deliver each four pounds of oil from the Persian Gulf to our Eastern Seaboard – halfway around the world – for less money than the government charges for delivering a one-ounce letter across the street![1]

Leave men be free
The lesson I have to teach is this: Leave all creative energies uninhibited. Merely organize society to act in harmony with this lesson. Let society's legal apparatus remove all obstacles the best it can. Permit creative knowhow to freely flow. Have faith that free men will respond to the "Invisible Hand". This faith will be confirmed. I, Pencil, seemingly simple though I am, offer the miracle of my creation as testimony that this is a practical faith, as practical as the sun, the rain, a cedar tree, and the good earth.

NOTE

1   *Ed.: Some things have changed since this essay first ran in 1958!*

Bibliography

Abramovitz, M. (1979), 'Rapid Growth Potential and Its Realization: The Experience of the Capitalist Economies in Post-War Period', in: E. Malinvaud and R.O.C. Matthews (eds), *Economic Growth and Resources*, vol. 1, London and New York: St. Martin's Press, pp. 1–50.

Acemoğlu D. and J. Robinson (2008), *The Role of Institutions in Growth and Development*, Washington, DC: World Bank/Commission on Growth and Development.

Acemoğlu D. and J. Robinson (2012), *Why Nations Fail: The Origins of Power, Prosperity, and Poverty*, New York: Random House.

Albert, H. (1979), 'The Economic Tradition. Economics as a Research Programme for Theoretical Social Science', in: K. Brunner (ed.) (1979), *Economics and Social Institutions, Insights from the Conferences on Analysis and Ideology*, Boston–The Hague–London: M. Nijhoff.

Albert, H. (1985), 'On Using Leibniz in Economics. Comment on Peter Koslowski', in: P. Koslowski (ed.) (1985), *Economics in Philosophy*, Tübingen: Mohr Siebeck, pp. 68–78.

Alchian, A. (1987), 'Property Rights', in J. Eatwell et al. (eds), *The Palgrave Dictionary of Economics*, London: Macmillan and New York: Stockton Press, pp. 1031–1034.

Alchian, A. and H. Demsetz (1972), 'Production, Information Costs, and Economic Organisation', *American Economic Review*, vol. 62, pp. 777–795.

Alchian, A. and H. Demsetz (1973), 'The Property Rights Paradigm', *Journal of Economic History*, vol. 33, no. 1, pp. 16–27.

de Alessi, L. (1969), 'Implications of Property Rights for Government Investment Choices', *American Economic Review*, vol. 59, pp. 16–63.

de Alessi, L. (1980), 'A Review of Property Rights: A Review of the Evidence', *Research in Law and Economics*, vol. 2, pp. 1–47.

de Alessi, L. (1982), 'On the Nature and Consequences of Private and Public Enterprise', *Minnesota Law Review*, vol. 67, pp. 191–209.

de Alessi, L. (1983), 'Property Rights, Transaction Costs, and X-Efficiency: An Essay in Economic Theory', *American Economic Review*, vol. 73, no. 1, pp. 64–81.

de Alessi, L. (1995), 'Institutions, Competition, and Individual Welfare', in N. Karlsson (ed.), *Can the Present Problems of Mature Welfare States such as Sweden be Solved?*, Stockholm: City University Press, pp. 76–87.

Aligica, G.P. and P.J. Boettke (2009), *Rethinking Institutional Analysis and Development: The Bloomington School*, London: Routledge.

Aligica, G.P. and K. Boudreaux (2007), *Paths to Property: Approaches to Institutional Change in International Development*, London: Institute of Economic Affairs.

Alston, L.J., T. Eggertsson, and D.C. North (1996), *Empirical Studies in Institutional Change*, Cambridge: Cambridge University Press.

Anderson, G. and P.J. Boettke (1993), 'Perestroika and Public Choice: the Economics of Autocratic Succession in a Rent-Seeking Society', *Public Choice*, vol. 75, no. 2, pp. 101–118.

Anderson, G. and P.J. Boettke (1997), 'Soviet Venality: A Rent-Seeking Model of the Communist State', *Public Choice*, vol. 93, no. 1–2, pp. 37–53.

Anderson, P.W., K.J. Arrow and D. Pines (1988), *The Economy as an Evolving, Complex System*, Redwood: Addison-Wesley.

Anderson, T.L. and D.R. Leal (1991), *Free Market Environmentalism*, San Francisco: Pacific Research Institute for Public Policy.

Anderson, T.L. and D.R. Leal (1997), *Enviro-Capitalists – Doing Good While Doing Well*, Lanham, MD: Rowman-Littlefield.

Anderson, T.L. and F.S. McChesney (eds) (2003), *Private Property Rights: Cooperation, Conflict, and Law*, Princeton, NJ: Princeton University Press.

Armentano, D.T. (1991), *Antitrust and Monopoly – Anatomy of a Policy Failure*, 2nd. edn, New York and London: Holmes & Meier.

Arrow, K.J. (1951), *Social Choice and Individual Values*, New York: John Wiley.

Arrow, K.J. (1962/1971), 'Economic Welfare and the Allocation of Resources for Invention', in D.M. Lamberton (ed.), *Economics of Information and Knowledge*, Harmondsworth: Penguin, pp. 141–160.

Arrow, K.J. (1969), 'The Organization of Economic Activity: Issues Pertinent to the Choice of Market versus Non-Market Allocation', in Joint Economic Committee (91st US Congress, 1st session), *The Analysis and Evaluation of Public Expenditure*, vol. **1**, Washington, DC: Congressional Printing Office, pp. 59–73.

Arrow, K.J. (1985), 'The Economics of Agency', in J.W. Pratt and R.J. Zeckhauser (eds), *Principals and Agents: The Structure of Business*, Boston: Harvard Business Books, pp. 31–57.

Arthur, W.B. (1995), 'Complexity in Economic and Financial Markets', *Complexity*, vol. **1**, no. 1, pp. 20–25 [reprinted in Drobak and Nye (eds) (1997), op. cit., pp. 291–304].

Axelrod, R. (1984), *The Evolution of Cooperation*, New York: Basic Books.

Banks, G. and J. Tumlir (1986), *Economic Policy and the Adjustment Problem*, London: Gower.

Barro, R.J. and X. Sala-I-Martin (1995), *Economic Growth*, New York: McGraw Hill.

Barzel, Y. (1982), 'Measurement Cost and the Organization of Markets', *Journal of Law and Economics*, vol. **25**, no. 2, pp. 7–48.

Barzel, Y. (1989), *Economic Analysis of Property Rights*, Cambridge, UK: Cambridge University Press.

Bates, R. (1990), 'Macropolitical Economy in the Field of Development, in J. Alt and K. Shepsle (eds), *Perspectives on Positive Political Economy*, Cambridge: Cambridge University Press, pp. 31–54.

Bauer, P.T. (1957). *Economic Analysis and Policy in Under-developed Countries*, Cambridge, UK: Cambridge University Press.

Bauer, P.T. (2000), *From Subsistence to Exchange and Other Essays*, Princeton, NJ: Princeton University Press.

Bauer, P.T. and A. Sen (2004), *From Subsistence to Exchange*, Princeton, NJ: Princeton University Press.

Baumol, W.J. (1952/1965), *Welfare Economics and the Theory of the State* (reprinted 1965), London: Bell and Sons.

Baumol, W.J. (1990), 'Entrepreneurship: Productive, Unproductive and Destructive', *Journal of Political Economy*, vol. **98**, pp. 893–921.

Becker, G. (1964), *Human Capital*, New York: National Bureau of Economic Research.

Becker, G. and R. Posner (2011), 'Deserving and Undeserving Inequality', available at Becker-Posner blog, www.e-axes.com/content/workingpaper, accessed 20 October 2011).

Becker, J. (1996), *Hungry Ghosts: China's Secret Famine*, London: John Murray.

Beckerman, W. (1974), *In Defence of Economic Growth*, London: J. Cape.

Bennett. J. (2012), *Little Green Lies: Twelve Environmental Myths*, Melbourne: Connor Court.

Bennett, J.T. (1990), 'Right to Work Laws, Evidence from the United States', in F. Mihlar (ed.), *Unions and Right-to-Work Laws*, Vancouver, BC: Fraser Institute, pp. 71–89.

Benson, B.L. (1989), 'The Spontaneous Evolution of Commercial Law', *Southern Economic Journal*, vol. **55**, pp. 655–661.

Benson, B.L. (1990), *The Enterprise of Law: Justice without the State*, San Francisco: Pacific Research Institute for Public Policy.

Benson, B.L. (1995), 'The Evolution of Values and Institutions in a Free Society: Underpinnings of a Market Economy', in G. Radnitzky and H. Bouillon (1995a), op. cit., pp. 87–126.

Benson, B.L. (1997), 'Institutions and the Spontaneous Evolution of Morality', in G. Radnitzky (ed.) (1997), *Values and the Social Order: Voluntary versus Coercive Orders*, Aldershot, UK and Brookfield, USA: Avebury Publishing, pp. 245–282.

Benson, B.L. (1998a), 'Law Merchant', in P. Newman (ed.), *The Palgrave Dictionary of Economics and the Law*, New York: Stockton.

Benson, B.L. (1998b), 'Economic Freedom and the Evolution of Law', *Cato Journal*, vol. **18**, no. 2, pp. 209–232.

Berger, P. (1987), *The Capitalist Revolution*, Aldershot, UK: Wildwood House and New York: Basic Books.

Berggren, N., N. Karlson and J. Nergelius (eds) (2002), *Why Constitutions Matter*, New Brundwick, NJ: Transaction Publishing.

Bergh, A. (2011), *The Rise, Fall and Revival of a Capitalist Welfare State: What are the Policy Lessons from Sweden*, Working Paper Series # 873, Research Institute of Industrial Economics, accessed at http://ideas.repec.org/pbe193.html, 18 March 2012.

Berle, A.A. and G.C. Means (1932), *The Modern Corporation and Private Property*, New York: Macmillan.

Bernholz, P. (1966), 'Economic Policies in a Democracy', *Kyklos*, vol. **19**, pp. 48–80.

Bernholz, P. (1982), 'Expanding Welfare State, Democracy and Free Market Economy: Are They Compatible?', *Journal of Institutional and Theoretical Economics*, vol. **138**, pp. 583–598.

Bernholz, P., M.E. Streit and R. Vaubel (eds) (1998), *Political Competition, Innovation and Growth – A Historical Analysis*, Berlin–New York: Springer.

Bethell, T. (1998), *The Noblest Triumph: Property and Prosperity through the Ages*, New York: St. Martin's Press.

Bhagwati, J. (2002), *Free Trade Today*, Princeton, NJ: Princeton University Press.

Bickenbach, F. and R. Soltwedel (1995), *Leadership and Business Organization: Findings from a Survey of Corporate Executives*, Gütersloh: Bertelsmann Foundation.

Bish, R. (1987), 'Federalism: A Market Economic Perspective', *Cato Journal*, vol. **5** (Fall), pp. 377–397.

Blandy, R. et al. (1985), *Structured Chaos – The Process of Productivity Advance*, Oxford and New York: Oxford University Press.

Block, W. (ed.) (1990), *Economics and the Environment: A Reconciliation*, Vancouver: The Fraser Institute.

Boettke, P.J. (1990), *The Political Economy of Soviet Socialism: The Formative Years, 1918–1928*, Dordrecht, Holland, London and Boston: Kluwer Academic Publishers.

Boettke, P.J. (1993), *Why Perestroika Failed: The Politics and Economics of Socialist Transformation*, London–New York: Routledge.

Boettke, P.J. (ed.) (1994), *The Elgar Companion to Austrian Economics*, Aldershot, UK and Brookfield, VT, USA: Edward Elgar.

Boettke, P.J. (ed.) (1998), *The Elgar Companion to Austrian Economics*, Cheltenham, UK and Lyme, NH, USA: Edward Elgar.

Boettke, P.J. (2001), *Calculation and Coordination. Essays on Socialism and Transitional Political Economy*, London: Routledge.

Boettke, P.J. (ed.) (2010), *Handbook on Contemporary Austrian Economics*, Cheltenham, UK and Northampton, MA, USA: Edward Elgar.

Boettke, P.J. (2012), *Living Economics, Yesterday, Today, and Tomorrow*, Oakland, CA–Guatemala City: The Independent Institute-University Francisco Marroquín.

Boettke, P.J. and C.J. Coyne, (2006), 'The Role of the Economist in Economic Development', *Quarterly Journal of Austrian Economics*, pp. 47–68.

Boettke, P.J. and P.T. Leeson (2004), 'Liberalism, Socialism, and Robust Political Economy', *Journal of Markets and Morality*, vol. 7, no.1, pp. 99–111.

Boettke, P.J., C.J. Coyne and P.T. Leeson (2008), 'Institutional Stickiness and the New Development Economics', *American Journal of Economics and Sociology*, vol. **67**, no. 2 (April), pp. 331–358.

Borner, S., A. Brunetti and B. Weber (1992), *Institutional Obstacles to Latin American Growth*, San Francisco: International Center for Economic Growth.

Bouillon, H. (ed.) (1996), *Libertarians and Liberalism – Essays in Honour of Gerard Radnitzky*, Aldershot, UK and Brookfield, USA: Avebury Publishing.

Boulding, K.E. (1956/1997), *The Image – Knowledge in Life and Society*, 11th edn, Ann Arbor: University of Michigan Press.

Boulding, K.E. (1959), *Principles of Economic Policy*, London: Staples Press.

Boulding, K.E. (1968/1962), 'Knowledge as a Commodity', *Beyond Economics – Essays on Society, Religion, and Ethics*, Ann Arbor: University of Michigan Press, pp. 141–150.

Boulding, K.E. (1969), 'Economics as a Moral Science', *American Economic Review*, vol. **59**, pp. 1–12.

Boyko, M., A. Shleifer and R. Vishny (1994), 'Voucher Privatization', *Journal of Financial Economics*, vol. **55**, no. 2, pp. 249–266.

Boyoko, M., A. Shleifer and R. Vishny (1997), *Privatizing Russia*, Cambridge, MA: MIT Press.

Braudel, F. (1981–84), *Civilization and Capitalism, 15th–18th Century*, 3 vols, London: Collins.

Brennan, G. and J.M. Buchanan (1980/1985), *The Power to Tax: Analytical Foundations of a Fiscal Constitution*, Cambridge and New York: Cambridge University Press.

Brennan, G. and J.M. Buchanan (1985), *The Reason of Rules: Constitutional Political Economy*, Cambridge and New York: Cambridge University Press.

Breughel Institute (2012), 'Lessons for Europe's Fiscal Union from US Federalism', *VoxEUorg* (25 January), accessed at http://www.voxeu.org/index.php?q/7559, on 13 March 2012.

Breyer, S. (1995), *Breaking the Vicious Circle; Toward Effective Risk Regulation*, new edition, Cambridge, MA: Harvard University Press.

Brunetti, A., G. Kisunko and B. Weder (1997), *Institutional Obstacles to Doing Business: Region-by-Region Results from a Worldwide Survey of the Private Sector*, Washington, DC: World Bank.

Brunner, K. and A. Meltzer (1971), 'The Uses of Money: Money in the Theory of the Exchange Economy', *American Economic Review*, vol. **61**, no. 5, pp. 784–805.

Buchanan, J. (1964), 'What Should Economists Do?', *Southern Economic Journal*, vol. **xxx**, no. 3 (Jan.), pp. 213–222.

Buchanan, J.M. (1965), 'An Economic Theory of Clubs', *Economica*, vol. **32**, pp. 1–14.

Buchanan, J.M. (1969), *Cost and Choice, An Inquiry in Economic Theory*, Chicago: University of Chicago Press.

Buchanan, J.M. (1975), *The Limits of Liberty – Between Anarchy and Leviathan*, Chicago: University of Chicago Press.

Buchanan, J.M. (1978), 'From Private Preferences to Public Philosophy. The Development of Public Choice', in Institute of Economic Affairs (1978), *The Economics of Politics*, London: Institute of Economic Affairs, pp. 3–20.

Buchanan, J.M. (1987), 'The Constitution of Economic Policy', *American Economic Review*, vol. **77**, pp. 243–250.

Buchanan, J.M. (1991), *Constitutional Economics*, Oxford, UK and Cambridge, MA: Basil Blackwell.

Buchanan, J.M. and A. di Pierro (1980), 'Cognition, Choice, and Entrepreneurship', *Southern Economic Journal*, vol. **46**, pp. 693–701.

Buchanan, J.M. and G. Tullock (1962), *The Calculus of Consent: Logical Foundations of Constitutional Democracy*, Ann Arbor: University of Michigan Press.

Buchanan, J.M. and R.E. Wagner (1977), *Democracy in Deficit: The Political Legacy of Lord Keynes*, New York: Academic Press.

Buchanan, J.M. et al. (eds) (1980), *Toward a Theory of the Rent-Seeking Society*, College Station: Texas A&M University Press.

Burton, J. et al. (1986), *Keynes's General Theory: Fifty Years On*, London: Institute of Economic Affairs.

Bush, P. (1987), 'The Theory of Institutional Change', *Journal of Economic Issues*, vol. **21**, pp. 1075–1116.

Butler, E. (2010), *Ludwig von Mises – a Primer*. London: Institute of Economic Affairs.

Carter, R.M. (2010), *Climate: The Counter-Consensus – a Scientist Speaks*. London: Stacey International.

Casson, M. (1993), 'Cultural Determinants of Economic Performance', *Journal of Comparative Economics*, vol. **17**, pp. 418–442.

Chenery, H.B. and M. Syrquin (1975), *Patterns of Development, 1950–70*, London: Oxford University Press for the World Bank.

Chenery, H.B., S. Robinson and M. Syrquin (1986), *Industrialization and Growth, A Comparative Study*, New York: Oxford University Press for the World Bank.

Cheung, S. (1983), 'The Contractual Nature of the Firm', *Journal of Law and Economics*, vol. **26**, pp. 1–21.

Ch'ng, D. (1993), *The Overseas Chinese Entrepreneurs in East Asia: Background, Business Practices and International Networks*, Melbourne: Committee for the Economic Development of Australia (CEDA).

Christainsen, G.B. (1989–90), 'Law as a Discovery Procedure', *Cato Journal*, vol. **9**, pp. 497–530.

Clark, G. (2007), *A Farewell to Alms: A Brief History of the World*, Princeton, NJ: Princeton University Press.

Clark, J.M. (1962), *Competition as a Dynamic Process*, Washington, DC: Brookings.

Clower, R.W. (ed.) (1969), *Monetary Theory: Selected Readings*, Harmondsworth: Penguin.

Coase, R.H. (1952/1937), 'The Nature of the Firm', in G.S. Stigler and K.E. Boulding (eds), *Readings in Price Theory*, Homewood, IL: Irwin, pp. 331–352.

Coase, R.H. (1960), 'The Problem of Social Cost', *Journal of Law and Economics*, vol. **3**, pp. 1–44.

Coase, R.H. (1988), 'The Nature of the Firm: Origin, Meaning, Influence', *Journal of Law, Economics and Organization*, vol. **4**, no. 1 (Spring), pp. 3–47.

Coleman, J.S. (1990), *Foundations of Social Theory*, Cambridge, MA: Belknap Press of Harvard University Press.

Cooter, R.D. (1996), 'Decentralised Law for a Complex Economy: The Structural Approach to Adjudicating the New Law Merchant', *University of Pennsylvania Law Review*, no. 144, pp. 1643–696.

Cooter, R.D. and T. Ulen (1997), *Law and Economics*, 2nd edn, New York: Addison-Wesley).

Cordato, R.E. (1994), 'Efficiency', in P.J. Boettke (ed.) (1994), op. cit., pp. 131–137.

Coughlin, C.C., A.K. Chrystal and G.E. Wood (1988), 'Protectionist Trade Policies: A Survey of Theory, Evidence and Rationale', *Federal Reserve Bank of St. Louis Review*, vol. **70**, no. 1, pp. 12–29.

Courtois, S. et al. (1999), *The Black Book of Communism: Crimes, Terror, Repression*, Cambridge, MA: Harvard University Press.

Cowen, T. (1988), 'The Marshall Plan: Myths and Realities', in Heritage Foundation, *US Aid to the Developing World – A Free Market Agenda*, Washington, DC: Heritage Foundation.

Cowen, T. (2002), *Creative Destruction, How Globalization is Changing the World's Cultures*, Princeton, NJ: Princeton University Press.

Cowen, T. and E. Crampton (2003), *Market Failure and Success: The New Debate*, Cheltenham, UK and Northampton, MA, USA: Edward Elgar.

Cox, M. (ed.) (1999), *Rethinking the Soviet Collapse: Sovietology, the Death of Communism and the New Russia*, London: Pinter.

Coyne, C. (2007), *After War*, Palo Alto, CA: Stanford University Press.

Coyne, C. and P. Leeson (2009), *Media, Development and Institutional Change*, Cheltenham, UK and Northampton, MA, USA: Edward Elgar.

Curzon-Price, V. (1997), 'International Commerce as an Instance of Non-Coerced Social Order', in G. Radnitzky (ed.) (1997), op. cit., pp. 425–438.

Cyert, R.M. and J.G. March (1992), *A Behavioral Theory of the Firm*, 2nd edn, Cambridge, MA: Blackwell Business.

Dahlmann, C.J. (1979), 'The Problem of Externality', *Journal of Law and Economics*, vol. **22**, no. 1, pp. 41–162.

Dahmén, E., L. Hannah and I.M. Kirzner (eds) (1994), *The Dynamics of Entrepreneurship*, *Crawford Lectures, no. 5*, The Institute of Economic Research, Malmø: Lund University.

Dean, J.W. (1981), 'The Dissolution of the Keynesian Consensus', in D. Bell and I. Kristol (eds), *The Crisis in Economic Theory*, New York: Basic Books, pp. 19–34.

Demsetz, H. (1964), 'The Exchange and Enforcement of Property Rights', *Journal of Law and Economics*, vol. **7**, pp. 11–26.

Demsetz, H. (1967), 'Toward a Theory of Property Rights', *American Economic Review*, vol. **57**, no. 2, pp. 347–359.

Demsetz, H. (1969), 'Information and Efficiency. Another Viewpoint', *Journal of Law and Economics*, vol. **13**, pp. 1–22.

Demsetz, H. (1970), 'The Private Production of Public Goods', *Journal of Law and Economics*, vol. **13**, pp. 293–06.

Demsetz, H. (1982), *Economic, Political and Legal Dimensions of Competition*, Amsterdam and New York: North Holland.

Demsetz, II. (1983), 'The Structure of Ownership and the Theory of the Firm', *Journal of Law and Economics* , vol. **26**, pp. 375–393.

Demsetz, H. (1988), 'The Theory of the Firm Revisited', *Journal of Law, Economics and Organization*, vol. **4**, no. 1 (Spring), pp. 141–161.

Demsetz, H. (1989/1982), *Efficiency, Competition and Policy: The Organisation of Economic Activity*, London and New York: Basil Blackwell.

Demsetz , H. (2003), 'Ownership and the Externality Problem', in T.L. Anderson and F.S. McChesney (eds), op. cit.

Denison, E.F. (1967), *Why Growth Rates Differ?*, Washington, DC: Brookings.

Dolan, E.G. (ed.) (1976), *The Foundations of Modern Austrian Economics*, Kansas City: Sheed and Ward.

Doti, J. and D.R. Lee (1991), *The Market Economy, A Reader*, Los Angeles: Roxbury Publications.

Downs, A. (1957a), *An Economic Theory of Democracy*, New York: Harper & Row.

Downs, A. (1957b), 'An Economic Theory of Political Action in a Democracy', in E. J. Hamilton (ed.), *Landmarks in Political Economy*, vol. **2**, Chicago: University of Chicago Press, pp. 559–582.

Drexler, K.E. (1986), *Engines of Creation, the Coming Era of Nanotechnology*, New York: Doubleday.

Drobak, J.N. and J.V. Nye (eds) (1997), *The Frontiers of the New Institutional Economics*, San Diego, CA: Academic Press.

Drucker, P.F. (1993), *Post-Capitalist Society*, New York: Harper Business.

Easterbrook, G. (2003), *The Progress Paradox: How Life Gets Better While People Feel Worse*, New York: Random House.

Easterly, W. (2006), *The White Man's Burden: Why the West's Efforts to Aid the Rest Have done so Much Ill and so Little Good*, New York: Penguin HC.

Edwards, C. (1995), *Crisis and Reforms in Latin America*, Oxford and New York: Oxford University Press.

Eggertsson, T. (1990), *Economic Behavior and Institutions*, Cambridge, UK: Cambridge University Press.

Eggertsson, T. (1998), 'Limits to Institutional Reforms', *Scandinavian Journal of Economics*, vol. **100**, no. 1, pp. 335–357.

Eisenstadt, S.N. (ed.) (2000), *Multiple Modernities*, New Brunswick NJ: Transaction Publishers.

Elster, J. (1989), *The Cement of Society: A Study of Social Order*, Cambridge, UK and New York: Cambridge University Press.

Epstein, R. (1985), *Takings: Private Property and the Power of Eminent Domain*, Cambridge, MA: Harvard University Press.

Epstein, R.A. (1995), *Simple Rules for a Complex World*, Cambridge, MA: Harvard University Press.

Epstein, R.A. (2007), *Economics of Property Law*, Cheltenham, UK and Northampton, MA, USA: Edward Elgar.

Epstein, R.A., G. Wood and G. Owens (2005), *Free Markets under Siege: Cartels, Politics and Social Welfare*, Stanford CA: Hoover Institution Press.

Erhard, L. (1960), *Prosperity through Competition*, 3rd edn, London: Thames and Hudson.

Eucken, W. (1992/1940), *The Foundations of Economics, History and Theory in the Analysis of Economic Reality*, New York and Heidelberg, Springer Publishers [first German edn 1940].

Fama, E.F. and M.C. Jensen (1985), 'Organizational Costs and Investment Decisions', *Journal of Financial Economics*, vol. **14**, no. 1, available at www.people.hbs.edu/mjensen/pub2.html, accessed 12 August 2011.

Ferguson, N. (2011), *Civillization – The West and the Rest*, London: Allen Lane.

Fields, G.S. (1984), 'Employment Income Distribution, and Economic Growth in Seven Small Open Economies', *Economic Journal*, vol. **94**, pp. 74–83.

Findlay, R. (1992), 'The Roots of Divergence: Western Economic History in Comparative Perspective', *American Economic Review*, vol. **82** (May), pp. 158–161.

Fisher, I. (1922), *The Purchasing Power of Money* available at www.econlib.org/library/Enc/bios/Fisher.htm, accessed 5 March 2011.

Flew, A. (1989), *Equality in Liberty and Justice*, London and New York: Routledge.

Foldvary, F. (1994), *Public Goods and Private Communities*, Aldershot, UK and Brookfield, VT, USA: Edward Elgar.

Fonte, J. (2011), *Sovereignty or Submission: Will Americans Rule Themselves or Be Ruled by Others?* New York: Encounter Books.

Freedom House (2011), *Freedom in the World 2011: The Authoritarian Challenge to Democracy* available at www.freedomhouse.org/template.cfm?page=70&release=1310, accessed 22 October 2011.

Freeman, D. (1983), *Margaret Mead and Samoa: The Making and Unmaking of an Anthropological Myth*, Canberra: Australian National University Press.

Freeman, R. and B. Berelson (1974), 'The Human Population', *Scientific American* (Sept.), pp. 32–49.

Friedman, D. (1979), 'Private Creation and Enforcement of Law: A Historical Case', *Journal of Legal Studies*, vol. **8**, no. 2, pp. 399–415.

Friedman, M. (1962), *Capitalism and Freedom*, Chicago and London: University of Chicago Press.

Friedman, M. (1968), 'The Role of Monetary Policy', *American Economic Review*, vol. **78**, (May), pp. 1–17.

Friedman, M. (1991), 'The Sources of Monopoly', in J.L. Doti and D.R. Lee (eds) (1991), op. cit., pp. 103–106.

Friedman, M. and R. Friedman (1980), *Free to Choose: A Personal Statement*, Harmondsworth: Pelican Books.

Fuglesang, A. and D. Chandler (1987), *Participation as Process: What we can Learn from Grameen Bank, Bangladesh*, Oslo: Ministry of Development Cooperation, NORAD.

Furubotn, E. (1994), *Future Development of the New Institutional Economics: Extension of the Neoclassical Model or New Construct?*, *Lectiones Jenenses*, Jena/Germany: Max-Planck-Institute for Research Into Economic Systems.

Furubotn, E. and R. Richter (eds) (1991), *The New Institutional Economics*, College Station: Texas A&M University Press.

Galbraith, J.K. (1967), *The New Industrial State*, Boston: Houghton Mifflin.

Gartzke, E. (2005), 'Economic Freedom and Peace', in Gwartney and Lawson, 2005, op. cit., pp. 29–44.

Gates, B. (1995), *The Road Ahead*, rev. edn, New York and London: Viking–Penguin.

Gerken, J. (ed.) (1995), *Competition among Institutions*, London: St. Martin's Press.

Gibbon, E. (1776–88/1996), *The History of the Decline and Fall of the Roman Empire*, London: Random House.

Giersch, H. (ed.) (1971), *Integration through Monetary Union?*, Tübingen, Germany: Mohr-Siebeck.

Giersch, H. (ed.) (1980), *Towards an Explanation of Economic Growth*, Tübingen, Germany: Mohr-Siebeck.

Giersch, H. (1989), *The Ethics of Economic Freedom*, Sydney: Independent Studies*.

Giersch, H. (1993), *Openness for Prosperity*, Cambridge, MA: MIT Press.

Giersch, H. (1996), 'Economic Morality as a Competitive Asset', in A. Hamlin et al. (1996), *Markets, Morals and Community*, Sydney: Centre for Independent Studies, pp. 19–42.

Giersch, H., K.H. Paqué and H. Schmieding (1992), *The Fading German Miracle*, Cambridge, UK and New York: Cambridge University Press.

Gigerenzer, G. (2006), 'Bounded and Rational', in R.J. Stainton, *Contemporary Debates in Cognitive Science*, London: Blackwell, pp. 120–135.

Gleeson-White, J. (2011), *Double Entry*, Sydney: Allen & Unwin.

Graham, A. and A. Seldon (1990), *Government and Economics in the Postwar World*, London: Routledge.

Green, D.G. (1996), *From Welfare State to Civil Society*, Wellington, NZ: NZ Business Roundtable.

Gregory, P.R. (1990/2006), *Restructuring the Soviet Economic Bureaucracy*, Cambridge, UK: Cambridge University Press.

Gregory, P.R. (2004), *The Political Economy of Stalinism*, Cambridge: Cambridge University Press.

---

* All publications of the Centre for Independent Studies cited here are available free of charge at www.cis.org.au/publications.

Gregory. P.R. (2008), 'Russia's Economy: Putin and the KGB State' available at www.econlib. org/library/Columns/y2011/Gregorykgbstate.html on 12 Nov. 2011

Gwartney, J.D. (1991), 'Private Property, Freedom and the West', in J.L. Doti and D.R. Lee, op. cit., pp. 62–76.

Gwartney, J. and R. Lawson (passim), *Economic Freedom of the World, Annual Report*, Vancouver: The Fraser Institute.

Gwartney, J.D. and R.E. Wagner (eds) (1988), *Public Choice and Constitutional Economics*, Greenwich, CT: JAI Press.

Gwartney, J., R. Lawson and J. Hall (2011), *Economic Freedom of the World, 2011 Annual Report*, Vancouver: The Fraser Institute.

Hahn, F.H. and R.C.O. Matthews (1969), 'The Theory of Economic Growth. A Survey', in: Royal Economic Society and American Economic Association, *Surveys of Economic Theory*, vol. **II**, London: Macmillan, pp. 1–124.

Harberger, A. (1984), *World Economic Growth*, San Francisco: Institute for Contemporary Studies.

Hardin, G. (1968), 'The Tragedy of the Commons', *Science*, no. 162, pp. 1243–1248.

Hardin, G. (1993/2008), 'The Tragedy of the Commons', in D. Henderson (ed.), op. cit., pp. 497–499.

Harper, D.A. (1996), *Entrepreneurship and the Market Process – An Inquiry into the Growth of Knowledge*, London and Florence: Routledge.

Hayek, F.A. (1933/2008), *Monetary Theory and the Trade Cycle*, reprinted in P.T. Salerno (ed.). *On Money, the Business Cycle and the Gold Standard*, Auburn, AL: Ludwig von Mises Institute [German original 1929].

Hayek, F.A. (1935), *Prices and Production*, 2nd edn, New York: Augustus Kelly (reprinted 1975).

Hayek, F.A. (1935/1948), 'The Nature and History of the Problem', in F.A. Hayek, *Individualism and Economic Order*, 2 vols, Chicago: University of Chicago Press, pp. 1–40.

Hayek, F.A. (1937), 'Economics and Knowledge', *Economica*, vol. **4**, 33–54.

Hayek, F.A. (1940), 'Socialist Calculation: The Competitive "Solution"', *Economica*, vol. **7**, pp. 125–149.

Hayek, F.A. (1944), *The Road to Serfdom*, Chicago: University of Chicago Press.

Hayek, F.A. (1945), 'The Use of Knowledge in Society', *American Economic Review*, vol. **35**, pp. 519–530.

Hayek, F.A. (1960), *The Constitution of Liberty*, London: Routledge Kegan Paul.

Hayek, F.A. (1967a), 'Notes on the Evolution of Systems of Rules of Conduct', in F.A. Hayek, *Studies in Philosophy, Politics and Economics*, London: Routledge Kegan Paul, pp. 66–81.

Hayek, F.A. (1967b), 'Kinds of Rationalism', in F.A. Hayek, *Studies in Philosophy, Politics and Economics*, London: Routledge Kegan Paul, pp. 82–95.

Hayek, F.A. (1973), *Rules and Order*, vol. 1 of *Law, Legislation and Liberty*, Chicago and London: University of Chicago Press.

Hayek, F.A. (1976), *The Mirage of Social Justice*, vol. 2 of *Law, Legislation and Liberty*, Chicago and London: University of Chicago Press.

Hayek, F.A. (1978a), *Denationalization of Money. An Analysis of the Theory and Practice of Concurrent Currencies*, London: Institute of Economic Affairs.

Hayek, F.A. (1978b), 'Competition as a Discovery Procedure', in F.A. Hayek, *New Studies in Philosophy, Politics, Economics and the History of Ideas*, London: Routledge Kegan Paul, pp. 179–190.

Hayek, F.A. (1979a), *The Political Order of a Free People*, vol. 3 of *Law, Legislation and Liberty*, Chicago and London: University of Chicago Press.

Hayek, F.A. (1979b), *Counter Revolution of Science: Studies on the Abuse of Reason*, 2nd edn, Indianapolis: Liberty Press.

Hayek, F.A. (1986/1978), 'Socialism and Science', in C. Nishiyama and K.R. Leube (eds), *The Essence of Hayek*, Stanford: Hoover Institution, pp. 114–127.

Hayek, F.A. (1988), *The Fatal Conceit: The Errors of Socialism*, London: Routledge and Chicago: University of Chicago Press.

Hazlitt, H. (1988/1964), *The Foundations of Morality*, Lanham, MD: University Press of America.

Henderson, D. (2001), *Misguided Virtue: False Notions of Corporate Social Responsibility*, Wellington: New Zealand Business Roundtable.

Henderson, D. (ed.) (2008), *The Concise Encyclopedia of Economics*, Indianapolis, IN: Liberty Fund.

Hessen, R. (2008), 'Capitalism', in D. Henderson (2008), op. cit., pp. 57–61.

Heyne, P., P.J. Boettke and D.L. Prychitko (2012), *The Economic Way of Thinking*, 12th edn, Upper Saddle River, NJ: Prentice Hall.

Higgs, R. (1997), 'Regime Uncertainty: Why the Great Depression Lasted So Long and Why Prosperity Returned After the War', *The Independent Review*, vol. 1, no. 4 (Spring), pp. 561–590.

Hirschman, A.O. (1977), *The Passions and the Interests – Political Arguments for Capitalism before its Triumph*, Princeton, NJ: Princeton University Press.

Hirschman, A.O. (1980/1970), *Exit, Voice and Loyalty: Responses to Decline in Firms, Organizations, and States*, Cambridge, MA: Harvard University Press.

Hobbes, J.T. (1651/1962), *Leviathan*, London: Collins.

Hodgson, G.M. (1988), *Economics and Institutions: A Manifesto for a Modern Institutional Economics*, Philadelphia, US: University of Pennsylvania Press and Cambridge: Polity Press.

Hodgson, G.M. (1989), 'Institutional Economic Theory: The Old versus the New', *Review of Political Economy*, vol. **1**, no. 3, pp. 249–269.

Hodgson, G.M. (1998), 'The Approach of Institutional Economics', *Journal of Economic Literature*, vol. **xxxvi** (March), 166–192.

Hodgson, G.M., W.J. Samuels and M.R. Tool (eds) (1994), *The Elgar Companion to Institutional and Evolutionary Economics*, 2 volumes, Aldershot, UK and Brookfield, VT, USA: Edward Elgar.

Hofstede, G. and R. Bond (1988), 'The Confucius Connection: From Cultural Roots to Economic Growth', *Organizational Dynamics*, vol. **16** (Spring), pp. 5–21.

Howitt, P. (2006), 'Growth and Development: A Schumpeterian Perspective', available at http://www.cdhowe.org/pdf/commentary_246.pdf, accessed 12 January 2011.

Huerta de Soto, J. (1998), 'The Ongoing *Methodenstreit* of the Austrian School', *Journal des économistes et des études humaines*, vol. **8**, no.1 (March), pp. 75–113.

Hume, D. (1965/1786), 'A Treatise of Human Nature', in D. Hume, *The Philosophical Works of David Hume*, edited by T.H. Green and T.H. Grose, Oxford: Clarendon.

Hutchison, T.W. (1981), 'On the Aims and Methods of Economic Theorizing', in T.W. Hutchison, *The Politics and Philosophy of Economics – Marxians, Keynesians and Austrians*, New York: New York University Press, pp. 266–307.

International Monetary Fund (1997), *World Economic Outlook, October 1997*, Washington, DC: IMF.

Jackson, K. et al. (2011), *International Property Rights Index, 2011 Report* (Washington, DC: Americans for Tax Reform Alliance/Property Rights Alliance), available at ATR–2011 Index–Web2.pdf, accessed 8 August 2011.

Jacobs, J. (1992), *Systems of Survival, a Dialogue on the Moral Foundations of Commerce and Politics*, New York: Random House.

James, J.J. and M. Thomas (eds) (1994), *Capitalism in Context*, Chicago and London: University of Chicago Press.

de Jasay, A. (1985), *The State*, Oxford and New York: Basil Blackwell.

de Jasay, A. (1993), 'Is limited government possible?' in H. Bouillon and G. Radnitzky (eds), *Government: Servant or Master?* Amsterdam–Atlanta, GA, USA: Editions Rodopi, pp. 73–97.

de Jasay, A. (1995), *Conventions: Some Thoughts on the Economics of Ordered Anarchy, Lectiones Jenenses*, Jena, Germany: Max-Planck-Institute for Research into Economic Systems.

de Jasay, A. (2002), *Justice and Its Surroundings*, Indianapolis, IN: Liberty Fund.

Jefferson, G.H. and T.G. Rawski (1995), 'How Industrial Reform Worked in China: The Role of Innovation, Competition and Property Rights', in World Bank (1995), op. cit., pp. 129–170.

Jensen, M.C. (1983), 'Organization Theory and Methodology', Accounting Review, vol. **58**, pp. 319–339.

Jensen, M.C. and W. Meckling (1976), 'Theory of the Firm: Managerial Behavior, Agency Costs, and Capital Structure', *Journal of Financial Economics*, vol. **3**, pp. 305–360.

Jensen, M.C. and R.S. Ruback (1983), 'The Market for Corporate Control: The Scientific Evidence', *Journal of Financial Economics*, vol. **11**, nos 1–4, pp. 5–50.

Johnson, P. (1983), *A History of the Modern World, From 1917 to the 1980s*, London: Weidenfeld and Nicholson.

Johnson, P. (1991), *The Birth of the Modern, World Society 1815–1830*, London: Weidenfeld and Nicholson.

Jones, CI. and P.M. Romer (2010), 'The New Kaldor Facts: Ideas, Institutions, Population, and Human Capital', *American Economic Journal: Macroeconomics*, vol. **2**, no. 1, pp. 224–245.

Jones, E.L. (1981/2003), *The European Miracle: Environments, Economies, and Geopolitics in the History of Europe and Asia*, 3rd edn, Cambridge, UK and New York: Cambridge University Press.

Jones, E.L (1988), *Growth Recurring. Economic Change in World History*, Oxford: Clarendon Press.

Jones, E.L. (1994), 'Patterns of Growth in History', in J.J James and M. Thomas (eds), op. cit., pp. 115–128.

Jones, E.L. (1995), 'Culture and Its Relationship to Economic Change', *Journal of Institutional and Theoretical Economics*, vol. **151**, no. 2, pp. 269–285.

Jones, E.L., L. Frost and C. White (1994), *Coming Full Circle: An Economic History of the Pacific Rim*, Melbourne: Oxford University Press.

Kahn, H. (1979), *World Economic Development: 1979 and Beyond*, London: Croom Helm and Boulder, CO: Westview Press.

Karlson, N. (ed.) (1995), *Can the Present Problems of Mature Welfare States such as Sweden be Solved?*, Stockholm: City University Press.

Karlson, N. (forthcoming), *Statecraft. How to Reform Modern Welfare States. Lessons from the Reform Processes of Sweden and Australia*, Cheltenham, UK and Northampton, MA, USA: Edward Elgar.

Kasper, W. (1970), 'European Integration and Greater Flexibility of Exchange Rates', in H.N. Halm (ed.), *Approaches to Greater Flexibility of Exchange Rates, The Bürgenstock Papers*, Princeton, NJ: Princeton University Press, pp. 385–388.

Kasper, W. (1981), 'The Sichuan Experiment', *The Australian Journal of Chinese Affairs*, no. 7, pp. 163–172.

Kasper, W. (1982), *Australian Political Economy*, Melbourne, Australia: Macmillan.

Kasper, W. (1994), *Global Competition, Institutions, and the East Asian Ascendancy*, San Francisco: International Center for Economic Growth.

Kasper, W. (1995), *Competitive Federalism*, Perth: Institute of Public Affairs, States' Policy Unit.

Kasper, W. (1996a), *Competitive Federalism Revisited: Bidding Wars, or Getting the Fundamentals Right?*, Perth: Institute for Public Affairs States' Policy Unit.

Kasper, W. (1996b), 'Responsibility and Reform, A Conversation with Ruth Richardson', *Policy*, vol. **12**, no. 3, pp. 25–31.

Kasper, W. (1998), 'Rapid Development in East Asia: Institutional Evolution and Backlogs', *Malaysian Journal of Economic Studies*, vol. **xxxv**, nos 1–2, pp. 45–65.

Kasper, W. (2002), *Sustainable Immigration and Cultural Integration*, Sydney: Centre for Independent Studies.

Kasper, W. (2005a), 'Human Progress – and Collapse?' *Energy & Environment*, vol. **16**, nos 3–4, pp. 441–456.

Kasper, W. (2005b), 'Can Islam Meet the Challenges of Modernity?', *Quadrant*, no. 516, vol. **xlix**, no. 5 (May), pp. 8–19.

Kasper, W. (2006), *Make Poverty History: Tackle Corruption, Issue Analysis*, no. 67. Sydney: Centre for Independent Studies, also available at wwwe.africanexecutive.com/development under the title 'Laws Create Thieves and Bandits'.

Kasper, W. (2007), "The Political Economy of Global Warming, Rent Seeking and Freedom", in Civil Society Coalition on Climate Change (2010), *Civil Society Report on Climate Change*, London: International Policy Press, pp. 77–97.

Kasper, W. (2008a), 'Competition', in D. Henderson (ed.) (2008), op. cit., pp. 468–471.

Kasper, W. (2008b), 'Spatial Economics', in D. Henderson (ed.) (2008), op. cit., 73–6.

Kasper, W. (2010), *What's Wrong with Neoclassical Orthodoxy? An Overdue* Methodenstreit, Wellington, NZ: New Zealand Business Roundtable, available at www.nzbr.org.nz/site/nzbr/files/Kasper%20paper%204.pdf, accessed 12 December 2010.

Kasper, W. (2011a), 'A Generation of Reform . . . and a Few Years of Backsliding', *Quadrant* , vol. **LV**, no. 4, pp. 49–58.

Kasper, W. (2011b), *The Merits of Western Civilisation*, Melbourne: Institute of Public Affairs.

Kasper, W. (2011c), 'No News on the Eurofront', *EconLib* (Dec.), available at http://www.econlib.org/library/Columns/y2011/Kaspereuro.html.

Kasper, W. and H.-M. Stahl (1974), 'L'intégration par unification monétaire: une vue pessimiste', in P. Salin (ed.), *L'unification monétaire européenne*, Paris: Calmann-Lévy, pp. 133–164.

Kasper, W. and M.E. Streit (1993), *Lessons from the Freiburg School. The Institutional Foundations of Freedom and Prosperity*, Sydney: Centre for Independent Studies.

Kasper, W. and M.E. Streit (1998), *Institutional Economics Social Order and Public Policy*, Cheltenham, UK and Lyme, NH, USA: Edward Elgar.

Kē Wŭgang and Xi Manfei (2000), *Zì Dù Jing Ji Xúe – Sè Hùi Zhi Xù Yu Gong Gòng Zèn Cè* [Institutional Economics: Social Order and Public Policy], Beijing: Commercial Press.

Kilby, P. (ed.) (1971), *Entrepreneurship and Economic Development*, New York: Free Press.

Kimminich, O. (1990), 'Institutionen in der Rechtsordnung', in E. Pankoke (ed.), *Institutionen und Technische Zivilisation*, Berlin: Duncker & Humblot, pp. 90–118.

Kirzner, I.M. (1960), *The Economic Point of View*, Kansas City: Sheed and Ward.

Kirzner, I.M. (1963), *Market Theory and the Price System*, Princeton, NJ: Van Nostrand.

Kirzner, I.M. (1973), *Competition and Entrepreneurship*, Chicago: University of Chicago Press.

Kirzner, I.M. (1985), *Discovery and the Capitalist Process*, Chicago: University of Chicago Press.

Kirzner, I.M. (1992), *The Meaning of the Market Process: Essays in the Development of Modern Austrian Economics*, London and New York: Routledge.

Kirzner, I.M. (ed.), (1994), *Classics in Austrian Economics, A Sampling in the History of a Tradition*, 3 vols, London: W. Pickering.

Kirzner, I.M. (1997), 'Entrepreneurial Discovery and the Competitive Market Process: An Austrian Approach', *Journal of Economic Literature*, vol. **xxxv**, no. 1 (March), pp. 60–85.

Kiwit, D. (1994), 'Zur Leistungsfähigkeit neoklassisch orientierter Transaktionskostenansätze', *Ordo*, vol. **45**, pp. 105–36.

Kiwit, D. (1996), 'Path Dependence in Technological and Institutional Change – Some Criticisms and Suggestions', *Journal des Économistes et des Études Humaines*, vol. 7, no. 1, pp. 69–83.

Klaus, V. (1991), *Dismantling Socialism, a Preliminary Report*, Sydney: Centre for Independent Studies.

Klaus, V. (1997), *Renaissance*, Washington, DC: Cato Institute.

Klaus, V. (2008), *Blue Planet in Green Shackles – What is Endangered: Climate or Freedom?*, Washington, DC: Free Enterprise Institute.

Kliemt, H. (1993), 'On Justifying a Minimum Welfare State', *Constitutional Political Economy*, vol. **4**, pp. 159–172

Klitgaard, R. (1995), *Institutional Adjustment and Adjusting to Institutions*, World Bank Discussion Paper no. 303, Washington, DC: World Bank.

Kreps, D. (1990), 'Corporate Culture and Economic Theory', in J.E. Alt and K.A. Shepsle (eds), *Perspectives on Positive Political Economy*, Cambridge, UK and New York: Cambridge University Press, pp. 90–143.

Krueger, A.O. (1994), *Political Economy of Policy Reform in Developing Countries*, Cambridge, MA: MIT Press.

Krueger, A.O. (1997), 'Trade Policy and Economic Development: How We Learn', *American Economic Review*, vol. **87**, no. 1 (March), pp. 1–22.

Krugman, P (2007), *How Countries Compete: Strategy, Structures and Government in the Global Economy*, Cambridge, MA: Harvard Business School Press.

Kukathas, C, (2003), *The Liberal Archipelago: A Theory of Diversity and Freedom*, New York: Oxford University Press.

Kukathas, C., D.W. Lovell and W. Maley (1991), *The Transition from Socialism: State and Civil Society in the USSR*, Melbourne: Longman Cheshire.

Kuran, T. (1997), *Private Truths, Public Lies. The Social Consequences of Preference Falsification*, Cambridge, MA: Harvard University Press.

Kuran, T. (2009), 'Explaining the Economic Trajectory of Civilizations: The Systematic Approach', *Journal of Economic Behavior and Organization*, vol. **71**, pp. 593–605.

Kuran, T. (2011), *The Long Divergence: How Islamic Law Held Back the Middle East*, Princeton, NJ: Princeton University Press.

Lachmann, L. (1943/1977), *Capital, Expectations, and the Market Process – Essays on the Theory of the Market Economy*, edited with an introduction by W.E. Grinder, Kansas City: Sheed and Andrews, pp. 655–680.

Lachmann, L. (1973), *The Legacy of Max Weber*, Berkeley, CA: Glendessary Press.

Lal, D. (2004), *In Praise of Empires. Globalization and Order*, New York: Palgrave-Macmillan.

Landa, J.T. (1994), *Trust, Ethnicity, and Identity: Beyond the New institutional Economics of Ethnic Trading Networks, Contract Law, and Gift-Exchange*, Ann Arbor, MI: University of Michigan Press.

Lange, O.R. and F.M. Taylor (1964/1939), *On the Economic Theory of Socialism*, New York: McGraw Hill.

Langlois, R.N. (ed.), (1986), *Economics as a Process: Essays in the New Institutional Economics*, Cambridge, UK and New York: Cambridge University Press.

Lawson, R.A. (2008), 'Economic Freedom', in D. Henderson (ed.), *The Concise Encyclopedia of Economics*, Indianapolis IN: Liberty Fund, pp. 124–127.

Leakey, R. (1994), *The Origin of Humankind*, London: Weidenfeld and Nicholson.

Leeson, P.T (2008), 'How Important is State Enforcement for Trade?', *American Law and Economics Review*, vol. **10**, no. 1, pp. 61–89.

Leeson, P.T. and J.R. Subrick (2006), 'Robust Political Economy', *The Review of Austrian Economics*, vol. **19**, nos. 2–3, pp. 107–111.

Leibenstein, H. (1966), 'Allocative and X-Efficiency', *American Economic Review*, vol. **76**, no 3, pp. 392–415.

Leibenstein, H. (1984), 'On the Economics of Conventions and Institutions: An Exploratory Essay', *Journal of Institutional and Theoretical Economics*, vol. **140**, pp. 74–86.

Leoni, B. (1961), *Freedom and the Law*, Princeton, NJ: Van Norstrand.

Levy, D.M. (2002), *How the Dismal Science Got its Name*, Ann Arbor, MI: University of Michigan Press.

Lindbeck, A. (1995), 'Welfare State Disincentives with Endogenous Habits and Norms', *Scandinavian Journal of Economics*, vol. **97**, no. 4, pp. 477–494.

Lucas, R.E. (1972), 'Expectations and the Neutrality of Money', *Journal of Economic Theory*, vol. **4**, pp. 103–124.

Lutz, F.A. (1935/1963), 'Goldwährung und Wirtschaftsordnung' (Gold Standard and Economic Order), *Weltwirtschaftliches Archiv*, vol. **41**, pp. 224–236, reprinted in an edited English translation in H.G. Grubel (ed.), (1963), *World Monetary Reform*, Stanford: Stanford University Press, pp. 320–328.

Machlup, F. (1981–84), *Knowledge: Its Creation, Distribution and Economic Significance*, 3 vols. Princeton, NJ: Princeton University Press.

Maddison, A. (1995), *Explaining the Economic Performance of Nations: Essays in Time and Space*, Cheltenham, UK and Brookfield, VT, USA: Edward Elgar.

Maddison, A. (2001), *The World Economy: A Millennial Perspective*, 2 vols, Paris: OECD.

Maddison, A. (2007), *Contours of the World Economy*, Oxford and New York: Oxford University Press.

Magee, S., W.A. Brock and L. Young (1989), 'The Invisible Foot and the Fate of Nations: Lawyers as Negative Externalities', in S. Magee, S. et al. (eds) *Black Hole Tariffs and Endogenous Policy Theory: Political Economy in General Equilibrium*, Cambridge, UK and New York: Cambridge University Press.

Malia, M. (1994), *The Soviet Tragedy*, New York: The Free Press.

Mankiw, N.G. et al. (1993), 'A Symposium on Keynesian Economics Today', *Journal of Economic Perspectives*, vol. **7** (Winter), pp. 3–82.

Martin, W. and P. Béguin (1980), *Histoire de la Suisse, avec une suite (L'histoire récente)*, 8th edn, Lausanne: Payot.

Matthews, R.C.O. (1986), 'The Economics of Institutions and the Sources of Economic Growth', *Economic Journal*, vol. **96** (Dec.), pp. 903–918.

Mauro, P. (1995), 'Corruption and Growth', *Quarterly Journal of Economics*, vol. **110**, pp. 681–712.

Mayhew, A. (1987), 'Culture: Core Concept under Attack', *Journal of Economic Issues*, vol. **21**, no. 2, pp. 587–603.

McChesney, F.S. (2006), 'Coase, Demsetz, and the Unending Externality Debate', *Cato Journal*, vol. **26**, no. 1 (Winter), pp. 179–200.

McCloskey, D, (2010), *Bourgeois Dignity: Why Economics Can't Explain the Modern World*, Chicago: University of Chicago Press.

McKenzie, R.B. (ed.) (1984), *Constitutional Economics – Containing the Economic Powers of Government*, Lexington: Lexington Books.

McKenzie, R.B. and G. Tullock (1975), *The New World of Economics, Explorations into the Human Experience*, Homewood, IL: Richard D. Irwin.

Meadows, D.H. et al. (1972), *The Limits to Growth*, New York: Universe Books.

Menger, C. (1963/1883), *Problems of Economics and Sociology*, Urbana, IL: University of Illinois Press.

Menger, C. (1981/1871), *Principles of Economics*, New York: New York University Press [German original 1871].

Menger, C. (1985/1883), *Investigations into the Method of the Social Sciences*, New York: New York University Press [German original 1883].

Metcalfe, S. (1989), 'Evolution and Economic Change', in A. Silberston (ed.), *Technology and Economic Progress*, London: Macmillan.

Milgrom, P.R. and J. Roberts (1976), *Economics, Organisations and Management*, Englewood Cliffs, NJ: Prentice-Hall.

Milgrom, P.R., and J. Roberts (1992), *Economics, Organisations and Management*, Englewood Cliffs, NJ: Prentice Hall.

Mises, L. von (1920/1994), 'Economic Calculation in the Socialist Commonwealth', in I.M. Kirzner (1994), op. cit., vol. **3**, pp. 3–30.

Mises, L. von (1922/1936), *Socialism: An Economic and Sociological Analysis*, London: Jonathan Cape [German original published in 1922].

Mises, L. von (1944), *Bureaucracy*, New Haven, CT: Yale University Press.

Mises, L. (1945/1952), 'Laissez Faire or Dictatorship', *Economic Planning*, New York: Dynamic America; repr. 1952: *Planning for Freedom and Other Essays and Addresses*, South Holland, IL: Libertarian Press.

Mises, L. von (1949), *Human Action: A Treatise on Economics*, New Haven, CT: Yale University Press.

Mises, L. von (1978), *Liberalism*, Kansas City: Sheed and Ward.

Mises, L. von (1979), *Economic Policy. Thoughts for Today and Tomorrow*, Chicago, IL: Regnery Gateway.

Mitchell, W.C. and R.T. Simmons (1994), *Beyond Politics. Markets, Welfare, and the Failure of Bureaucracy*, Boulder, CO: Westview Press.

Mix, M. (2011), 'The Right to Work: A Fundamental Freedom', *Imprimis*, vol. **40**, no. 5/6.

Mokyr, J. (2004), *The Gifts of Athena: Historical Origins of the Knowledge Economy*, Princeton, NJ: Princeton University Press.

Moss, L.S. (1976), *The Economics of Ludwig von Mises*, Kansas City: Sheed and Ward, .

Mueller, D.C. (1996), *On the Decline of Nations, Lectiones Jeneses*, Jena, Germany: Max-Planck-Institute for Research into Economic Systems.

Mueller, D.C. (2003), *Public Choice III*, Cambridge: Cambridge University Press.

Murray, C. (2003), *Human Accomplishment*, New York: Harper Collins.

Myers, R. (ed.) (1996), *The Wealth of Nations in the Twentieth Century: The Policies and Determinants of Economic Development*, Stanford, CA: Hoover Institution Press.

Naisbitt, J. (1994), *Global Paradox: The Bigger the World Economy, the More Powerful its Smallest Players*, New York: William Morrow.

Naishul, V. (1993), 'Liberalism, Customary Rights and Economic Reforms', *Communist Economies and Economic Transformation*, vol. **5**, pp. 29–44.

Nelson, R.R. (1970), 'Information and Consumer Behavior', *Journal of Political Economy*, vol. **78**, no. 2, pp. 311–329.

Nelson, R.R. (1995), 'Recent Evolutionary Theorizing about Economic Change', *Journal of Economic Literature*, vol. **33**, no. 1, 48–90.

Nelson, R.R. and S.G. Winter (1982), *An Evolutionary Theory of Economic Change*, Cambridge, MA: Belknap Press of Harvard University Press.

Némo, P. (2006), *What is the West?*, Pittsburg, VA: Duquesne University Press.

Nishiyama C. and K.R. Leube (eds) (1984), *The Essence of Hayek*, Stanford: Hoover Institutions Press.

North, D.C. (1981), *Structure and Change in Economic History*, New York: W.W. Norton.

North, D.C. (1990), *Institutions, Institutional Change and Economic Performance*, Cambridge, UK and New York: Cambridge, University Press.

North, D.C. (1992), *Transaction Costs, Institutions, and Economic Performance*, San Francisco: International Center for Economic Growth.

North, D.C. (1993), 'Institutions and Economic Performance', in Mäki, U. et al. (1993), op. cit., pp. 242–263.

North, D.C. (1994), 'The Evolution of Efficient Markets', in J.J. James and M. Thomas (eds), op. cit., pp. 257–264.

North, D.C. and R.P. Thomas (1973), *The Rise of the Western World: A New Economic History*, Cambridge, UK: Cambridge University Press.

North, D.C. and R.P. Thomas (1977), 'The First Economic Revolution', *Economic History Review*, vol. **30**, 2nd series, no. 2, pp. 229–241.

Nove, A. (1993), *An Economic History of the USSR*, London: Penguin.

Nowak, J.E. and R.D. Rotunda (2010), *Constitutional Law*, 8th edn (Hornbrook series), Thomson-Reuters: Westlaw.

Odell, J. (1990), 'Understanding International Trade Policies – An Emerging Synthesis', *World Politics*, vol. **453**, pp. 139–167.

O'Driscoll, G.P. (1977), *Economics as a Coordination Problem*, Kansas City: Sheed, Andrews and McNeel.

O'Driscoll Jr., G.P. and M.J. Rizzo (1985), *The Economics of Time and Ignorance*, New York: Columbia University Press.

OECD (Organisation for Economic Cooperation and Development) (1983), *Positive Adjustment Policies – Managing Structural Change*, Paris: OECD.

Oi, W.Y. (1990), 'Productivity in the Distributive Trades', Economic and Legal Organization Workshop, University of Rochester, *mimeo*.

Olasky, M. (1992), *The Tragedy of American Compassion*, Wheaton, IL: Crossway Books.

O'Leary, J. (ed.) (1995), *Privatization 1995*, Los Angeles: Reason Foundation.

Olson, M. (1965), *The Logic of Collective Action: Public Goods and the Theory of Groups*, New York: Schocken Books.

Olson, M. (1982), *The Rise and Decline of Nations: Economic Growth, Stagflation and Social Rigidities*, New Haven and London: Yale University Press.

Olson, M. (1993), 'Dictatorship, Democracy and Development', *American Political Science Review*, vol. **87**, no. 3, pp. 567–576.

Olson, M. (1996), 'Big Bills Left on the Sidewalk: Why Some Nations are Rich, and Others Poor', *Journal of Economic Perspectives*, vol. **10**, pp. 3–24.

Ostrom, E. (1990), *Governing the Commons: The Evolution of Institutions for Collective Action*, Cambridge, UK and New York: Cambridge University Press.

Ostrom, E. (2005), *Understanding Institutional Diversity*, Princeton, NJ: Princeton University Press.

Ostrom, E. and T.K. Kahn (eds) (2003), *Foundations of Social Capital*, Cheltenham, UK and Northampton, MA, USA: Edward Elgar.

Palmer, T.G. (2011), *The Morality of Capitalism*, Ottawa, IL: Jameson Books.

Papageorgiou, D., A.M. Choksi and M. Michaely (1991), *Liberalizing Foreign Trade*, Oxford, UK and Cambridge, MA: Basil Blackwell.

Pareto, V. (2009). *The Rise and Fall of Elites*, New Brunswick, Transaction Publishers (Italian original 1901).

Parker, D. and R. Stacey (1995), *Chaos, Management and Economics: The Implications of Non-Linear Thinking*, London: Institute of Economic Affairs.

Pennington, M. (2010), *Robust Political Economy: Classical Liberalism and the Future of Public Policy*, Cheltenham, UK and Northampton, MA, USA: Edward Elgar.

Pejovich, S. (1995), *Economic Analysis of Institutions and Systems*, Dordrecht, Holland and Boston, MA: Kluwer Academic.

Pejovich, S. (2003), *Understanding the Transaction Costs of Transition: It's the Culture, Stupid*, Arlington, VA: Mercatus Center, George Mason University, available at http://www.usaid.gov/our_work/economic_growth_and_trade/eg/forum_series/f6-session2-pefovich.pdf, accessed 15 January 2012.

Pethig, R. and U. Schlieper (eds) (1987), *Efficiency, Institutions and Economic Policy*, Berlin and New York: Springer Publishers.

Pirenne, H. (1969). *Medieval Cities: Their Origins and the Revival of Trade*, Princeton, NJ: Princeton University Press.

Polanyi, M. (1966), *The Tacit Dimension*, New York: Doubleday.

Popper, K.R. (1945/1974), *The Open Society and its Enemies*, 2 vols, London: Routledge Kegan Paul [reprinted 1974].

Popper, K.R. (1957/2002), *The Poverty of Historicism*, London: Routledge.

Popper, K.R. (1959), *The Logic of Scientific Discovery*, London: Hutchinson.

Porter, M.E. (1990), *The Competitive Advantage of Nation*, London, UK: Macmillan and New York: Free Press.

Porter, P. and G. Scully (1995), 'Institutional Technology and Economic Growth', *Public Choice*, vol. **82**, pp. 17–36.

Powelson, J.P. (1994), *Centuries of Economic Endeaavor*, Ann Arbor, MI: University of Michigan Press.

Prins, G. et al. (2010), *The Hartwell Paper - A New Direction for Climate Policy after the Crash of 2009*, London-Oxford, UK: London School of Economics/Institute for Science, Innovation and Society, Oxford University, available at http://eprints.lse.ac.uk/27939/1/HartwellPaper_English_version.pdf, accessed 12 December 2010.

Qian, Y. and B.R. Weingast (1995), *China's Transition to Market-Preserving Federalism, Chinese Style*, Stanford: Hoover Institution Press.

Quigley, C. (1979/1961), *The Evolution of Civilizations, An Introduction to Historical Analysis*, Indianapolis, IN: Liberty Press.

Rabushka, A. (1974), *A Theory of Racial Harmony*, Columbia, SC: University of South Carolina Press.

Radnitzky, G. (1987), 'An Economic Theory of the Rise of Civilisation and Its Policy Implications: Hayek's Account Generalised', *Ordo*, vol. **38**, pp. 47–90.

Radnitzky, G. (ed.) (1997), *Values and the Social Order, Volume 3: Voluntary versus Coercive Orders*, Aldershot, UK and Brookfield, USA: Avebury Publishing.

Radnitzky, G., and H. Bouillon (eds) (1995a), *Values and the Social Order, Volume 1: Values and Society*, Aldershot, UK and Brookfield, USA: Avebury Publishing.

Radnitzky, G. and H. Bouillon (eds) (1995b), *Values and the Social Order, Volume 2: Society and Order*, Aldershot, UK and Brookfield, USA: Avebury Publishing.

Radnitzky, G. and H. Bouillon (eds) (1996), *Government: Servant or Master?*, Amsterdam-Atlanta, GA: Rodopi.

Ratnapala, S. (1990), *Welfare State or Constitutional State?*, Sydney: Centre for Independent Studies.

Redding, S.G. (1993), *The Spirit of Chinese Capitalism*, Berlin: Walter de Gruyter.

Richardson, R. (1995), *Making a Difference*, Christchurch, NZ: Shoal Bay Press.

Ridley, M. (2010), *The Rational Optimist. How Prosperity Evolves*, London: Fourth Estate/HarperCollins.

Riedel, J. (1988), 'Economic Development in East Asia: Doing What Comes Naturally', in H. Hughes (ed.), *Achieving Industrialization in East Asia*, Melbourne, Australia: Cambridge University Press, pp. 1–38.

Robbins, L.R. (1976), *Political Economy: Past and Present. A Review of Leading Theories of Economic Policy*, London: Macmillan.

Robinson, C. (ed.) (2008), *Climate Change Policy: Challenging the Activists*, London: Institute of Economic Affairs.

Rockwell, L.H. (ed.) (1988), *The Free Market Reader*, Burlingname, CA: Ludwig von Mises Institute.

Roll, R. and J. Talbot (2003), 'Political Freedom, Economic Liberty and Prosperity', *Journal of Democracy*, vol. **14**, no. 3, pp. 75–89.

Romer, P. (1990), 'Endogenous Technological Change', *Journal of Political Economy*, vol. **98**, no. 5, pp. S71–102.

Romer, P.M. (2008), 'Economic Growth' in D. Henderson (ed.), op. cit., 128–131.

Rosenberg, N. (1988), 'Technological Change under Capitalism and Socialism', in A. Anderson and D.L. Bark (eds), *Thinking about America*, Stanford: Hoover Institution Press, pp. 193–202.

Rosenberg, N. and L.E. Birdzell (1986), *How the West Grew Rich, The Economic Transformation of the Industrial World*, New York: Basic Books.

Rostow, W.W. (1978), *The World Economy: History and Prospect*, London: Macmillan.

Rothbard, M. (1962), *Man, Economy and State*, Princeton, NJ: Van Nostrand.

Rozman, G. (ed.) (1991), *The East Asian Region, Confucian Heritage and Its Modern Adaptation*, Princeton, NJ: Princeton University Press.

Sachs, J. and A. Warner (1995), 'Economic Reform and the Process of Economic Integration', *Brookings Papers on Economic Activity*, vol. **86**, no. 1, pp. 1–118.

Sacks, D.W., B. Stevenvon and J. Wolfers (2010), *Subjective Well-Being, Income, Economic Development and Growth, National Bureau of Economic Research Working Paper* 16441 (October), Cambridge, MA: NBER. available at http://bpp.wharton.upenn.edu/betseys/papers/SWBIncomeEconomicGrowth.pdf, accessed 16 December 2010.

Sally, R. (2008), *New Frontiers in Free Trade*, Washington, DC: Cato Institute.

Sally, R. and R. Sen (2011), 'Trade Policies in Southeast Asia in the Wider Asian Perspective', *World Economy*, vol. **34**, no. 4, pp. 568–601.

Samuels, W.J. (ed.) (1988), *Institutional Economics*, 3 volumes, Aldershot, UK and Brookfield, VT, USA: Edward Elgar.

Scherer, F.A. (1984), *Innovation and Growth, Schumpeterian Perspectives*, Cambridge, MA: MIT Press.

Schuck, P. (1992), 'Legal Complexity: Some Causes, Consequences, and Cures', *Duke Law Journal*, vol. **1**, no. 3.

Schumpeter, J.A. (1908/1961), *The Theory of Economic Development: An Inquiry into Profits, Capital, Credit, Interest and the Business Cycle*, Oxford, UK and New York: Oxford University Press [first German edition, 1908].

Schumpeter, J.A. (1947), *Capitalism, Socialism and Democracy*, 2nd edn, New York: Harper.

Schumpeter, J.A. (1970/1991), 'Money and Currency', '*Social Research*, vol. **58**, no. 3, pp. 1–31 [posthumous publication of a German manuscript written ca. 1930, edited by A. Mack].

Scobie, G. and S. Lim (1992),' Economic Reform: A Global Revolution', *Policy*, vol. **8**, no. 3, pp. 2–7.

Scully, G.W. (1991), 'Rights, Equity and Economic Efficiency', *Public Choice*, vol. **68**, pp. 195–215.

Scully, G.W. (1992), *Constitutional Environments and Economic Growth*, Princeton, NJ: Princeton University Press.

Seldon, A. (1990), *Capitalism*, Oxford, UK and Cambridge, MA: Basil Blackwell.

Seldon, A. (2004), *The Virtues of Capitalism*, Indianapolis, IN: Liberty Fund.

Sen, A. (1999), *Development as Freedom*, New York: Anchor Books.

Shackle, G.L.S. (1972), *Epistemics and Economics – A Critique of Economic Doctrines*, Cambridge, UK: Cambridge University Press.

Shane, S. (1994), *Dismantling Utopia: How Information Ended the Soviet Union*, Chicago: Ivan R. Dee.

Siebert, H. (ed.) (1993), *Overcoming the Transformation Crisis – Lessons for the Successor States of the Soviet Union*, Tübingen, Germany: Mohr-Siebeck.

Siebert, H. (ed.) (1995), *Trends in Business Organization: Do Participation and Cooperation Increase Competitiveness?*, Tübingen, Germany: Mohr-Siebeck.

Simon, H.A. (1957), *Administrative Behavior*, New York: Free Press.

Simon, H.A. (1959), 'Theories of Decision-Making in Business Organizations', *American Economic Review*, vol. **49**, pp. 253–283.

Simon, H.A. (1976), 'From Substantive to Procedural Rationality', in S.J. Latsis (ed.), *Method and Appraisal in Economics*, Cambridge, UK and New York: Cambridge University Press, pp. 129–148.

Simon, H.A. (1982), *Models of Bounded Rationality and Other Topics in Economic Theory*, 2 volumes, Cambridge, MA: MIT Press.

Simon, H.A. (1983), *Reason in Human Affairs*, Oxford, UK and Cambridge, MA: Basil Blackwell.

Simon, J.L. (ed.) (1995), *The State of Humanity*, Oxford, UK and Cambridge, MA: Basil Blackwell.

Simons, H.C. (1948/1936), 'Rules versus Authorities in Monetary Policy', in H.C. Simons (ed.), *Economic Policy for a Free Society*, Chicago: University of Chicago Press.

Smith, A. (1976/1776), *An Inquiry into the Wealth of Nations*, 2 volumes, London: Dent.

Sohmen, E. (1959), 'Competition and Growth: The Lessons of West Germany', *American Economic Review*, vol. **49**, pp. 986–1003.

Solow, R.E. (1988), *Growth Theory, an Exposition*, Oxford, UK and New York: Oxford University Press.

de Soto, H. (1990), *The Other Path – The Invisible Revolution in the Third World*, New York: Harper & Row.

de Soto, H. (2001), *The Mystery of Capital: Why Capitalism Triumphs in the West and Fails Everywhere Else*, New York: Basic Books.

Sowell, T. (1987), *A Conflict of Visions*, New York: William Morrow.

Sowell, T. (1990), *Preferential Policies: An International Perspective*, New York: William Morrow.

Sowell, T. (1991), 'Cultural Diversity, A World View', *The American Enterprise* (May/June), vol. **5**, pp. 44–55.

Sowell, T. (1994), *Race and Culture*, New York: Basic Books.

Sowell, T. (1996), *Migration and Cultures – A World View*, New York: Basic Books.

Sowell, T. (1998), *Conquest and Cultures – A World View*, New York: Basic Books.

Sowell, T. (2009), *Intellectuals and Society*, New York: Basic Books.

Stigler, G.J. (1967), 'Imperfections in Capital Markets', *Journal of Political Economy*, vol. **75**, no. 2, pp. 287–292.

Stigler, G.J. (1971), 'The Theory of Economic Regulation', *Bell Journal of Economics and Management Science*, vol. **2**, no. 1, pp. 3–21.

Stigler, G.J. (1975), *The Citizen and the State. Essays on Regulation*, Chicago and London: University of Chicago Press.

Streit, M.E. (1981), 'Demand Management and Catallaxy. Reflections on a Poor Policy Record', *Ordo*, vol. **32**, pp. 17–34.

Streit, M.E. (1983), 'Modelling, Managing and Monitoring Futures Trading: Frontiers of Analytical Inquiry', in M.E. Streit (ed.), *Futures Markets*, Oxford, UK and New York: Basil Blackwell, pp. 1–26.

Streit, M.E. (1984), 'The Shadow Economy. A Challenge to the Welfare State?', *Ordo*, vol. **35**, pp. 109–119.

Streit, M.E. (1987), 'Economic Order and Public Policy – Market, Constitution and the Welfare State', in R. Pethig and U. Schlieper (eds) op. cit., pp. 1–21.

Streit, M.E. (1992), 'Economic Order, Private Law and Public Policy – The Freiburg School of Law and Economics in Perspective', *Journal of Institutional and Theoretical Economics*, vol. **148**, pp. 675–705.

Streit, M.E. (1993a), 'Cognition, Competition, and Catallaxy – In Memory of Friedrich August von Hayek', *Constitutional Political Economy*, vol. **4**, no. 2, pp. 223–262.

Streit, M.E. (1993b), 'Welfare Economics, Economic Order and Competition', in: H. Giersch (ed.), *Money, Trade and Competition – Essays in Memory of Egon Sohmen*, Berlin and New York: Springer Publishers, pp. 255–278.

Streit, M.E. (1995), *Freiburger Beiträge zur Ordnungspolitik*, Tübingen: Mohr-Siebeck.

Streit, M.E. (1996), 'Competition among Systems as a Defence of Liberty', in H. Bouillon (ed.), *Libertarians and Liberalism, Essays in Honour of Gerard Radnitzky*, Aldershot, UK and Brookfield, USA: Avebury Publishing, pp. 236–252.

Streit, M.E. (1998), 'Constitutional Ignorance, Spontaneous Order and Rule Orientation; Hayekian Paradigms from a Policy Perspective', in S. Frowen (ed.) (1998), *Hayek the Economist and Social Philosopher: A Critical Retrospect*, London: Macmillan.

Streit, M.E. and A. Mangels (1996), *Privatautonomes Recht und grenzüberschreitende Transaktionen, Jena Discussion Papers 07–96*, Jena, Germany: Max-Planck-Institute for Research into Economic Systems.

Streit, M.E. and G. Mussler (1994), 'The Economic Constitution of the European Community: From Rome to Maastricht', *Constitutional Political Economy*, vol. **5**, no. 3, pp. 319–353.

Streit, M.E. and S. Voigt (1993), 'The Economics of Conflict Resolution in International Trade', in D. Friedmann and E.-J. Mestmäcker (eds), *Conflict Resolution in International Trade – A Symposium*, Baden-Baden, Germany: Nomos Verlag, pp. 39–72.

Streit, M.E. and G. Wegner (1992), 'Information, Transaction and Catallaxy. Reflections on Some Key Concepts of Evolutionary Market Theory', in U. Witt (ed.), *Explaining Process and Change*, Ann Arbor: University of Michigan Press, pp. 125–149.

Sugden, R. (1986), 'Spontaneous Order', *Journal of Economic Perspectives*, vol. **3**, no. 4, pp. 85–7.

Syrquin, M. (1988), 'Patterns of Structural Change', in H.B. Chenery and T.N. Srinivasan (eds), *Handbook of Development Economics*, vol. **I**, Amsterdam–New York: North Holland, pp. 203–230.

Taleb, N.N. (2010), *The Black Swan*, 2nd edn Harmondworth: Penguin.

Tanzer, A. (1994), 'The Bamboo Network', *Forbes Magazine*, (18 July), pp. 138–45.

Tanzi, V. and L. Schuknecht (1995), *The Growth of Government and Reform of the State in Industrial Countries*, IMF Working Paper, Washington, DC: International Monetary Fund, mimeo.

Taverne, D, (2005), *The March of Unreason – Science, Democracy, and the New Fundamentalism*, Oxford: Oxford University Press.

Thurow, L.C. (1980), *The Zero-Sum Society: Distribution and Possibilities of Economic Change*, Harmondsworth: Penguin Books.

Tollison, R.D. (1982), 'Rent Seeking: A Survey', *Kyklos*, vol. **35**, 575–602.

Tu, W. (1996), *Confucian Traditions in East Asian Modernity*. Cambridge, MA: Harvard University Press.

Tu, W. (2000), 'Implications of the Rise of "Confucian" Asia', in S.N. Eisenstadt (ed.), op. cit., pp. 195–218.

Tullock, G. (1963), *Rent Seeking*, Aldershot, UK and Brookfield, VT, USA: Edward Elgar.

Tullock, G. (1967), 'The Welfare Costs of Tariffs, Monopolies and Theft', *Western Economic Journal*, vol. **5**, pp. 224–232.

Tullock, G. (1971), 'Public Decisions as Public Goods', *Journal of Political Economy*, vol. **79**, pp. 913–918.

Tullock, G. (1983), *Economics of Redistribution*, Boston: Kluwer-Nijhoff.

Tullock, G. (1992), 'The Economics of Conflict', in G. Radnitzky (ed.) (1992), op. cit., pp. 301–314.

Tumlir, J. (1979), 'International Economic Order and Democratic Constitutionalism', *Ordo*, vol. **34**, pp. 71–83.

Tylor, E.B. (1883), *Primitive Culture: Researches Into the Development of Mythology, Religion, Language, Art and Custom*, 2 volumes, New York: H. Holt.

United Nations Development Program, 2002, *Arab Human Development Report 2002*, New York: United Nations.

Vanberg, V.J. (1988), 'Ordungstheorie as Constitutional Economics – The German Conceptions of the Social Market Economy', *Ordo*, vol. **34**, pp. 71–83.

Vanberg, V.J. (1992), 'Organizations as Constitutional Systems', *Constitutional Political Economy*, vol. **3**, no. 2, pp. 223–253.

Vaubel, R. (1985), 'Competing Currencies. The Case for Free Entry', *Zeitschrift für die gesamten Staatswissenschaften*, vol. **105**, pp. 547–564.

Vickery, G. and G. Wurzburg (1996), 'Flexible Firms, Skills, and Employment', *OECD Observer*, no. 202 (Oct./Nov.), pp. 17–21.

Viscusi, W.K. (1993), 'The Value of Risks to Life and Health', *Journal of Economic Literature*, vol. **31**, no. 4, pp. 1912–1976.

Voigt, S. (1997), 'Positive Constitutional Economics: A Survey', *Public Choice* (Special issue on constitutional political economy), vol. **90**, pp. 11–53.

Wagener, H.J. (ed.) (1994), *The Political Economy of Transformation*, Heidelberg, Germany: Physica-Springer Publishers.

de Q. Walker, G. (1988), *The Rule of Law: Foundation of Constitutional Democracy*, Melbourne: Melbourne University Press.

Weaver, G.H. (1947/1974), *The Mainspring of Human Progress*, Irvington-on-Hudson, New York: Foundation of Economic Freedom.

Weber, M. (1904/1985), *The Protestant Ethic and the Spirit of Capitalism*, London: Unwin Paperbacks.

Weber, M. (1921/1978), *Economy and Society: An Outline in Interpretative Sociology*, 2 vols, Berkeley: University of California Press.

Weber, M. (1927/1995), *General Economic History*, 6th edn, New Brunswick: Transaction Books.

Weber, M. (1951), *The Religion of China: Confucianism and Taoism*, Glencoe, IL: The Free Press.

Weede, E. (1990), 'Ideas, Institutions and Political Culture in Western Development', *Journal of Theoretical Politics*, vol. **2**, no. 4, pp. 369–399.

Weede, E. (1995), 'Freedom, Knowledge and Law as Social Capital', in Radnitzky and Bouillon (eds) (1995a), op. cit., pp. 63–81.

Weede, E. (1996), *Economic Development, Social Order, and World Politics*, Boulder, CO: Lynne Rienner.

Weede, E. (2011), 'The Capitalist Peace', in C.J. Coyne and R. Mathers (eds), *The Handbook on the Political Economy of War*, Cheltenham, UK and Northampton, MA, USA: Edward Elgar, pp. 269–280.

Williamson, O.E. (1985), *The Economic Institutions of Capitalism: Firms, Market and Relational Contracting*, New York and London: The Free Press.

Williamson, O.E. (1987), 'Transaction Cost Economics. The Comparative Contracting Perspective', *Journal of Economic Behaviour and Organization*, vol. **8**, pp. 617–625.

Williamson, O.E. (1988), 'The Logic of Economic Organization', *Journal of Law, Economics and Organization*, vol. **4**, no. 1 (Spring), pp. 65–93.

Wills, I. (1997), *Economics and the Environment*, Sydney: Allen and Unwin.

Winiecki, J. (1988), *The Distorted World of Soviet-Type Economics*, Pittsburg, PA: University of Pittsburgh Press.

Witt, U. (1991), 'Reflections on the Present State of Evolutionary Economic Theory', in G.M. Hodgson and E. Screpanti (eds), *Rethinking Economics: Markets, Technology, and Economic Evolution*, Aldershot, UK and Brookfield, VT, USA: Edward Elgar, 83–102.

Witt, U. (1994), 'Evolutionary Economics', in P. Boettke (ed.), op. cit., pp. 541–548.

World Bank (1993), *The East Asian Miracle, Economic Growth and Public Policy*, Oxford and New York: Oxford University Press.

World Bank (1995), *Proceedings of the World Bank Annual Conference on Development Economics 1994*, Supplement to the World Bank Economic Review, Washington, DC: The World Bank.

World Bank (1997), *World Bank Atlas 1997*, Washington, DC: The World Bank.

World Bank (2011), *World Development Report 2011: Conflict, Security, and Development*, Oxford and New York: Oxford University Press for World Bank, available at http://wdr2011.world-bank.org/fulltext, accessed 30 October 2011.

World Bank (*passim*), *World Development Report 19*, Oxford and New York: Oxford University Press for World Bank.

World Economic Forum (1996), *The Global Competitiveness Report*, Geneva: World Economic Forum.

Yu, Tzong-shian and J.S. Lee (eds) (1995), *Confucianism and Economic Development*, Taipei: Chung-Hua Institution of Economic Research.

Index

Printed and bound by CPI Group (UK) Ltd, Croydon, CR0 4YY

16/04/2025

14658435-0001